War, Culture and Society, 1750–1850

Titles include:

Katherine Aaslestad and Johan Joor (*editors*)
REVISITING NAPOLEON'S CONTINENTAL SYSTEM: LOCAL, REGIONAL AND EUROPEAN EXPERIENCES

Richard Bessel, Nicholas Guyatt and Jane Rendall (*editors*)
WAR, EMPIRE AND SLAVERY, 1770–1830

Eveline G. Bouwers
PUBLIC PANTHEONS IN REVOLUTIONARY EUROPE
Comparing Cultures of Remembrance, c. 1790–1840

Michael Broers, Agustin Guimera and Peter Hick (*editors*)
THE NAPOLEONIC EMPIRE AND THE NEW EUROPEAN POLITICAL CULTURE

Oskar Cox Jensen
NAPOLEON AND BRITISH SONG, 1797–1822

Gavin Daly
THE BRITISH SOLDIER IN THE PENINSULAR WAR
Encounters with Spain and Portugal, 1808–1814

Charles J. Esdaile and Philip Freeman
BURGOS IN THE PENINSULAR WAR, 1808–1814
Occupation, Siege, Aftermath

Alan Forrest, Etienne François and Karen Hagemann (*editors*)
WAR MEMORIES
The Revolutionary and Napoleonic Wars in Modern European Culture

Alan Forrest, Karen Hagemann and Jane Rendall (*editors*)
SOLDIERS, CITIZENS AND CIVILIANS
Experiences and Perceptions of the Revolutionary and Napoleonic Wars, 1790–1820

Alan Forrest, Karen Hagemann and Michael Rowe (*editors*)
WAR, DEMOBILIZATION AND MEMORY
The Legacy of War in the Era of Atlantic Revolutions

Alan Forrest and Peter H. Wilson (*editors*)
THE BEE AND THE EAGLE
Napoleonic France and the End of the Holy Roman Empire, 1806

Rasmus Glenthøj and Morten Nordhagen Ottosen
EXPERIENCES OF WAR AND NATIONALITY IN DENMARK AND NORWAY, 1807–1815

Marion F. Godfroy
KOUROU AND THE STRUGGLE FOR A FRENCH AMERICA

Karen Hagemann, Gisela Mettele and Jane Rendall (*editors*)
GENDER, WAR AND POLITICS
Transatlantic Perspectives, 1755–1830

Janet M. Hartley, Paul Keenan and Dominic Lieven (*editors*)
RUSSIA AND THE NAPOLEONIC WARS

Leighton S. James
WITNESSING THE REVOLUTIONARY AND NAPOLEONIC WARS IN GERMAN CENTRAL EUROPE

Catriona Kennedy
NARRATIVES OF THE REVOLUTIONARY AND NAPOLEONIC WARS
Military and Civilian Experience in Britain and Ireland

Catriona Kennedy and Matthew McCormack (*editors*)
SOLDIERING IN BRITAIN AND IRELAND, 1750–1850
Men of Arms

Ralph Kingston
BUREAUCRATS AND BOURGEOIS SOCIETY
Office Politics and Individual Credit, France 1789–1848

Mark Lawrence
SPAIN'S FIRST CARLIST WAR, 1833–40

Kevin Linch
BRITAIN AND WELLINGTON'S ARMY
Recruitment, Society and Tradition, 1807–1815

J.R. Moores
REPRESENTATIONS OF FRANCE IN ENGLISH SATIRICAL PRINTS 1740–1832

Julia Osman
CITIZEN SOLDIERS AND THE KEY TO THE BASTILLE

Ute Planert (*editor*)
NAPOLEON'S EMPIRE
European Politics in Global Perspective

Pierre Serna, Antonino De Francesco and Judith Miller (*editors*)
REPUBLICS AT WAR, 1776–1840
Revolutions, Conflicts and Geopolitics in Europe and the Atlantic World

Marie-Cécile Thoral
FROM VALMY TO WATERLOO
France at War, 1792–1815

Mark Wishon
GERMAN FORCES AND THE BRITISH ARMY
Interactions and Perceptions, 1742–1815

Christine Wright
WELLINGTON'S MEN IN AUSTRALIA
Peninsular War Veterans and the Making of Empire c.1820–40

War, Culture and Society, 1750–1850
Series Standing Order ISBN 978–0–230–54532–8 hardback
978–0–230–54533–5 paperback
(*outside North America only*)

You can receive future titles in this series as they are published by placing a standing order. Please contact your bookseller or, in case of difficulty, write to us at the address below with your name and address, the title of the series and one of the ISBNs quoted above.

Customer Services Department, Macmillan Distribution Ltd, Houndmills, Basingstoke, Hampshire RG21 6XS, England

---

War, Demobilization and Memory

The Legacy of War in the Era of Atlantic Revolutions

Edited by

Alan Forrest
University of York, UK

Karen Hagemann
University of North Carolina at Chapel Hill, USA

and

Michael Rowe
King's College London, UK

palgrave
macmillan

Softcover reprint of the hardcover 1st edition 2016 978–1–137–40648–4

First published 2016 by
PALGRAVE MACMILLAN

Palgrave Macmillan in the UK is an imprint of Macmillan Publishers Limited, registered in England, company number 785998, of Houndmills, Basingstoke, Hampshire RG21 6XS.

Palgrave Macmillan in the US is a division of St Martin's Press LLC, 175 Fifth Avenue, New York, NY 10010.

Palgrave Macmillan is the global academic imprint of the above companies and has companies and representatives throughout the world.

Palgrave® and Macmillan® are registered trademarks in the United States, the United Kingdom, Europe and other countries.

ISBN 978-1-349-58038-5 ISBN 978-1-137-40649-1 (eBook)
DOI 10.1007/978-1-137-40649-1

This book is printed on paper suitable for recycling and made from fully managed and sustained forest sources. Logging, pulping and manufacturing processes are expected to conform to the environmental regulations of the country of origin.

A catalogue record for this book is available from the British Library.

Library of Congress Cataloging-in-Publication Data
Names: Forrest, Alan. | Hagemann, Karen. | Rowe, Michael, 1970–
Title: War, demobilization and memory: the legacy of war in the era of Atlantic revolutions / Alan Forrest, Karen Hagemann, Michael Rowe.
Other titles: Legacy of war in the era of Atlantic revolutions
Description: New York, NY: Palgrave Macmillan, [2016] | Series: War, culture and society, 1750–1850 | Includes bibliographical references.
Identifiers: LCCN 2015025958 | ISBN 9781137406484
Subjects: LCSH: Napoleonic Wars, 1800–1815. | Napoleonic Wars, 1800–1815—Influence. | Revolutions—History—18th century. | Revolutions—History—19th century.
Classification: LCC DC226.3 .F67 2016 | DDC 355.02/1809033—dc23
LC record available at http://lccn.loc.gov/2015025958

Typeset by MPS Limited, Chennai, India.

Contents

List of Figures, Graphs and Maps

Cover: Moritz Daniel Oppenheim (1800–1882), 'Return of the Volunteer from the Wars of Liberation to His Family Living According to the Old Customs (Heimkehr des Freiwilligen aus den Befreiungskriegen zu den nach alter Sitte lebenden Seinen) (oil on canvas, 1833–34). The Jewish Museum, New York.

Figures

Graphs

Maps

Series Editors' Preface

The century from 1750 to 1850 was a seminal period of change, not just in Europe but across the globe. The political landscape was transformed by a series of revolutions fought in the name of liberty—most notably in the Americas and France, of course, but elsewhere, too: in Holland and Geneva during the eighteenth century and across much of mainland Europe by 1848. Nor was change confined to the European world. New ideas of freedom, equality and human rights were carried to the furthest outposts of empire, to Egypt, India and the Caribbean, which saw the creation in 1801 of the first black republic in Haiti, the former French colony of Saint-Domingue. And in the early part of the nineteenth century they continued to inspire anti-colonial and liberation movements throughout Central and Latin America.

If political and social institutions were transformed by revolution in these years, so, too, was warfare. During the quarter-century of the French Revolutionary Wars, in particular, Europe was faced with the prospect of 'total' war, on a scale unprecedented before the twentieth century. Military hardware, it is true, evolved only gradually, and battles were not necessarily any bloodier than they had been during the Seven Years War. But in other ways these can legitimately be described as the first modern wars, fought by mass armies mobilized by national and patriotic propaganda, leading to the displacement of millions of people throughout Europe and beyond, as soldiers, prisoners of war, civilians and refugees. For those who lived through the period these wars would be a formative experience that shaped the ambitions and the identities of a generation.

The aims of the series are necessarily ambitious. In its various volumes, whether single-authored monographs or themed collections, it seeks to extend the scope of more traditional historiography. It will study warfare during this formative century not just in Europe, but in the Americas, in colonial societies, and across the world. It will analyse the construction of identities and power relations by integrating the principal categories of difference, most notably class and religion, generation and gender, race and ethnicity. It will adopt a multi-faceted approach to the period, and turn to methods of political, cultural, social, military, and gender history, in order to develop a challenging and multidisciplinary analysis. Finally, it will examine elements of comparison and transfer and so tease out the complexities of regional, national and global history.

Rafe Blaufarb, *Alan Forrest* and *Karen Hagemann*

Preface and Acknowledgements

With the bicentenaries of several key events of the Wars of Revolution and Liberation between 1775 and 1830 just past or soon approaching, many questions about the legacy and memory of these conflicts remain unanswered. While the wars and revolutions of this period have been studied extensively within their own national or broader regional contexts, relatively little has been done to understand them within a trans-national framework. Even less do we know about the short-term aftermath and long-term legacy of these wars, the problems incurred in demobilization, or their often bitterly contested memories.

Bringing together thirty scholars of Europe, Russia, and North, Central, and South America—from five countries and a variety of institutions—the international conference on 'War, Demobilization and Memory: The Legacy of War in the Era of Atlantic Revolutions', which took place in London from 30 May to 1 June 2013, revisited the Era of the Atlantic Revolutions. Among other issues, it explored the flow of ideas and material across the Atlantic during and after the wars and revolutions of the period, the cross-cultural dialogues that were created, the various attempts to come to terms with the violence and destruction wrought by warfare on an unprecedented scale, the impact of the demobilization that followed, and the contested memories of these conflicts.

Two years after the conference we are pleased to be able to present some of its findings as a volume of essays, and it is a timely moment to thank everybody who has contributed to this enterprise. First and foremost, thanks are due to the main sponsors of the conference: the Department of History and the Department of War Studies of King's College London; the College of Arts & Sciences, the Curriculum in Peace, War, and Defense, the Department of History and the Institute for Arts and Humanities of the University of North Carolina at Chapel Hill; and the host of the conference, the UNC Winston House European Study Center in London. We must also thank the two doctoral students who helped us with the conference organization, at Kings' College, Mark Edward Hay, and at UNC Chapel Hill, Gregory Mole, and all who took part in the conference, whether as paper presenters, commentators, moderators or participants in the general discussion. They all made an important contribution in helping the authors and editors to produce a more coherent book. Finally, we want to thank our authors for their cooperation in the rewriting of their papers. It has been a pleasure to work with them: indeed, this book can be seen as a shining example of transatlantic teamwork.

Notes on Contributors

Katherine B. Aaslestad is Professor of History at West Virginia University. Her main field of research and teaching is modern German history. She is the author of *Place and Politics: Local Identity, Civic Culture, and German Nationalism in North Germany during the Revolutionary Era* (2005). She has co-edited with Karen Hagemann special issues on war and gender in *Central European History* and *European History Quarterly* and published articles on republican political culture in the Hanseatic cities, gender and consumption, and the Napoleonic Wars in northern Europe as book chapters in a variety of edited volumes.

David A. Bell is Sidney and Ruth Lapidus Professor of the Era of North Atlantic Revolutions, in the Department of History at Princeton University. His research and teaching focuses on Modern French and European history. He is the author of *Lawyers and Citizens: The Making of a Political Elite in Old Regime France* (1994); *The Cult of the Nation in France: Inventing Nationalism, 1680–1800* (2001); and *The First Total War: Napoleon's Europe and the Birth of Warfare as We Know It* (2007), the last of which has been translated into French, Spanish and Portuguese. He is a member of the editorial board of *The American Historical Review*, and a Delegate for World History of the Oxford University Press (USA). He writes frequently for the general interest press, and is a contributing editor to *The New Republic*.

John Bew is Reader in History and Foreign Policy at the War Studies Department at King's College London and co-director of the International Centre for the Study of Radicalization and Political Violence. His research interest covers British foreign policy since 1789; national identity, state formation and political thought in the British Isles and state approaches to terrorism and political violence. His previous publications include *Castlereagh: A Life* (2012), which was named one of the books of the year by the *Wall Street Journal*, *Sunday Telegraph*, *Spectator*, *BBC Booktalk* and *Total Politics* magazine.

Rafe Blaufarb holds the Ben Weider Eminent Scholar Chair and is Director of the Institute on Napoleon and the French Revolution at Florida State University. His research interests are Revolutionary and Napoleonic France and Latin American Independence. His books include *The French Army, 1750–1820: Careers, Talent, Merit* (2002); and *Bonapartists in the Borderlands: French Refugees and Exiles on the Gulf Coast, 1815–1835* (2005). His current research is on property in the French Revolution, the transatlantic slave trade, and the naval dimensions of the Wars of Latin American Independence.

Matthew Brown is Reader in Latin American Studies at the University of Bristol. He was Director of the Centre for the Study of Colonial and Postcolonial Societies at the University of Bristol during 2009–2014. His research and teaching focuses on Modern Spanish American history. He is the author of *From Frontiers to Football: An Alternative History of Latin America since 1800* (2014); *The Struggle for Power in Post-Independence Colombia and Venezuela* (2012); *Adventuring through Spanish Colonies: Simón Bolívar, Foreign Mercenaries and the Birth of New Nations* (2006); and the editor of *Connections after Colonialism: Europe and Latin America in the 1820s* (with Gabriel Paquette, 2013); and *Informal Empire in Latin America: Culture, Commerce and Capital* (2008).

Kit Candlin is an Australian Research Council postdoctoral research fellow at the University of Sydney working on a project in collaboration with Cassandra Pybus and Robin Pettered entitled 'The Black Loyalist Project: Developing a Digital Repository to Enable E-Research'. His publications include *The Last Caribbean Frontier, 1790–1815* (2012); and together with Cassandra Pybus *Enterprising Women, Race Gender and Power in the Revolutionary Atlantic 1770–1830* (2015).

Sarah C. Chambers is Professor of History at the University of Minnesota, Twin Cities. Her research explores political culture and citizenship during Spanish America's transition from colonialism to independence. She is researching a book project on migrations spurred by the Wars of Independence in South America; in it she will trace the paths of internal refugees, political exiles and royalist émigrés, and analyse how these movements affected the formation of shifting colonial and new national identities. She is the author of *Families in War and Peace: Chile from Colony to Nation* (2015); *From Subjects to Citizens: Honor, Gender, and Politics in Arequipa, Peru, 1780–1854* (1999); and the co-editor with Sueann Caulfield and Lara Putnam, of *Honor, Status, and Law in Modern Latin America* (2005).

Catherine Davies is Professor of Hispanic and Latin American Studies and Director of the Institute of Modern Languages Research at the University of London. She has published on the literature, history and culture of nineteenth- and twentieth-century Spain and Spanish America, with particular focus on gender and politics. Her books include *Latin American Women's Writing: Feminist Readings in Theory and Crisis*, co-edited with A. Brooksbank Jones (1996); *A Place in the Sun? Women's Writing in Twentieth-century Cuba* (1997); and an edition of the Cuban abolitionist novel *Sab* [1841] by Gertrudis

Gómez de Avellaneda (2001). She is co-author with Claire Brewster and Hilary Owen of *South American Independence: Gender, Politics, Text* (2006).

John A. Davis holds the Emiliana Pasca Noether Chair in Modern Italian History at the University of Connecticut. He is also a senior research fellow at the Institute for Advanced Study, Paris, and Editor in Chief of the *Journal of Modern Italian Studies*. His research and teaching focuses on Modern Italian and European history. His book *Naples and Napoleon: Southern Italy and the European Revolutions (1780–1860)* (2006; Italian edition: 2013) won the American Historical Association's 2007 Helen & Howard Marraro Prize for the best book on Italian history in any period, the Premio Sele D'Oro and the International Napoleonic Literary Award: the Italian edition (Rubbettino Editore) won the 2014 Premio Sila '49. His most recent book is *The Jews of San Nicandro* (2010; Italian edition 2013), and he is working on the South and Italian unity from unification to the present.

Alan Forrest is Emeritus Professor of History at the University of York. His research and teaching focuses on Modern French and European history. His books include *Conscripts and Deserters: Napoleon's Men: The Soldiers of the Revolution and Empire* (2002); *Paris, the Provinces and the French Revolution* (2004); *The Legacy of the French Revolutionary Wars: The Nation-in-Arms in French Republican Memory* (2009); *Napoleon: Life, Legacy and Image* (2011); and *Waterloo* (2015). He is co-author with Jean-Paul Bertaud and Annie Jourdan, of *Napoléon, le monde et les Anglais: Guerre des mots et des images* (2004); and has co-edited several works on the French Revolutionary and Napoleonic period, including *War Memories: The Revolutionary and Napoleonic Wars in Modern European Culture*, with Etienne François and Karen Hagemann (2012); and *The Routledge Companion to the French Revolution in World History*, with Matthias Middell (2015).

Karen Hagemann is James G. Kenan Distinguished Professor of History at the University of North Carolina at Chapel Hill. She has published widely in Modern German, European and Transatlantic history, gender history and the history of military and war. Her books include *'Mannlicher Mut und Teutsche Ehre': Nation, Militär und Geschlecht zur Zeit der Antinapoleonischen Kriege Preußens* (2002); *Representing Masculinity: Citizenship in Modern Western Culture*, co-edited with Stefan Dudink and Anna Clark (2007/2012); *Soldiers, Citizens and Civilians: Experiences and Perceptions of the French Wars, 1790–1820*, co-edited with Alan Forrest and Jane Rendall (2009); *Gender, War, and Politics: Transatlantic Perspectives, 1775–1830*, co-edited with Gisela Mettele and Jane Rendall (2010); *War Memories: The Revolutionary and Napoleonic Wars in Modern European Culture*, co-edited with Alan Forrest and Etienne François, (2012/2013); and *Revisiting Prussia's Wars against Napoleon: History,*

Culture, Memory (2015). She is preparing, as general editor, the *Oxford Handbook on Gender, War and the Western World since 1650.*

Janet M. Hartley is Professor of International History at the London School of Economics and Political Science, Department of International History. She has published on the military, diplomatic, cultural, social and political history of Russia in the eighteenth and early nineteenth centuries. Her books include *Alexander I* (1994); *A Social History of the Russian Empire 1650–1825* (1999); and *Charles Whitworth: Diplomat in the Age of Peter the Great* (2002). She also published *Russia, 1762–1825: Military Power, the State, and the People* (2008), which studied the impact on Russia, a country which we would normally consider to be 'backward', of almost continual warfare in the late eighteenth and early nineteenth century. Her most recent book is *Siberia: A History of the People* (2014).

Mark Edward Hay is a doctoral candidate at the History Department of King's College London, funded by the Arts and Humanities Research Council. His topic of research is Dutch power projection and strategies of conflict resolution in the Revolutionary and Napoleonic period. He has published on Dutch military and political history, and his article on 'The House of Nassau between France and Independence, 1795–1814: Lesser Powers, Strategies of Conflict Resolution, Dynastic Networks' will appear in the *International History Review* (2015).

Christine Haynes is Associate Professor of European History at the University of North Carolina at Charlotte. A specialist in nineteenth-century French cultural history, she is the author of the monograph *Lost Illusions: The Politics of Publishing in Nineteenth-Century France* (2010); as well as several articles related to the history of publishing and authorship. She is now venturing into military history, for a new book project on the aftermath of the Napoleonic Wars, tentatively entitled '"Our Friends, the Enemies": The First Allied Occupation of France, 1815–1818'.

Leighton S. James is Associate Professor of European History at Swansea University. His work concentrates on German and European history and the culture of warfare in the late eighteenth and early nineteenth century. His publications include two monographs: *The Politics of Identity and Civil Society in Britain and Germany: Miners in the Ruhr and South Wales, 1890–1926* (2008); and *Witnessing the Revolutionary and Napoleonic Wars: German Central Europe, 1789–1815* (2013).

Gregory T. Knouff is Professor of History at Keene State College in New Hampshire. He teaches courses in Colonial North America, American Revolution, American Military History, Loyalist History, Native American

History, the African Atlantic World, and Gender in Early North America. He is the author of *The Soldiers' Revolution: Pennsylvanians in Arms and the Forging of Early American Identity* (2004/2012) and several published articles including, most recently, 'Masculinity, Race and Citizenship: Soldier's Memories of the American Revolution' in *Gender, War, and Politics: The Wars of Revolution and Liberation*, ed. by Karen Hagemann et al. (2010). His current book project is *A Seductive Sedition: Loyalists, Language, and Power in Revolutionary New Hampshire.*

Lloyd Kramer is Professor of History at the University of North Carolina, Chapel Hill. The focus of his research and teaching is on Modern European Intellectual History, the history of cross-cultural exchanges in the Atlantic World, and the history of modern France. He is the author of several books, including *Threshold of a New World: Intellectuals and the Exile Experience in Paris, 1830–1848* (1988); *Lafayette in Two Worlds: Public Cultures and Personal Identities in an Age of Revolutions* (1996); and *Nationalism in Europe and America: Politics, Cultures, and Identities since 1775* (2011).

Andrew Lambert is Laughton Professor of Naval History in the Department of War Studies at King's College London. He is a fellow of the Royal Historical Society and Director of the Laughton Naval History Unit in the War Studies Department. Lambert's research concentrates on the naval and strategic history of the British Empire between the Napoleonic Wars and the First World War, and the early development of naval historical writing. His work has addressed a range of issues, including technology, policy-making, regional security, deterrence, historiography, crisis-management and conflict. His many books include *The Crimean War: British Grand Strategy against Russia 1853–1856* (1990/2011); *'The Foundations of Naval History': Sir John Laughton, the Royal Navy and the Historical Profession* (1998); *Franklin: Tragic Hero of Polar Navigation* (2009); and *The Challenge: Britain against America in the Naval War of 1812* (2012), which won the Anderson Medal of the Society for Nautical Research in 2012.

John R. Maass is a historian with the US Army Center of Military History in Washington, DC. He teaches American military history. His publications include '"Humanity Mourns Over Such a Site": The Army's Disaster at Terre aux Boeufs, 1809', *Army History* (2012); 'Nathanael Greene and the Politics of Moderation, 1781–1783', in *General Nathanael Greene and the American Revolution in the South*, edited by James Piecuch and Gregory Massey (2012); '"The Cure for All Our Political Calamities": Archibald Maclaine and the Politics of Moderation in Revolutionary North Carolina', *The North Carolina Historical Review* (2008); and '"From Principles of Humanity and Virtue": Moderation and the Revolutionary Settlement in North Carolina', *Journal of Backcountry Studies* (2007). He is working on a book about North Carolina and the French and Indian War (1754–1763).

Alexander M. Martin is Professor of History at the University of Notre Dame. His research focuses on imperial Russia. He is the author of *Enlightened Metropolis: Constructing Imperial Moscow, 1762–1855* (2013); and *Romantics, Reformers, Reactionaries: Russian Conservative Thought and Politics in the Reign of Alexander I* (1997); and the editor and translator of Dmitrii Rostislavov's *Provincial Russia in the Age of Enlightenment: The Memoir of a Priest's Son* (2002). His next project, tentatively entitled 'Pastor Rosenstrauch's Secret: A German Life in Tsarist Russia', is an examination of the history of Germany and Russia through the lens of the experience of one German emigrant family.

Cassandra Pybus is an honorary professor at Sydney University, Department of History. She has published widely on Australian, American and Transatlantic history and her interests span as broadly as Australian social history, colonial history in North America, South East Asia, Africa and Australia, slavery and the history of labour. She has published several books, including *Epic Journeys of Freedom: Runaway Slaves of the American Revolution and Their Global Quest for Liberty* (2006); *Black Founders: The Unknown Story of Australia's First Black Settlers* (2006); and as co-editor with Emma Christopher and Marcus Rediker *Many Middle Passages: Forced Migration and the Making of the Modern World* (2007).

Michael Rowe is Senior Lecturer in Modern European History at King's College London, and a fellow of the Royal Historical Society. His research focuses on the history of Germany in the late eighteenth and nineteenth centuries and addresses a wide range of issues within this context, including especially the development of the state and government, and the emergence of national identities. His most important publications include *From Reich to State: The Rhineland in the Revolutionary Age* (2003/2007); and as an edited volume *Collaboration and Resistance in Napoleonic Europe: State-Formation in an Age of Upheaval* (2003). His current research focuses on the governance of the Napoleonic Empire and comparisons with other empires and polities of the period.

David Todd is Lecturer in World History at King's College London. His research focuses on three main themes: the origins and beginnings of the conquest of Algeria, between 1815 and 1840; ideas of economic and cultural informal empire, and their impact on France's engagement with the Arab world in the nineteenth century; and the rise of Anglo-French imperial cooperation between 1815 and 1914. In his book, *L'Identité économique de la France, 1814–1851* (2008), which came out in English as *Free Trade and its Enemies in France, 1814–1851* (2015), he examines early debates about international trade and globalization in post-Napoleonic France. He works on the reinvention of French imperialism after 1815.

List of Abbreviations

AAE	Archives des Affaires étrangères, Paris (La Courneuve)
AB	*Amts-Blatt der königlich kurmärkischen Regierung*
ADBR	Archives Départementales du Bas-Rhin, Strasbourg
ADG	Archives Départementales de la Gironde, Bordeaux
AGI	Archivo General de Indias, Seville
AHN	Archivo Histórico Nacional, Madrid
AHR	*American Historical Review*
AN	Archives Nationales, Paris (Pierrefitte-sur-Seine)
BN	*Berlinische Nachrichten*
CAOM	Centre des Archives d'Outre-Mer, Aix-en-Provence
CLS	Church of the Latter Day Saints Records, Utah
DB	*Deutsche Blätter*
DLAR	David Library of the American Revolution
GCR	Grenada Church Records
LRO	Liverpool Record Office
NCSR	The State Records of North Carolina
NHCS	New Hampshire State Archives, Concord, Folder, Loyalism Allegiance, Early Documents, General Court Records, Committee of Safety
NHPL	New Hampshire State Archives, Concord, NH, Petitions to the Legislature
NHSP	New Hampshire State Papers
ÖKA	Österreiches Hauptstaatsarchiv (Kriegsarchiv), Vienna
PSZ	*Polnoe sobranie zakonov Rossiiskoi imperii*
RGVIA	Rossiiskii gosudarstvennyi voenno-istoricheskiii arkhiv, Moscow
RM	*Rheinischer Merkur*
SHD	Service Historique de la Défense, Paris (Vincennes)
SP	*Schlesisches Provinzialblatt*
SPZ	*Schlesische Privilegierte Zeitung*
SRG	State Registry of Grenada

SRO	Suffolk Record Office, Ipswich
StAHbg	Staatsarchiv Hamburg
StAL	Staatsarchiv Leipzig
TG	*Tageblatt der Geschichte*
TNA	The National Archives, London
TNA, ADM	The National Archives, London, Admiralty
TNA, AO	The National Archives, London, Audit Office
TNA, CUST	The National Archives, London, Customs
TNA, FO	The National Archives, London, Foreign Office
VZ	*Vossische Zeitung*
WD	The Dispatches of Field Marshal the Duke of Wellington during His Various Campaigns
WSD	Supplementary Despatches, Correspondence, and Memoranda of Field Marshal Arthur Duke of Wellington, K. G.
ZFeW	*Zeitschrift für die elegante Welt*
ZVHG	*Zeitschrift des Verein für Hamburgische Geschichte*

Part I
Rethinking the Legacy of Conflict in the Era of Atlantic Revolutions

1
Introduction: War, Demobilization and Memory in the Era of Atlantic Revolutions

Alan Forrest, Karen Hagemann and Michael Rowe

The picture that appears on the cover of this book, Moritz Daniel Oppenheim's *The Return of the Volunteer from the Wars of Liberation to his Family still living in Accordance with the Old Customs*, may seem a strange choice for a volume that purports to speak to war, demobilization and memory in the Era of Atlantic Revolutions—starting in the 1770s and ending in the 1830s. The German-Jewish painter Oppenheim, born in 1800 in the Hessian town of Hanau, was too young to volunteer for the Wars of 1813–1815, the final struggle to liberate Germany and Europe from Napoleonic rule. But in this painting, which dates from 1833–1834, Oppenheim invoked the memory of these wars. He referred to the participation of young Jewish volunteers in what he saw as a fight for liberation *and* liberty.[1] His painting portrays the return of one of these victorious fighters after demobilization to the warmth of his family. Like many other Jewish families that had allowed their sons to participate in these 'people's wars', they had hoped to become part of the German people as a result of their patriotic support for the war. The Jewish volunteers also expected to get equal citizenship rights after the wars—as was promised by kings and princes—because they had done their military duty as men and protected family, home and country.[2]

Though for us today the painting seems to have little that is revolutionary about it, for Oppenheim's contemporaries it clearly spoke to the national myths of the uprising of the German people against Napoleon and their struggle for liberation, liberty and national unity. The painting is especially interesting for our subject because it represents broken promises in a dual sense: both the hopes of the population at large for German unification and greater political liberty and the hopes of the Jewish community for their own emancipation were crushed in the period of postwar restoration. For both reasons, the painting seems to have enjoyed considerable popularity in its time, as the many reproductions indicate.[3]

Oppenheim, who was the first academically trained Jewish painter in Germany, did not create a heroic history painting in the traditional sense of the term. National governments commissioned paintings that focused on events of high-political and military importance to hang in their national galleries and public buildings. Thus the US Capitol is decorated with John Trumbull's 1820 painting *Surrender of Lord Cornwallis*, commemorating a key moment of American pride in the Wars of Independence, and the Palace of Westminster with Daniel Maclise's 1861 painting of *The Meeting of Wellington and Blücher after the Battle of Waterloo*. Windsor Castle is endowed with an entire Chamber in memory of the battle and Allied military heroes, whilst the Winter Palace in Saint Petersburg boasts its Military Gallery containing the portraits of hundreds of generals who fought in the 'Patriotic War' of 1812. Napoleon, most famously, turned to the finest artists of the day—Jacques Louis David, Antoine-Jean Gros and Jean-Auguste-Dominique Ingres—to provide heroic images of his victories and portraits that would capture the imagination of a continent.[4]

Art remained a political weapon even after the guns fell silent, recording victories and emphasizing the martial qualities of nations. Almost unavoidably these were highly gendered images, highlighting the role of warriors and kings. Women were generally absent from such paintings, or were relegated to domestic scenes. Oppenheim's *The Return of the Volunteer* is very different, revealing subtly changing sensibilities about war and depicting soldiers and civilians, women as well as men, and people of every generation from the youngest to the oldest. It places emphasis on the idea of inclusion, on status that is related to ability and aspiration rather than to the old order of estates. It suggests the emergence of new nations bound together by the principle of citizenship, and equates that citizenship with the performance of military service.[5] It has left the world of the eighteenth century far behind.

Oppenheim's painting was a product of Germany in the period of the *Vormärz*. Painted in the years after the July Revolution of 1830 in France and the German Hambach Festival of May 1832, where thousands had demonstrated for national unity and liberty at Hambach Castle in present-day Rhineland-Palatinate, it expresses universal aspirations, too. On the one hand it represents the hope for more political rights and equal citizenship as recognition of the military service that many soldiers, especially volunteers and militias, had shared during the Era of Atlantic Revolutions. On the other hand it embodies the desire of soldiers everywhere to return to their families and the relief of their loved-ones upon their homecoming. It was a moment that had kept men going in the midst of terrible deprivations, and only accentuated the plight of those who emerged from the conflict with nowhere to go to, whose families had been killed, whose homes had been destroyed, and whose prospects had been ruined in the fighting.

This close entanglement of the political, social and personal was true of all the conflicts during the Era of Atlantic Revolutions: wars about empire and global hegemony as well as wars of liberation and decolonization. During this era the Atlantic became a highway for exchange not only of peoples and commodities but also of ideas and cultural practices. Improving literacy and the spread of the printed word meant that the public in both Europe and the Americas was made aware of events from across the ocean and the new ideas of fraternity, liberty and unity. For the new forms of mass struggle that characterize this era, patriotic-national propaganda attempted to mobilize soldiers and civilians, men and women, rich and poor, free and enslaved alike. This was most clearly seen in the American, French and Haitian Revolutions and in the Wars of Liberation in Spanish America.[6]

It is not the purpose of this volume to examine the processes of military, political and cultural mobilization for revolution and war—here many important studies have already been published.[7] Instead, it focuses on the much less explored theme of the military, economic, political, social and cultural demobilization after these conflicts, not only by states but also by local communities and individuals, and examines the long-term legacy of these conflicts and their collective memories, because the transition from war to peace was a huge challenge for all the states and societies involved. In the following pages we will first reflect on the specific character of war and postwar in the Era of Atlantic Revolutions, and then discuss the agenda of the book in more detail and explore the different areas of demobilization and collective memory construction.

Rethinking war and postwar

The decades between the 1770s and 1830s were scarred by war throughout the Atlantic world. The period began with the American Revolutionary Wars (1775–1783) (see Map 1.1), included the French Revolution (1789–1799) and its Wars (1792–1799) and the Napoleonic Wars (1803–1815) (see Map 1.2), the Haitian Revolution (1791–1804) and the conflicts in the Caribbean, and ended with the Spanish American Wars of Independence (1808–1833) (see Map 1.3). The Americas and Europe were part of an Atlantic world which shared a collective identity shaped by the twin forces of revolution and war. Earlier periods had, of course, been marked by lengthy periods of warfare, including such global conflicts as the War of the Spanish Succession (1701–1714) and the Seven Years War (1754–1763), the second of which had actually broken out in the Americas. But it is the linking of war and revolution that makes the half-century between the 1770s and 1830s distinctive, with its huge concentration of wars and the resultant dislocation which demobilization incurred.

Wars in these years were of unprecedented scale and extent, requiring a massive mobilization of men for the military. Mass armies were deployed, composed of conscripts, militias and volunteers, as well as long-service professionals. As revolutionary and conservative regimes alike used armies of increasing size across Europe and the Americas, the conduct of warfare was transformed, too. This was not so much through the introduction of new weaponry, which largely remained unaltered, but by the new demands of mass armies. These demands also imposed new burdens on the economy and society, which in turn transformed the political, social and gender orders on both sides of the Atlantic. Soldiers and civilians of all classes, races, and ethnicities—men and women—were mobilized for war with a greater intensity than ever before. Extensive financial and material support by civilians through taxes and tributes, requisitions and quartering, outfitting soldiers, medical care and war charity was badly needed by all war powers. Without these varied forms of civilian war support mass warfare on this scale would not have been possible. To mobilize this support, coercion alone was not enough. Even conservative governments used intensive patriotic-national propaganda that addressed civilians and soldiers alike. Often it promised soldiers—regardless of race—personal freedom and political rights in return for military service. When necessary, the armed forces on all sides admitted to their ranks groups of men that had previously been marginalized, including, in some instances, slaves.[8]

The global scale of warfare, the extent to which the wars of the era included civil society, and the close entanglement of war, politics and culture have led some historians of the period, among them David A. Bell and Jean-Yves Guiomar, to suggest that these were wars of a quite different kind from previous conflicts, to the extent that they should be thought of as the first instances in history of 'total war'—war that affected all classes of society, independent of their ethnicity, gender or race, and necessitated massive economic and cultural resources.[9]

The term 'total war' has been contested, of course, not least by historians of twentieth-century warfare. But there is no doubting the scale of these conflicts or the overarching ambition of the powers engaged in them. They were fought over continents and across oceans, involving India and the Orient as well as the Atlantic world. They were characterized by their maximalist war aims and by the huge systemic changes which they brought about. Wars were now fought to change social and political regimes and to free colonized peoples from the rule of multinational empires; they involved mass armies, armed populations and civilians, and already crossed the lines between 'front' and 'homeland'. The civilian population became a target long before the two World Wars, as the siege of a number of cities—including Boston (1775), Breslau (1806), Saragossa (1809), Moscow (1812), Hamburg (1813–1814) and Washington (1814)—and the destruction of thousands of towns and villages indicate.[10] War atrocities are also no invention of the twentieth century. They were quite common in the Era of Atlantic Revolutions, as several new studies have shown.[11] The civilian population was already being targeted, too, by economic blockades like the Continental System (1806–1814), declared by Napoleon with the Berlin Decree in November 1806 in response to the naval blockade of the French coasts enacted by the British government in May of the same year.[12]

As a result, the wars of this era fused the military and civilian worlds more closely than in previous generations: Oppenheim's image is unmistakably one of war fought in the period from the 1780s to 1830s, and would have been barely conceivable earlier, even during the 1750s. War now involved massive social and political changes: it helped forge larger states across Europe and beyond, states which extended their polity at the expense of those alternative structures which they had previously stood alongside: clerical states, city republics, composite monarchies, mercantilist-oceanic empires. These were increasingly sacrificed to the rise of more powerful territorial and nation states, united under a single ruler and establishing their undisputed monopoly of military force. The old order of corporate privilege was, often contemptuously, swept aside.[13]

These were transnational trends, which many see as exerting a global impact, yet they were not found everywhere in equal measure: by the very fact of European settlement and colonization, they were heavily concentrated in the Atlantic world. In recent years there has been some reappraisal of the term, both as a geographical entity and as a distinct political culture, as the Atlantic world has come to be understood as a region of commercial exchange and cultural transfer. European empires remain, of course, at its heart, since, in territorial terms, they spanned the Atlantic, and much of the dynamic of revolution and war was shaped by them, or followed in the wake of commercial shipping. Cultural and philosophical ideas, political and economic ideologies also spanned the Atlantic, so that a revolutionary movement on one side of the ocean soon impacted on those who lived on the other shore.

It was in large measure a European world, in cultural terms, with European liberalism, European commercialism, and European religious faiths at its core. But it was a space where the various European cultures came into contact, and often conflict, with other cultures and other races, and where, as a result of the European slave trade with the United States, the Caribbean, and Spanish and Portuguese South America, African cultures and traditions also came into play.[14] It was the space where these conflicts were most densely concentrated. But it was not, of course, the only place where cultures clashed or where recognizably new technologies were applied to war. In China the great armies of the Qing dynasty were undone by the superior western cannon their soldiers faced. In India the period was marked by the modernization of weaponry that followed the introduction of gunpowder.[15] In large parts of Africa the slave trade led Europeans to intervene in internal African wars, with the spread of guns and weaponry which that implied. And with Napoleon's invasion of Egypt, European Great Power politics were once again introduced into the eastern Mediterranean, where they helped to undermine the military pretensions of the Ottoman Empire. What happened in the Atlantic was only part of a wider global crisis that followed the decline of the old Asian regimes on the one hand and the American and French Revolutions on the other. If these years saw the British burn Washington, it was not the only political centre to fall to invading armies. So, around the globe, did Cairo, Moscow, Paris, Jogjakarta and Delhi.[16]

This extensive scale of warfare was experienced by contemporaries on both sides of the Atlantic as something new and challenging and it left an enduring mark in collective memory. Part of the contemporary perception of living in a 'time of upheaval and change' was not only the regional scale and intensity of the conflicts but also their diversity and complexity. New subjects became historical agents in these conflicts: workers and women, indigenous people and slaves, people of unknown regions. And this, too, would be important in the memories which these years created and the processes of identity formation they imposed. Indeed, one could plausibly argue that not only were new national identities crafted in this period against their respective 'others', but also that the notions of 'Europe' and 'the West' were very much the product of these years. Both were constructed against perceived others: the 'barbaric East' and the 'savages' in the colonies. They included the sense that the 'Western hemisphere' was united by ideas and values as well as by commercial interest, a world of constant interchange as merchants, planters and government officials passed seamlessly from one part of the globe to another.[17]

This new thinking was reflected in and fostered by international politics. It was in this period that many of the fundamental treaties were signed that shaped the Atlantic world as we know it, establishing, amongst other outcomes, the independence of the United States, the loss of France's first Atlantic empire, the creation in Haiti of the world's first black republic, and the succession of independence movements that ended Spanish domination in much of Central and South America. Revolution, too, was transnational, with its roots in trade and the economy.[18] The 'sinews of government', as Bailey Stone remarks, 'are its finances', and in the last years of the Ancien Régime in France, war, royal absolutism and the fiscal crisis were very closely entangled.[19] If the colonial struggles of these years left Britain as the dominant global power, they also had a unique role in forging a new territorial order that had particular resonance in the Americas. The War of 1812 was a key moment in the emergence of modern Canada and its future coexistence with the United States, while the years from around 1808 until the 1820s saw the arrival of a clutch of new states in South America, polities born of Napoleon's invasion of Spain and often brought into existence with the aid of European soldiers and European arms. Their emergence into statehood was often accompanied by violent struggle that generated powerful images and memories. These would subsequently be an inspiration to others, not least to peoples seeking liberation from colonial suzerainty. The Age of Atlantic Revolutions was also the first age of decolonization.[20]

Whilst recent scholarship has emphasized the importance of the transatlantic dimension in the history of this period, and has foregrounded the new character of warfare and its far reaching consequences, little has been said about the short- and long-term legacy of these large-scale conflicts. This is quite astonishing. The concept of 'postwar', which now appears widely in studies of the 'age of the two World Wars', has not been commonly applied to the period between the 1770s and 1830s. With this volume we want to change this. We hope to foster further research on the many postwars of the Era of Atlantic Revolutions, especially the military, economic, political and cultural demobilizations after the mass wars of this period, together with their long-term aftermath and their commemoration and memory.

Such an approach will provide us with new insights into how wars influence the economy, society, culture and politics long after combat ceases. The challenges that both Europeans and Americans eventually confronted, after the wars in the era of Atlantic Revolutions had ended, were unprecedented, not least because of the vast scale of the conflicts themselves. States and societies were ill-prepared to deal with the consequences of a style of warfare that was arguably now 'total'. One obvious problem was the need to de-mobilize mass armies and navies, and to re-integrate large numbers of ordinary combatants into civilian life. Beyond this, they had to deal with the economic consequences of warfare: the destruction of towns and villages, of fields and forests. Especially painful was the re-adjustment of the Atlantic economy following the dismantling of blockades and counter-blockades, the collapse of mercantilism and the abolition of the slave trade by several of the leading slaving nations. It was in this unpropitious context that communities and families needed to accommodate unprecedented numbers of physically and psychologically scarred veterans. Similar processes took place in the cultural sphere, which had been militarized during wartime through the celebration of heroism and martial virtues. Culture and the arts, which had been widely used as an instrument of war mobilization, had to adapt to an environment in which large-scale armed conflict was at an end and where bellicose rhetoric was no longer prized. This cultural aspect of demobilization cannot be detached from political and social issues. Rather, it had an integral role to play, as culture influenced narratives and memories, which were themselves contested by groups struggling to find a more advantageous social and political position in the new postwar order.

And indeed the wars of the Era of Atlantic Revolutions would leave a powerful memory, marked by emotive *lieux de mémoire*. For the United States the year 1789, with the Bill of Rights and the election of George Washington as the country's first president, would mark the beginning of a new era. In France the year 1789 would also have this function, while the countries France invaded had their own heroic dates to celebrate: 1798 for Ireland, 1808 for Spain, 1812 for Russia, or 1813 for Germany. The potency of these memories can be seen in public celebrations like Bastille Day (14 July) in France, in street names, and in monuments like Nelson's Column and Trafalgar Square in London, or the Butte du Lion at Waterloo, a Dutch memorial to the part played by the young Prince of Orange. In Moscow the Tsar ordered the construction of a huge cathedral in honor of Christ the Saviour as a memorial to the sacrifices of the Russian people in Napoleon's wars. In Leipzig a hundred years after the Battle of the Nations in 1813, a huge monument was erected to celebrate a victory hailed as the triumph of German nationalism. Yet, unlike in the Americas, it would be difficult to claim that these years lie at the root of Europe's modern state system. At best they could be remembered as the time when many European nations were born.[21]

The legacy of war, demobilizing and memory

This book has three main aims. It first examines how the processes of immediate military, economic, social and cultural demobilization were managed, not only by states but by local communities and individuals, all facing up to the major challenges that had to be overcome if a return was to be made to a peaceful and civil society. But there were much wider challenges for the postwar world, and the second aim of the book is to analyze these. It asks, how could the long-term economic, social and cultural legacy be resolved? How should the lasting political fall-out of the wars be addressed? Can we talk of a discrete postwar generation here, or, indeed, a recognizable postwar politics?[22] And thirdly, there is the question of the memories which the wars left behind and which, for some, scarred that entire generation. How were the wars remembered in different regions, different nations and different social, racial and ethnic groups? Who shaped these memories, and how were they used and turned to political advantage? Why did some of these uses endure while others rapidly faded? Was there, indeed, a critical difference between 'winners' and 'losers' in the ways they appropriated the memory of a period that for many conjured up images of pain and humiliation? Did it matter that a campaign had been won or lost?[23]

These questions are deliberately examined in a comparative transatlantic context, with one overarching issue in mind: what similarities and differences can we identify in the ways in which postwar societies on both sides of the Atlantic approached the problems of military, economic, social and cultural demobilization, and addressed their corollary, the construction of memory? This complex approach does much to establish the book's originality. It also leads us to give some thought to the longer-term legacies of war on the Atlantic world. What were the most important transnational legacies—and did these affect both sides of the Atlantic in equal measure? Or was it the case that for many in Europe and the Americas this was not principally an age of revolution, but an age of fracture, of paradoxes and ambiguities? Was it perceived as an age that united the Atlantic world or as a period that left this world increasingly split as Continental Europe turned away from the Atlantic, looking more to itself, to the Levant, to Asia and to Africa, and leaving Britain as the only unashamedly Atlantic power in Europe? Perhaps contemporaries recognized the parallelism of both developments? After around 1830 (with France's colonization of Algeria) Europe's second age of colonization would privilege Asia, the Maghreb and sub-Saharan Africa. The nineteenth century heralded a new era when colonial wars—still largely involving the traditional colonial powers—would be fought in India, the Middle East and Africa, and later also the Far East.[24] The Atlantic world of the late eighteenth century was visibly giving way to the global world of the nineteenth and its culture of militarism and imperialism.

David A. Bell opens the volume with a provocative essay in which he suggests that it is in the Atlantic world of these years, and most specifically in the shadow of the American and French revolutions, that modern militarism was born. 'Perhaps', he argues, 'the most common forms of modern militarism had their origins in the Age of Democratic Revolutions and Revolutionary Wars, and are symbiotically related to the revolutionary regimes that emerged in this period'.[25] It is certainly the case that in the American, French and Haitian revolutions a much larger percentage of young men were compelled to bear arms and that, especially in the Revolutionary and Napoleonic Wars, armies reached a size that consumed resources on a scale not previously known. One extreme example is Napoleon's Russian Campaign in 1812: The Grande Armée numbered 380,000 soldiers from 13 conquered and allied European states and 300,000 men of French departments. Only 120,000 of them survived.[26]

Military service, citizenship and masculinity were linked in the propaganda, not only of France and Prussia, but also of most other belligerent powers. Soldiering was now presented as a duty of male citizens, or, alternatively, as the precondition for gaining equal political citizenship rights.[27] The new mass armies rapidly acquired a high degree of professionalism, too, as the officers became increasingly specialized and their aspirations became focused on promotion and command. But how much evidence is there that the culture of societies was becoming more militaristic? In France the revolutionaries tried to maintain the primacy of the political, aware of the risks of a politicized army and of officers with political ambitions of their own. They ended up, of course, with Napoleon. In some political contexts army officers did play a leading role in revolutionary movements, whether in the Italy of the 1820s and 1830s or in South America in the years after 1820. Even in England, John Bew finds that a government honed in war could be more effective when it came to managing the problems of the postwar world. But this does not necessarily imply that these countries were becoming more militarized, only that the knowledge and skills gained in war could easily be switched to other, more pacific purposes.

For sure, the military leaderships in most countries involved in war were not quickly ready to step back from the limelight once peace returned. They expected their share of recognition and influence. But they were generally prepared to act within the confines of the political arena, to accept the constraints of civil governance, and to resist the temptation to seize power, militarily. More challenging was the integration of the many returning professional soldiers, militiamen and volunteers into civil society. They brought their military habits, and with them their often traumatic experiences, their scars of war, back to their families, villages and hometowns. They too, expected recognition for their military service and hoped to benefit from the political freedoms which their governments and army leaders had promised in their war propaganda.

Peace-making, occupation and military demobilization

The first thematic section, on peace-making, occupation and military demobilization, focuses on the very different circumstances in which wars ended and on the impact which the large-scale demobilization of armies had on societies at large and on individual soldiers and officers. Just as in the wars themselves, there is often a glaring discrepancy between the discourse of peace-making and the reality of what subsequently happened, which often fell short of the ideals that were held out to the soldiers. Janet M. Hartley's discussion of Russia after the Napoleonic Era is a telling case-in-point. Russia had, of course, a particular problem, in that those demobilized were in many cases serfs, and the agrarian infrastructure to which they could hope to return was notoriously underdeveloped. Tsar Alexander I dreamed of a much bolder solution, one that would integrate the army into the social fabric of Russia through the establishment of military colonies, which had first been set up in 1810 in western Russia. They involved one battalion and 4,000 state peasants (most of whom perished), but the outbreak of war in 1812 prevented their development. Now, with the war over, they were conceived of on a far greater scale in a bid, as Alexander I stated in the preamble to the decree which established the colonies, to make the soldiers' service 'less burdensome'. Hartley shows that, far from the colonies helping to ease the financial burden on the state, they cost a vast amount of money to set up and maintain. The reason for this was that the colonies were intended to do far more—to modernize agriculture, improve standards of life, and, in the process, to create new types of 'citizen' for the state.[28]

Perhaps predictably, this all turned out to be somewhat utopian, and the best intentions were to prove illusory. Similarly, Christine Haynes sees in postwar France the imposition of an Allied army of occupation after 1815 as being planned with some sensitivity, passing rapidly from the initial military invasion to a peace-keeping force. This occupation was, however, perceived quite differently by many people in the occupied territories of France who had to carry the burden. It did not help that the invasion was termed an 'Occupation of Guarantee', commissioned with the supervision of the demobilization of the troops who had served Napoleon in the Hundred Days. Wellington was determined to avoid unnecessary acts of violence against the civilian population, and the British convinced themselves that the occupation succeeded in punishing France without antagonizing the French population.[29] That may have been over-optimistic, though Haynes makes the case that the occupation years from 1815–1818 did contribute to stabilize the postwar order in the longer term, an order, which, Paul W. Schroeder argues, had already come together in the war years 1813–1814.[30] Meanwhile France demobilized after 1815: thousands of soldiers were put on half-pay, and officers loyal to Napoleon were discharged. In France the Bourbon Restoration was, for the moment at least, secure. The opportunity had been seized, though for many Frenchmen it still felt like an opportunity lost.

This highlights another important aspect of demobilization: the reputation enjoyed by those who had fought, and the reception they could expect to receive when they returned. Even for victorious armies demobilization might pose a challenge, especially where the political sympathies of the troops were perceived as an issue. As Leighton S. James shows for German Central Europe, different forms of military service were celebrated in markedly different ways after 1815, in a culture that drew sharp distinctions between those who had volunteered for service or were conscripted for the newly formed militias, and the men of the professional military units. Veterans' organizations had been discouraged in Prussia in the immediate aftermath of the Napoleonic Wars, and James suggests that there was even a certain antipathy in the army towards the formation of veterans' associations, particularly those of volunteers which were perceived as potentially tainted by radical national and democratic sympathies.[31]

Rafe Blaufarb turns to another key problem raised by demobilization on this scale: the process did not just involve decommissioning men, but also running down huge stockpiles of weaponry. What was to be done with the arsenals of guns, ammunition and artillery pieces left discarded after years of combat? Blaufarb shows how the end of one war provided opportunities for those fighting elsewhere, and how demobilization in Europe helped reignite conflicts in South America as speculators and privateers, often threatened with financial ruin with the return of peace, exploited the opportunity which a new arms trade provided. They were not alone in seeking profit in other people's wars. The flood of arms across the Atlantic in the years after 1815 provided many, in Europe and the Americas, with the chance to make their fortunes, as cash-strapped governments, military adventurers and arms traders joined forces to turn adversity into a new source of riches. Theirs was a truly transatlantic trade, linking the debris of one war to the destruction of others.[32]

The Aftermath of War in Politics and Political Culture

The following section discusses politics and political culture in the aftermath of war. How far did the war experiences continue to affect the values of societies once they had laid down their arms and reverted to a peacetime existence? How far, indeed, could they be said, as David A. Bell suggests, to have been 'militarized' by the experience and propaganda of the war years? All the chapters in this section address this question to a greater or lesser degree, and it is clear that the memories of the recent wars continued to weigh heavily on political leaders and citizens alike. It is true, for instance, of the Jewish experience in the German-Central Europe which Michael Rowe analyses in his chapter on the debates about citizenship for Jewish men that started during the Congress of Vienna and continued afterwards. In this fierce public discussion all sides agreed that military service was a vital measure of civic worth, with which the future civic status of Jews was intimately entwined. If they disagreed, it was not with the measure, but over whether there were other more important preconditions for becoming a member of the German nation and a citizen in one of the thirty-four territorial states of the newly founded German Confederation. The majority of the voices in the public debate concurred that only Christian men could be accepted as citizens. Thus conversion to Christianity became for Jewish men the only way to become legally equal to German men of their social rank; this was even the case when they had distinguished themselves in the battles of the Wars of 1813 to 1815, something not questioned at the time by most officers and generals.[33]

This does surely suggest that there was some militarization of values. Military service was now broadly accepted as *one* precondition for political citizenship, as scholars have observed of Prussia and other German states that after 1815 maintained a system of military conscription.[34] But next to military service other preconditions were required: a Christian faith, education and property, and, of course, being male. It was not only Jewish men, but also workers and women, who were excluded from equal rights of political citizenship. Even middle-class men had to fight in German Central Europe until the Democratic Revolution of 1848–1849 and its aftermath to get basic political rights. Universal suffrage was not introduced until the November Revolution of 1918.[35] In respect of the importance of military service as a precondition for male political citizenship, Britain might appear to be the outstanding exception, a country that resisted conscription until it faced, in 1916, an apparently insurmountable crisis of manpower. But that does not mean that Britain was unaffected by militarism in the post-1815 years.[36]

In his discussion of British high politics, John Bew concentrates more on the structures of government, essentially on the survival of wartime government and exceptional legislation into a postwar period that continued to be characterized by a sense of crisis. In particular, the British establishment lived in fear of revolution and insubordination, forces which they believed had been released by the war with France and which found their most concrete form in Luddism, machine-breaking, and mass demonstrations like that held at St Peter's Fields in Manchester in 1819. To the British Conservative ministers who remained in power for much of the postwar period the distinction between war and peace, between different sorts of struggle, remained somewhat fuzzy, and their instinctive answer to workers' demands was to treat them as a political challenge which had to be resisted by force. Domestic politics, like foreign war, justified a military solution. To that degree, British politics, too, emerged from the Napoleonic Wars tinged with a nascent militarism.[37]

John R. Maass, in his analysis of North Carolina after the American War of Independence, deliberately focuses on the local content of politics in a state which had always been hyper-conscious of its own interests and rights. But here, too, he finds that military participation in the war effort against Britain attained a particular significance in the postwar era, when it explained much of the political jockeying that marked relations between the North Carolinian state and the fledgling government of the Confederation. It was not just an issue of who paid for the conflict, but whether local autonomy could be adequately restored once the war was over. In the end it would appear that the states often ended up surrendering more sovereignty than they had imagined as a consequence of military mobilization. For, as Maass concludes, when Carolinians could see that 'the state's financial and commercial matters were improving; that western land issues had been resolved; and that the new Federal Union was more respectable than that which had waged war so disjointedly, they opted to align their state with it, and completed their revolutionary settlement'.[38]

Moving from the strictly political to the politico-cultural, John A. Davis examines the Italian context where the experience of the Napoleonic Empire left somewhat conflicting images and memories. His chapter underlines the French concern to produce the men who would provide administrators, judges and soldiers for the Napoleonic Empire, and notions of masculinity and martial virtue that were identified with France and the French.[39] This links with some of Michael Broers' writing on Italy, and especially with French contempt for the effeminate sons of Italian noble families, those who were unwilling to fill the leadership roles the French demanded. In this process Napoleon created what Broers calls a 'subaltern Italy'.[40]

Gender stereotypes played an important part in these derogatory images of Italian manhood. But constructions of a heroic and virile masculinity—and of effeminate male 'others'—were also used by many other governments to mobilize men for war at this time. They were called to arms as 'protectors' of their families, their homes and their countries. It was their task to liberate their nation or secure its independence. Only men who willingly fulfilled their 'manly' obligations could label themselves 'men' and could stay or become citizens. For young, single men military service became a 'rite the passage' to adult manhood. They could hope to marry after the war and become heads of households themselves.[41] What happened to these militarized masculine ideals after the wars ended? How did ideas about the gender order change after the wars? How did these changes affect politics? These are questions Catherine Davies discusses in her chapter on the gender order of postwar politics in Spanish South America and Spain. She compares the constructions of femininity and masculinity in the political discourse in Spanish America following the Wars of Liberation with those which they could expect to occupy in Spain itself, and identifies similarities, despite the fact that Spain in the 1830s and 1840s was ruled by a Queen. The focus in the debates was on women and the roles allowed to them and requested from them in the war and postwar times. Women had supported the war in many different ways—by collecting money, organizing war charity and offering medical service—, and they also played a symbolic role during the Wars of Independence, of course. Their support for war represented the unity of the entire nation. Individual heroines could even achieve a rare prominence.[42] But once the wars were over, Davies observes,

> in Spanish America, as in Europe and the rest of the Americas, it was considered self-evident that the political sphere should be restricted to men, of all classes and races, as long as they were literate to a degree and economically solvent, and to exclude all women, irrespective of class, race, education, or wealth.[43]

The gender dimension of demobilization and of the memory of the wars of the Era of the Atlantic Revolutions is a subject that needs further scholarly attention. War as a 'gendering activity'—one that ritually marks the gender of every member of a society in war propaganda, yet at the same time questions these discursively constructed gender lines in everyday practice because of the urgent need for female war support—destabilizes dominant prewar ideas about the gender order. Thus, in postwar periods, it becomes all the more necessary to stabilize the gender order and with it the social order. And one important instrument for this 'regendering' of postwar societies is the construction of national war memories that are themselves highly gendered.[44]

Restoring postwar economies and reordering societies

The book then moves to discuss the short- and long-term aftermath of war in economy and society and the related policies: the ways in which countries sought to restore their economies and to reorder their societies to take account of the return of peace. What is most interesting here, in a period that is often represented as one of aggressive state-building, is how relatively limited state power often seems to have been when compared to the contributions of individuals or the efforts of civil society. States might have had a monopoly of armed force in wartime, but they did not enjoy the same degree of social and fiscal control when war was over, with the consequence that civil society comes across in these chapters as a more powerful force than one is generally led to believe in the historiography of Restoration Europe. This is true even of that area, the economy, where the state might be assumed to have the greatest control.

The French restoration government, as David Todd shows in his chapter, tried to expand Atlantic trade and engineer a return to the commercial prosperity of the Ancien Régime. Ultimately this economic strategy would prove unsuccessful, as France's external trade stagnated in the face of broader economic forces and the ensuing commercial malaise helped to nurture disaffection for the regime. Yet the strategy was not irrational or doomed to fail. Hopes of a revival were informed by nostalgia for a better world, but also by memories of the rapid commercial recoveries that had followed previous returns to peace in 1763, 1783 and 1802. Past experience suggested that it might work again.[45]

The other chapters in this section all point to the importance of private initiative in tackling different aspects of a postwar world where the outreach of governments was still strikingly limited. Katherine B. Aaslestad examines the cost of the Wars of 1813–1815 on the urban societies of Hamburg and Leipzig and compares the role of civil society in the relief effort. Both cities had been devastated by war and occupation and by the diseases and plagues that accompanied passing armies. She emphasizes the importance of private initiatives, most especially those of the various patriotic associations, which, frequently led and inspired by women from the city's elite families, raised money for a host of charitable works.[46] There was a significant international element here, too, with the involvement of merchants and charitable groups from across Europe, not least from Britain, an involvement that only underlines the limited efficacy of government in social disasters on this scale.

The same reliance on individual initiative is evident in Sarah C. Chambers' chapter on the fate of refugees from the Wars of Independence in South America. These refugees included royal bureaucrats and magistrates who fled or requested a transfer to Cuba, where their pleas for assistance set off policy debates over where they should establish residence, what financial support they should receive until they could return to their posts and, later, whether they should be given preference in appointments to new positions. The Spanish government might wish to help them, but Chambers shows that the extent of that help was limited. Individuals—women as well as men—stepped in to fill voids created by the absence of meaningful government control. They often did so as merchants and entrepreneurs, seizing opportunities to profit from the war and its aftermath, and among those who did so were people who had previously been marginalized by their class, color or gender.[47]

One very interesting example is provided by Kit Candlin and Cassandra Pybus in a chapter that explores the entanglement of race, gender and power in the revolutionary Caribbean. It challenges the current understanding of the dynamic between gender, race and power by examining the role of entrepreneurial women of color as key actors in the contested, multinational colonies of the southern Caribbean. Such women were part of a highly successful and economically tenacious free-colored community that exploded after the American Revolutionary War to become a particular feature of this multicultural and volatile region, at a time when allegiances to Spain, France and England were in a state of flux. In discussions of the Caribbean in this period, free women of color are rarely noticed, except as manipulative or parasitic concubines of the white male elite. Candlin and Pybus argue that free women of color were often highly entrepreneurial, operating substantial colonial enterprises and exploiting extensive commercial connections, with business and kinship networks stretching across the West Indies and extending into Europe. Again, it is individuals, entrepreneurs and market forces that appear significant for the postwar recovery.[48]

Postwar cultures and contested war memories

But how, more generally, did the experience of war affect postwar political cultures and produce memories for future generations, memories which were often fiercely contested? This vital question provides the subject matter of the final section of the book. A key question here relates to the conditions under which contested collective memories of war tend to divide or to heal. One possible conclusion might be that with time there is an ineluctable healing process, in that time allows for a degree of forgetting and for the development of a single agreed narrative of events.[49]

Gregory T. Knouff develops this theme with respect to Loyalist experiences and memories of the American War of Independence in New Hampshire. Revolutionary authorities identified Loyalists as traitors—as much in terms of what individuals said as what they did. They were denounced in gendered and familial metaphors befitting the need to construct an image of a domestic enemy who refused to show fidelity to the new state. In response, Loyalists constructed a collective identity during and after the Revolutionary War that inverted this formulation. They fostered a view of themselves as faithful British subjects victimized by rebel traitors who seduced the masses with emotive propaganda coupled with the threat of brutal repression. Thus, the Loyalist memory of the war revolved around a just, yet lost cause that was overwhelmed by a small group of self-interested cynics who had seized power by manipulating imagery through language and intolerance of dissent.

But it is not only in a newly independent and mainly rural colony that memories of the wars became distorted.[50] Alexander M. Martin looks at the Russian memory of 1812 and of a Moscow that came to symbolize Russian identity. Moscow, Russia's largest city, was the principal site where European urban culture penetrated into the interior of the Russian Empire. The Napoleonic invasion of 1812 left the city physically ruined and socially divided, and dealt a severe blow to the effort to make Russia a fully-fledged

European country. In the immediate aftermath of the Russian campaign, and determined above all to restore social harmony, the regime eschewed prosecutions for wartime looters and collaborators and offered assistance to the economically devastated middle classes. In the decades that followed, it took a twofold approach to strengthening stability. On the one hand, it resumed the long-term project of Europeanization by restoring the spatial, social, and institutional structures created in Moscow in the age of enlightened absolutism. On the other hand, it departed from Enlightenment tradition. In the end, it was not the Moscow of western modernization, nor yet of the regime's urban policies: it was a Moscow—as in Tolstoi's *War and Peace*—peopled by aristocrats and peasants from which the middle strata and their Europeanized urban lifestyle were notably absent.[51]

Both Knouff and Martin approach the history and memory of the postwar years from a regional and national perspective, whereas Andrew Lambert offers a comparative approach in his analysis of the military, political and cultural legacy of the Anglo-American War of 1812–1815 in the United States and Britain. He shows how America's oceanic vision gave way to a new, transcontinental gaze. In 1812, America may have lost the war, but it secured cultural independence from Britain, and in the process acquired a new identity. Painters and illustrators vied in their bid to make the frontier, and with it western expansion, into the dominant theme of American culture. In Britain the war was quickly forgotten, peace had been greeted with relief by a nation exhausted by twenty-two years of world war, while statesmen devoted their efforts to rebuilding Europe, keeping France quiet, Russia as far east as possible, and setting up a balanced state system to avoid future problems.[52]

The final three chapters extend the chronology across the long nineteenth century. Matthew Brown examines the making of a Latin American hero in the person of Simón Bolívar, and shows how he was appropriated in the formation of national identity across the new nations of Spanish America. This appropriation continues to the present day, with Hugo Chávez exploiting popular memories of the Wars of Independence, their protagonists, victors and victims by casting Bolívar as his inspiration and thus seeking to tap into the broadly-held, popularly-constructed myth of Bolívar as national redeemer.[53]

In the old continent, too, memories of victories in the Napoleonic Wars came to enjoy a wide resonance in the countries that had fought in them. Karen Hagemann examines the construction of the collective memory of the Battle of Leipzig from 16–19 October 1813 and the contested recollections of the Wars of 1813–1815 in German Central Europe more generally. Her focus is on the celebrations commemorating this so-called 'Battle of the Nations' and on how they changed between 1813 and 1913. Hagemann argues that celebrations and rituals play a central role in the construction of the collective memory of wars, since they were holistic experiences, which addressed all the senses and were strongly shaped by emotion. Patriotic-minded contemporaries were well aware that events linked with strong emotions engrave themselves especially deeply in the memory. Their suggestions for patriotic-national celebrations were widely adopted. Despite all attempts to create national unity, however, the commemoration of the battle and the wars were highly contested and changed over time. Two main narratives emerged: a liberal German-national interpretation of the struggle as 'Wars of Liberty' by a people fighting for liberty and liberation, and a monarchic-conservative interpretation of the conflict as 'Wars of Liberation' led by the princes and generals. After the unification of Germany in 1871 by 'blood and iron', it was this second narrative that gained increasing influence.[54]

Similarly, as Alan Forrest infers, Napoleon's final defeat, at Waterloo, was then manipulated by politicians and writers to fit cultural stereotypes. Very different narratives were produced in the nations that had been engaged in the battle, and whereas nineteenth-century Britain was encouraged to wallow in a victory that Wellington claimed as his own, France remembered the battle as the epitome of a 'glorious defeat' that lent grandeur and a certain pathos to the Napoleonic legend. Over time, states began to shape these memories for their people. They increasingly controlled urban space and provided funding for monuments and memorials, which allowed them to impose their vision of the past and went some way to ensure the triumph of official narratives.[55]

If this volume demonstrates the diversity of the social and economic impact of demobilization and highlights some of the ways in which war memories were fostered, it also opens up other areas for discussion. Three questions, in particular, seem to us to cry out for further investigation. One is the role of religion in a generation dominated by war. How far did soldiers and their families turn to religion as a way of dealing with fear and grieving, as would most certainly happen in the First World War?[56] Or had the 'godlessness' of the Enlightenment and the French Revolutionary era turned people against the Church in sufficient numbers for grief to be something that they could deal with in other ways? In France this may have been partly so: it is interesting that Napoleon's armies had no place for religion, no posts for almoners in the regiments, but this was not the case in many other armies such as the Austrian, Prussian and Russian. The Prussian state even ordered that Catholic, Protestant and Jewish soldiers should attend the same religious services in the army and listen to the same sermons by field chaplains.[57] In the Prussian monarchy, as elsewhere in Europe, the era from 1780 to 1830 was characterized by something of a religious revival, perhaps even the beginnings of a second confessional age: was this simply a reaction to the Enlightenment, or should we seek an explanation in the adversity caused by the ravages of war?[58]

A second question concerns the social and individual costs of warfare and their gender dimension. In postwar societies that lacked a governmental and military infrastructure to heal the wounds of war, local communities, the churches, patriotic associations and, last but not least, families played an important role in postwar reconstruction. They had to support the thousands of war victims—unemployed soldiers returning from the front, prisoners of war, sick and disabled veterans, war widows and orphans, as well as impoverished refugees. Especially in the families, but also in the churches and associations, it was mainly women who were responsible for providing this service. It was their female task to integrate the returning soldiers into civilian life, heal the wounds of war and mourn the fallen soldiers. We know very little about the consequences of the wars of this period for families and individuals—men and women—back home.[59]

A third question is the degree to which veterans were able to reintegrate into civil society once peace was signed. Did their war service bring any social advantages, or did they languish on the margins of society, disabled by wounds and mental illness, and poorly equipped to make their way in civil society? Thanks to recent French research we know something of what happened to the old soldiers of Napoleon's armies in France, but our knowledge remains more fragmentary for much of the rest of Europe and the Americas.[60] One answer, of course, for those who were too unsettled to face the challenges of civilian life, was to seek adventure elsewhere, in other wars, often on different continents. British survivors of Waterloo might sign up for colonial service, some among them in the Australian convict settlements of New South Wales and Van Diemen's Land.[61] Napoleonic soldiers sought adventure in the Americas, whether in the South American Wars of Liberation or on the American frontier, in Texas and along the Gulf of Mexico.[62] We might well ask how far peripheral wars after 1815—on the American frontier, in the Caucasus, in the Balkans, in Algeria—provided an opportunity to soften the transition from war to peace, providing an outlet for veterans incapable of adjusting to the postwar world and for a new generation keen to share in the glory of their ancestors.

The perspective of postcolonial studies

In the wide-ranging and often provocative essay that concludes this volume, Lloyd Kramer offers some reflections on how the study of this period has evolved over the past half century, or 'several bicentennial historical generations'. He shows how historians have increasingly come to view the Atlantic world of the Age of Revolutions as a single entity, with commerce and political ideology passing back and forth between Europe and the Americas, and with each side influencing the other as country after country came to face the challenges posed by revolution and war. This approach not only questions many of the assumptions that have dominated national histories of the period; it also demands new thinking about historical sources and methods. Kramer shows how historians might develop new perspectives on the period by drawing on other disciplines, not least on the burgeoning field of postcolonial studies which has been such a growth area in the study of Europe's overseas empires. Postcolonial theory does not only insist that the world has been decisively shaped by empire. It emphasizes the enduring effects of the experience of colonialism in a postcolonial context, underlining the power of memory and the strength of historical continuities, and showing how the resentments produced by the colonial experience continue to leave a deep legacy in society and culture.

Kramer suggests that the value of this approach is not restricted to Europe's ex-colonies, and that postcolonial theory has lessons for European historians, too. It should, he says, be completely persuasive to anyone who studies the legacies of the revolutionary upheavals in the Atlantic world and of the Napoleonic Empire across Europe. For the legacy of the wars and revolutions of these years are still to be seen all around us. We still live within institutions, ideologies, economic systems, and national states that were constructed in the era between 1770 and 1830, and in this respect the Napoleonic Empire in mainland Europe may not be so different from the extra-European colonial systems that were being challenged in the United States, across the Caribbean, and in Central and South America. In Italy, in Holland, or in Dalmatia, the local elites were judged and given responsibility by the French in accordance with a cultural judgement: were they the sort of people who could be trusted to administer, to hand down justice, to collect taxes, the tasks that were required by a modern, secular empire? Were they, in other words, imbued with the same competences, the same values, the same sense of service to the polity as Napoleon would expect of his *notables* in France? It was, as Michael Broers has suggested, a form of colonialism within Europe, akin to that imposed by Britain on its overseas empire, where the colonized population were expected to act and to respond like Frenchmen.

Contemporaries across Europe referred to their wars against Napoleon's Empire as 'wars of independence', using the same language as in Britain's North American colonies and in nineteenth-century Latin America. But the idea of anti-colonial struggles within Europe can be extended further. The French historian Pierre Serna has recently suggested that the European revolutions of the later eighteenth century also had a strongly anti-colonial aspect, describing them as wars of independence by peoples against the authority structures imposed by Ancien Régime monarchies and empires. Eighteenth-century revolutions, he suggests—in Geneva, for instance, or in the Belgian provinces of the Austrian Empire—should be seen as struggles between the periphery and the center, between the outer margins and the locus of centralizing power. Warming to his theme, he takes the analogy to what may be its logical conclusion, and to France itself. Should not the French Revolution, too, be seen, at least initially, as a war of independence, an anti-colonial struggle fought by municipalities and provinces eager to free themselves from the tutelage of Versailles? Is it so ridiculous to revisit 1789 from this perspective, he asks, and see not the unitary state of the French monarchy but a country that had overlapping loyalties and identities, a state that contained a variety of *petites patries,* different administrations and jurisdictions each eager to assert its rights even as it made the necessary gestures of loyalty to the King? Seen in this light, Lyon and Marseille were not so different from Port-au-Prince or Basse-Terre, to say nothing of Naples or Boston.[63] This approach is still very much work in progress. But it clearly holds out considerable promise, and Lloyd Kramer is surely right when he suggests that the application of postcolonial theory opens up new and challenging research questions not only in the Americas but across the whole of the Atlantic world.

Notes

1. See Georg Heuberger and Anton Merk (eds), *Moritz Daniel Oppenheim: Die Entdeckung des jüdischen Selbstbewußtseins in der Kunst* (Cologne, 1999); and Maurice Berger and Joan Rosenbaum (eds), *Masterworks of the Jewish Museum* (New York, 2004), 42–43.
2. See Horst Fischer, *Judentum, Staat und Heer in Preussen im frühen 19. Jahrhundert: Zur Geschichte der staatlichen Judenpolitik* (Tübingen, 1968); and more recently Karen Hagemann, *Revisiting Prussia's Wars against Napoleon: History, Culture and Memory* (Cambridge, 2015), 113–129.
3. See Berger, *Masterworks.*
4. See, for instance, Timothy Wilson-Smith, *Napoleon and his Artists* (London, 1996); Holger Hoock, *Empires of the Imagination: Politics, War and the Arts in the British World, 1750–1850* (London, 2010); Todd Porterfield and Susan L. Siegfried, *Staging Empire: Napoleon, Ingres, and David* (University Park, PA, 2006); and David O'Brien, *After the Revolution: Antoine-Jean Gros, Painting and Propaganda Under Napoleon* (University Park, PA, 2006).
5. Donald Stoker et al. (eds), *Conscription in the Napoleonic Era: A Revolution in Military Affairs?* (London, 2008).
6. See for example, Christophe Belaubre et al. (eds), *Napoleon's Atlantic: The Impact of Napoleonic Empire in the Atlantic World* (Leiden, 2010).
7. See for example, Roger Chickering and Stig Förster (eds), *War in an Age of Revolution, 1775–1815* (Cambridge, 2010).
8. See Ibid.; and Alan Forrest et al. (eds), *Soldiers, Citizens and Civilians: Experiences and Perceptions of the French Wars, 1790–1820* (Basingstoke, 2009); and Richard Bessel et al. (eds), *War, Empire and Slavery, 1770–1830* (Basingstoke, 2010).
9. David A. Bell, *The First Total War: Napoleon's Europe and the Birth of Warfare as We Know It* (Boston, MA, 2007); and Jean-Yves Guiomar, *L'invention de la guerre totale, 18e –20e siècle* (Paris, 2004).
10. See for example, Erica Charters et al. (eds), *Civilians and War in Europe, 1618–1815* (Liverpool, 2012), 182–261.
11. Philip G. Dwyer and Lyndall Ryan (eds), *Massacre in the Old and New Worlds, c. 1780–1820,* special issue, *Journal of Genocide Research* 15/2 (2013).
12. Katherine B. Aaslestad and Johan Joor (eds), *Revisiting Napoleon's Continental System: Local, Regional and European Experiences* (Basingstoke, 2014).
13. Paul W. Schroeder, *The Transformation of European Politics, 1763–1848* (Oxford, 1994), 514–516.

14. See Tamar Herzog, 'Identities and Processes of Identification in the Atlantic World', in *The Oxford Handbook of the Atlantic World, 1450–1850*, ed. Nicholas Canny and Philip Morgan (Oxford, 2011), 480–495.
15. Peter Lorge, 'War and Warfare in China, 1450–1815', in *War in the Early Modern World, 1450–1815*, ed. Jeremy Black (London, 1999), 87–103.
16. Christopher Bayly, *The Birth of the Modern World, 1780–1914* (Oxford, 2004), 125–126.
17. For a striking instance of this global mobility see Linda Colley, *The Ordeal of Elizabeth Marsh: How a Remarkable Woman Crossed Seas and Empires to Become Part of World History* (London, 2008).
18. Lynn Hunt, 'The Global Financial Origins of 1789', in *The French Revolution in Global Perspective*, ed. Suzanne Desan et al. (Ithaca, NY, 2013), 32–43.
19. Bailey Stone, *The Genesis of the French Revolution: A Global-Historical Interpretation* (Cambridge, 1994), 99.
20. See David Armitage and Sanjay Subrahmanyam (eds), *The Age of Revolutions in Global Context, c.1760–1840* (Basingstoke, 2010); also David Armitage, *The Declaration of Independence: A Global History* (Cambridge, MA, 2007).
21. Alan Forrest et al. (eds), *War Memories: The Revolutionary and Napoleonic Wars in Modern European Culture* (Basingstoke, 2012), esp. 1–37; and Michael A. McDonnell et al. (eds), *Remembering the Revolution: Memory, History, and Nation Making from Independence to the Civil War* (Amherst, MA, 2015).
22. For France, for instance, see Alan B. Spitzer, *The French Generation of 1820* (Princeton, NJ, 1987).
23. Michael Broers, 'Civilized, Rational Behaviour? The Concept and Practice of Surrender in the Revolutionary and Napoleonic Wars', in *How Fighting Ends: A History of Surrender*, ed. Holger Afflerbach and Hew Strachan (Oxford, 2012), 229–238.
24. See, for instance, John Darwin, *The Empire Project: the Rise and Fall of the British World-System, 1830–1970* (Cambridge, 2009).
25. David A. Bell, 'The Birth of Militarism in the Age of Democratic Revolutions', in this volume, pp. 66–91.
26. On the Russian campaign, see Dominic Lieven, *Russia Against Napoleon: The Battle for Europe, 1807 to 1814* (London, 2009); and Adam Zamoyski, *Moscow 1812: Napoleon's Fatal March* (London, 2004).
27. Stefan Dudink et al. (eds), *Masculinities in Politics and War: Gendering Modern History* (Manchester, 2004), 3–40; and idem et al. (eds), *Representing Masculinity: Citizenship in Modern Western Culture* (Basingstoke, 2008).
28. See also Janet M. Hartley, *Russia, 1762–1825: Military Power, the State, and the People* (Westport, CN, 2008).
29. See also Christine Haynes, *'Our Friends, the Enemies': The First Allied Occupation of France, 1815–1818* (forthcoming).
30. Schroeder, *The Transformation*, 575–582.
31. See also, Leighton S. James, *Witnessing the Revolutionary and Napoleonic Wars in German Central Europe* (Basingstoke, 2013).
32. See also, Rafe Baufarb, *Bonapartists in the Borderlands: French Exiles and Refugees on the Gulf Coast, 1815–1835* (Tuscaloosa, AL, 2005).
33. See Hagemann, *Revisiting*, 113–129; and Fischer, *Judentum*.
34. See for example, Thomas Hippler, *Citizens, Soldiers and National Armies: Military Service in France and Germany, 1789–1830* (London, 2008), 163–189; more critical is Ute Frevert, *A Nation in Barracks: Modern Germany, Military Conscription and Civil Society* (Oxford, 2004).

35. Hagemann, *Revisiting*, 113–129 and 155–170.
36. Sonya O. Rose, '"Fit to Fight but Not to Vote?" Masculinity and Citizenship in Britain, 1832–1918', Dudink et al. *Representing Masculinity*, 131–150.
37. See also, John Bew, *Castlereagh: A Life* (Oxford, 2012).
38. John R. Maass is currently working on a book about North Carolina and the French and Indian War (1754–1763).
39. See also John A. Davis, *Naples and Napoleon: Southern Italy and the European Revolutions (1780–1860)* (Oxford, 2006).
40. Michael Broers, *The Napoleonic Empire in Italy, 1796–1814* (Basingstoke, 2005), 291–194.
41. Karen Hagemann et al. (eds), *Gender, War and Politics: Transatlantic Perspectives, 1775–1830* (Basingstoke, 2010), 93–168.
42. See also Ibid., 169–227; and Catherine Davies et al., *South American Independence: Gender, Politics, Text* (Liverpool, 2006).
43. Catherine Davies, 'The Gender Order of Postwar Politics: Comparing Spanish South America and Spain, 1810s–1850s', in this volume, 310–338.
44. See as an example, Karen Hagemann, 'Reconstructing "Front" and "Home": Gendered Experiences and Memories of the German Wars against Napoleon—A Case Study', *War in History* 16/1 (2009): 25–50.
45. See also David Todd, *Free Trade and its Enemies in France, 1814–1851* (Cambridge, 2015).
46. See also, Katherine B. Aaslestad, *Place and Politics: Local Identity, Civic Culture, and German Nationalism in North Germany during the Revolutionary Era* (Leiden, 2005).
47. See also, Sarah C. Chambers, *Families in War and Peace: Chile from Colony to Nation* (Durham, NC, 2015); and idem, *From Subjects to Citizens: Honor, Gender, and Politics in Arequipa, Peru, 1780–1854* (University Park, PA, 1999).
48. See also, Kit Candlin and Cassandra Pybus, *Enterprising Women, Race Gender and Power in the Revolutionary Atlantic 1770–1830* (Basingstoke, 2015).
49. Forrest et al., *War Memories*; and McDonnell et al., *Remembering*.
50. See also Gregory T. Knouff, *Soldiers' Revolution: Pennsylvanians in Arms and the Forging of Early American Identity* (Pennsylvania, PA, 2003); and idem, *A Seductive Sedition: Loyalists, Language, and Power in Revolutionary New Hampshire* (forthcoming).
51. See also, Alexander M. Martin, *Enlightened Metropolis: Constructing Imperial Moscow, 1762–1855* (Oxford, 2013).
52. See also, Andrew Lambert, *The Challenge: Britain, Against America in the Naval War of 1812* (London, 2012).
53. See also, Matthew Brown, *Adventuring through Spanish Colonies: Simón Bolívar, Foreign Mercenaries and the Birth of New Nations* (Liverpool, 2006).
54. See also, Hagemann, *Revisiting*.
55. See also, Alan Forrest, *Waterloo* (Oxford, 2015).
56. Most notably for World War I, perhaps, Annette Becker, *War and Faith: the Religious Imagination in France, 1914–1930* (Oxford, 1998).
57. See Karen Hagemann, *'Mannlicher Muth und Teutsche Ehre': Nation, Militär und Geschlecht zur Zeit der Antinapoleonischen Kriege Preußens* (Paderborn, 2002), 143–148.
58. See, for instance, Nigel Aston, *Christianity and Revolutionary Europe, 1750–1830* (Cambridge, 2002).
59. See Hagemann et al., *Gender, War and Politics*, 169–226 and 307–360.
60. Natalie Petiteau, *Lendemains d'Empire: Les soldats de Napoléon dans la France du dix-neuvième siècle* (Paris, 2003); and Stéphane Calvet, *Les officiers charentais de Napoléon au dix-neuvième siècle* (Paris, 2010).

61. Christine Wright, *Wellington's Men in Australia: Peninsular War Veterans and the Making of Empire, c. 1820–1840* (Basingstoke, 2011), 175–178.
62. Blaufarb, *Bonapartists*, 61–64 and 86–116.
63. Pierre Serna, 'Toute révolution est guerre d'indépendance', in *Pour quoi faire la Révolution?*, ed. Jean-Luc Chappey et al., (Marseille, 2012), 19–49, here 37–40.

Map 1.1 The United States of America, 1783
Source: Edmaps.com (free online cartographic resource): http://www.edmaps.com/united_states_america_1783.gif (Accessed, May 6, 2015).

Map 1.2 Europa after the Congress of Vienna, 1815

Source: Edmaps.com (free online cartographic resource): http://www.edmaps.com/europe_1815.gif (Accessed, May 6, 2015).

Map 1.3 The new nations of Latin America, 1830
Source: Judith G. Coffin and Robert C. Stacey, *Western Civilizations*, 2 Vols. Sixteenth Edition: W. W. Norton & Company Inc., 2008, Vol. 2.

2

The Birth of Militarism in the Age of Democratic Revolutions

David A. Bell

In the year 1813, as Napoleon Bonaparte's empire was crumbling, Benjamin Constant issued one of the earliest and most powerful condemnations of what we now call militarism. It was highly dangerous, he warned, 'to create in a country ... a large mass of men imbued with an exclusively military spirit'. Would these men, at the end of a war, shed their attitudes along with their uniforms? To the contrary, 'those without weapons strike them as an ignoble mob, laws as useless subtleties ... opposition as disorder and reasoning as revolt'. Constant insisted that in a modern world of constitutional regimes and commerce, a military 'spirit of conquest' was a menacing vestige of an earlier age.[1]

Two hundred years later, Constant's words still seem to ring true. Most modern observers have continued to see militarism not merely as a danger to modern democratic societies, but as antithetical to them, from both theoretical and historical perspectives. As Emile Durkheim wrote in *Suicide*: 'Military morality is a vestige; it resembles the morality of primitive societies'.[2] This remark would still find considerable support today, even among those otherwise uncomfortable with the adjective 'primitive'. The sociologist Hans Joas has argued that because of militarism's perceived anachronistic qualities, social scientists and historians have for the most part given it relatively little attention.[3] The historians who have done most to investigate the history of militarism are, for the most part, historians of Germany. They have concentrated their efforts heavily on the question of that country's 'special historical path' to modernity (*Sonderweg*), and the way that a supposedly precocious German militarism helps explain the pathologies of the twentieth century. In particular, they often trace this militarism back to a regime that made for one of the least imaginable seedbeds of modern democracy: absolutist Prussia.[4]

In this essay, I will propose a different account of the birth of modern militarism, looking closely at changes in what could be called the 'political culture of war' in the Age of Atlantic Revolutions, with a particular focus on the United States and France. Perhaps, I will suggest, militarism does not actually represent a vestige of an earlier age, one that has reared up only when modern constitutional regimes fail. Perhaps, indeed, the most common forms of modern militarism had their origins in the Age of Democratic Revolutions and Revolutionary War, and are symbiotically related to the revolutionary regimes that emerged in this period.

Militarism and the 'Military/Civilian' distinction

In 1921, a German essayist named Friedrich Sternthal offered the following, useful definition of militarism: 'the subordination of all other aspects of life to the military one, and the domination of civilian life by military ideas and values'.[5] Sternthal himself associated militarism particularly with Germany's Second Empire, but militarism defined in this way has played a central role in the histories of many societies across the world. Where it has flourished, it has also generally involved an assertion of the moral superiority conferred by military service, thanks to the association of this service with three distinct qualities: strength, discipline and selflessness, including especially the readiness of warriors to die for their countries.

Sternthal, like most students of the subject, assumed that militarism is a potentially universal phenomenon, capable of arising in any society with organized armed forces. But is this really the case? His definition assumes a distinction that we today see as natural and take utterly for granted, namely the division of human societies into distinct, separate 'military' and 'civilian' spheres. Past societies, however, have not always recognized this distinction in the same way, or organized themselves on this basis. In fact, in the modern West, the way we understand the distinction emerged only in the age of democratic revolutions. Only in this period did it become possible even to conceive of distinctly 'military' ideas, values and practices imposing themselves on 'civilian' life. And without this conceptual basis in place, the conditions under which militarism could develop simply did not yet exist. Militarism is by no means an *inevitable* product of the military/civilian distinction now recognized in most societies. But the distinction engenders a *potential* for militarism which can be very difficult to overcome, and which exists in most modern states. Obviously, I do not mean to argue that military forces did not yet exist as distinct institutions before the age of revolutions, or that they were not perceived as such. Nor do I mean to claim that military service was not identified as a distinct, honourable vocation long before the age of revolutions. What I mean to argue is something different, namely that society was not seen as divided into distinct, separate, and potentially opposed military and civilian spheres, each possessing its own distinct set of values and practices.

Language provides one of the most telling pieces of evidence for this proposition. We can, of course, look back at past societies and classify their inhabitants as 'military' or 'civilian' according to our own definitions. Yet in the English language the word 'civilian' did not exist with its modern meaning before 1794—until then, it signified only an expert in civil law, Roman law. A similar situation prevailed in German and French, where words with the meaning of 'civilian' made their first recorded appearances in 1790 and 1834, respectively (for French, I am referring to the noun, as opposed to the adjective 'civil'). The concept of 'civilian' life that we invoke easily today—for instance when we speak of civilian victims, or civilian control of armed forces—did not yet exist.[6]

The reason for this absence becomes somewhat clearer if we consider the difficulty of relating the modern concept of the 'civilian' to two of the most important models of social order that early modern Europeans had at their disposal. The first of these was the model of the three estates: clergy, nobility, and commons. In one sense, the second estate, also defined as 'those who fight' (*bellatori*) certainly amounted to a military sphere of sorts. It is therefore tempting to define the other two, in contrast, as civilian. True, by the eighteenth century, many male nobles did not serve in the military. Some countries, France most obviously, had entire formal categories of nobles attached to non-military callings. Still, the overall links remained strong and clear, and in many countries, a large majority of nobles did serve. Even in France, a large majority of those elected to the Second Estate of the Estates General in 1789 had military experience.[7] On the other hand, the second estate can hardly be equated with 'the military' in general, because of course it did not include common soldiers. And while the second estate had its distinct values and practices, these were not imagined in any way to be at odds with those of the other two estates, the clergy and the commons. The model of the three estates was a functional model of society—the three estates theoretically had complementary functions within the greater social body. To suggest that commoners should adopt the values and practices of the second estate was, at least in theory, nonsensical, equivalent to asking an arm to behave like an ear. In this model, quite clearly, a military leadership class was seen as an integral part of the larger social body. And so, this model did not define a distinct and separate 'civilian' sphere from which military personnel and military activity were absent.[8]

A second great model to which Europeans had access was the model of the ancient republic, and particularly the Roman Republic whose texts were foundational to early modern European elite education. In this model, every citizen was potentially a soldier, ready to sacrifice his life for the fatherland. Therefore, in theory, this model permitted no division whatsoever between what we would now term civilian and military spheres. There was simply a seamlessly united civic whole, all of whose members stood ready to take up arms to defend the fatherland. In this model, too, the military was integral to society as a whole, and in no sense could be classified as a separate sphere whose values and practices challenged those of 'civilians'.

It is worth discussing the republican model in greater detail, however, because republicanism matters greatly in the larger story addressed by this essay. In the early modern European imagination, the story of the ancient republics, and especially of the Roman one, was a story of corruption, decline and degeneration. The age of Junius Brutus and the Horatii gave way to the age of Sulla and Marius, Pompey and Caesar. As Rome expanded, so the story went, its armies became divorced from the civic life of the Republic; soldiers felt more loyalty to their generals than to the city; and finally, Caesar brought his army across the Rubicon, extinguishing republican liberty and the Republic itself. This process of degeneration, in other words, was also a project of distinction, of sorting out, as the life of the military became detached from the life of the city, until the two indeed existed as separate and opposed entities.[9]

This belief made up a crucial plank of what historians now think of as early modern classical republican language, going back to that unparalleled admirer of the Roman Republic, Machiavelli. To cite his 1520 *Art of War*: 'Many are of the opinion that no two things go less well with one another, or are less similar, than military life and civil life' (*vita militare* and *vita civile*).[10] But while Machiavelli recognized the distinction, as a good republican he saw it as an unnatural one—he called it 'bad and corrupt'. He linked it to the decadence of the Italian city states, and their practice of hiring foreign mercenaries, rather than forming true citizen armies. The idea that 'civil life', when divorced and separate from military activity, might have any coherence, unity and value to it, was in fact anathema to him. So, while Machiavelli's modern readers naturally liken his distinction of *vita militare* and *vita civile* to their own distinction between military and civilian spheres, the comparison is untenable. The point comes through graphically if we look at how Machiavelli has been translated over time. Modern translations consistently render his '*civile*' as 'civilian'. But in a translation from eighteenth-century England, in a single paragraph, the Italian '*civile*' is translated as 'civil', 'common', and 'of a Citizen'. Clearly the translator did not know exactly what to make of the word '*civile*', and had no concept of 'civilian life' at his disposal.[11] In short, neither of the two models of social organization I have just been discussing allowed Europeans to imagine a military/civilian distinction of the sort we are familiar with today existing in their own societies—although republicanism did contribute to the way patterns of thought changed.

It is important to stress that the absence of the modern way of making the distinction was not just a matter of semantics, but was related to very real social practices. Today, military forces possess what could be called an elaborate infrastructure of difference from civilian society: barracks, bases, educational institutions, legal systems, distinctive forms of dress, and so forth. It is this infrastructure that allows us to conceive of a wholly non-military 'civilian' sphere of life outside its (often literal) walls. But this infrastructure was only beginning to emerge in the seventeenth and eighteenth centuries. To be sure, armies and navies existed as distinct institutions with their own structures, rules, and even forms of speech. Yet officers in particular did not draw sharp lines between their professional military roles, and their social identities as nobles.[12] And while military service remained a crucial component of what it meant to be a noble, it was by no means the only component of noble identity, and the lines between the different components were not always clear. In Europe, most noble officers normally spent much of the year apart from their regiments, at court or on their estates. In some countries, until quite late in the century, officers disdained wearing military uniforms, even on campaign. Relatively few of them had formal, school-based military training. Values and forms of behaviour remained strikingly similar across what could be called the twin theatres of noble life that were royal courts and the officer corps on campaign. In practice, nobles slipped back and forth seamlessly between what we would now call their 'military' and 'civilian' roles.

Furthermore, before the age of revolutions, it was still almost impossible to think of European armies as sources of independent political power—as institutions that could exist, threateningly, 'outside' the normal parameters of political life. In our own intellectual universe, in which 'military' and 'civilian' values and practices not only exist side by side but stand in potential opposition to one another, it is possible to think of military figures acting to impose their values and practices on 'civilian' political life, most graphically through the means of a military coup d'état. Early modern Europeans were intellectually familiar with the idea of a military coup, thanks to their knowledge of Roman history, and Julius Caesar in particular. But this knowledge had little relevance to the societies in which they themselves lived. The aristocratic leaders of European armies saw the most important element of their vocation as absolute loyalty to the sovereign. Was a military coup imaginable in the France of Louis XIV? Would it have made the least sense there to talk of 'civilian control of the military'? Obviously not. Even in Prussia, where the military certainly played an outsized role in domestic government, it did so as part of the royal administration, under the firm control of the king and his ministers, and not as any sort of autonomous political force.

There was one obvious possible exception to this pattern in early modern Europe: Oliver Cromwell's New Model Army, which certainly did emerge as an independent political force during the British Civil Wars. But its political independence developed above all because of the independent political and religious groups that found a home in its ranks. It did not press its political claims *as an army*—that is to say, its defenders never argued that its legitimacy as a political actor derived from its specifically military qualities, in comparison with what we would now call civilian ones.[13]

For these reasons, I would take issue with the historians who have discerned the origins of modern militarism in Ancien Régime Europe, and particularly in Prussia.[14] Prussia's King Friedrich Wilhelm I certainly fetishized his army, and almost always wore a simple officer's uniform.

As just mentioned, Prussia also integrated military officers and practices into domestic political administration to an unusual extent. This last fact encouraged an older generation of German historians to conclude, as Hans Rosenberg once wrote, that 'martial concepts of authority and of military virtues' served as models for 'civil life in general' in early modern Prussia.[15] But more recent historians of Germany such as Peter Wilson have argued against this interpretation, and suggested that Prussian rulers did not make serious efforts to extend the regimentation of the state apparatus to society in general.[16] Rather, Prussian practices represented an extreme example of the so-called 'well-ordered police state' that flourished throughout absolutist Continental Europe, and that contained a complex mixture of what we would now distinguish as military and civilian elements. To put it in a phrase, Prussia was bellicose, but not yet militarist.[17]

The birth of the 'Military/Civilian' distinction in early modern Europe

Let us now turn to the large-scale changes which, in effect, scrambled the ways Europeans envisaged the relationship between military service and societies as a whole, and made possible the modern distinction between 'military' life and 'civilian' life—and therefore, also, modern militarism. These changes were both material and intellectual in nature.

The development of large standing armies certainly constituted an important piece of the background. Between 1500 and 1700, whether or not as a consequence of a 'military revolution', astonishing new military institutions came into being: the first modern armies. They could include hundreds of thousands of soldiers and officers, differentiated by ranks, wearing uniforms, and following a military law code and written rules of discipline. During the eighteenth century there followed barracks, military schools, and, at least where common soldiers were concerned, a recognizable infrastructure of difference. Most soldiers served for long periods, cut off from the rest of society. A discourse of military professionalism developed, with the goal of turning noble officer corps into something more closely resembling a full-time profession which one entered after formal training.[18]

This institutional change contributed to two crucial intellectual changes that were already underway. First, there was the continuing development of a classical republican language of political opposition, especially in the Anglophone world, although it had some echoes in France in the struggles between the judicial *parlements* and the crown. As John Pocock emphasized many years ago, from a classical republican viewpoint, nothing was more unnatural or abhorrent than a standing army of professional soldiers. This had been Machiavelli's view, and in the late seventeenth and eighteenth centuries British Whigs harped on the theme ever more relentlessly, as the British military expanded, and as fears grew that a despotic monarch might use a standing army to curtail the liberties of the people. John Trenchard's well-known pamphlets on the subject fed into a large literature that repeated his warnings ad nauseam.[19] In Britain's American colonies, the concerns became even more pointed as the authority of the British crown was challenged in the 1760s and 1770s—and as the British government responded by sending red-coated troops to American cities to restore order. In 1774, the future American revolutionary Josiah Quincy wrote at length on the theme, concluding: 'what a deformed monster is a standing army in a free nation'.[20]

The second intellectual development was of a different order. Over the course of the eighteenth century, an increasingly influential series of thinkers developed a new critique of war itself. Theirs was not the venerable Christian critique, which decried war as a sin but at the same time recognized its inevitability, given the sinful nature of humankind. It was a theoretical and historical critique, grounded in stadial theories of history according to which human societies naturally evolved away from martial, bellicose roots, and were becoming steadily more sophisticated, polite, commercial, and peaceful. The destructiveness of the wars fought by the period's new standing armies certainly contributed to and sharpened this critique. It provided material for Louis XIV's great critic Fénelon, for the Abbé Saint-Pierre, for Baron d'Holbach, for Kant in his *Project for Perpetual Peace*, and finally for Benjamin Constant, in the text quoted at the start of this essay.[21] Along the way, it frequently turned into a critique of the ideas of valour, honour and nobility associated with the second estate. Consider for instance d'Holbach's comments in his 1776 book *Universal Morality*:

> The glory associated with conquest, war and valour in almost all countries is visibly a remnant of the savage customs that prevailed in all nations before they were civilized ... the deadly profession of war has been reputed the most noble ... thanks to a series of opinions mistakenly handed down by our barbarian ancestors, ...[22]

This critique, and the stadial theories of history they derived from, have a particular importance for the history of militarism because their vision of polite, commercial and peaceful societies was also in effect a vision of *civilian* societies: societies in which war, and the martial values associated with it, had no place. The historical distinction these authors drew between primitive and modern societies was in fact, quite precisely, a distinction between military and civilian forms of life. Benjamin Constant made the point explicitly:

> It is not true that war is always an evil. During certain periods of human history it was in the nature of man ... But the world of our day is, from this perspective, the precise opposite of the ancient world ... A government that would today speak of military glory as a goal would be

> misunderstanding the spirit of the age ... It would be engaging in a crude and deadly anachronism.[23]

Taken together, the republican and pacifist discourses radically reframed the way Europeans understood the relationship between war and society in this new age of standing armies. Classical republicanism, and the Whig fears of a British king using an army to curtail the liberties of the people, prompted the realization that the fall of the Roman Republic, and Caesarism, were not simply pieces of ancient history that bore moral lessons, but salutary examples that bore directly on the experience of their own societies. With the development of stadial theories, and eighteenth-century Enlightened pacifism, it became possible to conceive of a new sort of society—civilian society—that existed in opposition to military society, with each operating according to its own driving principles, and with its own distinct values and practices.

The military in the American and French revolutions

The discourses played important roles at the start of the period's great political revolutions. These revolutions, in both America and France, directly challenged the sovereignty of the monarchs who had previously bound civil and military authority so tightly together in their own persons. They also challenged or even overthrew the aristocratic elites who had so seamlessly combined what we now think of as military and civilian roles. They posed, in the starkest possible terms, the problem of who would control the military forces necessary for the defence of large modern states. In facing these challenges, the leaders of the revolutionary movements drew heavily on the critiques just discussed, and the critiques were contested and modified in their turn.

In the Thirteen Colonies, from the very start of pre-revolutionary agitation in the 1760's, the actions of the British standing army appeared as one of the principal abuses justifying American resistance to British authority, and, ultimately, justifying independence. Consider only the Declaration of Independence, and the long line of charges that it hurled against King George III. 'He has kept among us, in times of peace, standing armies without the consent of our legislatures', wrote Jefferson. 'He has affected to render the Military independent of and superior to the Civil Power'.[24] While George Washington recognized the need for a professional military force, modelled on British forces, in order to wage the War of Independence successfully, it was not anticipated that a large standing army would need to remain in existence after independence.[25] And this belief did not simply stem from the classical republican conviction that the soldiers would return to their farms, along with their general, a modern Cincinnatus. Some Americans, like the European thinkers just mentioned, believed that the age of war was itself coming to an end. One of the most prominent was none other than George Washington himself, who discussed the issue at length with a French officer and *philosophe* who had written about it in a popular book: the Marquis de Chastellux. In 1788 Washington wrote to Chastellux:

> It is time for the age of Knight-Errantry and mad-heroism to be at an end ... for the sake of humanity it is devoutly to be wished, that the manly employment of agriculture and the humanizing benefits of commerce, would supersede the waste of war and the rage of conquest ...[26]

In 1787–1789, when the new American constitution was debated, the relationship of what we can now call civilian and military spheres was a central concern.[27]

In France, as soon as challenges to the sovereignty of the King developed in 1789, strikingly parallel developments occurred—especially after King Louis XVI responded to the actions of the new, revolutionary National Assembly by concentrating troops around the city of Paris. The fall of the Bastille on July 14, 1789 removed the immediate threat of a military strike, but from then on, most of the nascent revolutionary movement saw the royal army in the worst possible light. In December 1789, when the deputy Edmond Dubois-Crancé made a series of proposals to reform the armed forces, he characterized the army as 'men without a fatherland or fixed domicile, controlled only by a severe and often unjust discipline, governed by a despotic regime'.[28] The newspaper *Révolutions de Paris* warned almost daily about the dangers of a military coup. In one issue, after conjuring up the shade of Julius Caesar, it commented: 'The army is patriotic today, it is enlightened. But will it still be so a century from now?' After all, 'isn't a victorious leader almost always the idol of his soldiers?'[29] These passages bear witness to a much stronger perception of the military as a separate sphere—and potentially an independent political power—than had ever been the case in France before the Revolution. And the preferred solution to the problem was to replace the standing, royal army with a citizen army—in the often-repeated slogan of French military reformers of the period, to make every citizen a soldier, and every soldier a citizen.[30] In 1793, just a year after France went to war with Austria and Prussia, the revolutionary government actually tried to implement this principle with the *levée en masse*, the mass levy that in theory drafted every healthy adult male into the army.

The critiques of a professional, standing military did not stop with warnings about Caesarism. Many revolutionaries even denounced the project of forming a National Guard and a citizen army. When deputies proposed military-style uniforms for the new National Guard established in the summer of 1789, radical newspapers howled. Jean-Paul Marat attacked what he called the 'ridiculous project' of trying to transform the French into a 'people of soldiers'—surely, he insisted, the age of soldiers had passed.[31]

In France, as in the United States, control of the armed forces became a major point of contention in debates over the new constitution that the National Assembly slowly drafted between 1789 and 1791. Who had the right to declare war? Who had the right to approve military funding? Debates on this subject went even farther in France than they had done in the United States. In May, 1790, when the threat of war against Britain briefly loomed, and King Louis XVI asked the Assembly to approve new military spending, speaker after speaker, starting with none other than Maximilien Robespierre, declared that war itself was a relic of the past, and a fraternally-minded modern nation should abhor it. Commerce, they repeated, had changed the face of the world.[32] The particular issue of whether the king or the legislature should control France's armed forces was resolved by a muddy compromise, but it came accompanied by what revolutionaries quickly dubbed the Declaration of Peace to the World: a promise that France would never launch a war of aggression (the pledge was incorporated into the short-lived Constitution of 1791). The deputies were in effect committing themselves to making France a civilian society.

At this point in the Atlantic revolutions, in short, a somewhat paradoxical situation had emerged. A spectre was haunting the Atlantic world—the spectre of militarism. But it was only a spectre. Nowhere did militarism actually yet exist as a real political phenomenon. In the United States, Caesar indeed turned out to be Cincinnatus. George Washington gave up his military title, and this act of renunciation became a key element of his legend, later reinforced by his surrender of the presidency.[33] At only one moment did the new United States experience anything like an attempt by the military to intervene in politics: the muddy and abortive Newburgh Conspiracy at the end of the Revolutionary War.[34] In France, as well, during the first five years of the Revolution, no general came close to filling the role that the Cassandras of militarism had warned of. Lafayette may have contemplated leading the army against the revolutionary government, but never tried. General Charles-François Dumouriez repeatedly disobeyed the orders of the civilian government in Paris, and in 1793, as radical forces gained the ascendant in the capital, he incited his armies to march there and seize power. But they refused to obey him, and like Lafayette before him he fled across the lines to the enemy. During the Reign of Terror, no fewer than eighty-four French generals died on the guillotine. Some were executed for alleged incompetence, but many were accused of designs on power, and the names of Cromwell and Caesar appeared in indictment after indictment. The spectre of militarism produced many ghosts.[35]

Regenerative warfare

But in the course of the revolutionary period itself another intellectual development made itself felt and, finally, allowed the spectre to take on flesh. At this point, it had become conceptually possible to see the military as a distinct sphere of modern society, existing in diametrical opposition to the 'civilian' sphere—again, it is no coincidence that the word 'civilian' made its appearance at precisely this moment in history. But those who acknowledged the distinction did so in one of two ways, as suggested above. Either, in accordance with classical republicanism, they saw the distinction as a corrupt, unnatural cleavage in what should be a single, seamless, civic whole; or they saw the 'military' sphere as an anachronistic relic of barbarous times. But in the late eighteenth century, the idea had arisen that the military could in fact be a *redemptive* and *regenerating* force, a force that could, far from threatening civil society, become its salvation, and its renewal. The idea would eventually come to play a decisive role in French revolutionary politics.

This final transformation had begun principally as a reaction against the stadial theories that treated war as an anachronism. It owed a great deal to the question, posed most prominently by Jean-Jacques Rousseau, as to what might be lost, rather than gained, by the advance of peaceful civilization. It did not come from a new and distinct intellectual party, but from within the same Enlightenment universe as the critics of war. In fact, it was perfectly possible to prophesy perpetual peace one moment, and to worry about its consequences the next. Consider these words, first published in 1790:

> The sublime needs violence ... War itself has something sublime in it, and makes the disposition of the people who carry it on, only the more sublime, the more dangers they are exposed to ... By contrast, a long peace generally brings about a predominant commercial spirit, and along with it, low selfishness, cowardice, and effeminacy.[36]

The author was Immanuel Kant, in his *Critique of Judgment* of 1790, written five years before his call for a permanent end to war in his *Project for Perpetual Peace*. A decade earlier, the German scholar Johann Valentin Embser had praised war as a necessary phenomenon without which noble sentiments would wither and die: 'war ... rejuvenates the people'.[37] And in 1792, the writer and statesman Wilhelm von Humboldt called war 'one of the healthiest phenomena for the cultivation of the human race'. He continued: 'It is unwillingly that I see it disappearing more and more from the scene. It is the admittedly fearful extreme, through which active courage ... is tested and steeled'.[38] During the French Revolution, much the same language appeared in France, especially among the Girondin advocates for war against Austria. Madame Roland, for instance, criticized what she called the 'flighty character, and corrupt or frivolous mores' of the French ... 'peace is taking us backwards ... and we can only be regenerated by blood'.[39]

This exaltation of war as a source of moral regeneration was something quite new in European history. Although it invoked classical examples, it amounted to far more than the classical association of military service with civic virtue. And although it made uses of the languages of honour and glory, it went well beyond the languages of noble valour that had been central to the self-image of the second estate since the Middle Ages. It had, for lack of a better word, a mystical quality that characterized combat and sacrificial death as moments of transcendence. But this was not a religious transcendence, in the service of any divine plan or will. It was a secular transcendence, linked to that quintessential eighteenth-century word used by Kant in his *Critique of Judgment*: the sublime. Furthermore, it did not simply involve a distinction between military and civilian spheres, but something more: a deprecation of the latter. In early modern Europe, countless writers had eloquently praised military service as honourable, valorous, healthy, pleasant and virtuous, and compared it favourably to other professions. But they did not denounce civilian life as selfish, cowardly, effeminate and debased, as Kant would do—not surprisingly, since, as this essay has argued, the very concept of 'civilian life' did not yet exist. But hardly had the concept made its way into the world than it became the target of the sort of fierce criticism levelled by Kant, Embser and von Humboldt. To touch the face of the sublime, one could not be peaceful. One had to struggle, to fight, and to risk sacrificial death.

During the period of the Revolutionary and Napoleonic Wars, a virtual cult of regenerative warfare developed, which associated the sacrifice of one's life in combat not simply with civic virtue, but with sexual pleasure. No single image better expresses this idea than Jacques-Louis David's remarkable painting of 1794, 'The Death of Joseph Bara', commemorating a young revolutionary killed during the revolt of the Vendée, in western France. David stripped the scene of all particularity, and presented Bara as an androgynous object of desire. The same infusion of sexuality into representations of combat and sacrificial death would figure with particular intensity in the poetry of the German resistance to Napoleon, culminating with the Austrian poet Theodor Körner, who died fighting for Prussia in 1813, and who later became a favourite of the Nazis. 'Honour is the wedding guest, and the Fatherland the bride', Körner would write. 'He who lustfully embraces her has married death itself'. True happiness, Körner insisted, could only be found in sacrificial death: 'Nur in dem Opfertod reift uns das Glück'.[40]

Militarism in post-Thermidorian France

In France, after the end of the Terror, this developing mystique of war allowed new sorts of claims to be made for the moral superiority of actual military institutions. If war could rejuvenate, regenerate, heal and redeem a debased and degenerate civilian society, the principal vector of this process was the army. Between 1794 and 1799 it was the neo-Jacobin left that pressed these claims most strongly. In 1789, ironically, it had been the left which warned more loudly than any other political faction about the dangers of Caesarism, but eight years later the armies had been purged of their royalist elements; nearly all of the old noble officer corps had fled or been executed; and the old units of the line had been 'amalgamated' with revolutionary volunteers. Meanwhile, in Paris, conservative and even royalist forces were gaining the ascendant, winning elections in the summer of 1797. In that year the neo-Jacobin executive Director Louis-Marie de La Revellière-Lépeaux declared that the Republic barely existed outside of the armies. Radical newspapers went further, repeatedly denouncing civilian politics as corrupt and debased, and leading the country to ruin. As one of them insisted, 'The great flood was necessary to purge the earth. The armies will be necessary to purify France'.[41] There followed the first real military coup in western European history, the late summer coup of Fructidor. With soldiers marching into the capital, right-wing Directors and members of the Assembly were purged. Hundreds of political opponents were imprisoned or deported to French Guyana. And where the Left had once warned against militarism and Caesarism, now the Right took up the theme. Royalist newspapers repeatedly raised the spectre of military despotism, asked if the Rubicon had already been crossed, and predicted the coming of a 'military republic'.[42]

The great beneficiary of these developments was, of course, Napoleon Bonaparte. Already in 1797 and 1798, the young general ostentatiously disobeyed the government's orders, defying civilian control when it suited him, and sent units to support the Fructidor coup. His actions exemplified the new, independent role of a military conscious of its separation from, and superiority to, civilian politics. But in addition, Napoleon personified the new mystique of war. He was Humboldt's 'admittedly fearful extreme' in the flesh. In the Italian campaign of 1796–1797 he had acquired the most brilliant reputation of any French general in centuries. And he was supremely talented at using the press—including newspapers he personally founded or sponsored—to forge an image of himself as the exceptional man, perfectly suited for a new sort of exceptional, sublime warfare. The portrait that he commissioned from Gros of himself at the battle of Arcola provides one famous example. Or consider a 1797 description from his newspaper the *Courier of the Army of Italy*: 'He flies like lightning and strikes like thunder. The speed of his movements excludes neither precision nor prudence. He is everywhere, he sees everything. Like a shooting star streaking across the sky, he presents himself in the same moment on the banks of two different rivers'.[43] Very early on, Napoleon set his sights upon taking power in France, and presented himself as a possible political redeemer. During the parade celebrating Bastille Day in 1797 in Milan, he stage-managed a remarkable incident, which his newspaper the *Courier* duly reported. A soldier stepped out of the ranks and shouted: 'General, you have saved France. Your children, who glory in belonging to your invincible army, will make you a rampart of their bodies. Now go and save the Republic'.[44]

By 1797, in other words, Bonaparte had become precisely the sort of 'idol' that the *Révolutions de Paris* had warned about nine years before. And he was not just an idol of his soldiers, but of much of the French population. To them, he embodied what could be called an alternate form of revolutionary legitimacy, whereby his military qualities of strength, of discipline and of selflessness were held to supply what the 'political class'—the *civilian* 'political class', as it could now be called—was believed so sorely to lack. He, and his men, would be the agents acting to regenerate all of France through their glory. These qualities, it needs to be stressed, allowed Bonaparte to succeed not only where previous generals had failed, but where all previous revolutionary leaders had failed, namely in gaining a durable personal reputation without falling victim to charges of acting in the service of selfish personal ambition. Two years later, after further military exploits in Egypt, Bonaparte would in fact seize power. He did so through another military coup, and thereby established, for the first time in Western European history, what can fairly be called a militarist regime.

Napoleon's regime: not military, but militarist

The militarist nature of Napoleon's regime has been much disputed, especially in France. *Marxisant* historians who viewed Napoleon as the agent of the bourgeoisie, and right-wing historians who cast him as the heir of the Revolution could agree on little, but they did come together in stressing the civilian basis of his rule. They repeatedly quoted his assertion that he was 'the most civilian of generals'—*le plus civil des généraux*—and that he did not intend to govern as a general.[45] This remark, incidentally, shows that Napoleon himself now saw French society divided into distinct military and civilian spheres. The historians argued that he won power where other generals failed precisely because of his success in cultivating civilian support. The historian Patrice Gueniffey, in his recent biography, insists that Napoleon did not establish a 'dictatorship of the sword'.[46]

But other recent work suggests that denying the militarism of Napoleon's regime amounts to an exercise in wishful thinking. Napoleon stood out from other generals because of his superior military reputation, far more than because of his allegedly civilian qualities. His triumphal return to France from Egypt in the fall of 1799, which he himself remembered as one of the happiest episodes in life, amounted to one long celebration of his military triumphs—the extent to which the Egyptian campaign was a disaster had not yet become known. In Lyon, he was greeted with a stage play called 'The Return of the Hero'.[47] In Paris, the coup itself was accomplished by soldiers marching into the parliament. When deputies challenged him, he shouted: 'Don't forget, I walk with the God of war and the God of victory!'[48]

Of course, Bonaparte did not rule through the army. His was not a *military* regime. But a militarist regime is not the same as a military one. It is also true that especially in the first year after taking power, with his authority still fragile, Bonaparte continued assiduously to cultivate civilian support. But what confirmed him in power was not this civilian backing but the Battle of Marengo, in 1800, and the success of his second Italian campaign. And afterwards, as Robert Morrissey has argued, Bonaparte actively sought to ground his political legitimacy in his military glory.[49] He himself admitted as much, many times. 'A First Consul is not like kings ... who see their states as an inheritance', he remarked in May 1803. 'He needs brilliant deeds, and therefore war'.[50] Years later, in exile, he told his small entourage: 'I myself was the keystone of an edifice totally new and raised on a slight foundation! Its stability depended on each of my battles!'[51] During his years in power, Napoleon acted repeatedly to strengthen the position of the army, gave huge rewards to his most successful commanders, and imposed forms of military discipline (including uniforms) on the state administration, and also, significantly, in secondary schools.[52] He dreamed of reconstructing the city of Paris around a series of military monuments, including the Arc de Triomphe and the Church of the Madeleine, originally conceived of as a 'Temple of Glory'. Hired poets chanted the moral superiority of the military. Consider a poem read with great pomp before the Institute of France, by one of the regime's most prominent intellectuals, in 1800, soon after Marengo: 'Follow the generous example of our warriors. Life is nothing for them, and glory is all. Those who risk death are the masters of the world'.[53]

In Bonaparte, all the elements of modern militarism discussed in this paper came together. The French, or at least the politically active part of them, had learned to see their society as divided into two separate, complementary and opposing parts that could be labelled military and civilian. Thanks to the new mystique of war, 'the military' could now be seen both as a potential threat to civilian society, but also as a potential saviour of civilian society from itself—a force that could, by infusing values of strength, discipline and disinterestedness into civilian society, and by exposing it to the sublime experience of war, rejuvenate and redeem it. This militarism, in Napoleonic France, was bound up with a powerful, charismatic figure who seemed to incarnate all these military qualities, and to act as the agent through which they did their work.

Militarism in the western world would, of course, continue to evolve after the Napoleonic period. The further professionalization of armed forces and the standardization of peacetime systems of conscription would have crucial effects. The relationships between armed forces and civilian society in the German Second Empire, or in modern Latin America, would differ in important ways from the patterns described in this essay.[54] But in these cases as well, militarism could only develop because societies saw themselves as divided into military and civilian spheres—the conceptual development that took place in the West during the late eighteenth century. It was only with the modern military-civilian distinction in place that it became possible to assert the military's moral superiority to civilian society, grounded in its qualities of strength, discipline and selflessness. And it was only then that the military's right to shape and dominate civilian society and politics could be asserted.

Conclusion

This essay has looked at the place of war and the military in European culture in the age of Atlantic revolutions, to make an argument about the birth of militarism. Defining militarism as the imposition of ideas, values and practices conceived of as 'military' over others conceived of as 'civilian', it has argued that the phenomenon can only arise in societies that perceive and try to enact a clear distinction between 'military' and 'civilian' spheres. It has noted that until the age of Atlantic revolutions this distinction was not in fact generally recognized in Western societies. It traces the way the distinction arose, and the way the perception of military and civilian spheres was further developed and transformed in the course of the American and French Revolutions. It concludes by suggesting that the emergence of a powerful concept of 'regenerative warfare' at the very end of the eighteenth century proved crucial in allowing 'the military', now clearly defined as a separate sphere of society and associated with qualities of strength, discipline and selflessness, to be perceived as superior to 'civilian society'. These changes lay behind the rise of the first great militarist regime in modern history, that of Napoleon Bonaparte.

Notes

1. Benjamin Constant, 'L'esprit de conquête et de l'usurpation dans leurs rapports avec la civilisation européenne', in idem. *Œuvres* (Paris, 1957), 1001–1002.
2. Émile Durkheim, *Suicide, Study in Sociology* (New York, 1951), 238.
3. Hans Joas, *War and Modernity* (Cambridge, 2003); and Hans Joas and Wolfgang Knöbl, *War in Social Thought: Hobbes to the Present* (Princeton, NJ, 2013).
4. See Volker R. Berghahn, *Militarism: The History of an International Debate, 1861–1979* (New York, 1982); Alfred Vagts, *A History of Militarism* (Westport, CT, 1981); and Hans Rosenberg, *Bureaucracy, Aristocracy, and Autocracy; the Prussian Experience, 1660–1815* (Cambridge, MA, 1958).
5. Quoted in Berghahn, *Militarism*, 37.
6. See the Oxford English Dictionary (http://dictionary.oed.com), s.v. 'civilian', and the Trésor de la langue française (http://atilf.atilf.fr/tlf.htm), s.v. 'civil'. For German, Google ngrams search at https://books.google.com/ngrams/graph?content=Zivilist&year_start=1800&year_end=2000&corpus=20&smoothing=3&share=&direct_url=t1%3B%2CZivilist%3B%2Cc0 (accessed: 24 March 2015).
7. Timothy Tackett, *Becoming a Revolutionary: The Deputies of the French National Assembly and the Emergence of a Revolutionary Culture (1789–1790)* (Princeton, NJ, 1996), 32–34.
8. On the three orders see the classic work of Georges Duby, *Les trois ordres, ou l'imaginaire du féodalisme* (Paris, 1978).

9. On classical republicanism, see above all J. G. A. Pocock, *The Machiavellian Moment: Florentine Political Thought and the Atlantic Republican Tradition* (Princeton, NJ, 1975).
10. Niccolò Machiavelli, L'arte della guerra (1520) (http://www.classicitaliani.it/machiav/mac22.htm) (accessed: 24 March 2015).
11. Niccolò Machiavelli, *The Works of the Famous Nicholas Machiavel, Citizen and Secretary of Florence* (London, 1720), 433; see also idem, *The Works of Nicholas Machiavel, Secretary of State of the Republic of Florence*, 4 vols. (London, 1775), vol. 4, 7.
12. See the discussion in David A. Bell, *The First Total War: Napoleon's Europe and the Birth of Warfare as We Know it* (Boston, 2007), 21–37.
13. See Mark Kishlansky, *The Rise of the New Model Army* (Cambridge, 1979).
14. See especially Vagts, *A History of Militarism*; and Rosenberg, *Bureaucracy, Aristocracy, and Autocracy*.
15. Rosenberg, *Bureaucracy, Aristocracy, and Autocracy*, 41.
16. Peter Wilson, 'Social Militarization in Eighteenth-Century Germany', *German History* 18/1 (2000): 1–39.
17. See Marc Raeff, *The Well-Ordered Police State: Social and Institutional Change Through Law in the Germanies and Russia, 1600–1800* (New Haven, CT, 1983).
18. On the 'military revolution', see the essays in Clifford J. Rogers, ed., *The Military Revolution Debate: Readings on the Military Transformation of Early Modern Europe* (Boulder, CO, 1995).
19. John Trenchard, *An Argument Shewing: That a Standing Army is Inconsistent with a Free Government*, ed. Walter Moyle (Exeter, 1971); and Pocock, *The Machiavellian Moment*, 401–422.
20. Josiah Quincy, *Observations on the Act of Parliament, Commonly Called the Boston Port-Bill with Thoughts on Civil Society and Standing Armies. By Josiah Quincy, Junior* (London, N.E. printed. London, 1774), 39.
21. See discussion in Bell, *The First Total War*, 52–83.
22. Paul-Henri Thiry, baron d'Holbach, *La morale universelle, ou les devoirs de l'homme fondés sur sa nature*, 3 vols. (Amsterdam, 1776), vol. 2, 6.
23. Constant, *L'esprit de conquête*, 991, 993, 995.
24. Declaration of Independence at http://www.archives.gov/exhibits/charters/declaration_transcript.html (accessed: 24 March 2015).
25. See Caroline Cox, *A Proper Sense of Honor: Service and Sacrifice in George Washington's Army* (Chapel Hill, NC, 2004).
26. George Washington to François-Jean de Beauvoir de Chastellux, 25 April 1788, in *George Washington: A Collection*, ed. W. B. Allen (Indianapolis, IN, 1988), 479. Jean-François de Chastellux was the author of *An Essay on Public Happiness, Investigating the State of Human Nature, Under Each of its Particular Appearances Through the Several Periods of History, to the Present Times*, 2 vols. (London, 1774).
27. See Félix Blanc, 'L'organisation des pouvoirs de guerre et de paix aux origines du gouvernement représentatif: Essai sur l'invention du concours des pouvoirs en Angleterre, en France et aux Etats-Unis', thèse de doctorat (École des Hautes Études en Sciences Sociales, 2014).
28. *Archives parlementaires de 1787 à 1860. Recueil complet des débats législatifs et politiques des Chambres françaises*, dir. Jérôme Mavidal (Paris, 1879), vol. 10, 519 (12 December 1789).
29. Quoted in Wolfgang Kruse, *Die Erfindung des modernen Militarismus: Krieg, Militär und bürgerliche Gesellschaft im politischen Diskurs der Französischen Revolution, 1789–1799* (Munich, 2003), 59.
30. See Rafe Blaufarb, *The French Army, 1750–1820: Careers, Talent, Merit* (Manchester, 2002), 12–74.

31. Quoted in Kruse, *Die Erfindung*, 40.
32. See Bell, *The First Total War*, 84–109.
33. See François Furstenberg, *In the Name of the Father: Washington's Legacy, Slavery, and the Making of a Nation* (New York, 2006).
34. See Richard H. Kohn, 'The Inside History of the Newburgh Conspiracy: America and the Coup d'Etat', *William and Mary Quarterly* 27/2 (1970): 187–220.
35. See T. C. W. Blanning, *The French Revolutionary Wars, 1787–1802* (London, 1996), 126.
36. Immanuel Kant, The Critique of Judgment (1790), at http://philosophy.eserver.org/kant/critique-of-judgment.txt, ss. 28 (accessed: 24 March 2015).
37. Quoted in Wilhelm Janssen, 'Johann Valentin Embser und der vorrevolutionäre Bellizismus in Deutschland', in *Die Wiedergeburt des Krieges aus dem Geist der Revolution: Studien zum bellizisitischen Diskurs des ausgehenden 18. und beginnenden 19. Jahrhunderts*, ed. Johannes Kunisch and Herfried Münkler (Berlin, 1999), 43.
38. Wilhelm von Humboldt, *Ideen zu einem Versuch die Grenzen der Wirksamkeit des Staates zu bestimmen* (1792). http://gutenberg.spiegel.de/humboldw/wirksam/wirksam.htm, Chapter 5 (accessed: 24 March 2015).
39. Madame Roland to Bancal, Paris, 25 June 1791, in *Jeanne-Marie Roland de La Platière, Lettres de Madame Roland*, ed. Claude Perroud, 2 vols. (Paris, 1900–1902), vol. 2, 313.
40. Theodor Körner, *Leier und Schwert* (1814), http://www.gutenberg2000.de/koerner/leier/leier.htm, (accessed: 24 March 2015).
41. Quoted in Kruse, *Die Erfindung*, 317.
42. Quoted in Philip G. Dwyer, 'Napoleon Bonaparte as Hero and Saviour: Image, Rhetoric and Behaviour in the Construction of a Legend', *French History* 18/4 (2004): 379–404, 389.
43. *Courrier de l'armée d'Italie*, no. 48, 23 October 1797, 206.
44. Ibid., no. 1, 20 July 1797, 4.
45. Thierry Lentz, *Nouvelle histoire du Premier Empire: La France et l'Europe de Napoléon, 1804–1814* (Paris, 2007), 172.
46. Patrice Gueniffey, *Bonaparte, 1769–1802* (Paris, 2013), 496.
47. Bell, *The First Total War*, 220.
48. Ibid., 221.
49. Robert Morrissey, *The Economy of Glory: From Ancien Régime France to the Fall of Napoleon* (Chicago, 2014).
50. Quoted in Jean Tulard, *Napoleon, ou le mythe du sauveur* (Paris, 1987), 180.
51. Emmanuel de Las Cases, *Mémorial de Sainte Hélène* (Paris, 1862), 193
52. See Bell, *The First Total War*, 244–248.
53. Quoted in Morrissey, *The Economy*, 93.
54. See Berghahn, *Militarism*; Vagts, *A History of Militarism*; Alain Rouquié, *The Military and the State in Latin America* (Berkeley, CA, 1987); and Ute Frevert, *A Nation in Barracks: Modern Germany, Military Conscription and Civil Society* (Oxford, 2004).

Part II
Peace Making, Occupation and Military Demobilization

3

Making Peace: The Allied Occupation of France, 1815–1818

Christine Haynes

Two days after the Battle of Waterloo, from the town of Nivelles in what is now Belgium, the British Commander-in-Chief of the Allied forces, the Duke of Wellington, issued the following General Order:

> As the army is about to enter the French territory, the troops of the nations which are at present under the command of Field Marshal the Duke of Wellington, are desired to recollect that their respective Sovereigns are the Allies of His Majesty the King of France, and that France ought, therefore to be treated as a friendly country.

Thanking the army for its conduct in the 'glorious action fought on the 18th' of June, he insisted that in the upcoming campaign in France, 'nothing should be taken either by officers or soldiers, for which payment be not made'.[1] During the subsequent invasion of France in the summer of 1815, this order was followed mostly in the breach. Within two weeks of the Battle of Waterloo, some 150,000 British and Prussian troops had arrived in Paris, bivouacking in the Bois de Boulogne and on the Champs-Elysées. Over the next two months, soldiers from Great Britain, Russia, Prussia, Austria and most of the rest of Europe, including Denmark, Holland, Bavaria, Württemberg, Saxony, Hanover, Piedmont, and Spain, continued to stream into France. By September, two-thirds of the country was occupied by 1.2 million troops, the largest force gathered anywhere to that date. As they invaded, Allied troops ransacked the country, pillaging food and forage, appropriating valuables including artworks, destroying fields and forests, seizing weapons, raiding treasuries, and levying contributions, in complete violation of Wellington's order. For such behaviour, Wellington and other Allied leaders acknowledged some justification, especially among troops of those nations such as Austria and Prussia who sought revenge for their own experience of occupation during the Revolutionary and Napoleonic Wars. However, these leaders feared that such pillaging threatened the main hope of the campaign against Napoleon, 'permanent peace', as Wellington put it in a letter to his brother Henry on 19 July 1815.[2]

In the aftermath of Waterloo, how to attain such a peace was the main challenge for Allied military and political leaders. Little more than a year after the first defeat of Napoleon, these leaders faced the problem of how to demobilize not just the army of France, which had backed him in his return to power, but the coalition force of more than one million soldiers who had been sent by his enemies into France to defeat him, yet again. After several months of negotiation, during which they continued to occupy much of the country to enforce the disarmament of the French, the Allies confronted this challenge with a new approach to the termination of war: what they termed an 'occupation of guarantee'. Resisting demands for punitive measures including territorial concessions, particularly from the leaders of Austria and Prussia, they agreed to a more lenient settlement, employing a smaller, temporary occupation force to ensure political stability within France and hence general security in Europe. According to the peace treaty signed on 20 November 1815, the Allies would station 150,000 troops in the seven departments along the north-eastern frontier, at the expense of the French, until they were indemnified for the damages caused by the return of Napoleon. Lasting three years, until November 1818, this occupation played a pivotal role in the demobilization and reconstruction of France and Europe after 25 years of revolution and war.

Despite its significance, the importance of this occupation has been overlooked by historians even in France itself.[3] This essay revisits this neglected episode in the history of the Napoleonic Wars. Explicating the intentions and operations of the 'occupation of guarantee', it argues that this event was critical for the establishment of a new postwar order in France and across the continent. Although this occupation in some ways resembled a traditional military 'execution', it also represented a new approach to the age-old problem of how to end war. Extending the logic of the 'first total war' into the postwar period, it constituted part of a panoply of tools for effecting 'total' peace. This peace was forged not just in the cabinets of statesmen, as scholars such as Paul Schroeder have argued about this era's revolution in international politics, but also in military headquarters and garrisons.[4] Involving a number of innovations in the theory and practice of war termination, the 'occupation of guarantee' foreshadowed many aspects of the modern law of war, well before the Lieber Code or Hague Conventions later in the nineteenth century with which they are usually associated.

From military invasion to 'Occupation of Guarantee'

In the history of warfare, military occupation for the purpose of peacekeeping or regime change—as opposed to conquest or annexation—is a distinctly modern development. Rare before the late eighteenth century, it dates from the Revolutionary and Napoleonic Wars between 1792 and 1815. First employed in some of the territories defeated by France, it was in turn imposed upon the French themselves, first briefly in 1814 and then more extensively in 1815. In the spring of 1814 and then again (following the Hundred Days) in the summer of 1815, a coalition of forces from Great Britain, Russia, Prussia, Austria, and a number of smaller powers occupied French territory, to ensure the defeat of Napoleon and the establishment—in this case, the re-establishment—of a new government.[5]

Initially, this occupation took the form of a military 'execution'. During the summer of 1815, hundreds of thousands of soldiers from all over Europe marched into France. As they entered French territory, the invaders helped themselves to whatever they could find. Threatening local authorities who refused to cooperate with them with imprisonment and exile, they levied arbitrary 'contributions' on occupied communities. To alleviate abuses, in the month after Waterloo the Allies instituted a formal system for the initial military occupation. Divided into four zones, this preliminary '*occupation de guerre*' covered 61 departments, excluding only parts of Brittany and Cotentin, north and east of the Loire. To standardize requisitions in the occupied zones, both sides established commissions, to coordinate demands and transmit complaints back and forth between the Allied forces and local populations. Between July and November, the amount of such requisitions was estimated at two and a half million francs per day. In spite of this system, abuses continued.[6]

Unlike in 1814, when the Allies had issued a generous peace treaty and evacuated French territory very quickly, in 1815 they spent months negotiating a final peace treaty. While most Allied leaders agreed that this time France needed to be occupied for a more extensive period, they differed on a number of other questions, including how long the French should be subject to occupation, how much of a financial indemnity they should pay, and whether they should concede additional territory beyond the frontiers of 1792 imposed on them by the First Treaty of Paris in 1814. Some members of the Coalition, particularly Prussia and Austria but also the British Prime Minister Lord Liverpool, thought France needed to be punished for backing Napoleon in his return to power and war. From the French, they wanted to exact territorial concessions, particularly in Alsace and Lorraine, as well as heavy financial contributions. In part, these demands were motivated by a desire for revenge, for French behaviour especially in Austria and Prussia during the Napoleonic Wars; in part, they were devised as a pragmatic tool for financing their own remobilization upon the return of Napoleon.[7] However, such a punitive approach was resisted by other Allied leaders, including the Russian Tsar Alexander and, especially, Lord Castlereagh, as well as the Duke of Wellington, who maintained that it would destabilize France and peace in Europe even further. Although they acknowledged that the First Treaty of Paris had left France too strong, Castlereagh and Wellington argued that moderation was in the interests of the Allies.[8]

According to these more moderate Allied leaders, the main goal of any settlement, including the occupation, was to ensure a durable peace—as well as financial indemnification—for the nations of Europe. As Wellington wrote in a letter to Castlereagh on 11 August 1815, the object of the Allies in their campaigns against Napoleon 'has been to put an end to the French Revolution, to obtain peace for themselves and their people, to have the power of reducing their overgrown military establishments, and the leisure to attend to the internal concerns of their several nations, and to improve the situation of their people'. To achieve this object, in contrast to a permanent cession of territory, which would only unsettle France, Wellington advised a temporary occupation, at the expense of the French, which he saw as the best means of helping the monarchy to secure its power, as well as of enabling the Allied Coalition to recoup the cost of remobilization against Napoleon. Explicitly distinguishing the Allied approach from the French mode of occupation based on plunder and war, the Duke argued: 'These measures will not only give us, during the period of occupation, all the military security which could be expected from the permanent cession, but, if carried into execution in the spirit in which they are conceived, they are in themselves the bond of peace'.[9] In subsequent correspondence with Castlereagh, Wellington added that such an occupation would serve to protect, not usurp, the power of civil authorities in France. In a memorandum dated 31 August, he outlined what he saw as the goals of a temporary occupation:

> First, to give security to the government of the King, and to afford him time to form a force of his own with which he can carry on his government, and take his fair share in the concerns of Europe; secondly, to give the Allies some security against a second revolutionary convulsion and reaction; and, thirdly, to enable the Allies to enforce the payment of those contributions which they deem it just towards their own subjects to lay on France in payment of the expenses of the war.[10]

These goals shaped the settlement that was ultimately adopted by the Allies, in negotiation with the French foreign minister, the Duc de Richelieu, in the autumn of 1815.

On 20 November, the Second Treaty of Paris replaced the 'war occupation' with a more limited occupation 'for the purpose of guarantee' of security and indemnification, involving a smaller number of 150,000 troops (plus 50,000 horses) stationed around 18 garrisons in seven departments on the north-eastern frontier of France. These troops, of which there were 30,000 from each of the major powers and 5,000 from each of the small ones, were divided into national zones, with the Austrians headquartered in Colmar, the Prussians in Sedan, the Russians in Maubeuge and the British in Cambrai (see Map 3.1). Together, these troops were placed under the general command of the Duke of Wellington. Aside from these 150,000 troops, all other forces were to leave France by January 1816. To provide for the maintenance of the remaining troops, the French were forced to pay contributions

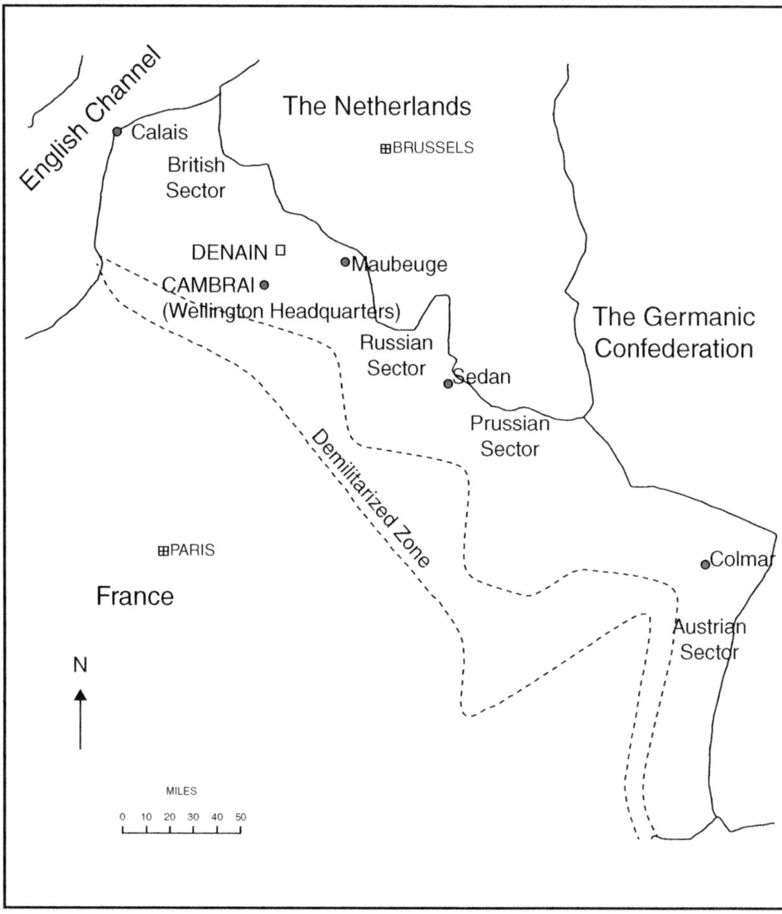

Map 3.1 The occupied territories in postwar France: major power locations, 1816–1818
Source: Thomas Dwight Veve, 'The Duke of Wellington and the Army of Occupation in France, 1815–1818', Ph.D. diss. (Marquette University, 1990). Courtesy of Thomas Dwight Veve, Dalton State College.

of 50 million francs per year in quarterly instalments, plus daily rations for 200,000 men and 50,000 horses, totalling another 100 million francs per year. In addition, they were required to pay indemnities to the Allies for the damages caused by the return of Napoleon. Set at 700 million francs (excluding sums owed to foreigners claiming damages prior to 1814, which the Duke of Wellington ultimately negotiated down from 1.6 billion to 240 million francs), these indemnities had to be paid in full before the occupying forces would leave, up to five years later. Throughout the occupation, the Allied forces were required to participate in a vigorous training programme, in small groups three times per week, and they were subjected to biannual inspections. They were also invited to participate in annual joint military exercises on the plains of Denain.

Ultimately, the occupation instituted by the Treaty of 20 November 1815 would last for three years. In February 1817, after the French temporarily suspended payments to the Allies, the coalition powers decided to reduce the army of occupation—and accompanying requisition burden—by 30,000 troops, beginning on 1 April. In October 1818, satisfied that the French had (with the help of foreign financiers) settled their debt and rebuilt a loyal army, the Allied powers agreed, in a treaty signed at the Congress of Aix-la-Chapelle, to end the occupation two years early. During the three years that it lasted, the 'occupation of guarantee' instituted a new approach to war termination, significantly different from previous military occupations, including the occupations of France in the spring of 1814 and again in the summer and fall of 1815. While it borrowed from a long-standing tradition of military punishment, the occupation of guarantee also departed from these previous occupations in significant ways.[11]

The old tradition of 'Making War Pay for Itself'

In practice, especially for those French men and women who lived in the occupation zone in the north-east, the 'occupation of guarantee' resembled earlier military 'executions' under the Ancien Régime and during the Revolutionary and Napoleonic Wars. Albeit on a larger scale, it was not that different from, say, the billeting of troops by one German power on another in the Holy Roman Empire, or the occupation by the French army of the Low Countries and the Italian lands in the 1790s or Spain, Austria, and especially Prussia in the following decade. It also had much in common with the military executions carried out by Revolutionary and Napoleonic armies in recalcitrant communities within France, for example in the Vendée. Like these earlier occupations, the 'occupation of guarantee' was motivated in part by the tradition, current since at least the time of Louis XIV, of 'making war pay for itself'. In spite of the revolutionary promise that war would be used to liberate peoples, states maintained the Ancien Régime practice of provisioning their armies and replenishing their treasuries on conquered countries, through billeting, requisitioning and pillaging, including of cultural trophies and luxury items as well as of necessities such as food, clothing and forage. In a more organized form of pillage, they routinely demanded monetary 'contributions' toward their costs. For example, in 1809, the Napoleonic regime levied a contribution of 250 million francs (of which 164 were paid) on occupied Austria; between 1806 and 1812, it demanded similar sums from defeated Prussia. Along with these exactions, the occupiers often inflicted considerable violence on the occupied.[12]

Like these earlier military executions, the occupation of 1815–1818 imposed considerable hardships on the French population, including requisitions of lodging, transport, and food, as well as financial contributions. After November 1815, these requisitions and contributions were all funded by the central administration, through extra taxation and credit. But the burden of procuring furnished lodgings in communal barracks or private homes and adequate food and forage from local suppliers still fell on the local communities where the foreign troops were garrisoned. For these communities, the occupation of guarantee was experienced as a traumatic violation of their physical space and daily routine as well as their material resources.[13]

As had been the case in earlier conquests, the occupied suffered from innumerable 'excesses', as they were characterized in contemporary language. Despite its goal of promoting order and peace, the 'occupation of guarantee' did not always differ much from the preceding military occupation, in its resemblance to a petty war. Violence was especially rampant in 1815–1816, during the initial invasion, and again in 1818, on the eve of liberation. In the beginning, the violence was most egregious among the Prussian forces, whose excesses were motivated by revenge for the cruel treatment of the German lands at the hands of the French. But such excesses continued long after the official shift from war-time to peace-keeping occupation in November 1815, across the national zones. During the three years of the 'occupation of guarantee', across the towns and villages where contingents of Allied troops were quartered, inhabitants suffered countless abuses, including destruction of property, arson, looting, theft, insults, brawls, assaults, murders and rapes.

Reports of such abuses are numerous in the archives of the ministries of war and police, especially in reports from stagecoach drivers and mail couriers in provincial France back to the ministry of police in Paris. These reports indicate that, well into 1816 and 1817, many French people felt that the Allies were still acting as 'enemies'. As one police informant remarked from the Russian zone around Rethel and Rocroi in mid-1816, Allied troops 'vexed the inhabitants, subjected them to various contributions, and often threatened to burn their villages', and the local civilian authorities were 'frequently powerless and unrecognized by these foreign soldiers, who behave absolutely as if in enemy territory'.[14] Such behaviour was not isolated to the Russians or the Prussians, but was observed among all of the Allied contingents, including the Saxons, Bavarians, Württembergers, and even British. Although Allied violence was spread throughout the occupied zone, it was especially severe in the department of the Ardennes, where resistance to the invasions had been greatest. In several reports to the minister of war, the local gendarmerie described this department as in complete despair.[15] In violation of the guidelines for the occupation negotiated between Allied and French authorities, the 'occupation of guarantee' often resembled a traditional military execution in its violence.

As the many reports in French archives suggest, as in earlier (and later) military occupations, one of the most egregious and symbolic excesses committed by the occupiers against the occupied was rape. Although definitive statistics on the crime of rape are elusive, during the three years the Allies remained in France, there were countless police reports and judicial records of sexual violence committed by all of the contingents of Allied troops, including the British, against French women and girls—as old as 60 and as young as six; married and unmarried; in homes, fields, and forests. To take just one of many reported incidents, in the commune of Cheppy toward the end of the occupation, two Prussian soldiers approached a girl of 17 who was gathering flax in a field, seized her by the throat and raped her, under threat of their bared sabres; according to the report of a brigadier of the gendarmerie of Varennes, who saw her afterwards in bed, this girl was sick as a result of the 'violences of every kind' she had suffered. As Jacques Hantraye has argued with regard to the invasions of the Seine-et-Oise in 1814 and 1815, for the occupiers, rape was a means of demonstrating power over the territory and people of France. This symbolic aspect of rape was understood by contemporary commentators, who characterized the whole 'occupation of guarantee' as a violation of the French nation. Employing a trope that is common in the context of military conquest, numerous texts and images produced in the 1810s depicted France—usually represented as a woman—prostituted and despoiled by its supposed 'allies'. This trope underscores the humiliation felt by the French in the face of what remained in some ways a brutal military execution.[16]

A new approach to the 'Bond of Peace'

But, if it shared much with the long tradition of military execution, the 'occupation of guarantee' also represented a significant departure in the law and practice of warfare. In its overall goal of peace-keeping and its institutional framework of multinational cooperation, this was a new type of occupation, for political reconstruction rather than territorial conquest. Establishing clear limits on exactions and interventions by belligerents against civilians, it marked a transition in international law from the old concept of 'just war' based in nature to a new view of war as one of the rights of nations, which had been emerging in the eighteenth century but was consolidated in the settlement of 1815. In the intentions of its architects if not always in the practices of its foot-soldiers on the ground, the 'occupation of guarantee' served, in Wellington's words, as the 'bond of peace'. Rather than a mere concomitant of war, it constituted part of the 'way beyond war' sought in international politics circa 1815, as described by Paul Schroeder. Based on mutual defence of independent and equal states, this 'way beyond war' involved a slew of new procedures and institutions in international law, of which the 'occupation of guarantee' was a key part.[17]

The departure represented by the 'occupation of guarantee' is seen in the terms of the treaty of 20 November 1815. The Second Treaty of Paris revised the formulae used in settlements at the end of wars since the seminal Treaty of Westphalia of 1648. With its emphasis on dynastic sovereignty and religious toleration, the Treaty of Westphalia had created a framework for a 'Christian and Universal Peace', which was reiterated in subsequent treaties between individual sovereigns over the next century and a half—including the Treaty of Tilsit between France and Russia in 1807—which focused on territorial boundaries, prizes, and prisoners.[18] In contrast, the Second Treaty of Paris aimed to ensure a secular and national order against the threat of revolution.[19] To enforce the terms of the Treaty, the signatories employed a number of different instruments, including defensive border fortresses, joint military exercises, financial reparations, mixed Franco-Allied commissions, Allied political observers, and regular international meetings, as well as occupation for peace-keeping. In contrast to the earlier type of military occupation employed by the French themselves throughout the revolutionary era, this 'occupation of guarantee' involved a truly international coalition: even after the troop reduction of the spring of 1817, the Allied leadership insisted on the involvement of the minor as well as major nations of Europe, to keep the power of the big four victors over Napoleon in check. Moreover, from the beginning, this occupation was defined as a *temporary* regime that did not confer sovereignty on the occupier. Although the Second Treaty of Paris has often been overlooked in histories of the law of war, it already anticipated many elements of modern international law regarding occupation, such as the Hague Regulations, especially in this respect for the sovereignty of government it was designed to install—or, in this case, re-install.[20]

One of the most significant innovations of the Second Treaty of Paris was the requirement that the defeated power pay to the victors indemnities, or reparations, different in nature from the 'contributions' levied in earlier conquests, including during the initial invasion in 1815. Although reparations are usually identified with the world wars of the twentieth century, they date from the Revolutionary and Napoleonic era, which saw an evolution in practice—if not always yet in terminology—from 'contributions' to 'indemnities', for the purpose not just of punishment but of recompense and security.[21] Prior to these wars, victors had appropriated prizes in money or kind and/or demanded repayment of debts, as a way of assigning responsibility for conflict. However, reparations for damages were a rare and recent practice, first instituted within France in a revolutionary decree of 11 August 1792 guaranteeing indemnities for citizens who lost property as a result of war and subsequently applied in some of the territories occupied by the French.[22] Following the first defeat of Napoleon in 1814, the only financial burden placed on the French was that they recognize the debts incurred by the imperial government through contracts signed with private entities outside France. In 1815, however, the Allies insisted upon additional indemnification for the damages they had suffered as a result of the return of Napoleon to power, as a condition of peace. In comparison to earlier war contributions, including those demanded by Napoleon, the 'indemnities' in the 1815 treaty were designed as a tool less for punishing the defeated power than for guaranteeing its fulfilment of the peace settlement with the international community. Payment of these reparations was hence the pre-condition for the end of the occupation of guarantee. In an effort, first, to reduce the number of troops stationed there and, second, to end the occupation ahead of schedule, the Duc de Richelieu and his finance minister, Count Corvetto, worked diligently to restore the political stability and hence the credit rating of France. After countering an Ultra-Royalist reaction in the fall of 1816, they were able to obtain a series of loans from Baring and Company of London and Hope and Company of Amsterdam, as well as French bankers and investors, which enabled them to fulfil their financial obligations to the Allies two years early, even if the final payments were not made until 1821, due to a last-minute financial crisis. As the economic historian Eugene N. White has concluded, these reparations imposed a high cost on the French economy in terms of lost output, consumption, and capital stock. However, they enabled France to be accepted once again as an equal among the great powers, thereby constituting a new mechanism for re-establishing peace among nations.[23]

To administer their occupation, the Allies relied not just on their military forces, but on a number of civilian institutions. Building on the practice of multinational cooperation employed in the campaign against Napoleon, including the Inter-Allied Commission and the Pact of Chaumont, they established several new international institutions, including a Council of Allied Ambassadors to oversee affairs in France, as well as the broader Concert of Europe, assembling on an ad hoc basis to address issues of common interest. The Council of Allied Ambassadors, which met at the British Embassy in the French capital at least once a week—or over 300 times—from the summer of 1815 through to the end of 1818, was the brainchild of the Duke of Wellington, who sought a 'permanent council' with whom he could consult on a regular basis.[24] Composed of the ambassadors of the major powers, including Charles Stuart (Great Britain), Pozzo di Borgo (Russia), General Baron von Vincent (Austria) and Count von der Goltz (Prussia), this council addressed such issues as requisitions, reparations, other financial claims by various Allies, exiled revolutionaries, various conspiracies and rebellions, liberal publications produced in France and abroad, the reduction of the occupation force in 1817, affairs in Spain and Portugal and their colonies, and especially the debates of the Chambers in France. Monitoring political developments for the Allied powers, it exerted an influence on the government in France, for example by encouraging the Duc de Richelieu to dissolve the Ultra-Royalist *Chambre Introuvable* in September 1816. It also helped to solidify perhaps the most significant institution of the post-Napoleonic settlement, the Concert of Europe, a loose diplomatic arrangement between the four major powers and, eventually, France, to promote unity and peace in Europe through regular consultation and cooperation. Although the

Concert did not stop disagreements between the powers of Europe, it was, in the words of the contemporary Austrian diplomat Friedrich von Gentz, 'a phenomenon without precedent in the world'.[25] The political accompaniments to the military forces commanded by Wellington, both the Council of Allied Ambassadors and the Concert of Europe played a key role in the revolution in international relations described by Paul Schroeder. Through such institutions, the occupation of France contributed to the development of the idea of 'Europe', as a political as well as a cultural entity.[26]

On the ground, the Allied authorities supplemented these institutions with a number of practices to encourage peaceful relations between occupying forces and local inhabitants. Following the example of Wellington, most Allied commanders insisted on tight discipline. If soldiers committed abuses against civilians, they were subject to trial by court martial. Such protection of the rights of civilians, which was a recent development in the law of war, was taken seriously by Allied leaders. For the British troops alone, there are dozens of records of courts martial for offences against civilians in France between 1815 and 1818; while not as numerous, references to such military court cases exist for all of the other Allied contingents, including the Russians. Although some offenders escaped trial, let alone punishment, this system helped to keep violence in check. Moreover, there existed a formal structure for conveying complaints from local authorities through the ministers in Paris, particularly the Duc de Richelieu, to the Duke of Wellington, who would then issue orders to the troops under his command. To promote what they termed good 'intelligence' or 'harmony' in the occupied zones, Allied commanders undertook a number of other measures, including organizing joint patrols with local National Guard regiments, providing manpower for grain and grape harvests, ordering deliveries of grain or forage from elsewhere to allay local shortages, and collecting monetary donations for the benefit of victims of disaster or famine. For their part, local authorities worked to cooperate with Allied officers and to maintain order among their subjects, to avoid any controversy that would increase the burden of the occupation. For offences against Allied troops, civilians were subject to trial before French courts. As a result of these efforts by both sides, occupier and occupied reached a state of accommodation, if not affection.[27]

Such practices provided a framework for the 'bond of peace' to be forged not just from above, but from below. Like other instances of military subjugation, including by the French armies during the Revolutionary and Napoleonic Wars, the 'occupation of guarantee' definitely provoked its share of conflict between occupiers and occupied, especially among the lower classes, who suffered most from the presence of foreign troops in their communities. However, given its multinational nature and its focus on security rather than conquest, it also promoted contact—if not understanding—across cultures. After 25 years in which French troops and their allies from several European states had marched through all parts of the continent, now France itself was inundated not just with occupying troops but with foreign sovereigns, statesmen, bureaucrats, servants, tradesmen, artists, and accompanying tourists. Tens of thousands came from Great Britain alone, profiting from the security provided by the occupation to service the troops or indulge their curiosity, ambition, or pleasure. By putting peoples from around Europe in such close proximity to one another, the 'occupation of guarantee' provided the context for what Jacques Hantraye has termed an 'apprenticeship of the Other'. While this sort of apprenticeship was not unprecedented, it does seem—as attested by countless contemporary memoirs, fictional representations, and images by French and foreign observers—to have been more widespread and enduring than in previous wars and occupations. During the occupation, occupiers and occupied traded a wide variety of words, foods, fashions, amusements, and ideas. Some of this cross-cultural fertilization left a legacy for years afterwards. Russian officers, for instance, who had frequented masonic lodges and read liberal publications while in France, exported revolutionary political ideas which would later fuel the Decembrist movement.[28]

As this example suggests, such cross-cultural exchange was promoted by 'fraternization' between occupiers and occupied, which was considerable throughout the occupied zones, especially among the upper classes. Such fraternization among elites, many of whom shared a knowledge of the French language, had a long tradition in early modern warfare. In the context of the occupation of guarantee, although there were tensions between Allied commanders and French officials, foreign dignitaries and their entourages tended to get along well with local bourgeois. In the occupied zone in the north-east as well as in the capital, Allied officers (and accompanying tourists) and French civilians socialized in masonic lodges, reading rooms, theatres, banquets, and balls, at which they alternated between French and foreign dance steps. Allied officers and local elites also hunted and dined together, and they attended each other's parades and festivals.[29]

Farther down the social scale, artisans and peasants tended to be less hospitable toward Allied troops, given that the burden of the occupation weighed heaviest on them. Nonetheless, in archival documents as well as published memoirs and histories, there is considerable evidence of fraternization between foreign soldiers and French men and women of the lower classes. Housed near or with the inhabitants of the communes where they were garrisoned, often for the full three years of the occupation unless they were among the 30,000 troops sent home in April 1817, occupying soldiers got to know their hosts, sometimes quite intimately—to the chagrin of local authorities, who worried about the 'demoralization' of their subjects, especially young women.[30] Sharing meals, playing games, harvesting fields, and celebrating holidays together, occupiers and occupied came to accommodate, if not always like, each other. On a regular basis, Allied soldiers also socialized with local men and, especially, women, in taverns, dance halls, and brothels. Such socialization sometimes led to more intimate relations between occupier and occupied, including not just prostitution, but also romance and marriage. When British troops re-embarked for England, they frequently took French women with them. Some of these relationships culminated in marriages. Such marriages were approved, in limited numbers, by the British authorities as well as some other governments. Although it is difficult to obtain precise statistics on marriages (or births or naturalizations) among foreign troops in France in this period, the occupation did promote cross-cultural relations of the most personal kind.[31]

Such amorous relations became common enough that they were satirized in popular culture, for instance in several plays produced on the occasion of the Congress of Aix-la-Chapelle at which the Allies agreed to end the occupation. In these plays, French girls in fortress towns along the north-eastern border reject foreign suitors in favour of returning French soldiers. For instance, in the one-act vaudeville 'The Route from Aix-la-Chapelle', three young women, who during the occupation have been courted by foreign troops, await the return of their lovers, French soldiers who have been stationed outside the occupied zone. When a Prussian sergeant named Tertef who has been courting her comes to say farewell, one of the girls, named Victorine, responds, '... How I love you ... but do not stay for that, I love even better to regret you a little than to see you so near to me'. When Tertef says, 'Adieu, Mamzelle, think of me a little, a lot from time to time; me, I will regret extraordinarily France, the women as pretty as anything and the wine so good like the women', Victorine ripostes, 'Adieu! Monsieur Tertef, bon voyage, and do not ever come back'. Following the return of Victorine's French lover, Toutcoeur (All Heart), everyone drinks to the Congress of Aix-la-Chapelle, and the local noblewoman concludes,

> Now that all credits are erased; | The times become calm and serene; | It is necessary for subjects to embrace each other | When kings extend to each other a hand. | No more enemy discord, | Peace succeeds fear; | Good faith, | The law is here; | And all of Europe exclaims: | It is necessary for each one to stay home.

Except, adds Victorine in the last line, 'to go to the theatre'.[32] Despite their often nationalistic tone, such satires reveal that the occupation did accomplish its ultimate goal: peace. Unlike a traditional military execution, the 'occupation of guarantee' effected at least grudging reconciliation between former enemies.

Conclusion

The Congress of Aix-la-Chapelle culminated in a treaty dated 9 October 1818 whereby, in exchange for payment in full of their financial obligations, the French obtained liberation from occupation. The following month, the foreign troops began to evacuate the territory of France and to march home to Russia, Prussia, Austria, Russia, Denmark, Saxony, and other German lands. At Calais, the British troops—along with a number of women—awaited transport across the Channel. The end of the 'occupation of guarantee' brought a massive de-, or re-, mobilization of a multinational force now totalling 120,000 men, many of whom were quite sad to leave their relatively cushy posts in France. Whether out of regret for the life they were leaving behind or out of worry for what they faced at home, many Russian and Prussian troops were reported to have actually shed tears upon their departure.

Long after these troops left French soil, however, both occupiers and occupied remained altered by the three-year occupation of guarantee. From France, the occupiers took new tastes, idioms, amusements, ideas, and even companions. For their part, despite the heavy burden imposed by the foreign presence, the French were able to reconstruct a stable government, military, and economy and to re-emerge as a world power. Above all, the occupation of guarantee succeeded not just in keeping but in actually *making*—in at least some hearts and minds—peace in Europe, for years to come. Following more than two decades of continent-wide war, this new approach to ending war proved remarkably effective at gradually demobilizing hundreds of thousands of soldiers, rebuilding the defeated state as a stable power, and reconciling bitter enemies. Although it did not eliminate conflict between individual nations, the settlement of 1815 did prevent another continent-wide war for a century. As Thomas Veve has concluded in respect of the British army of occupation, 'The final test of the success of the duke and his army lies in events after the departure of the allies. General war, which had engulfed Europe for a generation, was not renewed for another century'.[33]

When it was renewed, European war was even more 'total'. Following the next 'Great War', the example of the post-Napoleonic settlement, including the 'occupation of guarantee', was rejected out of hand by the victors. In contrast to the approach of Wellington and Castlereagh a century earlier, they insisted on a punitive approach to the losers, thereby destabilizing Germany to such an extent that this war was followed by an even more 'total' one only two decades later. In the aftermath of World War II, a new coalition of Allies took a more moderate approach to making peace, at least in the West. In the context of the mid-twentieth century, the Allied occupations of West Germany and Japan seemed innovative. However, whether they acknowledged it or not, they borrowed much from the type of multinational peace-keeping mission first tried in the long-forgotten 'occupation of guarantee' of 1815–1818.[34]

Acknowledgements

I would like to thank the editors for providing me with such provocative and thoughtful comments on the preliminary version of this piece.

Notes

1. 'General Order, Nivelles, 20 June 1815', in: *The Dispatches of Field Marshal the Duke of Wellington During His Various Campaigns*, ed. Lt. Col. Gurwood, 13 vols (London, 1834–1837) (hereafter *WD*), vol. 12, 493–494.
2. 'To the Right Hon. Sir Henry Wellesley, G. C. B., Paris, 19 July 1815', in: ibid., 566.
3. Notable exceptions include Marc Blancpain, *La vie quotidienne dans la France du Nord sous les Occupations, 1814–1944* (Paris, 1983); Thomas Dwight Veve, *The Duke of Wellington and the British Army of Occupation in France, 1815–1818* (Westport, CT, 1992); Volker Wacker, *Die allierte Besetzung Frankreichs in den Jahren 1814 bis 1818* (Hamburg, 2001); and Jacques Hantraye, *Les Cosaques aux Champs-Élysées: L'Occupation de la France après la chute de Napoléon* (Paris, 2005).
4. David A. Bell, *The First Total War: Napoleon's Europe and the Birth of Warfare as We Know It* (Boston, 2007); and Paul Schroeder, *The Transformation of European Politics, 1763–1848* (Oxford, 1994).
5. This point was made over a century ago by Raymond Robin, 'Des occupations militaires en dehors des occupations de guerre', doctoral thesis (University of Paris, 1913). On the evolution of occupation during the revolutionary era, see also Peter Haggenmacher, 'L'occupation militaire en droit international: Genèse et profil d'une institution juridique', *Relations internationales* 79 (1994): 285–301; and Philippe Burin, 'Writing the History of Military Occupations', in *France at War: Vichy and the Historian*, ed. Sarah Fishman et al. (Oxford, 2000), 77–90.
6. On the 'war occupation' of July to November 1815, see especially Roger André, *L'Occupation de la France par les Alliés en 1815 (juillet-novembre)* (Paris, 1924).
7. See for example, 'The Earl of Liverpool to Viscount Castlereagh, Fife House, 11th Aug. 1815', in Duke of Wellington, *Supplementary Despatches, Correspondence, and Memoranda of Field Marshal Arthur Duke of Wellington, K. G.*, ed. by his son, the Duke of Wellington, 15 vols (London, 1858–1872) (hereafter *WSD*), vol. 11, 114.
8. On these negotiations, see *WD*, vol. 12, and *WSD*, vol. 11; also Veve, *The Duke of Wellington*, Chapter 2, and Emmanuel de Waresquiel, *Le Duc de Richelieu, 1766–1822* (Paris, 1990), Chapter 8.
9. 'To Viscount Castlereagh, K.G., Paris, 11th August 1815', *WD*, vol. 12, 596–600.
10. 'To Viscount Castlereagh, K.G., Paris, August 1815' and 'Memorandum: On the temporary occupation of part of France, To Viscount Castlereagh, K.G., Paris, 31st August 1815', in *WD*, vol. 12, 600–601 and 622–625.
11. On the organization of the 'occupation of guarantee', see especially Veve, *The Duke of Wellington*, Chapter 2; and Blancpain, *La vie quotidienne*, 58–65.
12. On the tradition of 'making war pay' and occupation before 1815, see especially Peter H. Wilson, *German Armies: War and German Politics, 1648–1806* (London, 1998); Michael Rowe, *From Reich to State: The Rhineland in the Revolutionary Age, 1780–1830* (Cambridge, 2003); John A. Lynn (ed.), *Feeding Mars: Logistics in Western Warfare from the Middle Ages to the Present* (Boulder, CO, 1993); G. Jacquemyns (ed.), *Occupants, occupés, 1792–1815: Colloque de Bruxelles, 29 et 30 janvier 1968* (Brussels, 1969); and Jean-François Chanet et al. (eds), *Le Temps des hommes doubles: Les arrangements face à l'occupation, de la Révolution française à la guerre de 1870* (Rennes, 2013). On Austria in 1809, see Robert Ouvrard, *1809: Les Français à Vienne: Chronique d'une occupation* (Paris, 2009); on Prussia from 1806 to 1808, see Karen Hagemann, '"Desperation to the Utmost": The Defeat of 1806 and the French Occupation in Prussian Experience and Perception', in *The Bee and the Eagle: Napoleonic France and the End of the Holy Roman Empire*, ed. Alan Forrest and Peter Wilson (Basingstoke, 2008), 191–214.

13. This description of the burden of the occupation is based on records regarding requisitions in Archives des Affaires Etrangères (La Courneuve), Fonds France 692, and Service Historique de la Défense, Paris (Vincennes) (hereafter SHD), D3/16, as well as police records regarding the occupied departments in Archives Nationales, Paris (Pierrefitte-sur-Seine) (hereafter AN), F7/9899–9903, and extensive research in departmental and municipal archives in the Nord, Ardennes, Moselle, Meuse, Bas-Rhin and Haut-Rhin.
14. Report from stagecoach driver to ministry of police, departing from Mézières, 2 June 1816, AN, F7/3826.
15. 'Rapport sur la situation politique pendant le mois de janvier 1816 des Départements de la Moselle, la Meuse, la Marne, et les Ardennes formant ensemble la 23e Légion de Gendarmerie Royale' to Ministry of War, Metz, 2 February 1816, SHD D3/20.
16. Report from prefecture of the Meuse to ministry of police for September 1818, AN, F7/9900; and Hantraye, *Les Cosaques*, 41–42.
17. Schroeder, *The Transformation of European Politics*, especially Preface and 578. The evolution from a natural-law to a positivist concept of war is discussed in Stephen C. Neff, *War and the Law of Nations* (Cambridge, 2005). On the significance of this postwar peace settlement, see also Michael Howard, *The Invention of Peace: Reflections on War and International Order* (New Haven, CT, 2000); and Mark Mazower, *Governing the World: The History of an Idea* (New York, 2012).
18. On the Treaty of Westphalia, see the final chapters of Peter H. Wilson's *The Thirty Years War: Europe's Tragedy* (London, 2009).
19. For the text of the treaty, see Veve, *The Duke of Wellington*, Appendix A, 175–80; of the attached military convention, Ibid., Appendix B, 181–185.
20. On the development of the law of occupation, in addition to Neff, *War and the Law of Nations*, especially 190, see Eyal Benvenisti, *The International Law of Occupation* (Princeton, 1993); Geoffrey Best, *War and Law Since 1945* (Oxford, 1994); David Kennedy, *Of War and Law* (Princeton, 2006); and John Fabian Witt, *Lincoln's Code: The Laws of War in American History* (New York, 2012).
21. On the development of war reparations, in addition to Neff, *War and the Law of Nations*, 211–214, see John Torpey, '"Making Whole What Has Been Smashed": Reflections on Reparations', *The Journal of Modern History* 73/2 (2001): 333–358; and Luc Somerhausen, *Essai sur les origines et l'évolution du droit à réparation des victimes militaires des guerres* (Brussels, 1974). On the reparations required by the Second Treaty of Paris see André Nicolle, 'The Problem of Reparations after the Hundred Days', *Journal of Modern History* 25/4 (1953): 343–354, and Eugene N. White, 'Making the French Pay: The Costs and Consequences of the Napoleonic Reparations', *European Review of Economic History* 5/3 (2001): 337–365.
22. Somerhausen, *Essai sur les origines et l'évolution du droit à réparation*, 16, and Bell, *The First Total War*, 240.
23. Nicolle, 'The Problem of Reparations', 343; White, 'Making the French Pay', 361–362.
24. 'To Viscount Castlereagh, K.G., Paris, 19th Sept. 1815', *WD*, vol. 12, 638–639.
25. Quoted in Mazower, *Governing the World*, 17.
26. Carsten Holbraad, *The Concert of Europe: A Study in German and British International Theory, 1815–1914* (London, 1970), 1. On the multinational coalition against Napoleon, see Gordon A. Craig, 'Problems of Coalition Warfare: The Military Alliance against Napoleon, 1813–1814', in *War, Politics, and Diplomacy: Selected Essays* (New York, 1966), 22–46. On the Council of Allied Ambassadors, see the Protocols in The National Archives, London, (TNA) FO 146/ 6, 14, 15, 22, 23, 29,

and 30, as well as Pierre Rain, *L'Europe et la Restauration des Bourbons* (Paris, 1908). On the Concert of Europe, see Howard, *The Invention of Peace*, and Mazower, *Governing the World*, as well as Adam Zamoyski, *Rites of Peace: The Fall of Napoleon and the Congress of Vienna* (New York, 2007). On the emergence of the idea of 'Europe' as a political entity in this period, see Gerard Delanty, *Inventing Europe: Idea, Identity, Reality* (New York, 1995), esp. 74–79.

27. The following points are based on research in municipal and departmental archives in the Nord, Meuse, Moselle, Ardennes, Bas-Rhin and Haut-Rhin as well as archives of the ministries of police, justice and war in Paris, especially AN, F7/9899–9904, as well as numerous local histories, particularly Blancpain, *La Vie quotidienne*, and Jean Breuillard, 'L'occupation russe à Givet de 1816 à 1818, d'après les mémoires du Gen.-Baron V.I. Loewenstern', *Revue historique ardennaise* 12 (1977): 47–77. For British court martial cases during this period, see TNA, WO 71/242–247 and WO 90/1 (Register).
28. Hantraye, *Les Cosaques*, 169. On the influx of British travellers to France in these years, see Victoria Thompson, 'Foreign Bodies: British Travel to Paris and the Troubled National Self, 1789–1830', *Studies in Travel Writing* 15/3 (2011): 243–265.
29. For examples of such socialization, see invitations from French authorities to British officers in Records of Military Headquarters in Calais, TNA, WO 28/17, and François-Simon Cazin, *Les Russes en France: Souvenirs des années 1815, 1816, 1817* (Avranches, 1880).
30. See, for example, a letter from the mayor of the commune of Neiderbronn to the Prefect of the Bas-Rhin, 6 May 1816, expressing concern about the excessive familiarity between Württemberger soldiers and local girls, Archives Départementales du Bas-Rhin, Strasbourg, RP 1247.
31. For evidence of such intimate relations, see Veve, *The Duke of Wellington*, 77; William Lawrence, *Mémoires d'un grenadier anglais (1791–1867)*, (Paris, 1897), Chapter 23; and R. Wauthier, 'Les Russes à Givet, 1816–1818', *Revue historique ardennaise* 19 (1912): 155–161.
32. Armand d'Artois and Emmanuel Théanlon, *La route d'Aix-la-Chapelle: Tableau-Vaudeville, en un acte*, (Paris, November 1818), Bibliothèque Nationale de France, Arts du Spectacle, Rf-35836. For other examples, see *Le Retour de Valenciennes, ou Rentrons chez nous*, reviewed in *Galignani's Messenger*, 3 December 1818; and Jean-Baptiste Dubois and Nicolas Brazier, *Une heure sur la frontière* (Paris, 1819).
33. Veve, *The Duke of Wellington*, x.
34. On the rejection of the model of 1815 in 1919, in addition to Neff, *War and the Law of Nations*, and Mazower, *Governing the World*, see Margaret Macmillan, *Paris 1919: Six Months That Changed the World* (New York, 2003). On the relatively gentler settlements, including occupations, after World War II, see, among numerous other works, Ian Buruma, *Year Zero: A History of 1945* (London, 2013); and John Dower, *Embracing Defeat: Japan in the Wake of World War II* (New York, 2000).

4
The Experience of Demobilization: War Veterans in the Central European Armies and Societies after 1815

Leighton S. James

On 18 June 1815 the final act of the Napoleonic Wars was played on the field at Waterloo. In the hard-fought battle Napoleon's bid to restore himself to power was foiled by Coalition forces under the command of Wellington and Blücher. Victory cemented Wellington's place within the pantheon of British military heroes, while Waterloo became a key *lieu de mémoire* for British memories of the Napoleonic Wars. It was folded into a triumphalist British narrative in which French attempts to dominate Europe were halted once and for all, allowing Britain to concentrate on its maritime empire. The battlefield quickly developed into a tourist attraction. Early visitors were drawn from the British elite, but mass tourism in the later nineteenth century allowed working-class men and women to visit the battlefield. Tourism and the market in relics, both real and fake, ensured the battle's place in British cultural memory.

In Britain, therefore, Waterloo was and is widely commemorated and celebrated as a British victory. Yet, as Jasper Heinzen has shown, early commemorations of the battle in Britain also demonstrated striking awareness of the debt owed to non-British soldiers, particularly the King's German Legion. Hanover was still bound to Britain in a personal union until 1837, but the shared experiences of the veterans were also crucial in maintaining a transnational communicative memory of the battle. Philanthropic efforts in Britain provided for both British and Hanoverian veterans and war widows, while memorial architecture and decoration commemorated Anglo-Hanoverian sacrifice. Veterans of the King's German Legion were also awarded the Waterloo Medal, the first British military decoration for which all ranks were eligible. By contrast, veterans of the Peninsula were not similarly rewarded as proposals for a campaign medal were blocked by Wellington, who aimed to elevate Waterloo above other victories. This rankled with veterans of the Iberian theatre of war for more than symbolic reasons, as the Waterloo Medal entitled the bearer to a two-year pension enhancement. Veterans of Portugal and Spain had to wait until the creation of the Hanoverian Peninsular Medal in 1841 and the Military General Service Medal by Britain in 1847.[1]

The transnational nature of the Anglo-Hanoverian memory of the battle was in contrast to Prussian traditions. Although the Battle of Leipzig loomed larger in Prussian memories of the conflict, Prussian veterans also cultivated the memory of Waterloo. In June 1845, for example, veterans of *Landwehr*, regular and volunteer units gathered to celebrate the victory.[2] Veterans' organizations had been discouraged in Prussia in the immediate aftermath of the Napoleonic Wars. Indeed, there appears to have been official antipathy amongst the regular army towards the formation of veterans' associations, particularly those of volunteers which were perceived as potentially tainted by radical national and democratic sympathies. The career soldier and Chief of the General Staff, Friedrich Karl von Müffling, actively sought to prevent their establishment, believing that they represented the 'arrogance of young men brought too soon into the world by the War of Liberation'.[3] By the 1840s, however, associations had received official sanction and had begun to spread. Unlike the Anglo-Hanoverian memorial tradition, they emphasized the arrival of the Prussian army under General Blücher as the key turning point and claimed Waterloo as a German victory. Prussian historian Julius von Pflugk-Harttung reiterated this view of Waterloo as a German victory before and during the First World War, while Peter Hofschröer has made the same claim more recently.[4] These two traditions clashed following Prussia's annexation of Hanover in 1866. Eventually, following Emperor Wilhelm II's 'decree on tradition', Hanoverian battle honours were transferred to certain Prussian regiments and on 18 June 1915 thousands gathered at the Waterloo Column in Hanover to remember the battle as a German victory.[5]

The contested memory of Waterloo and the role veterans played within it hint at the diversity of their demobilization experiences and war memories in the nineteenth century. For veterans, issues such as recognition and pensions, association and commemoration, were played out against the backdrop of domestic and international politics. Yet while the experience of demobilization in Europe following later wars, particularly the World Wars, has been extensively examined, less attention has been devoted to the post-Napoleonic period, with the exception of France.[6] A social history of demobilization in the various German states that examines not only the political role of veterans, but also their impact on such diverse aspects as the labour market, criminality, social welfare and the provision for the disabled, is sorely lacking. This chapter throws some light on demobilization through reference to military memoirs. These texts have inherent limitations, not least due to the fact that many memoirists were officers. Many also focus exclusively on their wartime service.[7] Even where memoirists did cover the postwar period, the published versions are often limited to the war itself.

The memoirs, however, provide some insight into officers' reactions to the outbreak of peace and the challenges they faced reintegrating into civilian society. Here the focus is on two key areas: the diversity of experience for demobilized soldiers and officers during and after the Napoleonic Wars, and the reaction to the cessation of hostilities and their relation to the cultures of commemoration that emerged in the nineteenth century.

Officers' experience of demobilization

The Revolutionary and Napoleonic Wars witnessed a vast expansion of military experience in German Central Europe. Although the famous French *levée en masse* of 23 August 1793 might have differed more in rhetoric than in implementation from systems of recruitment in the Holy Roman Empire, the demand for manpower created by the Napoleonic Wars necessarily witnessed an expansion of military service across the German states.[8] Hundreds of thousands of German-speaking men were mobilized, both by the German states and as part of Napoleon's armies. Although substitutions were still allowed, at least in the armies of the Confederation of the Rhine founded in July 1806 by Napoleon, which included 20 German states (only Austria, Prussia, Danish Holstein, and Swedish Pomerania stayed outside), the myriad exemptions based on social status that had characterized older forms of recruitment and conscription were reduced and, consequently, thousands more men in German Central Europe received a taste of military life than had been the case in the wars of the eighteenth century.[9] To give just a few examples, it is estimated that around a third of the male population in the Rhenish regions directly annexed to the French Empire were conscripted, while almost 100,000 German soldiers participated in Napoleon's disastrous campaign in Russia in 1812 alone. As noted above, German-speaking soldiers also served in the armies of Great Britain, and also of Russia.[10] Indeed, during the period between 1792 and 1815 many served in the army of more than one state, either due to the shifting of political boundaries, the need for subsistence or as a means of escaping captivity as a prisoner of war.

Thousands of young men across the social spectrum were therefore required to adapt quickly to the rigours of military discipline, the deprivations of campaigning and the terrifying violence of the battlefield. To differing degrees these experiences loom large in the letters, diaries and memoirs of veterans from across Europe. Demobilization represented a part of that military experience. It was an urgent issue, not only for the German states, but also for individuals. At a state level, one of the most pressing concerns was the financial burden imposed upon treasuries across the continent by the mass mobilization that characterized the Napoleonic Wars. The Austrian army, for example, still consumed a half of state revenues in 1817.[11] This problem emerged long before the final climax to the conflict in 1815. The Habsburg Monarchy was plagued with financial difficulties throughout the 1800s because of its war effort. The economic dislocation caused by the war negatively impacted on state revenues, as did the loss of territories to the French Empire, its client states and allies. The Habsburgs were therefore required to reduce the size of their army on several occasions between 1800 and 1815, not least after the conclusion of the Treaty of Schönbrunn (1809), which limited the army to 150,000 men. Although it is common to see the period between 1793 and 1815 as a generation of warfare, the episodic nature of the struggle with France meant that demobilization occurred throughout these years at different times in different states, and not just following the ultimate defeat of Napoleon in 1815. Indeed, the eighteenth-century practice of keeping aged and invalid soldiers on the muster rolls out of charity meant that the Prussian mobilizations in 1792 also entailed the demobilization of those unfit for service.[12] Although the largest scale demobilization occurred after 1815, the period as a whole witnessed a series of mobilizations and demobilizations.

Demobilization was further complicated between 1813 and 1815 due to the extinction of the Napoleonic satellite states in German Central Europe, the Kingdom of Westphalia and the Grand Duchy of Berg, and also the existence of substantial auxiliary and volunteer forces. Alongside the regular army, both Austria and Prussia mobilized sizeable militia, or *Landwehr*, forces in 1809 and 1813 respectively. On the eve of the 1809 campaign the Austrian *Landwehr* numbered some 152,000, while in 1813 the Prussian *Landwehr* included some 151 infantry battalions and 113 cavalry squadrons, with a combined strength on paper of over 120,000 men, a substantial portion of the available Prussian military force. The Prussian armies of 1813 also included volunteer units, such as Major Lützow's famous Free Corps, which served alongside the Prussian regular army.[13] The Austrian and Prussian *Landwehr* had different terms of service from the regulars and, consequently, different expectations. The exact circumstances of demobilization often depended on which group a soldier belonged to. Following the abdication of Napoleon in 1815, for example, some 30,000 Prussian regulars, along with the same number of Austrian soldiers, remained stationed on France's eastern borders as part of the Allied army of occupation between 1815 and 1818. The smaller German states also contributed troops to what has been called the 'first joint multinational peacekeeping army'. Bavaria contributed 10,000 soldiers, while Württemberg, Saxony and Hanover contributed 5,000 each.[14] By contrast, the volunteers were among the first to be discharged. The majority of the Prussian *Landwehr* formations too were quickly demobilized against the background of a burgeoning struggle between Prussian War Minister Hermann von Boyen and Prince Wittgenstein, Minister of Police, over universal conscription and the nature of military service.[15] Thus the experience of demobilization for German-speaking soldiers up to and including 1815 varied greatly. Much depended on whether they were regulars, militia or volunteers. Some were demobilized because of reforms, others as a consequence of military defeat or political struggles over the meaning of military service.

Demobilization posed questions concerning the reintegration of soldiers into civilian society. For many soldiers and officers in the regular armies of the German states this meant returning to the more regular and mundane, but undoubtedly safer, existence of garrison duty and other peace-time operations. For example, after serving throughout the Revolutionary and Napoleonic Wars, Michael Pauliny von Köwelsdamm, an Austrian hussar officer, was posted to the Banat on the Habsburg Military Frontier with the Ottoman Empire. While Köwelsdamm's earlier 'diaries' were filled with his military exploits, the final volume, written during his peacetime service, is given over to ethnographic descriptions of the people of the Banat.[16]

While many other soldiers experienced a similarly straightforward transition from wartime to peacetime service as Köwelsdamm, military personnel discharged from the army faced more complex problems that typically revolved around career advancement or their reintegration into civilian society. As a consequence of the reduction in military establishments or the extinction of some German states, many soldiers and officers found their military career abruptly terminated. Many Prussian officers, for example, after the defeat of 1806–1807 and the Treaty of Tilsit of July 1807 that reduced the Prussian army from over 100,000 men to just 40,000, faced a choice between taking up a civilian profession or continuing their military service in the army of another state, often at a lower rank. While some sought commissions in armies independent of or hostile to Napoleon, others were forced to take service with his allies and satellites. One such satellite was the Kingdom of Westphalia, established from Hessian, Prussian and other territories in 1807, and counting 2.6 million subjects. Its army, which numbered some 25,000 troops, had an officer corps made up of ex-Hessian and ex-Prussian officers, and during its existence it received German soldiers discharged from other states.[17] Johann von Borcke was among those ex-Prussian officers. He sought to legitimize his decision to join the Westphalian army by claiming in his memoirs that he believed re-enlistment in the Prussian army to be impossible. Rubbing salt in the wound, he was also forced to accept the lowest officer's commission, that of *sous-lieutenant*, despite a 12-year period of military service.[18]

By February 1814, Borcke was back in Prussian uniform following the collapse of the Kingdom of Westphalia. But, whereas he welcomed the opportunity to return to Prussian service, others experienced a very abrupt demobilization and were less than enthusiastic when the state they served collapsed. This was the experience of officers such as Johann Friedrich von Gieße and Wilhelm von Conrady, both of whom had served with some distinction in the army of Westphalia. The collapse of this quintessential Napoleonic satellite state marked a major disruption in the military career of both men. Conrady had served in the Hessian Guards Regiment. Following the dissolution of Hesse-Cassel he joined the army of Westphalia where he rose to the rank of *Oberstleutenant*. He participated in the Russian campaign, during which he was captured and transported deep into the interior. By the time Conrady returned to Germany in 1813 following his captivity in Russia, Jérôme Bonaparte had fled and his kingdom was no more. Conrady thus found himself forcibly demobilized. His professional situation further deteriorated when it became clear that the restored Elector Wilhelm I of Hesse was intent, in Conrady's words, on turning back the clock by a decade. Conrady noted caustically in his memoir that the Elector 'would have liked to have erased the years 1806–1813 from history and begin again to reign where he had left off. Military and civil administration was established in the old manner and the army organized as it had been in 1806'.[19]

The restoration of William I of Hesse had dire implications for Conrady's military career, which had flourished under King Jérôme. Conrady's repeated requests for a military commission in the reformed Hessian army were denied. He was therefore forced to continue his military career elsewhere, eventually enlisting in the Prussian army. Like Borcke, Conrady sought to legitimate his decision in his memoirs by writing of his long-standing respect for the Prussian army and its traditions. He also seemingly adopted the official interpretation of Prussia's role in the Wars of Liberation. In a passage illustrative of the flexibility of concepts of patriotism in the period, he wrote that he 'was filled with a deep respect for the House of Hohenzollern which had first shown its greatness in its misfortune ... From the moment that I belonged to my new Fatherland, which had risen like a phoenix from the ashes, my fate took a surer path'.[20]

Conrady's experience mirrored those of other German officers who found themselves unemployed as a result of the fortune of war. Borcke corroborated Conrady's claim that the Hessian Elector sought to 'turn back the clock'. He wrote that although 'the foreign government was loved by no one, it had done some good, [and] had brought many people, officers and officials, rapid advancement'. The Elector, in contrast, was 'neither loved nor respected', and Borcke concluded he was lucky not to be born a Hessian.[21] It is probably too much to call this a purge of the Hessian state, but the restoration of German sovereignty was clearly not an unalloyed good, particularly for those whose careers had prospered under the French.[22]

One officer who particularly suffered from the collapse of the Kingdom of Westphalia was Friedrich Gieße. His experience was similar to Conrady's. Although Hessian-born, he had served exclusively in the Westphalian army and the collapse of the state destroyed his career. It was a particularly bitter pill to swallow since Gieße had not only advanced to the rank of captain, but had also been awarded the Order of the Crown of Westphalia, which had been established in 1809. Derisively referred to as *La Menagerie* because of the number of animals it depicted, the Order nevertheless included a yearly pension and other privileges.[23] Not only could Gieße no longer claim the pension. From February 1815 the wearing of the order was banned in Prussian territory. Gieße wrote sadly in his memoir that 'now there remains to me nothing of that [time], but proud and untarnished memories'.[24] After 1813, Elector Wilhelm I refused to accept Gieße into the reconstituted Hessian army. Like Conrady, he was forced to seek service in another army, in this case the army of Nassau. However, to Gieße's disappointment he received a commission as a lieutenant, rather than as a captain. Nevertheless, after a career fighting for the French Empire, he ultimately fought against Napoleon at Waterloo and marched victoriously into Paris.[25]

The multinational, or perhaps more precisely multi-state, nature of the German armies evident in the experiences of Borcke, Conrady and Gieße also led to other complications. The dramatic redrawing of political boundaries in 1813 as German states reclaimed lost territory, coupled with the continued demand for manpower, meant that many contained military contingents from different German states. Some soldiers had taken service in the Prussian or Austrian armies on an individual basis, but others had been attached en masse. This resulted in tensions between troops, sometimes exacerbated by the negotiations at the Congress of Vienna, which had direct implications for the soldiers. In an act reminiscent of Frederick the Great's forced incorporation of the Saxon army into the Prussian in 1757, in 1815 around 14,000 Saxons were to be absorbed into the Prussian military following the annexation of part of Saxony to the Prussian state. When news reached the Saxon contingent at Liège a group among them mutinied, temporarily forcing General Blücher to abandon his headquarters before the rebellion was brutally crushed and the ringleaders executed.[26] Werner von Herwig, a Prussian officer among those sent to put down the mutineers, wrote to his wife, 'this event made an unpleasant impression on me and my comrades since it was only their love for their Fatherland [Saxony] that had caused the Saxons to revolt'.[27]

The demobilization experience of soldiers

The rank and file's experience of demobilization is more difficult to reconstruct from personal documentation, not least because of its scarcity. Like the Austrian officer, Ignaz Berndt, some no doubt sought to continue their military service. Berndt gained a taste for army life after serving in the Austrian *Landwehr* in 1808 and subsequently enlisted with the regulars when the militia was reduced in size after 1809.[28] Even if the European states reduced their military establishment after 1815, there were still opportunities overseas. Of the 176,250 European soldiers recruited into the Dutch colonial army between 1814 and 1909, some 40 percent were non-Dutch, the majority of whom were of either Belgian or German origin.[29]

Others, such as Jakob Walter, a soldier from Württemberg, returned to their peacetime occupations, or, like Carl Schehl, a soldier from the Lower

Rhine region, began the careers they had prepared for before the wars intruded on their lives.[30] Josef Müller, the founder of the first veterans' association in Bohemia, returned to his trade as a journeyman clothworker after 14 years of military service.[31] This was particularly true of the volunteers and the *Landwehr*. Unlike the regulars, for these troops military service was a temporary situation, an interruption to their normal life course. Statistical analysis of the 30,000 or so Prussian volunteers has revealed that the majority were artisans, labourers and shopkeepers, occupations to which most presumably returned after the war.[32] For some, demobilization could not come soon enough as they chafed under the strictures of military discipline. The novelist Georg Häring served as a volunteer with the Kolberg Regiment in the 1815 campaign. In his memoirs of the campaign, published under his pseudonym Willibald Alexis, he records the growing discontent among the volunteers over their treatment. He complained that their 'volunteer status' (*Freiwilligtum*) seemed forgotten by the regulars. In a scene that encapsulated the sense of discontent, Alexis depicted an exchange at Buzancy when a general addressed them after parade. '"Well, *Jäger*, now you will go home. I thank you in the name of the King. Well, and if it starts again, you'll come again?" Only a few voices answered. The General is dead now. He had only recently become Prussian'.[33] Alexis concludes, 'I no longer wanted to play the soldier, I no longer wanted to press a shako on my head and to bind my hair up'.[34]

For their part, the regular soldiers were not always sorry to see the volunteers or the *Landwehr* depart. Throughout the so-called Wars of Liberation tensions existed between the regular army, the *Landwehr* and the volunteers. While some non-Prussians looked to the Prussian volunteers as an inspiring example of patriotic sentiment, others were scornful of their claims to be liberating Germany. Despite the nationalist discourse that accompanied the Wars of Liberation, regional patriotism (*Landespatriotismus*) and its loyalties often resulted in friction, as the Saxon mutiny illustrated. Even within the Prussian military establishment itself, doubts over the military efficacy of the volunteers and *Landwehr* were sometimes coupled with resentment at their perceived arrogance. The Prussian officer Thomas Gottschall, who had been in service since 1809, referred to the volunteers disparagingly as 'those thieving defenders of the fatherland [who] did their mischief excessively'.[35]

Veterans, military culture and postwar commemoration

The often tense relationship between the Prussian officers and the volunteers fed into competing commemorative cultures that emerged in the decades after 1815. Two variants were developed in Prussia. A monarchical interpretation emphasized the role of the Hohenzollerns and the state in spearheading the German struggle against the French, while a radical–democratic version celebrated 1813–1814 as a popular uprising.[36] Officers' and soldiers' narratives fed into this communicative and cultural memory.[37] Many soldiers' narratives depict the homecoming in a heroic light that fitted with the official commemoration that would later develop. Karl August Jordan, who served in the East Prussian National Cavalry Regiment, provides a typical example. He recorded his homecoming thus:

> Everywhere we were warmly received. We were delighted by the patriotic sentiments of the inhabitants of the areas we crossed. In one village in the Graffschaft Mark, I asked a peasant standing by the road, 'Is this village old Prussian?' 'Yes, we are old Prussians', he called, 'with body and soul!' The expression on this face spoke more feelingly than the words.[38]

These patriotic sentiments were not limited to Prussian officers or volunteers. The Austrian officer, Michael Pauliny von Köwelsdamm, was inspired by the patriotic discourse of 1813, which was itself foreshadowed by Austrian propaganda in 1809.[39] He drew a direct link between the patriotism he believed had inspired the Prussian population and the expansion of the Austrian army, claiming that the recruits he trained in 1813 were eager to step 'onto the field of glory, to make themselves good citizens and defenders'.[40] By contrast, he remembered his recruits of eight years earlier as convicts and murderers who served from fear of punishment.[41] Köwelsdamm, therefore, represented the campaigns of 1809 and 1813–1814 as a qualitatively different type of conflict to those which he had experienced in the 1790s and earlier 1800s, seemingly symptomatic of a shift from 'Kabinettskrieg' to the 'nation in arms' or 'people's war'.

It is the case that almost all officers' letters, diaries and memoirs refer to the celebrations with which they were received upon their return from France in 1814 and 1815.[42] Some of the volunteers, however, were less than enthused with the postwar settlement hammered out at the Congress of Vienna. Alexis believed that the dreams of German national unity and freedom had been betrayed at the Congress.[43] Similarly, the students who gathered at the Wartburg castle in Eisenach in 1817 to celebrate the tricentenary of Martin Luther's 95 Theses and the four-year anniversary of the Battle of Nations shared the disillusionment that Alexis felt. Prussian commemorations of the battle had become a tradition since 1813. Celebrations of the victory centred on the wearing of oak leaves and gatherings around a 'pillar of fire' on a nearby hilltop, or altars situated in town squares.[44] Jordan, for example, recorded in his memoir that he remained close to some of his old companions and saw others at festivals in 1833 and 1843, where they honoured the dead.[45] But the Wartburg Festival was not to be an uncomplicated celebration of Prussian military success over the French. Former volunteers, and their admirers, inspired by a romantic nationalist fervour expressed in the works of Arndt and Theodor Körner, the same literature that would be quoted so liberally on the occasion of the centenary in 1913, were frustrated by what they saw as the restoration of the status quo ante bellum and the failure to create a more unified Germany. Ludwig Rödiger, a student leader from Jena, claimed to speak for the veterans of war when he stated that 'those who are allowed to bleed for the fatherland also have the right to speak about how they can best serve the fatherland in peacetime'. Along with books deemed 'un-German' and a copy of the Napoleonic Code, various accoutrements of the German regular armies were committed to the flames of the bonfire: an Austrian corporal's stick, a Prussian Uhlan's tunic and a Hessian military braid.[46]

The works burnt at Wartburg may have been pre-arranged, and the book-burning in general was less enthusiastically endorsed by the attendees at the festival than was assumed at the time or has been since.[47] However, the immolation of symbols of the regular army was nevertheless symptomatic of the tensions that existed between the expectations of the former volunteers and the interests of German princes and their military establishments, both during and immediately after the war. While some ex-volunteers might criticize the army for upholding the conservatism of the postwar German regimes, regular army officers with years of experience of fighting the French resented volunteers' claims that they had liberated Germany, something that implicitly seemed to demean the regulars' past efforts.[48]

If the volunteers were mistrusted because of their nationalist ideas, other veterans were suspect for the opposite reason, for their seeming pro-Napoleonic sentiments. Much of the Rhineland had been incorporated into the French Empire for two decades before becoming a Prussian territory after 1815, and loyalties to the Hohenzollerns were weak. Despite the slew of anti-French literature that had accompanied the Wars of Liberation, Francophile and pro-Napoleonic songs continued to circulate in the Rhineland and south-western Germany during the first half of the nineteenth century, while new works appeared in the 1820s and 1830s. These songs apparently appealed particularly to veterans of the Napoleonic armies in the Rhineland, who continued to sing them into the mid-nineteenth century.[49] In fact, pro-Napoleonic works and slogans were utilized to express political opposition, both in the Rhineland and beyond. The Bavarian authorities, for example, feared that veterans of Napoleon's armies might throw their weight behind the liberal activists' demands for a free press at the Hambach Festival in 1832.[50] Even in Berlin, pro-Napoleon sentiments could be encountered. Shouts of 'Long live Napoleon' were heard during a riot between artisans and soldiers in the city in 1820.[51]

Veterans of Napoleon's armies also sought to honour their former comrades through processions and monuments. For example, every year in Cologne veterans of Napoleon's armies marched to church to hear mass for those who had fallen in battle.[52] Meanwhile, in Worms, an association was established in 1846 with the explicit goal of erecting a monument commemorating those who had died serving under Napoleon's banners. Its members, which encompassed both former infantry and cavalrymen, included veterans who had served in almost every theatre during the Napoleonic Wars. Most had been wounded, while some had been prisoners of war. The monument was unveiled in 1848 and the accompanying ceremony was remembered as a celebration of the camaraderie and honour of fallen 'brothers in arms' who died under the banners of their 'once great leader Napoleon'.[53]

It was these tensions and the resultant official antipathy, particularly in Prussia, which limited the growth of veterans' associations in the decades immediately after 1815. Consequently, associations grew slowly. The first Austrian veterans' association appears to have been established by Josef Müller in 1820 in the Bohemian town of Reichenberg and was intended to cover funeral and medical costs. Although precise figures are elusive, it seems that thereafter the number of Austrian veterans' associations grew only slowly in the 1830s and 1840s, before expanding more rapidly in the 1870s.[54] Meanwhile, in Prussia, of the 45 associations that existed in 1848, only two had been formed before 1828. The growth in veterans' associations in Prussia only occurred after 1842, following their sanction by Friedrich Wilhelm IV.[55] By then the Prussian state had made efforts to incorporate veterans into the official, monarchical commemoration of the wars through the production of memorabilia, such as teacups and medallions. The manufacture of the former was facilitated by the falling costs of production at the Royal Porcelain Works. Although guided by consumer demand, these objects were also aimed at promoting loyalty amongst former volunteers and members of the *Landwehr* to the Hohenzollerns, rather than more radical democratic and nationalist political visions.[56] By the last third of the nineteenth century, in the aftermath of the Wars of Unification and the Franco-Prussian War, veterans' associations had completed their journey from suspect organizations to seemingly patriotic institutions in the eyes of the authorities. By then, most of the Napoleonic veterans had passed away, and the membership was instead drawn from more recent wars and national service men. However, those still alive continued to play some role in the celebrations marking the creation of the Second Reich. For example, at Tuttlingen in Württemberg, five veterans of the Napoleonic Wars took part in a procession to mark the unification of Germany.[57]

Although all associations were committed to the commemoration of former comrades, it does appear that there was some difference between the volunteers' and the veterans' associations in the first half of the nineteenth century. While the latter drew from a wide cross-section of society, the former, such as the Association of Silesian Volunteers, the Pomeranian Detachment of Volunteers of 1813 to 1815, and the Volunteers' Association of Berlin, appear to have drawn their membership more from the propertied and educated in Prussian society. Certainly, at festivals of remembrance these social groups were more evident, partly as a consequence of the costs of travel. Of 339 former volunteers who gathered at a festival held in Berlin on 3 February 1841 over 40 percent were state officials of some kind, while a fifth were men of business.[58]

These symbolic functions aside, most veterans' associations across the German states were aimed at providing material benefits to their members. These included support for invalid veterans and funds to meet medical expenses and the provision of a decent burial. Indeed, Josef Müller was said to have been inspired to found his association after witnessing a former soldier receiving a pauper's burial.[59] Many associations also added to the ceremony of veterans' funerals by providing uniformed men, thereby reminding the community of the deceased's war service and raising his status.[60] Finally, the sociability that these associations, as well as less formal meetings of veterans, offered to former soldiers should not be overlooked. They offered the individual not only an opportunity to reminisce about his youth, but the chance of social interaction in convivial surroundings. The associations that emerged in the postwar decades were undoubtedly an attempt to recreate the elation and camaraderie among former comrades.[61] As the old order of corporate privilege continued to decline, veterans' groups, like masonic lodges and Carnival associations, fulfilled a social need and formed part of the associational life (*Vereinswesen*) that expanded in nineteenth-century Germany. As such, they had a role to play in reintegrating former soldiers back into civilian society, both in material and psychological terms.

Conclusion

Although few in German Central Europe shed tears at the final defeat of Napoleon, the transition to peace and the final military demobilization was a complex process. This was not least a consequence of the political fragmentation of Germany, the different troop types mobilized by the war effort, and the hopes that had been unleashed by the propaganda that characterized the campaigns of 1813 to 1815. All welcomed peace after a generation of warfare, but not all were happy with what followed, be that the exact circumstances of demobilization or the postwar political settlement.

For those officers whose military careers had been tied to the existence of the Napoleonic regime, the period after 1815 was often one of professional frustration, marked by a desperate search for a commission. This was not a new phenomenon in 1815. Demobilization was a periodic experience during the Revolutionary and Napoleonic Wars. The episodic nature of the conflict and the separate peace treaties signed before 1814/15 meant that armies of different German states were mobilized and demobilized at different times. Defeat and financial retrenchment meant slashing military budgets and manpower, only for armies to be remobilized for the next round of fighting. Each period of demobilization posed challenges of reintegration into the civilian society and economy. The enforced reduction of the Prussian army after Tilsit had been particularly traumatic, but although they were often forced to accept commissions at lower ranks than they had hitherto enjoyed, the expansion of military establishments of other German states and the likelihood of further campaigns at least held out hope of a position and possibly rapid advancement. Those opportunities were scarcer in the decades of peace after 1815.

Meanwhile, those who had invested their political hopes for a more united Germany in the campaign against Napoleon were to be disappointed. Their discontent was loudly proclaimed at Wartburg and Hambach. Official suspicions over veterans' political sympathies, particularly of those who had served under Napoleon or those who voiced radical national sentiment, coupled with the animosity towards the perceived arrogance of volunteers felt by some regular officers, dovetailed to hamper the development of veterans' associations immediately after 1815, particularly in Prussia. Attempts were made through commemorative memorabilia to draw former *Landwehr* and volunteers into the official monarchical narrative. How successful this was is unclear. In some regions, such as the Rhineland, pro-Napoleonic songs remained popular, especially among veterans, and became symbols of political opposition in the years before 1848.

Political sympathies aside, the veterans' associations that did emerge before 1848 offered their members tangible benefits. But the associations and the festivals also offered members sociability and were a part of the emerging associational life that was increasingly replacing corporate society. Above all, however, the associations revealed the desire among veterans to commemorate their war service. Whether it was the Worms Veterans' Association and their monument, the Cologne veterans at mass, or the former members of Lützow's Corps gathered at Körner's grave, all were engaged in the validation and remembrance of their war service. Although they might be separated by political sympathies, social origins and personal circumstances, for most veterans the Napoleonic Wars were the seminal experience of their youth, binding them together within the consciousness of having lived through a distinct epoch and providing a common frame of meaning through which they interpreted and understood their individual experience.[62]

Notes

1. Jasper Heinzen, 'Transnational Affinities and Invented Traditions: The Napoleonic Wars in British and Hanoverian Memory, 1815–1915', *English Historical Review* 529 (2012): 1404–1434. See also Brendan Simms, *The Longest Afternoon: The 400 Men Who Decided the Battle of Waterloo* (London, 2014).
2. Christopher Clark, *Iron Kingdom: The Rise and Decline of Prussia, 1600–1947* (London, 2006), 380.
3. Cited in Daniel Moran, 'Arms and the Concert: The Nation in Arms and the Dilemmas of German Liberalism' in *The People in Arms: Military Myth and National Mobilization since the French Revolution*, ed. Daniel Moran and Arthur Waldron (Cambridge, 2003), 49–74, 60.

4. Julius Pflugk-Harttung, *Belle-Alliance—verbündetes Heer* (Berlin, 1915); Peter Hofschröer, *1815, The Waterloo Campaign: The German Victory* (London, 1999).
5. Heinzen, 'Transnational Affinities', 1427–1431. On the different ways the battle was remembered by the participants see Alan Forrest, *Waterloo* (Oxford, 2015).
6. See, for example, Adam R. Seipp, *The Ordeal of Peace: Demobilization and Experience in Britain and Germany, 1917–1921* (Aldershot, 2009). For French veterans see Natalie Petiteau, 'Survivors of War: French Soldiers and Veterans of the Napoleonic Armies', in *Soldiers, Citizens and Civilians: Experiences and Perceptions of the Revolutionary and Napoleonic Wars, 1790–1820*, ed. Alan Forrest et al. (Basingstoke, 2009), 43–58; and Petiteau, *Lendemains d'Empire: Les soldats de Napoléon dans la France du XIXe siècle* (Paris, 2003).
7. For the use of *Ego-Dokumente* to study soldiers' experience see Mark Hewitson, 'I Witness: Soldiers, Selfhood and Testimony in Modern Wars', *German History* 28/3 (2010): 310–325.
8. See Peter H. Wilson, *German Armies: War and German Politics, 1648–1806* (London, 1998), 314–315.
9. For the southern German states see, Ute Planert, *Mythos vom Befreiungskrieg: Frankreichs Kriege und der deutsche Süden: Alltag–Wahrnehmung–Deutung* (Paderborn, 2007), 408–419.
10. Both the British and Russian armies included foreign units in the form of the King's German Legion and the Russian–German Legion respectively. Germans also served in the regular line army of the British Empire. See Mark Wishon, *German Forces and the British Army: Interaction and Perceptions, 1742–1815* (Basingstoke, 2013). The Russian-German Legion was financed by Britain. See Wishon, *German Forces*, 143.
11. Gunther Rothenberg, *The Army of Francis Joseph* (Purdue, IN, 1998), 10.
12. Willerd R. Fann, 'On the Infantryman's Age in Eighteenth Century Prussia', *Military Affairs* 41/4 (1977): 165–170.
13. Ernst Zehetbauer, *Landwehr gegen Napoleon: Österreichs erste Miliz und der Nationalkrieg von 1809* (Vienna, 1999), 50; and Dennis Showalter, 'The Prussian *Landwehr* and its Critics', *Central European History* 4/1 (1971): 3–33, 13.
14. Thomas Dwight Veve, *The Duke of Wellington and the British Army of Occupation in France, 1815–1818* (Westport, CT, 1992), 20. See also the chapter by Christine Haynes in this volume.
15. Gordon Craig, *Politics of the Prussian Army, 1640–1945* (Oxford, 1955), 69.
16. Österreiches Hauptstaatsarchiv (Kriegsarchiv), Vienna (hereafter ÖKA), Nachlässe und Versammlungen, B 1505, Michael Freiherr Pauliny v. Köwelsdamm, 'Historisch-Militär Tagebuch der Jahre 1813 to 1817', Part III, fo. 278. Although entitled diaries, his account was retrospective.
17. See Michael F. Pavokić, 'Recruitment and Conscription in the Kingdom of Westphalia: "The Palladium of Westphalian Freedom"', in *Conscription in the Napoleonic Era: A Revolution in Military Affairs*, ed. Donald Stoker et al. (London and New York, 2008), 135–148.
18. Johann von Borcke, *Kriegerleben des Johann von Borcke, weiland Kgl. Preuß. Obrestlieutenants, 1806–1815* (Berlin, 1888), 101 and 112.
19. Wilhelm von Conrady, *Aus stürmischer Zeit: Ein Soldatenleben vor hundert Jahren. Nach den Tagebüchern und Aufzeichnungen des weiland kurhessischen Stabskapitans im Leibdragoner-Regiment L. W. von Conrady* (Berlin, 1907), 400.
20. Ibid., 402.
21. Borcke, *Kriegerleben*, 287–290.

22. On the removal of French collaborators see Carl Haase, *Politische Säuberungen in Niedersachsen, 1813–1815: Eine Fallstudie zur Phänomenologie der Kollaboration* (Hildesheim, 1983).
23. Veit Veltzke (ed.), *Napoleon: Trikolore und Kaiseradler über Rhein und Weser* (Cologne, 2007), 352.
24. Friedrich Gieße, *Kassel-Moskau-Küstrin, 1812–1813: Tagebuch während des russischen Feldzuges geführt*, ed. Karl Gieße (Leipzig, 1912), 337.
25. Ibid., 339.
26. See Lawrence J. Flockerzie, 'Saxony, Austria, and the German Question After the Congress of Vienna, 1815–1816', *International History Review* 12/4 (1990): 661–687.
27. H. Hollender (ed.), *Erinnerungen und Briefe eines preußischen Offiziers aus den Jahren, 1805 bis 1815* (Kattowitz, 1913), 105.
28. ÖKA, Nachlässe und Versammlungen, B 683, Ignaz Berndt, 'Bemerkungen aus dem Leben eines Pensionierten Stabsoffiziers der österreichischen Armee', Heft 1, fo. 161.
29. Martin Bossenbroek, 'The Living Tools of Empire: The Recruitment of European Soldiers for the Dutch Colonial Army, 1814–1909', *Journal of Imperial and Commonwealth History* 23/1 (1995): 26–53.
30. Jakob Walter, *The Diary of a Napoleonic Foot Soldier*, ed. Marc Raeff (Moreton-in-Marsh, 1991); and Carl Schehl, *Vom Rhein zur Moskwa, 1812*, ed. Jürgen Olmes (Krefeld, 1957).
31. Laurence Cole, *Military Culture and Popular Patriotism in Late Imperial Austria* (Oxford, 2014), 126.
32. Rudolf Ibbeken, *Preussen, 1807–1813: Staat und Volk als Idee und Wirklichkeit* (Cologne, 1970), 442–450.
33. Willibald Alexis, *Als Kriegsfreiwilliger nach Frankreich, 1815: Blätter aus meinen Erinnerungen*, http://gutenberg.spiegel.de/buch/als-kriegsfreiwilliger-nach-frankreich-1815-4822/2 (accessed 9 May 2012).
34. Ibid.
35. Quoted in Thomas Hippler, *Citizens, Soldiers and National Armies: Military Service in France and Germany, 1789–1830* (New York, 2008), 202.
36. Christopher Clark, 'The Wars of Liberation in Prussian Memory: Reflections on the Memorialization of War in Early Nineteenth-Century Germany', *Journal of Modern History* 68/3 (1996): 550–576. See the chapter by Karen Hagemann in this volume and her monograph *Revisiting Prussia's Wars against Napoleon: History, Culture, Memory* (Cambridge, 2015).
37. On the memory and commemoration of the war see Alan Forrest et al. (eds), *War Memories: The Revolutionary and Napoleonic Wars in Modern European Culture* (Basingstoke, 2012), 1–40.
38. Karl August Jordan (ed.), *Zur Geschichte des ehemaligen ostpreußischen National-Kavallerie-Regiments in den Feldzügen von 1813 und 1814: Mittheilungen aus den Tagebüchern und Erinnerungen eines Freiwilligen* (Leipzig, 1846), 248.
39. Karen Hagemann, '"Be Proud and Firm, Citizens of Austria!" Patriotism and Masculinity in Texts of the "Political Romantics" written during Austria's Anti-Napoleonic Wars', *German Studies Review* 29/1 (2006): 41–62.
40. ÖKA, Nachlässe, B 1505, Köwelsdamm, 'Historisch-Militär Tagebüch der Jahre 1813', Dritte Theil, fo. 38.
41. Ibid. Köwelsdamm, 'Historisch-Militär Tagebüch der Jahre 1801 to 1811', Part II, fo. 43.
42. See on these celebrations Karen Hagemann, *'Mannlicher Muth und Teutsche Ehre': Nation, Militär und Geschlecht zur Zeit der Antinapoleonischen Kriege Preußens* (Paderborn, 2002), 475–481.

43. Alexis, *Als Kriegsfreiwilliger*, 7.
44. See, for the celebrations of the Battle of Leipzig starting in 1813, the chapter by Hagemann in this volume and Hagemann, *'Mannlicher Muth'*, 481–497.
45. Jordan, *Geschichte*, 256.
46. Matthew Bernard Levinger, *Enlightened Nationalism: The Transformation of Prussian Political Culture, 1806–1848* (New York, 2000), 111.
47. Steven Michael Press, 'False Fire: The Wartburg Book-burning of 1817', *Central European History* 42 (2009): 621–646.
48. See Leighton S. James, *Witnessing the Revolutionary and Napoleonic Wars in German Central Europe* (Basingstoke, 2013), 76–77.
49. James M. Brophy, *Popular Culture and the Public Sphere in the Rhineland, 1800–1850* (Cambridge, 2007), 62.
50. Michael Rowe, *From Reich to State: The Rhineland in the Revolutionary Age, 1780–1830* (Cambridge, 2003), 280.
51. Hagen Schulze, 'Napoleon', in *Deutsche Erinnerungsorte,* ed. Etienne François and Hagen Schulz, 3 vols (Munich, 2009), vol. 2, 28–46, 35.
52. Jonathan Sperber, *Rhineland Radicals: The Democratic Movement and the Revolution of 1848–1849* (Princeton, NJ, 1991), 6.
53. Margit Rinker-Oldbrisch and Torben Olbrisch, 'Der Wormser Veteranen-Verein und sein Denkmal von 1848 für die Kriegsteilnehmer in der Grande Armée Napoleons', *Die Wormsgau* 26 (2008): 53–74, 73.
54. Laurence Cole, 'Military Veterans and Popular Patriotism in Imperial Austria', in *The Limits of Loyalty: Imperial Symbolism, Popular Allegiances, and State Patriotism in the Late Habsburg Monarchy*, ed. Laurence Cole and Daniel Unowsky (New York, 2007), 36–61, 38.
55. Eckhard Trox, *Militärischer Konservativismus: Kriegervereine und 'Militärpartei' in Preußen zwischen 1815 und 1848/49* (Stuttgart, 1990), 55.
56. On teacups see Eva Giloi, *Monarchy, Myth and Material Culture in Germany, 1750–1950* (Cambridge, 2011), 27–28. On medals see Karen Hagemann, *'Männlicher Muth'*, 455–456 and 'National Symbols and the Politics of Memory: The Prussian Iron Cross of 1813, Its Cultural Context and its Aftermath', in Alan Forrest et al. (eds) *War Memories*, 215–244.
57. Alon Confino, *The Nation as a Local Metaphor: Württemberg, Imperial Germany and National Memory, 1870–1918* (Chapel Hill, NC, 1997), 50.
58. Trox, *Militärischer Konservativismus*, 44–45.
59. Cole, *Military Culture*, 126.
60. Clark, *Iron Kingdom*, 380.
61. Trox, *Militärischer Konservativismus*, 56.
62. Peter Fritzsche, *Stranded in the Present: Modern Time and the Melancholy of History* (Cambridge, MA, 2004), 43–44.

5

War, Economy and Utopianism: Russia after the Napoleonic Era

Janet M. Hartley

The Napoleonic Wars transformed the status of the Russian Empire within Europe. At the beginning of the campaigns the perception of the other major European powers was that Russia was not capable of inflicting a major defeat on Napoleon without allied support. Alexander I was humiliated at the Battle of Austerlitz on 2 December 1805, and almost suffered the indignity of being captured. Following a further defeat at the Battle of Friedland in June 1807, Alexander had to come to terms with Napoleon at Tilsit (7 July 1807) and had to recognize the dominant position of the French Emperor in central and eastern Europe. Relations between France and Russia deteriorated, particularly as a result of French influence over Poland and the implementation of the Continental System, and led to the invasion of Russia in June 1812 by a massive army of some 680,000 men. The presence of Napoleon's troops in the Russian Empire was brief compared with the experience of some other European countries, but traumatic in terms of casualties suffered in major battles (Smolensk on 16–18 August and Borodino on 7 September), and the occupation of Moscow. The retreat started in mid-October and the Russian campaign effectively ended on 14 December 1812, with the last troops of the Grande Armée leaving Russian soil. But by now Russia had established its military superiority and became the dominant partner of the coalition which pushed Napoleon back to the borders of France. Alexander I entered Paris in triumph on 30 March 1814 and subsequently dominated the peace negotiations at Vienna.[1] This new-found international status had, however, come at an enormous cost. This chapter looks at how the Russian Empire, which had many of the attributes normally considered to be 'backward' (political, social, cultural, economic), dealt with strains of war which tested far more modernized countries at the time.[2]

The costs of warfare

Russia suffered enormous human and material losses in the Napoleonic Wars. First, the immediate economic consequences of the invasion were severe. The occupation and fire in Moscow led to the destruction of roughly three-fifths of the city; almost all of Smolensk and smaller towns and villages were ravaged in the western provinces on the invasion route. Towns, villages and religious buildings had to be rebuilt after 1815. The state compensated nobles, merchants and other inhabitants of Moscow with over ten million roubles, and the Synod was given 3.5 million roubles to restore churches in Moscow and elsewhere.[3] Factories and workshops in the city and the province had been destroyed, and trade only resumed slowly. In Smolensk, nobles claimed that 710 houses had been destroyed, as well as goods and crops, to the total value of over 2.5 million roubles.[4] The invasion left rotting bodies and carcasses on the land, which had to be cleared when they thawed in the spring—in Smolensk province alone it was estimated in December 1812 that there were 172,566 corpses and 128,739 animal carcasses to be cleared.[5] Peasants had their lands laid waste, their livestock slaughtered, their grain seized by soldiers and their homes destroyed. Peasants in the provinces subjected to invasion had to be exempted from the poll tax, the main state tax on all peasants, sometimes for several years, which also meant a further loss of income to the imperial treasury.

Second, the costs of sustained warfare over the whole Napoleonic period were immense. It is difficult to be certain about Russian expenditure as figures are inaccurate and can be misleading. We know, however, that the proportion of the budget spent on the armed forces was always high, but surged during the Napoleonic Wars. In 1808, expenditure on the armed forces has been estimated at 93 percent of net revenue.[6] Expenditure covered pay, equipment, armaments, uniforms, food, fodder and military administration. There was also, however, massive capital expenditure on fortresses and on the garrisons which stretched in 'lines' across the frontiers of the country in the south and the east. It has been estimated that about 26 million roubles were spent on the building and repair of fortresses between 1803 and 1820. An additional 25.7 million roubles were spent on construction between 1822 and 1825, that is, in peacetime after the end of the Napoleonic Wars. The main expenditure was always on the army but Russia also had to build and then maintain ships and shipyards for its naval forces in the Baltic and the Black Sea. Millions of roubles had already been spent on reconstruction of the shipyards in Kronstadt and the Baltic ports in the 1780s and 1790s.[7]

Third, Russia sustained these extensive losses and expenditure without modernizing her internal structures. The Russian state developed few of the features of Napoleonic France, the most modern state at the time, or Britain, and war naturally put significant strains on both those countries too. Russia did not receive a French Revolutionary or Napoleonic-style constitution, unlike so many other countries in Europe (although not, of course, Britain). The Tsar retained powers unchecked by either an institutional or a legal framework, even if in practice he had to be wary of alienating the noble elite. The Russian legal system remained unmodernized; there was no 'civil code' in

Russia. The legal profession, and what we might call a 'legal consciousness', only developed slowly. The first Russian professor of jurisprudence in Moscow University, S. A. Desnitsky, had been trained at Glasgow University in the 1770s. The educational standards in the Russian Empire were low by western and central European standards. By the early nineteenth century there were six universities in Russia, but two of those—in Vilnius and Dorpat—were in non-Russian lands and one—Khar'kov—was in Ukraine.[8]

The Russian social structure also remained unchanged during the Napoleonic period. The institutionalization of serfdom in the mid-seventeenth century was based on the assumption that nobles gave, mainly, military service to the state in return for the exclusive privilege of owning serfs. The Russian army was not strictly speaking a 'serf army', as only roughly half of the peasantry were serfs, that is, peasants who lived on noble land, but it was an army of conscripts and not of free citizens. Over 1.6 million men were conscripted in the period 1796 to 1815.[9] Service in the army was for life, or 25 years after 1793, which often in practice meant for life. This was itself a reflection of Russia's rigid social structure as 'soldiers' left their social estate once they departed for the army and it was then almost impossible to re-integrate them. They were no longer responsible for collective obligations of their former social estate. Recruits left the village to the sound of funeral laments, not only bewailing their fate but reflecting that as far as the village was concerned they were 'dead', and would not return in any capacity. Their wives often married again, sometimes with the connivance of the Orthodox Church. A consequence of this was that soldiers were not 'demobbed' at the end of campaigns but remained in the army, either in barracks or in garrisons on the frontiers. The only exceptions to this were temporary militias levied during the Napoleonic Wars. These men were supposed to be demobilized at the end of the campaigns but the limited evidence that exists suggests that at least some of them were transferred to regular regiments, and, in any event, these were only a small number of soldiers.[10]

Moreover, Russia lacked a modern, entrepreneurial, or politically powerful business class, and the big factories in the Urals supplied goods for the armed forces at prices determined largely by the state. Most of these factories were run by nobles appointed by the state as a 'privilege'. The labour force was almost entirely serf labour, as the noble owners dispatched their serfs, either as individuals or as whole villages, to work in their factories. In the short term, warfare stimulated demand for iron, copper, weapons and cloth, but by the 1820s the low productivity and lack of innovation in Russian factories was beginning to set her apart from the productive processes becoming common in western Europe. The primitive transport system, coupled with the distances involved, furthermore inhibited the development of modern internal commerce.[11]

Russia retained an Ancien Régime taxation system. The 'privileged' (the nobles, wealthier merchants, members of the clergy) were not taxed and the burden of direct taxation fell on peasants and ordinary townspeople. As a result, receipts were small and arrears were high. The poll tax, the state tax on peasants and townspeople, was introduced by Tsar Peter the Great in 1718 specifically to fund the cost of the army, and was initially allocated based on the sum required to cover that cost. The level of the poll tax failed to rise over the eighteenth and early nineteenth centuries and could not defray the cost of warfare. Arrears on all taxation had reached over 20 million roubles by 1793, and rose to over 80 million roubles in 1814.[12] Indirect taxes were levied by the state on necessities—in particular on salt and alcohol—but the poverty of the majority of the inhabitants meant that this did not bring in enough income to fund warfare (unlike, for example, Britain). Exports increased as Britain in particular needed Russian raw material for her navy—masts, hemp, tar, pitch—but the increase in tariffs did not fill the gap left by arrears on internal taxation.

Banking was hopelessly undeveloped in Russia. The few banks which did exist had been set up by the Russian rulers in the second half of the eighteenth century to encourage investment by nobles and attempt to reduce their indebtedness (although in practice they only served to increase it). In 1810, in the peaceful interlude between the Treaty of Tilsit and the French invasion of Russia, Mikhail Speransky, the chief minister, put forward a plan to reform Russian banking, based on British and French models and the latest economic thinking in Western Europe, which would have established a state bank on the model of the Bank of England, run by shareholders, and supported by new private banks. The plan was, however, considered too radical to be implemented, and was then overtaken by events when Napoleon invaded Russia.[13]

The gap between income and expenditure in Russia continued to grow—something which also affected other states during the period of the Revolutionary and Napoleonic Wars like Prussia. In 1801 the deficit was 132 million roubles and this grew to over 143 million by 1809, and over 200 million in 1814.[14] Lacking the means to generate income from taxation or loans from its own banks, Russia had to resort to the two traditional ways of funding warfare; first, loans and subsidies from other countries; second, devaluation of the currency. Russia entered the Napoleonic Wars with debts on loans taken by Catherine II to fund her wars with Turkey. However, the Wars led to greater loans, from Amsterdam, and greater debt. The foreign debt (called the 'Dutch debt') reached over 100 million guilders in 1816. In the period after the war ended the situation only deteriorated. Russian external and internal debt rose by 383 million roubles in the period from 1821 to 1824.[15] The other short-term traditional solution to trying to cover the cost of wars was the printing of paper money and the debasement of the currency. By 1799, the paper rouble was only worth 69 copecks in silver.[16] The strains of the Napoleonic Wars exacerbated the situation further. By 1810, the paper rouble was only worth 29 copecks.[17] In 1810, Speransky introduced a number of reforms in an attempt to stabilize the rouble in the short term but the outbreak of war again in 1812 led to the further printing of money. The number of roubles in circulation increased from 580 million in 1810 to 836 million in 1817, and the value of the paper rouble continued to fall.[18]

The failure to increase income and reduce indebtedness had led Russia by the end of the Napoleonic Wars to, in the words of one historian, 'come to the end of her resources'.[19] Robert Walpole (the classical scholar and traveller) gave his general assessment of the European situation in 1814 to Secretary of State Viscount Castlereagh in which he noted that Russia had a 'deplorable state of finances' and could not pay for her enormous army.[20] Russia, put bluntly, was broke, yet she had to rebuild and compensate for the losses of the invasion of 1812, and the disruption of trade and industry. More fundamentally, she still had to pay for the support of the largest standing army in the world—some 750,000 men—in order to maintain her new-found position as a serious diplomatic player within Europe.

Military colonies

Russia had always stationed men in military or semi-military communities on its border for defence, as indeed did Austria in the Balkans. That was how Cossack communities originated on the southern borders of Russia. Cossack regiments and garrison troops continued to guard the frontiers of Russia in 'lines' of forts which stretched across the southern frontiers of Ukraine and the north Caucasus, and then followed the southern borders of Siberia. Some of these garrison troops were elderly and the army became almost a form of 'outdoor relief' caring for elderly and sick soldiers who could not be demobbed, and who had nowhere else to go.

In Alexander I's reign, however, a far more complex attempt was made to integrate the army into the social fabric of Russia through the establishment of military colonies. Alexander was influenced by the 'model villages' which his adviser Count Aleksei Arakcheev had set up on his own estates, where he particularly admired: '(1) the order which prevails everywhere; (2) the neatness; (3) the construction of roads and plantations; (4) a kind of symmetry and elegance which pervades the place'.[21]

Military colonies were first set up in 1810 in western Russia, involving one battalion and 4,000 state peasants (most of whom perished), but the outbreak of war prevented their development. After 1815, they were conceived of on a far greater scale. Alexander stated in the preamble to the decree which established the colonies that they would serve 'to ease [the peasants'] transition to the military state and make [the soldiers'] service less burdensome'.[22] The personal commitment of Alexander to the colonies is not in doubt, and Arakcheev was put in charge to ensure that his ideas would be fully implemented.

At one level, the military colonies were a simple solution to the costs of sustaining and re-populating this enormous standing army. Colonies were to comprise roughly equal numbers of soldiers and officers on the one hand, and peasants on the other hand. In peacetime, the soldiers—primarily of peasant stock and young—would live with and work with the peasants on the land and would feed themselves. In wartime, the soldiers would leave to fight and the peasants would maintain all the land, and all the soldiers' dependants, in their absence. Future recruits to the army would be drawn from the children of peasants and soldiers in the colonies. At a stroke, this would seem to solve the problems of having to maintain such a large standing army: it would dispense with the need to provide supplies to feed the army in peacetime; it would provide a constant supply of recruits as ordinary soldiers, and even non-commissioned officers; it would make best use of young, physically fit, soldiers, while continuing to fill garrisons with elderly ones; in the process this would reduce the burden of conscription and supporting the army on the rest of the population.[23]

The assumptions made by Alexander in the preamble to the decree raise a number of questions around the colonies, in particular relating to how they were set up and how they functioned in practice. However, it also leads to broader questions about the intentions surrounding the initiative, and about what Alexander and his ministers hoped to achieve in the longer term. Had the colonies worked fully, they would not only have saved money and supplied new recruits but would have transformed the relationship between soldiers and peasants in peacetime, and could have led to a fundamental change in the economic, social and legal relationship between the new colonists and the state. In effect, the colonies would have created new social groups and could have altered social and political relationships within the Russian Empire.

The total number of colonists is a matter of dispute but was probably in the region of three quarters of a million by the end of the reign, including army personnel, peasants and minors.[24] The colonies, however, comprised more than soldiers and peasants in practice. The colonist had to be looked after—physically and spiritually—and had to be educated and trained, not only to ensure the economic success of the colonies, but also to train the colonists and soldiers of the future. In the process, modern institutions were to be established, in an attempt to end what Arakcheev and Alexander regarded as the backward way of life in the Russian village.

No expense was spared to provide this support. Hospitals were established, and midwives appointed: in July 1819 Arakcheev demonstrated his personal commitment in correspondence over the appointment, and travel arrangements, of one Natal'ia Kulakova as midwife to a colony in Novgorod province (in the north-west of European Russia).[25] By 1826, there were 29 churches in the Staraia Russa colony (in Novgorod province, situated about 100 kilometres south of the town of Novgorod) alone, staffed by 175 clergy.[26] In 1827, it was estimated there were 157 schools in the colonies, employing almost 200 teachers and educating almost 17,000 pupils, using the

Lancastrian method of instruction, that is, the most modern method of the time copied from Britain.[27] Colonies were also supplied with specialists in agricultural methods, including foreign agronomists and artisans; an English agronomist was paid 4,000 roubles in 1824 to increase agricultural productivity.[28] The very 'best' was imported to make the colonies work—from within and outside the country. This could include anything from architects and designers, teachers, pedigree livestock, foreign tools, warm clothing, bells (for churches) and clocks (for timekeeping—something very unfamiliar to peasants). All the buildings had to be constructed in brick and to a strict design. A foreign visitor commented on the Novgorod colonies that:

> ...the double houses were very neat, and extended on one side of the road for several versts; the spire of the church rose amongst them; attached to each house was a small garden, and windmills with six sails were in front; the soldiers were employed in the fields, mowing (in line), dressed in forage-caps and jackets; also repairing the roads.[29]

Colonies required both the purchase of land and construction of houses and roads. The role of colonies as landowners is an interesting one. Local records show how in Novgorod province land was purchased from the local nobility at seemingly a fixed price per acreage. The soil in Novgorod province was not very fertile, and the establishment of colonies may have been a godsend for the local nobility as they could sell unprofitable land to an unlikely purchaser. In 1825, for example, a widow, Golenishcheva–Kutuzova sold land comprising ploughed and unploughed land and woods for a total 17,718 roubles 78 copecks to the colonies administration. Other local nobles sold houses as well as land—another widow, Akermana, sold her residence and outbuildings for 7,000 roubles.[30] Local merchants and state peasants in the region also sold and leased property, including houses, shops, mills and gardens. In total, these purchases were very significant and must have had a considerable impact on the local economy. The Second Uhlan Regiment paid almost 81,000 roubles for land and property for their colony in Ukraine.[31]

Not only, however, had land and buildings to be acquired and colonies constructed, but *people* also had to be purchased. In the long term, the colonies could be expected to reproduce themselves, but in the short term peasant families had to be purchased as colonists. This is another feature of the colonies which has received little scholarly attention. The costs were high and, on the other side, the revenue acquired by the sale—from noble serf-owners, or the state if they were state peasants—was also considerable. The price varied according to the age and sex of the peasants. In 1823, they were set by the state, ranging from 22 roubles for an infant (there was a risk of course, as the child might die) to 300 roubles for a ten-year-old boy (who could work) and 1,000 roubles for an 18-year-old boy, who could be a full colonist.[32] In practice, prices could vary. In one document dated 1824, 14 children were bought at what seems an almost arbitrary price which disguises the human cost of such purchases to the children, and their parents. To give some examples: Evgeniia Bolgul'ianova, aged ten, cost as little as 150 roubles; at the other end of the scale Aleksei Sinapalov, aged 17, cost 930 roubles; Mikhail Gur'ev, aged 11, cost 390 roubles; his sister, Praskov'ia, aged 14, cost 330 roubles; the brothers Spiridov, Efim aged nine and Zakhar aged 13, cost 258 and 430 roubles respectively.[33] This was at a time when 'substitutes' were regularly purchased as recruits for the army, either individually or collectively by peasants, or by noble landowners on behalf of their peasants, and when peasants were bought and sold as 'property'.[34] Nevertheless, these transactions not only demonstrate the financial commitment of the government to the colonies but are also significant for an examination of the more 'utopian' aims of the colonies.

The total cost of the colonies to Russia is impossible to calculate accurately but it was clearly very considerable. A recent study by a Russian historian estimates that the cost per year between 1820 and 1829 varied from 2.5 million to over four million roubles.[35] In addition, Arakcheev built up the capital of the colonies, to an estimated 30 million roubles by 1831. How could such expenditure possibly be justified, given the declared aim of the colonies to reduce the burden on the population? The burden on recruitment was not fully tested in the long term as the colonies underwent so much change in the 1830s and were never expanded to the extent that they could replace the normal recruitment procedures. Indeed, Nicholas I was obliged in the 1830s to consider other ways in which the levy could be made less burdensome. The military component of the colonies was small in reality. It was estimated that of the three-quarters of a million inhabitants of the colonies, only some 160,000 were officers and men. This was at a time when the standing Russian army numbered some 750,000 men.[36] So, at best, the colonies were feeding and supporting less than a quarter of the armed forces. The rest were quartered on peasant households, lodged in barracks (although there were relatively few of these in Russia compared with other European countries) or private houses in towns, or employed in the garrisons. If we also take into account that Russia had a navy of not inconsiderable size, then the military colonies only catered for a relatively small part of the total armed forces, and at considerable expense.

That expense could have been justified if the colonies had fulfilled their economic aims. The evidence for this is not clear cut, and, in any event, the colonies did not last long enough in the form envisaged by Alexander and Arakcheev to have their credentials tested to the full. All the indications are, however, that on economic grounds the colonies failed to justify the expenditure in establishing them. The colonies were supposed to introduce the most modern agricultural methods. New roads should have improved communications which should have stimulated trade. The 'discipline' of the colonies should have improved productivity. The presence of young and physically fit soldiers should have helped agricultural work. At the same time, their presence should have encouraged marriage with local peasant girls and procreation, which would have increased the population of the colonies. We know that new crops were introduced into Novgorod province, a region where productivity was traditionally low. These new crops included potatoes in 1818. Official reports from the colonies listed the 'successes' of agriculture by yields of crops and by the development of rural industries, like fishing. Some peasants clearly thrived: one colonist became so wealthy that he had bought land from a noble and owned 2,000 Spanish sheep.[37]

Other evidence, however, suggests that the military colonies were not an economic success, or at least not to the extent of justifying this vast outlay of resources. The poor quality of land in Novgorod meant that peasants needed large allocations of land to prosper. In practice, the colonies failed to provide enough land and so most peasant–colonists remained in poverty. Figures for yields are unreliable; in Novgorod colonies they rose but, according to a recent Russian historian, did not reach the levels needed to sustain the peasants.[38] Harvests were poor throughout this period in the Ukrainian colonies. Rigid adherence to new crops and arbitrary allocation of livestock to peasants irrespective of local conditions often distorted the traditional pattern of agriculture with poor results. Initiatives to develop new crops, the building of mills and local industry in colonies could disrupt local trade. Colonists were further diverted by the obligation on all colonists—including peasants—to perform drill and be subjected to inspections and other, hated, military obligations, as well as being forced to carry out construction work. Colonel I. Dibich (Diebitsch), in Russian service, commented in 1826 that: '...the soldier–farmers are scarcely able to feed their own families ... agriculture has been completely neglected and everything has been done for appearance's sake instead of for genuine effect'.[39] In addition, of course, peasants were supposed to feed extra mouths—the soldier and their officers living in the colonies. This simply proved to be impossible, and was not compensated for by exemption from the state poll tax for colonists. The burden was especially onerous if the peasant had to support not only a soldier but also a cavalry horse. The British traveller, Robert Lyall, estimated that it cost between 45 and 50 roubles a year to support a soldier and between 180 and 200 roubles a year to maintain a cavalry horse.[40] This made the colonies economically unsustainable.

The longer-term sustainability of the colonies could only be assured by maintaining their population, and, indeed, growing so that the pool of recruits could be maintained and increased. Marriages were certainly encouraged between soldiers and peasant girls, and there were contemporary rumours that these were forced by the authorities to stimulate population growth. There were tales of peasant girls being chosen by 'lot', and of soldiers being lined up by their officers and allocated brides on the spot.[41] These stories cannot be verified but there is evidence that many marriages did take place, doubtless stimulated by the reward of 25 roubles per wedding, a not inconsiderable sum at the time. In 1824, as many as 3,813 marriages took place in the one colony of Staraia Russa. At the same time, the colony sensibly employed a wet nurse![42] It is not clear whether this could be sustained; the reality was that such a burst of activity mopped up the single girls in a village. The following year only 423 marriages took place.

The colonies failed as economic units and as a pool for future recruits. Put this way, the enormous investment of money and time by the government and Alexander's personal commitment to the scheme simply seem bizarre. It can in fact only be understood not in these, practical, terms but as a wider, utopian, vision for Russian state and society. Tsar Alexander saw the military colonies as a new way of keeping soldiers in the army after the wars had ended and of not only improving the economic life of the peasants but creating a new type of peasant. He wanted all the colonies to be completely ordered in their layout in comparison with the scattered, disorganized, Russian village. As the British traveller, Sir Robert Ker Porter observed, the Tsar saw the scheme as: '...forwarding the civilization of the peasantry—by introducing a habit of order and cleanliness, as well as a more extensive knowledge of the ordinary acquirements of reading and writing'.[43] It would also, according to Ker Porter, stop peasants from 'passing a great deal of their lives in drunkenness and idleness'. Such thinking was behind the setting up of schools and other welfare institutions in the colonies. The aim was to eliminate not only the poverty, but also the superstition and ignorance of the Russian village.

The colonies aimed, however, to do more than this; not just to create a clean, tidy and literate peasant but a new type of citizen, and 'new man', legally as well as morally. Alexander hinted that he wanted a new type of property ownership in the colonies—not serfs, not state peasants, but a new legal category of 'colonists'. The colonies had not only their own new layout and economic priorities set out for them, but also their own educational system, and their own laws, which were outside and distinct from the laws and institutions of the land. Furthermore, had the colonies functioned in the way envisaged they would have created a new cadre of soldiers whose only loyalty would have been to the person of the Tsar, and who would have been completely detached from the rest of Russian society.

The ambitions of Alexander are so potentially far reaching that they can be seen as 'utopian'. That was certainly not lost on contemporaries, in Russia or abroad. Russian soldiers and Russian officers hated having to be located in colonies and saw themselves reduced to little more than the peasantry themselves. Moreover, officers were also members of the Russian nobility and nobles were more fearful of the creation of a new social group who were neither serfs nor state peasants, and who, Alexander had hinted, could 'own' the land of the colonies. Any change in the ownership of land could threaten the status of nobles as the only group in society entitled to own serfs, a right which had been originally granted in the mid-seventeenth century in return for service, mainly military, to the state. The colonies were a 'state within a state' and that was inevitably threatening to the existing social order.

Furthermore, the creation of a potential new military force, loyal only to the Tsar, was a threat to the political position of nobles. There were precedents for this which rightly worried nobles. Tsar Peter I had put down a revolt at the beginning of his reign employing a separate and special military force—the so-called *strel'tsy*, usually translated as 'musketeers'—whose loyalty was supposed to be to the Tsar alone rather than to the nobles as a social group. As one nobleman said at the time, the colonists 'are the new *strel'tsy* who, in time, will lead Russia to a revolution'.[44] This threat was also not lost on foreign commentators. Robert Lyall remarked in his account that the:

> ...gigantic system contains in its bosom the seeds which will spring up, and prove its own ... under a warlike sovereign it may operate the subversion of all the established dynasties of Europe; under a weak one, the partitions of Russia may be looked upon as likely to result from the explosion of its latent power.[45]

More explicit was a long memorandum on the colonies sent in 1826 by the British politician and diplomat Edward Disbrowe, Minister Plenipotentiary in Russia, to George Canning, the Foreign Secretary, in which his warning is clear:

> ...a mass of Military force would be formed in time beyond all calculation, and most dangerous to its neighbours ... In its present shape, the plan offers ... the anomaly of an half educated military population dependent on the Crown, placed in the Centre of an half savage peasantry slaves to a Nobility, who themselves tremble at the Nod of The Despot. There will thus be a complete 'Imperium in Imperio', which in my humble opinion must soon escape from the control of its chief, an event the accomplishment of which the present troubles in this Country may hasten but which, in the ordinary course of things, must change the whole face of the Empire.[46]

In the event the experiment with the colonies failed. They were hated by the soldiers, the officers and the peasants. As Viscount Strangford, British ambassador in Russia, reported to Canning in 1826: '...the soldier (and more particularly the officer) complains of being reduced to the level of the peasant, whilst the peasant complains of his privacy being disturbed; his little property invaded, and himself exposed to most of the inconveniences of the military service'.[47] Robert Lyall characterized the peasant resentment in more human terms: within a peasant hut, he wrote, 'Every thing bore an aspect of military regularity: the very water pail has its assigned place, and should it happen to be found in any other, by the inspecting subaltern officer, on his morning visit, a severe reprimand, if not a stroke of the cane is sure to follow'.[48] Peasants proved ungrateful for the introduction of cleanliness and civilization into their villages, including even the importation of English-styled latrines! Lyall summed up the colonies as 'held in utter abhorrence by the peasantry; ... detested by the regular army ... highly disapproved of by all classes of the nobility'.[49]

Resentment against the brutal discipline and lack of sensitivity to local customs (not least the requirement that peasants had to shave off their beards) led to a series of revolts in the colonies in 1818 and 1819. These were put down with great savagery in which all the humanitarian ideals of the colonies were forgotten. A revolt in Chuguev, in the south, involved over 27,000 people. Over 1,000 colonists and 899 soldiers were arrested and many subjected to severe punishments including running the gauntlet.[50] In 1831, in the early years of the reign of Tsar Nicholas I, a great revolt took place in Novgorod province which was suppressed so brutally that all the failings of the colonies were exposed. Some 200 protestors died and over 3,600 were tried and punished. Sixty men were sentenced to receive some 4,000 blows as they passed eight times through the ranks of 500 men; 50 died as a result.[51] One contemporary described the scenes as: '...hell ... clamour, weeping, cries, moans–flowed like a wave, and tore not only at the heart and the soul but, it seemed, at the very stones lying at the place of punishment'.[52]

Conclusion

The colonies failed in their practical aims: they could not sustain a standing army; they could not lessen the burden of the recruitment levy on the Russian population. Nor were Alexander's more utopian aspirations realized. The history of the colonies ended in bloodshed and savage reprisals for revolts. Where did that leave Russia? On the financial side, the experiment had failed to find a solution to the unsustainable cost of maintaining her army. Nicholas toyed with ideas about changing the recruitment levy but without success.[53] More fundamentally, this experiment, proposed by the Tsar, *within,* at least in his view, the social and political order, had failed. It demonstrated that there were no easy solutions to reforming and modernizing society or the economy without more fundamental change to the Russian political and social order.

Admittedly, in the short term there was no pressure on Russia to change her political or social system. She had been victorious in the Napoleonic Wars: traditional, unmodernized Russia had beaten the most modern nation in Continental Europe; peasant armies had triumphed over 'free' men. Russia—like the other victor in the Napoleonic Wars, Britain—was under no pressure to introduce modern, French-style, constitutions, let alone to change the social or political order. But the financial weakness of Russia had been fully exposed and the country was almost bankrupted by the Napoleonic Wars. The failure to resolve this within the political and social system either by the reforms introduced by Mikhail Speransky or by the newly established military colonies simply exposed this weakness further. The tsars and the government were fully aware of Russia's vulnerability but unable to address the issue without risking undermining the social system, and ultimately their own authority. While Russia was at peace, or while European conflicts could be localized, then the Ancien Régime could survive. However, tested again by war in the Crimea, the failure to transform from within was cruelly illustrated. Defeat in the Crimean War led to fundamental change to the social order, and the abolition of serfdom. It took defeat, or at least military failure, in further wars in the twentieth century to force political change and ultimately to result in the end of the tsarist system, which had been so successful on the field of battle in the early nineteenth century.

Notes

1. The literature on Russia during the Napoleonic Wars is too extensive to be listed in full. The excellent recent study by Dominic Lieven, *Russia Against Napoleon: The Battle for Europe, 1807–1814* (London, 2009) includes an extensive bibliography. The best recent biography of Alexander I is Marie-Pierre Rey, *Alexander I: The Tsar Who Defeated Napoleon* (Dekalb, IL, 2012), which is a translation of *Alexander Ier* (Paris, 2009). The proceedings of a recent, 2014, conference on Russia and the Napoleonic Wars which brought together scholars from North America, Western and Eastern Europe and Russia have now been published in a volume entitled *Russia and the Napoleonic Wars* (Basingstoke, 2015), ed. by Janet M. Hartley, Paul Keenan and Dominic Lieven.
2. This chapter draws heavily on my *Russia 1762–1825: Military Power, the State and the People* (Westport, CT, 2008), and in particular on Chapter 10 on the military colonies, 190–208. The methods Russia deployed to deal with the human and material costs of war, and the consequences of this for state and society, are the themes of the book. The conclusion is that Russia did so not by modernizing but by strengthening its traditional structures: of the state, of the economy and of society. Service in the army became the *raison d'être* of the nobility with serfdom and tax exemptions regarded as exclusive symbols of their privilege and reward for service. At the same time, the mechanism of conscription of peasants reinforced the traditional authority of the peasant commune, which selected the recruits, and preserved the collective responsibility of the commune. In addition, the culling of the least useful members of the peasant community, and the transfer of income from rich to poor peasants through the purchase of substitutes, helped to preserve the traditional economy and the social relationships of the village. The expansion of the

arms industry occurred within pre-modern economic and social relationships. Finally the image of the Tsar as the military victor asserted traditional values; soldiers fought to assert the superiority of Orthodox Christianity but also for the Tsar, and, by implication, for the existing social and political order which underpinned Tsardom.

3. *Polnoe sobranie zakonov Rossiiskoi imperii* (hereafter *PSZ*), vol. 32, no. 25, 275, 463, 26 November 1812.
4. I. P. Shcherov, *Zapadnoi region Rossii i Dekabrizm* (Smolensk, 2003), 66–71.
5. *Otechestvennaia voina v khudozhestvennykh proizvodeniiakh, zapiskakh, pismakh i vospominaniiakh sovremennikov,* compiled by A. V. Mezier (St Petersburg, 1912), 171. See also Janet M. Hartley, 'Russia in 1812: Part 1: The French Presence in the Gubernii of Smolensk and Mogilev', *Jahrbücher für Geschichte Osteuropas* 38 (1990): 178–198.
6. Frederick W. Kagan, *The Military Reforms of Nicholas I: The Origins of the Modern Russian Army* (London, 1999), 12.
7. L. G. Beskrovnyi, *The Russian Army and Fleet in the Nineteenth Century* (Gulf Breeze, FL, 1996), 256–257.
8. For a general survey of educational developments in the Russian Empire in the late eighteenth and early nineteenth century see Janet M. Hartley, *A Social History of the Russian Empire 1650–1825* (London, 1999), 125–145; the most thorough account of the establishment of universities can be found in James T. Flynn, *The University Reforms of Alexander I 1802–1835* (Washington, DC, 1988).
9. L. G. Beskrovnyi, *Russkaia armiia i flot v XVIII v (ocherki)* (Moscow, 1958), 294–297.
10. For more details on conscription and its consequences see Hartley, *Russia 1762–1825*, 29–46, and Janet M. Hartley, 'The Russian Recruit', in *Reflections on Russia in the Eighteenth Century*, ed. Joachim Klein, et al. (Cologne, 2001), 32–42. On militias see Janet M. Hartley, 'Patriotism in the Provinces in 1812: Volunteers and Donations', in *Russia and the Napoleonic Wars*, 148–162.
11. For more details on the operation of the Russian economy and its limitation in supporting the needs of the army and navy see Hartley, *Russia 1762–1825*, 88–99.
12. K. V. Sivkov, 'Finansy Rossii posle voin s Napoleonon', in *Otechestvennaia voina i russkoe obshchestvo*, ed. A. K. Dzhivelegov (Moscow, 1912), vol. 7, 124–137, 131.
13. Marc Raeff, *Michael Speransky: Statesman of Imperial Russia 1772–1839* (The Hague, 1957), 92, 97–98.
14. *Ministerstvo finansov 1802–1902 gg.* (official Ministry of Finance publication) (St Petersburg, 1902), vol. 1, 170–171; and Sivkov, 'Finansy Rossii', 132–133.
15. V. G. Sirotkin, 'Finansovo-ekonomicheskoe posledstvia Napoleonovskikh voin i Rossiia v 1814–1824 gody', *Istoriia SSSR* 4 (1974): 46–56, 56.
16. Beskrovnyi, *Russkaia armiia*, 379.
17. L. G. Beskrovnyi, *Otechestvennaia voina 1812 goda* (Moscow, 1962), 250.
18. Kagan, *Military Reforms,* 15.
19. Quoted in Ibid., 13.
20. The National Archives, London, Foreign Office, FO 65/94, Walpole to Castlereagh, St Petersburg, 29 April 1814.
21. Richard Pipes, 'The Military Colonies, 1810–1831', *Journal of Modern History* 22 (1950): 205–219, 211.
22. Quoted in John L. H. Keep, *Soldiers of the Tsar: Army and Society in Russia, 1462–1874* (Oxford, 1985), 284.

23. The section on military colonies is drawn largely from Hartley, *Russia 1762–1825*, Chapter 10, 190–208, which uses archival material in Russia. A good introduction in English is Pipes, 'Military Colonies', 205–219.
24. Keep, *Soldiers of the Tsar*, 286.
25. Rossiiskii gosudarstvennyi voenno-istoricheskiii arkhiv, Moscow (hereafter RGVIA), fond (hereafter f.) 405, opis' (hereafter op.) 3, delo (hereafter d.) 101, folios (hereafter fos) 1–2v, Military colonies, on the hiring of a midwife for the Prince of Prussia's Regiment, 1819.
26. *Novgorodskii sbornik* (Novgorod, 1865), Part III, 139–140.
27. K. M. Iachmenikhin, *Voennye poseleniia v Rossii: Istoriia sotsial'no-ekonomicheskogo eksperimenta* (Ufa, 1994), 56.
28. RGVIA, f. 405, op. 3, d. 348, Military colonies, payment of 4,000 roubles to an English agronomist.
29. James E. Alexander, *Travels to the Seat of War in the East, through Russia and the Crimea in 1829* (London, 1830), vol. 1, 142.
30. RGVIA, f. 405, op. 3, d. 364, fos 30, 60–60v, Military colonies, on the purchasing and leasing of land, 1824–1825.
31. Ibid., fos 116, 119, 179v.
32. *PSZ*, vol. 38, no. 29,312, 768–770, 13 February 1823.
33. RGVIA, f. 405, op. 3, d. 381, fos 1, 9–9v, 15–17, Military colonies, on moving women and children to the colonies.
34. For more details on the purchase of substitutes for the army see Hartley, *Russia 1762–1825*, 33–34, 79–81. See also Rodney D. Bohac, 'The Mir and the Military Draft', *Slavic Review* 47 (1988): 652–666.
35. K. M. Iachmenikhin, 'Ekonomicheskii potentsial voennykh poselenii v Rossii', *Voprosy istorii* 2 (1997): 34–48.
36. Beskrovnyi, *The Russian Army*, 2.
37. L. P. Bogdanov, *Voennye poseleniia v Rossii* (Moscow, 1992), 53.
38. Iachmenikhin, 'Ekonomicheskii potentsial', 39–43.
39. Keep, *Soldiers of the Tsar*, 289–290.
40. Robert Lyall, *An Account of the Organisation etc of the Military Colonies in Russia* (London, 1824), 38.
41. A. N. Petrov, 'Ustroistvo i upravlenie voennykh poselenii v Rossii', in *Materialy k noveishei otechestvennoi istorii: Graf Arakcheev i voennye poseleniia*, ed. M. I. Semevskii (St Petersburg, 1871), 85–207, 159; and S. I. Maevskii, 'Moi vek ili istoriia generala Maevskogo', *Russkaia starina* 10 (1873): 427–464, 435.
42. *Novgorodskii sbornik* (Novgorod, 1865), Part IV, 233–234.
43. Bodleian Library, Oxford, MS Eng. hist. c.409, fo. 25v, Notes to Sir Robert Ker Porter on the military colonies.
44. Quoted in Pipes, 'The Military Colonies', 217.
45. Lyall, *An Account*, 39, 40.
46. Alexander Bitis and Janet M. Hartley, 'The Russian Military Colonies in 1826', *The Slavonic and East European Review* 79 (2000): 323–330, 329.
47. The National Archives, London, Foreign Office, FO 65/157, Strangford to Canning, 23 January/4 February 1826, quoted in Bitis and Hartley, 'The Russian Military Colonies', 328.
48. Lyall, *An Account*, 43.
49. Ibid., 40–41.
50. V. A. Fedorov, 'Bor'ba krest'ian Rossii protiv voennykh poselenii, 1810–1818', *Voprosy istorii* 11 (1952): 112–124, 121.

51. P. Pavlov, 'Vospominaniia ochevidtsa o bunte voennykh poselian v 1831', *Istoricheskii vestnik* 3 (1894): 738–787, 786.
52. I. Radzikovskii, 'Epizod iz bunta voennykh poselian v 1831 godu', *Istoricheskii vestnik* 11 (1888): 434–447, 447.
53. Alexander Bitis, 'Reserves under Serfdom? Nicholas I's Attempt to Solve the Russian Army's Manpower Crisis under Serfdom', *Jahrbücher für Geschichte Osteuropas* 51 (2003): 185–196.

6

Arms for Revolutions: Military Demobilization after the Napoleonic Wars and Latin American Independence

Rafe Blaufarb

By the end of 1815, the Latin American independence movement was stalled. In New Spain (Mexico) the creole elites, who elsewhere led the movement, had been frightened by the spectre of social upheaval into supporting the royalist cause. The last major Mexican insurgent leader, Morelos, was executed in December 1815. His army disintegrated. On the Costa Firme, infighting and an effective, homegrown royalist military response hindered the insurgents' ability to resist the expedition of Spanish General Morillo when it arrived in mid-1815. Composed of over 10,000 veterans of the Peninsular campaign, it overwhelmed the insurgents. Their last bastion, Cartagena, surrendered on 6 December 1815. Only a few insurgents escaped, fleeing by boat to Jamaica or Haiti. Six months later, Morillo took Bogotá, the last major city in insurgent hands, which in turn prompted Quito to surrender. Only in Buenos Aires did independence seem secure. Yet, even there, all was not well. Repeated attempts by Buenos Aires to invade Peru, the centre of royalist power in South America, failed. In Buenos Aires itself, factionalism produced instability. At the same time, the provinces chafed at the city's centralizing ambitions. Trouble was also brewing across the River Plate, in the Banda Oriental (Uruguay), where a local independence movement was confronting Buenos Aires, Spain, and Portugal. The troops of the last-named power occupied the area in August 1816, probably with Argentine complicity. With the exception of beleaguered Buenos Aires, therefore, the movement for Latin American independence appeared to have been 'crushed'[1] by the end of 1815.

Within two years, however, insurgent hopes had been rekindled. In January 1817, the Argentine general San Martín led an army over the Andes into Chile, liberated it, and, by spring 1818, began his epic seaborne invasion of Peru. On the Costa Firme, Bolívar, who had returned to the continent in December 1816, won control of the strategic Orinoco River in 1817. Secure in this base and reinforced with volunteers, both local and European, as well as arms, Bolívar went on the offensive. Although his campaign in 1818 against Morillo's forces in Venezuela ended in stalemate, his surprise thrust on Bogotá the following year succeeded brilliantly. The tide had turned.

What explains the shift in insurgent fortunes? An older, nationalist historiography sought an answer in the deeds of the great liberators. With the emphasis on social-historical approaches and 'history from below' in the 1970s and 1980s, interest shifted away from explaining turning points such as this to uncovering the long-term, structural causes of independence. Since the 1990s, however, the pendulum has swung back toward political history, albeit with greater emphasis on constitutional and ideological contexts than on the day-to-day unfolding of events.[2] Nonetheless, the resurgence of political approaches, which has been energized by the beginning of the bicentennial cycle, has drawn new attention to the question of why insurgent fortunes revived after 1815.[3] Some have suggested that Morillo's harsh repression drove people into the arms of the insurgency.[4] Others have claimed that Fernando VII's abrogation of the Constitution of Cádiz led to mass disenchantment with the royalist cause.[5] The most sophisticated explanations identify a variety of factors—the inconsistency of Spanish pacification policies, disputes between royalist authorities, anonymous denunciations and the settling of old scores, and the inevitable civilian resentments generated by the presence of hungry, poorly-paid troops—that converged to undermine the reconquest.[6] Another possibility that has been raised in recent years is that the 1815 ebb in insurgent fortunes was just one of several troughs, not a particularly decisive moment, in a long struggle that had many ups and downs.[7]

Despite the recent revival of interest, however, the question of how a struggling insurgency was able to turn things around has remained on the historiographical margins. This may stem from the sense that Latin American independence was inevitable, that it was just meant to be. If viewed from this perspective, the dark years of 1815 and 1816 appear as no more than a historically-insignificant downturn, a stumble, in the drive toward a necessary independence. This chapter questions the assumption of inevitability. Instead it begins by recognizing that the progress of the insurgency had halted by 1815. Whether this was a temporary setback or a potentially more decisive development, we must still ask how this situation was reversed in the following two or three years. The answer does not lie entirely in the realm of ideas, nor in the sweep of military events. Related to both factors—indeed, tying them together—was a third ingredient in the reversal of revolutionary fortunes, the arrival of large quantities of European and North American arms from 1815 on. These not only reinvigorated the military efforts of the insurgents, but also helped garner political support for their cause.

Foreign volunteers

Military demobilization after the Napoleonic Wars and the War of 1812 made available military resources, both human and material, for service in

Spanish America. The presence of foreign volunteers in the armies of Bolívar and San Martín is well known. Most studies of these volunteers, most of whom were British, have claimed that they made up for their relatively small numbers by their military experience and technical expertise.[8] Their participation may have been decisive in several battles, notably Boyacá (7 August 1819) and Carabobo (24 June 1821). But were the volunteers really veterans? In the case of the French, who numbered only several hundred, they were. However, as Matthew Brown has demonstrated, the British were not. Of the 7,000 volunteers Brown identified, only one-third had previous military service. The rest were restless, idealistic young men living out a 'culture of adventure'.[9] Although the European taste for adventurism predated the Napoleonic Wars, those conflicts made the prospect of volunteering for the Spanish American insurgency especially attractive for the generation just too young to have participated in them.[10] In this sense, post-1815 volunteerism was a consequence of peace, demobilization and restoration.

Not all foreign volunteers served on land. Thousands served aboard the hundreds of privateers commissioned between 1810 and 1830 by the insurgent republics of Spanish America. Many were veterans of the Royal Navy, which downsized dramatically after 1815. Others had served in the Imperial French Navy or as privateersmen operating from Caribbean bases. When the last of these (Santo Domingo) was occupied by the British in 1810, some acquired Venezuelan commissions and then, in 1812, American ones. Others were American privateersmen caught short by the Peace of Ghent (1815). They had spent heavily on arming vessels and needed to continue commerce-raiding to recoup their investments. For privateer investors, agents, captains, and officers, the wars of Latin American independence were a godsend. Thanks to commissions readily obtained in Baltimore, New Orleans, and other American ports from agents of the insurgent republics, they were able to put to sea after all, albeit in search of Spanish rather than British prizes. The names of their vessels highlight continuity between American privateering during the War of 1812 and maritime conflict between Spain and its insurgent American provinces: the *4th of July* (re-baptized *Patriota*) under Captain Taylor, the *Mammoth* (later *Independencia del Sur*) under Captain Chaytor, and the *True-Blooded Yankee* (which operated under that name through to 1817) under Captain Jewett. With the winding-down of the Wars of Independence in the mid-1820s, some privateer chieftains became admirals in the Latin American navies. Thus, we find the ex-Royal Navy officer Guise heading Peru's navy, the former Imperial French naval officer Fournier as an Argentinian admiral, the former American captain Porter commanding Mexico's fleet, and the New Orleans-born privateer Beluche (who had held commissions from both France and the United States) as a general in the Venezuelan navy.[11] Demobilized seamen of the wars that ended in 1815 played a decisive role in the naval campaigns for Latin American independence.[12]

Foreign volunteers contributed to the military struggle for Latin American independence, probably more effectively at sea than on land. Volunteerism, however, was not responsible for the victory of the insurgents, nor does it explain the post-1815 resurgence. In the final analysis, Spanish Americans won their own independence through armed struggle. However, they could not have done this—nor would they have dared to try—without weapons. Surplus military equipment from the Napoleonic Wars and the War of 1812 provided them with the instruments of war they needed to fight and, more importantly, establish the credibility necessary to attract mass support.

The political impact of the arms trade

In 1815, a flood of military equipment began to pour onto the world market. Weapons of all kinds could be acquired at discount prices. Even warships, the most advanced weapons systems of the day, could be purchased by private individuals, especially in Britain where the Royal Navy was cut from 713 to 134 vessels between 1814 and 1820.[13] The Admiralty put these vessels up for auction, and there were many takers. During the period between 1814 and 1818, over 250 warships were sold to individual purchasers.[14] No one kept track of what buyers did with their warships, so it is impossible to state how many of them ended up sailing for insurgents in Spanish America. However, we do have evidence that this was the use to which some of these vessels were put. In 1814, the British launched a 16-gun brig called the *Imogen*, one of dozens of vessels of this type built for the Napoleonic Wars. Demobilized and offered at auction in Plymouth, the *Imogen* was sold in April 1817 to Joseph Ismay for £690.[15] Ismay then resold the vessel to Venezuelan agents.[16] These dispatched the *Imogen* to Amsterdam, where it was outfitted as a privateer. It then sailed to Margarita, an island near Venezuela and an insurgent privateering base. There, the *Imogen* was renamed *Libertador* and taken to sea by Walter Davis Chitty, a British naval veteran of the Napoleonic Wars, now turned privateer, who would later obtain high rank in the Venezuelan navy. On this cruise, however, Chitty was unlucky. His vessel was arrested off Jamaica by the Royal Navy for plundering a British merchantman and smuggling. Although a Kingston court acquitted Chitty, the *Libertador* was condemned for violating the Navigation Laws and auctioned off in 1820.[17] American vessels that had served in the War of 1812 also ended up sailing for the Spanish American insurgents. One was the former Boston privateer *Avon*, acquired by Chilean agents in the United States and commissioned in the Chilean Navy in 1818.[18]

Clearly the Spanish American naval insurgency depended heavily on demobilized men and materiel from Europe and the United States. Equally, its armies would have had trouble opposing the royalists—especially after the arrival of Morillo in mid-1815—without firearms, powder, shot and cannon from these same sources. Moreover, had the insurgents lacked arms, it would have been difficult for them to have won popular support and recruited their armies. Independence and republicanism were powerful ideas, but were they powerful enough to push unarmed people into open rebellion, especially in the presence of effective royalist forces such as Morillo's? The significance of arms was thus not primarily military. Weapons were a potent force which helped Spanish Americans make a risky political choice they might otherwise have avoided. 'Political power flows from the barrel of a gun', Mao explained, because 'having guns ... we can create political organizations ... We can also create cadres, create schools, create culture, create mass movements'.[19] If Mao was right, then the power of guns lies less in their ability to destroy counterinsurgent armies than in their ability to turn revolutionary ideas into revolutionary action. Spain certainly viewed the flow of arms to its rebellious provinces in this light. As its ambassador in London complained at the end of 1815, Britain was 'fanning the flames of war, particularly by the sale of arms'.[20]

The timing of the remark is significant, for it was at precisely this moment that arms began flooding into Spanish America. As soon as hostilities with Great Britain ended, the United States reduced its war-swollen army, releasing quantities of weapons into the market. In April 1815, the Spanish Ambassador to the United States, Don Luis de Onís, sent ominous reports to his government about the impact of this on the insurgency. 'The conclusion of peace with England', he wrote, 'has given new impulse to the speculators interested in fomenting revolution in our Americas'. He relayed intelligence of the formation of 'a company of merchants from this city [Philadelphia], Baltimore, and New York to purchase from the United States government 30,000 muskets from the reduction in its army' and dispatch them, via the West Indies, 'to all of our revolted provinces'.[21] In Europe, the end of war made available even greater quantities of weapons. Surplus from Austria, Britain, France and the Netherlands are known to have been sent either directly from Europe to Latin America or to the United States for re-export to the insurgents.[22] In one instance, a Philadelphia merchant named Allen was discovered by Spanish diplomats arranging a large arms shipment, presumably Austrian in origin, from Trieste to Spanish America.[23]

Size and circuits of the arms trade

There are several difficulties in quantifying the flow of weapons to the Spanish American insurgencies. First, this trade was often clandestine. Undeclared and unrecorded, successful smuggling voyages left no archival trace. We can only glimpse these activities on the rare occasions when authorities managed to detect them. We will never know the scope of this shadowy traffic. Second, quantifying the licit arms trade to Latin America poses methodological challenges. How should we treat exports to neutral destinations and known transshipment points like the West Indian islands of St Thomas, St Bartholomew and St Eustatius? How can we measure arms re-exports to Spanish America from ports in the United States and Brazil? Third, some of the arms may have been intended for the royalists, although their quantity could not have been great. For these reasons, we shall probably never have exact figures on the extent of the trade. For our purpose, however, rough estimates of the scale, geography and chronology of the trade demonstrate its role in reviving the fortunes of Latin American independence after 1815.

Much of the trade in military supplies from Europe and North America was clandestine. We would know nothing about it had it not been for the surveillance of Great Britain, the United States and Spain. Their diplomatic and naval reports convey a sense—admittedly impressionistic—of the nature of this business. The first British authorities heard of the arms trade to the insurgency was in August 1813, when customs agents learned that an English merchant ship, the *Marianne*, intended to sail to Buenos Aires with 2,000 muskets, 200 pistols and 700 swords. They detained the vessel and confiscated the arms on the grounds that their export violated wartime regulations. However, less than two weeks later, it was reported that another English vessel, the *Melville*, had left Portsmouth, full of muskets for the insurgents of Buenos Aires.[24] These are the only specific cases of arms smuggling which appear in the British Foreign Office records, but there were probably further attempts that went undetected. Although the British government eventually bowed to Spanish pressure and banned the shipment of arms to Spanish America, one gets the sense that it was more concerned to give the Spanish the sop of a legal prohibition than to stop the flow of arms. As we shall see, the official prohibition left open loopholes so gaping that its effect on the trade is doubtful. As for the United States, it resisted Spanish pressure to outlaw the arms exports. On at least one occasion, it even sold surplus military supplies directly to the insurgents.[25]

Spanish diplomats in Great Britain and the United States followed the activities of the clandestine arms exporters more closely than the customs officials of these two countries. Their dispatches and protests reveal an extensive underground arms trade to the Spanish American insurgents. In London, Ambassador Fernan Nuñez directed a stream of denunciations to the British government. Indeed, he provided it with more intelligence on the trade than it received from its own customs officials. For example, it was Fernan Nuñez who informed the Foreign Office that a Curaçao merchant, Luis Brión, had arrived in Britain, purchased a decommissioned American privateer, and intended to use it to ship arms to the insurgents.[26] Further denunciations followed in rapid succession. A vessel was set to sail from Liverpool with 4,000 muskets, eight cannon and 'other warlike stores' (20 April 1816).[27] Three others—the *General Blucher*, *Samuel Barnel* and *Nancy*—were on the point of sailing with over £12,000 worth of arms (18 December 1816).[28] Across the Atlantic, Fernan Nuñez's counterpart, Luis de Onís, was also busy uncovering the activities of American arms merchants. A vessel from New Orleans, the *Petit Milan*, was going to deliver 'arms and munitions' to the Mexican insurgents (4 November 1815).[29] Several vessels which had been fitted out as privateers in 'various ports of the Union' were going to transport arms to Buenos Aires and then turn to piracy (8 May 1816).[30] An American vessel, the *Ellen*, crammed with arms and British volunteers, was about to leave Philadelphia for the Orinoco (3 November 1817).[31] From 1814 through to 1817, Onís issued two formal protests about the arms trade and Fernan Nuñez no fewer than seven.

The American government ignored the complaints.[32] Fernan Nuñez had more success with the British, but the concessions he obtained proved illusory. In response to his prodding, the British government prohibited the export of arms to Spanish America. However, merchants could bypass the ban by petitioning the Privy Council for a special licence. It routinely granted these requests. From January through November to 1817, the critical period when insurgent fortunes in the Costa Firme began to revive, the Privy Council granted licences to export over 700 cannon, 60,000 muskets, 90 tons of gunpowder and over five million gunflints. In practice, therefore, the prohibition was nullified by the ease of obtaining a waiver from the Privy Council.

This was not the only loophole through which British arms flowed. Merchants could also send arms to the insurgents via intermediary destinations. This had a number of advantages, the most important of which was that it diminished the risk of seizure, confiscation and punishment by royalist authorities. The principal destinations of the British arms shipments to the western hemisphere were thus ports in the United States, Caribbean and Brazil. Some of these, particularly to the United States, were probably intended for re-export to Spanish America. During the period between 1815 and 1825, British customs recorded the actual export of over 300,000 muskets to the United States. Although it is impossible to discover exactly how many of these eventually reached Latin America, the sheer quantity sent to the United States—a country with its own vigorous arms industry—makes it unlikely that all entered the domestic American market. The stream of British arms probably helped swell the torrent of muskets—conservatively estimated at 150,000[33]—shipped from the United States to the insurgents. Nevertheless, given the current state of our knowledge, it is hazardous even to attempt a guess the size of Britain's contribution. Anecdotal evidence suggests that the re-export of arms from the United States to South America was a booming business. In an appendix to her dissertation, Caitlyn Fitz lists numerous instances of American merchants re-exporting British, Dutch, and French weapons to the insurgents.[34] The case mentioned above of the American merchant, Allen, discovered trying to purchase arms in Trieste, suggests that we might add Austria to the list of indirect suppliers. The insurgent governments of Spanish America also procured arms and military supplies by sending purchasing agents to likely markets. The best-known of these was Spanish-born Philadelphia resident Manuel Torres, Bolívar's principal purchasing agent in the United States. In late 1819, he was directed to obtain 10,000 muskets, a quantity increased to 30,000 soon thereafter. Between April and September 1820, Torres concluded several purchases with the Philadelphia merchant Jacob Idler. Idler ultimately supplied Bolívar with nearly 12,000 muskets (of which 4,360 were re-exported French pieces), 175,000 gunflints, 4,200 uniforms, and 4,000 pairs of boots for over $230,000. To guarantee the transaction, Torres assigned a quantity of Venezuelan tobacco to Idler until full payment had been made.[35] From the mid-1820s, the newly independent republics of Latin America—which lacked cash but needed arms to counter persistent threats—assigned national resources, conceded mining rights, and even alienated taxes to pay for foreign arms.[36]

The arms trade to insurgent Spanish America was thus intricate, mobilizing Atlantic mercantile networks, privateering alliances, and local fiscal structures. Here is an example. In 1817, the privateer *Adeline*, owned by Philadelphia merchants David Maffet and Andrew Curcier, left for Chile with arms—4,500 muskets and 3,500 barrels of gunpowder—which the partners had purchased in London. En route, the vessel stopped at Buenos Aires where it picked up 1,000 more guns before rounding Cape Horn to deliver its cargo and resume commerce raiding in the Pacific.[37] Further complicating this glimpse of a transnational subculture in which lines between arms trading and privateering were blurred, we should note that Curcier was also involved in the Vine and Olive Colony (1817), a settlement of Bonapartist exiles in Alabama, near the Gulf Coast of the United States. He also helped fund the 1818 invasion of Texas by Napoleon's former general, Charles Lallemand.[38]

Caitlyn Fitz's exemplary research has shown that east coast ports were conduits for European arms shipments to the insurgents. The most important, New York, received over 75,000 muskets from Britain alone between 1815 and 1825, some of which were probably re-exported. New York, however, was not the epicentre of the American arms trade to Spanish America. This was New Orleans. According to Spanish diplomats, the city's lawlessness had attained 'such a state of depravation' that piratical insurgents could do as they pleased, arming vessels, disposing of ill-gotten gains, and indulging in smuggling of all kinds.[39] New Orleans was not only a base of operations for filibustering expeditions against New Spain, but also home to some of the leading figures in the Bolivarian naval insurgency. We have already met one of them, Renato Beluche, but he was not alone. Others included Dominique You, Vincent Gambi, Charles Lominé and Nicholas Joly, to name a few.[40] Like privateers on the eastern seaboard, these men probably dabbled in the arms trade. The city was certainly awash with arms. Between 1815 and 1825, British merchants shipped nearly 150,000 muskets to New Orleans, about as many as they shipped to all east-coast destinations during that same period.

Close to the battlefields of New Spain and the Costa Firme, as well as boasting a population of privateers, smugglers, and adventurers connected to the insurgencies, New Orleans was an ideal point from which to send arms to the Spanish American insurgents.

There is only anecdotal evidence that British and other European arms exported to ports in the United States were intended for re-export to Latin America. British arms shipments to two other destinations, however, were definitely intended for the insurgency: the Caribbean islands of St. Thomas (Danish) and St. Bartholomew (Swedish). Their total white male adult population numbered in the hundreds. Yet British export records for the period between 1814 and 1825 indicate that they received 30,000 muskets, 1.5 million gunflints, 300 tons of cannon, 130 tons of gunpowder, 550 tons of shot, 2,750 pistols, and 4,500 swords. In 1817 alone, the Privy Council authorized the shipment to the islands of 190 tons of cannon, 67 artillery pieces, 22,600 muskets, over 40 tons of gunpowder, 5,450 pistols, 6,700 swords, and 1.4 million gunflints.[41] This was enough not only to provide each of the islands' residents with an arsenal at which even the National Rifle Association might blanch, but, more seriously, to equip a typical Bolivarian army several times over. Even at the critical battles of Boyacá and Carabobo, the Liberator commanded only 3,200 and 6,300 men respectively.[42] The islands lay within easy reach of insurgent privateers who would sail there to dispose of their prize goods (including slaves taken from illicit Spanish slave-trading vessels), purchase weapons, and then transport them to the insurgent armies. Although the islands' importance faded as the insurgents captured mainland ports, they resumed their role as privateering bases and arms depots during the Cisplatine War from 1825 to 1827 between Argentina and Brazil.[43]

There were other, lesser re-export points. One of these was Jamaica, home to a number of merchants sympathetic to Bolívar's cause. The most important was Maxwell Hyslop, a trader with business and family connections to Liverpool and New York City. During Bolívar's 1815 exile in Kingston, the two men became friends and allies. Bolívar appointed Hyslop his chief agent in Jamaica and urged him to obtain weapons. 'Costa Firme could be saved', Bolívar wrote, 'with six or eight thousand rifles, the necessary ammunition, and five hundred thousand duros to defray the costs of the early months of the campaign'.[44] Hyslop and his family threw themselves into the cause of independence, pressing for British recognition, acting as a prize agent for the Venezuelan privateer fleet, and almost certainly (given their own mercantile inclinations and the Jamaican tradition of smuggling into Spanish America) shipping arms to South America.[45] There were quantities of arms in Jamaica potentially available for re-export, for approximately 55,000 muskets and 215 tons of gunpowder were sent there from Britain during the period between 1815 and 1825. Other British possessions may have played a re-export role from time to time. Trinidad, near the Venezuelan theatre of war, may have been one such site.[46] Anecdotal evidence points to further conduits. In September 1817, for example, Captain Sharpe of HMS *Hyacinthe*, stationed in the River Plate, informed the Admiralty of covert arms traffic from Britain to Buenos Aires via Portuguese Madeira.[47]

Perhaps the greatest surprise disclosed by the official British arms trade figures to the Americas is the huge number of weapons shipped to Brazil, both before and after its independence from Portugal. During the years between 1815 and 1825, it received approximately 150,000 muskets and 4,500 tons of cannon, making it the principal American destination for British-made artillery. For much of this period, Brazil was involved in external war (the invasion of the Banda Oriental) and civil strife (the Pernambuco revolt of 1817, the Wars of Independence 1822–1824, and the post-independence military campaign to assert central control over several recalcitrant provinces). These operations absorbed many of the imported British arms, but some may have been re-exported to Buenos Aires. There are two reasons why this is likely. First, British Customs recorded only a tiny quantity of arms (about 5,700 muskets, 18 tons of gunpowder and 16 tons of cannon) sent directly to Buenos Aires during this period. It is hard to reconcile these negligible quantities with the fact that Britain was Buenos Aires's principal trading partner and that the Argentine army was well-equipped. Moreover, as we have seen in the case of the *Adeline*, it apparently had sufficient muskets to re-export some to Chile. Second, until their relations deteriorated in 1824, Buenos Aires was effectively allied with Brazil, bound by a common interest in preventing the Spanish from regaining Montevideo and in suppressing the movement for Uruguayan independence. The period between 1819 and 1820, when rumours reached a fever pitch that a Spanish expedition was about to sail against Buenos Aires, was when British arms imports to Brazil reached their height. These two years, when Brazil was at peace, saw it import over 57,000 muskets and at least 1,900 tons of artillery,[48] about 40 percent of the total quantity of those weapons Brazil imported from Britain during the period between 1815 and 1825. Were some of these arms passed on to Buenos Aires?

A final possibility is that some of the British arms exported to Brazil were exchanged by Brazilian slave traders for slaves in Africa. It was notorious in the eighteenth and nineteenth centuries that British manufactured goods nourished the Portuguese and Brazilian slave trades. In 1846 Henry A. Wise, the American ambassador to Brazil, observed that 'the largest interests in the world, next to those of Brazilian subjects, now favoring the slave trade, are those of a certain class of British manufacturers, merchants, and capitalists'.[49] In his now-classic study of the Angolan slave trade, *Way of Death*, Joseph C. Miller found that arms, particularly of British make, 'came in a strong third' after textiles and alcohol among the commodities brought to Africa by Portuguese and Brazilian slave traders.[50] This, together with other research into the economics of the slave trade, strongly suggests that some British arms exported to Brazil after 1815 were destined for that infamous traffic.[51]

It is probably impossible to map the circuits of the legal arms re-export trade, let alone provide even a reasonably accurate sketch of the pathways and extent of the clandestine arms trade. We do, however, possess official British arms export figures. These can establish a base line, a minimum figure of the arms potentially available to Spanish American revolutionaries. Between 1815 and 1825, the British government recorded the export to the Americas of 704,104 muskets, 35,617,854 gunflints, 4,508 tons of gunpowder, 10,254 tons of cannon, 100,637 pistols, and 209,846 swords.[52] There was clearly a large quantity of British-manufactured arms dispatched to the western hemisphere during the Wars of Latin American Independence. Into whose hands they fell was not clear then, nor is it clear now. The arms sent to the neutral islands of the West Indies were certainly intended for the insurgents. But which insurgents? The fact that they were picked up by privateers and paid for with contraband goods obscures these transactions still further. Both purchasers and sellers shunned publicity, so we shall probably never know exactly where these arms ended up. The weapons sent to other destinations—New York, New Orleans, Jamaica, Rio de Janeiro—may have remained in local hands, but they may have also been re-exported for military service in South America, probably with the insurgents, but possibly with the royalists. Anecdotal evidence sometimes makes explicit instances of re-export, but infrequently reveals the complete itinerary of the arms from original source to final destination. Rare are the cases, such as the voyage of the *Adeline*, where we get a hint of the full reach and complexity of the circuits of the re-export trade. We probably have to accept the impossibility of quantifying the flow of arms to the Spanish American insurgents and settle for anecdotal evidence.

Conclusion

With these caveats, let us draw what conclusions we can about the arms trade to Latin America from Graphs 6.1–6.3, based on the official British figures. The first finding is that Britain directed a veritable flood of arms to the Americas after the Napoleonic Wars and the War of 1812. Second, few of these exports went directly to Spain's revolted provinces, in all likelihood because the insurgents controlled only one significant port (Buenos Aires) during most of the period between 1815 and 1817. Instead, the arms went primarily to the United States, the West Indies and Brazil. Third, some of these arms were probably re-exported to insurgents on the Costa Firme and in the River Plate. These helped equip the armies of San Martín and Bolívar which regained the initiative from the royalists by the end of 1817. Fourth, there was a distinct temporal rhythm to the geographical distribution of the exports. Arms exports to the Gulf of Mexico and the Caribbean dropped

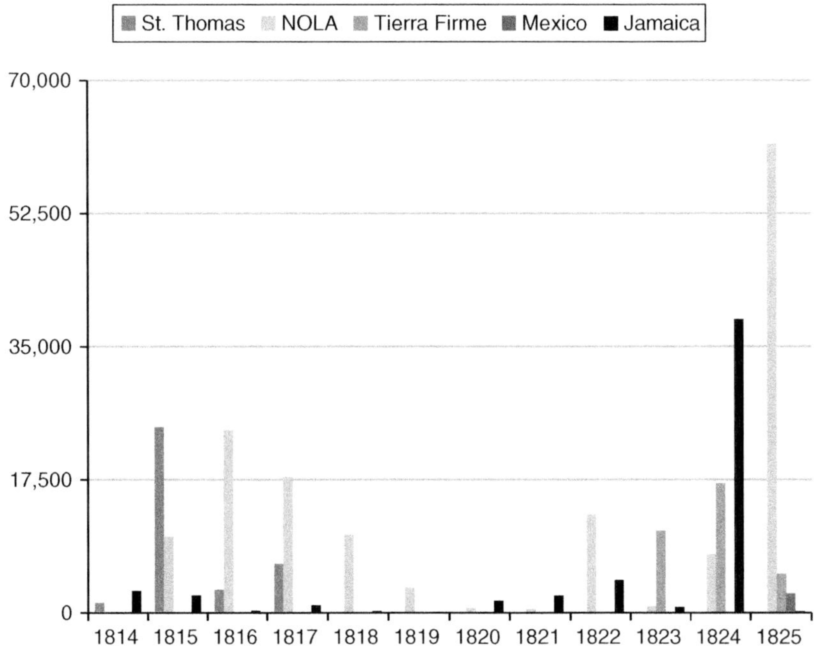

Graph 6.1 British gun exports to the Caribbean, 1814–1825
Source: British National Archives, Customs (Cust) 8, registers 2 through 30.

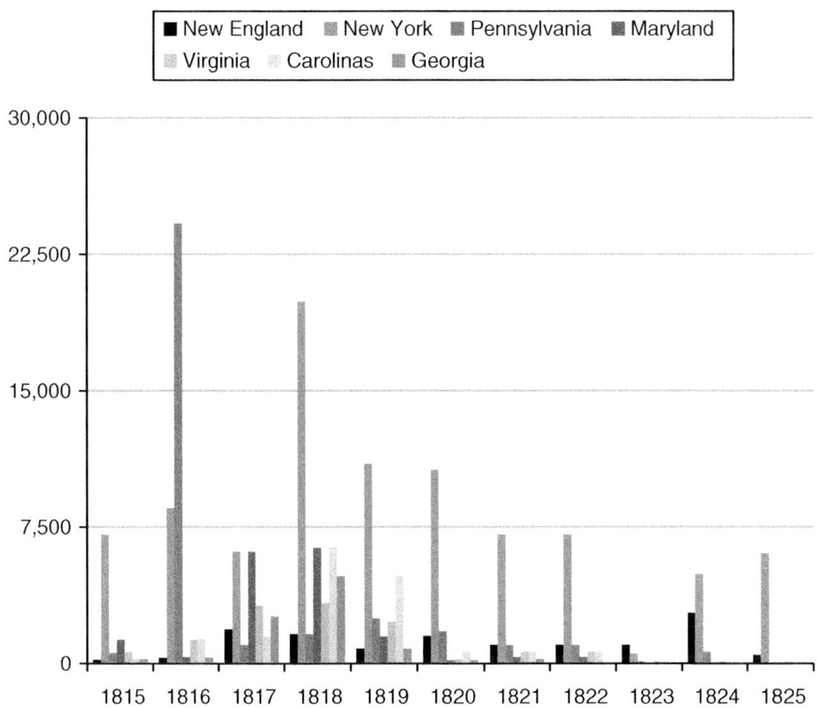

Graph 6.2 British gun exports to the United States, 1814–1825
Source: British National Archives, Customs (Cust) 8, registers 2 through 30.

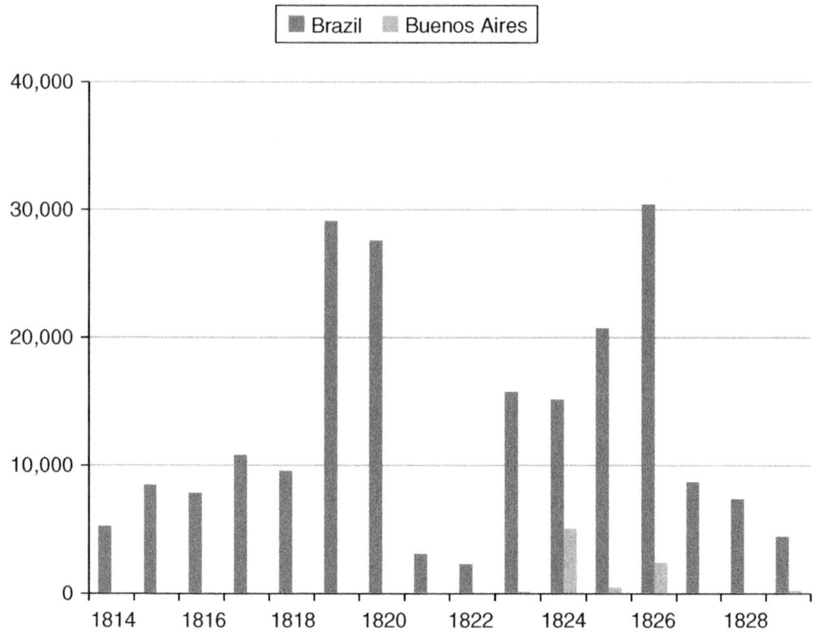

Graph 6.3 British gun exports to Brazil and La Plata, 1814–1829
Source: British National Archives, Customs (Cust) 8, registers 2 through 30.

sharply in 1818. However, they rebounded strongly in 1824–1825. Why this second surge? Since these arms were destined primarily for New Orleans and the Costa Firme, and considering that 1825–1826 saw the great offensive that drove the last royalist army from the continent, it is likely that these weapons were intended to equip Bolívar's final campaign and arm the new republics bordering the Caribbean (Gran Colombia and Mexico) against counterattacks from Spain. For, contrary to most accounts of the Wars of Latin American Independence, fighting did not end in 1826, with the ejection of the last Spanish garrisons from the continent. Spain massed land and naval forces in Cuba and raided the mainland while preparing a full-scale invasion. The republics responded by purchasing arms—including, for the first time, quantities of cannon—to re-equip their worn armies and by planning a joint invasion of Cuba. By 1830, however, this forgotten episode fizzled out in a farcical Spanish invasion of Mexico (1829) and what amounted to financial default by the republics.

Demobilization in Europe and North America in 1815 released a flood of military resources—both human and material—that inflected the course of the struggle for Latin American independence. This is both obvious and commonsensical, yet it is largely absent from the historiography of the independence movements.[53] The only historian who has foregrounded the impact of the arms trade on the struggle is Christon Archer. It is significant that Archer studies Mexico, the area of Spanish America least affected by the trade. For Archer, it was the *absence* of a flow of demobilized arms into Mexico that explains the Mexican insurgency's failure. It is worth quoting him at length.

> The revolutionaries of Venezuela, Columbia, and La Plata managed better than others because they could import arms from the enormous stocks available in the Atlantic economy following the defeat of Napoleon. They employed mercenary officers and soldiers who were looking for work and new adventures unobtainable in peacetime Europe. Strangely, given its geographic location, New Spain was more isolated despite the connections by some rebels with New Orleans and American maritime contrabandists.[54]

In the final analysis, Archer writes, the insurgents of Mexico failed because they were 'cut off from the market for muskets'.[55] Inverting Archer's observation, we might conclude that where arms were plentiful, they succeeded. Yet, historians have overlooked this phenomenon. This essay does not deny the importance of political ideas or military events, far from it. Rather, it seeks to add a third factor—the arms shipments—to the story of Latin American independence. These not only gave the insurgents the means to fight, but also lent them plausibility. Without this, their political ideas would have likely been less capable of mobilizing active support. Indeed, given the strength of popular royalism in Spanish America,[56] it is not clear if the cause of independence would have prevailed in a contest of pure ideas. If not, then the political significance of foreign arms to the insurgency after 1815 was great indeed. Perhaps Latin American independence was inevitable over the long term. But it is impossible to understand when and how it actually occurred without taking into account the wave of military resources which poured into South America after 1815. Post-Napoleonic demobilization nourished independence in Spanish America.

Acknowledgements

I should like to express my thanks to Matthew Brown, Rachel Crooks, Marcella Echeverri and Caitlyn Fitz for their invaluable suggestions and guidance.

Notes

1. The word is from Jaime E. Rodriguez O., 'The Process of Spanish American Independence', in *A Companion to Latin American History*, ed. Thomas H. Holloway (Malden, MA, 2008), 195–214, 200.

2. François-Xavier Guerra, *Modernidad e Independencias: Ensayos sobre las Revoluciones Hispánicas* (Madrid, 1992); and Jaime E. Rodriguez O., *The Independence of Spanish America* (Cambridge, 1998).
3. Among these works, a number offer sophisticated analyses of the political impact of military structures and events. See, in particular, Juan Luis Ossa Santa Cruz, 'Armies, Politics, and Revolution: Chile, 1780–1826', D.Phil dissertation (University of Oxford, 2011); and Clément Thibaud, *Républiques en armes: Les armées de Bolívar dans les guerres d'indépendance du Venezuela et de la Colombie* (Rennes, 2006).
4. Rodriguez, 'The Process', 206.
5. The impact of the Constitution of 1812 on the Spanish American revolutions is attracting more and more attention. Among the many recent publications, see Manuel Chus (ed.), *1812: El Poder de la Palabra. América y la Constitución de 1812* (Madrid, 2012).
6. For a particularly effective treatment of this kind, see Rebecca A. Earle, *Spain and the Independence of Columbia, 1810–1825* (Exeter, 2000).
7. This important idea was communicated to the author by Matthew Brown in an email of 17 October 2013.
8. For the British, see Alfred Hasbrouck, *Foreign Legionaries in the Liberation of Spanish America* (New York, 1928). For the French, see Walter Bruyère-Ostells, *La grande armée de la liberté* (Paris, 2009), 46–53.
9. Matthew Brown, *Adventuring through Spanish Colonies: Simon Bolivar, Foreign Mercenaries, and the Birth of New Nations* (Liverpool, 2006), 25 and 27. On government efforts to prevent volunteerism, see D. A. G. Waddell, 'British Neutrality and Spanish American Independence: The Problem of Foreign Enlistment', *Journal of Latin American Studies* 18/1 (1987): 1–18.
10. This is a recurrent theme in the fictional and memoir literature of the post-1815 period. For examples, see Stendhal's *Le rouge et le noir* (1830) and de Vigny's *Servitude et grandeur militaire* (1835).
11. Jane Lucas De Grummond, *Renato Beluche: Smuggler, Privateer, and Patriot, 1780–1860* (Baton Rouge, LA, 1999).
12. The maritime dimensions of the wars are at last beginning to receive attention. For the Spanish perspective, see Feliciano Gámez Duarte, *Del uno al otro confino: España y la lucha contra el corso insurgent hispanoamericano, 1812–1828* (Cádiz, 2008); for the American, see David Head, 'Sailing for Spanish America: The Atlantic Geopolitics of Foreign Privateering from the United States in the Early Republic', Ph.D. dissertation (University of SUNY Buffalo, 2009); and for the British, see Matthew McCarthy, *Privateering, Piracy, and British Policy in Spanish America, 1810–1830* (London, 2013).
13. Moises Enrique Rodriguez, *Freedom's Mercenaries: British Volunteers in the Wars of Independence of Latin America*, vol. 1, *Northern South America* (Lanham, MD, 2006), 68.
14. The National Archives, London (hereafter TNA), Admiralty (hereafter ADM) 106 3522.
15. TNA, Foreign Office (hereafter FO) 316 1, 'Affadavit as to the value of the Imogene', early 1830s.
16. TNA, ADM 106 3522. Ismay bought five other warships between September 1814 and April 1817.
17. TNA, FO 316 1, 'Dossier: Claim no.1'.
18. William L. Neumann, 'United States Aid to the Chilean Wars of Independence', *Hispanic American Historical Review* 27/2 (1947): 204–219, 214.

19. *Selected Works of Mao Tse-Tung*, 'Problems of War and Strategy' (6 November 1938), vol. 2 (Peking, 1965), 224–225.
20. TNA, FO 72 180, Fernan Nuñez to his government, 23 December 1815.
21. Archivo Histórico Nacional, Madrid (AHN), Estado, Legajo 5640, letter no. 34, 'Onis to Cevallos', Philadelphia, 17 April 1815.
22. Caitlyn A. Fitz, 'Our Sister Republics: The United States in an Age of American Revolution', Ph.D. dissertation (Yale University, 2010). Appendix III gives examples of all of these.
23. AHN Legajo 5642, letter no. 45, 'Onís to Pizarro', Washington, 11 March 1817.
24. TNA, FO 72 49 and 154.
25. This was a quantity of gunpowder sold by the US Ordnance Department to the purchasing agent of Venezuela in 1816. See Arthur Preston Whitaker, *The United States and the Independence of Latin America, 1800–1830* (New York, 1962), 197–198.
26. TNA, FO 72 182, Fernan Nuñez to Foreign Office, 27 May 1815. The ambassador's intelligence was correct. Brión indeed shipped a large quantity of arms to the neutral island of St Thomas, where they were presumably picked up by the insurgents. Shortly thereafter Brión himself took a Venezuelan privateer commission and within a year had been named overall commander of the insurgency's naval forces by Bolívar.
27. Ibid., FO 72 190.
28. Ibid., FO 72 191. The London Custom House subsequently reported that the *Blucher* and *Nancy* together carried 12,500 muskets, 2,650 swords, 2,400 pistols, 220,000 gunflints and assorted other equipment. The Privy Council had issued orders in council authorizing these shipments, so the two vessels were able to proceed to New Orleans in early December 1816. See TNA, FO 72 205, 'Report from London Customs House', 2 January 1817.
29. AHN, Estado, Legajo 5640, letter no. 96.
30. AHN, Estado, Legajo 5641, letter no. 47.
31. AHN, Estado, Legajo 5642, letter no. 186.
32. Fitz, 'Our Sister Republics', 194–195.
33. Ibid., 345.
34. Ibid., Appendix III.
35. Charles H. Bowman, Jr., 'The Activities of Manuel Torres As Purchasing Agent, 1820–1821', *Hispanic American Historical Review* 48/2 (1968): 234–246.
36. For example, in October 1826, the Intendancy of Cartagena was forced to take out a loan from 16 foreign and 16 local merchants resident in the city to pay for the subsistence of the garrison, upkeep of the hospitals and the 'maintenance of public order and tranquility'. To guarantee repayment of the loan, the Intendancy directed the port's customs officers to turn over all the duties they collected into the hands of the merchants. TNA, FO 18 32, 'Dispatch', 28 October 1826.
37. Neumann, 'United States Aid', 211 and 216, and Fitz, 'Our Sister Republics', 349.
38. See my *Bonapartists in the Borderlands: French Refugees and Exiles on the Gulf Coast, 1815–1835* (Tuscaloosa, FL, 2006).
39. AHN, Estado, Legajo 5640, letter no. 96, 'Onís to Cevallos', Philadelphia, 4 November 1815.
40. Stanley Faye, 'Privateersmen of the Gulf and their Prizes', *Louisiana Historical Quarterly* 22/4 (1939): 1012–1094. On the transfer of former imperial French privateers to the cause of Latin American independence, see Faye, 'Privateers of Guadeloupe and their Establishment in Barataria', *Louisiana Historical Quarterly* 23/2 (1940): 428–444.

41. TNA, FO 72 208, Council Office, 'Whitehall, to Foreign Office', 29 November 1817.
42. Robert L. Scheina, *Latin America's Wars: The Age of the Caudillo, 1791–1899*, vol.1, (Washington, DC, 2003), 36–7.
43. TNA, FO 73 138, 'Lord Bloomfield, British Ambassador to Stockholm, to Count de Wetterstadt, Swedish Foreign Minister', Stockholm, 20 March 1829.
44. *Selected Writings of Bolivar*, ed. Harold A. Bierck, Jr., 2 vols (New York, 1951), vol.1, 98: letter no. 38, 'To Maxwell Hyslop, Merchant of Jamaica', Kingston, 19 May 1815.
45. On the circuits of trade, both licit and illicit between the British West Indies and Spanish America, see Adrian J. Pearce, *British Trade with Spanish America, 1763–1808* (Liverpool, 2007).
46. In 1817, Britain exported 2,500 swords to Trinidad. TNA, Customs (CUST), 8/6.
47. TNA, FO 72 208, 'Sharpe to Croker', Hyacinthe, Buenos Aires, 18 September 1817.
48. In addition, there were 75 individual artillery pieces of undisclosed weight.
49. Cited in Robert Edgar Conrad, *World of Sorrow: The African Slave Trade to Brazil* (Baton Rouge, LA, 1986), 126.
50. Joseph C. Miller, *Way of Death: Merchant Capitalism and the Angolan Slave Trade, 1730–1830* (Madison, WI, 1988), 75.
51. David Richardson, 'West African Consumption Patterns and their Influence on the Eighteenth-Century English Slave Trade', in *The Uncommon Market: Essays in the Economic History of the Atlantic Slave Trade*, ed. Henry A. Gemery and Jan S. Hogendorn (New York, 1979), 303–330.
52. Figures based on TNA, CUST 9. The registers for 1821 and 1822 are missing, so I estimated these years according to the median figure for each particular category of arms.
53. A recent exception is Brown, *Adventuring*, 18.
54. Christon I. Archer, 'Introduction', *The Wars of Independence in Spanish America*, ed. Christon I. Archer (Wilmington, DL, 2000), 3–42, 36.
55. Ibid.
56. Marcela Echeverri, 'Popular Royalists, Empire, and Politics in Southwestern New Granada, 1809–1819', *Hispanic American Historical Review* 91/2 (2011): 237–269.

Part III
The Aftermath of War in Politics and Political Culture

7

North Carolina and the New Nation: Reconstruction and Reconciliation Efforts in the 1780s

John R. Maass

In November 1789, delegates at a state convention in Fayetteville, North Carolina voted to adopt the United States Constitution, ratification having failed the year before. North Carolina was the second to last state to vote for the Constitution due to a number of concerns and reservations its political leaders raised about the terms of the new union. The state's history during the 1780s shows a pattern of disinclination on the part of Carolinians to wed their interests with the larger enterprise of American unity. Carolinians exhibited a strong desire to protect their own interests over national political goals. Their focus included possession of valuable western territory and the burden of financial debts; jealous concerns over the potential loss of state sovereignty; the traumatic wartime experiences of the state's citizens; and a localism that emphasized the importance of their own communities. All of these issues came directly from the trying experience of the American War for Independence between 1775 and 1783, the rebellion of the American settlers against the British authorities. In the context of this conflict the Continental Congress declared the colonies free and independent states in July 1776. One year later these 13 states became the United States of America, a loose union under the Articles of Confederation (commonly referred to as the 'Confederation government'). The war ended in 1783 with a peace treaty that confirmed the new nation's separation from the British Empire.[1]

Many historians have concluded that after the receipt of numerous petitions from those in support of the Federal Union in North Carolina, the state's leaders began to consider their disadvantageous situation outside the new national government. Carolinians were also favourably influenced by their observation of the orderly operation of the new Federal system, improved postwar economic conditions, and the effort by James Madison, the 'Father of the Constitution', to amend it with a bill of rights. In the Carolina backcountry numerous Anti-federalists decided to support the Constitution because of the 'ill policy of separating themselves from the Union, and from the excellency of our Constitution', as Federalist William R. Davie, a military officer and North Carolinian statesman, opined.[2]

Additionally, some historians suggest that support developed for the Constitution in North Carolina by 1789 due to a perceived need for increased southern influence in the Congress, and to press for a national seat of government on the Potomac River.[3] Some westerners in the state saw a need for strong protection from the Indians and Spanish intrigues over shipping on the Mississippi River, as well as stability for their land investments, all of which would be more effectively handled by the United States government than that of North Carolina. There was also an expectation that state debts would be assumed by the Federal Government under the Constitution, which would be to North Carolina's benefit as a member of the union. Moreover, Anti-federalists hoped to add limiting amendments to the Constitution.[4]

Given the central place the Constitution has in the story of the American nation's founding, and the unparalleled impact it has had in American politics over the past two centuries, scholars have focused on the exertions of the North Carolina Federalists to ratify this novel plan of government. Less scholarly attention has been paid to the political 'losers' in this struggle, the Anti-federalists. Nevertheless, the reasons for opposition to the Constitution are almost always given as a fear of a strong central government, the initial lack of a bill of rights, and a jealous defence of individual liberties and freedoms.[5]

Yet this is only part of the story. The 1780s were not just about reaching agreement on the Constitution; they were also about the effects of war on society. Carolinians had just been through a bitter struggle within their own divided communities during the Revolutionary conflict. Between 1776 and 1782, North Carolina suffered through a brutal civil war between pro-British Tories and American Whigs, who favoured independence; a devastating British invasion of the state in 1781; violent relations with its hostile Indian neighbours on the western frontier; and the occupation of its most important shipping port, Wilmington, on the Cape Fear River. In many counties across the state, the destruction from the conflict was severe in terms of homes burned, farms destroyed, property lost or confiscated, soldiers killed, and civilians attacked. These concurrent conflicts created great difficulties for military and civilian leaders in their lengthy struggle to establish political and social legitimacy for the cause of independence through the restoration of order and stability. To a large extent, this backdrop has been unduly minimized or ignored by previous studies of the period.

The story of the 1780s is that of a reaction to the Revolutionary War and how it influenced the decade. The question to be asked is not why North Carolina did not ratify the Constitution, but 'why would they?'

Reluctance to join the Union in North Carolina

Some opposition to the Federal Union was the natural result of the state's colonial past. Those within the state with a local outlook, and a number of 'cosmopolitans' as well, were likely to have been reluctant to accept the authority of a central power after they had just endured so much suffering and destruction in throwing off the yoke of a British monarch. They were not about to replace a distant 'tyrant' with a 'tyrannical' Congress close to home. The three decades prior to the outbreak of the Revolutionary War in 1775 had witnessed the significant rise in power of the elected provincial lower house of the Assembly, the curtailment of the King's prerogative, and an effective opposition to royal governors. This hard-won authority was not to be given up in the 1780s, and neither were the state's new powers of appointment, the limits on the executive, the power of impeachment, monetary control, and other capacities assumed by the state during the conflict.

The issue of state-owned western lands between the Appalachian Mountains and the Mississippi River that North Carolina ceded to the Federal Government in 1789 also seems to have driven a wedge between the national government of the Articles of Confederation and the state. This transmontane territory was tied to state veterans' benefits and the 1783 emission of North Carolina paper currency was to be retired (paid off) by the land sales. Giving these tracts of lands to Congress would impair the state's own financial soundness and undermine its credibility in the eyes of those to whom it had promised land in return for military service. Keeping western lands was financially and politically necessary—a powerful incentive to shun the union directly related to the effects of the Revolutionary War.[6]

Apparently many North Carolinians saw little benefit in supporting the Confederation government or espousing the Constitution due to the dismal performance of the Continental war effort. Carolinians may have looked negatively on the nationally coordinated mobilization, logistical endeavours and military campaigns of the war years to the point that association with this government had little appeal. The Continental Army's few clear-cut victories in the south and its inability to prevent the British from marching almost at will through the Carolinas, Georgia and Virginia in the period up to September 1781 could not have made North Carolinians any more inclined to flock to the national colours or to sustain their faith in ultimate victory until late in the war.[7]

The state also found itself opposed to the national government for financial reasons. Within a few years of the end of the war, Congress began to settle accounts with the 13 states, to determine the contributions of each, in order to reduce the national debt. This process was complicated because some states had paid for expenses associated with the war out of state funds and sought reimbursement for these outlays from Congress, or at the very least, demanded credit for these expenditures against the contributions Congress required. It became a disputatious matter between North Carolina, which was convinced it was being burdened unfairly, and the Confederation government which was desperate for money from the states.[8]

According to the reckoning of state officials, North Carolina should have been entitled to an offset of what it owed Congress because it had partially financed several frontier campaigns against hostile Indians and spent large sums fighting Loyalists within its borders. Moreover, the state had sent several relief expeditions of militia forces into South Carolina and Georgia during the war, at its own expense. Carolinians pointed out that other states such as New Jersey and Rhode Island did not have to pay for frontier defences and that others were not as burdened by Loyalists.

Because it had received criticism from Congress and other states for its lack of financial contributions during the latter years of the struggle, the state was emphatic about proving its military contributions to the Continental war effort, noted above.[9] Congress also pointed out that North Carolina had not fulfilled its wartime quota of Continental troops. Carolina officials hoped that 'all militia service that has been performed in consequence of recommendations of Congress' or by the order of a Continental military commander would be 'charged to the account of the United States', which would enable Congress to 'reason mathematically' on the amount of service Carolinians performed in relation to the quota assigned to the state.[10] Given the chaotic nature of the war, however, the state's records of expenditures and military service were often in a terrible condition, 'confused, imperfect and unintelligible'.[11] This issue of sorting out war-related accounts with Congress, as all states were obliged to do, was burdensome for North Carolina in the 1780s. Western land cession, contributions toward the Confederation coffers, and other financial challenges were frustrating questions that often placed North Carolina in an antagonistic relationship with the Confederation government. No two issues more clearly highlight this adversarial relationship than that of the Treaty of 1783 and the debate on ratification of the Federal Constitution. Looking at these matters of dispute more broadly, the battles over the Treaty and the Constitution were in essence a conflict over sovereignty, that is to say, who would rule at home in North Carolina.

The question of state sovereignty

The Treaty of Paris, signed by representatives of Great Britain and of the United States of America on 3 September 1783, ended the War of American Independence. The Confederation congress pressured the 13 American states to heed the Treaty's provisions. As an independent state, however, North Carolina concluded that it was not bound to honour it. This problematic interpretation was not universally shared. The importance of state sovereignty was accepted by American negotiators in Paris at the time the details of the accord were settled, hence the precise wording of the Treaty in which Congress was to 'recommend' to the states their compliance with it. This stipulation recognized that while the Congress of the Confederation would actually ratify the Treaty, it could not compel the states to abide by it, a tacit recognition of state sovereignty. Yet the fact that the Treaty was not sent to each state to debate and ratify (as was the new Constitution several years later) signified that the states as individual entities were not fully sovereign, at least in terms of deciding issues of war and peace.

The United States Congress ratified the Treaty of Paris on 14 January 1784. Congress felt justified signing the Treaty because, in fact, no state constitution written and adopted during the war claimed authority in matters of diplomacy or national defence, sovereign powers they reserved to the Confederation government. Already by 1776, the Congress had issued recommendations to the people to organize state governments, rather than the states having formed first and then created Congress. American independence was proclaimed on 4 July 1776 in an 'act of paramount and sovereign authority' by Congress, not a collection of state governments. Likewise, the petitions and memorials sent to the King and the British people in the war's early years emanated from Congress, not the states. Many contemporaries recognized an 'external sovereignty' of the Continental Union of States, as opposed to the 'internal sovereignty' exercised by the states. As historian Richard B. Morris put it, the Congress 'was viewed by the former colonies, by most of the Revolutionary leaders, and by itself as exercising the substance of national sovereignty'.[12]

For North Carolina, the issue of sovereignty was linked to the 1783 Treaty of Paris that ended the war. The state legislature, called the Assembly, with some conservative dissent, ignored the articles of the Treaty preventing banishment of Loyalists and confiscation of Loyalist property, a policy that endured until 1787, when the state of North Carolina finally made the Treaty of Paris the law of the land. Until that time, confiscations of Loyalist property, mostly in the form of land, proceeded with vigour, and Loyalists and British creditors were typically barred from entering the state, which smothered their opposition to the practice. The state resold the confiscated property to pay off its debts, which also allowed many Carolina Whigs to purchase good lands at a discounted price. Thus for many North Carolina citizens, a close association with the Confederation government would likely mean that the state would be forced to comply with the Treaty and its stipulations preventing continued confiscation, interference with prewar debts, and the recovery of both. With the state's currency tied to the sale of confiscated property and the perpetual lack of specie in the former colonies a bar to the payment of foreign debts, North Carolina was unwilling to concur with these treaty provisions, which drove another wedge between ideas of state sovereignty and national authority.

During the postwar period, many Carolinians espoused sentiments of vengeance and retribution toward the Loyalists who had just been their fierce foes, and these Patriots were strongly averse to restoring forfeited Loyalist property to their former enemies and supported continued seizures well into the 1780s. Moreover, it appears that a number of North Carolina Patriots objected to paying debts they incurred to either Loyalists or British creditors, in light of the massive depredations committed by British forces and their allies in North Carolina during the war, and for which London authorities offered no compensation. Patriots remained bitter in the years after the war against those Carolinians who had supported the British crown in what had been a violent ordeal. For the majority of people within the state, the war had brought numerous hardships endured at or near home in the form of small skirmishes, Tory attacks, house burnings, whippings, and what one Continental general referred to as 'the most horrid Murders and plunder', much of which the state was powerless to prevent.[13]

In addition to the persistent concern over the Tory menace, almost all North Carolinians saw the war significantly intrude upon their lives in the form of impressment officials, whose job it was to confiscate private property for the use of military forces. These officers were unwelcome visitors to hard-pressed farming families in the midst of war, chaos, financial disorders, taxes, and scarcity of all kinds of goods and property. As the war dragged on, the needs became more pressing, and as a result, more intrusive and burdensome. The forced collection of all manner of things by the state and the new national government impoverished many Carolinians, no doubt making them bitter towards authorities and vengeful against their Loyalist enemies.

Thus, bitter feelings against their enemies and the pressing need for the financial resources derived from confiscated property led the state to reject the Treaty and to maintain its rejection for a number of years, a decision which put it at odds with the Federal Government. It also shows that North Carolina did not subscribe to the idea of limited state sovereignty at the expense of national sovereignty under the Federal Government of the Confederation. North Carolina, by eschewing compliance with the Treaty, retained its own sovereignty long enough to defeat its Tory foes, not on the field of battle, but in the social, legal, and political realm. In order to buttress this claim of state sovereignty, Carolinians need have looked no further than the text of the Articles of Confederation, the second of which stated that 'each state retains its sovereignty, freedom, and independence, and every power, jurisdiction, and right, which is not by this Confederation expressly delegated to the United States, in Congress assembled'. It was not coincidental that the congressman responsible for inserting this language into the Articles was a prominent North Carolinian, former state governor Thomas Burke.[14]

The impact of the war years

Just as issues related to the 1783 Treaty of Paris were influenced by the recently concluded war, the military struggle of the American Revolution shaped the state's debate over the Constitution as well. This can be seen clearly with regard to monetary issues, a constant concern for North Carolina during the 1780s. When across the state, men debated the document's provisions, they, of course, read Article 1, Section 10 of the Constitution, which stated in part that the states were prohibited from coining their own money, emitting bills of credit, and were barred from making 'any Thing but gold and silver Coin a Tender in Payment of Debts'. In North Carolina, still suffering from the war's devastation and resultant financial hardships, the Constitution's prohibitions meant that no more paper currency could be issued, and that debts would have to be paid in specie. With a chronic lack of money, this last provision would create significant difficulties for debtors who were already hard pressed. With these concerns in mind, North Carolina recommended an amendment to the Federal Constitution forbidding Congress from interfering 'with any one of the states in the redemption of paper money already emitted and now in circulation, or in liquidating and discharging the public securities of any one of the states'.[15]

Anti-federalists in North Carolina also worried about federal taxes. One of their chief objections to the proposed plan of union was the power of Congress to levy direct taxes, which was held to be a danger to the states' own ability to tax their citizens. With all of the painful wartime and postwar troubles related to money and taxes, these Carolina Anti-federalists seemed unwilling to allow a national government such powers. Moreover, they worried that Federal taxes would be due in specie, not paper bills.[16]

Another issue for North Carolina's Anti-federalists was the Constitution's strong executive, based on colonial experiences with chief magistrates' propensity to engage in war against the people in their own province. They could hardly have forgotten the 'War of the Regulation', an uprising in the British North Carolina colonies that had lasted from about 1765 to 1771, in which citizens took up arms against corrupt colonial officials. The rebellion was not successful, but nevertheless some historians consider it as one catalyst to the American Revolutionary War. The uprising was crushed by William Tryon, since 1770 the province's Royal Governor, who led a military expedition that defeated the Regulator movement in 1771 and hanged several of its leaders for their role in the insurrection. Tryon's successor, Josiah Martin, was also seen as a military despot for his highhandedness in 1775 and 1776. He became the symbol of British tyranny and oppression during the waning days of the colonial period in which he acted to suppress popular meetings and foment Indian hostilities against the Whigs on the frontier. Even more threateningly, this official—a former British soldier, no less—had raised the King's standard in January 1776 to encourage Loyalists to embody in arms and crush what he called an insurrection of the Whigs. Thus it is evident why Carolinians already fearful of executive abuses had the lessons of recent history to convince them that the Constitution's creation of a strong magistrate was potentially dangerous. Perhaps this is why the state suggested an amendment to the United States Constitution in 1789 that 'no person shall be capable of being president of the United States for more than eight years in any term of sixteen years'.[17]

Some North Carolina opponents of the Federal Constitution also seem to have feared the power of the new government to raise a national standing army. 'Standing armies in time of peace are dangerous to Liberty, and therefore ought to be avoided, as far as the circumstances and protection of the community will admit', stated the North Carolina Declaration of Rights, adopted in 1789.[18] While Carolinians should have been the first to recall the wastefulness, inefficiency and poor performance of their militia during the war, they could with some irony point out that the war was in fact won without the state having to raise much of an army at all. No doubt most of these men did not fool themselves into thinking that the militia system was faultless. What these radicals actually opposed was the enormous expense of a national military force and the certainty that taxes would be needed to maintain it. They need only have looked back to the war years, and to see how burdensome the support of Continental forces had been from 1780 to 1783, to convince themselves of this point. Others looked to the war's battles and saw no need for a permanent army. A 1787 letter in the *Pennsylvania Packet* made this point: 'Had we a standing army when the British invaded our peaceful shores? Was it a standing army that gained the battles of Lexington and Bunker Hill, and took the ill-fated Burgoyne [at Saratoga]?'[19] No doubt North Carolina opponents of a permanent force would have added the battles at Moore's Creek Bridge, Kings Mountain and Ramsour's Mill to this list. Upon the adoption of the Constitution in 1789, the state suggested to Congress an amendment to the Federal Charter stating that 'no standing army or regular troops shall be raised or kept up in time of peace, without the consent of two-thirds of the members present in both houses'.[20]

Carolina localism

Finally, it is possible that opposition to the Federal Constitution was strongly rooted in localism, an outlook which, if not born in North Carolina during the war, was certainly strengthened by it. For North Carolina, the War of the Revolution was intensely local for the inhabitants. While generals, governors and other military and civil leaders looked on the war as a struggle for economic, political or constitutional rights against Great Britain, many Carolinians looked on it as an intrusion into their local communities. North Carolina was divided by local concerns, in terms of both geography and interest. There were former Regulators in the backcountry and foothills who were distrustful of eastern elites; immigrant Scots along the Cape Fear with loyalties to the British Crown; Pietists in the Albemarle Sound (Quakers) and the backcountry (Moravians) desperate to avoid the demands of the war; backcountry men and women focused primarily on securing their lands and defending their families from speculators and Indians; lawyers and planters, many of whom sought independence from British rule; and a huge number of Loyalists all over the state intent upon keeping their property. Many of these communities and groups had little to drive them into war with Britain, a distant enemy. Rather, they sought to protect themselves and their localities from invasion, Indian attacks, and violence from their neighbours, be they Tory or Whig. Most importantly, these localists sought to resist the demands of the state, which were far more intrusive in the forms of the draft, impressment and militia duty than was the red-coated enemy. They also wanted order in the form of debt relief, tax relief and effective courts that would secure their rights and maintain public order in their communities.

North Carolina's localist Weltanschauung thus contributed collectively to a disinclination to support the war effort and abide by the Treaty. While some historians have argued that the experience of waging the war made many involved with it Federalists, North Carolinians could look at the chaotic Continental war effort in their own state (including a wretched army that physically embodied it) and incline the other way.[21] This might be called 'centrifugalism', a movement tending away from the centralization of national authority, which was a response to the events during the war years.

As the decade of the 1780s drew to a close, state governor Alexander Martin addressed the members of the Assembly as they prepared to leave Fayetteville, having just adopted the Federal Constitution. Martin recalled that back in 1776, North Carolina 'had embarked with our sister states in one bottom, making one common cause, which by the effusion of kindred and united blood spent in its support, hath cemented our mutual interests in one great family'. But now, as they made preparations to end the session and go their separate ways, the governor reminded them of their great responsibility. They were to 'return to the citizens you represent, to reconcile those jarring sentiments, if any remain, that seemed unfortunately to prevail in different parts of the state'. Although he noted that the 'public peace' remained undisturbed, he did worry that 'invidious distinctions have arisen'. He urged the delegates to squelch such distinctions among their constituents: 'Let hereafter the federal and antifederal name be no more heard as a reproach; let the people be told that the government of the United States is still in the power of their citizens', so that all could 'enter the union, now fixed on firmer ground, with joy, and with united efforts'. For Martin, and presumably others, this was the end of the Revolution, but for many Carolinians, only after the state had confiscated the property of its domestic foes and banished them, extracted the value out of its western lands before ceding them to the new United States government, and finished the reconstructive process of rebuilding its institutions and structures, was there a revolutionary settlement.[22]

Conclusion

North Carolina's experience during the American Revolutionary War was traumatic. With scant resources and dangerous internal enemies, this southern state was ravaged during the conflict's last several years, saw its commerce destroyed, its people killed or displaced, and its institutions disrupted. The wartime experience of Carolinians clearly shaped the postwar reconstruction. The revolutionary struggle also informed the 1780s in terms of how North Carolina's people perceived themselves in relation to the other American states, all of which were deeply in debt and searching for an effective plan of union once their independence had been won by 1783.

The significant number of Loyalists within the state and their violent battle against the Whigs led to a dominant spirit of enmity against these Carolina Tories in the postwar period. Despite the opposition of some prominent moderate and conservative leaders, the bitterness aroused by the savagery of the Whig/Tory conflict ensured that the last few years of the war and its aftermath were marked by vengeance, retribution and punishment. This manifested itself in various punitive acts against the Tories in the 1780s, including banishment and property confiscation. These retaliatory measures did not simply serve to punish the disaffected. Sales of Loyalist property shored up the state's financial foundation, while banishment had the salutary effect of removing many obnoxious Tories from the state, and thereby bringing at least some order and stability to North Carolina by their absence.

More significantly however, this penchant for revenge led the state to refuse to abide by the terms of the peace accord that finally ended the war in 1783, so that property confiscation could continue, and so that British collection of prewar debts could be avoided. North Carolina declined to allow the provisions of the Treaty of Paris to become the law of the land within the state's boundaries; consequently the sale of seized property continued unabated until 1787. The failure to abide by the terms of the Treaty is strongly indicative of a 'centrifugalism' that characterized North Carolina for much of the 1780s. Matters such as the 1783 Treaty, in so far as the state decided not to abide by it, demonstrate that the majority of Carolinians—or at least of those in the elected Assembly—did not regard the Confederation government as either authoritative or indispensable for the postwar years. In fact, many Carolinians seem to have regarded a national government as an impediment to reconstruction, and held it in low regard.

A strong national union would not only mean having to abide by the Treaty terms, but also the potential loss of the state's trans-Appalachian lands, upon which North Carolina based (in part) its currency, and bounties for its military veterans. Many Carolinians came to regard the Continental Congress, and later the Confederation government, as weak and ineffective due to its wartime performance, and thus refused to support North Carolina's active allegiance to it. A national government unable to provide for an effective defence of the South and which made incessant demands for men and money may well have inclined many Carolinians to look inward, not toward a union with the other states.

Finally, this perspective of opposition to confederation or union was based to a large extent on the localist outlook which characterized North Carolina inhabitants during the war, and apparently afterwards as well. Men refused to serve in arms far from home, or when they saw little or no threat to their families, farms or communities. They bitterly resented and opposed a draft for this very reason, as conscripted men typically served for extended periods far from home. Much more popular were local militia tours of just a few months, but even these were often eschewed, and they were vehemently objected to by army commanders desperate to have troops for more than a few weeks at a time. The unwillingness of many men to serve militarily, and opposition to impressment, combined to pit families, settlements, and communities against the insatiable demands of state and Continental authorities, and must have further buttressed this sense of local attachment.

The postwar era of the 1780s in North Carolina was a critical period that can only be understood in connection with the trying times of the war. When Carolinians could see that most of the Tories were no longer inhabitants of the state; that the state's financial and commercial matters were improving; that western land issues had been resolved; and that the new Federal Union was more respectable than that which had waged war so disjointedly, they opted to align their state with it, and completed their revolutionary settlement.

Notes

1. Norman K. Risjord, *Chesapeake Politics, 1781–1800* (New York, 1978), 5. Risjord argues that geography was also a factor in North Carolina's continued provincialism during and after the war. 'It is clear that North Carolina was the most isolated of the thirteen states', for the most part due to the Outer Banks and high sand bars at harbour entrances, both of which inhibited trade and commerce.
2. See Blackwell P. Robinson, *William R. Davie* (Chapel Hill, NC, 1957), 213–215; and Gordon DenBoer et al. (eds), *The Documentary History of the First Federal Elections, 1788–1790,* 4 vols (Madison, 1989), vol. 4, 303–309.
3. 'David Stuart to George Washington', 12 September 1789 in *Documentary History of the First Federal Congress of the United States of America, March 4, 1789–March 3, 1791*, eds Charlene Bangs Bickford et al., 20 vols (Baltimore, 1972), vol. 17, 1519; 'Robert Morris to Richard Peters', 13 September 1789, ibid. vol. 15, 1535; and 'Pierce Butler to James Iredell', 11 August 1789, ibid. vol. 16, 1289.
4. See John R. Maass, '"A Complicated Scene of Difficulties": North Carolina and the Revolutionary Settlement, 1776–1789', dissertation thesis (The Ohio State University, 2007); Samuel A. Ashe, *History of North Carolina,* 2 vols (Raleigh, NC, 1925), vol. 2, 100; Hugh Talmage Lefler and Albert Ray Newsome, *North Carolina: History of a Southern State* (Chapel Hill, NC, 1954), 285; John C. Cavanagh, *Decision at Fayetteville: The North Carolina Ratification Convention and General Assembly of 1789* (Raleigh, NC, 1989), 13, 20 and 22; DenBoer, *Documentary History,* vol. 4, 306 and 313–312; Alan D. Watson, 'States' Rights and Agrarianism Ascendant', in *The Constitution and the States: The Role of the Original Thirteen in the Framing and Adoption of the Federal Constitution*, eds. Patrick T. Conley and John P.

Kaminski (Madison, 1988), 255–256; and 'James Madison to Anthony Wayne', 31 July 1789, Bickford, *First Federal Congress,* vol. 16, 1185–1186. Federalist leader Hugh Williamson feared that if the Constitution were not adopted in 1789, several counties in the Albemarle Sound region would seek to be admitted to the union 'as a separate state under some other Name'. 'Hugh Williamson to Nicholas Gilman', undated, ibid., vol. 15, 648.

5. See Jackson T. Main, *The Antifederalists: Critics of the Constitution, 1781–1788* (Chapel Hill, NC, 1961); Forrest McDonald, 'The Anti-Federalists, 1781–1789', in *The Reinterpretation of the American Revolution, 1763–1789,* ed. Jack P. Greene (New York, 1968), 365–378; Jackson T. Main, *Political Parties before the Constitution* (Chapel Hill, NC, 1973); Saul Cornell, *The Other Founders: Anti-Federalism and the Dissenting Tradition in America, 1788–1828* (Chapel Hill, NC, 1999); and Ronald Hoffman and Peter J. Albert (eds), *The Bill of Rights: Government Proscribed* (Charlottesville, VA, 1997).
6. 'Benjamin Hawkins and Hugh Williamson to Alexander Martin', 26 September 1783, in *The State Records of North Carolina,* ed. Walter Clark, 16 vols (Winston, NC, 1895–1905), vol. 16, 888–889 (hereafter NCSR); and 'Alexander Martin to North Carolina Congressional Delegation', 8 December 1783, ibid. vol. 16, 919–920.
7. E. Wayne Carp, *To Starve the Army at Pleasure: Continental Army Administration and American Popular Culture, 1775–1783* (Chapel Hill, NC, 1984); James Kirby Martin and Mark Edward Lender, *A Respectable Army: The Military Origins of the Republic, 1763–1789* (2nd edn, Wheeling, IL, 2006), 148–154, 160; and Jack Rakove, *The Beginnings of National Politics* (New York, 1979), 288–295.
8. Merrill Jensen, *The New Nation: A History of the United States during the Confederation, 1781–1789* (New York, 1950), 375–398.
9. 'Alexander Martin to William Bryan', 21 September 1782, NCSR, vol. 16, 711–712.
10. 'Hugh Williamson to Alexander Martin', 30 September 1784, NCSR, vol. 17, 95–97.
11. NCSR, vol. 24, 679–680; 'Hugh Williamson to Alexander Martin', 30 September 1784, NCSR, vol. 17, 95–97; and 'Joshua Potts to Thomas Burke', 9 March 1782, NCSR, vol. 16, 226.
12. Richard B. Morris, *Forging the Union, 1781–1789* (New York, 1978), 58–63, 87–91 and 196–197; Rakove, *The Beginnings of National Politics,* 145–147; and Jensen, *The New Nation,* 25 and 43–46, 399–421. Jensen argues that 'the Articles of Confederation ... left ultimate power in the hands of the states', as does Gordon Wood, who concludes that 'the Confederation was intended to be, and remained, a Confederation of sovereign states'. Gordon S. Wood, *Creation of the American Republic, 1776–1787* (Chapel Hill, NC, 1969), 357.
13. 'Nathanael Greene to Robert Morris', 9 March 1782, *Papers of Nathanael Greene,* 10: 469.
14. Rakove, *The Beginnings of National Politics,* 164–176; Wood, *Creation of the American Republic,* 355–357; and John Sayle Watterson, *Thomas Burke: Restless Revolutionary* (Washington, DC, 1980), 61–64.
15. Forrest McDonald, *Novus Ordo Seclorum: The Intellectual Origins of the Constitution* (Lawrence, KS, 1985), 275.
16. See John R. Maass, '"All This Poor Province Could Do": North Carolina and the Seven Years' War, 1757–1762', *The North Carolina Historical Review* 79/1 (2002): 50–89; and William S. Powell, *North Carolina through Four Centuries* (Chapel Hill, NC, 1989), 226.
17. Marvin L. M. Kay, 'The North Carolina Regulation, 1766–1776: A Class Conflict', in *The American Revolution: Explorations in the History of American Radicalism,* ed. Alfred F. Young (DeKalb, IL, 1976), 71–123.

18. See Robert L. Gaynard, *The Emergence of North Carolina's Revolutionary State Government* (Raleigh, NC, 1978), 82–83, 88.
19. 'A Democratic Federalist', *The Pennsylvania Packet*, 23 October 1787.
20. 'North Carolina Declaration of Rights', 1789, text at http://www.learnnc.org/lp/editions/nchist-revolution/4286 (accessed 18 March 2015).
21. McDonald, 'The Anti-Federalists, 1781–1789', 365–378; Stanley Elkins and Eric McKittrick, 'The Founding Fathers: Young Men of the Revolution', *The Political Science Quarterly* 76 (1961): 181–183 and 200–216; and Thomas P. Slaughter, *The Whiskey Rebellion: Frontier Epilogue to the American Revolution* (New York, 1986), 4, 22–23 and 26–27.
22. 'Alexander Martin to the General Assembly', 22 December 1789, DenBoer, *Documentary History*, vol. 4, 349–351.

8

The Issue of Citizenship: Jews, Germans and the Contested Legacy of the Napoleonic Wars

Michael Rowe

> This general animosity against the Jews is quite inconceivable. From every quarter we have accounts of the same scandalous scenes. At Reinbart [sic], a village near Wurtzburg [sic], the peasants not only plundered the houses of the Jews, but demolished the synagogue, trampled on the *Ihoza* or Ark, in which were the Books of Moses; threw the whole into the street, broke the chandeliers, and committed the most reprehensible excesses. In some little towns in Franconia, there have been very serious tumults, occasioned by the same hatred of the Jews. At Berlin, a Jew, being pursued by a crowd of idle people, had no means of saving himself but to join in the cry of 'Hep! Hep!' which has become so terrible to the Jews in Germany.[1]

The so-called 'Hep-Hep' riots of 1819 are surprisingly neglected in general histories of nineteenth-century Germany, though they are the subject of the more specialized studies on the history of German antisemitism.[2] The riots have been overshadowed in particular by the passage of the Carlsbad Decrees, which occurred at the same time and confirmed the reactionary course that German politics would take for at least a generation. This paper will examine the anti-Jewish riots of 1819 in the context of the Napoleonic Wars and their immediate aftermath. It will consider how the legacy and memories of these Wars not only created the conditions which made the riots possible, but also bolstered German Jews and their supporters in their argument for acceptance and equality.

The contested status of Jews in Napoleonic and restoration Germany

The Napoleonic Wars terminated the thousand-year old Holy Roman Empire, whose final demise in 1806 was an important turning point in

German history. Its dissolution allowed the individual German states to implement radical change without encountering resistance from the now defunct imperial courts. The reforms varied in extent and detail, but generally tended towards weakening existing privileges and strengthening the state. The Wars not only provided the opportunity for change, by destroying the Empire. They also supplied an incentive, by creating an unparalleled need to mobilize resources for the conduct of war. Reform and war were therefore inextricably linked in Germany. Napoleon's final defeat in 1815 modified this dynamic and diminished the impetus for further innovation. Yet references to the Napoleonic Wars greatly informed political discourse after 1815, as various groups jockeyed for advantage in a world that apparently remained in flux.[3]

One such group was Germany's Jews. Prior to the Napoleonic period, Jews had confronted a variety of restrictions and legal disabilities, as was generally the case in the rest of Europe. However, in order to encourage economic development, some enlightened absolutist rulers started to ease these restrictions in the 1780s. Most prominent among them was Austria's ruler, Emperor Joseph II, who in order to make his Jewish subjects 'more useful to the state', issued a series of patents in 1781, 1782 and 1783 that abolished the need for Jews to wear identifying marks, diminished fiscal inequalities, and opened up employment prospects in previously forbidden trades. Other smaller German states, like the Electorate of Mainz, enacted similar measures, for the same reasons.[4]

However, it was the upheaval caused by the Napoleonic Wars that fundamentally undermined the existing order governing Jewish existence in Germany. Generally, the period saw moves towards emancipation and greater equality, though the trend was by no means universal, uncontested or indeed irreversible. Within France itself, which served as a model for many of the German states, Napoleon issued decrees in 1808 that undermined the equality assured Jews by earlier revolutionary legislation passed in the 1790s. Within Prussia, whose defeat at the hands of France in 1806–1807 created an impetus for reform, calls for Jewish emancipation encountered much resistance, including from individuals associated with progress. Freiherr vom Stein, for example, though praised in the literature as a great reformer on account of his ministry's abolition of serfdom (1807) and liberalization of urban government (1808), was extremely ill-disposed towards Jews, whom he regarded as parasites living off the peasantry. His vision for reform remained wedded to the older notion of society divided into separate estates, each with its distinctive character.[5]

Fundamental reform, based on the principle of civic equality, was confined to the later government of Karl August von Hardenberg, who served as chancellor from 1810 to 1822. Hardenberg was the Prussian statesman most committed to Jewish equality, a position that his critics at the time linked to his personal dependence upon Jewish businessmen for financial support.

It was Hardenberg more than anyone else who drove through the famous 'Edict Concerning the Civil Status of the Jews in the Prussian State' of 11 March 1812, a measure that accorded Jews greater equality than most other German states. Part of the impetus for this reform was the need to encourage Jewish financiers to purchase Prussian crown domains that the state was selling off in order to pay the war reparations imposed by Napoleon. Under existing legislation, Jews were restricted from acquiring such property. The edict of 11 March removed these restrictions, though King Friedrich Wilhelm III's amendments to Hardenberg's draft watered down those provisions promising Jews equal access to positions within the civil service and military. The edict fell short of full equality, but nonetheless extended the right to Jews legally resident in Prussia to acquire citizenship rights, and this was progressive in the context of the period. Jewish communities in Prussia certainly greeted the edict of 11 March 1812 with enthusiasm. For their part, opponents of emancipation claimed that the edict was essentially purchased by wealthy Jews from a regime that was associated, not without some reason, with financial corruption.[6]

Opponents of Jewish emancipation produced a similar narrative to explain reforms undertaken in the neighbouring Kingdom of Westphalia. Unlike Prussia, Westphalia as a state was an entirely novel creation, cobbled together by Napoleon in 1807 out of a variety of territories in order to anchor more securely French power in northern Germany. Napoleon named his youngest brother Jérôme king of this new polity, which he intended to serve as a progressive 'model state' that would provide an example for German princes allied to France to follow, whilst also putting the Prussians to shame.[7] Both for this reason, and in order to create a coherent whole out of a multiplicity of territories with a variety of laws and customs, Napoleon imposed a constitution that abolished discrimination on grounds of religious affiliation and instead guaranteed civil equality. This principle was explicitly extended to the Kingdom's Jewish minority in the *Emanzipationsdekret* of 27 January 1808. Westphalia thereby became the most progressive state in Germany, in terms of the equal status accorded to Jews, and even surpassed France itself, which under Napoleon reapplied discriminatory legislation in 1808. At the opposite end of the spectrum from Westphalia lay Saxony, and the Mecklenburg duchies, where the status of Jews underwent no meaningful change in this period.[8]

In Bavaria, the largest German state apart from Austria and Prussia, a growing consensus in favour of tolerance between Christian confessions, as laid out in Maximilian von Montgelas's important 'Ansbach memorandum' (1796), did not extend to Jews, who were deemed morally unripe to be considered as citizens (*Staatsbürger*). Bavaria's subsequent annexation of territories in Swabia and Franconia increased the number of Jews living in the kingdom to approximately 37,000 by 1812, a ten-fold increase over the pre-Napoleonic situation. Most lived in relative poverty in rural areas, as they were generally not allowed to settle in towns, though their legal status varied in the different parts of the newly-enlarged kingdom. The Bavarian government's paramount aim was to create uniformity across the kingdom, and it was this rather than a desire for greater equality between Jews and non-Jews that shaped policy. This policy found expression in a new edict on the status of the kingdom's Jews, the *Edikt über die Verhältnisse der jüdischen Glaubensgenossen im Königreiche Baiern,* promulgated on 10 June 1813.[9]

As seen from the above, the status of Jews across the German states varied considerably when the Napoleonic Wars ended, but the tendency over the previous decade had been towards emancipation and greater equality. The Congress of Vienna that convened in the Austrian capital in September 1814 included much discussion about the future of Germany. This encompassed the issue of the relationship between confessional groups, something previously regulated minutely by the now defunct Treaty of Westphalia (1648) ending the Thirty Years War. Confessional politics, more even than territorial arrangements, was an area that attracted considerable public attention in Germany. Commentators debated about the balance of power between Catholics and Protestants, and how this had changed as a consequence of the Revolutionary and Napoleonic Wars, and how it might develop in the future.[10] The final settlement on German affairs, concluded at the Congress and enshrined in the German Federal Acts passed on 8 June 1815, included article 16 stipulating that confessional differences between Christian faiths should no longer impair an individual's enjoyment of civic and political rights. The signatories considered this essential in that the new territorial order created a situation where large numbers of Protestants and Catholics found themselves incorporated into states in which they constituted a minority. However, this principle was not extended to Jews, where the Federal Acts in practice confirmed existing inequalities. Further attempts at improving the status of Jews were blocked by some of the states, including notably the kingdoms of Bavaria, Hanover and Württemberg.[11]

The flood of publications generated by the Congress of Vienna and its aftermath on the whole welcomed the provisions guaranteeing equality between the Christian confessions, but no such consensus existed with regards to the status of Jews. Rather, to quote the German-Jewish writer, Ludwig Börne, writing in Frankfurt in 1819 at the time of the 'Hep Hep' riots, and referring back to the city's liberation from Napoleonic rule in 1813:

> After the expulsion of the French, one started to view the civic freedom granted to Jews as something corrosive. To this was added the view that Jews were supporters of French rule because they, though no less oppressed by it than other Germans, nonetheless also derived some benefit from it. It is excusable when a feeling develops in us against those who derive some advantage from the same source as our misery—I mean, it is an excusable weakness.[12]

How this resentment played out on the ground, in rural and small-town Germany, is revealed in Robert von Friedeburg's recent study of communal antisemitism in the region between the rivers Eder and Werra. Here, it was widely believed that Jews in particular had benefitted financially from the Napoleonic Wars. Typical, in this context, was the complaint of the parish priest of Völkershausen, near the Wartburg, that Christians found themselves indebted to Jewish creditors on account of French billeting and requisitioning, and hence were exposed to their usury.[13]

The costs of the Napoleonic Wars added to longer-term factors to create something of a socio-economic crisis in much of rural Germany in the years after 1815. These factors included a rising population, a growing gap between rich and poor, and greater competition for communal resources. The colossal damage inflicted by the wars on Germany's forests and woodlands exacerbated the situation. These problems were directly tied to the Jewish emancipation debate, in that full emancipation promised Jews equal access to communal resources. To a large extent, Jews were caught up in a conflict between central government, whose officials generally favoured greater uniformity, and local communities, who resented loss of control over the disposition of what they regarded as their resources. Jews found themselves in the unfortunate position of becoming associated with central government interference, something that was well-nigh inevitable given their historical status as essentially crown property. The fact that politicians, including most prominently Austria's chief minister Klemens von Metternich, blamed for the political reaction that set in after 1815, were generally seen as supportive of Jewish demands only increased in the public mind the connection between Jewish interests and oppression. The reverse of the coin was that many opponents of the so-called 'Metternich System', including the student fraternities, exhibited a strong grain of antisemitism, as was demonstrated by the infamous book burning episode at the Wartburg Festival in 1817. Authors sympathetic to the Jewish position saw their works consigned to the flames, alongside writers allegedly supportive of reactionary politics.[14]

The 'Hep-Hep' riots of 1819

August von Kotzebue was one of the authors whose works were allegedly burned at the Wartburg, and it was his assassination two years later that provoked passage of the Carlsbad Decrees suppressing student fraternities and restricting press freedom. The year 1819 also witnessed the worst wave of anti-Jewish violence in Germany to be experienced in over a century. There was a direct connection between the violence, known as the 'Hep-Hep riots', and the public debate about the status of Jews.[15] The ongoing bleak economic context of the postwar period, together with dissatisfaction at the growth of the state and loss of local autonomy, were further factors behind the violence which started in the Franconian city of Würzburg in August 1819, before spreading to other areas.[16]

Würzburg's experience during the Revolutionary and Napoleonic Wars can be viewed as a microcosm of the upheaval confronting all Germany. Its strategic location and fortifications insured that it had witnessed much military activity, including a full-scale battle in September 1796 between French and Austrian armies each numbering in excess of 40,000 troops, a month-long siege at the end of 1800, and an even longer siege lasting from October 1813 to May 1814. In October 1806, Napoleon visited the city accompanied by at least 10,000 of his imperial guard, who needed to be supported by the city's population which at the time numbered only about 20,000 souls. Political turmoil accompanied these military campaigns. Historically, Würzburg and the surrounding region constituted an independent prince-bishopric. As a consequence of Napoleon's reordering of Germany, it was ceded in 1803 to Bavaria before regaining its independence in 1806 as a Grand Duchy awarded to a Habsburg prince in compensation for his loss of Tuscany. It then reverted back to Bavaria in 1814.[17] This change in territorial status was final, but from the perspective of the immediate post-Napoleonic period there was no reason to believe that the Vienna settlement should prove any more durable than previous re-orderings. For Würzburgers, like the other estimated 60 percent of Germans who changed sovereigns at least once in this period, it can be assumed that their allegiances in the years immediately after 1815 were influenced by the consideration that their new status might prove short-lived. Within Würzburg, Bavarian rule was resented by many as alien and destructive of the independence enjoyed previously. That some prominent Jews in the region were known to have supported the Bavarian state with the provision of military supplies during the Napoleonic Wars, and to have purchased secularized church property sold by the government, in part to finance the war effort, only encouraged the association of Jews as a whole with the loss of local independence.[18]

The spark that caused the 'Hep-Hep' riots to ignite in Würzburg in 1819 was provided by polemics in the local press about Jewish emancipation, an issue at the time being debated in the Bavarian parliament (*Landtag*) in Munich. The Bavarian government had initiated the debate, as it intended to harmonize the status of Jews across the kingdom including provinces recently acquired at the Congress of Vienna.[19] According to contemporary accounts, the trouble in Würzburg started on 2 August when a crowd, including students, gathered to welcome upon his return from Munich Professor Wilhelm Behr, who had served as a deputy at the *Landtag*. Also present was Sebald Brendel, a professor at the University of Würzburg, known as a supporter of 'Jewish emancipation', who had recently engaged in polemics against the Würzburger jurist and anti-Jewish writer Thomas August Scheuring. Earlier in the year, Scheuring had published a piece, *The Citizenship of Jews*, in which he argued against Jewish equality, a line that Brendel publicly opposed.[20] The polemics in the local press between Scheuring and Brendel had continued in the days before Behr's return. Brendel, as a consequence, now became the target of the hostility of the crowd, whose sympathies lay with Scheuring. Brendel was forced to flee, whereupon the crowd, now chanting 'Hep! Hep!', turned upon the city's Jewish minority. The balance of evidence suggests that no Jews were killed, despite some reports to the contrary, but that the violence was directed mainly at Jewish property, including shops and warehouses. These the rioters proceeded to wreck, scattering their contents onto the streets. The tumults continued into the following days, forcing the Jewish community to flee into the surrounding countryside. Eventually, the Bavarian army deployed in sufficient force to quell the riots, and Würzburg's Jews could return to the city before the end of the month.[21]

As news of the tumults in Würzburg spread, so did a wave of copycat riots. These eventually engulfed various cities across the Germanic Confederation and even beyond. Frankfurt, which like Würzburg had witnessed considerable change in the Napoleonic period including to the status of Jews, was especially afflicted. The same was true of other cities that similarly enjoyed a tradition of independence, like Hamburg. Here, the civic authorities were slow to react or even blamed Jews for the trouble. In the larger territorial states, in contrast, including notably Prussia, a swift and determined response prevented major trouble.[22] For many Jews at the time the riots obviously fell within a longer tradition of anti-Jewish persecutions stretching back to the medieval period. This made them no less shocking, given the belief entertained by many, especially within the elite, that they were living in an age characterized by enlightenment and progress. According to this world view, the outbreak of a medieval-style pogrom simply did not fit, which is why after the initial shock one can detect a tendency of commentators—both Jewish and non-Jewish—to dismiss the riots as something of an aberration, caused by a minority of 'riff-raff'. Conservative politicians like Metternich, in contrast, were less sanguine. For them, the riots provided one more argument against democracy, thereby deepening the unfortunate association of Jews not only with the loss of civic autonomy, but with reaction.

Jewish soldiers in the Napoleonic wars

The Napoleonic Wars reinforced prejudices against Jews as outsiders and profiteers not only in Germany, but elsewhere. For example, British prints of the period show Jews in an unflattering manner, portraying them as unscrupulous loan sharks preying upon sailors dependent upon them because of the Royal Navy's habit of deferring payment of their wages.[23] However, just as the Napoleonic Wars could provide ammunition for opponents of Jewish emancipation in Germany and elsewhere, so the same Wars could equally supply arguments in favour of the Jewish cause. In Germany,

Jews and non-Jews supportive of equality could and did highlight the Jewish contribution to the struggle against the French. In doing so, they were rebutting not only the accusation that Jews had supported Napoleon, but also challenging the stereotype that Jews were profoundly unfit for military service, and hence unworthy of citizenship.[24]

The stereotype of the un-soldierly Jew, cowardly and physically feeble, long predated the Napoleonic era. It found expression in eighteenth-century satirical prints.[25] Even proponents of Jewish emancipation at the turn of the eighteenth and nineteenth centuries, and some Jews themselves, tacitly supported this stereotype in their argument that compulsory military service was essential for the 'regeneration' of Jews, and hence their emancipation. This argument was, for example, posited by Christian Wilhelm Dohm, in his famous book, *On the Civil Improvement of the Jews,* first published in 1781. Dohm wrote emphatically that, 'so long as Jews do not prove themselves as willing and capable in the performance of military service, then they cannot claim the same rights as the rest of society'.[26] Similar sentiments were later expressed in France, at the time of the Revolution.[27] The Abbé Grégoire shared the view that Jews were weak, but noted that this did not matter in modern armies where physical effort was less important than dexterity. Military service, so Grégoire believed, would break down their prejudices and peculiar practices by exposing them to the peer-pressure of non-Jewish recruits.[28] Such arguments continued into the Napoleonic period, including in Germany. Here, the Prussian early-liberal writer Friedrich Buchholz, in a pamphlet published in 1803 titled *Moses and Jesus,* claimed Jews would shed their cowardice only through military training and discipline, something that should be possible given that they had fought well enough in antiquity. Buchholz went on to praise military service more generally, as encouraging physical fitness, honesty, a disdain for excess wealth, comradeship, and self-sacrifice. Armies, said Buchholz, have a unique capacity to unite different types, and to engender tolerance.[29]

German armies had started openly admitting Jews on the eve of the Napoleonic Wars. Joseph II's Austria was the first to do so, despite hostility from the officer corps and from Orthodox Jews. In total, approximately 36,200 Jews served in the Austrian forces during the Napoleonic Wars, with the majority recruited from Bohemia and Galicia.[30] The Napoleonic satellite states in Germany, through their agreements with France, were obliged to mobilize sizeable military contingents, and this caused them to grapple with the issue of subjecting their Jewish inhabitants to military conscription. In the Grand Duchy of Hesse, the government minister Karl Wilhelm Heinrich du Bos du Thil prepared a memorandum in 1809 that linked the issue of military service to emancipation, which he favoured. Only citizens of the state (*Staatsbürger*), claimed Thil, could be expected to demonstrate the necessary patriotism demanded of military service, but extension of this status to Jews would yield an additional 200 conscripts.[31] In Bavaria, the government extended compulsory military service to Jews in 1804, but with the special provision that they could purchase their exemption for 180 florins. Non-Jews viewed this facility as government favouritism towards Jews, whilst some Jews insisted on doing military service anyway. Other Jews opposed military service on the grounds that they did not enjoy equality with other Bavarians. In 1808, the Bavarian government extended the conscription of Jews to the militia, and the king publicly praised the service Jews performed in this formation.[32]

It was above all the extent of Jewish participation in the Prussian war effort of 1813 that would inform subsequent debates about the place Jews should occupy in German society. This was hardly surprising given the importance that the year 1813 quickly assumed in wider arguments about Germany's redemption and regeneration. For many, the mobilization of 1813 was a general uprising of the *Volk*, based upon voluntary engagement, and hence fundamentally different from Napoleonic-style conscription in armies subordinate to French interests. Jewish involvement in the so-called 'Wars of Liberation', including the involvement of some Jewish women, served as a demonstration of inclusion in the nation, in the same way that participation in the defence of England against the anticipated Napoleonic invasion (in 1803–1804) provided a marker of inclusion in Britain.[33]

King Friedrich Wilhelm III's famous proclamation *An mein Volk*, issued on 17 March 1813, was viewed subsequently as marking the start of the 'Wars of Liberation', at the centre of which stood the alliance between throne and nation. The Prussian government decreed that the proclamation be read out in all churches, forgetting to include synagogues, but these nonetheless organized their own special events to associate themselves with the occasion. The authorities, recognizing the omission, then stepped in to officially include them as well. Prussia's Jews from the outset understood the importance of engagement in the war effort, both through military service, and also through patriotic publications. Some of these directly addressed accusations that Jews were unfit for military service.[34]

The actual extent of Jewish engagement in the 'Wars of Liberation' is of less concern here than the importance the issue assumed after 1815. Jews argued at the time that their status was *de facto* transformed by their contribution to the war against Napoleon. An early formulation of the argument came from the jurist Carl August Buchholz from Lübeck, who represented the Jewish communities at the Congress of Vienna, and who wrote in a pamphlet in 1815,

> It is a fact that the sons of the wealthiest Jewish families in the capital cities voluntarily marched forth, weapon in hand, with loyalty and determination, and fought and bled like other citizens. It is a fact that Jewish doctors and surgeons risked their lives in the hospitals.... It is a fact, that Jewish women and girls spared no effort and avoided no risk

> in providing help and comfort to the wounded. It is a fact, finally, that all Jewish citizens proved their attachment to King and Country through the numerous donations of treasure they volunteered. Thanks and glory to the exalted Prussian government, that all these efforts are accepted as having come from citizens, and not from Jews, as these are no longer considered a separate category.[35]

A review of Buchholz's text in the Jewish periodical *Sulamith* in 1816 pressed home the point: 'Jews throughout Germany have done their duty in defending the Fatherland and with weapon in hand have proved themselves citizens; as a consequence, they have actually become citizens, and it would be unfair, indeed unjust, to deny them the rights of citizens.'[36]

Such arguments were far from attracting universal agreement, but instead provoked further debate between proponents and opponents of Jewish equality. Vocal opponents of Jewish equality included the philosopher Jakob Friedrich Fries and the historian Friedrich Rühs.[37] Fries was especially violent in his attacks on Jews, whom he portrayed as cowardly, lazy and given over to speculation. He identified them as beneficiaries of the era of 'French disorder', which had caused the abolition of previous restrictions, and had provided opportunities for profiteering. Fries dismissed the participation of Jews in the Wars of Liberation, and instead accused Jews of buying their way out of military service.[38] Rühs, for his part, argued that Jews had above all distinguished themselves as French spies and collaborators working for Napoleon's secret police.[39] Some young Jews had contributed to the good cause in 1813, he admitted, behaving 'in a Christian way', but he went on to comment that if Jews were to be believed, they had won the war against Napoleon single-handedly. 'On the whole', he continued, 'Jewish involvement was notably marginal and one-sided; this was the case even in numerical terms, according to officers whom I have asked; the best service they performed was as commissaries, requisitioning and such like'.[40] In making this last point, Rühs turned around the experience of military service to reinforce existing prejudices about the alleged Jewish predilection for speculation and greed. More fundamentally, Rühs argued that military service was now an honourable civic duty, unlike under the Ancien Régime when it had been based upon monetary reward and compulsion. Hence, it was now especially inappropriate for Jews to serve.

Not surprisingly, these anti-Jewish arguments provoked a response. One such, published in 1816 by the Protestant theologian Johann Ewald from Baden, employed extracts from newspapers produced during the 'Wars of Liberation' to bolster its case that Jews had played an important and patriotic part.[41] These extracts included an article originally published in the *Nationalzeitung der Deutschen* of 8 February 1815, which praised the efforts of Salomon Löb Sondheimer, a Jewish businessman from Mannheim, in organizing a field hospital in the city. These efforts, so the article claimed, won recognition not only from the Catholic, Orthodox and Protestant soldiers cared for in the hospital, but, significantly, from the Coalition military authorities including the Russian city commandant.[42] Other examples cited by Ewald included an article from the *Badischen Staatszeitung*, concerning Amalie Beer, the wife of the Berlin banker and industrialist Jacob Herz Beer, who, on the recommendation of Princess Wilhelm of Prussia, was awarded the *Luisenorden* for her wartime charity.[43] Amalie Beer's receipt of the *Luisenorden* attracted much attention at the time. It highlighted how Jewish women could join with Christian women in engaging in patriotic philanthropy, and also receive royal recognition for their efforts. The fact that Amalie Beer was awarded a special version of the *Luisenorden* medal, without a cross, in order to take account of her religious sensibilities, was celebrated as exemplifying the tolerance of the Prussian state.[44] This patriotic engagement by Jews, said Ewald, was especially pronounced in Prussia, which had surpassed other states in its enlightened treatment of Jews. Ewald, in making this argument, was claiming Prussia for the cause of Jewish emancipation, just as anti-Jewish romantic-nationalists initially attempted to enlist the Hohenzollern monarchy for their cause.[45]

Eventually, the Prussian government would disappoint both, opposing the nationalist agenda, but also in part reversing the earlier trend towards Jewish emancipation. A litmus test of the attainment of equal civic status in post-Napoleonic Prussia was access to civil service jobs. In 1813, as part of the mobilization effort of that year, the Prussian government promised that every volunteer would have the chance of a civil service position. The promise was made without specific consideration of Prussia's Jewish subjects, whose status was regulated by the Emancipation Edict of March 1812, a measure that, whilst comparatively progressive, nonetheless postponed a definitive regulation of Jewish access to public office. After the war, Jews in Prussia who had volunteered quite naturally assumed that their military service entitled them to public office. This sense of entitlement is reflected in their petitions, written in the same patriotic, martial language as those submitted by non-Jewish applicants. The Prussian authorities, whilst not questioning the patriotism and military engagement of these Jewish applicants, nevertheless refused their applications on the grounds that they were not Christian. Should they convert, then their military service would indeed provide the necessary entitlement.[46] This conclusion was very much in keeping with the new postwar ethos of Prussia as a Christian 'missionary state'.[47]

This remained the state of affairs so far as Jewish veterans of the Napoleonic Wars were concerned until the death of Friedrich Wilhelm III in 1840. The accession of his successor, Friedrich Wilhelm IV, brought with it the prospect of long-delayed reform, including to the status of Prussia's Jews. The issue again became the subject of lengthy public debate, and despite the passage of a quarter of a century, the extent of Jewish participation in the 'Wars of Liberation' figured prominently during the discussions on the issue. This can be seen, for example, in the debates held within the newly-convened all-Prussian *Landtag* that met in 1847.[48] The government even drafted a special memorandum for the benefit of the *Landtag*, containing statistics on the number of Jews who had served in the Prussian forces in 1813–1815. The memorandum concluded by lauding Jewish service in the Prussian army both during the final stages of the Napoleonic Wars, and subsequently. The memorandum in turn developed a life of its own, and was cited by later generations of German Jews whenever their status was questioned. Such was especially the case in the final years of the nineteenth century, the period which saw the spread of racial antisemitism. For example, the memorandum was cited in *The Jews as Soldiers*, a 167-page book published in 1897 by a committee for defence against antisemitic attacks in Berlin. *The Jews as Soldiers* includes other primary source material, including newspaper extracts from the Napoleonic era referring to Jewish participation in the wars against the French, and combines this with a mass of statistical data on Jewish soldiers who had served in the 1813–1815 campaigns.[49]

Despite its detail, *The Jews as Soldiers* did not remain the last word in the debate. As another publication devoted to the subject of Jewish involvement in the 'Wars of Liberation' put it only nine years later, the issue remained a 'much contested question'.[50] By this stage, German Jews had refined an alternative narrative of the Napoleonic period, one that refuted the conservative nationalist version that portrayed Jewish emancipation as a French imposition. In this alternative version, Napoleon had attempted to reverse the progress made earlier towards greater Jewish equality, through his so-called 'Infamous Decree' of 17 October 1808. From this point onwards, Jewish hopes rested with the Prussian reformers, but their progress was in turn stymied by the repressive Restoration era, with its reactionary princelings and conservative bureaucrats.[51]

Conflicting accounts of the Napoleonic Wars, and of the German Jewish experience during them, continued even after the First World War, and into the National Socialist period. The weight still lent to the issue can be seen with Heinz Bender's *The Struggle for the Emancipation of the Jews*, published in 1939. This reflected the new official ideology in its rubbishing of Jewish involvement in the Napoleonic Wars: Bender admits that a few Jews did well, but insists that the majority sought to buy themselves out of military service. Quoting from Friedrich Rühs, he claims that Jews only really distinguished themselves in managing supplies and requisitioning, gleefully profiteering whilst Christians killed each other.[52] The preferred Nazi version of the Napoleonic Wars was of course that presented in the epic film *Kolberg* (1945), which portrayed the conflict in terms of a *Völkisch* uprising in which Jews could play no constructive role.

Conclusion

The experience of German Jews in the Napoleonic Wars and their aftermath can be located within the broader historical span of the Jewish experience in Germany. However, comparisons might also be made 'laterally', with Jews elsewhere in Europe, and indeed, with other marginalized groups throughout the Atlantic World striving for recognition or preferment as a consequence of their contribution to recent war efforts. In this context, one might look across the North Sea, to Britain, where the issue of Catholic equality came on to the political agenda in the post-Napoleonic years. As with Germany's Jews, the degree and nature of Catholic participation in the Napoleonic Wars formed a sub-component of the debate. As in Germany, opponents of reform levelled accusations at Catholics that they had tended to side with Napoleon.[53]

That said, though important in helping forge a greater sense of 'Britishness', the Napoleonic Wars never came close to playing the seminal role as a redemptive moment that was the case in Germany. Accordingly, though the contribution of particular groups during the Napoleonic Wars was occasionally raised in the British emancipation debates after 1815, the issue hardly took on the same importance as in Germany. In Germany, and especially in Prussia, in contrast, an individual, group or even region's conduct during the Napoleonic Wars assumed considerable importance in the political discourse of the postwar years. The enlistment of the so-called 'Wars of Liberation' for sectarian purposes could be seen already at the Wartburg Festival in 1817. The whole conception of the festival sought to link the climax of the Wars (the Battle of Leipzig) with the Protestant Reformation. This was reflected in the timing of the event, which combined the fourth anniversary of the Battle with the tri-centenary of the beginning of the Reformation, and the locale—the Wartburg had served as a refuge for Martin Luther following his excommunication. In terms of the actual choreography of the event, it resembled as much a Protestant religious service as a political event.[54] Not surprisingly, Catholics constituted only a very small minority of participants in the Festival.

However, the status of German Jews after 1815 remained more precarious than that of adherents of the Christian confessions. To an extent, the Revolutionary and Napoleonic Wars encouraged a trend that had already started towards greater equality for Jews. The territorial upheaval caused by the wars, the requirement to integrate new provinces and create legal uniformity across enlarged states and, not least, the need of governments to mobilize manpower and money to wage war on the whole worked in favour of Jewish emancipation. Yet, unlike in Revolutionary France in the 1790s, the German states failed to embrace full equality out of principle, with the possible exception of Westphalia. Even in Prussia, which went relatively far, the Emancipation Edict of March 1812 was hedged with qualifications. At the same time, important factors were working against the acceptance of Jews by wider society. The hardship created by war exacerbated longer-term trends, including population increase and inflation, and lay behind the 'pauperism' that distinguished the years after 1815 in Central Europe. Jews, newly visible and often prominent, though not especially numerous, served as scapegoats for communities facing not only economic crises, but also a loss of autonomy as the bureaucratic state reinforced its authority.

The 'Hep-Hep' riots occurred against the background of this postwar crisis. This is not to deny the important ideological component of the 1819 riots, namely, the widespread opposition to the extension of the principle of civic equality to Jews. It was this contested status, as something less than full citizens, that made the issue of Jewish participation in the struggle against Napoleon in the campaigns of 1813, 1814 and 1815 so important. Had German Jews acquired equality in 1815 with the Federal Acts, and been accepted by the rest of society, then the issue of Jewish participation in the 'Wars of Liberation' would have faded in importance. Instead, it remained very much a live one, becoming more prominent whenever the position of German Jews was reassessed or challenged. Both those in favour and those against Jewish equality refined their own distinct narratives of the 'Wars of Liberation' after 1815, narratives that remained surprisingly stable in terms of content. These competing narratives ran in parallel, with both ultimately reinforcing the conviction that the Napoleonic Wars constituted a vital redemptive moment for Germany.

Notes

1. *The Times* (London), 11 September 1819, 2. It is possible that 'Ihoza' is a mistranscription of 'achuza' meaning usually '(treasured) possession', and sometimes 'stronghold'. I am grateful to Adam Sutcliffe for this explanation.
2. For German nationalism and citizenship in the period during and after the Napoleonic Wars see, Karen Hagemann, *'Mannlicher Muth und Teutsche Ehre': Nation, Militär und Geschlecht zur Zeit der antinapleonischen Kriege* (Paderborn, 2002), 242–271, esp. 255–271, and also her *Revisiting Prussia's Wars against Napoleon: History, Culture, Memory* (Cambridge, 2015), 113–129; the most important earlier works on the subject are: Eleonore Sterling, 'Anti-Jewish Riots in Germany in 1819', *Historia Judaica* 12 (1950): 105–142; Sterling, *Judenhaß: Die Anfänge des politischen Antisemitismus in Deutschland (1815–1850)* (Frankfurt/M. 1969); Nicoline Hortzitz, *'Früh-Antisemitismus' in Deutschland (1789–1870/72): Strukturelle Untersuchungen zu Wortschatz, Text und Argumentation* (Tübingen, 1988); Rainer Erb and Werner Bergmann, *Die Nachtseite der Judenemanzipation: Der Widerstand gegen die Integration der Juden in Deutschland 1780–1860* (Berlin, 1989); Stefan Rohrbacher, *Gewalt im Biedermeier: Antijüdische Ausschreitungen in Vormärz und Revolution (1815–1848/49)* (Frankfurt/M., 1993); Jacob Katz, *Zur Assimilation und Emanzipation der Juden* (Darmstadt, 1982); idem. *Vom Vorurteil bis zur Vernichtung: Der Antisemitismus 1770–1933* (Munich, 1989); idem. *Die Hep-Hep-Verfolgungen des Jahres 1819* (Berlin, 1994); and Stefan Rohrbacher, 'The "Hep Hep" Riots of 1819: Anti-Jewish Ideology, Agitation, and Violence', in *Exclusionary Violence: Antisemitic Riots in Modern German History*, ed. Christhard Hoffmann, et al. (Ann Arbor, MI, 2002), 23–42.
3. The literature on the reforms implemented in the various German states in the Napoleonic period is extensive. For an overview, see: Michael Rowe, 'Napoleon and

the "Modernization" of Germany', in *Napoleon and his Empire: Europe, 1804–1814*, ed. Philip Dwyer and Alan Forrest (Basingstoke, 2006), 202–220.

4. For Joseph's policy towards the Jews, see: Derek Beales, *Joseph II*, 2 vols, vol. 2: *Against the World 1780–1790* (Cambridge, 1987-2009), vol. 2, 196–213. For Mainz, see: T. C. W. Blanning, *Reform and Revolution in Mainz, 1743–1803* (London, 1974), 184–185. For a contemporary account of the position in Bavaria up to 1799, see: Johann Christian Freiherrn von Aretin, *Geschichte der Juden in Baiern* (Landshut, 1803), 61–96.
5. Albert Bruer, *Geschichte der Juden in Preussen (1750–1820)* (Frankfurt/M., 1991), 258–264.
6. Ibid., 289–305.
7. The intended role of Westphalia, as a tool for France's moral conquest of Germany, is famously stated in Napoleon's letter to Jérôme of 15 November 1807. *Correspondance de Napoléon Ier: publiée par ordre de l'empereur Napoléon III*, 32 vols (Paris, 1858–1869), vol. 16, No. 13361, 196.
8. Helmut Berding, 'Die Emanzipation der Juden im Königreich Westfalen, 1807–1813', *Archiv für Sozialgeschichte* 23 (1983): 23–50.
9. Hannes Ludyga, *Die Rechtsstellung der Juden in Bayern von 1819 bis 1918: Studie im Spiegel der Verhandlungen der Kammer der Abgeordneten des bayerischen Landtags* (Berlin, 2007), 36–42; see also, Stefan Schwarz, *Die Juden in Bayern im Wandel der Zeiten* (Munich, 1963), 107–124.
10. See, for example, Gottlieb Jakob Planck, *Ueber die gegenwärtige Lage und Verhältnisse der katholischen und der protestantischen Parthey in Deutschland und einige besondere zum Theil von dem deutschen Bundes=Tage darüber zu erwartende Bestimmungen* (Hannover, 1816); also, Franz Andreas Frey, *Frage: Ist der westphälische Friede vom J. 1648 den Bestimmungen des Art. V. nach in Bezug auf den Religionszustand der christlichen Hauptkonfessionen in Deutschland durch die rheinische und Wiener Bundesakten abgeschafft und aufgehoben?* (Bamberg, 1816), 14–19.
11. Ludyga, *Rechtsstellung*, 38–42. For a very recent study of the Congress of Vienna, including the issue of religion and the 'Jewish question', see Brian F. Vick, *The Congress of Vienna: Power and Politics after Napoleon* (Cambridge, MA, 2014), 223–277.
12. Ludwig Börne, *Gesammelte Schriften: Vollständige Ausgabe*, 12 vols (Vienna, 1868), vol. 2, 30. The translation is my own, as is the case with other quotations in this chapter unless otherwise stated.
13. Robert von Friedeburg, 'Kommunaler Antisemitismus: Christliche Landgemeinden und Juden zwischen Eder und Werra vom späten 18. bis zur Mitte des 19. Jahrhunderts', in *Jüdisches Leben auf dem Lande: Studien zur deutsch-jüdischen Geschichte*, ed. Monika Richarz and Reinhard Rürup (Tübingen, 1997), 139–173, 162.
14. For a recent analysis of the book burning, see Steven Michael Press, 'False Fire: The Wartburg Book-Burning of 1817', *Central European History* 42/4 (2009): 621–646. Press argues that the actual book burning was rather marginal to the main proceedings at the Wartburg, in terms of the number of participants, but was exploited by the authorities to justify oppression.
15. See Hagemann, *Mannlicher Muth*, 267–270.
16. For the disturbances, see: Katz, *Hep-Hep-Verfolgungen*; Sterling, 'Anti-Jewish Riots'. Katz disagrees with Sterling's argument that the riots were primarily displaced social protest, and instead emphasizes the widespread opposition to Jewish equality.
17. For more on Würzburg in this period, see Ulrich Wagner (ed.), *Geschichte der Stadt Würzburg*, 3 vols (Stuttgart, 2001–2007), vol. 2: *Vom Bauernkrieg 1525 bis zum Übergang an Bayern 1814* (2004).

18. Ursula Gehring-Münzel, 'Die Würzburger Juden von 1803 bis zum Ende des Ersten Weltkrieges', in Ibid., vol. 3/1: *Vom Übergang an Bayern bis zum 21. Jahrhundert* (Stuttgart, 2007), 499–528, 499 and 502–503. See also her study *Vom Schutzjuden zum Staatsbürger: Die gesellschaftliche Integration der Würzburger Juden 1803–1871* (Würzburg, 1992), 121–177.
19. Ludyga, *Rechtsstellung*, 45–50.
20. On Sebald Brendel's *Das Staatsbürgerrecht der Juden*, see Rohrbacher, 'The "Hep Hep" Riots of 1819', 36–39.
21. Katz, *Hep-Hep-Verfolgungen*, 14–39; also Hoffmann, *Exclusionary Violence*, 36–39.
22. Katz, *Hep-Hep-Verfolgungen*, 39–71.
23. Geoffrey L. Green, *The Royal Navy and Anglo-Jewry 1740–1820: Traders and Those who Served* (London, 1989), 32–40. In particular, see the etching by George Cruikshank, 'Pay day in port aboard a Man-of-War: Seaman and others skylarking with a Jewish pedlar', dated circa 1820. This is reproduced on page 32.
24. See Horst Fischer, *Judentum, Staat und Heer in Preussen im frühen 19. Jahrhundert: Zur Geschichte der staatlichen Judenpolitik* (Tübingen, 1968), 32–62.
25. Eduard Fuchs, *Die Juden in der Karikatur: Ein Beitrag zur Kulturgeschichte. Mit 307 Textillustrationen und 31 schwarzen und farbigen Beilagen* (Munich, 1921). See especially the insertion, located between pages 48–49, entitled 'Deutsche Karikatur auf die Juden als Soldaten. 18. Jahrhundert'.
26. Christian Wilhelm Dohm, *Ueber die bürgerliche Verbesserung der Juden: Zweyter Theil. Mit Königl. Preußischer Freyheit* (Berlin and Stettin, 1783), 222–246.
27. Derek J. Penslar, *Jews and the Military: A History* (Princeton, NJ, 2013), 41.
28. Abbé Grégoire, *Essai sur la régénération physique, morale et politique des Juifs: ouvrage couronné par la Société royale des sciences et des arts de Metz, le 23 août 1788* (Metz, 1789), especially Chapter 18, 'Il est possible de former les Juifs à l'art militaire. Résumé de ce chapitre et des deux précédents', 120–125.
29. Friedrich Buchholz, *Moses und Jesus, oder über das intellektuelle und moralische Verhältnis der Juden und Christen: Eine historisch-politische Abhandlung* (Berlin, 1803), 217–254. For the wider context of the debate over the status of Jews in Prussia at this time (1803–1804), of which Buchholz's pamphlet was a component, see: Bruer, *Geschichte der Juden in Preussen*, 206–210. For Buchholz's ideas more generally, see: Hans Gerth, 'Friedrich Buchholz—Auch ein Anfang der Soziologie', *Zeitschrift für die gesamte Staatswissenschaft* 110 (1954): 665–692.
30. Erwin A. Schmidl, *Juden in der K. (u.) K. Armee 1788–1918: Jews in the Habsburg Armed Forces* (Eisenstadt, 1989), 98–106 and 112.
31. J. Lebermann, 'Aus der Geschichte der Juden in Hessen am Anfang des 19. Jahrhunderts: Gutachten des Staatsministers [Karl Wilhelm Heinrich Freiherr] Du Bos Du Thil über "die Verbesserung des bürgerlichen Zustandes der Juden" [1809]', *Jahrbuch der Jüdisch-Literarischen Gesellschaft* 6 (1909): 105–152. Also, more broadly, Anton Maria Keim, *Die Judenfrage im Landtag des Großherzogtums Hessen 1820–1849: Ein Beitrag zur Geschichte der Juden im Vormärz* (Darmstadt, 1983).
32. Ludyga, *Rechtsstellung*, 32–33 and 35–36.
33. See, for Prussia, the extensive analysis of the debate on military service and male citizenship in, Hagemann, *'Mannlicher Muth'*, 271–350; for Britain, the reference to Jewish participation in the British mobilization effort of 1803 in *The Times* (London), 20 October 1803.
34. Erik Lindner, *Patriotismus deutscher Juden von der napoleonischen Ära bis zum Kaiserreich: Zwischen korporativem Loyalismus und individueller deutsch-jüdischer*

Identität (Frankfurt/M., 1997), 57–80; Hagemann, *'Mannlicher Muth'*, 281–289; Fischer, *Judentum*, 32–110. The prejudice that Jews were cowards, terrified of suffering even the slightest physical discomfort or pain, is reflected in a popular German theatre piece of the Napoleonic period, namely Karl Alexander Sessa, 'Unser Verkehr: eine Posse in einem Akt', in *Deutsche Schaubühne: Oder dramatische Bibliothek der neuesten Lust- Schau- Sing- und Trauerspiele* vol. 30 (Augsburg, 1815), 195–242.

35. Carl August Buchholz, *Actenstükke, die Verbesserung des bürgerlichen Zustandes der Israeliten betreffend: Herausgegeben und mit einer Einleitung begleitet durch Carl August Buchholz, bey der Rechte und der Philosophie Doctor, ausübenden Rechtsgelehrten zu Lübek* (Stuttgart, 1815), 30.
36. *Sulamith* 4/2 (1816): 180.
37. For more on the antisemitism of Fries and Rühs, including the differences between them, see Hagemann, *'Mannlicher Muth'*, 263–268.
38. Jakob Friedrich Fries, *Über die Gefährdung des Wohlstandes und Charakters der Deutschen durch die Juden: Eine aus den Heidelberger Jahrbüchern der Litteratur besonders abgedruckte Recension der Schrift des Professors Rühs in Berlin."Über die Ansprüche der Juden an das deutsche Bürgerrecht: Zweyter verbesserter Abdruck"* (Heidelberg, 1816), 19–22.
39. Friedrich Rühs, *Die Rechte des Christenthums und des deutschen Volkes: Vertheidigt gegen die Ansprüche der Juden und ihrer Verfechter* (Berlin, 1816), 31–32, 35–36 and 73.
40. Ibid., 76–78. See also Friedrich Rühs, *Ueber die Ansprüche der Juden an das deutsche Bürgerrecht: Zweiter, verbesserter und erweiterter Abdruck. Mit einem Anhange über die Geschichte der Juden in Spanien* (Berlin, 1816), 24–30. Here, Rühs takes particular exception to what he claims is Jewish arrogance in claiming to have contributed significantly to the German side in the 'Wars of Liberation'.
41. Johann Ludwig Ewald, *Ideen, über die nöthige Organisation der Israeliten in Christlichen Staaten* (Karlsruhe, 1816), 139.
42. Ibid., 140–143.
43. Ibid., 144–145.
44. Deborah Hertz, *How Jews Became Germans: The History of Conversion and Assimilation in Berlin* (New Haven, CT, 2007), 119–121; see also, Jean H. Quataert, *Staging Philanthropy: Patriotic Women and the National Imagination in Dynastic Germany, 1813–1916* (Ann Arbor, MI, 2004), 30.
45. Ewald, *Ideen* 154. Also, see Michael Hess, *Freimüthige Prüfung der Schrift des Herrn Professor Rühs, über die Ansprüche der Juden an das deutsche Bürgerrecht* (Frankfurt/M., 1816), 75–76. For a brief overview of the immediate postwar debate, see: Fischer, *Judentum*, 84–88.
46. Lindner, *Patriotismus*, 111–115.
47. Christopher Clark, *Iron Kingdom: The Rise and Downfall of Prussia* (London, 2006), 424–427.
48. Landtag (Prussia), *Vollständige Verhandlungen des Ersten Vereinigten Preußischen Landtages über die Emancipationsfrage der Juden* (Berlin, 1847), 75, 78, 100, 191–192, 196, 227, 230, 235–237, 240, 456 and 457.
49. Comite zur Abwehr antisemitischer Angriffe in Berlin, *Die Juden als Soldaten* (2nd edn, Berlin, 1897). The *Comité zur Abwehr antisemitischer Angriffe* was founded in 1892, on the initiative of Julius Isaacs. Christoph Jahr, *Antisemitismus vor Gericht: Debatten über die juristische Ahndung judenfeindlicher Agitation in Deutschland, 1879–1960* (Frankfurt/M., 2011), 155; Jacob Borut, 'Die jüdischen Abwehrvereine zu Beginn der neunziger Jahre des 19. Jahrhunderts', *Aschkenas* 7/2 (1997): 467–494.

50. Martin Philippson, 'Der Anteil der jüdischen Freiwilligen an dem Befreiungskriege 1813 und 1814', *Monatsschrift für Geschichte und Wissenschaft des Judentums* 50 (1906): 1.
51. Wolff, 'Die Juden in den Ostmarken: was haben sie dem Preussischen Staat und was hat er Ihnen geleistet?', *Ost und West: Illustrierte Monatsschrift für das Gesamte Judentum* 9/12 (1909): 709–726.
52. Heinz Bender, *Der Kampf um die Judenemanzipation in Deutschland im Spiegel der Flugschriften 1815–1820* (Jena, 1939), 26–27.
53. For more on the context of the Catholic emancipation debate, see: Michael Tomko, *British Romanticism and the Catholic Question: Religion, History and National Identity, 1778–1829* (Basingstoke, 2011), 27–28, 35–36.
54. Étienne François, 'Die Wartburg', in *Deutsche Erinnerungsorte*, ed. Étienne François and Hagen Schulze, 3 vols (Munich, 2001), vol. 2, 154–170.

9

The Costs of War: The Impact of the Revolutionary and Napoleonic Wars in Italian Postwar Politics

John A. Davis

From 1796 until the fall of Napoleon's Empire in 1815 the public and private lives of many, perhaps most, Italians were filled with war, rumours of war and preparation for war. While they cannot be compared with twentieth-century experiences of 'total war', the impact of the Revolutionary and Napoleonic Wars on the security, economies, politics, lives and culture of Italians of all classes was considerable. However, measuring the impact of war is complicated. War was experienced more often indirectly than directly, affecting different social groups in different ways, while the consequences that are specific to war are not easily distinguished from the broader burdens imposed by the imperial project. Bearing these qualifications in mind, this chapter will begin by considering the human and material costs of the Revolutionary and Napoleonic Wars in Italy. It will then explore the many different ways in which the experiences and memories of war weighed on Italian politics and political culture, from the closing years of Empire (1812–1815), including the Legitimist Restorations (1814–1815), to the liberal revolutions of 1820–1821 and their aftermath.[1]

The Italian states in the emperor's wars

When the armies of the French Republic invaded northern Italy in 1796 they brought to a close an unusually long period of relative peace and freedom from foreign invasion. For nearly two decades, from 1796 to 1815, the Italian peninsula would be, either directly or indirectly, almost constantly engaged in war. Between 1796 and 1799, armies of the French Republic invaded northern and central Italy and penetrated as far south as Rome (1798) and Naples (1799) before an Allied counter-offensive forced them to abandon their short-lived Italian sister republics to the fury of popular counter-revolutionary insurrections. In 1800 French armies returned to Italy, this time with an agenda that reflected the new political order in France following the coup of Brumaire on 9 November 1799 that had brought General Bonaparte to power as the First Consul of France. The former Cisapline

Republic was reconstituted in 1802 as the Italian Republic, incorporating Lombardy, much of the former Venetian Republic and the northern parts of the Papal State. Piedmont, Liguria and the former Grand Duchy of Tuscany (after a brief existence as a Spanish Bourbon principality) were administered directly from France, as were the temporal dominions of the Papacy when Pope Pius VII was forced into exile in 1809.

The political reorganization of the Italian states after 1800 anticipated the imperial project that was proclaimed in 1804, after which the Italian states tracked the Empire's dynastic turn and provided thrones for members of the imperial family. In March 1805 the Italian Republic became the Kingdom of Italy, with its capital in Milan, and was ruled on Napoleon's behalf by his stepson, Prince Eugène Beauharnais. Napoleon's sister, Elisa Baciocchi, ruled as Princess of Piombino and Duchess of Lucca (1805), and then as the Grand Duchess of Tuscany (1809). After the defeat of the Austrians at the Battle of Austerlitz (December 1805) Napoleon deposed the Bourbon rulers of the Kingdom of the Two Sicilies and placed his brother Joseph on the throne of Naples. In 1808 Joseph was moved to Spain, and the Emperor's brother-in-law and commander of the imperial cavalry, Joachim Murat, became King of Naples. French rule in Italy would reach its geographical peak in 1809 when French forces occupied Rome. Only the islands of Sardinia and Sicily, the refuges respectively for the former rulers of Piedmont and Naples, remained outside French control, and the failure of Joachim Murat to drive the Bourbons and their British allies out of Sicily in 1810 meant that Napoleon and his opponents were separated only by the narrow Straits of Messina until the fall of the Empire in 1815.[2]

From the start, the Italian states were engaged in the military enterprises of an empire that had been founded in Italy, and until the end they formed its most southerly Mediterranean frontiers. From 1796 to 1799, in 1800 and again in the last years of the Napoleonic Empire (1812–1815), the peninsula was the theatre of major campaigns, but the burdens imposed by rumours of war and preparations for war were no less disruptive. Uninterrupted warfare in the Mediterranean, for example, resulted in prolonged commercial recession that damaged merchants, deprived landowners of commercial outlets for their products, exacerbated the chronic underemployment of the rural poor and made coastal navigation and fishing hazardous occupations.

The conditions were further aggravated by imperial policies that subordinated the commercial interests of Italian producers to those of France or were designed to exclude British goods from the Continent. The outcome was not always negative, and Sicily, for example, experienced a prolonged commercial boom thanks to the presence of the British navy. On the mainland, imperial protectionist policies provided incentives for various experiments in import substitution, especially new textile and metal working industries and the introduction of new crops. The export of silk cocoons (Italy's principal export commodity down to the First World War) to France from northern Italy boomed, although this went hand in hand with the demise of the older silk textile industries of Lombardy and the Veneto, and was a clear sign of colonial subordination to French and especially Lyon manufacturers.[3]

The most direct, albeit unintended, consequence of the Berlin Decrees, issued by Napoleon in November 1806 with the aim of ending all trade between Britain and Continental Europe, was the unprecedented increase in the scale, volume and variety of smuggling throughout Italy. The contraband trades offered lucrative openings for speculators and investors, rich bribes for public officials, policemen and army officers (many of them French) and not least jobs for the armies of men and women who carried and distributed the illicit goods. It is unlikely that these operations offset the damage done to legitimate trade, but they did contribute to the lawlessness that became a feature of the final years of French rule in Italy. The activities of brigand bands were noted from the Alps and Illyrian frontiers in the northeast to the Po Valley and from central Italy to the south. Although by no means new to Italy, the rapid expansion of brigandage in these years was a direct consequence of commercial recession and unemployment, rising taxes on the poor, and above all conscription. As in France itself and in many other parts of the Empire, conscription was of course a major cause of brigandage and disorder, and brought home to many families the human costs of the imperial wars. Alexander Grab estimates that between 1802 and 1814, 155,000 men were conscripted in the Kingdom of Italy alone. Of more than 200,000 conscripts raised from the different Italian states before 1815, as many as 125,000 died either in combat or, and in much greater numbers, from disease.[4]

All of these burdens were direct consequences of the imperial wars and imperial policies, but the increase in brigandage was perhaps only the most visible index of the erosion of public order that in many other ways undermined what had originally been one of the greatest attractions of the Napoleonic regimes in Italy: the promise of order. Many Italians had welcomed French rule after 1800 as an alternative to the anarchy and upheavals of the previous decade of revolution and counter-revolutionary wars. Many believed, too, that the new order imposed by Napoleon would lay the foundations of new political and financial stability, so it was ironical that in its final stages the Empire should have proved to be the greatest threat to the new order that Napoleon had brought to Italy.

When the French armies arrived for the second time in Italy and occupied large parts of the peninsula after Napoleon's victory at Marengo in June 1800, virtually all of the Italian Ancien Régime states, like their counterparts across Europe, were bankrupt. As in the rest of Europe, the causes were deep-rooted and structural, but the final straw had been the costs of preparations for war after the Revolution in France. So the first task of the French administrators in the regions subsequently integrated into the French Empire, as well as the Kingdom of Italy and the Kingdom of Naples, was to repair public finances. For this purpose the French administrators had to hand a set of now well tested templates. Feudalism was abolished, the new codes of civil law were introduced, and the lands of the former rulers and the religious houses were sold off to liquidate and refloat the debts of the former rulers.[5] The skill shown by the French administrators in fixing the financial chaos of the Ancien Régime principalities was a political triumph that secured the support of the principal creditors of the Ancien Régime monarchies: the propertied classes and corporations. At least part of their assets was salvaged, and, as the prime beneficiaries of the massive sales of public and church lands at knockdown prices that funded the debt conversion, their support for the new regimes was assured.[6]

By 1812, however, the incessant financial demands generated by Napoleon's wars were threatening new financial disaster. In addition to satisfying the needs of the imperial bureaucracy in Paris, Napoleon's rulers in Italy were now obliged to maintain almost permanent military preparedness. As taxes continued to rise, so did popular protest and resistance. The punctilious determination of Count Prina, the Milanese finance minister of the Kingdom of Italy, to meet all the Emperor's demands made him the most hated face of empire in Italy and one of its conspicuous martyrs when he was stabbed to death by an enraged mob in the centre of Milan in April 1814. However, there were signs of crisis everywhere, and when he was asked to finance another military campaign in January 1815, Joachim Murat's closest and most trusted financial adviser informed his master that the kingdom was bankrupt and resigned.[7]

By 1812 the high material costs of Napoleon's wars had undermined the political and financial stability that had been the promise of the imperial order in Italy. Although Napoleon's defeat at Waterloo in June 1815 lifted many of these burdens, the imperial wars and the subordinate place of the Italian states in the imperial project had generated other and more lasting political legacies.

The closing campaigns, 1813–1815

Between 1814 and 1815, the collapse of Napoleon's Empire in Italy was uncertain, slow, contradictory and the cause of great political, no less than military, confusion. In these final years, the Italian peninsula was once again a major theatre of war, with almost constant manoeuvres, marches and counter-marches that were devastating for many communities. The final campaigns began in the summer of 1813 when the Austrians moved against the French outposts in the Illyrian provinces. Eugène Beauharnais first organized his defence of the French Kingdom of Italy on the Isonzo River before making tactical withdrawals to the Adige. The Austrian advance was contained, but Prince Eugène's position became more exposed when

Joachim Murat defected to the Allies in January 1814 and brought 20,000 Neapolitan soldiers to support the Austrian offensive in the Po Valley. Prince Eugène was still able to prevent the Austrians crossing the Mincio river, but when he learned of Napoleon's abdication (6 April 1814) he began negotiating with the Allies in the hope of retaining his throne. This was never likely and some of his own generals were already plotting to take his place before these political manoeuvres were cut short when the Austrian commander Field Marshal Bellegarde agreed to an armistice.

The Austrians occupied the Veneto, Lombardy and Piedmont, and when on 24 May Pope Pius VII returned from captivity to Rome it seemed that the wars in Italy were finally over. Such expectations were premature, however. Like Prince Eugène, Joachim Murat also hoped that in return for his defection the Allies would allow him to retain his Kingdom of Naples after the fall of Napoleon. Incensed by their refusal, when he learned of Napoleon's escape from Elba in February 1815 Murat switched sides again. Raising the imperial standard once more, he declared war on Austria on 15 March and led an army of 30,000 men to join the 20,000 Neapolitan troops that had remained in the Po Valley since the previous year. After invading the Papal States and causing the Pope to flee once more, on 30 March Murat called from the Adriatic port of Rimini for a general uprising of all Italians to drive out the Austrians and reclaim their independence. But he failed to divide the larger Austrian forces opposing him and as a result was decisively defeated at the Battle of Tolentino on 2 May 1815. After the defeat Murat fled to France, leaving his generals to negotiate the Treaty of Casalanza, signed on 20 May 1815, that set out the conditions for the return of the Bourbon dynasty to Naples.[8]

The Treaty of Casalanza brought the fighting in Italy to a close, but the final campaigns had provoked new episodes of protest and lawlessness. Everywhere hostility to the French was strong, and in the spring of 1814 Napoleon's former Minister of Police Joseph Fouché (1759–1820), who had been sent to persuade Murat to return to his allegiance to the Emperor, reported from Rome on the widespread hostility to the Empire and everything French amongst the masses. For Italians, he wrote, France meant two things only: 'taxes and conscription'.[9]

However, contemporary accounts indicate that popular discontent was directed indiscriminately against all the warring armies.[10] Prince Eugène's decision to increase conscription quotas in 1813 had provoked widespread resistance in Lombardy and the Veneto, multiplying the numbers of *réfractaires* and deserters.[11] The presence of Murat's armies in central Italy in 1814 and 1815 similarly gave rise to popular protest and resistance, including violent attacks on the minority Jewish communities in Tuscany. In Florence, Napoleon's sister Elisa Baciocchi, who had been deposed by her brother-in-law, complained to the Emperor that her subjects were outraged by the presence of the Neapolitans whom they despised and would resist with violence if they did not quickly leave.[12]

The appeals for popular risings against the French met with no response, but they did cause consternation among the propertied classes. Even before Murat's proclamation from Rimini, similar appeals had been made both by Prince Eugène and by Lord William Bentinck, the commander of a small British force that had landed on the Tuscan coast to join the campaign against Murat. Bentinck had in mind the model of the Spanish *guerrilla* war against Napoleon, but his action infuriated Lord Castlereagh who was outraged that a British general should have invoked the spectre of revolution precisely at the moment when the Allies were determined to restore the principles of order and hierarchy in Italy.

In Italy, the propertied classes were still mindful of the anarchy that had accompanied the popular counter-revolutions during the fall of the Jacobin republics a decade earlier and favoured a peaceful transition of power. So did the Austrian Chancellor, Prince Metternich, who repeatedly warned the returning Legitimist rulers not to indulge in excessively vindictive measures against the supporters of the former French regimes. Even the Neapolitan Bourbons were persuaded to forego a replay of the bloody purges that had followed the collapse of the Neapolitan Republic in 1799, and in 1815 by contrast Naples offered a model of peaceful transfer of power. To the astonishment of contemporaries like Luigi Blanch, the Italian Legitimist rulers regained power without any major unrest or disturbance, 'as though all these events were taking place in some cold northern country like Holland'.[13]

The restoration of 1815: the Italian rulers and their armies

Notwithstanding the apparently peaceful transition of power in 1814 and 1815, Napoleon's wars had left powerful political legacies that would undermine the Restoration settlement in the Italian states. The term 'restoration' is something of a misnomer, since even in the Kingdom of Piedmont–Sardinia and Papal Rome, where the rhetoric of counter-revolution was loudest, there were few serious attempts to undo the administrative and financial reforms carried through during the years of French rule, let alone restore feudalism or reverse the sales of the lands of the churches and the monasteries. The restored rulers were happy to preserve the greatly enhanced powers of the states they had been forced to abandon a decade earlier. They were open to rapprochement where possible with those who had supported the French regimes, although they were determined to check the subversive ideas embodied by the Revolution and the Empire.

The problem was that nowhere were those subversive ideas more firmly embedded than in the armies that had once served Napoleon and now served the Legitimist rulers. The challenges were the greater because rebuilding their armies was a high priority for the rulers of the larger dynastic states. That task was complicated by the ruinous financial legacies of Napoleon's wars and by the huge cash indemnities, bribes and preferential commercial treaties the Legitimist rulers had been forced to pay to the Allies in compensation for regaining their thrones. After 1815 the financial and economic situation was aggravated by a prolonged period of commercial depression that was another consequence of the wars, exacerbated by the devastating global climatic changes resulting from the massive eruption of Mount Tambora on the Indonesian peninsula of Sumbawa in April 1815 that in Italy brought harvest failures, catastrophic falls in the living conditions of the poor, major epidemics and, in 1816, possibly the last outbreak of the plague in Europe.

Rebuilding the Italian armies posed political as well as financial problems. When Prince Eugène unsuccessfully tried to persuade the Allies to allow him to keep his throne in April 1814, without his knowledge some of his generals were on their own account planning to continue resistance to the Austrians after Napoleon's abdication. Although the 'conspiracy of the former generals' was thwarted by Habsburg sympathizers and came to nothing, many of those suspected of involvement were later charged with treason by the Austrians. Those arrested included General Teodoro Lechi, who, with his brothers Giuseppe and Angelo, were the founders of the famed Lechi Division that had fought with great distinction in Spain and Russia. Napoleon had honoured all three brothers, but when the Austrians returned the fact that they had begun their careers as staunch republicans made them easy targets. Teodoro Lechi was sentenced to death but then reprieved and joined the hundreds of other Italian officers in exile.[14]

Similar problems faced the rulers of the two principal independent dynastic states, the Savoyard Kingdom of Sardinia–Piedmont and the Bourbon Kingdom of the Two Sicilies. For both King Victor Emanuel I in Piedmont and King Ferdinando I in Naples, reconstituting their armies was a high political priority. Both rulers reduced the heaviest burdens imposed by the French and abolished the French model of obligatory conscription in favour of older systems of voluntary enlistments.[15] However, as in Milan, the major problem was not the enlisted men but the officers, and in both the Piedmontese and the Neapolitan armies there were deep animosities between those who had followed the rulers into exile and those who had served the French. In Naples, for example, Pietro Colletta, whose career had flourished in Murat's army, protested that the officers who returned with the king from Sicily in 1815 were 'bloated and aged', yet they were preferred when it came to promotion and honours.[16]

As well as questions of preferment and promotion, there were deeper differences that resulted from the changing composition and training of the officer corps and dated from well before the Revolution. Eighteenth-century advances in military technologies demanded new technical skills, and the rulers had responded by adapting the curricula of the Ancien Régime military academies accordingly and curtailing the monopolies over military commissions previously enjoyed by a small circle of noble families.

Their efforts were applauded by Enlightenment writers who decried the inability of the Ancien Régime aristocracies to display the military qualities that had originally justified their privileged status. By contrast those writers looked to the modern soldier as a paragon of manly virtues, science and public service.[17] These changes in attitude pre-dated the Revolution, but they were accelerated during the Empire, whose militaristic values set the tone of the courts of the Napoleonic rulers while civic life came to be dominated by endless military parades and public celebrations of imperial victories.[18] Army officers enjoyed unprecedented prestige while service in Napoleon's wars offered significant employment for growing sections of the propertied classes.

Many of those who served in the armies of the French satellite rulers would have recognized themselves in Pietro Colletta's memoirs. The son of a Neapolitan attorney, Colletta had nothing but contempt for the self-seeking ambitions of his father's profession and considered the modern soldier to be a paragon of martial and civic virtues, equally prepared for battle, building bridges, running civil administration and maintaining order. In Naples, he later recalled, Joseph Bonaparte and Joachim Murat had created 'a new nobility consisting of military men who were influential supporters of the new order of things'.[19]

The French frequently complained that young Italians were reluctant to serve in the imperial armies, and often their families were coerced. But even many of those like Colletta who responded with enthusiasm kept their political distance from Napoleon. For Colletta, Napoleon Bonaparte was in most respects the very model of the modern soldier but he believed that the Brumaire coup had saved the Revolution at the cost of transforming it into the despotic, centralized and hierarchical imperial structure that had been imposed on Italy. The poet Ugo Foscolo, who served loyally in the imperial armies, was likewise unable to forgive Bonaparte for depriving the Venetian Republic of its independence in 1797, and remained even more hostile than Colletta.[20]

In their hostility to Napoleonic despotism, Foscolo and Colletta reflected the political disillusionment of the many young Italians who, like Stendhal's Fabrizio Del Dongo, had once dreamed of glory in the Emperor's service. There were many reasons why early admirers became fierce critics, not least resentment at the privileged positions retained by French nationals in Napoleon's armies and in those of his satellite rulers. However, those frustrations increasingly found expression in opposition to an imperial project that consistently subordinated the interests of the Italian states. For many of the Italians who served in the Grande Armée in the Peninsular Campaign, the Spanish war of resistance against Napoleon and the liberal constitution that the Spanish king was forced to concede to the Cortes of Cadiz in 1812 finally gave that opposition articulate political form and objectives.[21]

The empire, the military and the liberal revolutions of 1820–1821 in Italy

In both Milan and Naples in 1815, the most likely sequel to the collapse of the Empire might have been some form of military *pronunciamiento*. That this did not happen was a result in part of the resolute action taken by the Allies, and in part of the deep political divisions among the officers. Although its outlines were already visible in the events of 1814 and 1815, the discontents of the officer corps found expression in the liberal revolutions of 1820–1821. In Piedmont, many of the officers who had served under Napoleon were sympathetic to the liberals' demands for constitutional government. In the Neapolitan army, the influence of the liberals and the secret societies was even greater and grew after 1815. In Piedmont, Lombardy and in the south the secret societies played a critical role in promoting the liberal programme within the armies. The societies were an offshoot from the masonic lodges that had played important roles in the circulation of Enlightenment ideas and reform projects in the eighteenth century. In the early years of French rule in Italy the lodges were again promoted and encouraged since freemasonry was considered to offer an important political base for the new French regimes in Italy.[22]

As signs grew that the lodges were becoming centres of opposition, however, the French moved to shut them down, only to see them reappear in the form of secret societies. Of these, the best known was the *Carbonari*, a clandestine organization originally transplanted to Italy by dissident pro-Jacobins and republican sympathizers in Napoleon's armies—another export of the imperial wars.[23] Although the *Carbonari* drew its members from many branches of civil society and the professions, its most significant supporters were officers serving in the armies of Napoleon's satellite rulers. These included the officers who had plotted against Prince Eugène in Milan in April 1814, while the secret societies had spread even more openly in Joachim Murat's army. When Murat defected to the Allies in 1814, his generals made the concession of a constitution the condition of their support. Murat refused, but when in the following year he rallied to the Emperor his generals repeated the same demands; Murat finally agreed, but only after he had been defeated.[24]

After the Restorations, the secret societies continued to proliferate in all the Italian states and especially in southern Italy and Sicily. Contemporary estimates are unreliable, but the social reach of the secret societies was considerable and they played a direct part in planning the liberal revolutions of 1820. In 1818, the *Carbonari* formally adopted the Spanish Constitution of 1812 as their political objective and took responsibility for planning the outbreak of the revolutions not only in Naples and Turin, but also in Spain.[25]

The cue for the Italian revolutions of 1820 was the military *pronunciamiento* of March in Seville, after which King Fernando VII of Spain agreed to reinstate the 1812 Constitution that had been abolished after the Restoration. Following demands in favour of the Spanish constitution staged by non-commissioned officers in the Neapolitan army, Ferdinando I of the Two Sicilies also agreed to adopt the Spanish Constitution. In Turin, the liberal officers did not move until March 1821, but although their insurrection proved to be short-lived, they too demanded the adoption of the Spanish Constitution. For Italian liberals that constitution now embodied the principles of liberal government and national sovereignty and an explicit rejection of Napoleonic imperialism. This political programme was widely admired by liberals throughout Europe and Spanish America and gave the revolutions of 1820–1821 a transnational platform that has led some to describe the *trienio liberal* as a 'liberal international'.[26]

For Italian liberals, 'the myth of Spain' was perhaps the most important of all the legacies of the Empire and offered the example of a struggle for national independence that contrasted in important ways with their own experiences. In Italy foreign invasion had provoked internal divisions and the anarchy of popular counter-revolutions, but Spain seemed to offer an alternative model of national solidarity. However, the failure of the revolutions would quickly discredit that model, while the rise of Carlism revealed that Spanish realities were not so different. The liberal revolutions in Naples and Turin collapsed almost without resistance when in the spring of 1821 an Austrian army was despatched to restore the King of Naples to his throne with full absolutist powers, before making a brief intervention in Piedmont once the insurrection had collapsed. The *trienio liberal* ended when in 1823—to the delight of the French Romantic writer and politician Francois-René de Chateaubriand (1768–1848) and French royalists more generally—the French King Louis XVIII dispatched an army of a 'hundred thousand sons of St Louis' to restore the Spanish King Fernando VII to his full absolutist powers. By then, the liberal revolution in Portugal had already collapsed into civil war.

Militarization and Napoleonic memories

Despite the prominence of militarism in the political culture of the Napoleonic Empire, its legacies in Italy were deeply contradictory. The officers who had led the liberal revolutions of 1820–1821 saw themselves as opponents of the Napoleonic model and as agents of political changes that would result in constitutional government. Hence the figure of the 'crowned soldier' aroused suspicion, and most Italian nationalists remained hostile to Napoleon. Those like Pompeo Litta who defended Napoleon had to make the tortuous case that he had always wanted to create an independent national state in Italy but had been prevented by the French who were only interested in turning Italy into a colony.[27]

No one expressed more fully the contradictory reactions in Italy to the Emperor than the Milanese writer Alessandro Manzoni, who had spent long periods in Paris where he developed close contacts with many of Napoleon's liberal critics. On returning to Italy, Manzoni maintained his liberal views and initially showed enthusiasm for the liberal revolutions of 1820. However, in the ode *Il Cinque Maggio* (5 May) written within days of Napoleon's death in July 1821 (but not published until 1823), Manzoni applauded Napoleon for his reconciliation with Christianity before his death but decried the delusions of power and the human horrors that are inseparable from war, whether its causes be just or unjust. Those themes were developed more fully in works like his stage play *Adelchi* (1822) and above all in his great novel *The Betrothed* (*I Promessi Sposi*, 1827)[28] but were shared much more widely. Many Italian Romantics, for example, considered the monumental tomb for the poet Vittorio Alfieri in the Basilica of Santa Croce (1806–1810) in Florence by the Venetian sculptor Antonio Canova to be the finest artistic expression of Italian nationalist aspirations.[29] Yet Canova's neo-Classical masterpiece depicts *Italia* mourning for her children and the casualties of war; it pays tribute to Italian sufferings and sacrifices during the Empire, but is certainly not a celebration of war.[30]

Manzoni's emphasis on the horrors of war reminds us that Italian Romanticism was not associated only with the more aggressive forms of Risorgimento nationalism.[31] Indeed, Manzoni insisted that 'a dispersed people that does not even have a common name' ('*un volgo disperso che nome no ha*') could not expect to make effective resistance to foreign aggressors and must instead learn the arts of patience and Christian resignation. Such views had been reinforced by the experience of the Napoleonic Wars that many believed had once again called into question the warlike propensities of Italians.

When Italy was invaded in 1796, the Ancien Régime rulers had offered no effective opposition. Indeed, opposition to the French and their Italian Jacobin allies had come not from regular soldiers but from the popular counter-revolutionary movements organized and directed by the priests. In 1800, Italians had again been onlookers as Napoleon and the Austrians fought out the fate of the peninsula. In 1814, only Prince Eugène put up effective resistance to the Austrian offensive, while in 1815 the principal protagonists were Murat and the Austrians.

Italians were left without a triumphal Borodino, Leipzig or Waterloo to celebrate, or even a glorious defeat to mourn and avenge. They could claim to have performed feats of great valour, but even these were accomplished in the service of the French Emperor and against his enemies. Or against other Italians, as in the battles and campaigns that led to the fall of the Empire and the Legitimist Restorations between 1813 and 1815. Like Germans, Italians had participated on both sides, and in 1815 it had not been Italians but foreign generals—an Austrian (Bellegarde), an Englishman (Bentinck) and a Frenchman (Murat)—who had launched appeals for an Italian national uprising.

Those appeals met with no response and few Italians by then showed any desire to prolong the imperial enterprise.[32] Then came the liberal revolutions of 1820–1821 that had also collapsed in military confusion. There was no resistance to the Austrians and in Naples the generals openly quarrelled over tactics and disobeyed orders. There was no popular mobilization, although the internal disputes between the Neapolitans and the Sicilians had brought Italians into conflict with other Italians. After the revolutions, the reputations of the protagonists were subsequently diminished by the recriminations and duels that became the principal occupation of many of the exiles.

The warlike qualities of the Italians were an issue of great sensitivity, however, as became evident when it was rumoured that the French poet Alphonse Lamartine had described Italy as 'the land of the dead'. Although not exactly his words, Lamartine had indeed claimed that modern Italians no longer showed the warlike qualities of their Roman forebears, a calumny that provoked outraged responses including a furious rebuttal of the Frenchman's senseless 'brayings' against the Italians by Guglielmo Pepe, one of the leaders of the 1820 liberal revolution in Naples and now in exile in London.[33] Historian Silvana Pariarca has argued that these spats exposed collective doubts about Italian masculinity and virility that had deep cultural roots. Such doubts had been accentuated by the revival of militarism during the Revolutionary and Napoleonic Wars and would play a critical role in the nationalist literature of the Risorgimento.[34]

After 1815 the censors in Italy banned any reference, direct or indirect, to Napoleon or the Empire. This, as well as the often awkward questions posed by more recent military history, encouraged Italian nationalist writers to follow Scottish Romantic novelist Walter Scott and turn instead to the Middle Ages to seek examples of Italian bravery and military glory. Those in exile were less guarded, and from London the Milanese writer Giuseppe Pecchio (1785–1835) could cite the Napoleonic Army of Italy as a precocious model of Italian national unity that had 'cost many families many tears, but nevertheless promised to bring about the Kingdom's emancipation—its independence'.[35] But although Napoleon's Army of Italy remained a potent symbol in Italian nationalist literature, this was more than a little fanciful since in 1814 most of Eugène Beauharnais's Italian officers were offered and accepted commissions in the Habsburg imperial army.[36]

Many others who served in the imperial wars went on to serve in the armies of the Italian Restoration rulers, and their memoirs constituted the principal record of the imperial campaigns. These included the three-volume *History of the Campaigns and Sieges conducted in Spain by the Italians*, published in 1823 by Baron Camillo Vascani, a Milanese nobleman who had served with the French in Spain before becoming a general in the Austrian imperial army. Cesare de Laugier de Bellecour's 11-volume *Military Triumphs and Fortunes of the Italian People from 1801 to 1815* recounted his service in the French campaigns in Spain and in Russia and then as a battalion commander in Murat's army in 1815. After seven years as a prisoner of war in Hungary, de Laugier had resumed his military career in the Grand Ducal army in his native Tuscany where the memoirs were published between 1829 and 1838.[37]

Conclusion

Tales of military glory in the imperial wars were not absent from Italian nationalist literature in the 1830s and 1840s, but memories of the Empire and perceptions of the political role of the military remained contradictory. Giuseppe Mazzini (1805–1872), who founded the revolutionary and democratic nationalist association *Young Italy* in 1832, explicitly repudiated the example of the liberal generals of 1820, calling instead for a genuinely popular nationalist movement that would engage and represent the people, not just the elites. Like Carlo Bianco di Saint Jorioz (1795–1843), a Piedmontese soldier and liberal, Mazzini drew on the Spanish *guerrilla* as the model of a popular nationalist war.[38] In the meantime, the methodical political purges that had followed the Italian revolutions of 1820–1821 had created a new generation of professional army officers whose dynastic loyalties to the Restoration rulers were beyond question and would prove unswerving during the revolutions of 1848 and 1849.

By then the nationalist cause had found a new heroic symbol in the non-professional soldier epitomized by the revolutionary irregular leader Giuseppe Garibaldi (1807–1882), who came to represent the whole generation of Italian soldiers in political exile in the 1830s and 1840s.[39] But alongside the new and younger generation of political exiles who, like Garibaldi and the democrat ex-Neapolitan army officer, Carlo Pisacane (1818–1857), had earned their keep as soldiers of fortune fighting in the causes of others, many veterans of the Napoleonic Wars did return to serve during the revolutions. In Milan, Teodoro Lechi came out of retirement to command the National Guard, while the Neapolitan Guglielmo Pepe, who had been a leader of the liberal revolution of 1820–1821, commanded the Neapolitan army that fought the Austrians in the Po Valley before coming to the assistance of the Venetian Republic. Cesare de Laugier had little sympathy with the political aims of the revolution but was fiercely loyal to his native Tuscany and commanded the Tuscan forces during the defence of Curtatone and Montanara in May 1848, two of the bloodiest battles fought against the Austrians.

The veterans of the Napoleonic Wars still had a part to play in the revolutions of 1848, but the initiative had now passed to a younger generation of Italian nationalists amongst whom suspicion of France's imperial ambitions remained high, not least when in 1849 the French Republic and its newly elected President, Napoleon's nephew Louis Napoleon, sent an army against the Roman Republic to restore Pope Pius IX to his throne. Although the cause of Italian independence won many fervent supporters in France, when Louis Napoleon became the Emperor Napoleon III in 1852 his subsequent attempts to promote Joachim Murat as a champion of Italian independence and launch a carefully orchestrated attempt to legitimize the claims of Murat's descendants to the throne of Naples in the 1850s were met with deep suspicion in Italy. But even though the initiative was unsuccessful, it serves nonetheless to illustrate how memories of the Empire and its wars still remained alive, albeit in contradictory and contentious form, even in the final phases of the Italian Risorgimento.[40]

Acknowledgements

I wish to express my thanks to the *Institut d'Etudes Avancées* (IEA, Paris) for generous support of the research on which this chapter is in part based.

Notes

1. For recent studies on Napoleonic Italy, see Stuart J. Woolf, *Napoleon's Integration of Europe* (London, 1991); Paul W. Schroeder, *The Transformation of European Politics, 1763–1848* (Oxford, 1994); Luigi Mascilli Migliorini, *Napoleone* (Rome, 2001); Michael Broers, *The Napoleonic Empire in Italy, 1796–1814: Cultural Imperialism in a European Context?* (Basingstoke, 2005); John A. Davis, *Naples and Napoleon: Southern Italy and the European Revolutions, 1780–1860* (Oxford, 2006); and Renata De Lorenzo, *Murat* (Salerno, 2010). On Risorgimento nationalism, see Alberto Mario Banti, *La Nazione del Risorgimento: Parentela, santità e onore alle origini dell'Italia unità* (Turin, 2000); and Silvana Patriarca and Lucy Riall (eds), *The Risorgimento Revisited. Nationalism and Culture in Nineteenth Century Italy* (Basingstoke, 2012). There are as yet no Italian counterparts for the studies of Natalie Petiteau, *Lendemains d'Empire: Les soldats de Napoléon du XIXe siècle* (Paris, 2003); or Walter Bruyère-Ostells, *La Grande Armée de la Liberté* (Paris, 2009) on France.
2. See Alexander Grab, *Napoleon and the Transformation of Europe* (Basingstoke, 2003); and Piero Pieri, *Storia militare del Risorgimento* (Turin, 1962).
3. Pasquale Villani, *L'Italia Napoleonica* (Naples, 1978).
4. Alexander Grab, 'Army, State, Society: Conscription and Deserters in Napoleonic Italy, 1802–14', *Journal of Modern History* 67/1 (1995): 25–54; also Frederick C. Schneid, 'The French Revolutionary and Napoleonic Wars', *European History Online (EGO)*, published by the Institute of European History (IEG), Mainz 2011-01-27. See, http://www.ieg-ego.eu/schneidf-2011-en URN: urn:nbn:de:0159-20101025334 (accessed 15 March 2015); and idem, *Soldiers of Napoleon's Kingdom of Italy: Army, State and Society 1800–1815* (Westport CT, 1995). On brigandage, see Davis, *Naples and Napoleon*, 209–231.
5. Villani, *L'Italia Napoleonica*.
6. See Woolf, *Napoleon's Integration of Europe*.
7. On Prina, see Marco Meriggi, *Il Regno Lombardo-Veneto* (Turin, 1987); on Naples, see Davis, *Naples and Napoleon*.
8. Pieri, *Storia militare*; John Rath, *The fall of the Napoleonic Kingdom of Italy, 1814* (New York, 1975); Meriggi, *Il Regno*; and Schneid, *French Revolutionary and Napoleonic Wars*.

9. Cited in Davis, *Naples and Napoleon*, 260–261.
10. Ibid.
11. Grab, 'Army, State, Society'; and also Grab, 'Conscription and Desertion in France and Italy under Napoleon', in *Napoleonische Expansionspolitik: Okkupation oder Integration?*, ed. Guido Braun et al. (Berlin, 2013), 102–119.
12. Cited in Davis, *Naples and Napoleon*, 261.
13. Ibid., 272.
14. Pieri, *Storia militare*, 20; and Maria Casella (ed.), *Armi e Nazione: Dalla Repubblica Cisalpina al Regno d'Italia, 1797–1814* (Milan, 2002).
15. Pieri, *Storia militare*, 36–38. The strength of the Piedmontese and the Neapolitan armies was between 20,000–30,000 men, with reserves of 20,000.
16. Pietro Colletta, *History of the Kingdom of Naples, 1780–1860* (first published 1832), ed. John A. Davis, 2 vols (London, 2009), vol. 2.
17. Anna Maria Rao (ed.), *Esercito e società nell'età rivoluzionaria e napoleonica* (Naples, 1990).
18. Broers, *The Napoleonic Empire*; and Davis, *Naples and Napoleon*.
19. Colletta, *History of the Kingdom*, vol. 2, 134.
20. On Foscolo, see Peter Brand and Lino Pertile, *The Cambridge History of Italian Literature* (Cambridge, 1996), 412–416.
21. See Jean-Philippe Luis (ed.), *La Guerre d'indépendance espagnole et le libéralisme au XIXe siècle* (Madrid, 2011).
22. On Piedmont, see Walter Barberis, 'L'elmo di Scipio', in Storia d'Italia, Annali. 18, (Torino, 2002), 5–46; on Lombardy Rath, *The Fall of the Napoleonic Kingdom;* and Meriggi, *Il Regno*; on Naples Davis, *Naples and Napoleon*; and De Lorenzo, *Murat*.
23. Davis, *Naples and Napoleon*, 265–267. Guglielmo Pepe claimed that the membership of the Carbonarist lodges in southern Italy in 1818 was 300,000; Pietro Colletta gave an even higher figure of 800,000. See Pieri, *Storia militare*, 58.
24. Meriggi, *Il Regno*; and Davis, *Naples and Napoleon*.
25. Davis, *Naples and Napoleon*, 298–299; and Pieri, *Storia militare*, 54–76.
26. See Maurizio Isabella, *The Risorgimento in Exile: Italian Emigrés and the Liberal International in Post-Napoleonic Europe* (Oxford, 2010); and Giorgio Spini, *Il mito della Spagna nel Risorgimento italiano* (Rome, Perrella, 1954).
27. Roberto Bizzocchi, 'Immagini della nazione nelle Famiglie Celebri di Pompeo Litta', in *Immagini della nazione nell'Italia del Risorgimento*, ed. A. M. Banti and Roberto Bizzocchi (Rome, 2002), 60–73, 63. See also Adrian Lyttelton, 'The National Questions in Italy', in *The National Question in Europe in Historical Contest*, ed. Mikuláš Teich and Roy Porter (Cambridge, 1993), 63–105; Lyttelton, 'Creating a National Past: History, Myth and Image in the Risorgimento', in *Making and Remaking Italy: The Cultivation of National Identity Around the Risorgimento*, ed. Albert Russell Ascoli and Krystyna von Henneberg (Oxford, 2001), 27–76.
28. Alberto Asor Rosa, 'L'epopea tragica di un popolo non guerriero', in *Guerra e Pace: Storia d'Italia. Annali 18*, ed. Walter Barberis (Turin, 2002), 843–863, 848. On censorship, see John A. Davis, 'Italy', in *The War for the Public Mind: Political Censorship in Nineteenth Century Europe*, ed. Robert Justin Goldstein (Westport, CT, 2000), 81–124; and John A. Davis, 'Italy', Chapter 5 in *The Frightful Stage: Political Censorship of the Theatre in Nineteenth-century Europe*, ed. Robert Justin Goldstein (New York, 2009), 190–227.
29. Fernando Mazzocca, 'L'iconografia della patria tra l'età del Regno e l'Unità', in *Immagini della nazione nell'Italia del Risorgimento*, ed. A. M. Banti and Roberto Bizzocchi (Rome, 2002), 89–103, 89–100. That view was shared by the

correspondent for *Blackwood's Magazine* (Edinburgh, 1823), vol. 13, 27: 'But Santa Croce, despite its beggarly front, is the real cynosure of travellers. What wretched tomb-builders we are in England! ... The figures of any of Canova's monuments might furnish forth marble sufficient to record and illustrate a million of our illustrious dead....'

30. Napoleon had also been perturbed by the not very martial or even manly features of Canova's statue in which the Emperor posed nude as 'Mars the Peacemaker'. The work remained demurely draped in Paris until it was sold to the British government and donated to the Duke of Wellington: it still stands in Apsley House.
31. On Risorgimento nationalism and Romanticism, see Banti, *La Nazione del Risorgimento*; Patriarca and Riall, *The Risorgimento Revisited*; and Lucy Riall, *Garibaldi: Invention of a Hero* (New Haven, 2007).
32. See Pieri, *Storia militare*; and Asor Rosa, 'L'epopea tragica', 843–844.
33. The offending passage was in Lamartine's *Dernier Chant du Pèlerinage d'Harold: 'Je vais chercher d'ailleurs (pardon, ombre romaine!)/Des hommes et non par la poussière humaine'*. Pepe's protest against '*Le baie contro l'Italia*' was published in Paris in 1826.
34. Asor Rosa, 'L'epopea tragica', 843–856; and Silvana Patriarca, *Italian Vices: Nation and Character from the Risorgimento to the Republic* (Cambridge, 2010), 23.
35. On Pecchio, see Isabella, *The Risorgimento*.
36. Pieri, *Storia militare*, 19–22.
37. Ibid., 118–120; and Asor Rosa, 'L'epopea tragica', 847–856.
38. On Carlo Bianco di Saint Jorioz *Della Guerra Nazionale d'insurrezione per bande applicata all'Italia* (1830), see Pieri, *Storia militare*, 108–109.
39. On Garibaldi, see Riall, *Garibaldi*; on the Italian soldiers in exile, see Gilles Pécout (ed.), 'International Volunteers and the Risorgimento', *Journal of Modern Italian Studies* 14/4 (2009): 413–490; and Isabella, *The Risorgimento*.
40. De Lorenzo, *Murat*.

10

The Challenges of Peace: The High Politics of Postwar Reconstruction in Britain, 1815–1830

John Bew

In the wake of the Napoleonic Wars, as the glow of success from victory at the Battle of Waterloo faded, the United Kingdom encountered a series of challenges which were similar to those faced by many other European states. Taking a long view of how Britain developed during the nineteenth century, it is reasonable to conclude that the transition after more than 20 years of warfare was comparatively well managed. Britain was spared the instability that beset many other European nations (and indeed, America) during the next 60 years. Underpinned by unprecedented economic growth in the postwar period and the growth of Empire, such exceptionalism became the centrepiece of the 'Whig narrative' of non-revolutionary political progress, peaking with the publication of Thomas Macaulay's *The History of England from the Accession of James the Second* published in 1848. Mid-Victorian British patriotism was largely constructed around a liberal constitutional ideal, bolstered by comparison with the instability and despotism which beset so many other states.[1]

In 1815, however, things looked very different to those charged with the country's governance. Optimism was in short supply. Britain had triumphed over what was regarded by leading figures in the government as an existential threat to the country's survival. Yet few within the governing class were blessed with much confidence that the path ahead would be smooth. Over the next ten years, the government faced a series of domestic political challenges: an increasingly vociferous opposition in parliament; a rising tide of 'out-of-doors' radical agitation (including, in some extreme cases, plans for insurrection and plots to kill the cabinet); widespread social disorder and economic distress; bitter debates within the governing elite over what role the state should play in the spheres of economic and social life; the emergence of a Catholic-nationalist mass protest movement in Ireland; a challenge to the structures of the Anglican constitution from groups outside the Established Church; and assertive provincial elites whose strength was particularly pronounced in rapidly industrializing areas of the country. Not without reason is the Oxford History of England for the period entitled *A Mad, Bad, and Dangerous People*.[2]

That the British state rode this wave of challenges—and ultimately widened the basis of its legitimacy—is not contested. The question is how it managed to do so. One way of looking at the postwar period in Britain is in terms of a 'liberal awakening', both in terms of popular attitudes and approaches to governance.[3] Changes in the structures of governance followed along these lines as Britain made the transition from a 'fiscal-military' to a 'laissez-faire' state.[4] Although the increasing importance of 'liberal' ideas cannot be denied, there were other important ideological currents at work. Evangelical revivalism and other religious trends have also been identified as important influences on the thinking of elites, particularly on social and economic policy.[5]

A new generation of statesmen emerged in the period from 1815 to the Great Reform Act of 1832, which signalled something of a changing of the guard. The first manifestation of this was the appearance of a more 'liberal' form of Toryism in the early 1820s. It was embodied in men such as Robert Peel and George Canning (two future Prime Ministers), whose approach to social and economic policy is sometimes distinguished from those more closely associated with the wartime state, such as Lord Castlereagh and the Duke of Wellington.[6] The second phase of this 'awakening' played out in the revival of the Whig party in the late 1820s and the subsequent emergence of the Liberal Party in the 1830s, which was to become the dominant force in nineteenth-century British politics.[7]

Most of the scholarship on postwar Britain shares, as its starting point, a recognition of the factors that made the British experience unique—whether they be religious, social, ideological, political or economic. Rather than attempt a complete reinterpretation of this period—or to challenge the existing paradigm—the intention of this chapter is to offer further explanation as to what made the British state comparatively robust. Without dismissing the existence of forms of 'awakening' or 'revival' (liberal or religious, elite or popular), the chapter aims to weave more conventional notions of 'statecraft' back into the story. It emphasizes the importance of the period from 1793 to 1815 as a crucible of British political thought, rather than seeing it as a period of stagnation or 'arrested development'. In other words, there is more to the story than the 'soft' revolution in governance which came after 1815.

The first part of the chapter aims to re-establish the importance of considerations that might typically fall into the bracket of *raison d'état* and *realpolitik*. Such terms, with their respective French and German origins, are more commonly used in descriptions of other European states.[8] They have been given short shrift in British intellectual history. Rather than implying any theoretical framework, this is how the rather unfashionable term 'high politics' should be understood in the chapter title: as referring to the decisions taken, and policies formulated, by those with responsibility for the management of affairs of state.

The second part of the argument flows from the first: it is that Britain was better prepared for postwar challenges because of the lessons that a generation of statesman learned during a tumultuous period of total war and state formation. In the last third of the eighteenth century, Britain had experienced a series of traumas comparable to the experiences of other European states. These included the humiliating loss of its American colonies, a major rebellion in Ireland in 1798 and a series of invasion scares. Above all, to an extent that is sometimes forgotten, the country also underwent a process of blood-spattered state formation. It was in 1801 that the United Kingdom was created by Act of Union between Britain and Ireland—in a highly ambitious attempt to solve pressing internal difficulties within the British Isles, which had played out in the Irish rebellion of 1798. These experiences of both fracture and formation precipitated a process of deep critical thinking about statecraft among the ruling elites. Out of these debates and discussions came a series of new ideas about effective governance which do not easily fall into the bracket of 'liberal' or 'conservative'.

In some respects, the late eighteenth and early nineteenth centuries might be understood as an epilogue to the 'Machiavellian moment', first described by historian J. G. A. Pocock in 1976. By this phrase, Pocock implied a moment in which a state confronted problems of maintaining the stability and effectiveness of its institutions by reconsidering the civic basis of society—and the relationship between the state and the citizen.[9] As with Machiavelli's response to the challenges of Renaissance-era statecraft, the ideas of classical civic republicanism were revived as an attempt to bolster and stabilize the state. Pocock's book was primarily a study of Puritan England and Revolutionary and Federalist America. However, there were residues of similar strains of thought in the period of the Revolutionary and Napoleonic Wars, albeit in an altered form.

Related to this, another way of looking at this period is through the prism of the 'primacy of foreign policy'—an idea only recently applied to British history.[10] This applies to the extent that the period from 1793 to 1815 gave added urgency to questions of domestic governance because of the fear of French invasion and the need to harness the full energies of the state for the war effort. A final point made in the last part of the chapter is that this experience was not simply one of internal reflection and recalibration. After 1815, British understanding of 'good governance' was heightened by increased interest in—and interaction with—other European states.

Such lessons learned did not always translate into effective action at the legislative or political level. However, they did provide statesmen with a fund of experience as to mistakes to avoid and best practices to pursue. The most important of these included: decoupling Jacobinism from the concerns of confessional or socio-economic interest groups; broadening the basis of civic participation in the state by showing more toleration and thereby preempting organized campaigns for political change; 'managing party warfare' within the state; and acquiring general public acquiescence for government strategy, even in the field of foreign affairs (though how public acquiescence was to be measured remained a matter of contention).

The challenges of demobilization

In 1816, the British Foreign Secretary and the leader of the government in the House of Commons, Lord Castlereagh, identified the two great sources of instability in Europe as the huge standing armies bequeathed by 20 years of warfare and 'the Debts which hang about all the States of Europe, as Millstones dragging them to the bottom'.[11] The problems that Britain faced in 1815 were similar to those faced by many other states. The size, cost and purview of the British state had grown exponentially in the period from 1793 to 1815 in response to the demands of war.[12] The country was undergoing a period of explosive population growth, coupled with an industrializing economy and the associated ills of rapid urbanization, the spread of disease and social disorder. Ireland, which had been incorporated into the domestic political system in 1801, remained a source of constant concern, having experienced attempted rebellion in 1798 and 1803.

On the one hand, Britain had some advantages over its European counterparts. It was wealthier and its empire had been preserved over the course of the European war, giving it access to new resources and markets. It had not been subjected to the plunder of invading troops, notwithstanding a small French incursion into Ireland in 1798. Over the course of the war, Britain had created an army which was bigger than at any time in its history. By 1817, nearly 90 percent of commissioned naval officers were unemployed or on half-pay. The armaments industry which had sprung up in the Midlands was severely hit and the government was forced to try to alleviate conditions there with the Poor Employment Act of 1817.[13] However, the challenge of British demobilization still paled in comparison with that faced by other European states.

The fact that Britain's main strength was on the sea rather than in land forces also provided it with an important advantage. Even in peacetime, the Royal Navy remained a useful guarantor of markets and trade. This meant that the political and financial pressure to wind it down was much reduced, as many exponents of free trade and smaller government recognized the commercial advantages it brought. It was widely agreed, as Castlereagh told the House of Commons, that the 'unsettled state of the world' made it necessary 'to keep up a very considerable naval force'.[14]

Britain had by far the most open political system of any of the European states after 1815. On occasion, this could be a source of frustration and difficulty. The existence of a vociferous parliamentary opposition, a relatively free press and a lively regional political scene meant that the government faced pressure, scrutiny and criticism. Even before victory was secured, as

Britain and the Allies pushed into France in 1814–1815 to finally bring Napoleon to heel, the government came under pressure to scale down their Continental commitments. 'Many of our best friends think of nothing but the reduction of taxes and war establishments', complained the Prime Minister Lord Liverpool as Britain entered the last few critical months of the war, 'The country at this moment is peace mad.'[15]

The government was far from blind to the need for retrenchment, following the extravagant use of the public purse during the war years. As Foreign Secretary, Castlereagh—one of the more profligate spenders—expressed one of the foundational notions of British foreign policy, writing in March 1816:

> I am so thoroughly satisfied that a sound State of Finance is the true lever of our power, and that our Credit is the Real Basis of our Influence abroad and means of doing good, that nothing shall be wanting on my part to bring our Expenditure within our Income and to make an Effective progress during peace in the Reduction of Debt.[16]

Debt could not be reduced before it was serviced, however. For that, the government needed new sources of income. As every major spending measure went before parliament, it was not long before certain interest groups began to push back against new levies which they felt they would bear the burden of. 'Economy is more the order of the day, than War ever was', complained Castlereagh in March 1816, who feared that, if the government could not pass any new taxation measures, it would 'not have a Clear Revenue of above 9 Millions to meet an Expenditure in this year of 30, and in future years of 20 Millions'. Ministers regularly commented that parliament was a more difficult place to conduct than at any time during the war.[17]

Particularly troubling for ministers was the fact that their most reliable supporters—those who represented the 'agricultural interest', chiefly large landowners—were increasingly suspicious of the government. Following the ending of the Continental Blockade imposed by Napoleon in November 1806, the influx of cheap corn from other European markets caused a severe dip in prices. The government's inclination to move towards the repeal of the Corn Laws—by which prices were regulated to prevent their collapse—inevitably caused alarm for this interest group.[18] Known as the 'country gentlemen', they had been strongly supportive of William Pitt and his ministers during the war. From 1816, they became increasingly concerned about the government's postwar programme, as it shifted its priorities towards 'Peace, and retrenchment'.[19] Tellingly, the first major postwar parliamentary defeat for the government came over the implementation of a new property tax, signalling the end of its natural majority and leading to some speculation that it might fall.[20]

With the 'agricultural interest' deflecting the blow, those in the commercial and industrial middle classes were concerned that the burden would be shifted to them. Thus there was widespread opposition to income tax, both inside and outside parliament. Income tax had been introduced by William Pitt in 1799 specifically as a wartime measure. However, in February 1816 the Chancellor, Nicholas Vansittart, proposed to extend it into peacetime, albeit on a reduced rate. The Whig opposition, despite its own aristocratic heritage, capitalized on the issue as one which would allow them to build a broader coalition, with more support from the commercial and industrial middle classes. Significantly, as ministers were aware, the extension of income tax was not only opposed in the usual anti-government newspapers such as the *Morning Chronicle* and the *Leeds Mercury*. It also became a rallying cause for those portions of the press which had been sympathetic to the war effort, such as *The Times,* demonstrating the further fracturing of the government coalition.[21]

Managing discontent: learning from Ireland

As in many other European states, fear of Jacobinism and insurrection outlasted the defeat of France in 1815. There was hypersensitivity to any manifestation of popular agitation to which Britain was far from immune. This was particularly true in late 1816 and throughout 1817 as the severity of the postwar depression became apparent. A combination of a high tax burden and high bread prices contributed to the poisoning of the domestic political atmosphere. While the majority of protests against the government were peaceful, the conditions also created room for a flowering of radical political activity. In February 1817, a Secret Committee of the House of Commons reported that there were several active plots in the country which aimed at the 'overthrow of all existing establishments'. Among the plots uncovered were plans to storm the Bank of England and the Tower of London, attack army barracks and explode bombs on the bridges on the River Thames, infiltrate the army with radicals, and to establish a revolutionary tribunal along the lines of France's infamous Committee of Public Safety.[22] At the time when the Secret Committee reported its findings, the Duke of Wellington, in France as part of the occupying Allied force, suggested that violence and social disorder were now more likely in London than Paris.[23]

In dealing with these concerns, the government was not slow to adopt coercive measures, if not quite on the scale of Metternich's Carlsbad Decrees. Following an attempt on the Prince Regent's life—in which a shot was allegedly fired at his carriage—ministers passed an Act suspending *Habeas Corpus* in February 1817. This was decried as an aberration in British constitutional history. 'It is peculiarly painful to find that after having passed through all the dangers and pressures of war, it has become necessary, notwithstanding the return of peace abroad, to require the adoption of proceedings that might insure [sic] the continuance of tranquillity at home', claimed Castlereagh when introducing the measure.[24] That such acts became so infamous in British political culture underlines the fact that they were the exception rather than the rule. It is worth noting, though, that coercive legislation usually received the backing of parliament. In fact, *Habeas Corpus* was suspended with the concurrence of a large majority, including most of the Whig opposition.

The occasional resort to repressive measures obscures a larger fact about what made the British experience different from that of many other European states. As Mark Jarrett notes, the British state largely resisted the temptation to fall into systematic repression, as practised by the autocratic states in Europe. They could agree 'on the substance' of the threat from Jacobinism, but even in private communications with other states they made it clear that they differed significantly in their approach to the 'management' of the problem.[25] The overriding concern of the government was not the existence of Jacobinism or political radicalism *per se*. The government recognized that determined radicals were an established fact of political life, and that revolutionary plots were difficult to extinguish entirely. What it did do, however, was make an important distinction between individual (often idiosyncratic) plots and the prospect of general insurrection and disorder.

The result of this was an approach to governance concentrated on preventing the fusion of Jacobinism, or political radicalism, with other sources of popular grievance. Other types of grievance could include, of course, social and economic deprivation. The Secret Committee report of 1817, for example, made the point that radical political protest was 'confined to the principal manufacturing districts where the distress is more prevalent'. 'Great allowance', it was claimed, was made for those 'who, under the pressure of urgent distress, have been led to listen to plausible and confident demagogues'.[26]

More disconcerting was the prospect that Jacobinism could become entwined with the grievances of self-identifying communities of peoples (such as religious or clearly defined socio-economic groups). Such a perfect storm had already occurred in Ireland in 1798. In many ways, the Irish rebellion represented the nightmare scenario of the British ruling classes. A combustion of socio-economic grievance, sectarian tension and Jacobinism had led to the collapse of governing authority and the outbreak of violence at the cost of 30,000 lives. It had also provided an opening for France to attempt to land troops on the British Isles. William Pitt described the situation in parliament in 1799: 'Rent by party distraction, torn by the division of sects, subject to the revival of inflamed hostility ... the scene of constant prejudices proceeding from superstition and ignorance. Add, sir, to this true colouring, the infusion of that deadly poison, Jacobinism'.[27]

While conditions in England were not so combustible, it was not immune to some of the ingredients that fed the Irish rebellion. Historians have long debated the extent to which 'class consciousness' existed within the British working classes.[28] Certainly, British politics in this period was shaped by the increasing assertiveness of the middle classes, who attempted to tie up their own interests with the general cause of 'public opinion' in the years following the Napoleonic Wars.[29] Tied to this, and of greater concern to those charged with the protection of the state, was a growing body of Dissenting Protestants, particularly prominent in the manufacturing districts of Britain, with a clear set of both grievances and political demands. To a great extent, it was around such groups that English society was structured.[30] Edmund Burke's *Reflections on the Revolution in France*, published 1790 and sometimes forgotten, was partly an answer to the admiration for the Revolution expressed by radical Dissenters in the British Isles.[31]

In Ireland, as Burke noted two years after *Reflections*, much of the radical agitation had been initiated and led by Dissenters, particularly those in Ulster. He pointed out that the Irish Catholic hierarchy was both highly hostile to Francophile radicalism and favourably disposed to an accommodation with the British state (including state endowment for Catholic education).[32] As another representative of the Irish Protestant elite, Sir Henry Parnell, observed, the fact that Jacobinism found a receptive audience among Irish Catholics later in the 1790s was an anomaly in Europe. Anywhere else the French Revolutionary armies marched, 'armed peasants were their most formidable enemies'. Ireland presented 'the only instance where this religion existing in its full force, has been found leagued in resistance to the civil power, and inculcating, at the same time, the dogmas of religious superstition, and the principles of democratic enthusiasm'.[33] The failure of the Irish parliament to pass sufficient measures of reform to ameliorate Catholic grievances had contributed to the radicalization of the Irish reform movement in the 1790s, and its lurch towards revolution.

The 1801 Act of Union was seen as an opportunity to reset the relationship between the state and the Catholic and Presbyterian communities in Ireland by incorporating them into the civic fabric. The leading advocates of the Union saw an opportunity to do this through a dual process of emancipation (the lifting of civil and legal disabilities) and endowment (of both the Catholic and Irish Presbyterian churches). In practice, this ambitious scheme proved abortive. While the Act of Union was passed through both parliaments, the objections of King George III to Catholic emancipation meant that the scheme was only half implemented. Nonetheless, although the experiment was a failure, it was a spur to thinking about the function and the role of the state—the significance of which has yet to be given its full weight by British historians.[34]

The realist case for toleration

Ireland provided a poignant test case for the management of popular agitation in mainland Britain. Again, the lesson learned—and the priority of the architects of the United Kingdom in 1801—was the need to decouple radical politics and confessional identity. For this, the state had to show a greater degree of toleration. Rather than seeing this as a manifestation of benevolence, however, it is important to stress the primacy of security in such considerations. The fact that a portion of citizens could have a hostile attitude to the state in time of war was a matter of national weakness. As one leading government advisor put it, it entailed an 'alarming weakness in the British dominion ... for our foreign enemies to make use of—and will not Buonaparte feel this?'[35] 'Holding Ireland on our present tenure', asked General Charles Cornwallis, the Lord Lieutenant in December 1800 in a letter to Castlereagh, 'how are we to make head against all Europe leagued for our destruction?'[36] Cornwallis, who had first-hand experience of British difficulties in America (at the time of the War of Independence) and India (after the turbulent tenure of Warren Hastings), was particularly attuned to the challenge of popular violence. When it came to the security of the Empire, tough lessons had been learned over the previous 30 years.[37]

Following on from this, it is no coincidence that the strongest exponents of religious toleration at the turn of the century—William Pitt, George Canning, General Cornwallis and Lord Castlereagh—were among the most committed to the defeat of Napoleon. The lengthy document that Castlereagh presented to Pitt's cabinet in favour of Catholic emancipation made its case in the name of 'expediency' rather than 'justice'. Significantly, however, it also made the case that the principles of emancipation, toleration and endowment should be applied to all non-Establishment religions:

> Should it be thought that the dissenting interests of the empire at large (the Catholics being so admitted) have not weight, through their lawful operation, to shake the establishment, there can be no question that, in a state of exclusion, they are more naturally open to an alliance with Jacobinism, the enemy of the present day, than in a state of comprehension.[38]

It is in this re-imaging of the civic basis of society that one can see a version of Pocock's 'Machiavellian moment'. British unionism drew from a pool of ideas which included civic humanism, the Scottish Enlightenment and utilitarianism.[39] Pitt and his followers also owed a certain debt to Burke. A long-term advocate of Catholic emancipation, he had warned in 1795 that a 'half citizen' will become the 'whole Jacobin'.[40] However, Burke's hostility to Dissenters as uniquely 'seditious' meant that his writings were problematic when it came to applying the logic beyond Ireland.[41] Pitt, Castlereagh and a number of pro-Union intellectuals believed the formation of the United Kingdom presented an opportunity to broaden the civic basis of the state as far as possible without, of course, extending the franchise. Government should 'adopt a line of conduct towards the sectaries of less distrust, and thereby to put an end to questions affecting the constitutional rights of large classes of the community', Castlereagh told the cabinet in 1801.[42]

Although these dreams were unfulfilled, here was a vision of corporate, conciliatory and civic governance. The essence of good statecraft was to determine 'what system, without hazarding the powers of the State itself, is best calculated, if not warmly to attach at least to disarm the hostility of those classes in the community who cannot be got rid of, and must be governed'.[43] In this spirit, one influential government advisor, who had pushed hard for Catholic emancipation, also compared the Test Act, which restricted the access of Protestant Dissenters to high office, to 'a clog, hung, as I have sometimes seen, about a dog's neck to keep him at home, which did not prevent his running where he pleased but only made him every now and then growl and grumble, and bite it'.[44]

There was, of course, a fatal gap between intention and implementation. The Repeal of the Test and Corporation Act and the Catholic Relief Act were not passed until 1828 and 1829 respectively. Nonetheless, it is unsurprising that the legacy of these ideas outlasted 1801. 'The sensible operation of power', as Castlereagh put it in 1811, was 'the only resource to manage insensible masses'.[45] As he reiterated to a public audience in 1816, religious toleration was 'a question of policy', not a 'question or claim of right'.[46] In 1827, the novelist Walter Scott summed up this approach to religious toleration as a 'strong belief in the influence of common sense, when it gets the permission to act, in silencing party spirit, even at the expense of concessions'.[47]

John Bull's compass

A final area in which the government faced severe and intensifying pressure after 1815 was in the field of foreign affairs. External and domestic politics were more difficult to disentangle in postwar Britain than in many other European states, where diplomacy was largely the preserve of the court. Often to their frustration, those charged with the management of British foreign policy were forced to reconcile traditional conceptions of the national interest with the dictates of parliamentary pressure and public opinion (usually in the form of press criticism, public petitions and town hall meetings).

The extent of parliamentary scrutiny was incomparable to any European state. Crucially, though, the requirements and costs of the campaign against Napoleon meant that the government learned to live with public pressure during the white heat of war. The robustness and stability of the state were ultimately strengthened by the experience. Even in the conduct of military affairs, the government profited from the requirement to justify failures as well as claim successes. For example, the early phases of the Peninsular campaign were severely criticized to the extent that Arthur Wellesley, the future Duke of Wellington, was mocked by Byron and William Cobbett's *Weekly Political Register*, which demanded his recall.[48] Such was the outrage following the Convention of Cintra in 1808 that the government was forced to accede to a public inquiry and haul the country's highest-ranking generals back from the frontline to face the prospect of court martial.[49] Similarly, the disastrous Walcheren expedition of 1809 almost led to the collapse of the government and it was forced to put all related correspondence before a parliamentary committee composed of its enemies. Open to the press, every single piece of government correspondence relating to the campaign was released for public consumption.[50]

Even as the war finally turned in Britain's favour, following Napoleon's retreat from Moscow in 1812, ministers were given no respite. At this critical juncture, the Whig opposition renewed their calls for a negotiated peace with France and attempted to oppose rises in taxation designed to pay for increased British subsidies to the Allies.[51] As the cabinet drew up instructions for the Foreign Secretary to travel to the Continent to build a Grand Alliance at the end of 1813, they did so under constant external pressure from the anti-slavery movement and commercial interests (often in conflict with each other). William Wilberforce objected directly to the Prime Minister, Liverpool, that it was 'irreligious and immoral' not to use the opportunity to lobby for abolitionism.[52] The Foreign Secretary complained that 'in every small town and village, a meeting was held to advance the cause of the abolition of the slave trade, which, compared to the settlement of and adjustment of the equilibrium of Europe was at that moment a somewhat minor detail'.[53] Meanwhile, the government also came under attack from the mercantile interest because of its willingness to give up new colonial possessions (and therefore markets) that Britain had gained during the war.[54]

Having been criticized by the opposition for not seeking a peace deal with Napoleon in late 1813, by early 1814 the Prime Minister complained that public opinion was highly suspicious that Britain would now sue for peace. 'You can scarcely have an idea how Insane people in this Country are on the subject of any Peace with Buonaparte', he wrote. So exasperated was Liverpool that he did not put it past the Whig opposition to take up the cause of the Bourbon monarchy. Ultimately, though, after so many sacrifices, the Prime Minister recognized that final settlement had to be 'acceptable to the country, which can alone insure its continuance'.[55] Napoleon's exile to Elba in 1814 bought the government some respite. However, the public soon grew impatient with the extended negotiations at the Congress of Vienna, as attentions turned to reducing taxes. 'Now very few persons give themselves any anxiety about what is passing at Vienna, except in as far as it is connected with expense', wrote Liverpool in January 1815, just before Napoleon's escape from Elba.[56]

For all the frustrations that such pressures caused, there was a recognition that public opinion was also something that could be harnessed in support of the national interest. It was an asset that many other states did not have. The requirements of total mobilization meant that the acquiescence of the population was more important than ever. This was a lesson that ministers learned over the course of the war. Indeed, Castlereagh even went so far as to criticize Pitt, his mentor, for failing to recognize the significance of this at the outset of the conflict in 1793. Thus, the state was 'weakened for the first ten years of the War by a divided schism of publick opinion'. After 1803, the government 'profiting by experience ... never exposed ourselves to a question of this nature' again, and 'were supported in the War under all its accumulated burthens by the whole energy and voice of the Nation'.[57] The ministers believed that the public recognized that the country was engaged in 'a struggle for resistance' rather than 'a struggle for colonial aggrandisement'. Thus, 'His Majesty's ministers did not lead the people, the people led the Ministers'.[58]

Conclusion

As Castlereagh articulated in his famous State Paper of 1820, the successful operation of British foreign policy was predicated on a high level of public acquiescence, if not universal approval: 'if embarked in a War, which the Voice of the Country does not support, the Efforts of the strongest Administration which ever served the Crown would be unequal to the prosecution of the Conquest'.[59] The fate of the Congress system established after 1815 illustrated the point. Public mistrust of the other powers and dislike of the autocrats meant that systematic cooperation was doomed. It was impossible for Britain to act without 'the national sentiment' behind it:

> This is our compass, and by this we must steer; and our Allies on the Continent may be assured that they will deceive themselves if they suppose that we could for six months act with them unless the mind of the nation was in the cause. They must not therefore press us to place ourselves upon any ground that John Bull will not maintain ....[60]

Finally, and perhaps counter-intuitively, British understanding of what constituted effective governance was heightened by its interaction with other European states after 1815. Countless examples of instability and self-defeating political behaviour elsewhere encouraged an emerging sense of British exceptionalism. In France, for example, it was felt that the restored Bourbon monarchy was its own worst enemy—failing to broaden its basis of legitimacy or conciliate and incorporate former opponents. This was contrasted, for example, to the way in which George III had overcome his personal objections to bringing the Whig leader Charles James Fox into government in 1806 so as 'not to suffer a personal question to expose the public safety to hazard'.[61]

A recurrent motif in British foreign policy was that reactionary systems of government were just as likely to endanger security as Jacobinism (to the extent that ultra-loyalists were called 'White Jacobins').[62] British officials repeatedly lobbied the Bourbons to include former Bonapartists in government, to strengthen the moderates in the court and avoid relying on 'a feeble, odious and exclusive party ... [and] the idle clamour of *Vive le Roi*'.[63] In Spain also, it was feared that the restored King Fernando VII, also a Bourbon, had no conception of the 'temper of the times'. He must learn to 'speak to the nation' to survive.[64] The genius of the British constitution was its moderate (Polybian) balance of powers within the country. In much of the Continent, by contrast, the pendulum swung from one extreme to another. Both ultra-royalists and Jacobins had a tendency to construct 'the main authorities of the Constitution in hostility, instead of alliance with each other'.[65]

Ultimately then, while Britain shared many of the same concerns of other European states in the postwar period, the British governing classes linked national security and stability to balanced, moderate governance. A robust state was one which could pre-empt and absorb social and political conflict. As the British Foreign Secretary put it 1815:

> Tyrants may poison or murder an obnoxious character, but the surest and only means a constitutional sovereign has to restrain such a character is to employ him ... the essence of a free state is to manage the party warfare, as to reconcile it with the safety of the sovereign ... to do this, the King must give the contending parties facilities against each other, and not embark himself too deeply with any.[66]

Notes

1. Jonathan Parry, *The Politics of Patriotism: English Liberalism, National Identity and Europe, 1830–1886* (Cambridge, 2006).
2. Boyd Hilton, *A Mad, Bad, and Dangerous People? England, 1783–1846* (Oxford, 2006).
3. Élie Halévy, *The Liberal Awakening, 1815–1830* (London, 1931).
4. Philip Harling and Peter Mandler, 'From "Fiscal-Military" State to Laissez-Faire State, 1760–1850', *Journal of British Studies* 32/1 (1993): 44–70. See also Philip Harling, *The Waning of 'Old Corruption': The Politics of Economical Reform in Britain, 1779–1846* (New York, 1996).
5. Boyd Hilton, *The Age of Atonement: The Influence of Evangelicalism on Social and Economic Thought, 1785–1865* (Oxford, 1988). See also Boyd Hilton, 'Whiggery, Religion and Social Reform: The Case of Lord Morpeth', *Historical Journal* 4/37 (1994): 829–859.
6. William R. Brock, *Lord Liverpool and Liberal Toryism, 1820 to 1827* (London, 1967); and Stephen J. Lee, *George Canning and Liberal Toryism, 1801–1827* (London, 2008).
7. William Anthony Hay, *The Whig Revival, 1808–1830* (Basingstoke, 2005). See also Jonathan Parry, *The Rise and Fall of Liberal Government in Victorian Britain* (New Haven, CT, 1993).
8. While 'raison d'état' is normally said to have originated in the Renaissance era, 'realpolitik' was actually not coined until 1853, by the German publicist Ludwig

von Rochau in his book, *Grundsätze der Realpolitik* (Stuttgart, 1853). See J. Bew, 'The Real Origins of Realpolitik', *National Interest* (March–April, 2014).

9. J. G. A. Pocock, *The Machiavellian Moment: Florentine Political Thought and the Atlantic Republican Tradition* (Princeton, NJ, 1975).
10. For a classic statement of the 'primacy of foreign policy', see Brendan Simms, *The Struggle for Mastery in Germany, 1779–1850* (New York, 1998), 1–6 and 75–90. For its application to British history, see William Mulligan and Brendan Simms (eds), *The Primacy of Foreign Policy in British History, 1660–2000* (Basingstoke, 2010).
11. 'Castlereagh to Charles Stewart', 5 July 1816, Castlereagh Papers, (Public Record Office of Northern Ireland, Belfast), D3030/Q2/1. See also John Bew, *Castlereagh: A Life* (Oxford, 2012).
12. Roger Knight, *Britain Against Napoleon: The Organization of Victory, 1972–1815* (London, 2013).
13. Ibid., 467–474.
14. 14 February 1816, in *The Parliamentary Debates from the Year 1803 to the Present Time*, published by T.C. Hansard (London, 1816), vol. 32, 566–568.
15. Élie Halévy, *A History of the English People in 1815* (London, 1987), 92.
16. 'Castlereagh to Charles Stewart', 19 March 1816, Castlereagh Papers, D3020/Q1.
17. Ibid.
18. For the most authoritative account of the debates over protectionism, see Boyd Hilton, *Corn, Cash and Commerce: The Economic Policies of the Tory Governments, 1815–1830* (Oxford, 1977).
19. 'Charles Stewart to Lord Londonderry', 16 March 1816, Castlereagh Papers, D3020/Q1.
20. Hilton, *A Mad, Bad, and Dangerous People?*, 251.
21. Hay, *The Whig Revival*, 56–72.
22. Henry Bulwer-Lytton, *Historical Characters: Talleyrand, Cobbett, Mackintosh, Canning*, 2 vols (London, 1868), vol. 2, 294.
23. 'Duke of Wellington to Castlereagh', 3 February 1817, Castlereagh Papers, D3030/5234.
24. Marchioness of Londonderry, *Robert Stewart: Viscount Castlereagh* (London, 1904), 60.
25. Mark Jarrett, *The Congress of Vienna and its Legacy: War and Great Power Diplomacy after Napoleon* (London, 2013), 220–223.
26. Arthur Aspinall et al. (eds), *English Historical Documents* (London, 1996), vol. 11, 325–332.
27. Paul Bew, *Ireland: The Politics of Enmity, 1789–2006* (Oxford, 2007), 56.
28. For the classic study, see Edward P. Thompson, *The Making of the English Working Class* (London, 1963).
29. See Dror Wahrman, *Imagining the Middle Class: The Political Representation of Class in Britain, c. 1780–1840* (Cambridge, 1995).
30. J. C. D. Clarke, *English Society 1688–1832: Ideology, Social Structure and Political Practice During the Ancien Regime* (Cambridge, 1985).
31. Edmund Burke, *Reflections on the Revolution in France* (London, 1790).
32. Edmund Burke, 'Letter to Sir Hercules Langrishe', 1792, in *The Writings and Speeches of Edmund Burke, vol. 9, I: The Revolutionary War, 1794–1797, II: Ireland*, ed. R. B. McDowell (Oxford, 1991), 594–639.
33. Sir Henry Parnell, *An Enquiry into the Causes of Popular Discontent in Ireland* (2nd edn, London, 1805), 2–4.
34. For an important recent exception, see Douglas A. Kanter, *The Making of British Unionism, 1740–1848* (Dublin, 2009).

35. 'Alexander Knox to Castlereagh', 9 February 1801, in *Memoirs and Correspondence of Viscount Castlereagh*, ed. Charles Vane-Tempest Stewart, 12 vols (London, 1848–1853), vol. 4, 29–30.
36. 'Cornwallis to Castlereagh', 29 December 1800, in *Correspondence of Charles, first Marquis Cornwallis*, ed. Charles Ross, 3 vols (London, 1859), vol. 3, 316–317.
37. J. Bew, 'The Case for Cornwallis', *National Interest* (November–December, 2014).
38. 'On the expediency of making further concessions to the Catholics', *Correspondence of Castlereagh*, vol. 4, 392–400.
39. Kanter, *The Making of British Unionism.*
40. Bew, *Ireland*, 28.
41. Burke, 'Letter to Sir Hercules Langrishe'.
42. *Correspondence of Castlereagh*, vol. 4, 392–400.
43. Ibid.
44. 'Alexander Knox to Castlereagh', 9 February 1801, in *Correspondence of Castlereagh*, vol. 4, 29–33.
45. 'Castlereagh to Alexander Knox', 30 March 1811, Castlereagh Papers, D3030/3317.
46. *Belfast Newsletter*, 26 April 1816.
47. 'Walter Scott to Rev. S. M. Turner', 27 October 1827, in *Letter to the Lord Brougham and Vaux*, by the Marquis of Londonderry (London, 1839), 20–23.
48. Richard M. Schneer, 'Arthur Wellesley and the Cintra Convention: A New Look at an Old Puzzle', *The Journal of British Studies* 19/2 (1980): 93–119.
49. Peter Spence, *The Birth of Romantic Radicalism: War, Popular Politics and English Radical Reformism, 1800–1815* (Aldershot, 1996), 103.
50. Gordon C. Bond, *The Grand Expedition: The British Invasion of Holland in 1809* (Athens, GA, 1979), 144–146; and 'Minutes of Evidence taken before the Committee of the whole House, appointed to consider the policy and conduct of the late expedition to the Scheldt', 5 February 1810, in *The Parliamentary Debates from the Year 1803 to the Present Time*, published by T.C. Hansard (London, 1812), vol. 15, appendix no. 1.
51. Quoted in Rory Muir, *Britain and the Defeat of Napoleon, 1807–1815* (New Haven CT, 1996), 258–261.
52. Harold Nicolson, *The Congress of Vienna: A Study in Allied Unity, 1812–1822* (London, 1946), 65–67.
53. Marchioness of Londonderry, *Robert Stewart*, 56.
54. William H. Robson, 'New Light on Lord Castlereagh's Diplomacy', *The Journal of Modern History* 3/2 (1931): 198–218.
55. 'Lord Liverpool to Castlereagh', 12 February 1814, Castlereagh Papers, D3030/3794.
56. 'Liverpool to Castlereagh', 16 January 1815, in *British Diplomacy, 1813–1815: Select Documents Dealing with the Reconstruction of Europe*, ed. Charles K. Webster (London, 1921), 290.
57. 'Castlereagh to Lord Stewart', 24 February 1820, Castlereagh Papers, D3030/5814.
58. *Belfast Newsletter*, 3 November 1816.
59. 'The State Paper of 5 May 1820', in *Foundations of British Foreign Policy from Pitt (1792) to Salisbury (1902)*, ed. Harold Temperley and L. M. Penson (London, 1966), 48–63.
60. 'Castlereagh to Lord Stewart', 24 February 1820, Castlereagh Papers, D3030/5814.
61. 'Castlereagh to Sir Charles Stuart', 8 May 1815, in *The Foreign Policy of Castlereagh, vol. 1, 1812–1815, Britain and the Reconstruction of Europe*, ed. Charles Webster (London, 1931), 545–548.
62. *Belfast Newsletter*, 23 January 1816.

63. 'Castlereagh to Sir Charles Stuart', 8 May 1815, in *The Foreign Policy of Castlereagh, vol. 1*, 545–548.
64. 'Castlereagh to Liverpool', 10 May 1814, in *British Diplomacy*, 182–183.
65. Ronald Fraser, *Napoleon's Cursed War: Popular Resistance in the Spanish Peninsular War* (London, 2008), 470.
66. 'Castlereagh to Sir Charles Stuart', 8 May 1815, in *The Foreign Policy of Castlereagh, vol. 1*, 545–548.

11
The Gender Order of Postwar Politics: Comparing Spanish South America and Spain, 1810s–1850s

Catherine Davies

The Spanish American Wars of Independence, triggered by the Napoleonic invasion of the Iberian Peninsula, the forced abdication of the Spanish King, and the Spanish War of Independence (known in English as the Peninsular War), resulted in the fall of the Spanish Empire and a wave of violence, social upheaval and political experimentation on a vast scale. The Wars of Independence in Spanish America—affecting an area from California in the north to Patagonia in the south—lasted some 16 years, from 1810 to 1826, and were arguably the most profound consequence of the Napoleonic Wars. These liberation wars were civil wars, and although belligerence against Spain ended in the 1820s, the wars continued through to the 1830s and in some regions into the 1870s and beyond. The new Spanish American republics did not take their final shape regarding borders, systems of government and institutions until after the mid-nineteenth century.[1]

In Spain, the devastating effects of the struggle against Napoleon, lasting until 1814, are well known. The return of King Fernando VII, who rejected constitutional rule—for which the Cortes of Cadiz had legislated the Constitution of 1812—led to 15 years of tyranny relieved by three years of constitutional rule (1820–1823) imposed by a liberal army which, by denying reinforcements to the Americas, guaranteed a negotiated independence for Spanish America. After Fernando's death in 1833, the restoration of a constitutional monarch in the person of the Queen Regent María Cristina and the baby Queen, the future Isabel II, provoked a dynastic conflict with Fernando's brother, Carlos, and a bloody civil war in Spain—the Carlist Wars from 1833 to 1840—that recurred twice in the 1840s and in the 1870s.[2] The consequences of these events on both sides of the Atlantic were at least 50 years of violence, the ascendancy of a military officer corps with a range of political views prepared to take political leadership, the importance of the irregular militia and guerrilla forces, banditry and popular rebellions, and a preponderance of military officers in government until the middle of the century. These developments did not preclude the steady growth of political and civil society but they did hinder stability and the establishment of state governing institutions.[3]

As women were excluded from the regular military profession, bar notable exceptions in war time, it was the growth of civil society and alternative areas of influence such as philanthropy, education, cultural institutions and above all print culture, where there was evidence of change in the gender order during these times of political conflicts and military struggles. In all areas of the Hispanic world moves towards more or less universal suffrage, restricted to men of more or less property and economic solvency, irrespective of race, ethnicity, social status or wealth, meant that gender became the only criterion for total exclusion from political affairs and to a lesser degree from public life. As elsewhere, state and church attempted to 'normalize' gender relations to keep the gender hierarchy intact. With the aim to reserve politics and war exclusively to men, they set up politics, laws and institutions accordingly and fostered an ideology that defined home and the family as the 'female sphere'. The first Spanish American country to give women the right to vote was Ecuador, in 1929, some 100 years after independence, and two years before Spain—quite similar to many other countries that introduced women's suffrage in the decade after the First World War. But in the first half of the nineteenth century political participation of women took other forms in Spain and Spanish America, like elsewhere. It complemented male participation in the struggle for liberation and postwar politics.

This chapter discusses salient aspects of the aftermath of war on the gender order in immediate post-independence Spanish America and Spain in a comparative perspective. It will argue that to understand this aftermath, consideration should be given to the immediate context: prolonged conflict, social and economic disruption, material destruction and militarization.

Gendering state formation and politics

Elizabeth Dore and Maxine Molyneux draw attention to the fact that state formation is itself a gendered process and ask how republican states in Latin America responded to the existing gender order and how they sought to influence it. Dore's insightful discussion of the relationship between state formation and gender politics throughout the independence period concludes that for women 'the general direction of change was regressive rather than progressive' and that 'changes in state policy increased more than decreased gender inequalities'.[4] Late eighteenth-century colonial society was indeed a strictly hierarchical 'corporate patriarchy' divided into castes defined by gender, race and status (whites, mestizos, *pardos* [mulattos] indigenous and blacks) with deeply embedded male prerogatives. However, elite (white) women, especially single adult females and widows, enjoyed certain privileges and property rights.[5]

Despite political experimentation, patriarchy continued after independence, assumed by republicans and royalists; moreover, the liberal revolutions on both sides of the Atlantic privatized land and secularized society, which worsened the position of women. The liberal undoing of hereditary and historical privileges adversely affected above all the indigenous communities, the Church, and women. In the colonial period women, many of whom were heads of households, could sign contracts, make wills and were guaranteed an equal share of their parents' estate. In the highly unstable 'interregnum' between the colonial state and the new republics some of these rights remained. However, after independence women were expected to restrict their activities to the domestic sphere to ensure social stability, and the republics were modelled on the hierarchical patriarchal family. The liberal view was that 'the right to rule derived [not from class privilege or God but] from the social superiority of elite males'.[6]

Correspondingly, Sonia Salazar Garcés and Alejandra Sevillano Naranjo conclude in their study of women in revolutionary Quito (in the Viceroyalty of New Granada), one of the first cities to rebel against Spain in 1810, 'neither the Quito Revolution nor independence itself extended what today we refer to as women's rights'.[7] After independence was first celebrated, in 1822, elite Quito women returned to their traditional roles of strengthening their families by arranging advantageous marriages, a task which was more important than before the wars as there were now fewer men. Most army generals, irrespective of their own family's social status, secured advantageous marriages, demonstrating that elite women were the instruments by which traditional gender relations continued in state formation, property ownership and social rank. The study by Garcés and Naranjo also demonstrates that in the first years after independence women's scope for action was severely curtailed and their important contribution in the Wars of Independence was either discounted by state officials and historians, or remembered only within the parameters of prescribed codes of conduct expected from women at the time of remembering. A woman was only celebrated if her participation in the wars was considered extraordinary and masculine, 'because then she would be converted as if by magic into a man and therefore into a hero, negating herself, and leaving to one side her personal life, her home and her family, just like the male heroes'.[8] The authors blame women themselves, as nowhere do they find claims for women's rights.[9] But this is an 'ahistorical' argument that measures female involvement in politics and war by male standards.

Women in the Spanish-American struggles for independence

The first period of independence in the Colombian Caribbean town of Cartagena (between 1810 and 1812) brought little gain for women, irrespective of race or class, a situation which continued after the founding of the First Republic of Gran Colombia (1819–1831): 'legal equality regardless of race had little impact on them, as it did not affect gender inequalities'.[10] One of the few signs of progress was that racial barriers to legal marriage were weakened, allowing creole men to marry *pardo* women. In her study of the African-Caribbean populations of Colombia in this period Aline Helg traces the notable strides made to redress racial inequalities. The 1812 Constitution of the State of Cartagena granted legal equality and suffrage to all adult men, regardless of race, who lived from their rents or labour. The same egalitarian principles were embedded in Simón Bolívar's Constitution of Gran Colombia (Venezuela, Colombia, Ecuador and Panama) of 1821 which gave all officers and soldiers of the Gran Colombian army voting rights. Despite this legislation, however, most constitutions in Spanish America up to the mid-nineteenth century disenfranchised men without property or an independent income (namely waged labourers and servants), the vast majority of whom were not white—similar to the constitutions in Europe or the United States.[11] Women's status did not improve either in Gran Colombia. The only consequences of the war for women were widowhood and poverty.[12]

Yet women of all classes and ethnicities played a vital role in the Wars of Independence in Spanish America, as they did concurrently in the Spanish Peninsular War against Napoleon (1808–1814).[13] They provided the infrastructure for military operations (medical, intendancy, propaganda, espionage), they were effective political operators, they helped finance the wars, as mothers they provided the troops and kitted them out, they gave wise counsel and moral support, and often accompanied their menfolk to the battle lines to care for their needs. On the home front, many women took over men's roles as heads of households, property holders and managers of estates. Many actively fought in the wars, defending their besieged towns and cities. Some were even military leaders and fought with the irregular militia or guerrilla groups.[14] The male army leaders were fully aware of the power of women's influence. Revolutionary General José de San Martín, for example, appealed to the women of Lima in July 1821 to join the war effort and a year later he awarded almost 200 women the Order of the Sun to acknowledge their contribution in the struggle for independence.[15] However, once they had played their part, women were largely forgotten, erased from history, or remembered and misrepresented after their death, in order to meet specific political agendas and 'normalize' the gender order and with it the gender hierarchy, which had been challenged by the need for female war support.

One such woman was Javiera Carrera (1781–1861), an important figure in the early independence of Chile. Javiera was the eldest child of a distinguished family, loyal servants of the Spanish Crown. Both her husbands were members of the royalist elite. After ten years of peaceful married life, she and her three brothers, one of whom served in the Spanish army in the Peninsular War, took over the Chilean government after the Declaration for Independence in 1811. Her *tertulia*, or salon, was at the centre of revolutionary plans. José Miguel Carrera, the middle brother, ruled Chile in 1812. However, patriot forces were defeated by the royalists in 1814, and the situation was only saved by Bernardo O'Higgins, also a veteran of the Peninsular War. O'Higgins went on to be the Director of Chile while the rival José Miguel Carrera fled to exile in Argentina. In 1817, Javiera Carrera orchestrated a bold plan to remove O'Higgins from power which involved two of her brothers, Juan José and Luis, returning to Chile in disguise. They were caught, charged with conspiracy and executed in Mendoza, Argentina, in 1818. José Miguel Carrera was caught and executed three years later. Javiera escaped to Montevideo and, after the fall of O'Higgins, returned to Chile in 1824 to live a secluded life.[16]

All three Carreras were ostracized in Chile for their political activities, but criticism of Javiera was particularly harsh and clearly biased by the dominant gender norms. In his 1863 biography of the by then reinstated national hero José Miguel Carrera, Tomás Iriarte blamed Javiera entirely for the downfall of her brothers. She was a 'strong and manly [*varonil*] woman whose soul was tempered to a degree perhaps too highly for her sex'.[17] She was the cause of her brothers' mistakes and had led them astray, even though the two eldest were in their mid-30s at the time of their execution. In his biography of Bernardo O'Higgins, published more than one hundred years later in 1968, Stephen Clissold criticized her equally for being a woman of 'imperious character', a domineering and vindictive fanatic, the 'heart and soul of the Carrerista faction'.[18]

Even more sympathetic characterizations of Javiera Carrera were highly gendered. One example is the 1904 short biographical study written by the Chilean politician and historian Benjamín Vicuña Mackenna, whose grandparents had resisted the Carreras, published nearly 20 years after his death. For him Javiera was the 'venerable Chilean matron' whose 'docile' brothers had followed her advice 'until the last moment'. Keen to portray her as a fitting mother figure for the nation, he describes how she cared for her brothers when they were living in poverty in Argentina. In his view, this was by far the most commendable period of her political life, 'the most beautiful and the most appropriate for her mission as a Chilean woman'. Her letters of advice to her brothers demonstrate 'the evident intelligence of their author: a precise, sustained and vibrant diction, and above all they are full of warm spontaneity, without the deceitful digressions and thousand tricks of style and bewitching lies which are the epistolary art of women'. In other words, Javiera wrote like a man. However, Vicuña Mackenna adds that Javiera possessed 'the two greatest virtues of her sex: resignation in God and the denial of herself in the trials of life'. Ultimately she was largely forgotten when Vicuña Mackenna wrote his study, and though buried with state honours in Santiago in 1862, the public showed little interest.[19]

Although little changed for women in the political sphere after the struggle of independence, there were indications of wider opportunities for women in the immediate postwar period, especially in the 1840s. Pamela S. Murray argues that 'despite women's exclusion from the public sphere in formal government and politics, Spanish American women were far from strangers to the larger world of power and influence'.[20] This was the case for Javiera Carrera, as demonstrated above, and for Bolívar's long-term partner, Manuela Sáenz. After Bolívar's death in 1830, Sáenz was imprisoned and lived in exile in Peru until she died in a diphtheria epidemic aged 59. She was buried in a common grave outside the town of Paita. Thanks to Sáenz, who saved Bolívar's life on at least one occasion, many of Bolívar's documents and correspondence survived. Bolívar appointed her as his personal archivist and as such she has served historians well. She later became a rallying point for Bolivarians in Venezuela and for the women's movement in Ecuador.[21] Although her remains could not be found, she was given a symbolic state burial in Caracas in July 2010. This undeniable informal influence, however, was not translated through legislation into political duties and rights for women until the twentieth century, and was long ignored in historiography and forgotten in public memory. Instead women played a more important role in political representations of the new nations.

Political representations of women in the post-independence period

In the immediate post-independence period, women came to symbolize the embodiment of goodness and virtue, or of degeneracy and moral corruption. This is evident in 1820s Buenos Aires print culture where women's wellbeing signified the progress or backwardness of modern republican government. In Buenos Aires, largely unscathed by the wars, an effort was made to improve women's health and education, although women themselves were seldom the instruments of change. Women did not openly criticize patriarchal society but as a social sector they held 'huge symbolic power'.[22] The anonymous *Letters on the Education of the Fair Sex*, published in Buenos Aires in 1824, argued that women of polite society were duty bound to maintain the moral order and to ensure social progress.[23] Respectable elite wives should do this in those areas of civil society in which they had been traditionally involved: the family, the Church, philanthropy and education. Elite women became a key component of the social reform programme of Bernadino Rivadavia, the first President of the Argentine Republic. In 1823, he established the Charity Society (*Sociedad de Beneficencia*) to set up and manage girls' schools, the city orphanage and the women's hospital. He appointed an executive committee of high-status Buenos Aires women, captained by the iconic and much celebrated Mariquita Sánchez de Thompson (1786–1868) whose patriotic salon had existed since before 1810. From 1826, she was involved in the running of the Society, often acting as its president or secretary. Although these women were not proactive and tended not to make difficult decisions, they did learn how to manage public finances and direct publicly accountable institutions. Informally, they were influential. For example, in 1828 Mariquita used her diplomacy and contacts to broker peace with Brazil.[24] The appropriate social role for women and their education was much debated in Buenos Aires, fuelled by the influx of foreign publications including the British and French newspapers in the city. Macintyre quotes a review of a pamphlet entitled *Ladies' Miscellany* published in *The British Packet* in March 1833. The pamphlet is lost but *The British Packet* summarizes its radical preface. It is 'devoted to the service of Ladies, to redeem them from that obscurity to which the unjust tyranny of lordly men condemns them ... In order that they may break the chains imposed upon them by despotic man: woman being, to all intents and purposes, the most perfect workmanship of the Supreme Architect'.[25] The culmination of this debate was the publication of the first Latin American periodical edited by a woman: *La Aljaba*. Published twice weekly, it lasted only three months (until January 1831), but attempted to reshape elite gender ideology to incorporate republican ideas of active citizenship and progress. The editor, Petrona Rosende de Sierra, born in Uruguay, was the daughter of Spanish parents. Her second husband had fought in the Spanish American Wars of Independence. Her two sons were killed in the civil wars. In 1835, she established a school for girls in Montevideo. Her efforts were officially recognized in 1861 and she was given a state pension.[26]

The traumatic impact of the wars on the lives of elite women and their gradual accommodation within the new republican order is demonstrated by Inés Quintero's biographical studies of Bolívar's eldest sister, the staunchly royalist aristocrat, María Antonia Bolívar's. During the first Wars of Independence in Venezuela (1811–1816), despite her loyalty to the Crown on the one hand and protection by Bolívar on the other, María Antonia lost the vast majority of her properties and wealth and was forced to flee with her children to Cuba in 1817 for several years. When she returned to Caracas in 1821 she used her political contacts and writing skills to initiate several legal cases to regain her estates and privileges. However, a particular episode of her later life shows the extent to which her former status and influence were hardly relevant in republican government. In 1836, María Antonia, a wealthy, respected widow of 59 years of age, embarked on a torrid affair with a 22-year old tortoise-shell comb maker. Her subsequent vindictive attempts to have him imprisoned, with bogus accusations of theft, were unsuccessful and proved that women of the Venezuelan elite could no longer take for granted direct personal influence on judges and legal authorities. They were expected to behave according to the norms of society and to be treated on an equal basis as all other citizens of the newly established republic.[27]

Even more ambivalent was the perception and recollection of women who fought in the army during the War of Independence. Due to the pervasive militarization in Spanish America, modes of conduct and the social-conceptual space traditionally considered feminine were overwhelmed by an encroaching masculinity that made it acceptable for women to dress in men's uniform, bear arms, fight with weapons on the front line, to be incorporated into irregular and regular fighting troops, recognized as warrior heroines rather than as victims of war, and, exceptionally, to be remembered as such. After the Wars of Independence, as already discussed, women were expected to contribute to the re-ordering of civil society. However, the civil wars raged on and it took some time for fighting women—similar to the men who had fought—to readjust. One example is that of the much celebrated and derided Francisca Zubiaga. Zubiaga was the Peruvian daughter of a Spaniard. In 1825, she married the *mestizo* Agustín de Gamarra who fought with the royalists and then switched sides and joined the Argentinian army leader José de San Martín. Later Simón Bolívar appointed him prefect of Cuzco and in 1829 he became President of Peru. His wife, Francisca, who dressed in military uniform, saved him from an attempted coup and brought him troops to resist dismissal from office. Both went into exile, and she died in 1835 in Chile. Contemporary accounts describe her as an excellent horsewoman who could use pistols and sword with skill. However, she was also represented as an aggressive and imperious schemer, and was said to dominate her 'weaker' husband, which led to his downfall. The French writer Flora Tristan met her in Chile shortly before her death and describes her in her 1838 publication, *Peregrinations of a Pariah, 1833–1834*, as 'intoxicated by her power'.[28] Unlike the *mestiza* Juana de Azurduy, who also wore military uniform and led the guerrillas in the independence wars alongside her husband Manuel Padilla in Upper Peru in the 1810s, Zubiaga was not acclaimed a national heroine and very little is known about her life.[29] Her representation and demeanour challenged the constructed gender binaries and with it the dominating ideas of masculinity.

Changing ideals of masculinity

Turning to shifting concepts of masculinity in Spanish America in the independence period, Matthew Brown demonstrates that during the wars ideal masculinity was signified by 'military rank, facial hair, horse-riding and publicly acknowledged ... sexual prowess'.[30] Bravery and competency in battle was crucial. The ideally masculine officer was strong, tall and handsome, courteous, educated, loyal and honourable. Honour consisted of being true to one's beliefs, having self-respect and eliciting trust and respect in society. Dishonour was above all cowardice, shame and pretence.[31] While genealogy and race still mattered, particularly at the beginning of the wars, bravery and military skills could offset non-whiteness and humble origins the longer the struggle went on. General José Prudencio Padilla, the creator of the Colombian navy and a hero of Trafalgar, was a dark mulatto. He was greatly respected in Caribbean Colombia, but was executed in 1828 accused of conspiring against Simón Bolívar—allegedly due to Bolívar's fear of a 'pardocracy', the rise of the *pardo* elite. The mulatto General Manuel

Carlos Piar, who rose through the ranks of the Venezuelan liberating army, was also executed in 1817 accused of conspiring against Bolívar. General Agustín de Gamarra was defeated and killed by Bolivian forces during the Battle of Ingavi in 1841. José de San Martín, whose dark skin was according to contemporary gossip inherited from an indigenous mother, moved to Europe in 1824.

In many ways the perfect man of independent Spanish America was Bolívar himself: rich, white, reputed to be an excellent leader, good on horseback, a fine dancer, well-read, loved by the ladies but perhaps just too short and flamboyant.[32] San Martín had an imposing physical presence and was well-mannered and congenial, but he was considered too austere and (unlike Bolívar) held a deep hatred of luxury and ostentation. Many of the qualities of the ideally masculine that Bolívar embodied were shared, no doubt, in Europe during war time. Influenced by the Carrera family, the Scottish traveller Maria Graham disliked San Martín. She found him hypocritical and accused him of cowardice—the worst sin for a soldier. Although she described the Director of Chile, Bernardo O'Higgins, whom she also met, as brave, modest and looking good in uniform, she thought he was too short and fat and his hands and feet too small.[33] The greatest slur on O'Higgins's character was not his physique but the fact that he was constantly referred to by his enemies as a *huacho*, that is, a bastard born out of wedlock. He found this insult offensive, which demonstrated the continuing power of legitimate birth into a good family. O'Higgins's father, Ambrosio O'Higgins, of Irish descent, had been a general in the Spanish army and was the former viceroy of Peru. His mother, Isabel de Riquelme, belonged to a distinguished Chilean family, but the pair had never married. O'Higgins himself sired a child, Demetrio, out of wedlock with his partner Rosario Puga y Vidaurre, who had been married at an early age against her wishes. Rosario's father, General Puga Córdova, was living not with his wife but with another woman. Adultery was not looked on favourably but it was common in the pre-independence period as most marriages were arranged and divorce was difficult and expensive to achieve.[34] Even though O'Higgins was the Director of a newly independent Chile, he could not or would not try to change the law so that he could marry Rosario Puga and he exerted his paternal right by taking Demetrio with him into exile in Peru in 1823, although he did not officially recognize him as his son. Rosario never saw Demetrio again.

By the 1830s and 1840s, however, a change had taken place: the strongest and bravest men were no longer the ideally masculine. In the postwar era, their place was taken by patriarchal fathers of families and good providers.[35] The patriarchal family became the institution on which the secular republics were modelled. This shift to a different masculine ideal can be traced in Bolívar's later political writings. In the 'Speech to the Constituent Congress of Bolivia' of May 1826 he refers to himself as a mere soldier who cannot and should not aspire to the status of legislator, but he acknowledges his role as political strategist and encourages the legislators to find a balance between strong rule and representative government.[36] In his later speeches, Bolívar repeatedly calls for the force of arms to be made subject to the rule of law. His aim is to achieve stability, peace and security. For him, three years later, in 1828, the legislator is more important than the soldier and the values according to which the republics should be governed are strength, duty and obedience to the law. Only legitimate government will end the chaos brought about by uncontrolled aggression, the unregulated use of arms, personal ambition, and weakness rather than tolerance from a position of strength. Military law should not be confused with civil law; for example, civil legislation allowing soldiers to marry without a licence had compromised the army.[37] In his message to the Constituent Congress of the Republic of Colombia, in 1830, Bolívar refuses to take the position of President but exhorts Congress to choose a President who will be a magistrate, with implicitly feminine qualities. The new President will be 'a shining light [*iris*] of domestic concord, a bond of fraternity, a consolation for the defeated parties'. He should model the republic in the image of a family, with himself as the friendly but firm *pater familias*:

> All Colombians will gather round this fortunate being; he will embrace them in the arms of friendship, he will form from them a family of citizens. I will obey this legitimate magistrate with the most cordial respect. I will follow him like the angel of peace; I will sustain him with my sword and with all my strength ... From today I am no more than a citizen armed to defend the nation and obey the government.[38]

By modelling the public sphere on the patriarchal family in which ideal masculinity subsumes the domestic qualities of care and protection usually attributed to women, the republican leaders left little space for women's authority and autonomy. Simón Bolívar did not explicitly exclude women from politics in his rhetoric and writing. In his projected constitution for Bolivia the sole requirements for electors are the ability to write the name of choice, to sign one's name, to read the law and to have a means of earning a living. Only criminals, vagabonds and those with no education at all were explicitly excluded; 'knowledge and honour, not wealth, is what is needed for the exercising of public power'.[39] However, Bolívar took for granted that politics was 'men's business'; men were the new politically enfranchised citizens, not women. One example is a letter from 13 September 1829 which Bolívar wrote to his aide-de-camp, Daniel O'Leary. Here he rejects the idea of a monarchy for Colombia on the grounds that it is fundamentally undemocratic. He believed that 'legal equality is indispensable where there is physical disability, to correct the injustices of nature', but he refers to race and class. Good laws will redress racial and social inequalities, not gender inequalities. A republic is necessary because the majority, 'the inferior classes', reclaim their political prerogative 'with unchallengeable rights'.[40] Here too, Bolívar implicitly refers only to the rights of men. When he wants to refer to women, he does so explicitly, as in the decree of Chuquisaca of 14 December 1825 which distributes state owned land to the local people, to any individual 'of any sex or age', or in his founding of a school for girls of all classes in Cuzco (decree of 8 July 1825) because the education of girls is the 'basis of the morality of families'.[41] With this kind of rhetoric he constructed 'men' as the 'universal' and women as the 'specific'.

Towards the end of his life, Bolívar was embittered by the chaotic outcome of more than 20 years of revolutionary struggle. His emotive *An Overview of Spanish America*, written in 1829, is an angry cry of despair about the state of affairs in the former empire now overwhelmed by uncontrolled violence.[42] In the 'Overview', he deplores the seeking of personal ambition at the expense of the collective good, and calls on men to consider their duties as well as their rights. He rejects the law of the strongest who break the law of the state, so that, as in Buenos Aires, 'almost all the magistrates have been replaced by bloody conquerors'. He accuses the Argentine military officers of insubordination and 'parricidal rebelliousness'. He accuses the Carreras in Chile of banditry in the name of liberation, and in Mexico he denounces the actions of Vicente Guerrero, today hailed as Mexico's first black Indian President, whom Bolívar alludes to with a strong streak of racism as 'a barbarian from the southern coasts, the vile abortion of a savage Indian woman and a ferocious African'.[43] By the late 1820s, the enemy for Bolívar is no longer the monstrous mother Spain, as in the *Jamaican Letter* of 1815, but the collapse of order.[44] In his rhetoric he uses an explicitly sexual metaphor to emphasize his argument: the Colombians fell in love with Liberty, 'dazzled by her powerful attractions; but liberty is as dangerous as the beauty of women, who seduce and court everyone for love or vanity, and you have not conserved her pure and innocent as when she descended from the heavens'.[45] Liberty, fashioned as an otherworldly feminine ideal, has been corrupted by the *realpolitik* of men. This is just one of many examples of women figured as tropes signifying virtue and moral fibre, outside the business of nation-building in historical time.

Related developments in post-independence Spain

Bolívar died on 17 December 1830. Two months earlier, on 10 October 1830, in Spain, the future Queen Isabel II was born. Her father, King Fernando VII, had restored absolutism to Spain at the end of the Napoleonic Wars, revoking the liberal Constitution of 1812. Spain continued under absolutist rule until Fernando's death in 1833, despite several attempts by the liberal officer corps of the Spanish army to restore the Constitution. The most successful was General Rafael Riego's revolt of 1820 which gave rise to three years of constitutional rule, put down by the invading French troops led by the son of the future King of France, Charles X. During the Liberal Triennial from 1820 to 1823 progress was made to incorporate women into the public and political sphere. Accordingly, in 1821, a letter was published by a female citizen (*ciudadana*), arguing that the new Constitution did not exclude women from public office and government.[46] That same year Emilia Duguermeur, the widow of liberal General Luis Lacy, veteran of the Peninsular War against Napoleon, led a group of women in Madrid demanding to be allowed into the public gallery of the Spanish parliament. The majority of the deputies opposed this, but not all, and the matter was debated in parliament. Several deputies argued in favour of women's capacity to reason and their natural tendencies towards philanthropy and justice. Months later, the radical press denounced corruption among the deputies and published a pamphlet entitled *The Female Spanish Congress* which proposed that all the Spanish deputies should be women. They argued that women were more sensitive and more disposed to alleviate suffering. The tract was ironic, of course, although its author, Antonio Solano, made the serious point that the deputies had forbidden women to observe their sessions so that women would remain ignorant of their rights 'and therefore not be able to demand or enjoy them'. The pamphlet was considered so seditious that the author was condemned to six years' imprisonment.[47]

By the 1820s women's military heroism during the Peninsular War had become the stuff of legend. The most celebrated heroine was Agustina de Aragón (1786–1857), who had defended Zaragoza in July 1808 against the French and was awarded military honours.[48] Her bravery was much celebrated, for example in Francisco de Goya's sketches, *The Disasters of War* (1810–1815) and in Lord Byron's *Childe Harold's Pilgrimage* (1812).[49] But at the same time Agustina de Aragón was naturalized and domesticated in the recollection; she represented the nation fighting the foreign invader, moved by love for her soldier companion. As Byron wrote, 'Yet are Spain's maids no race of Amazons/ But form'd for all the witching arts of love'.[50] Nevertheless, using this historical precedent, in 1823 Emilia Duguermeur established a battalion of militia women to defend Barcelona once again from the invading French.[51] The women marched through the city armed with pikes and knives, but on this occasion their actions were not seen as heroic but as a demonstration of the degeneracy of the liberal regime. A newspaper warned humorously that the very idea of young ladies learning to use weapons was dangerous: 'we are giving due notice to the ugly sex so that they take measures against this abuse which could in time start a revolution against the empire of men'.[52]

In 1833, the baby Isabel, not yet aged three, was declared Queen. The resulting dynastic dispute with Fernando's brother Carlos resulted in the first Carlist Wars of 1833 to 1840. During these years, Spain was ruled by a woman, the Queen Regent, María Cristina. As a constitutional monarch, she was only able to do so with the support of the men of the liberal army. When she attempted to wield power outside the Constitution of 1812, as in 1836, she was promptly reminded by her Royal Guard of the pact with the military. The 1836 coup by sergeants of the Royal Guard at La Granja de San Ildefonso in the Province of Segovia led to the liberal Constitution of 1837, which applied until 1845. Its major aim was to restore the most liberal features of the Spanish Constitution of 1812 and to secure the ideas of constitutionalism, parliamentarism, and separation of powers in Spain. Thus, the four years between 1833 and the 1837 marked a period of transition in Spain from absolutist to constitutional monarchy. After that date, Spain never returned to absolutism again. In 1836, Spain also recognized, finally, the independence of Mexico. [53]

This course of events was important for the gender order in Spain. Liberal government and national progress were symbolized not by army generals and the 'fathers of the patria' as in the Spanish American republics, but by the figure of a young woman (the Queen Regent) and her baby daughter (the Queen). When liberal General Baldomero Espartero assumed the function of Regent, between 1841 and 1843, he was ousted and Isabel swiftly crowned, aged 13. Isabel was a monarch who reigned in accordance with constitutional rule until she was forced to abdicate in 1870. Her succession was disputed by the Carlists, who ardently refused to recognize a female sovereign. Their resistance led to the Second Carlist War from 1846 to 1849, when they tried to install a man, Carlos VI, on the throne. After a troubled reign, Queen Isabel was finally deposed in the Glorious Revolution of 1868.[54]

The political iconography of the 1830s and 1840s shows the figures of the three young women (including Isabel's younger sister, Luisa) representing the Spanish liberal nation-state, protected by the burly masculine figures of the liberal army officers. The images resonate with the Marian tradition of the Catholic Church (the young Virgin Mary with her mother Saint Anne). Isabel was the very embodiment of new beginnings under Catholic constitutional rule. The preamble of the first significant political document of the regime, the 1837 Constitution, reiterated the symbolic and to some extent real political power of these women, women made powerful by the grace of God, birth and genealogy, but powerful nonetheless—as long as they ruled within the parameters prescribed by the exclusively male parliament and army. On the front page of the Constitution the Queen Widow María Cristina is referred to as the 'august mother' and 'Restorer of Spanish liberty', and Isabel as the 'Queen of the Spains'.[55] The most important legal document in the land underwrites the power of roles exclusive to women: queen, mother and widow.

The 1837 Constitution refers throughout not to 'Queen' but to the allegedly neutrally gendered 'King' (*Rey*), yet there are specific mentions of women's rights. For example, all children born of Spanish fathers and of Spanish mothers will be considered Spanish even if born abroad (Article 1). The phrases 'all Spaniards' and 'every Spaniard' clearly refer to both sexes in most articles, although in Article 5 'All Spaniards can be admitted to public employment and positions', not in practice applicable to women, is qualified by the ambiguous phrase 'according to their merits and capacity'. Similarly ambiguous is Article 6, that 'every Spaniard is obliged to defend the nation when the law requires and to contribute to the expenditure of the state'; single women and heads of household would certainly be expected to pay taxes, but they were not expected to defend the nation bearing arms. In the laws of succession both males and females can succeed to the throne (Article 50), and, 'When a female reigns her husband shall have no part in the government of the kingdom' (Article 55).[56]

Important, too, was the fact that the young Queen was educated between 1841 and 1843 by a liberal woman: Juana de la Vega, Countess of Espoz y Mina, widow of the hero of the Peninsular War, General Espoz y Mina, the enlightened, middle-class daughter of a Galician commercial family who taught the Queen to be charitable and considerate towards her subjects.[57] Whether this symbolic connection of the female figure with political power in the 1830s and 1840s affected the gender order in Spain in any substantive way is the subject of another study. What is clear, however, is that Isabel did not live up to expectations. Her failure to uphold a public front of good conduct and decorum, which her contemporary Victoria so successfully deployed in Britain, brought the throne, the liberals and powerful women into serious disrepute. She was the last woman to sit on the Spanish throne. Forced to abdicate by military officers leading a liberal revolution, she was replaced by a series of kings and military dictators. In short, despite the emergence and even commemoration of warrior women and women of status in Spanish America and Spain, militarization was certainly not conducive to women's rights.

Conclusion

In summary, in the 1830s and 1840s in Spanish America, as in Europe and the rest of the Americas, it was considered self-evident that the political sphere should be restricted to men, of all classes and races, as long as they were literate to a degree and economically solvent, and to exclude all women, irrespective of class, race, education, or wealth. Women were subject to civil legislation, of course, and were encompassed, like old men, the infirm and children, in the notion of the people. According to historian Rina Villars, gender was not explicitly referred to as a criterion for exclusion in any of the nineteenth-century Spanish American constitutions, apart from the Colombian after 1843 which restricted citizenship to 'men [*varones*] over the age of 21'.[58] There was, as in Europe, an obvious distinction between political and civil rights, active and passive citizenship.

It is in the sphere of cultural citizenship, which, as Bryan Turner has suggested, goes far beyond the legal limitations of citizenship, having more to do with 'cultural empowerment' and the 'capacity to participate effectively ... within a national culture', that women were able to make their mark.[59]

This was the case with Mariquita Sánchez de Thompson in Buenos Aires, as we have seen. More generally it was the second-generation daughters of independence who took advantage of the new opportunities for women, especially in the press and print culture, women such as the Argentine writer and early feminist Juana Manso (born 1819), the Chilean *femme de lettres* Mercedes Marín Del Solar (born in 1804), and the Colombian writer Josefa Acevedo (born in 1803).[60] In an absolutist state neither men nor women enjoyed political rights, but some professions and elites were granted privileges. Status and wealth could override gender and afforded some elite women privilege and power. The new republics responded to the existing gender order by removing status and wealth as prerequisites for political power, giving one gender—most men—full political rights irrespective of class or race, and at the same time removing women, the other gender, entirely from formal political power and state formation.

In 1830s Spain, the liberal order was gendered female, in the real figure of a mother (the Regent, Queen Mother María Cristina) who upheld the rule of constitutional law with the support of military men. The accession to the throne in 1843 of Isabel II, known as the Catholic Queen, consolidated the maternal line as symbolic of national progress and modernity but at the same time confirmed the traditional power of the Catholic Church, motherhood and domesticity. In terms of cultural citizenship, it is perhaps surprising that the most celebrated woman of the 1840s, in Spain and Spanish America, was the poet, novelist and dramatist Gertrudis Gómez de Avellaneda (1814–1873). Ironically, she was born in a part of the Americas that was not independent from Spain: Cuba; and her phenomenal success was due partly to royal patronage. Once Isabel was deposed, Avellaneda was largely forgotten.[61] Ultimately, women fared no better in monarchic Spain than in republican Spanish America. A Spanish woman could be a Queen or a Regent but she had no other access to politics; she had no access to higher education, and an unwritten moral code made her the repository of the family's honour while failing to protect her against personal violence. The nineteenth-century Spanish constitutions, from 1812 on, did not further the cause of women; indeed, legislation impeded women from gaining positions of responsibility and made them more dependent on fathers and husbands.[62] By mid-century, on both sides of the Atlantic, the exemplary model for women to follow was no longer the activist but the domestic angel, the *ángel del hogar*, as propagated in Spain by, among others, María del Pilar Sinués with her 1850 book *The Angel in the Home: A Moral and Recreation Book Dedicated to Women*,[63] and in Spanish America by Josefa Acevedo with her 1848 *Treatise on Domestic Economy for the Use of Mothers and Housewives*.[64]

Notes

1. John Lynch, *The Spanish American Revolutions 1808–1826*, 2nd edn (New York, 1986); Robert L. Scheina, *Latin America's Wars, Vol. 1: The Age of the Caudillo*

(Washington, DC, 2003); and John Charles Chasteen, *Americanos: Latin America's Struggle for Independence* (Oxford, 2008).

2. Raymond Carr, *Spain 1808–1939* (Oxford, 1966); Eric Christiansen, *The Origins of Military Power in Spain 1800–1854* (Oxford, 1967); Charles Esdaile, *Spain in the Liberal Age: From Constitution to Civil War, 1808–1939* (Oxford, 2000); and Josep Fontana, *Historia de España, vol 6: La época del liberalismo* (Barcelona, 2007).
3. Leslie Bethell (ed.), *The Cambridge History of Latin America, Vol. 3, From Independence to c. 1870* (Cambridge, 1984); and Wayne H. Bowen and José E. Alvarez, *A Military History of Modern Spain: from the Napoleonic Era to the International War on Terror* (Westport, CT, 2007).
4. Elizabeth Dore, 'One Step Forward. Two Steps Back: Gender and the State in the Long Nineteenth Century', in *Hidden Histories of Gender and the State in Latin America*, ed. Elizabeth Dore and Maxine Molyneux (Durham, NC, 2000), 4–32, 5.
5. Ibid., 12.
6. Ibid., 9.
7. Sonia Salazar Garcés and Alejandra Sevillano Naranjo, *Mujeres en la revolución de Quito* (Quito, 2009), 243. My translation. All further translations are my own unless stated otherwise.
8. Ibid., 242.
9. Ibid., 239.
10. Aline Helg, *Liberty and Equality in Caribbean Colombia, 1770–1835* (Chapel Hill, NC, 2004), 262.
11. Ibid., 242.
12. Evelyn Cherpak, 'The Participation of Women in the Independence Movement in Gran Colombia, 1780–1830', in *Latin American Women: Historical Perspectives*, ed. Asuncion Lavrin (Westport, CT, 1978), 219–234, 221.
13. See the database 'Gendering Latin American Independence' (Genderlatam) for 3000 examples: http://www.genderlatam.org.uk (accessed 21 January 2015). See also Sara Beatriz Guardia (ed.), *Las mujeres en la independencia de América Latina* (Lima, 2010).
14. Catherine Davies et al., *South American Independence: Gender, Politics, Text* (Liverpool, 2006), 131–158.
15. Claire Brewster, 'Women and the Spanish-American Wars of Independence: An Overview', *Feminist Review* 79 (2005): 20–35, 21. See Decretos de San Martín, *British Library* (London, catalogue number 8179e20), no page.
16. Sergio Vergara Quiroz, *Cartas de mujeres en Chile, 1630–1885* (Santiago de Chile, 1987), xxv.
17. Tomás Iriarte, *Biografía del Brigadier General D. José Miguel Carrera* (Buenos Aires, 1863), 13; and Davies et al., *South American Independence*, 164–182.
18. Stephen Clissold, *Bernardo O'Higgins and the Independence of Chile* (London, 1968), 123 and 165.
19. Benjamín Vicuña Mackenna, *Doña Javiera de Carrera: Rasgo biográfico* (Santiago, 1904), 5, 17, 21, 24 and 37.
20. Pamela S. Murray, *For Glory and Bolívar: The Remarkable Life of Manuela Sáenz* (Austin, TX, 2008), 162.
21. Ibid., 159.
22. Iona Macintyre, *Women and Print Culture in Post-Independence Buenos Aires* (Woodbridge, Suffolk, 2010), 199.
23. Anon., *Cartas sobre la Educación del Bello Sexo* (Buenos Aires, 1824).

24. María Sáenz Quesada, *Mariquita Sánchez: Vida política y sentimental* (Buenos Aires, 1998), 138–140.
25. 'Miscelánea de Damas' (1833), in: Macintyre, *Women and Print*, 21 and 58.
26. Ibid., 167–168.
27. Inés Quintero, *La criolla principal: María Antonia Bolívar, la hermana del Libertador* (Caracas, 2008); and by the same author *El fabricante de peinetas: Ultimo romance de María Antonia Bolívar* (Caracas, 2011). Research on royalist women is scant.
28. Flora Tristan, *Peregrinations of a Pariah, 1833–1834*, ed. Jean Hawkes (London, 1986), 302.
29. Berta Wexler, *Juana Azurduy y las mujeres en la revolución Altoperuana* (Villa Constitución, 7th edition, 2011) and Mary G. Berg, 'Ficciones de la historia: Zubiaga de Gamarra', in *Las mujeres en la independencia de América Latina*, 413–420.
30. Matthew Brown, 'Soldiers and Strawberries: Questioning Military Masculinity in 1860s Colombia', *Bulletin of Hispanic Studies* 87/6 (2010): 725–744, 728.
31. Matthew Brown, *Adventuring through Spanish Colonies: Simon Bolívar, Foreign Mercenaries and the Birth of New Nations* (Liverpool, 2006), 91.
32. For a repudiation of Bolívar's bravery, see José Rafael Sañudo, *Estudios sobre la vida de Bolívar* (Pasto, 1925).
33. Maria Graham, *Journal of a Residence in Chile During the Year 1822 and a Voyage from Chile to Brazil in 1823* (London, 1824), 27, 34 and 42–43.
34. Giomar Dueñas Vargas, *Los hijos del pecado: Ilegitimidad y vida familiar en la Santafé de Bogotá colonial* (Bogotá, 1997).
35. Brown, *Adventuring*, 192.
36. Simón Bolívar, 'Discurso al Congreso Constituyente de Bolivia', in *Simón Bolívar: Discursos, proclamas y epistolario político*, ed. M. Hernández Sánchez-Barba (Madrid, 1975), 299–312, 300.
37. Simón Bolívar, 'A los representantes del pueblo en la Convención Nacional (Mensaje a la Convención de Ocaña), 1828', in Ibid., 323–334, 330.
38. Simón Bolívar, 'Al Congreso Constituyente de la República de Colombia en 1830', in Ibid., 353–360, 359–360.
39. Bolívar, 'Discurso al Congreso', 301.
40. Simón Bolívar, 'Carta al General Daniel O'Leary', in *Simón Bolívar Fundamental*, ed. Germán Carrera Damas, 2 vols (Caracas, 1993), vol. 1, 588–594, 590.
41. For the land, see Vicente Lecuna (ed.), *Documentos referentes a la creación de Bolivia* (Caracas, 1975), no page numbering. For the school, see Cristóbal Mendoza (ed.), *Decretos del Libertador*, 3 vols (Caracas, 1961), vol. 1 (1813–1825), 420–421.
42. Simón Bolívar, 'Una mirada sobre la América Española', in Simón Bolívar: *Discursos, proclamas y epistolario político* ed M. Hernández Sánchez-Barba, Madrid 1975, 343–352.
43. Ibid., 344–345.
44. Davies et al., *South American Independence*, 40–41.
45. Bolívar, 'Una mirada sobre la América Española', 352.
46. Jordi Roca Vernet, 'Emilia Duguermeur de Lacy, un liderazgo femenino en el liberalismo español', in *Heroínas y Patriotas. Mujeres de 1808*, eds Irene Castells et al. (Madrid, 2009), 371–397, 390.
47. La Congresa Española restablecimiento de la libertad y prosperidad de España (Madrid, 1822). No author. Cited in Roca Vernet, 'Emilia Duguermeur', 371–397, 383–385.
48. See John L. Tone, 'A Dangerous Amazon: Agustina Zaragoza and the Spanish Revolutionary War, 1808–1814', *European History Quarterly* 3 (2007): 548–561.

49. Lord Byron, *Childe Harold's Pilgrimage. A Romaunt (cantos 1 and 2) and Other Poems* (Philadelphia, 1812), Canto I, verses LIV–LVIII,
50. Ibid., Canto I, LVII.
51. Enric Ucelay Da Cal, 'Agustina, la dama del cañón: el *topos* de la heroína fálica y el invento del patriotismo', in *Heroínas y Patriotas*, 193–265.
52. Roca Vernet, 'Emilia Duguermeur', 390.
53. Rafael Muñoz Saldaña, *México independiente: El despertar de una nación*, vol. 1 (México DF, 2009), 140–141.
54. Fontana, *Historia de España*, vol. 6, 404.
55. Constitución de la Monarquía Española (Madrid, 1837).
56. Fernando González-Doria, *Historias de las constituciones españolas de Godoy a Suárez* (Madrid, 1986), 350.
57. Isabel Burdiel, *Isabel II: No se puede reinar inocentemente* (Madrid, 2004), 171–177.
58. Rina Villars, 'Exclusión e inclusión de la mujer en el concepto de ciudadanía política en las constituciones hispanoamericanas', *Revista de Derecho de la Pontificia Universidad Católica de Valparaíso* 27/2 (2006): 291–310, 294.
59. Bryan Turner, 'Outline of a General theory of Cultural Citizenship', in *Culture and Citizenship*, ed. Nick Stevenson (London, 2001), 11–32, 11.
60. Davies et al., *South American Independence*, 183–209 and 241–267.
61. Ibid., 270–273.
62. María Victoria López-Cordón Cortezo, 'La situación de la mujer a finales del Antiguo Regimen 1760–1860', in *Mujer y Sociedad en España (1700–1975)*, ed. Rosa María Capel Martínez (Madrid, 1982), 51–107, 79–80.
63. María del Pilar Sinués, *El Angel del Hogar: Obra moral y recreativa dedicada a la mujer* (Madrid, 1859)
64. See Josefa Acevedo, *Tratado sobre economía doméstica para el uso de las madres de familia y de las amas de casa* (Bogotá, 1848), in English: *A Treatise on Domestic Economy, for the Use of Mothers and Housewives*, translated by Sarah Sanchez, introduced by Catherine Davies (Nottingham, 2007).

Part IV
Restoring Postwar Economies and Reordering Societies

12

Remembering and Restoring the Economic Ancien Régime: France and Its Colonies, 1815–1830

David Todd

Neither economists nor historians have paid much attention to the influence of memory on economic policy and economic change. Modern economics are not unconcerned with the passage of time, but have instead placed an emphasis on the role of anticipations as a key factor in the behaviour of economic agents. Economic historians have proved more sensitive to the influence of past events on the present, but their reliance on quantifiable data has led them to focus on path dependency as a result of objective factors rather than the more subjective role of personal or collective memories. Such neglect is particularly apparent in the classical debate about the consequences of the 1789 Revolution on French and European economic development. Following Ernest Labrousse, supporters of a Marxist interpretation insisted on the limitations of the Ancien Régime's economy and viewed the Revolution as an accelerator of capitalist development.[1] Their adversaries, led by François Crouzet, insisted instead on the catastrophic consequences of hyperinflation and of the disruption of Atlantic commerce, even though Crouzet conceded that Napoleon's Continental Blockade facilitated the emergence of a modern manufacturing sector in north-eastern France, Belgium and the Rhineland.[2] Even the so-called revisionists, who gave a more optimistic account of the growth of per capita incomes in nineteenth-century France, still used the negative consequences of the Revolution as an excuse for the slow pace of French economic growth after 1815.[3] With the notable exception of Jeff Horn, who attributed the French industrialists' reluctance to replace workers by machinery to a 'fear from below' inherited from the Revolution, few scholars have examined what contemporaries thought about the economic significance of the years between 1789 and 1815, and how their views might have influenced economic policy and development in subsequent decades.[4]

Focusing on the commercial and colonial projects of the Bourbon Restoration (1814–1830), this chapter explores the role of economic memory in shaping France's economics and politics after 1815. Its main purpose is to highlight the existence of a widespread nostalgia for pre-revolutionary commercial prosperity and to examine how the restored monarchy sought to resuscitate it, and in particular its colonial Atlantic dimension. François Furet and others underlined the extent to which the Restoration endeavoured to revive the political institutions, practices and *moeurs* of the Ancien Régime.[5] Similarly, this chapter argues that the Restoration's foreign and colonial trade policy was unabashedly reactionary. The measures adopted were often more stringent than the old monarchy's legislation, in the hope of rolling back the changes of the revolutionary period. This policy of economic reaction achieved some successes, such as the resurrection of colonial prosperity in the slave plantations of France's remaining colonies. However, overall it was a disappointment, as French external trade stagnated between 1815 and 1830.

Secondly, the chapter analyses the influence of these economic memories on political attitudes. Whereas the views of the participants in the twentieth-century debate on the economic consequences of the Revolution were largely determined by their political leaning, in the years 1815 to 1830 it was often the contemporary interpretations of the Revolution's economic significance that shaped political preferences. In the aftermath of the fall of Napoleon, economic grievances linked to the collapse of maritime trade in the south and the west nurtured support for royalism, while nostalgia for the growth of continental trade under Napoleon in the north and the east favoured the liberal opposition. However, after the mid-1820s, as the experience of eighteenth-century prosperity became more distant and the commercial strategy of the Restoration seemed to falter, these memories became more malleable. Special attention is paid here to the case of the Bordelais merchants, whose simultaneous conversion from royalism to liberalism and from mercantilism to free trade was justified by new memories of the Revolution as a process of systematic exploitation of the southern agricultural provinces by the manufacturing north.

Memories of Ancien Régime prosperity: political battles over the re-export trade, 1815–1820

The prosperity of the late Ancien Régime primarily relied on the re-exportation of colonial produce from the French West Indies, especially Saint-Domingue, 'la perle des Antilles', to the rest of Continental Europe. In addition to this *entrepôt* trade, demand from the French and Spanish colonies encouraged the growth of a wide range of light industries in the west and the southwest, from linen cloth in Brittany to sugar refining in Bordeaux.[6] During the revolutionary and Napoleonic wars, British blockading and the loss by France of all its colonies dealt a fatal blow to these long-distance exchanges. However, Silvia Marzagalli has recently shown that the collapse of France's overseas trade was more gradual than previously thought. Using neutral American or Scandinavian flags, French merchants maintained a substantial level of activity in French ports throughout the 1790s, making possible the abrupt resurgence of colonial trade in official statistics during the peace of Amiens in 1802–1803.[7] It was only at the end of the Napoleonic era, especially after the draconian British Orders in Council of 1807, that French colonial trade was obliterated.

At the fall of Napoleon, the collapse of the French Atlantic trade was still relatively recent, which explains why the advent of a regime intent on preserving peace with Britain elicited widespread hopes of a commercial revival. Significantly, the first city to celebrate the return of the Bourbons was Bordeaux, when it opened its gates to the Duc d'Angoulême, the nephew of Louis XVIII, on 12 March 1814. A leading port for colonial trade in the eighteenth century, Bordeaux had been one of the main economic victims of the Napoleonic era, and it remained a stronghold of the Bourbon regime until the mid-1820s.[8] The restored monarchy was keen to reward and cultivate the royalism of Atlantic merchants. In April 1814, it repealed the legislation that underpinned the Continental Blockade and a few months later reintroduced a preferential tariff for French colonial goods. After the Hundred Days, in April 1816, the ultra-royalist *Chambre introuvable* adopted more vigorous measures to revive the Atlantic trade: the duty free storage of goods or *privilège de l'entrepôt* was confined to a handful of Atlantic cities (Bordeaux, Nantes, Le Havre, Dunkirk), while the importation of colonial goods (including sugar, cotton and coffee) via land borders was banned. This was to facilitate the repression of smuggling, rife on the north-eastern borders since the days of the Blockade, and also to prevent Antwerp, Amsterdam and Hamburg from supplying the French market. The measures were adopted amidst a concert of laments over the demise of the French Atlantic trade and their chief goal was to revive it. Supporting the new legislation, a royalist representative of the Gironde department reasserted the mercantilist primacy of the *entrepôt* trade:

> Commerce prospers by exporting the goods of other countries, and by speculating on foreign goods, by anticipating foreign needs, by keeping such goods in storage, and by re-exporting them with a profit when such needs make themselves felt; merchants turn a profit thanks to either the price [of the reselling] or a fee, and such profits increase the balance of trade in our favour.[9]

In subsequent years, the Bordeaux chamber of commerce clamoured for ever more stringent restrictions that would again make the port 'a warehouse for the products of the East and West Indies, which from here can be re-expedited to the rest of Europe'. In 1820, it demanded the implementation of France's 'Act of Navigation', the law of 3 September 1793, a measure inspired by Britain's ban on foreign shipping, but which had been suspended on 27 Vendémiaire Year II (18 October 1793) lest it disrupt supplies to revolutionary armies.[10] In 1821, the chamber of commerce's decision to build a vast warehouse, at the substantial cost of 1.2 million francs, testified to Bordeaux's faith in the resurrection of its re-export trade. The *Entrepôt des denrées coloniales*, an imposing building which today houses one of France's largest museums of contemporary art, the *Centre d'Arts Plastiques Contemporains*, was inaugurated in 1824.[11]

Memories of commercial splendour under the Ancien Régime therefore had substantial consequences, both at a national and at a local level. The strict legislation also infuriated merchants on land borders, especially in Alsace where it clashed with another set of pre-revolutionary economic memories: those of the lucrative transit of colonial goods along the Rhine Valley, from the Low Countries to Central Europe. Before 1789, colonial goods unloaded in Antwerp or Amsterdam were hauled in barges as far as Strasbourg and then, as the Rhine ceased to be navigable, by carriages along the left French bank of the river. Alsatian merchants were the main beneficiaries of the traffic because the province remained *à l'instar de l'étranger effectif* or beyond French customs lines, and effectively a free trade area.[12] When the Constituent Assembly extended France's commercial border to the Rhine, it maintained an exception for the transit of colonial goods, but the Convention abolished the Alsatian privilege in July 1793. Maritime warfare further disrupted the trade. However, French conquests in Germany and a large-scale contraband trade in colonial goods during the Continental Blockade helped preserve Alsace's economic ties with the rest of the Rhine valley. A licit transit trade resumed after 1815, but as a result of the1816 ban on the introduction of colonial goods by land borders, goods from the Low Countries were now transported along a slightly longer route, on the right German bank of the Rhine.

Alsatian merchants then launched a virulent campaign to restore the right of transit across Alsace. What might appear as an obscure and technical piece of commercial legislation caused one of the bitterest controversies on economic policy after the fall of Napoleon. In the winter of 1818, delegates from the Strasbourg chamber of commerce in Paris circulated over 10,000 copies of three pamphlets: *On transit across Alsace, A few observations in favour of transit across Alsace*, and *Yet another word about transit across Alsace*.[13] The pamphlets described the issue in simple yet patriotic terms as an alternative between leaving the transit trade to the German merchants of Baden or allowing Alsatian merchants to recapture it. They insistently recalled the benefits that Alsace derived from the transit of colonial goods before 1793 or, as yet another pamphlet put it in 1819, the 'splendour' of this trade 'in the times when there were ten to twelve carriages going [every day] from Basel to Frankfurt, and as many going from Frankfurt to Basel'.[14] A folding out map in *On transit across Alsace* offered a specific representation of Alsace's role as a commercial conduit between the Rhineland and Switzerland, evoking the times when the province was still commercially integrated with the Holy Roman Empire.

Liberal newspapers reproduced extracts from the pamphlets, while in the Chamber of Deputies, royalist representatives from the seaports denounced the campaign as an 'extraordinary phenomenon' inspired by 'political motives'.[15] Conversely, a delegate of the Strasbourg chamber of commerce rejoiced that the 'transit across Alsace has become a popular issue in Paris': 'everyone is talking about it, in the salons and in the antechambers, in trading firms as well as in small shops'.[16] The Alsatian campaign elicited strong emotions partly because it stirred economic memories of the Ancien Régime and the Napoleonic era. Although most Alsatian deputies sat on the centre-left benches of the chamber, they tried to gain royalist sympathies by describing Alsace as an economic victim of the Revolution. They recalled the alleged concern of the monarchy's successive ministers, from Colbert to Vergennes, for the preservation of the right of transit across Alsace, and insisted that it was a 'représentant du peuple en mission', a type of revolutionary official synonymous with republican zealotry, who abolished the Alsatian privilege: 'Wishing to punish this city for its courageous opposition to the suspension of Louis XVI, his blind fury made him suppress the transit, to which Strasbourg owed in part its prosperity'.[17]

Such professions of royalism from the Alsatian liberal deputies failed to persuade their right-wing colleagues from the Atlantic ports, who instead, and probably correctly, portrayed Alsace as one of the main economic beneficiaries of the Revolution. It was at the expense of the seaports, implied a deputy for Nantes and former Vendéen insurgent, that merchants from the land borders had prospered:

> For twenty-five years, the sea was forbidden to our ships and maritime commerce suspended. For twenty-five years, funds could not be used due to the lack of opportunities, ships remained idle and rotted in the harbours. Trade was redirected to the [land] borders, where the proximity of armies attracted the riches and the gold of Europe, while in the ports, the ruin of our colonies, the vain attempts to re-conquer them, the lack of activity resulting from protracted wars, the perfidious illusions of ephemeral peace altered—nay, annihilated!—commercial wealth.[18]

Resentment was compounded by the scale of smuggling in the eastern provinces during the Continental Blockade, especially in Alsace. The leading defender of transit at the Chamber of Deputies, Jean-Charles Magnier-Grandprez, was a former customs inspector whose vast personal wealth was rumoured to originate from his involvement in the Alsatian contraband trade.[19] Jean-Georges Humann, a delegate of the Strasbourg chamber of commerce in Paris, reported back to Strasbourg that 'Monsieur Grandprez ... harms our interests more than he serves them', because he was 'so notorious for having been a smuggler that his name has become proverbial', and that his support lent credence to the claims of their opponents that the campaign for transit was really intended to facilitate smuggling.[20] Royalists viewed the Alsatian campaign for transit as an attempt by revolutionary *parvenus* to consolidate their new wealth at the expense of honourable maritime merchant houses. For that reason, on 27 March 1818 'the entire right [royalist] side of the assembly stood up in order to reject transit', and the ban on the importation of colonial goods by land borders was not lifted until after the 1830 Revolution.[21]

Reviving the colonial economy and colonial trade, 1815–1825

In addition to the extraordinary measures taken to encourage the resurgence of the re-export trade of Atlantic ports, the Bourbon Restoration endeavoured to resurrect one of the main sources of the trade, the tightly regulated French colonial economy. With regard to the colonies returned to France at the Peace of Paris in 1814, the old *Exclusif* legislation was upheld and even reinforced by new tariffs that secured a monopoly for colonial producers on the metropolitan market.[22] Desperate efforts were also made to restore some form of French sovereignty over, and encourage trade with, the breakaway colony of Saint-Domingue.

In the colonies recovered after the fall of Napoleon (Martinique, Guadeloupe, Bourbon, Senegal), political reaction often went further than in the metropole, notably with the reintroduction of severe racial discrimination. As for trade regulations, the minister of the Navy and Colonies, Victor Malouet, a former administrator at Saint-Domingue and defender of slavery in the Constituent Assembly, pronounced himself for the restoration of the 'commercial ... old regime'. The recommendations to the Intendant and the Gouverneur of Martinique on 16 August 1814 were typical: the 'rules to follow' were 'the regulations of 24 March 1763, the ordinances of 25 January 1765 and 20 December 1783, the Code de la Martinique and the 1777 instructions to the Marquis de Bouillé and the Président de Tascher', in addition to the 'decision of 30 August 1784' on the *Exclusif* legislation. More succinct instructions enjoined the new administrators of Bourbon to 'uphold strictly the prohibitive regime' and the administrators of Senegal to 'uphold the prohibitive regime'.[23]

At the 1814 Peace of Paris, the Restoration had also obtained the continuation of the French slave trade for five years. The opportunistic abolition of the trade by Napoleon—to gain British and domestic liberal sympathies—during the Hundred Days, which the weakened Bourbons were in no position to repeal after Waterloo, dealt a severe blow to the hopes of reviving the plantation economy. Yet abolition was not sincerely implemented by the Bourbon regime. It is telling that in the 'correspondance générale' of the Bureau Central of the Ministry of the Marine and Colonies between 1815 and 1824, there are no apparent instructions on the repression of the slave trade. Serge Daget has shown that the illegal French slave trade thrived after 1815 (see Figure 12.1):

with the average annual number of slaves transported reaching 17,000 in the years 1821–1825, the French slave trade matched the numbers of the 1770s and only ranked second in post-Napoleonic Europe, after that of Portugal.[24] The main centre of French slave trading remained, as before the Revolution, Nantes, and even though the illegality of the resurgent French slave trade limits the number of available sources, it is difficult to imagine that it was not nurtured by the memories of its high profitability in the 1780s.[25]

Yet the relaxation of restrictions on colonial trade in other empires and the emergence of new producers triggered, after 1820, a long-term decline in the price of sugar, coffee and other colonial goods on world markets. Combined with the depletion of the slave labour force, and other damages inflicted during the wars of 1793–1815, these global transformations made the colonial products of Martinique, Guadeloupe and Bourbon unable to withstand foreign competition. In order to revive colonial production, it became necessary to shield French colonial producers from their Cuban, Brazilian or Asian competitors by means of a preferential tariff on the French metropolitan market. The *surtaxe* or additional tax on foreign sugar increased from 25 francs per 100kg in 1816 to 55 francs in 1822 and 75 francs in 1826, by which date overall duties on foreign sugar (120 francs) were nearly three times as high as the duties on French colonial sugar (45 francs) and tantamount to a

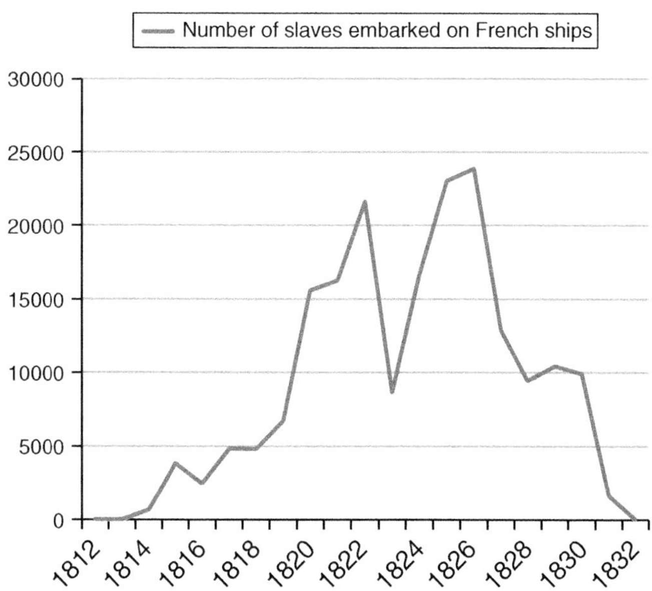

Figure 12.1 The French slave trade, 1812–1832
Source: 'The Transatlantic Slave Trade Database: Voyages', http://www.slavevoyages.org Accessed: 11 April 2013).

prohibition. Whereas the old *Exclusif* mainly benefited the metropole at the expense of the colonies, its revamped version after 1815 encouraged colonial producers to the detriment of metropolitan consumers.

This increase in the *surtaxe* on sugar gave rise to fierce debates in the Chamber of Deputies which again pitted royalist deputies from the Atlantic ports against liberal deputies from the north and the east. Even more than the Atlantic seaports, the colonial lobby had strong ties with reactionary royalism. Its most influential spokesmen were the Comte de Vaublanc, a plantation owner and minister of the interior during the White Terror of 1815–1816, and the Comte de Villèle, a former navy officer and Bourbon *colon*, who was premier from 1821 until 1828. Led by Benjamin Constant, liberal representatives described the increase in the 1822 sugar tariff as a 'privilégiaire' measure that would resuscitate in a new guise 'the greedy monopoly of commercial companies'.[26] The *surtaxe* reduced tax receipts on sugar imports as well as consumption, but it brought about what has been described as a last 'golden age' of the plantation economy in France's remaining Antilles, and spurred the development of Bourbon in the Indian Ocean.[27] It also resulted in an extraordinary revival of French colonial trade between 1815 and 1825 (Figure 12.2):

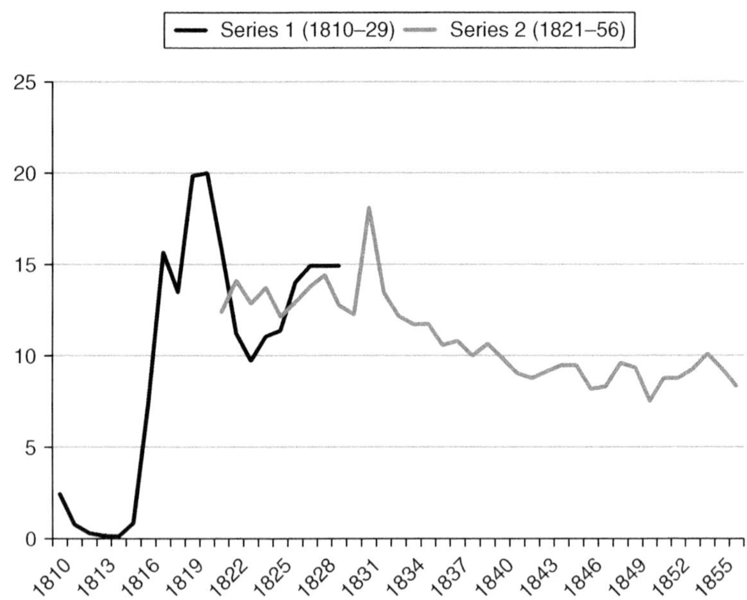

Figure 12.2 Share of colonial imports in total French imports, 1810–1856 (official values, percentage)
Source: David Todd, 'A French Imperial Meridian, 1814–1870', *Past & Present*, 210 (2011): 155–186, Figure 1; series 1 is based on data from the *Direction du commerce* at the Ministry of the Interior and series 2 on data from the Customs administration.

despite the loss of Saint-Domingue, the share of colonial imports in France's overall imports reached approximately 15 percent in the 1820s. Even though such a proportion remained well below the 35–40 per cent achieved by colonial imports before 1790, it would not be matched again until the 1910s.

The Restoration also endeavoured to recapture the legendary trade with Saint-Domingue, over which the 1814 peace treaty had confirmed France's sovereignty. Former planters relentlessly lobbied in favour of measures to restore effective control. In just six months, between April and October 1814, the Ministry of the Marine and Colonies received no fewer than 53 memoranda by former *colons* and administrators. The memoranda ceaselessly retold the story of the colony's fabulous wealth and were adamant that its prosperity could be revived, thanks to the re-imposition of slavery or another form of coerced labour. They urged the government to undertake a military expedition, attributing the disastrous outcome of the attempt made in 1802 to poor leadership. 'Saint-Domingue was a Peru [an El Dorado] before the French Revolution', wrote a planter, 'it can become again what it was, for its own benefit and the metropole's'.[28] They often exaggerated the riches they had lost during the Haitian Revolution, either honestly or with the hope of obtaining a larger indemnity.[29] Racial prejudice about the alleged incapacity of coloured insurgents to govern themselves and the lack of reliable information on the actual condition of former plantations further encouraged the perpetuation of fantasies about the economic advantages to be derived from the reassertion of French control.

In 1815, after the disaster of the Hundred Days, ministers refused to undertake what would have been a costly and hazardous military expedition. However, in subsequent years, the Restoration repeatedly offered Haitian rulers political autonomy in return for the acknowledgement of French sovereignty or suzerainty.[30] In order to encourage even a partial reintegration in the French colonial economy, an ordinance in 1816 authorized the resumption of trade with Saint-Domingue. The new legislation subjected imported goods to only half of the *surtaxe* on foreign colonial goods, in effect treating Haitian products as semi-French colonial goods.[31] The number of licences granted to French ships bound to Saint-Domingue rose from 11 in 1816 to 82 in 1821, before falling back to 44 in 1823. About a third of the ships departed from Bordeaux, also the main seat of direct trade with Saint-Domingue before 1789.[32] The incomplete data that is available suggests a modest resurgence of Franco-Haitian trade as a result of the measure, with imports in the early 1820s reaching approximately a tenth of their pre-revolutionary level (Figure 12.3).

The preferential treatment did not entice Haitian rulers to come to an arrangement about the status of the island, while the customs administration suspected that a large proportion of imports from Saint-Domingue were in fact re-exported Cuban products, so the 1816 ordinance was repealed in 1824. The following year, the Villèle government launched a limited naval

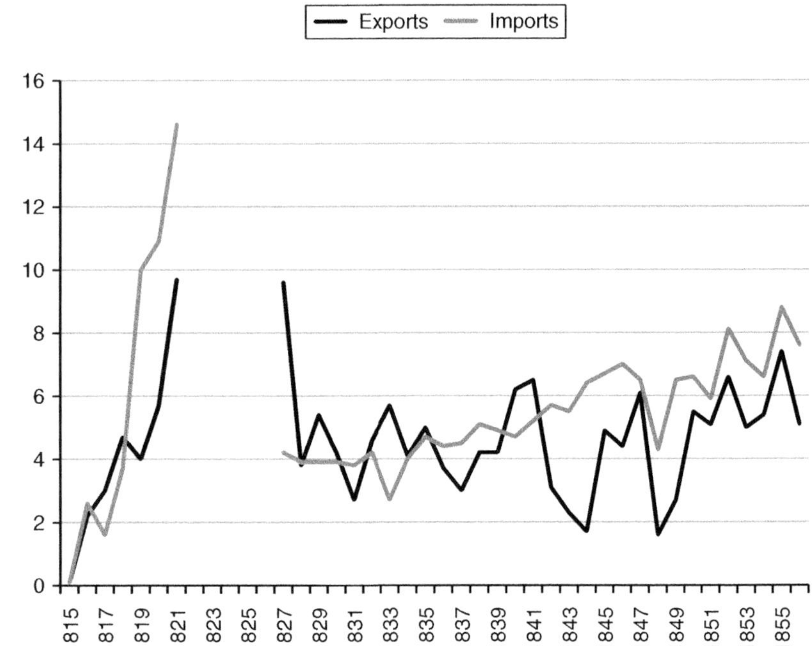

Figure 12.3 French trade with Haiti, 1815–1856 (official values, in millions of francs)
Source: AN, F12 251, *balance du commerce and tableaux* for the years 1815–1821; and Direction générale des douanes, *Tableau décennal du commerce de la France avec ses colonies et les puissances étrangères*, 7 vols (Paris, 1838–1898) for the years 1827–1856. The figures here are drawn from volumes 1, 2 and 3.

expedition to present Jean-Baptiste Boyer, the Haitian president, with an ultimatum: France would recognize Haiti's independence, but in return for significant commercial privileges and a 150 million franc indemnity as compensation for the expropriated planters.

Threatened with a permanent blockade if he rejected the offer, Boyer caved in. Secret clauses also banned Haitian citizens from travelling to French colonies and forced the Haitian government to contract the loans for the indemnity on the Paris market, with a view to making the island financially dependent on France. Even the recognition of Haitian independence amounted not so much to a renunciation of its fabled riches, but an attempt to regain them by other means. According to the officer at the head of the 1825 expedition, Haiti would become again 'a Province of France, which will yield a lot and cost nothing'.[33] New disillusions would rapidly ensue, as Haitian rulers evaded the commercial provisions of the treaty and as the country proved unable to pay the indemnity.[34] However, it took more than 20 years after the proclamation of Haitian independence on 1 January 1804 for the mirage of Saint-Domingue's riches to be finally dispelled.

In addition to economic nostalgia and geopolitical considerations, such as solidarity with the Spanish Bourbons' efforts to reassert control over their own breakaway colonies in the Americas, memories of the extraordinary violence of the Saint-Domingue insurgencies contributed to the Restoration's reluctance to concede political legitimacy to the Haitian regime. After a meeting of the cabinet rejected the recognition of independence in January 1821, Charles Esmangart, the chief negotiator with Haitian rulers and himself a warm supporter of recognition as a means of reviving France's Atlantic trade, admitted to the Duc de Richelieu, then Premier, that 'no one, however, would not take fright at the responsibility [of such a decision] when opinions as important and as respected as those of Monsieur Lainé and Monsieur de Villèle [both members of the cabinet] make you fear a general massacre of the whites in our other colonies'.[35] Joachim Laîné and Villèle, two major political figures, had been in Saint-Domingue in the early 1790s, the former as the legal representative of several Bordeaux merchants and the latter as a naval officer. Such personal experiences of the Ancien Régime's colonial economy and its discomfiture were rarely far below the surface of the Restoration regime's persistent attempts to bring it back to life.

Disillusions and the reconfiguring of economic memories, 1825–1830

In the second half of the 1820s, the commercial strategy of the Restoration reached its limits. After its rapid recovery in the late 1810s, trade with the old colonies grew slowly or stagnated. The paucity of official statistics about re-exports until 1825 makes it difficult to determine its trend before that date, but existing figures show a decline for the last years of the regime, from 123 million francs in 1825 to 104 million in 1829. Most damning for a mercantilist policy intent on increasing the surplus of the balance of trade was the latter's decline from a yearly average of 196 million francs between 1816 and 1820 to 35 million between 1826 and 1830, due to the stagnation of exports and a steady rise in imports.[36]

Attempts at reviving France's Mediterranean trade had been, if anything, more disappointing than the efforts to resuscitate Atlantic prosperity. In 1814, the Restoration had reinstated Marseille's *franchise*, a free port status conceded in 1669 and repealed on 11 Nivôse Year III (31 December 1794). The *franchise* failed to revive trade with the Levant and was replaced by warehousing privileges in 1817. The Bourbon government also sought to restore the privileges of French merchants in the Ottoman Empire. For example, in 1817, it bought back a set of commercial privileges—the 'concessions d'Afrique'—from the Dey of Algiers, which had been acquired by Britain in 1806. The government hoped to confer the privileges upon a resuscitated *Compagnie d'Afrique*, a monopoly company abolished by the Convention. However, Marseille merchants proved reluctant to invest capital in the venture and the *concessions* were attributed to the *Agence d'Afrique*, run by the Ministry of Foreign Affairs. Trade with the Regency of Algiers stagnated well below its pre-revolutionary level, while the *Agence d'Afrique*, in contrast to the highly profitable *Compagnie* before 1789, posted an average yearly loss of 50,000 francs between 1821 and 1823. An 1825 report on this unsatisfactory state of affairs suggested the transformation of the *concessions* into 'a kind of colonial regime', which would encourage the cultivation of tropical products in the Regency.[37] In this exceptional instance, commercial frustration would contribute to the outbreak of a military conflict in 1827 and formal colonization after 1830.[38]

The poor performance of French external trade after 1820 cannot be solely attributed to the Restoration's reactionary commercial policies. At most, one might argue that these policies proved ill-adapted responses to the deflationary context of the 1820s and the severe financial and commercial crisis set off by the bankruptcy of several newly-independent Latin American countries in 1825. Nonetheless, it was tempting for contemporaries to blame the regime, and commercial disillusionment helped to undermine support for the Restoration in the late 1820s.[39]

Disappointment was particularly acute in Bordeaux, where it encouraged a reinterpretation of the economic past and the adoption of more liberal political and economic ideas. An important figure in this local reconfiguration of economic memories was the liberal publicist Henri Fonfrède, also the owner of a small vineyard and partner in a commercial firm that went bankrupt in 1827.[40] Fonfrède's family history was entangled with the bloodiest phase of the Revolution: his father was Jean-Baptiste Boyer-Fonfrède, a representative of the Gironde at the Convention, who voted for the death of Louis XVI, but was executed in October 1793 after he contested the legality of the Montagnard coup of 31 May–2 June. A report from the Restoration prefect of the Gironde described Fonfrède *fils* as the 'son of a Regicide' and 'a boundless fanatic in terms of his political opinions'.[41] After 1825, Fonfrède took advantage of local commercial discontent to promote a more subtle economic interpretation of the Revolution, which blamed the decline of the southwest not on the entire revolutionary period, but on its most illiberal moments, 1793 and the Napoleonic regime. His diagnosis pointed to free trade rather than neo-mercantilism as the appropriate remedy for Bordeaux's commercial decay, combined with radical political change if necessary.

Fonfrède devised his interpretation in response to the claims of Charles Dupin, a former engineer in the Napoleonic navy and statistician, who attributed the growing economic superiority of France's northern provinces to higher levels of school enrolment and a more solid work ethic. Fonfrède retorted that the south was much richer than the north before 1789 and that it was the economic policies of the Terror and the First Empire that caused its decline. In 1793, the southern and moderate Girondin party, which supported only 'relative equality', was defeated by the northern and fanatical Montagnards, who stood for 'absolute equality'. Then, 'as the terror extended its iron fist, ... proscriptions fell hardest on the South. We cannot forget the accusations of *fédéralisme, modérantisme* and *négociantisme* levelled against us. Nantes, Bordeaux, Marseille, Lyon will remember them for a long time'. The wealthy south had been the main victim of the Maximum laws and the hyperinflation caused by the *assignats*. Fonfrède was less hostile to Napoleon than Jacobin extremism, but he argued that the Emperor's determination to wage economic war on Britain had sealed the commercial fate of France's southern provinces: as a result of 'permanent maritime warfare' and 'the necessity of a continental blockade to try and make commercial ruin mutual', 'the decay of the agricultural departments of the south was thoroughly completed'. By contrast, manufacturing in the northern provinces enjoyed an 'immense development', thanks to the ban on British goods and the extension of French rule across the Continent.[42] The Restoration's decision to maintain high tariffs on imported manufactured goods after 1815 explained the failure of attempts to revive maritime trade. Only free trade, an essential component of what he called 'veritable liberalism', could revive Bordeaux's commercial fortunes.[43]

Fonfrède's reinterpretation of the economic consequences of the years between 1789 and 1815 facilitated the conversion of merchants and vineyard proprietors to political liberalism and free trade. Whereas in the March 1824 general election all eight deputies of the Gironde were royalists, at the November 1827 election the department returned seven liberals and a single royalist—a much wider swing in favour of liberals than in the rest of the country.[44] Fonfrède's press articles also redirected nostalgia for pre-revolutionary prosperity towards demands for the liberalization of trade policy. In April 1828, a petition by 12,000 winegrowers from the Gironde against 'the prohibitive system of customs' was addressed to the Chamber of Deputies. The text combined Fonfrède's arguments with memories of the pre-revolutionary prosperity and the traditional language of the balance of trade: 'The balance of [our] exchanges [before 1789] was very advantageous because it was paid for in silver and amounted every year to more than 80 million francs'.[45]

In 1829, the winegrowers of 71 other departments or *arrondissements* petitioned in support of the Gironde's laments. The winegrowers of the Landes department, for example, complained that 'exportation from the port of Bayonne before 1790 amounted to, on average, 25,000 barrels of three hectolitres, whereas it has only been, on average over the past ten years, 5,597 barrels'.[46] However, in continental regions such as Burgundy, demands for the repeal of high tariffs expressed nostalgia for the Napoleonic era rather than the Ancien Régime, as for instance in a petition by the winegrowers of the Beaune *arrondissement*:

> Nothing is better remembered among tradesmen than the vast number of shipments then made by vineyards in Burgundy, Champagne and Lorraine beyond France's current borders! Who could compare the

> consumption that was then at our disposal in Belgium and Germany with today's smaller opportunities for our exports in the same countries, as a result of the more or less repulsive character imparted upon their tariffs by the French tariff? Can one forget that [under Napoleon] there were no more barriers for our products because Europe was a military dependency and France numbered 150 [*sic*] departments, peopled by fifty million consumers![47]

The protests of the wine industry, one of France's largest with approximately two million workers, played an often underestimated role in the process which led to the downfall of the Bourbons in 1830.[48] However, the new, more flexible use of references to the economic past in debates about commercial policy also reflected the growing temporal distance of the revolutionary era and the greater malleability of economic memories. Fonfrède was born in 1788 and could not have had many recollections of Bordeaux's commercial splendour under the Ancien Régime. The author of the Beaune petition, the magistrate Théophile Foisset, was born in 1800 and could not have had much direct experience of the wine trade's alleged prosperity under Napoleon.

The fading of economic memories accelerated after the advent of the July Monarchy in 1830. The *Orléaniste* regime abolished the restrictions on transit and warehousing in 1831 and did little to prevent the growth of the domestic beet sugar industry from inflicting fatal damage on the economy of the plantation islands. At the same time, the July Monarchy maintained high tariffs on imports of foodstuffs and manufactured goods. However, such protectionism was intended to encourage the growth of the domestic market rather than the re-exportation of colonial goods. The 1830 Revolution thus smothered hopes of reviving the economic as well as the political past. As the controversy over the level of protection against foreign competition superseded debates about specific commercial regulations, free traders and protectionists continued to invoke the past. The former often described themselves as the heirs of the 1789 Constituents, intent on abolishing privileges, while the latter attributed the downfall of the Ancien Régime to the allegedly disastrous 1786 commercial treaty with Britain, or celebrated Napoleon's Continental Blockade as a model of economic patriotism.[49] These were more or less dishonest uses of the past to provide legitimacy to present goals rather than instances of the influence of memory.

Conclusion

It is difficult not to agree with François Crouzet that the main long-term economic consequence of the revolutionary era for France was a shift from Atlantic commerce to continental manufacturing. However, long-term consequences can take a long time to become apparent and they are not always the product of linear and continuous processes. In the aftermath of the fall of Napoleon, a large number of contemporaries were confident that the old channels of colonial trade could be revived, from the slave trade with Africa to the importation of colonial goods from Saint-Domingue. Such hopes helped to shape the Bourbon Restoration's commercial policies, which in turn facilitated a brief and partial resurgence of the colonial economy. Economists might interpret this sequence as illustrating the short-term influence of anticipations on economic activity, but historians will be inclined to stress the role of past experiences and memories in fashioning anticipations.

Ultimately the economic strategy of the Restoration proved unsuccessful, as France's external trade stagnated and the ensuing commercial malaise helped to nurture disaffection for the regime. Yet it would be unfair to dismiss this strategy as irrational or doomed to fail. Hopes of a revival were informed by nostalgia, but also by the experience of the rapid commercial recoveries that followed previous returns to peace in 1763, 1783 and 1802. Crouzet argued that the extraordinary intensity of Anglo-French commercial warfare between 1805 and 1813 resulted in irreversible changes in the patterns of European commerce and economic growth. The initial partial success of the Restoration's policies suggests that such conclusions need to be nuanced and that these changes should be attributed to a broader set of causes. Only after about 1820 did the price of colonial goods on world markets decline steeply, making the French colonial economy uncompetitive. What rendered the effects of the British and Napoleonic blockades on European economies irreversible was the global economic transformations of the years from 1780 to 1825, ranging from the collapse of European mercantilist empires in the Americas to the emergence of new producers of colonial goods in Asia.[50]

Notes

1. Ernest Labrousse, *La crise de l'économie française à la fin de l'Ancien Régime* (Paris, 1943).
2. François Crouzet, 'Les conséquences économiques de la Révolution: A propos d'un inédit de Sir François d'Ivernois', *Annales historiques de la Révolution française* 168 (1962): 182–217, and 169 (1962): 336–362; and idem.,: 'Wars, Blockade and Economic Change in Europe, 1792–1815', *Journal of Economic History* 24 (1964): 567–588.
3. Patrick O'Brien and Caglar Keyder, *Economic Growth in Britain and France, 1780–1914: Two Paths to the Twentieth Century* (London, 1978), 178; and François Crouzet, 'The Historiography of French Economic Growth in the Nineteenth Century', *Economic History Review* 56 (2003): 215–242.
4. Jeff Horn, *The Path not Taken: French Industrialization in the Age of Revolution, 1750–1830* (Cambridge, MA, 2006).
5. François Furet, *La Révolution: de Turgot à Jules Ferry, 1770–1880*, 2 vols (Paris, 1988), vol. 1, 21–112; and Alain Laquièze, *Les origines du régime parlementaire en France, 1814–1848* (Paris, 2002), 59–76.

6. Guillaume Daudin, *Commerce et prospérité: La France au XVIIIe siècle* (Paris, 2005).
7. Silvia Marzagalli, 'Le négoce maritime et la rupture révolutionnaire: Un ancien débat revisité', *Annales historiques de la Révolution française* 352 (2008): 183–207.
8. André-Jean Tudesq, 'La Restauration: Renaissance et déceptions', in *Bordeaux au XIXe siècle*, ed. Louis Desgraves and Georges Dupeux (Bordeaux, 1969), 35–59.
9. Jérôme Mavidal and Emile Colombey (eds), *Archives Parlementaires*, 126 vols (Paris, 1862–1912), vol. 17, 257.
10. 'The chamber of commerce to the director general of the customs administration', 16 June 1818 and 27 October 1820, Archives Départementales de la Gironde, Bordeaux (hereafter ADG), 02/081/277, register 1818–1822, fols 7–10, 108–112.
11. 'The chamber of commerce to the mayor', 7 August 1821, ADG, 02/081/277, register 1818–1822, fols. 135–136; and 'Minutes', 19 July 1824. ADG, 02 /081/305, register 1823–1825, fol. 46.
12. John Bosher, *The Single Duty Project* (London, 1964), 5–7.
13. Anonym, *Du transit d'Alsace* (Strasbourg, 1818); Anonym, *Quelques observations en faveur du transit d'Alsace* (Strasbourg, 1818); and Anonym, *Encore un mot du transit d'Alsace* (Strasbourg, 1818); numbers of copies printed in: Archives Nationales, Paris (Pierrefitte-sur-Seine) (hereafter AN), F18*II 4, impressions 3933, 4247 and 4334.
14. J. Schott and Christian Hiller, *Transit par l'Alsace: réclamations des communes situées depuis Lauterbourg jusqu'à Strasbourg* (Strasbourg, 1819), 3.
15. *Archives parlementaires*, vol. 21, 464.
16. Charles Henri Schattenmann, a delegate of the chamber, of commerce, to Jean-Georges Schertz, its vice-president, 5 April 1818, Archives Départementales du Bas-Rhin, Strasbourg (hereafter ADBR), 79 J 70.
17. *Archives Parlementaires*, vol. 21, 368.
18. Ibid., 488.
19. Paul Leuilliot, *L'Alsace au début du XIXe siècle*, 3 vols (Paris, 1959–60), vol. 2, 257–258; and Geoffrey Ellis, *Napoleon's Continental Blockade: The Case of Alsace* (Oxford, 1981), 207–208.
20. Jean-Georges Humann to Jean-Georges Schertz, 7 January 1818, ADBR, 79 J 71.
21. Jean-Georges Humann to Jean-Georges Schertz, 27 March 1818, Ibid.
22. Jean Tarrade, *Le commerce colonial de la France à la fin de l'Ancien Régime: L'évolution du régime de 'l'Exclusif' de 1763 à 1789*, 2 vols (Paris, 1972).
23. 'Instructions' X (15 August 1814), XI (16 August 1814), XVIII (10 October 1814) and XXV (9 January 1815), Centre des Archives d'Outre-Mer, Aix-en-Provence (hereafter CAOM), 11 COL 61.
24. Serge Daget, *Répertoire des expéditions négrières françaises à la traite illégale, 1814–1850* (Nantes, 1988).
25. Guillaume Daudin, 'Profitability of Slave and Long-Distance Trading in Context: The Case of Eighteenth-Century France', *Journal of Economic History* 64 (2004): 144–171.
26. *Archives Parlementaires*, vol. 36, 733 and vol. 37, 94.
27. Paul Butel, *Histoire des Antilles françaises, XVIIe–XXe siècles* (Paris, 2002), 246–259.
28. 'Sur St Domingue', by Le Dué-Rouleau, July 1814, CAOM, CC9a 47.
29. Jean Hébrard, 'Les deux vies de Michel Vincent, colon à Saint-Domingue, c.1730–1804', *Revue d'histoire moderne et contemporaine* 57 (2010): 50–78.
30. Jean-François Brière, *Haïti et la France, 1804–1848: Le rêve brisé* (Paris, 2008), 47–157.
31. 'Décision prise le 27 mars 1816 relativement au commerce avec St Domingue', CAOM, 11 COL 61, CLXII, fol. 72.

32. 'Etat général des navires dont l'expédition pour St Domingue a été autorisée', 11 April 1820 and 'Etat', n.d. [1824], CAOM, CC9c 7.
33. 'Extrait du rapport du Baron de Mackau', n. d. [1825], Archives des Affaires étrangères, Paris (La Courneuve) (hereafter AAE), Correspondance politique, Haiti, 1, fols 25–26.
34. Frédérique Beauvois, 'L'indemnité de Saint-Domingue: "Dette d'indépendance" ou "rançon de l'esclavage"?', *French Colonial History* 10 (2009): 109–124.
35. 'Esmangart to Richelieu', 6 January 1821, AAE, Correspondance politique, Haiti, 2, fols 67–69.
36. Ministère des travaux publics, de l'agriculture et du commerce, *Statistique de la France*, 10 vols (Paris, 1838), vol. 7, 8–12.
37. 'Rapport sur les concessions d'Afrique', 16 September 1825, AN, F12 2620.
38. David Todd, 'Retour sur l'expédition d'Alger: les faux semblants d'un tournant colonialiste français', *Revue d'histoire moderne et contemporaine* 63, 1 (2016).
39. Maurice Lévy-Leboyer, *Les banques européennes et l'industrialisation internationale dans la première moitié du XIX*[e] *siècle* (Paris, 1964), 464–488; and Ronald Findlay and Kevin O'Rourke, *Power and Plenty: Trade, War, and the World Economy in the Second Millenium* (Princeton, 2007), 369–378.
40. On Fonfrède's economic ideas and influence, see David Todd, *L'identité économique de la France: Libre-échange et protectionnisme, 1814–1851* (Paris, 2008), 121–159.
41. 2 July 1827, AN, F7 6769, file 7.
42. 'Des départements du Nord et du Midi', 2nd and 3rd articles, *L'indicateur bordelais*, 4 January and 11 January 1827.
43. 'Des départements', 7th article, *L'indicateur bordelais*, 7 December 1827.
44. Sherman Kent, *The Election of 1827 in France* (Cambridge, MA, 1975).
45. [Etienne Hervé], *Pétition des propriétaires de vignes du département de la Gironde* (Bordeaux, 1828), 5–6.
46. 'Propriétaires de vignes des Landes', 1 February 1829, AN, C 2097.
47. 'Mémoire à l'appui de la pétition', n. d. [1829], Archives Départementales de la Côte d'Or, Dijon, 34 J 41.
48. Pamela Pilbeam, 'The Economic Crisis of 1827–1832 and the 1830 Revolution in Provincial France', *Historical Journal* 32 (1989): 319–338.
49. Todd, *Identité économique*, 331–379.
50. On transnational and global perspectives in the revolutionary era, see David Armitage and Sanjay Subrahmanyam (eds), *The Age of Revolutions in Global Context, c.1760–1840* (Basingstoke, 2010); and Suzanne Desan et al. (eds), *The French Revolution in Global Perspective* (Ithaca, NY, 2013).

13

Postwar Cities: The Cost of the Wars of 1813–1815 on Society in Hamburg and Leipzig

Katherine B. Aaslestad

'The years 1813 and 1814 are happy years indeed in deciding the inner independence of Europe [from French rule]. But they have also cost tears'.[1] With this bittersweet observation Pastor Karl Zimmerman began his account of the destruction of Hamm, his village outside Hamburg. The clergyman celebrated the Allied defeat of Napoleon in 1814, but stressed the burdens of war bequeathed to the postwar period. Merchant and shipowner Peter Godeffroy recounted these hardships in a series of letters in 1814. Godeffroy's letters to his daughter in England from his estate in Dockenhunden on the Elbe outside Hamburg, describing the destruction of Hamburg's suburbs, villages and gardens, provide lengthy accounts of requisitions by the occupying French military, and enumerate the fiscal cost and the miseries of those inside and outside of occupied Hamburg. His letters narrate the daily burden of billeting large numbers of soldiers as Russians replaced the French on his estate, the physical destruction of occupied Hamburg under Marshal Davout, and the many impoverished expellees who sought shelter on his property. Godeffroy's greatest loss, however, was beyond calculation; his son Jack, a second lieutenant in the cavalry of the Hanseatic Legion, a volunteer unit formed from citizens of the Hanseatic cities, fell in the Battle of Dutzow in Mecklenburg-West Pomerania.[2] The social trauma and costs of the war continued after the fighting ceased and armies moved on, as Godeffroy's case reveals. New armies of occupation as well as local militias appeared, expecting housing and provisions. A quarter-century of unremitting war between 1792 and 1815 produced non-combatants driven from their homes, war refugees dependent on charity, shattered commerce and infrastructure, mounting debt and thousands of soldiers, some wounded, returning home to resume civilian life. Transition from war to peace, from combat to stability, remained complex and socially tense.

The Napoleonic period has attracted much attention for its wars and politics, but scholars have neglected to examine the social and economic costs of the wars that affected German states between 1805 and 1815 and their aftermath. The decades after 1815 should be conceptualized more systematically as a postwar period. This approach provides new insights into how wars influence society long after combat ceases. The small number of studies that address the years after the Napoleonic Wars demonstrate the immediate consequences of the war: destruction and violence, economic, political and social disorder, and the construction of postwar memory.[3] They underscore that the postwar period is more than just a transition from a wartime to peacetime society. Rather, the postwar period comprises the staggering consequences of war, including collective experiences of violence, economic disruption, social and political collapse, and the longing for stability, prosperity and normalcy.

This chapter explores the immediate aftermath of the Wars of 1813–1815 on the civilian populations of Hamburg and Leipzig to reveal the conflicts' lingering legacy. By exploring the consequences of military occupation and combat on non-combatants and the efforts to aid them, it expands the reach of the war to raise the question: who carries the cost of the war? Focusing on material losses, displaced civilians, and those who assisted them in two cities, the chapter studies the effects of war and reconstruction on a local level and reveals the process by which groups lost, gained or expanded levels of social legitimacy during the transition from war to peace. The republican city-state of Hamburg, a port and trading *entrepôt* with well over 100,000 inhabitants in 1800, and the Saxon city of Leipzig, a commercial hub with about 32,000 residents in 1800, together with their surrounding towns and villages, are excellent subjects for a comparative local study of war. They were two of the regions in German Central Europe most afflicted by the Wars of 1813–1815. Moreover, prior to those campaigns, they shared experiences of economic decline due to the Continental System and to military requisitions and billeting. During the wars they suffered severe destruction and violence with the siege of Hamburg from 1813 to 1814 and the Battle of Leipzig in 1813. Residents faced material loss, displacement, epidemic illness and occupation by Russian liberators following the withdrawal of French forces. Republican Hamburg, annexed to the French Empire in early 1811, emerged from the wars with its sovereignty intact, whereas the Saxon Kingdom, Napoleon's last German ally, lost two-thirds of its territory to Prussia. A comparative study of the two cities, with different wartime and postwar allegiances and dissimilar economic and political structures, reveals the way in which different regions and states—a republican city-state and an Ancien Régime monarchy—responded to common post-conflict conditions.

War destruction in Hamburg and Leipzig, 1813–1814

The postwar history of the two cities begins with the trauma they experienced during the last years of war in 1813–1814.[4] The siege of Hamburg, which lasted until Napoleon's final defeat in April 1814, brought new hardships to the north German population. During a brief period of liberation in the spring of 1813, Hamburg and Lübeck united to form two voluntary militias, the Hanseatic Legion and Hanseatic Citizens' Guard, to defend their autonomy. These militias depended on civilian mobilization to outfit and provision them, but even with assistance from the Russian army and Cossacks, the militias could prevent neither Hamburg nor Lübeck from falling again to the French by late May. Holding Hamburg became the main goal of French operations in north Germany, and Napoleon demanded that the city be transformed into a military stronghold able to withstand both surprise attack and extended siege. This process changed the face of the city and caused hitherto unknown misery for its population. Along with heavy requisitions of buildings, food and wagons, the French finally emptied the Bank of Hamburg. Marshal Davout also required all of Hamburg's inhabitants to provision their households with enough food and fuel to last six months. Most Hamburgers, living from one week to the next in the dire economic situation, found it impossible to meet these expectations, and hundreds fled the city seeking refuge in neighbouring areas. During the Christmas season, Davout drove up to 25,000 of Hamburg's poorest and weakest residents out of their city and into the cold winter. Davout defended the expulsion as a military necessity and considered civilian distress of secondary importance.[5]

To clear fields of fire for the artillery, Davout levelled all the towns, gardens and farms surrounding the city, and burned the remaining suburbs of Hamburger Berg (Saint Pauli), Schulterblatt, Pöseldorf, Grindel and Hamm. Davout's policies led to the displacement of thousands of civilians across northern Germany and wide-scale destruction within Hamburg and in its environs. Between December 1813 and January 1814, the French destroyed over 1,207 structures at a cost of over 35 million francs.[6] The French burned the city's old *Pesthof,* a hospital, necessitating refuge for 800 patients and 60 insane inmates, and closed the Foundling Orphanage, expelling over 360 children from the city. In Hamburger Berg, Davout's soldiers destroyed at least 484 buildings that included over 1,000 residences, and in Hamm burned and levelled over 400 buildings, including schools, workshops, large summer residences and small village cottages.[7] Residents often had only a few days, and in some cases only hours, to vacate their homes and remove their belongings before the entire village was burned. French soldiers harassed the frantic villagers and looted at will, and in many cases they destroyed structures to retrieve firewood for the city.

In Hamburg, the French destroyed buildings near the main gates and requisitioned numerous public and private buildings for use as barracks, military hospitals and magazines. The cost of the demolished buildings was estimated at 10.5 million francs and requisitioned buildings, food, wood, beds, straw, linen and other assorted goods amounted to nearly 11 million francs.[8] Food and wood became scarce once the siege began in earnest, and the military hospitals demanded straw, beds and linen. Requiring space to stable over 5,000 horses, the French procured the Exchange and four of the city's five main churches. During the siege, dead horses littered the streets, filth and excrement fouled canals, and increasingly desperate soldiers foraged for food, whilst the ill and wounded filled the growing number of military hospitals. After the French left the city in May 1814, the Russians moved in with over 6,000 horses and another expensive and exhaustive period of occupation began.[9]

In May 1813, the population of Leipzig and its environs encountered combat conditions during the nearby Battle of Lützen, when soldiers, the wounded, and field hospitals filled the city and burdened the population. Furthermore, the region suffered from Napoleon's 'scorched earth policy', the destruction of livestock, agriculture and all means of subsistence to deprive the Allied armies moving towards Leipzig of resources. Between 16 and 19 October, the decisive Battle of Leipzig forced Napoleon and his troops into retreat and generated catastrophic conditions in the area for at least the following year. A coalition of Britain, Russia, Prussia, Sweden and Austria, comprising over 301,000 men from a variety of nationalities, faced the 171,000 strong Grande Armée in a 'Battle of the Nations', the largest European battle prior to the Great War. In the course of combat, Napoleon lost his last allies from the Confederation of the Rhine, which he had founded in 1806, as they defected to the coalition forces fighting under the leadership of Austrian Prince Schwarzenberg. The opposing armies fought for four days in the villages surrounding Leipzig before the Allies attacked on 19 October, compelling the French to fall back and generating widespread destruction, loss of life and civilian displacement.[10]

The destruction of the villages surrounding Leipzig in the heat of battle was far less methodical and more violent than in Hamburg. From 16 to 18 October, villages outside the city faced bombardment and gunfire, and more than 20 villages were burned and plundered.[11] Fires illuminated the advance of the victorious Allied armies and the destruction of battle.[12] During and after the mêlée, marauding troops of all nations pillaged ruthlessly, leaving nothing for returning residents.[13] Farmers reported losses of entire harvests, including seeds for spring planting, horses, cattle, sheep, pigs and geese, along with property damage and the complete loss of homes, barns, schools and churches.[14]

On 19 October Leipzig itself faced bombardment, as the French refused to surrender the city without a fight. Although cannon fire destroyed or damaged several buildings, most of the destruction remained directly outside the city gates. Despite ferocious urban fighting and resistance by the French, the Allied forces won the day and paraded into a battle-worn city to a cheering populace. Contemporaries welcomed Prince Schwarzenberg and the Russian and Prussian monarchs, who ordered strict military discipline and spared Leipzig from the plunder and pillage that the surrounding villages faced.[15] Yet, the city endured tremendous challenges, including refugees seeking shelter, and vast numbers of wounded and dead. Corpses and horse carcasses rotted on the streets and filled the river. Prisoners of war and conscripted Leipzig citizens toiled over two weeks to retrieve and bury most of the dead. Over 15,000 French prisoners of war remained in the city, requiring food, shelter and clothing. Indeed, bread remained scarce until deliveries arrived from outlying towns. Material losses within the city amounted to approximately two million thaler, and the total sum for the damages in 63 villages came to another 3.5 million thaler.[16] In the aftermath of French defeat, the Russians occupied Leipzig for two years, and a deadly epidemic plagued the city until late spring following Napoleon's surrender in April 1814. In both Hamburg and Leipzig, material destruction, though colossal, remained secondary to the enormous problem of disease and homelessness.

Epidemics, displaced civilians and the emergence of relief associations

Hamburg and Leipzig experienced severe epidemics during the winter of 1813–1814, though they had more fatal consequences in Leipzig. In Hamburg, typhus caused high death tolls among the French by mid-winter. More and more homes and buildings were transformed into hospitals for sick French soldiers and additional beds, mattresses, dressings, bedding and clothing were requisitioned from the city's residents. Davout obliged Hamburg's doctors, surgeons and pharmacists to serve the French or face confinement. In February and March, between 60 and 100 soldiers died daily; the French dug their own mass grave in St Georg, where 11,000 imperial soldiers were ultimately laid to rest.[17] After departing in May 1814, the French abandoned almost 8,000 sick soldiers in military hospitals.[18] Illness spread from Hamburg to the smaller neighbouring cities, as thousands of expellees travelled to Altona and Lübeck. In makeshift hospitals volunteers sought to contain the epidemic by imposing a quarantine in Lübeck, but over 1,000 died, approximately one-fifth of the refugees in the city, despite the efforts of the voluntary medical personnel of the newly founded relief associations.

In Leipzig the scale of the epidemic and related deaths were far greater. At the start of the battle, over 20,000 wounded soldiers convalesced in Leipzig, and by the end, an additional 45,000 required care. The city hosted 56 military hospitals and an additional 2,000 wounded sought relief in the churches, schools and public buildings.[19] Of the 13,500 residents infected with epidemic fevers, 2,700 died during the winter months and an additional 1,000 when it reappeared in the spring. In a city where fewer than 20 people normally died a week, the death toll rose to over 200 a week. The *Leipziger Tageblatt* listed weekly the death and burial of prominent citizens, foreign soldiers and unknown refugees. The majority of the wounded and sick soldiers remained in the city until late 1814. By early 1814, 17 homes in Leipzig continued to serve as hospitals and contributed to the shortage of quarters for Russian soldiers, who stayed in Leipzig until 1816.[20]

In Hamburg's hinterland and the neighbouring cities, the need to provide shelter, food, clothing and medical care for over 45,000 displaced civilians, along with provisioning the local militias besieging the city, became the most pressing problem during the last months of the war for Hamburg's interim government in exile. After Davout expelled Hamburg's un-provisioned population during the Christmas season, additional expulsions continued into January. Due to the bitter cold weather, many expellees perished of exposure, hunger, and illness; 1,138 were buried in a mass grave outside Altona. By early 1814, one report estimated the number of expellees from Hamburg at 26,000, with an additional 20,000 displaced from Hamburg's decimated suburbs: 'on the streets leading to Lübeck and Bremen, one sees lines of hungry, half frozen children, women and elderly of all social groups'.[21]

A number of civilian relief organizations and women's associations emerged to meet the challenges of the distressed and uprooted civilians. The Crown Prince of Sweden offered 40,000 Reichsthaler to assist the expellees; he directed all expelled men to join the Hanseatic Citizens' Guard, and women, children and the elderly to seek refuge in Bremen and Lübeck. As the expellees poured into Hamburg's Danish neighbour Altona, the city's chief administrative officer, *Oberpräsident* Conrad Daniel von Blücher, and a number of wealthy Hamburgers, including merchant Otto von Axen, organized a Support Committee (*Unterstützungs-Committee*) to feed, house and clothe the growing numbers of civilian refugees. With the assistance of the Schleswig Holstein Patriotic Society, von Axen established a Fund for the Support of the Needy Residents from Hamburg (*Kasse zur Unterstützung der hülfsbedürftigen Einwohner aus Hamburg*), raising 20,000 *Mark Courant* by 3 January 1814.[22] He also called for a commission to distribute funds.[23] By early January, the lawyer and former mayor Amandus Abendroth of Hamburg, a freemason like von Blücher and von Axen, directed the Central Commission for the Support of Hamburg's Expellees (*Centralkommittee zur Unterstützung der ausgewanderten und vertriebenen Hamburger während der Belagerung der Stadt*) and coordinated efforts with subcommittees from Altona, Bremen and Lübeck to meet the needs of mounting numbers of refugees from the Hamburg region.

The expellees and war refugees in northern Germany represented a huge burden for their host communities. Those with means and contacts lodged in private homes, but most of the refugees required public support to meet their basic needs. Altona, part of the Kingdom of Denmark, faced a dire situation, surrounded by the French on one side and the Russians on the other, and cut off from its supplies in Danish Holstein. It experienced great shortfalls of all necessities. In early January 1814, the *Neue Bremer Zeitung* reported the arrival of at least 1,100 expellees in that city and a further 1,600 in Lübeck.[24] Amidst wartime deficiencies and hardship, assistance societies managed to feed, clothe and house the needy. By the middle of January 1814, 3,550 individuals had found food and lodging in an array of public buildings in Altona, including the small Church of the Brethren that housed over 125 individuals.[25] Even though most of the refugees travelled on to Lübeck and Bremen, Altona still hosted 3,019 refugees, cared for 592 in hospitals, and assisted 16,134 with food and travel money by May 1814.[26] Lübeck sheltered 5,495 Hamburgers, 3,663 in five quickly improvised public buildings, providing food, clothing, bedding and medical care.[27]

Relief organizations also coordinated with the women's organizations originally formed in 1813 to support the militias.[28] They collected money for the expellees at churches, concerts, lotteries and handicraft bazaars. The women's associations of Hamburg, Altona, Bremen and Lübeck collected and distributed food, clothing, shoes, linens and medicine to war refugees. In Lübeck, women established a Clothing Board and fed and nursed the 5,495 refugees who arrived there between January and June 1814.[29] Women from prominent Hamburg families established a hospice for refugees in Blankenese and coordinated with the Altona Commission to assist the refugees.[30] Anna Parish, of the prosperous and well-known Parish family, provided shelter, food, medical care, bedding and clothing to the cost of 21,630 marks for expellees at her home on the Elbe.[31] Friederike Godeffroy, the daughter of the wealthy merchant Pierre Godeffroy, one of ten women on the Altona Committee, provided food for the old, sick and abandoned children, and with other women contributed to a hospital for the refugees in Altona.[32]

In Saxony, the main battle ground of the campaigns of 1813, a Saxon Help and Reconstruction Committee (*Hilfs- und Wiederstellungskommission*) emerged in December 1813, less than two months after the Battle of Leipzig, for which each province and district had its own commission. This organization took subscriptions throughout Saxony to support the devastated parts of the kingdom, and distributed funds until April 1814.[33] In Leipzig, the Support Association for Leipzig Environs (*Unterstützungsverein für Leipzig's Umgebungen*) undertook a variety of tasks to address post-battle conditions by distributing funds raised abroad for the region. In addition, ten influential Leipzig residents organized the Support to the Distressed and Needy (*Unterstützung der Unglücklichen und Hilfsfbedürftigen*) in early January. These volunteers distributed alms and endeavoured to ensure uniform distribution of donations for the restoration of the former battlefields, in particular for the transmission of seed for spring planting in 1814.[34]

As in Hamburg, Leipzig's women's association collected money, clothing and household goods for the displaced and needy. Members of the Young Women's Association (*Jungfrauen-Verein*), established in February 1814, sold handiwork at a local coffee shop and raised 3,025 thaler. Women also undertook the urgent task of collecting and distributing clothing and bedding during the bitterly cold winter. In April and again in May, the Support Association held fundraising performances featuring Haydn in the Nikolai church. Likewise, the Committee of Art Friends encouraged residents to loan their private works to an art exhibition fundraiser.[35] These organizations attended to the very worst of the hardships for the needy, and embodied efforts within Leipzig's civil society to address wartime destruction as the Allies concluded the war.

In both cities, new relief organizations, mainly funded by educated and wealthy upper-class men and women, provided impressive leadership during the transition from war to peace, and they raised money from an array of international and local donors. Contributions arrived to assist Altona from Hamburgers in exile in Holstein and Denmark. Assistance for Bremen and Lübeck came from all parts of Prussia, Austria and the German South and West, but also from Great Britain, Russia and Sweden. Many benefactors were merchants from Hamburg or associated with Hanseatic commerce.[36] Press reports garnered wide material support for both Hamburg and Leipzig. German newspapers and pamphlet literature graphically recounted the fate of the expellees from Hamburg and the grisly aftermath of the Battle of Leipzig to generate sympathy and contributions. Members of Hamburg's interim government, in particular Jonas Ludwig von Hess in England and Karl Sieveking on the Continent, worked hard to gain international support and material aid by drawing attention to the siege.[37] Indeed, von Hess's arrival in London was announced in *The Times* and *The Examiner* which reported the fate of Hamburg amidst the 'unexampled tyranny of an implacable enemy'.[38] The most generous support came from Great Britain, where the events of the war in the German states had been well documented in merchant correspondence, and disseminated in the public sphere.[39]

The Committee for Relieving the Distress in Germany, founded in 1805 in London, reconvened in January 1814 'to send immediate succour to the places in the greatest need' through subscriptions and contributions. An example of nineteenth-century cosmopolitan humanitarianism, the Committee also contributed to public awareness of the hardships in German states through translated and published letters outlining civilian suffering in particular.[40] Funds were collected from donations at coffee shops and taverns, subscriptions, and contributions from a variety of local and denominational associations that included the London Committee, the elite Westminister Association and the Committee of Ladies at Clapham. A few days after the Battle of Waterloo, the Westminister Association organized a fundraising concert at Whitehall Chapel that included Prince Blücher, the Duke of Wellington, members of the royal family and the Speaker of the House of Commons.[41] Clergy, bankers and merchant networks communicated news and allocated the funding for each German region. There, local committees, clergy, or nobles distributed either the money or supplies among the needy. For example, between 14 January and 17 March 1814, the London Committee donated approximately £8,000 to assist the displaced from Hamburg and entrusted local Hanseatic committees to spend the funds appropriately.[42] The Lübeck Commission justified its expenses and reported to the committee in Britain that between 31 December and 28 February it spent £500 feeding expellees; the Commission established three cooking houses, served 119,148 meals, and distributed 20,285 loaves of bread.[43] Many leading members in the British Committee were merchants and bankers, Quakers and Nonconformists, abolitionists (including William Wilberforce) and expatriate Germans motivated by business and humanitarian concerns. Appeals to the general public also emphasized Britain's obligation to German lands, where Germans suffered for Britain's benefit: 'our battles have been fought and our victories have been won ... and English blood had been spared'.[44] The committees in Britain raised money for distressed Germans throughout the summer of 1814, and Parliament provided £100,000 for humanitarian assistance.

Like Hamburg, Leipzig benefited from the generosity of the international community, in particular the Committee for the Relieving the Distress in Germany. Several Leipzig merchant houses, Free and Co., Reichenback and Co., and Küstner and Co., turned to London to entreat patrons and friends to open a subscription to assist the inhabitants of the villages and hamlets in the vicinity of Leipzig ruined by war. In letters from Leipzig addressed to Rudolf Ackermann, a successful London bookseller originally from Saxony who became the central organizer in the Committee, Count Schönfeld and local clergy emphasized loss and destruction of livelihoods following the Battle of Leipzig. Schönfeld's letter, for example, reflected the sentiments of Pastor Karl Zimmerman from Hamm, cited at the start of this chapter; in his appeal he noted that 'while millions now are raising to the sound of triumph, there are in Saxony alone a million souls reduced to such misery too severe to be capable of taking part in the general joy'. These combined accounts of Saxon sacrifice and misery amidst Allied military success generated generous assistance from the Committee which awarded Saxony more funds than any other German region, ahead of Hamburg and northern Germany.[45] Indeed, Saxony received more than one-third of the parliamentary grant.[46]

Ongoing quartering, lack of compensation, and continuing poverty

Although the French had fled Saxony after the Battle of Leipzig, the city and its environs continued to quarter and provision Allied forces. The cities and towns in northern Germany experienced a similar fate during and after the siege of Hamburg, in particular the Duchies of Schleswig and Holstein. Saxony experienced Russian occupation, and King Friedrich August I faced house arrest near Berlin for his loyalty to the French. Although Leipzig suffered severe overcrowding due to the number of refugees, wounded soldiers and French prisoners of war, it became the administrative seat of the interim military administration, the General-Government, under a Russian lieutenant general, Count Repnin-Wolkonski. The General-Government charged locals to contain the epidemic, form a subscription to gain wood and other necessities from neighbouring areas, and clear the battlefields of the dead and wounded. It also demanded a forced contribution of two million thaler.[47] Despite the Russian administration's humanitarian efforts to import food for Leipzig's population in the weeks following the battle and efforts to quarantine sick soldiers, its main task was to raise money within Saxony to pay for the ongoing war. To that end, Leipzig had to establish a Central Tax Commission to support garrisons, military hospitals and Allied soldiers, and to access funds from provincial surpluses and commercial loans to address wartime losses.

The costs of occupying armies weighed heavily on communities struggling to return to normality following the defeat of Napoleon. The case of a French military hospital in Leipzig demonstrates the number and variety of soldiers, and the destruction involved in post-combat quartering. In the course of 1814, the former French hospital served wounded Russian, Prussian and Saxon soldiers. The owner of the building documented carefully the damage each group caused; whilst the Russians wrecked chairs, tables and wash bowls, the Prussians were by far the most destructive, causing 236 of the 383 thalers' damage.[48] Depending on the size of armies on the move through Saxony and garrisoned in Leipzig, quartering imposed new levels of hardship until 1816. The numbers of soldiers assigned to private homes increased and even the poorest were expected to quarter. The poor with annual rents between 30 and 50 thaler, once exempt from the duty, could expect to house between one and six men in 1814. Many appealed their billeting assignments, especially widows with young children barely able to sustain themselves, much less additional soldiers.[49] In January 1814, the King, from his house arrest in Berlin, sent money to assist the poorest, who faced impoverishment due to ongoing quartering.[50] Despite the destruction of the countryside around Leipzig, surrounding towns were still expected to provision passing armies with oats, straw, hay and corn until 1816.[51]

Lübeck suffered a similar fate in early December 1813, when it was liberated from the French. It had to billet 5,000 soldiers from the Swedish army, as it struggled to meet the basic needs of Hamburg's refugees. In Hamburg, the French drew on confiscated bank funds and required the 55,000 citizens left in the city to provide supplies for 44,230 soldiers and 5,330 horses until they finally departed in late May 1814. Following the French retreat, Russian General Bennigsen's 9,000 men and 4,000 wounded and the two Hanseatic militias arrived in the city. The reconvened Hamburg Senate unsuccessfully attempted to reduce these numbers and the demands they placed on the population. As a result, the relations between the population and their occupying 'liberators' became increasingly tense. Many more soldiers remained quartered in Altona and Holstein, and when the Russians finally left the region in January 1815, they still numbered 39,000 men with 17,010 horses.[52] Supplying Benningsen's army alone cost 1,737,484 Reichsthaler.[53] The mayor of Bergedorf, a small town at the gates Hamburg, put it best in December 1814: 'What the French have left us, the Russians take, to the last piece of bread and firewood'.[54]

Townspeople and villagers elsewhere in northern Germany faced a similarly dire situation, provisioning and quartering Russian, Prussian and Swedish troops, and also local militias between 1813 and 1815. Locals in Schleswig and Holstein remembered the harsh winter of 1813–1814 as *Kossakenwinter* or *Russenwinter* as a way to summarize the privation they faced from demanding and often violent foreign soldiers. All troops, even local Hanseatic or Mecklenburg divisions, generated hardships on towns and communities, requiring precious food, drink, forage, animals and wagons.[55] Civilians located outside Hamburg continued to petition the city for compensation for Russian requisitions, or 'theft', until 1830.[56]

Compensation for war losses remained a frustrating disappointment for Hamburgers and an impossibility for Leipzig, since a defeated and diminished Saxony would not be compensated for its losses as Napoleon's last German ally. The Allies cancelled any repayment of state losses due to war conditions; only private demands could be made for compensation, and these were only partially fulfilled. In May 1814, one publicist estimated that the French occupation between 1806 and the end of 1810 cost Hamburg 188 million francs, and that the last year of occupation alone under Davout cost the city 75 million francs, including the 15 million francs 'stolen' from the Bank of Hamburg.[57] The city tallied the costs of material requisitions from civilians between May 1813 and 1814 at 17,835,116 francs.[58] Although Hamburg formed a Reclamation Commission and petitioned the new French monarchy to return the bank holdings taken by Marshal Davout in 1813 and 1814, along with other wartime losses, their efforts proved only partially successful. France refused to pay the full amount removed from the Bank and reimbursed only 20 million of the requested 52 million francs of private damage.[59] The compensation process advanced in 1818, moreover, privileged large businesses over average residents.[60] Residents also had to pay higher and more direct taxes to support the necessary loans taken out to help Hamburg rebuild following the French defeat. Most of the compensation claims uncovered in the archives apparently went unfulfilled, and the numerous repeated petitions illustrate civilian frustration at the authorities' failure to recognize and repay their losses. Compensation also required proof in the form of receipts or French *bons,* indicating what and how much had been taken and by whom.[61] Without this evidence, repayment proved impossible.

The majority of common people, who lost so much during the war, therefore, faced an impoverished future in the postwar years. If the wealthy struggled to regain their losses, and middling social groups fought off impoverishment following the war, the working poor were destitute. Rents remained artificially high, and the cost of living continued to rise. In Hamburg, the numbers requesting assistance from the General Poor Relief rose steadily during the months following liberation; 883 applications for support in July 1814 rose to 1,389 by December 1815.[62] The city's poor relief programmes became leaner and meaner after 1815, cutting back on medical and educational programmes originally designed to prevent total impoverishment among working people. The shift in the fiscal priorities of the city state and the change in the management of its poor relief left numerous needs beyond simple survival unmet.

By spring 1814, relief organizations originally formed to help the expellees shifted their attention to the social reintegration of war refugees, veterans and their dependents. Between May 1815 and June 1816, the Hamburg Women's Association, for example, sent 10,002 *Mark Courant* to military hospitals in Neuwied, Brussels, Frankfurt and Cologne and raised and donated over 17,500 *Mark Courrant* to meet an array of needs. These included support for war widows and children, food and medicine for the sick and injured, provisions for a volunteer unit for the 1815 campaign, and funds for start-up costs for the returning expellees to re-establish or start trades.[63] In contrast, the re-established local governments generally ignored injured and unemployed veterans following demobilization. Only after the military campaign of 1815 did Hamburg's Senate agree to offer pensions to those crippled by war. It fell, therefore, to societies like the Hamburg's Women's Association, the 1819 Hanseatic Association, and the 1827 Friendship Club of Hanseatic Veterans of 1813 and 1814 to provide for invalid veterans and their widows and orphans.[64]

Wartime women's associations in particular expanded their efforts to aid those impoverished by the war. During the thanksgiving service at St Michaelis Church, sisters and other female relatives of the soldiers collected donations at the church doors and later went house to house soliciting contributions for the families of missing and dead soldiers.[65] The women of Hamburg petitioned the Senate to take up a collection for war widows, orphans and disabled veterans on the anniversary of the Hanseatic Legion's return, and in 1817 this collection became an annual state practice that continued until 1863.[66] After the war, the Hamburg Women's Association expanded its support for veterans, their families, and refugees, to include others who suffered during the conflict, in particular the so-called 'worthy poor'. In 1816, the Women's Association reported: 'The recent happy success of our endeavours, the feeling that there is yet more healing to do ... compels us to desire to further continue our effectives. Peace also brings strong urgent demands for charity'.[67] They opened a school, where daughters of veterans and other 'worthy poor' were clothed, fed and educated for domestic service. In Bremen and Lübeck the wartime Women's Associations also moved to support the 'worthy poor'.[68]

Likewise, as the war ended in Leipzig, wartime voluntary associations continued and new civic organizations emerged to respond to hardships caused by the war, including the wartime Support Association for Leipzig's Region, the 1816 Patriotic Relief Association (*Vaterländischen Hilfs-Verein)* and the Society of the 19 October. As in Hamburg, the wives and daughters of leading Leipzig merchants continued their work in charitable organizations.[69] In the case of the villages around Leipzig, the Ladies Committee at Leipsic [*sic*] distributed £500 from England to destitute families and orphans in June 1814, detailing the amount provided to each family.[70] Like other Women's Associations across Germany, Leipzig's association raised resources to support the widows, orphans and wounded soldiers.[71] In both cities, civilian relief efforts expanded civic activism to address the social legacy of the wars.

Conclusion

For both Hamburg and Leipzig, the last years of the war increased suffering and completely disrupted families, work and everyday life. Civilians understood the enormous cost of the war, and they knew that peace would not bring immediate relief. Hamburg and Leipzig shared many wartime experiences; they endured the destruction of their surrounding villages and hamlets, war trauma and epidemic illness, the dilemma of sheltering and feeding war refugees, and the demands of ongoing requisitions and of quartering foreign troops following the end of hostilities. The poverty, illness, death and despair that characterized the final year of French occupation left scars; even as each city recovered physically, hardship remained etched on the inhabitants' faces.[72] The population of Hamburg shrank. By 1815, its population was about 58,000, less than it had been in 1787, and it only recovered the population level of 1800 after 1825.[73] In contrast, Leipzig supported new residents: 25,000 wounded and ill soldiers and refugees.[74] Both cities suffered from lingering illness and the spectre of large numbers of orphaned children.[75] Both cities also carried large public war debts for decades into the postwar period.[76]

Significantly, they also shared the experience that during the worst possible conditions, members of civil society—merchants, artisans, civic leaders, clergy, professionals, and their wives, sisters and daughters—rose to meet the needs of the desperate and needy within their communities. They acted like responsible state authorities finding social and economic solutions to such traumatic wartime experiences as epidemic illness and civilian displacement. They drew on professional and personal contacts and networks to raise money for war refugees, the displaced, and needy veterans of the returning militias and volunteer units. Indeed, it was the war and its consequences that drew them to offer their time, effort and talents to address social problems. It is not surprising that they continued to see a role for their associations in the postwar decades to assist victims of the war amidst poverty, social hardship, and a remote state.

The Napoleonic Wars mobilized more than local militias and patriotic support for the war effort which included collecting money for the outfitting and equipping of the militias and the medical care of sick and wounded soldiers. They also rallied civil society to address non-combatant hardships on the local and international level. Research on twentieth-century relief organizations acknowledges the 1863 forerunner of the International Committee of the Red Cross as the first organized relief effort, and sees twentieth-century relief efforts as a 'modern phenomenon' related to total war. Distinctive features of this approach to modern war relief include responding to the linkage between war and epidemic disease, the importance of planning and coordination, internationalism, and the importance of publicity.[77] These basic criteria also characterize the organizations that assisted distressed and displaced non-combatants during and after the Napoleonic Wars, evidenced in the case studies of local and international associations that supported residents in Hamburg and Leipzig.

Two historiographical narratives converge in these case studies of the postwar era. The *Sattlezeit* narrative that features the increased presence and activities of civil society, as shown in urban associational life and utilitarian networks, intersects with the 'new military history' narrative of the Napoleonic Wars that characterizes the conflict as comprising mass armies, economic warfare, civilian mobilization and ideological passions on a new unprecedented scale. The civic activism embodied in the voluntary relief associations that emerged from the war connects these approaches. Together, they contribute to our understanding of how contemporaries perceived war as a 'new, enduring, and defining feature of their lives'.[78]

Notes

1. Karl Gottfried Zimmerman, *Hamms Verwüstung in den Jahren 1813 und 1814* (Hamburg, 1909), 9.
2. H. Nirrnheim (ed.), 'Briefe von Peter Godeffroy und George Parish aus den Jahren 1813 und 1814', *Zeitschrift des Verein für Hamburgische Geschichte* (ZVHG) 18 (1914): 115–169.
3. See for example, Ute Planert, *Der Mythos vom Befreiungskrieg: Frankreichs Kriege und der deutsche Süden: Alltag—Wahrnehmung—Deutung, 1792–1841* (Paderborn, 2007); Alan Forrest et al. (eds), *Soldiers, Citizens and Civilians: Experiences and Perceptions of the Revolutionary and Napoleonic Wars, 1790–1820* (Basingstoke, 2009); Leighton S. James, *Witnessing the Revolutionary and Napoleonic Wars in German Central Europe* (Basingstoke, 2012); Katherine B. Aaslestad, 'Krieg, Demobilisierung und Erinnerungskultur in den republikanischen Stadtstaaten Hamburg, Bremen und Lübeck, 1813–1830', in *Kriegsenden, Nachkriegsordnungen, Folgekonflikte: Wege aus dem Krieg im 19. und 20. Jahrhundert*, ed. Jörg Echternkamp (Freiburg/Br., 2012), 53–74; and Karen Hagemann, *Revisiting Prussia's Wars against Napoleon: History, Culture, Memory* (Cambridge, 2015).
4. See Katherine B. Aaslestad, 'Paying for War: Experiences of Napoleonic Rule in the Hanseatic Cities', *Central European History* 39/4 (2006): 641–675, and Karen Hagemann, '"Unimaginable Horror and Misery": The Battle of Leipzig in October

1813 in Civilian Experience and Perception', in Forrest et al. (eds), *Soldiers, Citizens and Civilians*, 157–178.

5. John G. Gallaher, *Iron Marshal: A Biography of Louis N. Davout* (Carbondale, Ill, 1976), 287–289. Davout justified his severe treatment of Hamburg's population in his *Mémoire de M. le Maréchal Davout, Prince d'Eckmühl, Au Roi* (Paris, 1814).
6. Tilman Stieve, *Der Kampf um die Reform in Hamburg, 1789–1842* (Hamburg, 1993), 49.
7. Bernhard Mehnke, *Armut und Elend in Hamburg: Eine Untersuchung über das öffentliche Armenwesen in der ersten Hälfte des 19. Jahrhunderts* (Hamburg, 1982), 114; and Zimmerman, *Hamms Verwüstung*, 64.
8. Herman Friederich Rust, *Erläuterung einer kleinen Schrift, betitelt Kleines Licht auf dunkeln Wegen* (Hamburg, 1814), 43–45.
9. Carl Mönckeberg, *Hamburg unter dem Drucke der Franzosen, 1806–1814* (Hamburg, 1864), 231–232.
10. See Hagemann, 'Unimaginable Horror and Misery'.
11. Thomas Nabert (ed.), *Zeugen des Schreckens: Erlebnisberichte aus der Völkerschlachtzeit in und um Leipzig* (Leipzig, 2012), 64.
12. Theodor Apel, *Tabellarische Zusammenstellung der Kriegsereignisse bei Leipzig im October 1813* (Leipzig, 1866), 48–54.
13. Nabert, *Zeugen des Schreckens*, 75.
14. 'Kriegsverlustanzeigen vom Jahr 1813–1814 in Kreisamt Leipzig', Staatsarchiv Leipzig (StAL), Amt Leipzig, 1.6.4 Kriegsfolgen, 5984.
15. Hagemann, 'Unimaginable Horror and Misery', 168.
16. Dieter Walz, *Sachsenland war abgebrannt: Leipziger Völkerschlacht, 1813* (Leipzig, 1993), 165.
17. Gallaher, *Iron Marshal*, 289–291; and Renate Hauschild-Thiessen (ed.), 'In der belagerten Stadt: Tagebuch Aufzeichnungen von Henriette Brock aus dem Jahre 1814', *Hamburgische Geschichts- und Heimatblätter* 10 (1977): 57–59.
18. Mönckeberg, *Hamburg*, 292.
19. See Hagemann, 'Unimaginable Horror and Misery'; Nabert, *Zeugen des Schreckens*, 73; Walz, *Sachsenland*, 164; and Heinrich Eduard Maukisch, *Leipzig vor einem Vierteljahrhundert: Eine Denkschrift zur Erinnerung an die Octobertage des Jahres 1813* (Leipzig, 1838), 56.
20. Nabert, *Zeugen des Schreckens*, 81.
21. Frederich Perthes, *Die Vertriebenen Hamburger im Januar 1814* (no place, c. 1814).
22. Mönckeberg, *Hamburg*, 221.
23. 'An die vertriebenen Hamburger', Staatsarchiv Hamburg (hereafter StAHbg), 111–1 Senate Cl VII Lit Qa Nr 3 Vol 13 Conv. n.
24. *Neue Bremer Zeitung*, 17 January 1814.
25. *Allgemeiner Bericht über den Zustand, der während der Belagerung aus Hamburg Vertriebenen, und über die, zur Milderung ihres Schicksals angewandten Mittel: Erster Bericht, bis Ende März 1814. Den Wohlthätern dieser Unglücklichen vorgelegt von der Central-Commission* (Altona, 1814), 11; and Committee for Relieving the Distress in Germany and Other Parts of the Continent, 'Third Report of the Committee for Relieving the Distresses in Germany', in *Reports of the Committees formed in London in the Year 1814 for the Relief of the Unparalleled Distressed in Germany and other parts of the Continent, occasioned by the War which terminated in the Treaty of Paris 31 March 1814* (London, 1814), 6.
26. 'First Report of the Committee for Relieving the Distresses in Germany', *in Reports of the Committees*, 1–3.

27. *Allgemeiner Bericht über die Wirklichkeit der Unterstützungs-Commission zu Lübeck für die vertriebenen Hamburger vom 1sten Januars bis Ende Juli 1814* (Lübeck, 1815); and Anjekathrin Grassmann, '"Es bedarf keiner weiteren Schilderund des Elendes. Es war namen- und beispiellos": Die Aufnahme der vertriebenen Hamburger in Lübeck, 1814. Eine erfolgreiche Form von Krisenmanagement', *ZVHG* 83 (1997): 323–342.
28. Katherine B. Aaslestad, 'Citizenship in Action: Hanseatic Women's Wartime Associations', in *Gender in Urban Europe: Sites of Political Activity and Citizenship, 1750–1900*, eds Krista Cowman et al. (New York, 2014), 124–140. More general studies include Karen Hagemann, 'Female Patriots: Women, War and the Nation in the Period of the Prussian-German Anti-Napoleonic Wars', *Gender & History* 16/3 (2004): 396–424; Jean H. Quataert, *Staging Philanthropy: Patriotic Women and the National Imagination in Dynastic Germany, 1813–1916* (Ann Arbor, MI, 2001), 21–52; and Dirk Alexander Reder, *Frauenbewegung und Nation: Patriotische Frauenvereine in Deutschland im frühen 19. Jahrhundert* (Cologne, 1998).
29. *Allgemeiner Bericht über die Wirklichkeit.*
30. Anne-Charlott Trepp, *Sanfte Männlichkeit und selbständige Weiblichkeit: Frauen und Männer im Hamburger Bürgertum zwischen 1770 und 1840* (Göttingen, 1996), 277.
31. Letters dated February 1814, StAHbg, Bestand Familien Sieveking, E5 Band 3.
32. *Allgemeiner Bericht über den Zustand,* 39; and Mönckeberg, *Hamburg,* 229.
33. 'Verordnungen und Verfügungen der Hilfs-und Wiederherstellungs-Kommission, 1814', StAL, Amt Leipzig, 1.6.4 Kriegsfolgen, 5982.
34. Johannes Orzschig, 'Das russische General-Governement in Leipzig, Oktober 1813–November 1815', Phil. diss. (University of Leipzig, 1934), 13.
35. Orzschig, 'Das russische General-Governement', 12–15.
36. 'Sixth Report of the Committee for Relieving the Distresses in Germany', in *Reports of the Committees,* 13–14.
37. 'Karl Sieveking, Denkschriften über die politischen Lage der Hansestädte', December 1813, StAHbg, 622–1, von Hess, 2 Briefwechsel; and StAHbg, 622–1 Karl Sieveking. E5, Bd. 1.
38. 'Mr. von Hess', *The Examiner,* 1 August 1813.
39. See for example, Hannibal Evans Lloyd, *Hamburgh, or a Particular Account of the Transactions Which Took Place in that City During the First Six Months of 1813* (London, 1813), which was added to and reprinted several times in 1814; and Frederick Schoberl, *Narrative of the Most Remarkable Events Which Occurred in and Near Leipzig, Immediately Before, During and Subsequent to, the Sanguinary Series of Engagements Between the Allied Armies and the French from the 14th to the 19th October 1813* (London, 1814), also reprinted in at least ten editions.
40. Norbert Götz, 'Rationales of Humanitarianism: The Case of British Relief to Germany, 1805–1815', *Journal of Modern European History* 12/2 (2014): 186–199.
41. Ibid., 195.
42. 'First Report of the Committee for Relieving the Distresses in Germany', 1–3.
43. 'Fourth Report of the Committee for Relieving the Distresses in Germany', in *Reports of the Committees,* 16.
44. Henry George Watkins, *'Distress in Germany': A Sermon Preached in the Church of the United Parishes of St Swithin and St Mary Bothaw* (London, 1814), 13–14.
45. See 'Fourth Report of the Committee for Relieving the Distresses in Germany', in *Reports of the Committees,* 2.
46. Götz, 'Rationales of Humanitarianism', 197.

47. Robert Beachy, *The Soul of Commerce: Credit, Property, and Politics in Leipzig, 1750–1840* (Leiden, 2005), 165–168.
48. StAL, LVII B. Krieges des 19th Saeculi, 140 Acta.
49. 'Dr W. Ritzow, Einquartierung: Ihre Aufgabe und ihre Last', StAL, Amt Leipzig, 524, fols 22–25.
50. Ibid., 32.
51. 'Verfügungen bei Durchmärschen fremder Truppen und zur Beseitigung der Kriegsfolgen', StAL, Amt Leipzig, 1.6.4 Kriegsfolgen, 0156.
52. Mönckeberg, 310.
53. Jürgen Huck, *Das Ende der Franzosenzeit in Hamburg: Quellen und Studien zur Belagerung und Befreiung von Hamburg, 1813–1814* (Hamburg, 1984), 70.
54. Ibid., 48.
55. Dieter Kienitz, *Der Kosakenwinter in Schleswig-Holstein, 1813–1814* (Heide, 2000), 113–119 and 147–155.
56. For samples of claims see: StAHbg, 611–1 Sankt Johanniskloster auch Kloster Harvestehude: 1370, December 1816; 602, 1818; and 607, December 1830.
57. Rust, *Erläuterung einer kleinen Schrift*, 14–15 and 41–45.
58. 'Übersicht, der durch die Einwohner der Stadt Hamburg während der französischen Besitznahme von 30 May 1813 bis zum May 1814 geleisteten Requisitionen in Waren und anderen Gegenständen' StAHbg, 112–113: Marie Hamburg, 156.
59. Mönckeberg, *Hamburg*, 326–333.
60. Stieve, *Der Kampf*, 48–49.
61. Kienitz, *Kosakenwinter*, 166–172.
62. Mary Lindemann, *Patriots and Paupers: Hamburg, 1712–1830* (Oxford, 1990), 206.
63. 'Bericht des Hamburgischen Frauen-Vereins über seine bisherigne Wirksamkeit und Plan zur Fortsetzung derselben, im September 1816', StAHbg, 111–1 Senate Cl VII Lit Qa Nr 3 Vol 14.
64. 'Der Hamburgische Frauen-Verein, zum Besten verwundeter und hülfsbedürftiger Krieger', *Gemeinnützige Nachrichten von und für Hamburg*, 4 May 1815; 'Hamburger Frauenverein', Ibid., 29 July 1815.
65. StAHbg, 111–1 Senat Cl VIII Lit Ha Vol 1 6b, No 4.
66. StAHbg, 111–1 Senat Cl VII Lit Gb No 9. Vol O, Fasc 1 and Fasc 2; and 'Der Hamburgische Frauen-Verein, zum Besten verwundeter und hülfsbedürftiger Krieger', *Wöchentliche gemeinnützige Nachrichte von und für Hamburg*, 4 May 1815.
67. 'Bericht des Hamburgischen Frauen-Vereins über seine bisherigne Wirksamkeit und Plan zur Fortzetzung derselben, im September 1816', StAHbg 111–1 Senate Cl VII Lit Qa Nr 3 Vol 14.
68. Elisabeth Meyer-Renschhausen, *Weibliche Kultur und soziale Arbeit: Eine Geshichte der Frauenbewegung am Beispiel Bremens, 1810–1927* (Cologne, 1989), 51–53; and 'Die Lübecker Frauenvereine, ihr Entstehen, ihre Entwicklung und ihr Wirken in der Gegenwart', *Lübeckische Blätter* 44 (1902): 269–271, 269.
69. Thorsten Maentel, 'Stadtbürgerliche Elite im Spannungsfeld zwischen Bürgerlicher Selfständigkeit und Monarchisch-Bürokratischer Herrschaaft Leipziger Profile 1750 bis 1850', in *Eliten um 1800: Erfahrungshorizonte, Verhaltensweisen, Handlungsmöglichkeiten*, ed. Anja Victorine Hartmann et al. (Mainz, 2000), 267–297, 284–285.
70. 'Sixth Report of the Committee for the Relief of Distress in Germany', 9–11.
71. Orzschig, 'Das russische General-Governement', 12–15.
72. 'Karl Gries to Diederich Gries', July 1813, quoted in Heinrich Reincke (ed.), 'Aus dem Briefwechsel von Karl Gries und Diederich Gries 1796 bis 1819', *ZVHG* 25 (1924): 226–277, 265.

73. Lindemann, *Patriots*, 205 and Stieve, *Der Kampf*, 21.
74. Beachy, *The Soul of Commerce*, 163.
75. 'Bürgermeister Amsinck to Wilhelm Amsinck, 8 June and 14 June 1814', StAHbg, 622–1 Familie Amsinck, I. 11 f.
76. Gerhard Ahrens, 'Staatsverschuldung und Wirtschaftswachstum: Hanseatische Anleihepolitik im 19. Jahrhundert', *Hansische Geschichtsblätter* 112 (1994): 247–257; and Beachy, *The Soul of Commerce*, 165–196.
77. Jessica Reinisch, 'Introduction: Relief in the Aftermath of War', *Journal of Contemporary History* 43 (2008): 317–404.
78. Mark Hewitson, 'Princes' Wars, Wars of the People, or Total War? Mass Armies and the Question of a Military Revolution in Germany, 1792–1815', *War in History* 20 (2013): 452–490, 490.

14

Rewarding Loyalty after the Wars of Independence in Spanish America: Displaced Bureaucrats in Cuba

Sarah C. Chambers

At the beginning of the nineteenth century, Spaniard Francisco de Paula Vilches was on the verge of a promising career in royal administration. After serving four years in Spain as legal counsel for the navy, he was appointed as a magistrate on the High Court (*Audiencia*) of Caracas. However, a posting to Venezuela in 1811, the year that an assembly in Caracas had declared the colony's independence, was much riskier than it would have been a few years earlier. Although the separatists were expelled from Caracas by the time Vilches arrived in 1812, war continued to rage throughout this province of the Viceroyalty of New Granada, twice forcing members of the *Audiencia* to evacuate. 'During those turbulent and calamitous times', in the words of Treasury Official Juan Muñoz, 'was when Mr Vilches energetically deployed all possible measures in favour of the public good'.[1] Muñoz and a few other witnesses went so far as to conjecture that had more authorities acted like Vilches, advocating the rule of law rather than military repression, Spain might not have lost the colony to revolution. Having risen to the rank of Dean in the Caracas court, in 1818 Vilches was promoted to Regent, the highest position, of the *Audiencia* of Guatemala. Although his new posting was calm in comparison to Venezuela, in 1821 leading citizens in Guatemala also declared independence from Spain, and Vilches joined a growing number of displaced colonial administrators seeking refuge on the island of Cuba. Having risen quickly through the ranks of the judicial system, Vilches was frustrated to find his career on hold as he lived off unemployment benefits for several years. When that stipend was reduced in 1826, he penned a strong if respectful protest:

> We [émigrés] are not working because we are not being employed, but we deserve to be because we have left everything behind for Your Majesty; losing our belongings and the income that sustained us, we have faced all kinds of dangers and made enormous expenditures in our travels ... without having been compensated for anything....[2]

As part of a larger project on population displacement during the Spanish American Wars of Independence, this chapter explores primarily the case of royal bureaucrats and magistrates like Vilches who fled or requested a transfer to Cuba, where their pleas for assistance set off policy debates over where they should establish residence, what financial support they should receive until they could return to their posts and, later, whether they should be given preference in appointments to new positions. Initially, Fernando VII and his councillors were sympathetic to the émigrés, but tensions on the island grew as civil servants competed for scarce resources and employment. Although few in royal administration, even in the 1820s, would openly admit that Spain had definitively lost its mainland possessions, the passage of years made it clear that these were no short-term sojourns. Increasingly, therefore, metropolitan authorities had to balance the claims of multiple loyal subjects, both those colonial bureaucrats who had lost so much during the revolutions and the long-term residents of the 'ever faithful' isle of Cuba, Spain's most valuable remaining colony.[3]

Waves of warfare, waves of emigration

The Wars of Independence in Spanish America went through two major phases.[4] First, in response to Napoleon's capture in 1808 of Fernando VII, autonomist assemblies (*juntas*) in cities throughout the empire asserted their authority to govern during the King's absence. Some *juntas* even deposed royal authorities such as viceroys and high court magistrates, and a very few like that of Caracas openly declared independence. Restored to the throne in 1814, Fernando VII turned royal troops from the war against France to the suppression of insurgency in the colonies. By 1815, royal authorities maintained power in Lima and Mexico City and had re-established their control over many rebellious territories in Chile, New Spain and the Viceroyalty of New Granada (Ecuador, Colombia, Venezuela, and Panama). Although separatists in Buenos Aires retained the upper hand in much of what would become Argentina, they had been unable to assert their authority throughout all the Viceroyalty of Río de la Plata. During the second phase of warfare over the subsequent decade, however, the tide turned against Spain. The retributions exacted upon local populations by reconquering Spanish commanders turned previously neutral or vacillating subjects against the Crown and, as demonstrated by Rafe Blaufarb in this volume, demobilization in Europe freed up arms for purchase by rebels in the Americas. By 1826, the last Spanish troops on the mainland capitulated and only the islands of Cuba, Puerto Rico and the Philippines remained of Spain's overseas empire. Waves of émigrés and refugees corresponded to these phases of warfare.

Throughout the initial phase, control over territories across the mainland shifted back and forth between royalists and separatists, with rivals frequently in close proximity. Therefore, people could often move relatively short distances to take refuge with the side they supported.[5] When the *Junta* of Bogotá began requiring officials to swear an oath of independence in 1810, for example, Royal Accountant Carlos de Espada Andrés Martínez reported that he fled to the city of Santa Marta 'which upheld the just cause and sheltered good émigrés'.[6] The newly appointed Viceroy of New Granada, Benito Pérez, established his government in Panama in 1812, where he was joined by some members of Bogotá's *Audiencia*, but his successor the following year, Francisco Montalvo, based himself in Santa Marta until a royal expedition recaptured Bogotá in May 1816.[7] Residents of Venezuela, whether separatists or royalists, depending upon the fortunes of war tended to seek asylum on various Caribbean islands, Curaçao being a particularly close destination.[8] Capuchin Father Atanasio de Albalate had been working in the Indian missions in Cumaná, Venezuela, when he was arrested and expelled by insurgents, forcing him into a three-year pilgrimage 'through foreign islands relying only upon the charity of the faithful'.[9] Indeed, as Cassandra Pybus points out in this volume, war and rebellion triggered high levels of mobility throughout the Caribbean from the late eighteenth into the early nineteenth centuries.

Confident that rebellions in the colonies would soon be suppressed and appreciative of officials who demonstrated their loyalty by refusing to remain in territories held by insurgents, the Spanish Parliament (*Cortes*) agreed on 22 July 1811 to continue paying two-thirds of their salary to bureaucratic employees 'who have emigrated from towns in America that have risen up in insurrection'.[10] In October 1812, Viceroy Benito Pérez reported from Panama that he had received the instructions on payments to émigrés in his recommendation of the case of Martínez reported above.[11] Juan Hernández de Alva had been working as a judicial official in Guadalajara in 1810, when insurgents seized the city; he reported that he managed to make his way through San Blas and Acapulco to Mexico City, where he survived on his émigré salary until Guadalajara was retaken by royal forces in 1812.[12] As his case indicates, financial support to displaced bureaucrats was meant to be a temporary measure until they could return to their posts. The Regency made this explicit in a royal order dated 16 August 1812, that 'those employees who have fled from their provinces must present themselves there as soon as the enemy has been dislodged and prove their patriotic conduct or they will be dismissed from their positions'.[13] Treasury Official Juan Muñoz relocated several times as Caracas changed hands between 1810 and 1821, fleeing once to Puerto Rico via North America and a second time all the way to Spain, but each time returning to Venezuela to fulfil his duties in Cumaná, La Guayra and Puerto Cabello.[14]

During the 1810s, colonial officials moved varying distances to remain in Spanish-controlled territories and frequently were able to return to their posts after 're-conquest' by the Spanish army. Between 1819 and 1821, however, separatists won several key battles. The Battle of Boyacá in August

1819 led to a disorderly evacuation of royal authorities from Bogotá to Cartagena where, after a blockade of several months, they surrendered in October 1821. In Venezuela, Simón Bolívar's forces captured Caracas in May 1821 and decisively defeated the Spanish army the following month at the Battle of Carabobo, triggering a royalist emigration to Puerto Cabello. Assemblies in Mexico and Central America also declared independence in 1821, prompting some royal officials to flee.[15] With the exception of Peru and Upper Peru (later Bolivia), therefore, royalists were confined to pockets along the coasts where they tried to survive on low supplies. With few areas to which to flee, especially on the Atlantic side of the Americas, émigrés set sail. Although civilian refugees found in Puerto Rico a society that still had land to be settled and welcomed slave owners, career bureaucrats set their sights on either Spain or the closer destination of Cuba, the most cosmopolitan of Spain's remaining island possessions.[16] Given the experiences of the 1810s, authorities in Madrid planned once again to reconquer the mainland and therefore preferred to have displaced bureaucrats close at hand and ready to relocate. Long-term residents of Cuba, on the other hand, were alarmed by the growing numbers of émigrés who expected to receive financial aid on the island.

Policy debates on war émigrés in Cuba and Spain

From 1821 to 1824, Cuban and Peninsular officials skirmished over policies toward émigrés. Displaced bureaucrats from Venezuela complained that they received no assistance in Cuba, prompting the King, on 29 November 1821, to remind the Intendant of Havana to pay two-thirds of their salaries, as had been decreed in 1811.[17] Presumably this royal order had not yet reached the island on 12 December 1821, when the local government newspaper noted that all displaced military and civilian personnel with no official post in Cuba would be transported to Spain, there being insufficient funds on the island to support them.[18] Joaquín Ribera, Court Reporter for the *Audiencia* of Bogotá, had been receiving his stipend in Panama before a change in government forced him to flee via Jamaica; upon arriving in Cuba he requested the continuation of his partial salary, but on 12 February 1822 the Intendant, citing a lack of funds, refused to pay without an express order from his superiors.[19] By the time Ribera's petition reached Spain, an official there noted that the Intendant of Havana had since acknowledged the November order to pay the émigrés' pensions, but the King reiterated the order in the following August.

Until at least 1824, repeated complaints from émigrés and orders from Spain to pay them suggest that compliance by Cuban officials was lax.[20] José María de la Ferga, who had worked in the colonial administration of New Granada for 30 years until the surrender of Cartagena in 1821, requested that he not be sent to Spain as ordered by Cuban officials, but rather be allowed to collect his partial salary in Havana. The secretary charged with summarizing his case noted that the resolution by the Provincial Assembly in Havana to transport émigrés to Spain directly contradicted royal orders that civil servants should stay as close to their posts as possible and be ready to return as soon as those regions were pacified. Therefore, on 18 April 1823, the King ordered yet again that Ferga and all other displaced bureaucrats should stay in Cuba.[21] Nevertheless, on 14 July 1823, Romualdo Joaquin and Antonio Morales, a father and son who worked as colonial officials in their birthplace of New Granada, wrote from Santiago de Cuba to the King of their loyal service and wartime losses. 'But My Lord!', they protested, 'Who could believe that they have wanted to oblige us to continue on to the Metropolis, abandoning our families, and without sufficient means since our properties have been occupied and only our transportation would be paid'.[22] It is not clear whether the order from April had not reached Cuba or whether the Intendant interpreted it to apply only to Havana, but the official in Madrid charged with advising the King was clearly frustrated and recommended that the Intendant of Havana be ordered to stop harassing émigrés and to circulate the directive to officials throughout the island. On 31 March 1824, therefore, the King commanded the Intendant in no uncertain terms

> that the protection of loyal émigrés is not a mere consideration but an obligation of strict justice and of sound and rigorous policy, and therefore Your Lordship should not only desist from bothering them by requiring them to continue on to Spain, but also you should provide for them without interruption including the time in which such support stopped, and you should place them according to their merit and skills until the Kingdom of Santa Fé [New Granada] is pacified and they can return to their posts or they are appointed elsewhere. And His Majesty wishes that all that is mandated in this order is extended to all the other loyal émigrés who are now on or [will] later arrive at the Island of Cuba....[23]

Royal concern for the émigrés was undoubtedly sincere, but the recommendation that prompted this order also advocated that public finances on the Peninsula should not be further overwhelmed with the arrival of displaced bureaucrats from the colonies.[24]

Indeed, shortly before the royal order issued on behalf of the Morales and all other displaced officials in Cuba, budgetary concerns surfaced in a policy discussion in Madrid over high-level administrators who had fled all the way from the colonies to Spain. In the final days of 1823, the Minister of Grace and Justice sent an inquiry from the King to the Council of Indies:

> One of the things that has especially attracted the attention of His Majesty and moves the sensitivity of his paternal heart is the fate of so

> many *Magistrates, Ecclesiastical Prelates, and Civil Employees from America* who have taken refuge in the Peninsula fleeing the revolution and anarchy that are stirring up those unfortunate Regions. (Emphasis in the original)[25]

A pension might seem insufficient to an individual émigré, he continued, but added together pensions constituted a fiscal burden at a time when the populace would not react well to tax increases. The King, therefore, was considering reassigning displaced bureaucrats to vacant posts in the Peninsula in order to reduce the payment of pensions, but was concerned that these experienced officials would then not be available to send back to the colonies when they were regained. The Crown Attorney (*fiscal*) on the Council was in favour of such a policy; indeed, he asserted that displaced *audiencia* magistrates should be preferred over all other candidates for open positions. Although he acknowledged that making these appointments interim would make it easier to respond to the changing political context of the Americas, he advocated permanent assignments particularly for those 'of advanced age and those whose health and fortunes have been greatly damaged during long and costly peregrinations through such diverse and unhealthy climates'.[26] He was confident that should the situation change, those who were younger and had smaller families would be willing to relocate again in order to best serve the interests of the Crown. The Council, concurring with the *fiscal*, nominated the high-level officials in Spain at the time for particular vacancies.[27]

The advice of the Council of Indies applied specifically to the case of *audiencia* judges and bishops, who had travelled all the way to the Peninsula, but the principle of rewarding loyalty and saving on pensions was extended to Cuba where numerous émigrés at various ranks found themselves in limbo. On 16 January 1825, the King ordered that displaced judicial personnel in Cuba be placed in any appropriate vacancies on the island.[28] Although authorities in the metropole had been adamant that émigrés in Cuba stay on that island, they also recognized the financial burden it placed on the local treasury. On 1 July 1824, the governing board of the Cuban treasury reduced compensation for displaced bureaucrats to half salary. In confirming that decision and extending it to Puerto Rico in early 1826, the Council of Indies and the King placed a cap of 1000 pesos even on those who were working in temporary positions at two-thirds salary.[29] Émigrés complained that they could not subsist adequately on such stipends, and so, throughout the 1820s and into the 1830s, they repeatedly applied to both Cuban and Peninsular officials for permanent positions in which they could earn a full salary.[30] Émigrés certainly called attention to their merits and the accolades they had received in the performance of their duties, but tended to emphasize even more their service, made all the more valuable given the troubled times.

From pensions to positions: emigrés compete for employment

In their employment applications, émigrés portrayed themselves in dramatic terms as the King's most loyal and deserving vassals. Vicente Díaz y García, who until 1810 had been posted to Cartagena de Indias, asserted, 'He considers as an extraordinary service his emigration to Havana, fleeing from the disloyal Party, having lost his household goods, valuables and all his belongings which he had to abandon in order to maintain his fidelity and escape with his life'.[31] 'Resolute in sustaining and conserving the sentiments of religion and fidelity that he inherited from his Christian and loyal parents', claimed Bartolomé Guanche, a native of Tenerife who had served in Venezuela, and 'in order to defend the just cause of Your Majesty, he has had to make sacrifices and exert himself to an unusual degree since the anarchy and impiety began to break out in the unfortunate provinces of Venezuela'. He pointed to his service record as evidence of his 'sacrifices and losses'.[32] Thus, in the course of calling attention to the extraordinary nature of their services, émigrés added an additional category to the standard résumé called a 'report of merits and services'. Petitioner after petitioner added suffering or losses (*padecimientos*) as a third reason why they should be rewarded with appointments and promotions.[33]

Ildefonso José de Medina offers a particularly telling example of using appointments to compensate émigrés for their 'merits, services and losses', as he termed it in an employment application. Medina began his career in Cádiz before being appointed to serve as a judge on the *Audiencia* of Caracas where he ascended to the rank of dean. In 1815, he was promoted to the post of Criminal Judge on the *Audiencia* of Mexico, 'owing to his sufferings and good conduct during the revolution of Caracas'.[34] Mexico was calmer than Caracas in 1815, but did not remain so for long, and Medina claimed that he was among those, 'with arms in hand', trying to defend the capital from the rebels. Refusing offers to remain and work for the new national government, Medina returned via Cuba to Spain where he was awarded a pension in July 1823. A year later, he complained that other loyal officials had either been restored to their posts or rewarded with others, while he 'bewails his sad fate in obscurity having spent three full years crossing land and sea, abandoning lucrative posts in order to remain loyal to Your Majesty'.[35] Having been turned down in repeated requests to return to service in vacant posts, Medina indicated that he would be willing to serve as the Crown Attorney for the Royal Treasury of Havana, even though it was a step down from his former position, so long as he would not have to take a reduction in pay from his salary in Mexico. He pointed out that although that salary might be higher than usual for the position, the royal treasury would still gain by not having to pay his pension for which he did no work. The Minister of Grace and Justice concurred with the request, noting that he knew Medina personally as both loyal and meritorious and that his career advancement had suffered from his wartime appointments.[36] The King overturned an objection from the Council of Indies to the high salary, and in February 1825, Medina began to serve in his new position. He served for eight months, after which he was appointed as a magistrate on the *Audiencia* of Puerto Principe.

The expectation of rewards for loyalty and sacrifice could also extend beyond one generation. In 1839, Lucas Bayo, who applied for employment after his job with the semaphore telegraph was eliminated, cited the service of his father who had been Treasurer in San Luis de Potosí in New Spain and had been killed during the independence war there.[37] Miguel Bataller was a third generation colonial bureaucrat. His grandfather had been a magistrate in New Spain and his father served on *audiencias* in both Guatemala and Mexico City. Bataller himself had worked in various posts in the Peninsula for ten years since abandoning his 'homeland and fortune' to remain loyal to the Crown, and in 1836 applied for an opening in Havana.[38] Josefa Arcaya, from a wealthy family in Venezuela that had made significant donations to the royalist cause and the widow of Lieutenant Colonel Bernardo de Mijares, repeatedly stood out for the fulfilment of a royal order to find employment for her son. In 1831, the Intendant of Havana pointed out that the boy was only ten, but four years later finally agreed to appoint him as a supplementary scribe in the General Accounting Office of Santiago de Cuba despite his youth and poor showing in a test. Although the King agreed to a probationary period of six months – after which Mijares could be removed if he had not shown signs of improvement, 'so that a salary is not paid to a useless employee' – the appointment was clearly aimed at compensating losses rather than rewarding merits.[39]

By highlighting in employment applications their extraordinary sacrifices, all émigrés implied that they were more deserving than their colleagues who had enjoyed stable careers in Cuba. Some went further to draw an explicit contrast. Émigré Ildefonso de Medina, who lived through revolutions in both Venezuela and Mexico, pointed out that only those 'who had endured the same upheavals' could understand how much he had suffered in terms of 'considerable losses and damages across so many thousands of leagues'.[40] Francisco de Paula Vilches protested that capping the pension for émigrés put their earnings on a par with a mere artisan in Cuba, in contrast to the 'abundance and prosperity' enjoyed by bureaucrats earning their full salaries. 'And so my Lord', he asked, 'those of us who have abandoned our careers and with them our subsistence and comfort in order to be loyal to Your Majesty, do we deserve less than those who have never left their homes, their belongings, their repose, nor have had their courage tested...?'[41] The legal representative of José Teodoro Martínez, a cleric who had fled New Spain and was serving in 1828 as Secretary to the Archbishop of Cuba, similarly argued that this position did not sufficiently compensate his losses. In advocating that he be granted the sinecure (*ración*) of the Cuban Cathedral, valued at 1000 pesos annually, he acknowledged that another applicant had seniority, but that Martínez had not yet been rewarded for his 'uncommon services and sacrifices'.[42] It was one thing to advance through one's career during peacetime, he continued, and quite another to be prepared to sacrifice one's life for one's King. The King apparently agreed, appointing the middle-aged Martínez to the post over the candidate recommended in the first place, an elderly native of Cuba.

Giving émigrés priority in Cuban appointments allowed the Crown to reward their loyalty and to compensate their sacrifices while economizing on funds that would otherwise have gone into pensions. Not surprisingly, however, this was unpopular among native-born or long-time residents of Cuba, who considered themselves among the most loyal subjects of the Spanish empire. Such opposition was not frequently expressed openly, but did receive a full airing during a reorganization of the Department of Revenue in Matanzas. In 1824, there were four applicants for the position of Commander of the Guards of the Department of Revenue: three émigrés and one native son. Initially, the Cuban Ramón de Cozar, who had worked within the treasury division for 16 years before being laid off, was ranked first. Juan Bautista Ordaz came in second; although he had been in royal service longer, he had worked mostly in the navy with only an appointment of not quite five years in the tobacco monopoly in New Granada before fleeing to Cuba in 1817. The two other émigrés clearly had fewer qualifications: José Joaquin Muñoz had an entirely military career behind him, and Joaquin Reyna Capetillo had only a brief, temporary post in the customs house of Maracaibo, Venezuela.

Before sending on the recommendations to Madrid, however, the Intendant of Havana temporarily appointed the émigré Ordaz rather than Cozar to the post in order to fulfil a royal order that Ordaz be placed and 'since the former [Ordaz] has nine more years of service than the latter [Cozar], he has been active and has all the necessary qualifications to do a good job; he has proven his integrity and zeal while temporarily working in the subaltern office in the town of Los Güines'.[43] Cozar protested that he had been unemployed since March of 1822, because for each position to which he applied 'generally preference has been given to the émigrés from distant parts of America who are here, with notable harm to the laid-off bureaucrats [*cesantes*] on this Island, who have always been deserving of your Royal consideration for their fidelity and love for Your Majesty'.[44] In this case, the King overturned the Intendant's recommendation and appointed Cozar.

The Matanzas case reveals the frustration with the influx of émigrés among bureaucrats who had been gradually advancing through their career tracks in Cuba. The summary of the Council of Indies noted that the Intendant had earlier been urged to place Ordaz as the Revenue Administrator in Güines, but the chief of that division had objected that 'the placement and subsistence of these merely transient émigrés are not the responsibility of this province and it is not fair that they should be put ahead of those who are serving productively here'.[45] The Secretary of the Council concurred:

> It is true that there are orders to place the émigrés, but the same is true of those who have been laid off. The émigré bureaucrat has found in Havana half the salary he had without any obligation other than to hang around, or two thirds if he is attached to some office ... and it would be rash for the émigrés, after having received this favour, ... to also aspire to occupy all the vacancies that come up in a foreign land, so to speak.[46]

To appoint only émigrés to vacancies, the Secretary concluded, would mean that other bureaucrats would find themselves permanently unemployed. A year later, reports claiming that 'since Don Ramón de Cozar entered into service he has been developing ideas to give new energy to the division that he heads', seemed to confirm the wisdom of his appointment.[47]

The Cozar case suggests a shift from the favouritism shown toward émigrés to a consideration of the needs of various subjects and greater latitude for local officials to make appointments. Royal orders in 1826 and 1836 reiterated the priority to appoint to vacancies bureaucrats who were drawing either pensions or partial salaries, but extended this preference explicitly to both émigrés and *cesantes* who had been laid off for reasons other than the wars.[48] In 1827, José Blanco Pegazo, who had worked as a guard at the Tobacco Monopoly in Mérida, wrote to the Council of Indies requesting a similar position in Cuba. The Council's note recognized his merits and loyalty but expressed reservations about making low-level appointments which were generally the purview of local officials; moreover, they acknowledged a letter from the Intendant of Havana outlining 'the damages that can ensue from appointing people recommended by royal orders since there are so many meritorious subjects here that are taxing the public funds and awaiting the moment to put in an application'.[49] The authorities in Madrid sat on the application for over seven months before simply sending it along to the Intendant without any recommendation one way or the other. Certainly, some officials in Cuba took their responsibilities to both local and imperial needs seriously. In 1830, for example, the Intendant of Havana proposed a reorganization of the Maritime Revenue Administration that he claimed would improve efficiency without additional expense. It would do so by offsetting the payment of retirement pensions to employees who were too old or ill to be productive through the appointment of both émigrés and *cesantes* who would henceforth collect a salary for working rather than as unemployment assistance.[50]

Émigrés persisted in applying for positions on the grounds of their special sacrifices, but their record of success in the 1830s was mixed. In 1832, the Council of Indies forwarded a split ranking for a sinecure in Havana

Cathedral; each member had different recommendations for first and second place, but none were strictly émigrés. In the absence of a clear recommendation, the King chose the third-placed candidate, a native of Toledo who had been captured on his way to a post in Upper Peru in 1816 and had subsequently made his way to Puerto Rico.[51] In 1834 and 1836, Queen Regent María Cristina ordered temporary paid positions for émigrés Vicente Gayoso y Burk and José Santos González, who had fled New Spain and Río de la Plata respectively, until they were successful in attaining permanent posts.[52] However, royal favour was not bestowed on other supplicants. Almost 11 years after the 1825 royal order to favour émigrés in judicial appointments, Francisco Sánchez Chamorro cited it in his request for placement as a magistrate. He had served as Treasury Attorney and Judge Advocate in Veracruz and was one of the last royal officials to hold out in the fort of San Juan de Ulúa in New Spain.[53] The Minister of Grace and Justice simply sent his petition along to the Intendant of Havana without a recommendation. José Gutiérrez del Rivero was on a pension in 1837 after having served for 20 years in Caracas, Mexico City and Zaragoza; he applied for an opening in Havana where he could reunite with his wife and children, pointing out that by putting him back on salary the government would be relieved of paying his pension, but no response to his petition was recorded.[54]

Conclusion

The career path of Francisco de Paula Vilches, whose case opened this chapter, reflects the ongoing vicissitudes in the fortunes of displaced colonial administrators, as well as their general preference for employment in Cuba. After unsuccessfully appealing the reduction in his unemployment pension in 1826, Vilches began to apply for numerous posts in Cuba, some at lower ranks than his title of Regent. In 1828, the King named him Regent of the *Audiencia* of Manila, but Vilches declined on the grounds that he did not have the necessary funds to transport himself and his family such a great distance. The following year, he was appointed the Lieutenant Governor and Legal Counsel of Havana, over the application of native son Manuel Gómez de Avellaneda, in order to economize on the funds necessary to pay Vilches's pension. In 1831, the Council of Indies proposed Vilches to serve as Regent of the newly created *Audiencia* of Puerto Rico, noting that he could bring his experience to organizing the new court and end the power conflicts that had resulted from his appointment as a high-ranking magistrate to a lower-level post.[55] Within a year, nonetheless, Vilches began requesting leaves of absence, alleging health problems and hoping to reunite his family, which was divided between Cuba and Puerto Rico. In December 1833, he received the highest promotion possible in the judicial track – a place on the Council of Indies – but once again he suffered from bad timing as that body was dissolved a few months later. As of 1834, therefore, Vilches found himself again laid off on half salary, but at least he was granted permission to reside in Havana where 'he desired only to attend to the recovery of his health, in the midst of his family whose care and assistance he needs, and without exposing himself to renewed voyages and hardships'.[56] Despite his claim to lack other 'aspirations', he applied, unsuccessfully, for the Regency of the *Audiencia* of Havana in 1837 and 1841 because, in the words of his representative, 'recalling these services and all manner of losses suffered during the difficult periods of war and revolution in America, it is very distressing to find himself without a post in the class of *cesante* through no fault of his own...'.[57] In 1843, Vilches finally requested to be officially retired with a pension that would pay more than the half salary he was drawing as unemployment benefits, but the last note in his lengthy dossier indicated that a decision on his latest request should be postponed until rumours of his death could be verified.[58]

Colonial bureaucrats like Vilches, fleeing rebellions on the American mainland, created fiscal and employment pressures in Cuba for several decades. During the first phase of the wars, temporary pensions supported the émigrés until many could return to their posts. In the 1820s, however, as years passed without Spanish military victories, displaced administrators increasingly complained that partial salaries were insufficient to maintain themselves and failed to compensate the financial and familial losses they had suffered in order to remain loyal subjects. As the King and Council of Indies responded to their pleas with appointments to new permanent posts in Cuba, long-term residents of the island protested the interruption of their own career paths. Although some émigrés were successful in their requests to be rewarded for their special sacrifices into the 1830s, as a group they no longer benefited from an automatic preference over other candidates for employment. In this decade, especially after the death of Fernando VII in 1833, Spanish officials were more preoccupied with the Carlist Wars over succession to the throne than with recovering their former colonies. Although members of the royal family might still dispense patronage, they granted greater discretion to the authorities in Cuba to staff the island's administration. And in Cuba, governors did nominate émigrés whom they believed were well qualified (and possibly well connected), but also attended to the applications of locals who had been laid off. By adjusting policies in order to balance the needs of bureaucrats displaced by war with those who were native to or had made their careers in Cuba, metropolitan officials reduced the tensions arising from the flood of refugees to the island and reinforced loyalties to Spain in what remained its most important colony until 1898.

Acknowledgements

The research from which this chapter is drawn was supported by the Imagine Fund at the University of Minnesota and from fellowships awarded by the Fulbright

Commission (Spain) and the National Endowment for the Humanities. Any views, findings, conclusions, or recommendations expressed in this publication do not necessarily reflect those of the NEH.

Notes

1. Documents were consulted in the following archives: Archivo Histórico Nacional, Madrid (AHN) and Archivo General de Indias, Seville (AGI). Archival documents will be cited as follows: title, the abbreviation of the archival repository; followed by the document group (*ramo*), the *legajo* (bundle, hereafter leg.), and when applicable, a number (num.), box (caja), folder (expediente, hereafter exp.), or document (doc.). 'Don Francisco de Paula Vilches, Regente de la Audiencia de Guatemala emigrado en la Havana, pide colocación o pensión equivalente a dos tercios de su sueldo', testimonies taken in Cuba in 1827, AHN, Ultramar 1636, caja 1.
2. Petition dated 4 August 1826, AHN, Ultramar 1636, caja 1.
3. The historiography for Cuba in the early nineteenth-century focuses more on the rising sugar economy than on issues of governance; in terms of the movement of people, most attention has been on the dramatic rise in Spanish troops on the island with the withdrawals from the former colonies on the mainland, the growing importation of African slaves, and the immigration of Spaniards from the peninsula. For a recent analysis of race and Cuban loyalty, see David Sartorius, *Ever Faithful: Race, Loyalty, and the Ends of Empire in Spanish Cuba* (Durham, NC, 2013). On the influx of soldiers, see Manuel R. Moreno Fraginals and José J. Moreno Masó, *Guerra, migración y muerte (El ejército español en Cuba como vía migratoria)* (Colombres, 1993). For the demography of slaves and immigrants from Spain, see María Dolores Pérez Murillo, *Aspectos demográficos y sociales de la isla de Cuba en la primera mitad del siglo XIX* (Cádiz, 1988). For an overview of the relationship between Spain and Cuba, see Christopher Schmidt-Nowara, '"La España Ultramarina": Colonialism and Nation-Building in Nineteenth-Century Spain', *European History Quarterly* 34/2 (2004): 191–214; Josep M. Fradera, *Colonias para después de un imperio* (Barcelona, 2005); and Alfonso W. Quiroz, 'Implicit Costs of Empire: Bureaucratic Corruption in Nineteenth-Century Cuba', *Journal of Latin American Studies* 35/3 (2003): 473–511.
4. See also Rafe Blaufarb's chapter in this volume.
5. For an overview, see Edmundo A. Heredia, *Los vencidos: Un estudio sobre los realistas en la guerra de independencia hispanoamericana* (Córdoba, Argentina, 1997), 65–89. Mark Burkholder's work on *audiencia* judges includes some who were forced to flee during the independence wars: Mark Burkholder, *From Impotence to Authority: The Spanish Crown and the American Audiencias, 1687–1808* (Columbia, 1977), especially 139–144, and also Mark Burkholder and D. S. Chandler, *Biographical Dictionary of Audiencia Ministers in the Americas, 1687–1821* (Westport, CT, 1982).
6. AGI, Audiencia de Santa Fé, leg. 933.
7. Rebecca Earle, *Spain and the Independence of Colombia, 1810–1825* (Exeter, 2000), 41–43 and 64–66. For the case of Archdeacon Miguel María de Yarza y Olazarán, who accompanied the vice-regal court as it moved from Bogotá to Cartagena to Santa Marta to Panama, back to Santa Marta, and finally to Jamaica, see AHN, Ultramar, leg. 1607, caja 1, exp. 8, doc. 6.
8. For the cases of several royalists in Curaçao in 1814, see AGI, Audiencia de Caracas, leg. 386.

9. Report dated 26 November 1816, AGI, Audiencia de Caracas, Leg. 386. See also Report dated 15 August 1814, AGI, Audiencia de Caracas, leg. 386.
10. Spain, *Colección de los decretos y órdenes que han expedido las Córtes general y extraordinarias desde su instalación*, 10 vols (Cádiz and Madrid, 1813–1823), vol. 1 (Cádiz, 1813), 171.
11. 'Pérez to the Treasury Minister', 31 October 1812, AGI, Audiencia de Santa Fé, leg. 933.
12. 'Relación de Méritos de Juan Nepomuceno Hernández de Alva', AHN, Ultramar, leg. 1619, caja 1, exp. 20, doc. 40.
13. Natividad Moreno Garbayo, *Colección de reales cédulas del Archivo Histórico Nacional: Catálogo*, 2 vols (Madrid, 1977), vol. 2, 161.
14. Petition dated 31 August 1838 in Havana, AHN, Ultramar, leg. 2852. See also the case of Tomás de Francia in AGI, Audiencia de Caracas, leg. 386.
15. On Mexico, see Harold Dana Sims, *The Expulsion of Mexico's Spaniards, 1821–1836* (Pittsburgh, PA, 1990); and Jesús Ruiz de Gordejuela Urquijo, *La expulsión de los españoles de México y su destino incierto, 1821–1836* (Sevilla, 2006).
16. On Puerto Rico, see Raquel Rosario Rivera, *Los emigrantes llegados a Puerto Rico procedentes de Venezuela entre 1810–1848* (Hato Rey, 1992); Rosario Rivera, *La Real Cédula de Gracias de 1815 y sus primeros efectos en Puerto Rico* (San Juan, 1995); and Ivette Pérez Vega, 'El efecto económico, social y político de la emigración de Venezuela en el Sur de Puerto Rico (Ponce), 1810–1830', *Revista de Indias* 47/181 (1987): 869–885.
17. A copy of the order was attached (attachment num. 3) to 'Don Francisco de Paula Vilches, Regente de la Audiencia de Guatemala emigrado en la Havana, pide colocación o pensión equivalente a dos tercios de su sueldo' (1826), AHN, Ultramar, leg. 1636, caja 1.
18. Ildefonso José de Medina included a copy of the 12 December 1821 order in his petition to the Minister of Grace and Justice; AGI, Ultramar, leg. 137, num. 12.
19. AGI, Ultramar, leg. 137, num. 26.
20. In addition to the cases cited below, see AGI, Ultramar, leg. 137, num. 38 and 50; and AGI, Ultramar, leg. 158, num. 7.
21. AGI, Ultramar, leg. 137, num. 50. The order was also cited in the case of Pedro Ramírez, a royal accountant displaced from Bogotá; AGI, Ultramar, leg. 137, num. 60.
22. AGI, Ultramar, leg. 138, num. 11.
23. AGI, Ultramar, leg. 138, num. 11 indicates the King's agreement with the recommendation, but the full text of his order to the Intendant was included as an attachment in the case of Francisco de Paula Vilches in AHN, Ultramar, leg. 1636, caja 1, attachment 2.
24. AGI, Ultramar, leg. 138, num. 11.
25. 'Consulta del Consejo de Indias sobre la colocación de los empleados que han emigrado de Indias', 18 December 1823, AHN, Ultramar, leg. 1602, exp. 75, doc. 3.
26. Opinion of *fiscal* dated 28 December 1823, Ibid. doc. 2.
27. Similarly on 10 March 1824, the Council of Indies recommended that émigrés in the Peninsula be favoured over bureaucrats resident in the colonies for open positions; see the copy in the case of Vilches, AHN, Ultramar, leg. 1636, caja 1.
28. Ibid.
29. AHN, Ultramar, leg. 3304, exp. 27.
30. For a list of high-ranking officials still living in Cuba on pensions in 1836, see 'El Capitán General remite nota de sueldos y pensiones', AHN, Ultramar, leg. 1615, exp. 25.

31. 'Don Vicente Díaz y García pide los honores de Intendente de Provincia', 13 September 1838, AHN, Ultramar, leg. 2852.
32. 'Representación de Bartolomé Guanche y su hoja de servicio', 8 August 1827, AGI, Ultramar, leg. 142, exp. 45.
33. See 'Don José Vicente de la Huerta pide los honores de oidor', AHN, Ultramar, leg. 1608, exp. 22; 'Expediente de don Juan Jurado, oidor emigrado de Cartagena', Ibid. leg. 1608, exp. 15; 'Expediente sobre sugetos para el Arcedianato Vacante en la Santa Iglesia Catedral de la Habana', petition of Ramón Otero, 18 September 1827, Ibid. leg. 1612, caja 2, exp. 39, doc. 17; and 'Se recomienda al Intendente de la Habana á don José Pezuela para que procure colocarlo', 25 April 1835, Ibid., leg. 2939.
34. 'Al Señor Intendente de la Habana para que se liquiden los sueldos del oidor don Ildefonso Medina', 10 November 1835, AHN, Ultramar, leg. 2940, caja 2.
35. Ibid.
36. Ibid. See the note on the case summary. For details on procedures for appointments, which sometimes but not always involved consultation, see Burkholder and Chandler, *Biographical Dictionary*, xi–xxiii.
37. 'El Ministro de Marina, de Comercio, y Gobernacion de Ultramar remite al Ministro de Hacienda la instancia de Don Lucas Bayo, oficial cesante de las suprimidas lineas telegráficas, solicitando se le destine a las órdenes del Intendente de la Havana', 15 March 1839, AHN, Ultramar, leg. 2852.
38. 'Miguel Bataller pide la plaza vacante en el Tribunal Mayor de Cuentas de la Havana', 7 June 1836, AHN, Ultramar, leg. 2852. See also 'Minuta sobre instancia de don Juan Basadre, hijo de don Vicente Basadre, Intendente que fue de Caracas, pide alguna colocación en cualquiera de los dominios de Indias', 19 July 1832, AHN, Ultramar, leg. 2939, caja 2.
39. 'Al Intendente de la Habana para que dé colocación a don Bernardo Miyares', 1 March 1835, AHN, Ultramar, leg. 2939. But Ramón Hernández, an émigré twice over from first Santo Domingo and then Venezuela, was unsuccessful in his request that the six months of practice remaining for his son to be certified as a lawyer be waived given the delays caused by revolution and emigration; 'El Señor Secretario del Despacho de Marina recomienda por cuarta vez el mérito y servicios de don Ramón Hernández de Armas, Auditor de Marina de Caracas', AHN, Ultramar, leg. 1607, exp. 1, doc. 4.
40. 'Al Señor Intendente de la Habana para que se liquiden los sueldos del oidor don Ildefonso Medina', 24 August 1824, AHN, Ultramar, leg. 2940, caja 2.
41. 'Don Francisco de Paula Vilches', AHN, Ultramar, leg. 1636, caja 1, unnumbered exp. See also 'Expediente de don Francisco Hernández de la Joya, emigrado de Caracas', AHN, Ultramar, leg. 1619, exp. 19, doc. 24.
42. 'Recomendación para la ración de la Santa Iglesia vacante por la muerte de don Francisco Tomás Martínez Zaldivar', 20 September 1828, AHN, Ultramar, leg. 1606, exp. 51, doc. 2.
43. 'Arreglo de la administración y resguardo de Rentas de Matanzas y nombramientos de sus empleados', 24 June 1825, AHN, Ultramar, leg. 2939.
44. Ibid. Indeed, in another file, there is a royal order rejecting Cozar's application for a post in the Postal Service on the grounds that that division was already full of both regular employees and temporary appointments of émigrés; AHN, Ultramar, leg. 2940, 9 November 1822.
45. Ibid.
46. Ibid.

47. Ibid. Report dated 10 May 1826.
48. Cited in 'Petición de Juan de Arredondo y Santelices', 29 October 1836, AHN, Ultramar, leg. 2852.
49. 'Dirigiéndole una solicitud de don José Blanco Pegazo', AGI, Ultramar, leg. 142, exp. 47.
50. Report dated 29 October 1830, AHN, Ultramar, leg. 2940, caja 1. In 1836, the Intendant highly recommended émigré José Morote for a position as accountant in the local treasury; AHN, Ultramar, leg. 2940, caja 2, 10 July 1836.
51. It is also possible that the King chose the third-placed candidate because there was unanimity in his recommendation, and one of the first-placed candidates had once been captured by Colombians during naval service; AHN, Ultramar, leg. 1610, exp. 19. In 1829 and again in 1833, émigrés were both ranked first and appointed for the post of Legal Counsel in the new Colony of Fernandina de Jagua; the first was aged 69 in 1829 and it is not clear whether he ever took office before his death, and the second continued to petition for a different post on the grounds that the climate of Jagua was bad for his health. 'Expediente del Doctor Don Pantaleón Rosillo, emigrado de Venezuela en Cuba', AHN, Ultramar, leg. 1630, exp. 15.
52. AHN, Ultramar, leg. 2939, caja 2.
53. 'Al Intendente de la Habana que se ha remitido a Gracia y Justicia la solicitud de Don Francisco Sánchez Chamorro que pretenda una plaza de oidor', 10 December 1835, AHN, Ultramar, leg. 2940, caja 2.
54. 'Instancias sin curso, José Gutiérrez del Rivero, Magistrado Cesante de la Audiencia de Zaragoza pide se dignase agraciarle con la Asesoría en comisión de la Intendencia de la Havana que se halla vacante', 2 January 1837, AHN, Ultramar, Hacienda de Cuba, Leg. 2852. See also 'Don Ramón Martínez Téllez pide alguna plaza de Hacienda de las Provincias de Ultramar en la Isla de Cuba', 12 April 1838.
55. AHN, Ultramar 1636, caja 2, 8 August 1831.
56. AHN, Ultramar 1636, caja 1, 31 July 1834.
57. Ibid., 18 September 1841.
58. AHN, Ultramar 1636, caja 2, 24 August 1843.

15
Enterprising Women and War Profiteers: Race, Gender and Power in the Revolutionary Caribbean

Kit Candlin and Cassandra Pybus

War profiteers have long been a theme in conflict studies. Profiteering was as much a feature of the wars that tore through the Caribbean at the end of the eighteenth century as it was for later wars in the nineteenth and twentieth centuries. The age of democratic revolutions in the Atlantic World, beginning roughly with the end of the Seven Years War in 1763 and continuing through the American, French, and South American revolutions, brought upheaval to the Caribbean that lasted decades. In this turbulent world of slave rebellion and imperial contest a new group of people emerged to complicate further the social demography of the region. This chapter focuses on free women of colour, who perhaps more than any other social group were able to navigate the revolutionary turmoil in the Caribbean, self-fashion their own lives and profit from division and conflict. These were women who were descended from slaves and yet they themselves became slave owners with little inclination to manumit any of their chattels unless they happened to be family. By the time these conflicts came to an end, their mark on networks of power would be an indelible, often denigrated, part of afro-Caribbean identity. Their presence is an important legacy in the history of war, demonstrating that conflict and insecurity could create important entrepreneurial opportunity to be seized upon by marginalized or displaced civilians.

Free women of colour have increasingly caught the eye of scholars working on the Atlantic World, and we are not the first to notice their increased presence in late eighteenth century sources. There are several works that explore the rising visibility of such women.[1] These are important contributions to the study of this Caribbean group, but very little has been written to explore the relationship that free women of colour had to war and conflict and how some were able to successfully navigate the conflict in the Caribbean to enrich themselves and gain considerable social advancement.

In this chapter we focus on a case study of one particular woman, Dorothy Thomas, who most personified the possibilities for free women of colour in a complex, insecure and shifting war zone. Throughout her long life she maintained a sharp business sense, seeking out new avenues for profit and new contacts, and central to her entrepreneurial activity was her attachment to family, which was part and parcel of her modus operandi. Mixed-race women like Dorothy Thomas, driven from island to island by the fortunes of war, could be seen as refugees, a major theme in conflict studies, and yet Dorothy Thomas seemed to thrive in transience and uncertainty. Her restless ambitions and the deft way she dealt with ongoing international crises challenge the stock image of the refugee.

Revolution and war in the Caribbean and their legacy

The Treaty of Paris signed by the kingdoms of Great Britain, France and Spain, with Portugal in agreement, after Britain's victory over France and Spain formally ended the Seven Years War of 1754–1763 (known also as the French and Indian War in North America), was a watershed in Atlantic history. It really begins the age of democratic revolution. The ink on the treaty was barely dry as a motley collection of British speculators, financiers, merchants and other hopefuls fell to dividing the spoils from defeated France. Bringing great fortunes and even greater credit to bear, they inundated the British government with proposals, suggestions and advice in order to secure a share in the new prosperity.[2] Most eyes were on the Caribbean. In the age of King Sugar, it was an easy choice to make and the most sought-after new land was therefore to be found in the Windward Caribbean territories of Grenada, St Vincent, Dominica and Tobago that collectively became known as the Ceded Islands.

With the imperial gains of 1763 began a second phase of British expansion into the Caribbean, pushing the power base out from colonies like Jamaica, Antigua, Montserrat, Nevis and St Kitts in the north, and Barbados in the south, to fill much of the space in between. By the end of the eighteenth century, under external pressure from war, revolution and migration, this second phase of Caribbean growth led to a third and final phase, when the frontier colonies of Trinidad and Demerara, at the very south of the archipelago, were conquered and occupied in the 1790s. These new colonies were a magnet to free people of colour, relocating from colonies such as French Saint-Domingue, Martinique and St Lucia or else abandoning their existence in older British colonies where they were relegated to the margins of white society. The British exercised far less strict regimes in the fledgling colonies of the Ceded Islands, and here they could buy land, often without caveat, and suffer no restrictions on their movement, or on whom they could marry. Such were their numbers that by 1783 free people of colour on Grenada stood at 53 percent of the total free population, and the majority of these free coloureds were women.[3]

Colonies born of conquest and with porous borders were inevitable sites of contestation, and colonial governors in the ceded colonies had to negotiate their authority against a backdrop of disruption and unrest. Looming over these internal disputes was the threat of slave revolt—especially as the numbers of slaves brought into these colonies completely dwarfed those arriving in older possessions. With resident French Catholic populations in all these new islands, and well-populated French dominions like Guadeloupe and Martinique just a short sail away, British governors found themselves embroiled in contests over religion and custom.[4] In this space of compromise and accommodation a comparatively permissive culture arose that was free from many of the ingrained restrictions blighting other colonies. Free people of colour were quick to take advantage of this permissiveness.[5] As the century progressed in the southern Caribbean, whites found that they did not enjoy an exclusive hold on land tenure, slave ownership and influence in this fluid, frontier world where new British conquests sat uneasily beside the other great empires in the region.

More than once these islands changed hands as wars, revolution and revolt tore across the Atlantic World. The American Revolution and its War of Independence (1775–1783), followed closely by the French Revolution and the Revolutionary Wars (1792–1799), triggered a series of lesser, but no less disruptive colonial revolutions fought largely around the Caribbean. The French retook Grenada, St Vincent and Tobago during the American War of Independence, along with the Dutch colony of Demerara, accelerating animosity between original French inhabitants and newer arrivals from Britain. However, with the British destruction of the French fleet in the Caribbean in the closing stages of the American War of Independence and mounting financial difficulties at home, France was forced to return these colonies in the peace of 1783.[6] Every time a colony changed hands like this, a new group of people would be unsettled by the conflict. This transience made the southern Caribbean—with the close, interconnectedness of its islands—an ethnic polyglot, very different from the homogeneity distinctive of older European possessions. Here, on the edges of America, people of colour found they could exploit the gaps in the imperial framework.

The end of the American Revolution in 1783 did nothing to ease tensions between the French and the British, the latter retaking the Ceded Islands with renewed vigour and sense of righteousness. Tensions were most pronounced on Grenada, the wealthiest of the new British colonies in the southern Caribbean. Rafts of legislation were aimed at the complete disenfranchisement of French settlers who chose to remain in the colony.[7] Eventually, with so few European French left, this attack on the rights of the Francophone Catholic community fell squarely on the Francophone free coloureds, whose success was jealously coveted by new settlers from Britain.[8] Further laws attempted to curtail their influence in society and their prominence in the commercial life of the colony. Insulting this emergent community reflected imperial hubris, and it brought an enormous cost.

The Fedon Rebellion in British Grenada in 1795–1796 coming as it did right in the middle of the French Revolutionary Wars, was the most violent expression of conflict that erupted between 'revolutionary' France and Great Britain in the Caribbean between 1793 and 1815. It would only be surpassed in magnitude by the revolution on Saint-Domingue, better known as the Haitian Revolution (1791–1804). Both wars had free people of colour at their heart. However, such conflict was not unique. The war with France spawned several interconnected struggles during the age of revolutions in the southern Caribbean, played out through the 1790s and into the new century with shifting alliances complicating matters as the fighting drew in other imperial allies and combatants. With so many nations having colonies in such close proximity, the war with France rapidly turned the Caribbean into a cauldron of invasions and counter-invasions, while waves of refugees and migrants wandered from island to island looking for sanctuary or opportunities.

By 1796, the situation for the British had become dire. On St Lucia the British army of occupation experienced deadly guerrilla fighting by bands of armed free coloureds.[9] On Martinique, the situation was little better, with the invading British holding back an increasingly aggressive insurgency. This was also the case on Grenada, where a pro-republican insurrection led by Julien Fedon, a mixed race planter turned military officer, destroyed most of the island, leaving many whites killed, estates burned and towns ransacked, whilst slaves deserted their plantations en masse to join the rising. Another ugly war broke out on St Vincent, with Black Caribs and free coloureds finding common cause with white republican French against the British settlers.

The rise of the free people of colour in the revolutionary Caribbean

It was 1795, the year in which the British campaign in the southern Caribbean faltered, that marked a turning point in Atlantic history, as it saw free coloureds emerge as a new political player positioned between European rivals. Until that point, free people of colour were a statistic, occasionally showing themselves as subordinate players in the social demography of the Caribbean, or walk-on actors in a drama centred on slaves and masters. They were always targets for discrimination and abuse, as in Grenada, but 1795 changed all that. The upheaval of 1795 saw these people collectively flex their muscles across the Caribbean. As the war progressed on different islands, large engagements took place in which there were virtually no white people fighting on either side. Free coloured assertion was boosted by the anonymity and confusion provided by war and revolution. With easy passage between the islands, and Europeans distracted by either the Revolutionary War or, later, the Wars of Independence that rocked the Spanish empire, free coloureds could readily slip into neighbouring colonies and take on new identities.

The Revolutionary Wars created opportunities for thousands of refugees, white and black, moving from island to island as conflicts washed over communities. Increasingly, the slave revolts that shook the Caribbean in the last years of the eighteenth century and the first decades of the nineteenth pushed people further from one colony to the next. Whether forced or voluntary, these migrations had a profound effect on the development of the colonies in the southern Caribbean. In the years following 1795, these colonies would remain some of the most unstable in the Atlantic World as well as the most multicultural.

Assertive people of colour keep appearing to confound and confuse the narrative of Caribbean history. What had been a race war between slaves and free, black and white, became complicated by their presence; a conflict for global domination between European rivals and their allies became a confusing war where not all French were republican and not all British subjects were loyal. As generals sent to the region found, not all whites could be trusted and not all blacks were enemies. The appearance of the free coloured community on the world stage is not so much a story of a struggle against European colonial power, or a fight against slavery, or complicity in the colonial project, but rather, it is about how these people confuse, complicate and upset the delicate racial balance of the Caribbean. Free coloureds blurred the boundary between freedom and servitude and between politics and class. Their presence threw into stark relief the contradictions and hypocrisy of chattel slavery, and caused the strict racial lines to crumble and eventually give way.

In the 50 years from 1780 to 1830, free coloured numbers exploded to completely dwarf the white population on islands like Trinidad, Grenada, St Vincent and Tobago. Even on Barbados, Britain's oldest colony in the Caribbean and the only colony to have a majority of whites consistently in the free population until the end of slavery, free people of colour still represented a third of the free population by 1829.[10] On Trinidad, their numbers continued to grow, from 4,000 in 1797 to just under 16,000 by 1829, while the white population of 2,000 only doubled in the same period, making free coloureds almost four times as numerous.[11] Even though many free people of colour were removed from Grenada after the Fedon Rebellion, by 1829 Grenada had 3,786 free people of colour while the white population numbered just 801.[12] In Dominica, it was a similar story, where 703 whites lived alongside 3,590 free coloured people by 1830. Even the aggressive development of Demerara's slave society at the end of the eighteenth century still did not stop the rapid rise in the free population of colour, with over twice as many as there were whites in the colony in 1830.[13] Women of colour manumitted at a much greater rate than their male counterparts, and therefore constituted a much greater presence in the freed community. It was free women of colour who seized the moment.

The prominence of free women of colour in the local economies of colonies as diverse as Demerara and Grenada testifies to the powerful position to which some free coloured women had risen by the end of the Napoleonic Wars in 1815.[14] Wealthy in their own right, such women needed no white male partner to be a significant player and source of influence in the business culture. Certainly, many free coloured women cohabited with merchants and imperial powerbrokers, but increasingly they were drawn from a group of independent, articulate and entrepreneurial creole women, often able to manipulate situations and individuals to their own advantage and to fashion their own existence. These women were savvy and socially mobile, maintaining networks of contacts and associates (many of whom were other free coloured women) to maintain themselves and each other in turbulent times. They were careful to have their children educated in good schools in Britain, and in the process become the epicentre of a large network of family relations, which by the second and third generation had gained a noticeable amount of colonial authority. What follows is the story of just one of these women.

A free woman of colour, entrepreneur and war profiteer

Dorothy Thomas (née Kirwan) was born a slave in the Leeward Islands, in about 1756. She first came to the attention of colonial record keepers in the colony of Dominica in the spring of 1784. The War of the American Revolution had finally ended and Dominica was booming, with more merchant vessels in the port of Roseau than had visited the island over the previous five years of French occupation.[15] Before the war, Roseau was a free port that operated as an *entrepôt* for a lucrative re-export slave trade, and cash-strapped merchants were flocking back to the newly-restored colony to recoup the fortunes that had been lost to war and trade embargoes. Doubtless this inter-island slave trade was the mercantile activity that engaged Joseph Thomas, who owned a quarter of a trading vessel, the *Mary* out of Lancaster, based in the colony of Grenada. On 10 July 1784 Joseph Thomas was at the Roseau offices of Thomas Brayshaw and Charles Bates, who acted as executors of the estate of the late William Foden and were responding to an application from a mulatto woman named Dorothy Kirwan for a formal deed of freedom, in accordance with the intention expressed in Foden's will. Joseph Thomas was one of the four witnesses to the deed of manumission.

For an enslaved woman to purchase her own freedom and then insist upon receiving a formal deed of manumission was unusual and impressive, and it was apparent to at least one of the four men who signed the document that Dorothy was a very canny young woman, as well as highly desirable. The late William Foden had been the father of her children, William and Charlotte, but it was Joseph Thomas who had fathered her baby daughter, named Nan in the document, but thereafter known as Ann Thomas. Joseph Thomas would become the most significant man in her eventful life, but in 1784 he was just one of several white men Dorothy enlisted in her project to obtain freedom from the dehumanizing indignity of chattel slavery, along with her six children, her mother and her sisters.

Dorothy was a recent arrival in Dominica, having been taken by Foden from the nearby colony of Montserrat, where she was born a slave of the prominent Kirwan family, who also had landholdings on Antigua, Nevis and St Kitts, with business interests that stretched across the Caribbean.[16] Dorothy was almost certainly the daughter of one of the Kirwan men and in 1780 she was the property of Andrew Kirwan. By that time, she had already given birth to at least three children, Elizabeth Kirwan, Catherina Cells and Edward Isles, who were also Andrew Kirwan's property, and their surnames indicate that each of them had a different white father.[17] At some stage, all three children were manumitted, presumably on the payment of their purchase price to Andrew Kirwan. That was certainly the case for 'the mestee boy slave called Ned—son of a mulatto slave called Doll Kirwan' who was manumitted by Andrew Kirwan on 24 July 1781 on receipt of £40 from Ellis Iles.[18]

Since Edward appears to have stayed with his mother after this transaction, it is a reasonable presumption that Dorothy intervened to have Isles buy the freedom of her youngest child at the same time as she arranged for her purchase by William Foden, and that the monies paid by both men actually belonged to her. How did she get the money for these purchases, given that she was the property of the Kirwan family and her labour belonged to them? Perhaps she was permitted the mobility and independence to sell her person as an enslaved courtesan to the planter class.

Joseph Thomas did not enjoy an exclusive relationship with Dorothy. At some time around 1786, she gave birth to a daughter, whom she later had baptized as Frances Owen(s), most likely the child of Captain John Owens from Barbados, the skipper of the sloop *Nelly,* owned by William Barrow, the employer of William Foden.[19] However, by August 1786 Joseph Thomas had re-established his intimacy with Dorothy and on 1 June 1787 her daughter Eliza was baptized in the town of St George's, Grenada, registered in the church records as 'daughter of Joseph Thomas by Dorothy a free mulattress'.[20] The birth of Eliza Thomas was followed by the birth of a son named Joseph in 1789, and in the following year another son, Harry. All three children were properly baptized in the parish church of St George's with the father named as Joseph Thomas. The last child, Dorothea Christina Thomas, was born in June 1796.[21]

Joseph Thomas's economic fortunes were on the rise after St George's was declared a free port in 1787. The following year, he and his British partners purchased a second vessel, a sloop called *Jack,* sailing out of Liverpool. To all intents and purposes, he and Dorothy had become husband and wife. In her later years, Dorothy would insist on being called Mrs Thomas, which is not to say that Dorothy was the dependant of Joseph Thomas. They were never married according to English law, so she was free to keep her own surname and, more importantly, to keep her money and property completely separate from Thomas. It is a moot point which of the couple was the more economically secure at the time when she moved to Grenada, but certainly after a resumption of the war with France in 1793 she was doing much better financially than he was. It is unclear what the nature of Dorothy's business in Grenada was, but if her later life is any indication she was involved in huckstering, that is to say she was employing enslaved women to sell merchandise from door to door and to outlying plantations. She owned at least one hotel in St George's, and presumably she also had an involvement in the provision of housekeeping and sexual services for white men in the colony.

There is no doubt that Dorothy Thomas was making money after 1793, whereas Joseph Thomas was losing his. The resumed war with France meant that inter-island trade in which he was engaged had become an extremely risky business and in 1794 his ship *Mary* with its cargo was taken as a prize, which would have been a huge economic blow. In addition, the Fedon Rebellion of 1795 destroyed the plantation economy of Grenada for several years and had a seriously negative impact on Thomas's mercantile activity from which he never really recovered. He died a short while later, and there is no evidence of a will, which probably meant he died intestate.

During the years when Dorothy Thomas was building her business enterprise on Grenada, she had not lost sight of her two oldest children, nor her mother and sister. It can be established that in 1793 her daughter Catherina was living in Demerara as a free woman, married to a planter and longstanding resident named D. P. Simon, while her other daughter, Elizabeth Kirwan, was also a free woman by 1794, living in Grenada as the common-law wife of John Coxall, the son and heir of English merchant John Cavalero Coxall. How the manumission of the two daughters was accomplished is a matter of guesswork because there are no extant records for Demerara before 1795, and the Grenada records provide no evidence of the manumission of Elizabeth Kirwan. It is not far-fetched to speculate that Dorothy organized for the purchase and subsequent manumission of her older daughters, because that is what she did for other members of her family.

Over a period of 16 years, Dorothy Thomas managed to buy freedom for herself, for her children and for several other members of her family. An insight into her modus operandi can be found in a transaction on 1 December 1794 when she purchased 'the mulatto slave Mary Rose' whom she sought to manumit, claiming that Mary Rose had 'fully repaid' the sum.[22] This woman must have been a close relative, perhaps a sister, later described a free coloured woman named Mary Thomas, 'kinswoman' to Dorothy's daughter Frances Owens.[23] Dorothy Thomas also purchased her mother Betty whom she manumitted on 24 October 1797.[24]

In 1797, Grenada had just emerged from the brutal and economically catastrophic Fedon revolution and the British authorities were especially anxious about freed slaves.[25] A prominent and successful free coloured woman, who was the common-law wife of an Englishman, presented a problem for the British community in post-Fedon Grenada. For this reason, Dorothy Thomas kept her Catholic religion to herself and had her children baptized and buried in the Anglican Church, while her relationship with Joseph Thomas provided her with immunity from deportation. However, once Joseph Thomas died, she found it prudent to leave this maelstrom of heavy-handed, arbitrary reprisal and economic desolation, relocate to the more prosperous colony of Barbados and re-establish her business in Bridgetown, a thriving maritime centre, and home to British naval forces in the Caribbean.[26]

Like many free coloured entrepreneurs, she conducted her business outside the official channels and was a supplier of accommodation and services to feed the voracious appetite of the British military. The war economy centred on Barbados, the oldest and most established colony in the region, and the island's principal anchorage was a forest of ships. Throughout the 1790s, Barbados experienced unprecedented numbers of troops passing through Carlisle Bay. From Barbados, commanders launched successive expeditions against French islands. As one observer commented, Bridgetown became the epicentre of this military activity, with hundreds if not thousands of troops in port at any one time. Commanders, fearing the spread of disease, normally took troops off ships for shore leave. Women like Dorothy Thomas were an integral part to this movement of men and material, with a leading stake in service provision, as a provider of accommodation. Perhaps the most famous such establishment was the Royal Naval Hotel, which was set up by Rachael Pringle Polgreen and during the war run by Nancy Clarke. There were many other such establishments, run by free women of colour, where soldiers and sailors could find accommodation food, domestic service and sexual indulgence.

Across the Windward Islands, British attempts to conquer foreign colonies such as Martinique and Guadeloupe, and retain British ones in the wake of the republican threat, meant more reliance on free people of colour, thereby opening more opportunities for them as soldiers in the West Indian regiments, pilots for shipping, cooks, cleaners and washerwomen. Free coloured women feature significantly in this scenario, especially as the British military refused to allow white women to accompany the army. As a series of republican wars and slave rebellions engulfed the region in three successive waves in 1793, 1795 and 1797, the normal channels of supply were disrupted, and to feed the army's enormous appetite the British bought specie from whoever was willing to sell, providing a unique opportunity for free coloured women such Dorothy Thomas to thrive. When the British decided to pre-empt a French invasion of Dutch Demerara by taking the colony for themselves in 1796, she saw a new opportunity. Demerara had nothing like the metropolitan character of Bridgetown and could boast no hotels or places of amusement to service the British military. She was one of several women from Barbados to take advantage of the wind of change to establish a hotel and a huckstering business in Demerara. By 1807, she was listed as running a rooming house or hotel on the southern edge of the capital, Georgetown. That she was in the business of supplying accommodation, and much more, was suggested by a runaway notice posted July 1808 for a 'tall, good looking, full breasted Negro girl named Sarah' who took with her 'a few articles for sale'. Huckstering and the provision of personal services were a key element of her business success, as remarked upon in the later recollections of a resident who remembered that Doll [Dorothy Thomas] had by 'huckstering and hiring out negroes, accumulated an immense fortune'.[27] Sporadic advertisements in the *Demerara Gazette* draw attention to a range of enterprises: several runaway notices for women, and notices for the sale of male slave artisans, such as painters and carpenters. There were also notices for the rent of various substantial properties in Georgetown and Cumingsburg, and goods for sale at her 'dwelling-house'.[28]

Dorothy Thomas was certainly well-placed to make a successful mercantile business. She had connections to extensive merchant networks, including the two prominent Grenada merchants John Garraway and John Coxall who were her daughters' husbands. She also appears to have had a familial connection to William King, the son of the prominent London merchant Thomas King. As well as owning plantations in Demerara, Thomas and William King were slave traders, and they remained Dorothy's business associates all of her life, named in her 1843 will as the London correspondents who invested her money in 'government and other securities' in Britain.[29] Dorothy's mercantile connections in Demerara were given a further boost when her daughter Charlotte Foden became the common-law wife of John Fullerton, a Scottish merchant heavily involved in speculation in Demerara.[30] At about the same time, her daughter Eliza Thomas made a common-law marriage with Gilbert Robertson, the Demerara agent for the enormously influential company, Robertson, Sandbach and Parker, major players in the trade of the southern Caribbean, and well-known to Dorothy from her time in Grenada.[31]

Dorothy Thomas was not carrying crippling debt, nor was her enterprise subject to the vagaries of shipping convoys, or vulnerable to attack and seizure by French privateers, so she enjoyed considerable financial advantage over her white sons-in-law. Her business flourished during the long war with France, whereas their mercantile operations were under huge strain and their debt level rose exponentially. Circumstantial evidence points to Dorothy Thomas providing money to support these white men, an ironic reversal of the stereotype of the parasitic free coloured concubine.[32]

Her daughter Catherina's husband, D. P. Simon, was deeply in debt as early as 1794, and by 1807 he had lost his entire estate. He and Catherina had at least six children to support in much reduced circumstances where Simon eked out a living as the official translator for the colony. The eldest child,

Henrietta, went to a private school in England after 1813, apparently paid for by her grandmother.[33] Catherina Simon was recorded as dealing in land and slaves in her own right, presumably with the financial backing of her mother.[34] D. P. Simon's neighbour, Gilbert Robertson, the husband of Eliza Thomas, was another man mired in debt.[35] It is significant that he came to be listed as a joint owner of slaves on Dorothy Thomas's Kensington plantation, which suggests that Gilbert Robertson and Dorothy Thomas were in business together.[36] John Gloster Garraway, husband of Ann Thomas, was also in serious financial trouble in December 1824 when he lost his entire business and all his Grenada property to merchant creditors in Bristol and London.[37] A much-diminished man, Garraway was compelled to work as an attorney, with his slave property reduced to a mere two or three slaves. Yet over the next decade the number of Garraway slaves grew to around 40, all of them listed as the property of his wife Ann, and probably paid for by her mother.[38] Moreover, Garraway was able to regain his property in St George's because Dorothy Thomas purchased the indentures from his English creditors.[39] It was Dorothy, not her white sons-in-law, who paid for the education of their children in Britain. By the time she was established in Demerara, her youngest children and grandchildren were all enrolled at elite schools in Britain.[40]

By the end of the Napoleonic Wars, Dorothy Thomas had become something of a grande dame, who was no longer referred to as the diminutive Doll, but always as Mrs Dorothy Thomas. The size and status of her hotel in Cumingsburg reflected her enhanced standing. In February 1817, she was able to boast a restaurant with haute cuisine, having secured the services of a 'traiteur et Restaurateur' and a few months later she had an even more exotic offering in the form of a live African lion to amuse the guests.[41] She regularly bought and sold property along the waterfront and had interests in plantations in Mahaica and in Berbice. According to the Demerara Slave Registers, by 1820 she owned 83 slaves and was joint owner of another 17 on the Kensington plantation.[42] Her workforce was largely skilled, including housekeepers, seamstresses, nursemaids, boatmen, painters and carpenters. When compensation was paid after emancipation, she was granted £3,413, the largest sum of money paid to a free coloured person in the colony.[43]

Her flamboyance and prominence caught the eye of nearly every visitor to the colony. In 1822, a merchant in Demerara described Mrs Dorothy Thomas as the head of the free coloured community, with 'the deportment of an empress', living in 'a splendidly furnished house in Georgetown with a cotton plantation up the coast'.[44] A visiting American army officer remembered 'the celebrated Mrs Thomas, the free negress' who 'had a water-cistern capable of holding 5,000 or 6,000 gallons'.[45] Marianne Pemberton Holmes, a long-time white resident of the colony, was fascinated by her, observing that 'tho' totally illiterate yet she was a very clever woman; she used to have the management of all the grand entertainments'. Grand balls laid on for the garrison were only part of her offering. Fresh water was the lifeblood of the slave economy but also of the army. With her water cistern and skilled slaves for hire, the military relied on Dorothy Thomas for a great deal in addition to her lavish entertainment.

Matthew Henry Barker, a naval officer, was also fascinated by 'the well-known Doll Thomas' from whom he hired his slaves and for whom he felt grudging admiration, acknowledging that she 'was at this time, the richest person in the colony'. He could not help but be impressed that not only had she successfully petitioned the Colonial Secretary to change a law that discriminated against free coloured women, but she had been honoured with a private interview with the King, of which she was hugely proud.[46] Marianne Pemberton Holmes also reported this audience with the King, who apparently remembered that years earlier she had 'danced with him when he was a Reefer', a midshipman.[47]

The story about Dorothy's royal audience is probably fanciful. Yet it does have some elements of credibility. She may well have met Prince William Henry, the Duke of Clarence, later to become King William IV, who was once a midshipman in the Caribbean.[48] It is quite plausible that Dorothy may have danced, or otherwise cavorted, with the Prince when he was cutting up during his tour of duty in the Caribbean, given both the young Prince's schedule and his proven reputation for licentiousness.[49] Dorothy's granddaughter was the theatrical diva Madame Sala who had a very close connection to William Henry's illegitimate family, the Fitzclarences. Perhaps, in order to impress her fabulously wealthy grandmother, she had engineered a meeting with the man who would be king.

By the time these stories about Dorothy Thomas were in circulation, she was enjoying the final act of her life drama, playing the role of the 'Queen of Demerara', always extravagantly dressed and followed around by a slave carrying a box of gold coins while dispensing advice and patronage on the streets of Georgetown.[50] The American Consul to Demerara remembered that Doll Thomas was not only very wealthy, but also highly respected, and she took it upon herself to represent the interests of the free coloured community of Demerara.[51] The consul recalled that it was 'her custom to make formal calls on all officials and distinguished strangers arriving in the city ... After passing the compliments of the morning', he recalled, 'she introduced, very naturally, topics upon commercial affairs and the political state of the country'. Her networks spread around the southern Caribbean and even into the heart of empire, where she also had important friends. When she died in 1846, the names of the witnesses to her mark on the extensive will and the various codicils reads like a roll call of the influential white men in the colony.[52]

Conclusion

It might be tempting to argue that such an audacious black woman is sui generis, except that during the same period there were other women—perhaps not quite as flamboyant—who also amassed considerable fortunes, held many slaves and owned thousands of acres, and made demands on white men. As the age of revolutions spread war throughout the Caribbean, the transient insecurity of the fluid, contested colonies of the Windward Islands allowed enterprising black women to reach dizzying heights of success. These audacious, enterprising women present an extraordinary story that confounds and complicates much of what we understand about race and gender in the Atlantic World.

The age of revolutions brought changes to the Atlantic World, and especially to the Caribbean, the scene of some of the most intense fighting. Running in tandem with warfare was the amelioration of slavery, particularly in the British and French world, changes in colonial governance and changes in demography. New centres of power emerged, empires fell away or were replaced. Some of these changes were the result of warfare, others were forced from below, like these free women of colour who challenged the social order with startling entrepreneurial success. To be sure, they would again be marginalized once peace was established. In peacetime it was not easy to find the kind of entrepreneurial opportunities in supplying and supporting the military that had once been such an important part of their profits, nor was it so easy to exploit networks of white power based on slavery in the age of emancipation. It is telling that free women like Dorothy Thomas did less well from peace and emancipation than they had done in war. By the mid-nineteenth century the influence of a woman like Dorothy Thomas was effectively over.

Notes

1. See, for example, Pedro Welch, *'Red and Black Over White': Free Coloured Women in Pre-Emancipation Barbados* (Bridgetown, 2000); Verene Shepherd et al. (eds), *Engendering History: Caribbean Women in Historical Perspective*, (London, 1995); and D. B. Gaspar and Darlene Clark Hine (eds), *Beyond Bondage: Free Women of Color in the Americas* (Chicago, 2004).
2. D. H. Murdoch, 'Land Policy in the Eighteenth-Century British Empire: The Sale of Crown Lands in the Ceded Islands, 1763–1783', *Historical Journal* 27/3 (1984): 549–574.
3. Kit Candlin, *The Last Caribbean Frontier, 1795–1815* (Basingstoke, 2012), 43.
4. Andrew O'Shaugnessy, *An Empire Divided: The American Revolution and the British Caribbean* (Philadelphia, 2000), 117, 186 and 192–193.
5. Jerome Handler, *The Unappropriated People: Freedmen in the Slave Society of Barbados* (First edition: Baltimore, MD, 1974, reprint: Mona, 2009), 32–33.
6. Jonathan R. Dull, *The French Navy and the Seven Years' War* (Lincoln, NE, 2005).
7. See Raymund P. Devas, *The History of the Island of Grenada, 1650–1950* (Justin James Field, St George's, 1964); and Edward Cox, *Free Coloureds in the Slave Societies of St. Kitts and Grenada, 1763–1833* (Knoxville, TN, 1984).
8. Candlin, *The Last Caribbean Frontier*, 11–12.
9. Michael Duffy, *Soldiers, Sugar and Seapower: The British Expeditions to the West Indies and the War Against Revolutionary France* (Oxford, 1987), 255 and 337.

10. Handler, *The Unappropriated People*, 18–19.
11. 'Trinidad Questionnaire on Population and Climate 1830', report for the Royal College of Physicians, The National Archives, London (hereafter TNA), RCP/OFFIP/4022/1–2, 1829–1831.
12. George I. Brizan, *Grenada: Island of Conflict* (Basingstoke, 1998), 118.
13. Barry W. Higman, *Slave Populations of the British Caribbean, 1807–1834* (Mona, 1995, first published: Baltimore, MD, 1984), 77.
14. See Kit Candlin and Cassandra Pybus, *Enterprising Women: Race, Gender and Power in the Revolutionary Atlantic* (Athens, GA, 2015).
15. Hansard, *Parliamentary Register* (London, 1784), vol. 12, 92 50.
16. Kirwan Family Papers, Records 1780–1900, University of West Florida Archives, M 1991–13.
17. Elizabeth Kirwan is so named in Grenada Church records 10 October 1796, 2 July 1797, 3 March 1798, 12 December 1801 and 14 August 1803. mf 1523656, Church of the Latter Day Saints Records, Utah (CLS). Catherina Simon is also called Catherina Cells in the *Demerara Gazette*, 14 December 1805 and 13 February 1813.
18. Grenada Church Records (GCR), St Georges mf, 14 October 14 1792, mf 1523656, CLS. 'Montserrat deed of manumission for Ned', July 24, 1781, transcribed into Grenada 2 March 1787, Deed WI, RSG.
19. Baptized as 'infant daughter' in Grenada in December 20, 1789, GCR, mf 1523656 CLS.
20. Baptism Eliza Thomas, 1 June 1787, GCR, mf 1523656 CLS.
21. Baptized 9 September 1797, born 26 June, GCR, mf 1523656, CLS.
22. Benjamin Webster and Dolly Kirwan, 24 November 1794, 10 September 1795, Grenada Deed Book, E2, State Registry of Grenada (SRG) St Georges.
23. 'Land transfer in Grenville', 13 July 1829, entered 20 December 1830 into the Grenada Register of Wills, Indentures, MF1563329, 1829–1831 p. 449, CLS, Utah.
24. 24 October 1897, GCR, mf 1523656, item 2, p.55, CLS, Utah.
25. 'Governor Green to Portland', 27 May 1797, TNA, CO 101/35. See also Grenada Act of 27 December 1797, Ibid. 103/10.
26. There is no evidence for Dorothy Thomas/Kirwan in Barbados, except for the testimony of her daughter Dorothea Christina, see 'Bill of Advocation: Mrs Dorothea Gordon v. Major John Gordon', 1829, National Archives of Scotland, Edinburgh, CS 271/66510.
27. 'Marianne Pemberton Holmes, Notes on Demerara', University of Virginia Library, Charlottesville, Special Collections, 14748, Box Number 3.1. 1837–1859.
28. *Demerara Gazette*, 15 June 1811; 15 August 1812; 11 February 1815; 8 August 1815; and 1 July 1815.
29. 'Last Will and Testament of Dorothy Thomas', TNA, Prob.11/2007.
30. Fullerton later returned to Scotland and married. See Fullerton's genealogical record at http://www.thepeerage.com/p17018 (accessed 25 January 2015).
31. For more information on the company of Robertson, Sandbach and Parker, as well as Gilbert Robertson; see Liverpool Record Office (hereafter LRO), The Parker Family Papers, 920 PAR I–IV.
32. Dorothy Thomas's 1843 will, proved in 1846, subtracted the money she had already laid out on her daughters and their families.
33. Henrietta Simon went to England in 1813. 'Letter of D. P. Simon to Henrietta Simon', 25 March 1813, in personal possession of the authors.
34. *Demerara Gazette*, 14 December 1805; 30 May 1807; 10 February 1810; and 7 January 1812.

35. 'C. S. Parker to E. Parker', 28 June 1810, Liverpool Record Office (LRO) 920 PAR, 1/53.
36. 'Kensington Plantation–Gilbert Robertson and Charlotte Fullarton–56 slaves', Demerara Slave Returns, 1820, TNA T–71/407.
37. Deed Book R2, SRG, St Georges.
38. Grenada Slave Returns, TNA T-71/301.
39. 'Transaction', 29 August 1837, entered 4 April 1839, Grenada Deeds, 1839–1861 mf 1563330, 1836–1861 Ent. 2–4, p. 447, CLS, Utah.
40. Mixed-race children were present at Paisley Grammar School, Tain Academy and Inverness Royal Academy. After 1818, she sent the children to Dollar Academy, outside Glasgow.
41. *Demerara Gazette*, 6 May 1817.
42. 'Dorothy Thomas–82 slaves', TNA, Demerara Slave Returns, 1826, Index, no. 834. T–71/420.
43. 'Dorothy Thomas', Guiana Slave Holder Compensation, nos. 1400 and 1402, TNA NDO 4/8.
44. Christopher C. Thornburn (ed.), *No Messing: The Story of an Essex Man. The Autobiography of John Castelfranc Cheveley*, 2 vols (Chichester, NH, 2001 and 2012), vol. 2.
45. Anon, 'The Climate of Demerara', *The United Service Journal and Naval and Military Magazine* 3 (1838): 542–543.
46. Matthew Henry Barker, *The Victory, or, The Wardroom Mess* (London, 1844), 191.
47. 'Holmes, Notes on Demerara'.
48. Ibid.
49. Neville Connell, 'Prince William Henry's Visits to Barbados in 1776 and 1789', *The Journal of the Barbados Museum and Historical Society* 1 (1958): 157–164.
50. 'Holmes, Notes on Demerara'.
51. S. T. Masters, *Auburn Morning News: Official Paper of the County*, 6 January 1874, 191.
52. Dorothy Thomas's will, TNA Prob.11/2007.

Part V
Postwar Cultures and Contested War Memories

16
Seductive Sedition: New Hampshire Loyalists' Experiences and Memories of the American Revolutionary Wars

Gregory T. Knouff

On 12 May 1778, during the American Revolution, the *New Hampshire Gazette* reported the murder of Brookfield, Massachusetts resident, Joshua Spooner. William Brooks, James Buchanan and Ezra Ross were charged with Spooner's murder. Spooner's wife, Bathsheba, was charged as an accessory. All four were convicted and sentenced to death. Mrs Spooner engaged Ross, a 17-year-old Continental army veteran with whom she was having an affair, to kill her husband. Impatient with Ross's progress she recruited Buchanan and Brooks, British soldiers from General John Burgoyne's captured army, to participate in the plot in exchange for 'the deceased's watch, buckles, and a thousand dollars'. Brooks eventually beat Spooner to death and the three men hid his body in his well. They were apprehended with money and Spooner's goods. Bathsheba was soon arrested for complicity.[1]

The article in the *New Hampshire Gazette* was published in the midst of the years of the struggle for American Independence (1775–1783). It portrayed the domestic conflict largely, but not solely, as caused by the disorderliness of the wife, who plotted to kill her husband, a man whose 'only fault appears to be not supporting a manly importance as head of his family, and not duly regulating the government of it'.[2] Thus, a combination of a disloyal wife and weak husband at the head of a household led to domestic calamity. The story inverted eighteenth-century seduction narrative gender stereotypes by showing a woman manipulating men for her advantage, thus emphasizing a view of the particularly pathological nature of the crime.[3] The account suggests many possible readings, including a metaphor for the 'Loyalist threat', namely the fear that the colonists who remained loyal to British authority during the American Revolutionary War would undermine the new republic. This fear was not unsubstantiated, because many Americans in the 13 rebellious colonies opposed the Revolution. Paul H. Smith estimates that there were slightly over 500,000 Loyalists. He calculates this as 16 percent of the overall Revolutionary American population.[4] Maya Jasanoff has shown that about 60,000 Loyalists migrated to Britain and other parts of the British Empire as a result of the outcome of the American War of Independence.

This number includes approximately 8,000–10,000 black Loyalists who sought freedom from slavery through serving the British military and about 2,000 free blacks.[5]

New Hampshire was the first of the 13 rebellious British North American colonies to create a new state government and revolutionary constitution in January 1776. It preceded the United States Declaration of Independence by six months, but many in New Hampshire were critical of the new state government.[6] Concern over continued dissent led New Hampshire revolutionaries to emphasize obedience to their authority. In this light, the 1778 case of Joshua Spooner was a cautionary tale about the dangers of not upholding domestic government. For them, the case spoke to how internal dissent threatened authority. Traitors lured residents from their rightful duty to the state. Joshua was the head of a weak 'domestic government'. Bathsheba seduced Ezra Ross, 'and told him that if he would kill her husband, she would become his lawful wife'. Ross then insinuated himself with his intended victim, Joshua, who 'treated him with great civility'. The British regulars were paid mercenaries in the plot.[7] Bathsheba's role in the murder evoked English legal traditions of petit treason.[8] The implication was that infidelity should be dealt with harshly at the earliest stages. Had Joshua governed his family properly, Bathsheba would have received punishment before she plotted treason and seduced others. Not mentioned in the account, but well-known to readers, was the fact that Bathsheba's father was the notorious Loyalist, Timothy Ruggles, who earlier fled to the British army.[9]

The account drew upon assumptions about the mutually constitutive relationships between government, social and family hierarchy that were prevalent in the eighteenth-century British Empire, as well as during the age of transatlantic revolutions. The concept of 'domestic government' stressed consistency between obedience to household and political patriarchs. While revolutionaries initially challenged these notions by suggesting that cruel, tyrannical patriarchs should be resisted, their emergent states reconstituted new forms of patriarchal authority premised on unquestioned obedience. Evoking the language of seduction and infidelity was a central political trope of American revolutionary political discourse and it shaped the Loyalist memory of the war. According to revolutionaries, disloyal citizens and their seductive language were perhaps more dangerous than the armies of Great Britain. Conversely, New Hampshire Loyalists remembered the rebels as treasonous seducers within the political family. In the revolutionary Atlantic, many people within both empires and republics challenged authority, but equations between domestic patriarchy and government remained in reconstituted forms.[10]

Historians have approached the study of Loyalists variously by focusing on their ideologies, wartime experiences, and postwar migration within the British Empire. Recent scholarship has revived interest in Loyalists by showing them as active historical agents, rather than one-dimensional conservative opponents of change. Examining the experiences and memories of those North Americans who opposed U.S. independence informs a broader understanding of emerging republican and evolving imperial concepts of revolutionary wars as domestic struggles for power and legitimacy. Also, it invites comparisons with the resolution of postwar internal conflicts in the revolutionary transatlantic world. This chapter will analyse the creation of a coherent postwar New Hampshire Loyalist memory by relating it directly to their experiences in the U.S. War for Independence.

The first part will address their actual wartime experiences. The diverse peoples who opposed the Revolution and were labelled 'Tories' often had little in common other than their treatment by new state and local authorities. While some New Hampshire men did in fact fight alongside British forces, not all shared this experience. Unique among the rebellious 13 colonies, New Hampshire had no significant conventional military operations on its soil or internal civil warfare. The primary conflict among state residents in New Hampshire was over controlling and defining seditious speech. Political criticism was portrayed as a subversive threat to the new state. As the revolutionaries marginalized their opponents, including neutrals under the rubric of suspected 'Tories', they fostered—unintended—a unified 'Loyalist' identity during and after the war.[11]

The second part of the essay addresses how these experiences were evaluated immediately after the war as an overarching Loyalist memory. As evidenced particularly in the Loyalist Claims Commission records, deponents viewed themselves as faithful British subjects persecuted by an unlawful, repressive regime. The Commission was established by Parliament in 1783 to hear claims by Loyalists. Deponents needed to document their loyalty and verify the value of their lost property. The Commission then made a recommendation on compensation to Parliament.[12] New Hampshire claimants inverted the imagery of the Spooner case and explained that rebels seduced the masses from their rightful duty to proper authority. They homogenized their varied critiques of the Revolution into a narrative of heroic fidelity to British government. New Hampshire Loyalists' civil war was over control of language and perception, and they were still trying to affect that contest with their memories. Rejecting the rebels' label of them as traitors and a British view of them as unfortunate provincials, they asserted a story of themselves as patriotic defenders of the Empire. As Loyalists demobilized from the war, they mobilized newly constructed memories to bolster their claims to rights as British subjects.

The persecution of Loyalists by the revolutionary regulation of 'seductive speech'

Loyal British subjects in New Hampshire had known the dangers of treasonous seduction since the 1760s. During the Stamp Act crisis of 1765–1766,[13] a writer in the *New Hampshire Gazette* warned in March 1766 in an essay: 'At a time when the torrent runs high, and the state is unsettled, self-designing men will push themselves forward at all adventures, hoping for nothing more than self-promotion, tho' at the ruin of the public'.[14] This essay evoked the traditional image of the male rake in the form of self-interested demagogues exploiting passion to alienate people from proper loyalty. The colonial resistance movement utilized another seduction metaphor of its own, evoking the political dangers of embracing effeminate consumerism offered by imperial trade. Such a tie suggested a detrimental union.[15] In 1775, the same year that the American Revolutionary War began, recent English immigrant and political writer Thomas Paine published an essay entitled 'Reflections on Unhappy Marriages'. It extolled Native American marriages based on 'mutual affection' and spouses' 'liberty to separate'.[16] In 1776, Paine called for dissolving ties to Britain through marital analogy in his essay, 'Common Sense', which proved to be enormously popular and influential in bringing about American independence. Here he asserted: 'Bring the doctrine of reconciliation to the touchstone of nature, and then tell me, whether you can hereafter love, honour, and faithfully serve the power that hath carried fire and sword into your land ... Your future connection with Britain, whom you can neither love nor honour, will be forced and unnatural'.[17] As Paine used marriage as a political metaphor, he suggested a companionate ideal in which both spouses had rights. He ridiculed blind obedience to cruel patriarchal power and asserted that when governments violated natural rights, ''tis time to part'.[18] Upon attaining power, however, revolutionaries were no longer concerned with companionate marriage as a political metaphor. They emphasized unquestioned obedience to patriarchal authority. Those who challenged the validity of the new republican state were dealt with ruthlessly.

The rapid revolutionary seizure of power in provincial New Hampshire by 1776 was jarring to those who opposed or questioned it. With the exception of significant protests over the 1765 Stamp Act, Governor Benning Wentworth, who served from 1741 to 1767, was able govern the province through patronage networks with little internal opposition. His nephew and successor, John Wentworth, in office from 1767 to 1775, faced more unrest over Parliament's attempts to legislate for and raise revenue in the North American colonies. The situation became a crisis over the Tea and subsequent Coercive Acts in 1773–1774. While opposition to the Wentworth faction and parliamentary policy was simmering, it exploded on the eve of the Revolution. On 8 June 1774, unable to prevent a newly elected House of Representatives from appointing a Committee of Correspondence to coordinate interprovincial resistance, Wentworth dissolved it. Members of this Committee called legislators back into session who, in turn, called on towns to elect members of a Provincial Congress. Here, revolutionaries created an extra-legal government that coordinated New Hampshire's response to the outbreak of war in April 1775. On 24 August 1775, John Wentworth fled the province. The Provincial Congress declared itself the House of Representatives and charged a committee with drafting a constitution. The New Hampshire revolutionary government adopted its constitution in January 1776, thus creating its own formal power. Authorities then had to get New Hampshire residents to recognize their legitimacy.[19]

This was a daunting task. As critics pointed out, the new government and constitution were extra-legal. The revolutionaries acted quickly by exercising power, rather than justifying it. The state government portrayed dissent as 'dangerous'. A public broadside announcing the creation of the new government in 1776 was accompanied by a stern warning: 'It is earnestly recommended, that in this distressing day of public calamity, when our enemies are watching all opportunities to ensnare and divide us, everyone would strive to prevent, and if possible, to quell all appearance of party spirit'.[20] Revolutionary General John Sullivan soon acted against 'that infernal crew of Tories who have laughed at the Congress' by ordering suspect persons to surrender themselves to the authorities. William Start was 'apprehended by order of General Sullivan ... expecting some person to appear and charge him with some crime committed against somebody, he knows not who or what, but no one appeared'. He was stunned when a committee banished him from his home in order to prevent him from influencing neighbours. The arbitrary power exercised against Start and the ambiguity regarding what merited his punishment, sent a warning to those who questioned the new order. The face of Revolutionary power was not benign and paternal, but harsh and patriarchal.[21]

During this period, state and town Committees of Safety policed language and orthodoxy.[22] They also created the imagery of authority through exercise of sweeping discretionary powers that were eventually codified into law. In April 1776, the state of New Hampshire ordered one of the most aggressive association tests in revolutionary America. It required adult men to swear to oppose the British with arms. Like other states' test acts, it gendered the active political subject as male. Local committees were instructed to record the names of men who refused the oath, allowing them to monitor dissenters.[23] During the 1777 British campaign of General John Burgoyne, who invaded the nearby Lake Champlain-Hudson River area from Canada, more draconian measures emerged. The state government passed an act to allow the state Committee of Safety to imprison anyone whom they 'shall deem the safety of the commonwealth requires should be restrained of his personal liberty'. Such prisoners were to be held 'without bail' until released by state authority. The Committees of Safety had sweeping powers to arrest, examine and detain suspicious persons for an indefinite period based on hearsay evidence.[24]

This 1777 act, unlike the association test, applied to 'persons', suggesting the capacity of women to betray the state. The assumed political seducer was usually male, but women and men made accusations of seditious speech. As was the case when pre-war non-importation boycotts necessitated the participation of all ordinary colonial Americans, both men and women were politicized by taking action. As a consequence, unsubstantiated testimony by anyone could lead to detention of potential Loyalists because their words influenced people's political fidelity, regardless of intention. In such a heated situation, local gossip became a form of political power. Indeed, the significance of gossip in influencing the perceptions of neighbours' political identities revived the informal public sphere described by historian Mary Beth Norton in the colonial period in which women were central to policing the community. As was later the case in the years leading up to the French Revolution, women and common people spoke to frame public opinion for political means.[25] Indeed, anyone was encouraged to come forward with charges of seditious speech, often without ever having to testify to it in a hearing. One example is the case of Margaret and Sarah Dickey, who approached the New Hampshire Committee of Safety. They claimed that, 'We ... did hear one John Hicke of Boston say ... that the bulwarks of England would make the oak and stones of America to tremble'.[26]

The regulation of seditious speech became more acute as the war continued. A typical incidence is the following case. At a 1777 court session, John Butrick testified against Samuel Smith that 'he never heard him speak in favour of the Americans but in favour of the King'. Butrick continued, 'I said to him if you cannot think as other people do you had better not speak'.[27] Even those who evidenced a desire to remain peacefully in the revolutionary community if they could avoid military service were punished or confined for what they said to their neighbours. Breed Batcheller, for instance, was a notorious opponent of the Revolution, but even his enemies reported his repeated statements that he disavowed violent resistance to the new regime. John Farwell stated that he heard Batcheller say 'that he would not fight on either side but would stay at home and raise potatoes'.[28] Most damning against Batcheller was the accusation that he used verbal seduction. A local Committee of Safety reported that he 'used his influence' to discourage enlistments and encourage desertions from the Continental Army'. Eventually Batcheller felt so persecuted by local mobs and committees that he left his home to join the British army.[29] Given the actions of people such as Batcheller, suspicion of seductive intent of those not warmly attached to the Revolution grew. An essayist warned in *Freeman's Journal* that 'the baneful example of the neutral is not only dangerous, but infectious. When a few of the principal men in a country pursue such a conduct, it creates caution and distrust, suspicion and fear, in the inferior rank'.[30] Victims of such scrutiny conversely came to see it as tyrannical. Jonathan Warner answered a witness of his purported seditious intent in reporting that British regulars had occupied Philadelphia by exclaiming, 'you may be damned, 'tis high time for people to speak their minds, they had been long enough restrained'.[31]

The revolutionary New Hampshire government consolidated its authority over those who joined the British in the 1778 Proscription and Confiscation Acts, but the obsession with divining seditious seduction continued.[32] In 1779, an essay in the *New Hampshire Gazette* warned: 'Beware of those who, under the *mask of Whiggism*, are now hand in glove with persons strongly suspected to be *inimical* to our cause'.[33] The same year, William Whipple, a New Hampshire Continental Congress delegate warned that 'great dangers may arise from placing too good confidence in men who are not heartily attached to the independence of America. Such characters should be watched with the most jealous eye'.[34] Essays appearing in 1780 in the *New Hampshire Gazette* entitled the 'New Hampshire Crisis' developed this theme. The author argued that leniency toward suspected Tories would be the death of the state and warned: 'Our open and avowed enemies who have been indulged to speak and act agreeable to their infernal principles, have cooled or brought over to the side of opposition all those whose minds were not proof against the deceitful wiles of those unpardonable Traitors'. The essayist called for renewed vigilance, asking, 'where are your Committees of Safety?' and 'why have we suffered those unrelenting parricides to remain among us?'[35]

As these essays suggested, policy on policing disloyalty was contested even among revolutionaries. In the case in the French Revolution, over time, more centralized authorities attempted to exert control over local bodies.[36] However, in revolutionary America, local authorities remained strong and, even at the state level, no entity comparable to the Committees of Public Safety of 1793–1794 was able to extend absolute authority over local issues. The persistent tension showed that it was still not entirely clear where all new sources of power resided. In an extraordinary private letter, New Hampshire State Representative John Langdon stated:

> The confidence of the people out of doors was going fast. And that their [New Hampshire State Government's] acts and resolves would have but little force, soon, unless more spirited conduct in appointing men who have influence, and who the people will follow, and not suffer themselves to be turned about by their own servants at pleasure. And in short to do the necessary business of the colony, instead of hearing Tory matters ... before the people's minds are too much possessed, with that levelling spirit.[37]

Langdon feared that 'Tory matters' brought by local committees disrupted the authority of the state and might be a way in which the people exerted their 'levelling' desires.[38] The letter suggests that local and class conflict shaped accusations of sedition. Indeed, local committees often disagreed with the state. For example, the Surry Committee was outraged when the state Committee of Safety ordered Breed Batcheller and Robert Gilmore released on bail. They stated 'that however good your authority, your aims, and ends might be in liberating the said Gilmore and Batcheller ... [their release] in our opinion has no good effect but quite the reverse as it tends to weaken the hands of the Committees of Safety and strengthen the bonds of the enemies of the glorious cause of liberty'.[39]

It was in this context of local and class conflict that the abovementioned 1780 essays on the 'New Hampshire Crisis' appeared in the *New Hampshire Gazette*, which demanded that the state take harsher action against those who spoke against Revolution.[40] The state government responded in April 1781, and passed a revised Treason Act. It finally codified the informal practice of punishing seductive speech by stipulating that any person who 'shall seduce or persuade any inhabitant or inhabitants of this state to renounce his or their allegiance to this state and government thereof ... shall be adjudged guilty of high treason against this state and be put to death'.[41] The long-term durability of the seduction metaphor suggests the continuing connection between domestic order and government in the new American republic. Revolutionary politics both challenged and affirmed traditional gender and familial politics. The case of Rebecca Davis illustrates this process. She petitioned successfully for divorce from her husband, Elezar, in 1780 by informing the New Hampshire General Court that he 'hath cohabited with several other women by whom he hath had children. ...And to add to his guilt towards her, he hath voluntarily joined himself to the enemies of America and been in arms against his country'.[42] His lack of marital fidelity was amplified by his lack of fidelity to the revolutionary state. She bolstered her case for freedom from an oppressive marriage by implying her loyalty to the state.

Loyalists' memories of the American revolutionary wars

After the American War of Independence, New Hampshire Loyalists responded to their wartime experience by telling similar stories that downplayed subtle gradations of opposition to the Revolution as well as local and economic issues. They created a memory centred on the experience they shared: the application of the New Hampshire revolutionaries' seditious seduction metaphor. In their Loyalist Claims, petitioners went beyond the general requirements of proving loyalty and demonstrating the loss of property.[43] After asserting their clear fidelity to the British Empire, New Hampshire Loyalists manifested their acts of dissenting speech toward the revolutionary government as patriotic actions that led to brutal persecution. They also insisted that the dangerous seducers of the masses were the self-interested leaders of the rebellion who used a combination of appointments coupled with the threat of repression to hold their illegitimate power. Loyalists shared many of their opponent's assumptions about the dangers of political seduction. Yet, they modified them to emphasize their view of the coercive, tyrannical nature of the Revolution. Their memories articulated a vision of domestic government in New Hampshire usurped by seducers.

Formulaic statements of unambiguous fidelity were central pillars of Loyalist Claims depositions. While necessary for financial compensation, such narratives also countered glaring questions about the loyalty of those who remained among the revolutionaries for years. Breed Batcheller, for example, recalled that he 'has always been a Loyal faithful subject to his majesty and uniformly attached to the British Government. That at the call of his Sovereign and from a sense of duty to the government he was born under, he left his family and estate in the year 1777 and joined the British army'.[44] What was obvious to the Claims Commission was that he did not heed 'the call of his Sovereign' until over two years into the war. As noted, despite his outspoken opposition to the Revolution in his community, he gingerly tried to remain. Indeed, a petition by Batcheller to the New Hampshire General Court just before he joined Burgoyne's army suggested that his dispute was with local, not state revolutionaries. He explained: 'The treatment I received is hard though undeserved and the evidence taken on but one side, who were prejudiced persons chiefly. Could the court be rightly informed of the provocations and insults I have received from those my enemies, and the evidence heard on the other side, they would not pay any regard to the evidence against me'.[45] Local persecution was more important in motivating Batcheller than a direct call from his sovereign. Nonetheless, it was vital for Loyalists to establish continuous faithfulness to the Empire. They admitted of no flirtation with the rebel regime and erased much of the war's ambiguity.

Regardless of accuracy, this memory of faithful service to the British Crown was ubiquitous. It gave a common vocabulary to diverse people who opposed rebellion. In response to revolutionaries' charges of seduction, they asserted their constant 'fidelity' to Empire, suggesting that the rebels were seditious seducers of domestic government. In professions of loyalty, deponents often offered a three-part statement. They assured their audience first and foremost of their fidelity to the patriarchal head of state, the King. Second, they noted their unwavering support for the British constitution and government. Last, they stated their steadfast opposition to any rebel measures that might have led them astray. Typical was Enos Stephens, who stated, in a phrase repeated verbatim by other New Hampshire Loyalists, that he 'was uniformly and steadily attached to his Majesty's person, and the British Government, and was opposed to the measures of the American Congress'.[46] Josiah Pomeroy even tried to use this imagery to explain why he served as a judge well past independence, saying he 'was appointed judge of the county court and did employ his best endeavours to keep the county in due obedience to the King and Constitution till 1777 when his loyalty rendered him obnoxious to the rebels'.[47] Within this trope, Loyalists pointed to their particular attachment to the British King, George III. Deriving from colonial north American traditions of venerating the monarchy, these statements were also meant to answer Thomas Paine's emotive argument in his 1776 essay 'Common Sense' that it was 'unnatural' to 'love and honour' Britain.[48]

Historian Brendan McConville has uncovered a pattern of colonial British North American veneration of the monarch as the head of the nation presiding over various representative legislatures. Even during the height of the crisis, colonists asserted their loyalty to what they assumed was a benign, paternalistic King. By 1775, rebellious colonists came to believe that the King had betrayed them to the tyrannical policies of Parliament and the ministries, and renounced him with particular virulence as the war broke out. They asserted that it was George III, not themselves, who did not show fidelity in the union. Loyalists rejected this view in their depositions by asserting their 'steadfast' faithfulness to the King.[49] Loyalist Bartholomew Stavers emphasized, for example, 'his zeal and attachment to his Majesty's person' as a key reason for being persecuted by the rebels.[50] Robert Trail declared himself 'a true and faithful subject of his majesty' and firmly asserted that it was the rebellion that was 'unnatural'.[51]

Women who applied for benefits under the Loyalist Claims because of their husbands' actions evoked a modified image of familial fidelity to the state. Isabella Nevin argued, for instance, that she 'was obliged to leave America', because of 'her husband's immediate connections with government, the known attachment and inviolable fidelity of her family and relations to the King and the mother country left her no prospect of living with any comfort in a country which had thrown off all ties of allegiance'.[52] Her statement went further than most men's by implying that her entire family, including herself and possibly other women, were Loyalists rather than simply *femmes covert.* Nevin gendered the state as female, as the 'mother country', after asserting fidelity to the King. She suggested an irrational rebel mob that threw off the ties of a nurturing government and condemned them for acting against her in a 'spirit of anarchy'. Nevin shrewdly evinced her political consciousness in the language of familial obedience to the state.[53]

Loyalist men, in contrast, emphasized political speech against the rebels as active patriotic exertion on behalf of government. Asa Porter, argued for example that he had 'used all his influence both in a public and private capacity (which was very considerable) to support the King's authority in America. In consequence of which his person was seized upon by order of the body which then usurped the powers of government'.[54] And Benjamin Whiting similarly insisted that he was 'exerting his utmost influence to prevent the people joining in the violences then pervading the continent'.[55] In their postwar rhetoric Loyalists thus insisted that they were doing exactly what the revolutionaries had feared: using persuasion to undermine faith in the republican regime. They explained residence among the rebels and evoked a civil war that did not necessitate taking up arms. What the revolutionaries viewed as seditious speech, Loyalists portrayed as principled, active fidelity to Britain. Underscoring this claim, they recalled their persecution as central events in their war. Accordingly, a witness for Stephen Holland stated that Holland 'became very obnoxious to what was at that time called the Whig Party, who threatened to set fire to his house and burn him and his family to death'.[56] And likewise Joanna Dix recalled a mob attack on her household when in 1775, she 'had a quantity of tea goods etc. and household furniture stripped from her in a riotous manner, by reason of her husband, fleeing into Boston under the protection of his Majesty's arms'.[57] In addition to cataloguing property losses for reimbursement, such accounts bolstered claims for compensation by offering carefully constructed ideological statements about patriotic loyalty. They emphasized the suffering and sacrifice of Loyalists on behalf of the Empire.

In order to invert seditious seduction metaphors for use against the revolutionaries, Loyalists addressed their view of rebel motives. During the war, the Loyalist refugee community in New York built upon the longstanding image of the revolutionaries as self-interested figures who seduced the masses to aggrandize their own power. Accordingly, an essayist in New York's *Rivington's Loyal Gazette* lamented that America was ruined 'by the ambition of a few factious demagogues'.[58] Also advertising in the paper, Lieutenant Colonel Rudolphus Ritzema, who served in the Continental army before switching sides, sought to recruit rebel soldiers to his Loyal American Reformers by explaining how 'it must be evident to all men, that the contest has not been for the liberties of America, but for the AGGRANDIZEMENT OF INDIVIDUALS UPON THE RUINS OF THEIR COUNTRY'.[59] Here, Ritzema echoed the critique of leaders of the Stamp Act protests in the *New Hampshire Gazette* in 1766. In this classic Loyalist view, the Revolution was driven by power-hungry deceivers seeking office. The people of America were not to blame, but they were susceptible to verbal seduction.

New Hampshire Loyalists reinforced this view in their memories. They portrayed themselves as faithful to domestic government and unmoved by the rebels' allures of seditious appointments. Loyalist George Glen noted, for instance, that 'the insurgents being extremely pressed for officers as well as soldiers offered your memorialist a commission as a major in the Continental army, which he, however obnoxious he might become thereby, absolutely refused to accept'. Likewise, Stephen Little asserted 'that prior to his escape he had frequently the most pressing offers to be employed by them in a most profitable line of his profession in their army if he would take the oaths of allegiance to the states and abjuration to the King, which he constantly refused'.[60] And Loyalist Samuel Hale 'refused all the allurements held out by disloyalty, exerted all the little influence his connections and his profession of a lawyer gave him in support of his Majesty's government'. He also noted in a 1780 letter which he included with his claim how he 'refus[ed] all overtures of disloyalty'. [61] Former Royal Governor John Wentworth himself evoked such imagery when writing letters in support of Loyalist Claims. Praising Thomas McDonough for his 'fidelity to his Majesty's service', Wentworth went on: 'Still persisting to reject any flattering attempt to seduce him into the service of disloyalty, he was thence deprived of his property and means of subsistence'.[62] Here Wentworth explicitly articulated the metaphor of seduction from fidelity and, unsurprisingly, laid its charge on the rebels.

Conclusion

The price of fidelity to the British Empire was high. Not only did Loyalists lose the war, but tens of thousands migrated from their former homes in the United States. Those who stayed behind tried to reintegrate and did not assert their suffering or their loyalty to empire. In fact, they sometimes were forced to renounce former positions. Indeed, as North Americans tried to make sense of civil war and loyalty in terms of domestic government, the conflict sometimes separated families. While most women and children left with the male heads of their households and went into exile, a few wives sought to remain in their homes and retain some limited control over parts of family estates confiscated by the state.[63] In all cases, opponents of the Revolution who remained were forced to accept the authority of the United States. The nature of both political and familial power was challenged from multiple perspectives over the course of the war, but patriarchy re-emerged in modified republican forms.[64] There was no formal place for a Loyalist memory in postwar New Hampshire.

In contrast, expatriate New Hampshire Loyalists never repented their 'crime'. To them, the image of the seductive 'Tory' enemy to the state, spectacularly successful as it was in securing rebel power, was patently absurd. They would have dismissed a revolutionary reading of the Joshua Spooner case as ridiculous. From their perspective, the case of the adulterous, scheming Bathsheba, introduced at the start of this chapter, embodied the Revolution itself. Loyalists could liken Bathsheba Spooner's attempts to offer money, goods, or marriage to her co-conspirators as comparable to republican demagogues offering power and positions to the King's subjects. In their memories, Loyalists offered their own image of seductive sedition. It was not dissent from the Revolution that was dangerous. Indeed, not only was it rational political discourse, it was evidence of active fidelity to rightful authority. Their 'exertions' to influence people were portrayed as heroic counterpoints to the insidious schemes and coercion of self-interested tyrants who undermined proper domestic government. Derided as traitors by traitors and as seducers by seducers, New Hampshire Loyalists defended themselves as they did during the war: by continuing to speak against the Revolution. Thus, they forged a memory that valued political dissent and resistance to arbitrary power. Rebels were not the only ones to question the legitimacy of power. Indeed, they shared with Loyalists a common vocabulary and set of assumptions about the nature of domestic authority. In postwar Loyalist communities, emphasis on obedience to all patriarchal authority re-emerged.[65] Yet, many Loyalists continued to insist on their rights as British subjects within the Empire. As Maya Jasanoff shows, the Loyalist ideology or 'the spirit of 1783' was able to 'join liberal principles with hierarchical rule'.[66] Ideas about the nature of power flowed in many directions in the era of transatlantic revolutions and could reshape empires. The experiences and memories of New Hampshire Loyalists underscore how central the contested equation between domestic and state authority remained in the revolutionary and counter-revolutionary Atlantic World.

Notes

1. *New Hampshire Gazette*, 12 May 1778.
2. Ibid.
3. Katherine Binhammer, *The Seduction Narrative in Britain, 1747–1800* (Cambridge, 2009), 1–19.
4. Paul H. Smith, 'The American Loyalists: Notes on Their Organization and Numerical Strength', *William and Mary Quarterly* 25 (1968): 259–277.
5. Maya Jasanoff, *Liberty's Exiles: American Loyalists in the Revolutionary World* (New York, 2011), 357.
6. Jere R. Daniell, *Colonial New Hampshire: A History* (Millwood, NY, 1981), 240–244; and Jere R. Daniell, *Experiment in Republicanism: New Hampshire Politics and the American Revolution, 1741–1794* (Cambridge, MA, 1970), 109–112.
7. *New Hampshire Gazette*, 12 May 1778.
8. On petit treason, see Linda K. Kerber, *Women of the Republic: Intellect and Ideology in Revolutionary America* (Chapel Hill, NC, 1980), 119–120.
9. On the Ruggles's family's loyalism, see Deborah Navas, *Murdered By His Wife: A History With Documentation of the Joshua Spooner Murder and Execution of His Wife, Bathsheba, Who Was Hanged in Worcester, Massachusetts, 2 July 1778* (Amherst, MA, 1999), 14–28 and 93.
10. 'To Sir William Howe', *New Hampshire Gazette*, 12 May 1778. On the fusion of familial and governmental authority, see Kathleen Wilson, 'Rethinking the Colonial State: Family, Gender, and Governmentality in Eighteenth-Century British Frontiers', *American Historical Review (AHR)* 116/5 (2011): 1294–1322; Carole Shammas, *A History of Household Government in America* (Charlottesville, VA, 2002), 52–82; and Lynn Hunt, *The Family Romance of the French Revolution* (Berkeley, CA, 1992), 17–52 and 151–191. On the threat to the American republic and virtuous marriage presented by the 'vile seducer', see Jan Lewis, 'The Republican Wife: Virtue and Seduction in the Early Republic', *William and Mary Quarterly* 44 (1987): 689–721.
11. Classic studies of Loyalist ideology and experiences include: Robert McCluer Calhoon, *The Loyalists in Revolutionary America, 1760–1781* (New York, 1973); and Bernard Bailyn, *The Ordeal of Thomas Hutchinson* (Cambridge, MA, 1974). Important recent studies that focus on Loyalist diversity and identity formation include Ruma Chopra, *Unnatural Rebellion: Loyalists in New York City during the Revolution* (Charlottesville, VA, 2011); and Liam Riordan and Jerry Bannister (eds), *The Loyal Atlantic: Remaking the British Atlantic in the Revolutionary Era* (Toronto, 2012).

Some of the most dynamic new scholarship focuses on the Loyalist diaspora and its effects on the subsequent development of the British Empire in the late-eighteenth and early-nineteenth centuries. See Jasanoff, *Liberty's Exiles*.

12. On the Loyalist Claims Commission, Jasanoff, *Liberty's Exiles*, 120–123.
13. The Stamp Act Crisis (1765–1766) was the result of a tax imposed by the British Parliament on its American colonies that required a stamp issued by the Treasury office on paper used for certain legal transactions, recreational goods, and materials printed in the colonies. See Edmund S. Morgan and Helen H. Morgan, *The Stamp Act Crisis: Prologue to Revolution* (3rd edn, Chapel Hill, NC, 1995), 72.
14. 'Remarks on the Times', *New Hampshire Gazette*, 16 March 1766.
15. On the revolutionary linking of 'luxury, effeminacy and corruption', see Kerber, *Women of the Republic*, 31.
16. Thomas Paine, 'Reflections on Unhappy Marriages', in *Common Sense and Related Writing*, ed. Thomas P. Slaughter (Boston, 2001), 71–72.
17. Thomas Paine, 'Common Sense', in ibid., 91.
18. Ibid., 90.
19. Daniell, *Experiment in Republicanism*, 74–112; and Paul W. Wilderson, *Governor John Wentworth and the American Revolution: The English Connection* (Lebanon, NH, 1994), 221–265.
20. Public broadside, 19 March 1776, reprinted in Daniell, *Experiment in Republicanism*, 113.
21. 'John Sullivan to George Washington', 29 October 1775, in *Letters and Papers of Major General John Sullivan, Continental Army*, ed. Otis G. Hammond, 3 vols (Concord, NH, 1930), vol. 1, 119; and 'Petition of William Start to New Hampshire Committee of Safety', 5 December 1775. New Hampshire State Archives, Concord, NH, Petitions to the Legislature (NHPL).
22. As shown by T. H. Breen, *American Insurgents, American Patriots: The Revolution of the People* (New York, 2010), 166–167 and 203–206; these committees, originally called for by the Continental Congress to enforce a plan of boycotts (called 'the Association') in protest of the 1774 Coercive Acts, were truly Revolutionary bodies constituted at the provincial (later state) and local level that enforced Revolutionary policy and authority.
23. 'Association Test', in *New Hampshire State Papers (NHSP)*, ed. Nathaniel Bouton, 10 vols (Concord, NH, 1867–1877), vol. 8, 204–205.
24. Quotes from 'An Act for Taking Up, Imprisoning or Otherwise Restraining Persons Dangerous to This State', in NHSP, vol. 8, 592–593. Generally, on the power of Committees of Safety, see Daniell, Experiment in Republicanism, 99–128.
25. Mary Beth Norton, *Founding Mothers and Fathers: Gendered Power and the Forming of American Society* (New York, 1996), 252–277; on women and boycotts, see Kerber, *Women of the Republic*, 37–41; on Revolutionary France, see Arlette Farge, *Subversive Words: Public Opinion in Eighteenth-Century France* (University Park, PA, 1994); and Carla Hesse, *The Other Enlightenment: How French Women Became Modern* (Princeton, NJ, 2001), 3–30.
26. 'Deposition of Margaret and Sarah Dickey', 20 May 1777, New Hampshire State Archives, Concord, Folder, Loyalism Allegiance, Early Documents, General Court Records, Committee of Safety, Record Group 111 (NHCS).
27. 'Depositions and Order of Justices in the County of Cheshire Relative to Tories', 3 June 1777, NHSP, vol. 8, 594.

28. 'Evidence Against Breed Batcheller taken at a Special Session at Keene', 10 June 1777, Massachusetts Historical Society, Boston, Folder, Petitions: Tory: Packersfield: Breed Bacheller, NHPL.
29. 'Surrey Committee to Meshech Weare', 10 March 1777, Meshech Weare Papers, 1776–1785, 1 reel, microfilm, Massachusetts Historical Society, Boston.
30. *Freeman's Journal*, 23 August 1777.
31. 'Testimony of John Salter, Portsmouth Mariner, to Committee of Safety', 4 February 1777, NHCS, Folder, Investigation of Persons in Exeter.
32. 'New Hampshire Proscription and Confiscation Acts of 1778', in NHSP vol. 8, 810–814.
33. 'Essay by "A Whig"', *New Hampshire Gazette*, 23 November 1779.
34. 'William Whipple to Josiah Bartlett', 28 March 1779, Josiah Bartlett Papers, 1743–1795, Microfilm (originals housed in various repositories), (Concord, New Hampshire Historical Society, 1976) ed. Frank C. Mevers, Item D 298, F1603.
35. *New Hampshire Gazette*, 5 August 1780; and New Hampshire Gazette, 12 August 1780.
36. On the centralization of power in Revolutionary France at the expense of local authority, see Alan Forrest, *The French Revolution* (Cambridge, MA, 1995), 62–70; on the Committee of Public Safety, see R. R. Palmer, *Twelve Who Ruled: The Year of Terror in the French Revolution* (Princeton, NJ, 1989), 28–32 and 108–110.
37. 'John Langdon to Josiah Bartlett', 24 June 1776, Josiah Bartlett Papers, microfilm item D831, F882.
38. Ibid.
39. 'Letter from Surry Committee', 10 March 1777, Meshech Weare Papers, microfilm, Massachusetts Historical Society
40. *New Hampshire Gazette*, 5 August 1780; and New Hampshire Gazette, 12 August 1780.
41. 'Treason Act passed by General Assembly, 6 April 1781', *New Hampshire Gazette*, 21 May 1781.
42. 'Divorce Petition of Rebecca Davis', 13 April 1780, NHPL.
43. On provisions of Loyalist Claims, see Wallace Brown, *The Good Americans: The Loyalists and the American Revolution* (New York, 1969), 181.
44. 'American Loyalist Claims Commission Papers, 1780–1835', Great Britain, Audit Office, vol. 90, 78–79, microfilm edition, 1973 housed at David Library of the American Revolution (DLAR), Washington Crossing, PA (originals are in the The National Archives, London (TNA), hereafter AO13, followed by volume and pages: AO 13/90/78–79).
45. 'Deposition of Breed Batcheller', 14 July 1777, Box 1775–June 1776: Folder, Petitions: Tory: Packersfield: Breed Batchelor, NHPL.
46. AO13/83/573.
47. 'Records of the American Loyalist Claims Commission, 1776–1831', Great Britain, Audit Office, vol. 12, 85, microfilm edition, 1972 housed at DLAR (originals are in TNA, hereafter AO12 followed by volume and pages: AO12/12/85).
48. Thomas Paine, 'Common Sense', in *Common Sense and Related Writing*, 91.
49. Brendan McConville, *The King's Three Faces: The Rise and Fall of Royal America, 1688–1776* (Chapel Hill, NC, 2006), 249–311;
50. AO13/52/545.
51. Trail: AO13/53/349–350 and AO13/74/718–725.
52. AO13/53/196.
53. Ibid.
54. AO13/70B/330–331.

55. AO13/53/509.
56. AO13/53/100–102.
57. AO13/80/134–135.
58. Rivington's *New York Gazette* and *Advertiser* or *Loyal Gazette*, 6 March 1779.
59. Ibid., 9 May 1778.
60. A013/52/392–393.
61. AO13/53/82–83 and 86–87
62. AO13/53/142–143
63. Kerber, *Women of the Republic*, 119–136.
64. Ibid., 269–288. See also, Lewis, 'Republican Wife.'
65. Nancy Christie, '"He is the master of his house": Families and Political Authority in Counterrevolutionary Montreal', *William and Mary Quarterly* 3/2 (2013): 341–370; and Janice Potter-MacKinnon, *While the Women Only Wept: Loyalist Refugee Women in Eastern Ontario* (Montreal, 2003), 128–160
66. Jasanoff, *Liberty's Exiles*, 13.

17

Moscow after Napoleon: Reconciliation, Rebuilding, and Contested Memories

Alexander M. Martin

When Napoleon's army withdrew from Moscow in the middle of October 1812, it left behind a disaster of staggering magnitude. This was a situation no one had anticipated just a few months earlier. Napoleon had embarked on his ill-fated Russian campaign expecting a few decisive battles and a rapid victory, but the Russians had retreated and he had pursued them deep into the country's interior. After the bloody but indecisive battle of Borodino, the Grande Armée had arrived in Moscow, where it hoped to resupply itself and settle in for the winter. But these hopes were soon dashed. Nearly the entire population had fled as the French approached, leaving the city an empty shell. In the first days of the occupation, an enormous firestorm reduced much of Moscow to cinders. Houses that survived were looted by Napoleonic soldiers and Russian peasants, and the city was strewn with corpses and animal carcasses that rotted in the unusually warm weather. One of the great cities of Europe was left a stinking, lifeless field of rubble, and as the season turned to winter, the remnants of Napoleon's army were forced into a retreat that few survived.[1]

Moscow's destruction changed the course of two great imperial projects: Napoleon's bid for European hegemony and Empress Catherine II's attempt to bring Russia into Europe. Napoleon never recovered from the retreat from Moscow. The legacy of Catherine was likewise changed by the fire. During her reign (1762–1796) she had tried to secure a place for Russia as one of Europe's leading powers by pursuing expansion abroad and state-building at home, but she was stymied in part because Europeans perceived Russia as an unenlightened 'Asiatic' country, and because Russians were reluctant to embrace alien European ways. To overcome these obstacles, she sought strategies to disseminate European ways of living more widely in the Russian heartland. Moscow, Russia's historic capital and the undisputed metropolis of its interior, had a crucial role to play in this strategy. These policies were continued by her immediate successors, Paul I (1796–1801) and Alexander I (1801–1825).[2]

When Moscow burned in 1812, however, the trajectory of Catherine's project was profoundly altered. After the war, as the regime had hoped, Russia's educated public became larger and increasingly 'European' in its way of life. However, the fire also energized an anti-Western Russian nationalism, and the war indirectly led the government to adopt policies that rendered the city's institutions and infrastructure ever more backward. In the decades that followed, Russian memories of the occupation of Moscow, which form the subject of this chapter, were therefore shaped by two conflicting dynamics: the regime's success in fostering a Europeanized educated public, and its increasing inability to win that public's support for its own urban policies.

The eighteenth-century background

The Napoleonic occupation marked a dramatic transition between two eras in Moscow's history. In the period from 1812 to 1917, Moscow grew into a modern, albeit socioeconomically troubled, city and a symbol of Russian nationalism. This represented a departure from the direction in which Moscow had developed in the previous century. Moscow's eighteenth century had begun in 1703, when Emperor Peter the Great founded St Petersburg. This new city, which soon became the seat of government, gave Russia a twofold connection with the West: its port created a maritime outlet to the Baltic, and its urban design allowed Russians to visualize the European culture that Peter wished to implant in Russia as a whole. For the next two centuries, until the Bolsheviks moved the government back to Moscow in 1918, Russia had two 'capitals'. St Petersburg was the centre of government, foreign trade and a cosmopolitan elite culture—as the Italian Count Algarotti put it, it was Russia's 'window to Europe'—but it was culturally and geographically remote from the Russian heartland. Moscow, on the other hand, remained the hub of Russia's internal trade and communications, the residence of much of its merchant class, clergy and aristocracy, and a symbol of national tradition. Russian writers in the nineteenth century thought the tension between the two cities reflected the ambivalence of the Russian soul, but the view in the eighteenth century, at least at court, was that Moscow embodied Russia's backwardness and ought to be transformed along the lines of St Petersburg. The effort to do this acquired critical mass under Catherine II.[3]

One of her concerns was foreign policy. European visitors frequently depicted Moscow as 'Asiatic' and suggested that it, not St Petersburg, was representative of Russia as a whole. Casanova, for example, wrote in the 1790s that

> One has not seen Russia if one has not seen Moscow, and whoever has known only the Russians of St Petersburg does not know the Russians of the real Russia. The inhabitants of the new capital are viewed here [in Moscow] as foreigners. For a long time to come, the true capital of the Russians will be holy Moscow. ... Moscow clings to the past: city of

> traditions and memories, city of the tsars, she is a daughter of Asia and most surprised to find herself in Europe.[4]

This kind of Orientalizing rhetoric undermined Catherine's, and later Alexander I's, attempts to persuade Western opinion-makers that, as she put it, 'Russia is a European power'.[5] Ever since Peter the Great, Russians had sought acceptance as full members of the European system of states and cultures, and they were keenly sensitive to intimations that Europeans regarded them as Asiatic—the sentiment encapsulated by the apocryphal saying, 'Scratch a Russian and find a Tatar'. If Russia was to be accepted in Europe, Moscow had to be rebranded as an enlightened European metropolis.

Catherine also worried that Moscow's lack of enlightenment was a threat to state security. In 1771, Moscow was struck by a plague epidemic that killed 50,000 people. Guided by modern medical principles, officials imposed a quarantine and forbade public gatherings, but these policies only alienated the population without containing the disease. Things came to a head when despairing worshippers congregated near a miracle-working icon to pray for divine succour. Attempts by the police to remove the icon triggered a bloody popular uprising that was suppressed only when artillery opened fire in downtown Moscow.[6] Catherine wrote to Voltaire that this was proof of the people's benighted 'fanaticism'.[7] A new threat to the regime arose in 1774, when Russia's south-eastern frontier rose in revolt under the Cossack Emelian Pugachev, and it seemed likely that the people of Moscow would give the rebels a hero's welcome if they succeeded in capturing the city.[8] When Pugachev was finally captured, Catherine made her point to Moscow's 'fanatical' inhabitants by choosing their city as the site for his execution.

In addition to foreign opinion and internal security, the third concern of Catherine and her successors was the opportunity represented by Moscow's central position in the networks that tied together the sparsely settled Russian heartland. This centrality could endanger the regime if it allowed the otherwise diffuse forces of unrest in the Russian interior to concentrate at one point, but the same effect could work in reverse by giving the regime a site from which its influence could reach into the provinces. Transform Moscow, so Catherine evidently reasoned, and the hundreds of thousands of migrants who passed annually through the city—officials, merchants, clerics, peasant labourers, noble landlords—would carry the regime's ideology back into provincial Russia. Thus, from the 1770s onward, Catherine and her successors tried to reconstruct Moscow. The goal was to acculturate the city's 'middling sort'—the term used in both Russia and Europe for the various middling strata of society—into a European way of life, and to persuade public opinion at home and abroad that Moscow was an enlightened European metropolis. These efforts proceeded, without significant discontinuity, until the death of Nicholas I in 1855.

Moscow's infrastructure and institutions were reconstructed. Schools were opened for the children of the middling sort (mainly clergymen, officials and merchants), and these groups were drawn more deeply into participation in local government. European arts, consumer culture and sociability arrived in the form of coffeehouses, elegant shops, a theatre and tree-lined promenades, and enjoying these after one's workday became easier thanks to streetlights and the safety provided by a corps of watchmen. The aesthetic experience of the city was enhanced by neoclassical architecture and the removal of cemeteries, foul-smelling industries, and other sources of filth and stench from the city centre. All of this made little difference to the rich aristocratic elite or the labouring masses, but for the middling sort, who made up (depending on which groups are included) about 14–29 percent of the population, it made possible a life that resembled that of the urban middle classes in northwestern Europe. Moscow was also re-'constructed' on a cultural level. The city became the subject of maps, cityscape paintings, fiction, journal articles, statistical surveys and medical topographies. All of these increasingly depicted Moscow as a place that, for all its 'Russian' peculiarities (onion domes, log houses and the like), was fundamentally a city like others in Europe.[9]

The Napoleonic occupation

The Napoleonic occupation was a horrific calamity. Almost 98 percent of Moscow's 275,000 inhabitants had fled as the French approached.[10] Over two-thirds of all residential buildings were destroyed.[11] When, in 1813, the government offered to provide financial assistance to Moscow residents, it received over 18,000 petitions from people who reported that they had lost houses, possessions and merchandise worth 250 million rubles.[12] By comparison, the government's total tax receipts for the entire Empire for 1805 had been only 147 million rubles.[13] Behind these aggregate numbers lay heart-rending individual stories. For example, the petition from the widow Sofia Bolgarova, drafted no doubt (judging from its uninflected prose) by some government clerk, stated that

> I had my residence in the 4th Ward of Presnenskaia District in the house of the Moscow townswoman Anna Elagina together with my father the retired collegiate councilor Iakov Alekseevich Maksimov and my mother Elisaveta Vasilevna and during the enemy's invasion of Moscow my parents burned and both their and my possessions burned and were looted.[14]

The disaster of October 1812 struck the middling sort, those whom Catherine had sought to elevate, especially hard. The large labouring classes had—in terms of material wealth—little to lose, and the aristocratic elite could recoup its losses with revenue from its landed estates. The middling sort, on the other hand, derived its status in large part from the fact that they owned a house, a shop, a set of nice clothes, or other possessions that were hard to replace on their owner's modest income. Moreover, most labourers were migrant peasants and most aristocrats were landowners, so both had rural homes where they could wait out the occupation. The middling sort, on the other hand, were rooted in the city, so they often had either to remain in the city, or leave and become homeless refugees.

The war brought home to the middling sort the precariousness of their social position. Reading between the lines of the eyewitness accounts,[15] one senses that many felt that in their hour of need they were denied the respect and solidarity to which their semi-privileged status, genteel way of life and civic loyalty entitled them. One target of resentment was Governor-General Fedor Rostopchin, the government's top man in Moscow. Rostopchin treated Muscovites not as loyal citizens, but as a volatile rabble. To forestall disorders, he issued propaganda bulletins that painted a reassuring picture of the progress of the war and that, many later thought, encouraged people to remain in Moscow until it was too late for an orderly evacuation. The bitterness that this engendered was long-lived. At the end of the century, a deacon's son born shortly after the war recounted what he had heard from his parents: after the battle of Borodino,

> people who were prudent and affluent began leaving the city; people who were not affluent were forced either to stay in Moscow and throw themselves on the mercy of fate, or else run in despair wherever their legs took them. My father, being among the latter, tarried to leave, for he lacked accurate information about the enemy's approach and trusted Rostopchin's promises not to let Napoleon into Moscow—promises that confused everyone.[16]

As this quotation suggests, feelings also ran high against the aristocratic elite, who before the war had served as models of enlightened culture to the middling sort. The aristocrats, many thought, had bought up the remaining horses, fled to their country manors, and cravenly abandoned their less affluent fellow-citizens to their fate. According to one priest's son, 'The people grew agitated and said that the nobles were saving their own skins while surrendering them [the people] and the metropolis itself to Napoleon'.[17] The peasantry, meanwhile, refused to show the genteel urban classes the respect and deference that were owed to them. Instead, as the urban population fled, they poured into the city to loot whatever was not taken by the French. One priest recalled in the 1830s that 'They were merciless in pillaging Moscow and proffered all sorts of insults against the inhabitants of Moscow, calling them runaways and traitors, and declared resolutely that whatever the enemy had left behind in Moscow belonged to them'.[18]

As for Napoleon's army, it was the living embodiment of the European civilization that Russians were supposed to emulate, but in 1812 its encounter with the people of Moscow was a disaster. Memoirists recalled that Napoleon's men were filthy and ragged, lacked all military discipline, and assaulted civilians, vandalized homes, desecrated churches and otherwise behaved appallingly. In only two contexts did Russians refer to them sympathetically: they were grateful when French officers acted to restrain the greed and brutality of their men, and they sometimes felt pity at the sheer squalor and misery of Napoleon's troops. As we have seen, an enlightened, Europeanized middling sort played an important role in the government's strategy for transforming the Russian heartland. If the occupation was a stress test for this project, the results were disheartening. The middling sort felt abandoned by the governor-general and the aristocracy who were supposed to be their patrons, assaulted by peasants who were supposed to be deferential, and treated with contempt by the Europeans whose civilization they were supposed to emulate.

The second aspect of Moscow's reconstruction, the city's transformation into an enlightened European metropolis, did not fare much better. Fire, the bane of Russia's mostly wooden cities, made a calamitous comeback. So did public violence: the French shot suspected arsonists or hanged them from lampposts, while Russians attacked isolated Frenchmen, often using axes, the all-purpose tool of the peasantry, to smash their skulls as they slept.[19] In the absence of police or streetlights, it became dangerous again to go out after dark. According to the noblewoman Anna Khomutova, 'wandering among the snow-covered ruins, we did not hear the rumble of carriages, or for that matter, any noise at all: it was the silence of a burial vault. In the evenings, all of a sudden, a pistol shot would ring out; whether it was a chance occurrence or a crime, no one knew'.[20] Decades of environmental improvements were reversed as buildings smouldered, corpses and animal carcasses rotted, and soldiers and civilians suffered from diarrhoea. The fetid air was suffocating; one Russian reported that 15 km from Moscow 'it is already hard to breathe'.[21] Once the French were gone, peasants conscripted by the Moscow police reportedly collected the remains of 11,955 humans and 12,360 horses;[22] an eyewitness recalled that 'for several weeks, the police were burning them by the banks of the river and sweeping the ashes into the water'.[23]

Initial responses to the war

The war left Moscow and the other areas touched by the war in a state of acute social crisis. To cope with this situation, the Russian government adopted measures that emphasized pragmatism and reconciliation. This outcome was not a foregone conclusion. From the government's perspective, one problem was how to quash the apparently widespread expectation that serfs who fought in the war would be granted their freedom. Another problem, more directly relevant to the situation in Moscow, was how to deal with the violence and class hatred that the war had unleashed. In the panic and confusion of the war, when people were quick to suspect others of treason, patriotic francophobia easily escalated into hostility toward the Europeanized elites. As we saw earlier, nobles who fled Moscow were accused of desertion by commoners too poor to leave, and peasants cited the mass exodus from the city as justification for looting the homes that Muscovites had abandoned. Nobles and foreigners who were overheard speaking French risked being denounced as spies,[24] and refugees from Moscow were harassed by peasants for having surrendered the city to Napoleon.[25] In the villages that Napoleon's troops had ransacked on their march into and back out of Russia, the peasants avenged themselves on enemy prisoners in ways that Russian nobles found chilling. One noblewoman recalled with horror the story of a group of peasant women who had paid money to be allowed to torture a prisoner to death. She had heard the story from a male peasant who had witnessed the scene and who commented: 'What, is that women's business? ... They torture him and torture him, until it starts making you feel bad to watch it; so you go and give him a proper blow to the head with an axe. Then they start cursing, asking why you didn't let them do the killing themselves'.[26]

How would the regime respond to the social crisis? Massive repression was not really an option. In the plague revolt and the Pugachev rebellion in the 1770s, once military operations had ended, the public executions that followed had been spectacularly staged but they were few in number. In 1812, as Napoleon approached, Moscow's Governor-General Rostopchin followed a similar course. He invited the people to watch as his policemen herded allegedly disloyal foreign residents on to a boat and transported them into exile. When the emperor met with gatherings of Moscow nobles and merchants, Rostopchin stationed police carriages in conspicuous places as a warning to anyone who might think of asking critical questions. As the French were about to enter the city, he turned over a young merchant named Mikhail Vereshchagin, who was accused of possessing Napoleonic propaganda, to a lynch mob. Rostopchin admitted that his methods were publicity stunts; it does not seem that he or anyone else in the Russian government had the stomach for mass repression.[27]

Nor did they have the means for it, as the aftermath of the occupation showed. Rostopchin instructed the police to investigate all residents who had stayed in the city and might have collaborated with the enemy, but no attempt was made to carry out mass arrests. Stolen goods were another problem. Moscow had been thoroughly sacked, but the French were unable to take their loot with them, so the city and surrounding villages were awash with plundered goods. The police tried to collect these, but identifying the owners was often impossible, the police were themselves accused of embezzling goods,[28] and the revival of lawful trade was slow because of uncertainty about ownership claims.[29] The government also worried about the countless weapons from Napoleon's army that had ended up in the hands of Russian commoners. The government had only limited means of coercion to address these challenges because most of the army was campaigning abroad.

Under these circumstances, the regime did the only rational thing: it sought to restore social peace through reconciliation rather than retribution. In March 1813, Rostopchin announced that by order of Emperor Alexander I, goods henceforth belonged to whoever currently had possession of them.[30] The government's strategy to aid Muscovites' economic recovery thus did not rely on helping people recover their looted possessions, a futile undertaking that would have caused no end of disputes. Instead, the government offered assistance to Muscovites who had lost their homes and possessions. The sums available were, of course, paltry next to the population's needs. As noted earlier, in 1813 around 18,000 petitions were submitted that reported 250 million rubles' worth of losses; in response, the government awarded around 16.5 million rubles in aid, mostly in the form of loans. A further 21,000 petitions were submitted between 1816 and 1819; these led to the award of around 1.4 million rubles in aid.[31] It is hard to know what difference this aid made in people's lives, but at least it allowed the government to show its goodwill and made it easier to move beyond the property disputes that the war had engendered.

Similarly pragmatic attitudes prevailed in other areas. Worried about the many guns captured by peasants, the government launched a gun buy-back programme in the areas affected by the war. Recovering these arms was important, so the provincial governors were informed, because 'in the normal course of affairs, peasants should not be keeping arms in their homes'. To avoid antagonizing the peasants, however, they should be told that the army needed the weapons to fight against the French.[32] There was also no sustained effort to bring looters and other wartime offenders to justice; instead, a general amnesty was announced in 1814.

The long-term legacy

Once the immediate effects of the war had passed, Moscow continued, in important ways, on the same trajectory as before. Demographically the recovery was swift. According to the official statistics, which probably undercounted the large population of transients and migrants, the city had 275,000 inhabitants at the beginning of 1812. Despite the war, the population rose to 347,000 in 1840. By 1863 it had reached 462,500, and by 1897 it passed the one-million mark.[33] Moscow's position as the metropolis of the Russian interior was never in doubt, and no Russian city save St Petersburg ever rivalled it in population size.

The government's policies toward the city likewise remained much as they had been since Catherine's time. When the city was rebuilt, and decisions had to be made about the layout of major streets and squares, zoning regulations for different neighbourhoods, and the like, the main principles of Catherine's so-called General Plan of 1775 were kept intact.[34] This reflected the continuing usefulness of this plan, but there was also much inertia: virtually nothing had been done by the middle of the nineteenth century to modernize the increasingly antiquated infrastructure bequeathed by Catherine, whether by improving the water supply, building a sewer system, upgrading the streetlights from hempseed oil to coal gas, or replacing the ageing army veterans who served as city watchmen with a force of professional police officers.[35]

Another element of Catherine's system that remained intact was the decision to base urban institutions on the ascriptive social estates (nobility, merchants, clergy, peasantry and so on) to which Russians and other Ancien Régime Europeans belonged by law. Schools reserved to the middling estates grew rapidly, whereas public schools, which were open to all estates, did not. The right to vote in municipal elections continued to depend on one's estate, not, as in many countries, on one's wealth and the tax one paid. Much of the population continued to lack any rights of municipal citizenship, because labourers—that is, the majority of the inhabitants—were mostly peasants who legally resided in their home village or their master's household and worked in the city only on temporary work permits. Laws passed in the 1820s and 1830s made it easier for them to register as urban residents, but even so, the proportion of Moscow residents in 1835–1839 who were serfs or crown peasants was 45 percent (compared with 66 percent between 1789 and 1793).[36]

In its institutions and infrastructure, postwar Moscow, like Russia as a whole, thus continued on its earlier trajectory. Its place in the larger economic and political networks of the empire was also little changed; it suffered no long-term decline, but neither did it gain greater economic dynamism or political clout as a result of the war. What did change fundamentally, however, was the ideological prism through which Moscow was perceived. One development of broad importance, which made Moscow's archaic qualities appear in a much more favourable light than before, was a new respect among educated Russians for Russian national traditions. Religion was one reason for this. Like many other European countries, Russia experienced a religious revival during the Napoleonic Wars. At first, the imperial court tried to channel this revival in a Pietist-inspired ecumenical direction, but from the early 1820s on the emphasis was placed firmly on Russian Orthodoxy, the historic centre of which was Moscow.

The resurgence of Orthodoxy was related to the rise of nationalism, which also drew new attention to Moscow as the repository of Russian history and tradition. Educated society in the eighteenth century had thought of itself, naturally enough, as 'Russian', but what this meant was poorly defined—to be a 'Russian' noble meant to live in an Italianate mansion, read French and

English novels, attend lectures by German professors and imagine oneself as a part of 'enlightened' Europe. After 1812, Russians increasingly worked out a coherent conception of national identity. Before, there was little knowledge of pre-Petrine history, no agreement on how to write proper literary Russian, and no consensus about what was meant by 'Russian' folklore, character traits, landscape, architecture, or cuisine. By 1850, all of this had been resolved, and a conception of Russian nationality had crystallized that largely prevails to this day.[37] According to this conception, 'Russia' was two things: a multi-ethnic dynastic state that formed part of Europe, but also a unique nation that embodied a civilizational alternative to 'the West', that is, what Russians imagined as the bloc formed by the nations of central and western Europe.

The war played an important role in the emergence of this new vision of a national identity. Before 1812, the Russian elites had worried that an invasion by Napoleon might trigger an uprising by peasants and common Muscovites. This fear dissipated when the population not only failed to rebel but in fact offered active resistance to the French. Like its counterparts in Germany and Spain, the 'people's war' in Russia was variously interpreted as proof that the people were worthy of civil liberty or, on the contrary, that they were loyal to the Ancien Régime. Either way, 1812, when the peasants fought back against the French and the people of Moscow (supposedly) let their city go up in flames rather than yield it to Napoleon, became a symbol of a national solidarity embracing all social classes. As we have seen, survivors of the war preserved memories of bitter class antagonisms; the contest to shape the larger public discourse, however, was won by the proponents of the myth of heroic national unity.

Orthodoxy and nationalism contributed to a reassessment of pre-Petrine Muscovy's legacy of autocratic rule. Catherine II had presented herself as an enlightened absolute monarch in the European mould, and Alexander I endorsed constitutionalism, at least in theory. The upheavals of the post-Napoleonic period, however—the European revolutions of 1820–1821, the Decembrist revolt in Russia in 1825, and the revolutions in Europe and Russian Poland in 1830–1831—led the regime and its supporters to the novel assertion that autocracy formed a morally superior form of government with roots deep in the era before Peter the Great. The immensely influential *History of the Russian State*, first published in 1818, by the Russian writer and historian Nikolai Karamzin, argued for example that from the Middle Ages onward, Russia's peace and prosperity had depended on a strong autocratic power to fend off civil discord and foreign invasion. Mikhail Pogodin, professor of history at Moscow University, and the Slavophile intellectuals of the 1840s developed the thesis that Russians had always embraced autocratic rule because their national character was inclined to peace and social harmony, unlike the warlike peoples of the West. In this quite influential view, the embodiment of Western aggression was Catholic

Poland-Lithuania, historically a state with a constitutional monarchy and that ruled over vast, mostly Orthodox Belorussian and Ukrainian lands that Russians considered part of their own national patrimony. Polish forces had occupied Moscow in 1612 during Russia's Time of Troubles, and again as part of Napoleon's army in 1812. The way Russian nationalists saw it, the Polish uprising of 1830–1831, which aimed to restore Polish independence, was a renewal of a relentless Polish (and thus, Western) aggression that only a Russia united under an autocratic tsar could fend off.[38]

These developments—religious revival, nationalism, the ideological embrace of autocracy, distrust of the Poles—coloured how 1812 was remembered. Nationalist intellectuals portrayed the fire of Moscow as a collective self-sacrifice by a people who were not morally corrupted by European civilization; tellingly, they were proud to point out similarities between the anti-French resistance of the Russian common people and what they called the *gveriliasy* (guerrillas) of Spain. The most prominent monument erected in central Moscow in the war's immediate aftermath honoured Minin and Pozharskii, the leaders of the Russian army that expelled the Poles in 1612. It was also in Moscow that Alexander I proposed to build his own preferred monument, a grandiose cathedral, to give thanks to God for the victory over Napoleon. In keeping with Alexander's religious ecumenism, the initial plans called for it to be constructed in neoclassical style, but the cathedral's builders ultimately paid tribute to Orthodoxy and nationalism by adopting a design inspired by Byzantine and pre-Petrine Russian traditions.[39]

Thanks in part to the memory of 1812, the culture of the Russian elites became less exclusionary toward the religious and folk traditions of the middle and lower strata. At the same time, the middle strata gained in wealth, education and political influence, and hence engaged increasingly with the elite culture. The statistician Vasilii Androssov noted in 1832 that since the war, which had damaged many nobles' estates, fewer nobles owned property in Moscow or came for the annual winter season, and that economic dominance in Moscow was passing from them to 'the middle estate'.[40] Politically as well, the middle strata acquired greater weight. The coup attempt by liberal aristocratic officers in December 1825 (the Decembrist revolt) had left the new Emperor, Nicholas I (1825–1855), distrustful of the court aristocracy. Instead, he placed his trust in his rapidly expanding bureaucracy, which was staffed in large part by men from the clergy or other middle strata. These strata also provided a rapidly growing audience for patriotic, politically conservative, culturally middlebrow newspapers and periodicals. Before 1812, a Russian journal with a circulation over 1,000 had been considered very successful; by contrast, the daily *Northern Bee* reached 4,000 subscribers in the early 1830s and 10,000 in the 1850s, and the monthly *Library for Reading* had 7,000 subscribers by the late 1830s.[41] These numbers were not especially high by West European standards, but they nonetheless indicated a significant increase in circulation.[42]

A new social type emerged in Moscow and St Petersburg, sometimes called *raznochintsy* ('people of various ranks') because they did not fit comfortably into the Ancien Régime hierarchy of estates. They were Europeanized in their manners and external appearance, and exhibited cultural and consumer habits similar to the middle classes of Western countries. On the other hand, they were nationalistic and distrustful of the ostentatious cosmopolitanism of the aristocracy, and they retained a connection to the social estate of their origin; for example, sons of priests often retained the puritanical, service-oriented ethos of the Orthodox clergy.[43]

Had Moscow's transformation into an enlightened metropolis, with a middling sort that shared the regime's ideological vision, succeeded? Yes and no. The eyewitness accounts of 1812 suggest that Moscow's middle strata were deeply attached to the urban civilization that had been created since the 1770s. During the very time when their war memories were crystallizing, what Muscovites read about current urban affairs was likely to reinforce these sentiments. The Russian press in the 1820s to 1850s frequently reported that bourgeois greed, proletarian alienation and a general atmosphere of moral anomie were turning London and Paris into hellholes of pauperism, despair, criminality and revolutionary violence. By contrast, they claimed, Moscow and St Petersburg were blessed with a state-of-the-art urban infrastructure, a wise monarchical administration, and a population imbued with old-fashioned morality and common sense.[44] Judging from the memoirs of 1812, Moscow's middle strata had a less sanguine view of their city's class relations, but there is little doubt that they otherwise shared the regime's general conception of what constituted a successful urban community.

The memory of Napoleon's occupation of Moscow did not, however, ultimately cement public support for the regime's urban policies. Commemorations of 1812 reached a crescendo around the 50th anniversary in 1862, but by a twist of fate, Russia was then in a deep crisis that coloured recollections of the war.[45] The defeat in the Crimean War had shattered educated Russians' confidence in their country's social and political structures. The government responded by liberalizing public debate and launching ambitious social reforms, most prominently the abolition of serfdom, to transform Russia's Ancien Régime into a modern society of citizens. The 1860s and 1870s were therefore a period of national soul-searching and political polarization. By that time, the great cities of the West, especially London and Paris, were beginning to find solutions to their urban problems, such as the construction of the underground railway in London, or Haussmann's reconstruction of Paris. By comparison, Moscow's institutions and infrastructure began to seem obsolete, and when newly emancipated peasants began pouring into the city after 1861, Moscow developed the same pathologies that had plagued London and Paris in the 1820s to 1840s. Thanks to their much increased press freedom, educated Russians became keenly aware of these issues.

Conclusion

Understanding the long-term legacy of the Napoleonic occupation requires an appreciation of the timeframes in which change occurred in three areas: the sociopolitical domain, culture and collective memory. Moscow's social order and its urban institutions and infrastructure had experienced dynamic development between 1771 and 1812. The decades after 1812, however, were a period of stasis, by contrast with the Western cities (especially London and Paris) that served Russians as points of reference. For a long time, educated Russians took comfort in what they believed was their country's order and stability. By the 1860s, however, a consensus had developed that Moscow had become backward vis-à-vis 'the West' and was unprepared for the demographic and economic changes that lay ahead.

In the area of culture, the counterpart to the city's social and institutional transformation was the emergence of a culture that was simultaneously 'European' and 'Russian' and that reached beyond the aristocratic elite to include a broad middle stratum. While sociopolitical modernization stagnated after 1812, cultural change powered ahead. By the 1860s and 1870s, Russia had a broad, socially diverse educated public, and Russians were using European artistic forms—novels, symphonies, landscape painting, journalism—to express a vision of the world that was uniquely and recognizably 'Russian'.

Awkwardly for the regime, this culture trained its gaze on urban affairs just as the dynamism of the Catherinean era was fading from memory and Russia's authoritarian Ancien Régime started to look dysfunctional. The only way forward, Russians of all persuasions increasingly felt, lay in overcoming the Ancien Régime fragmentation of society and constructing a unified nation by empowering educated society and uplifting the masses. These concerns inspired intensely critical depictions of Russian urban modernity and commemorations of 1812 that foregrounded the common people, not the imperial elites. One of the literary sensations of the 1860s, Fedor Dostoevskii's *Crime and Punishment* (1866), explored the spiritual crisis of educated urban youth; another, Leo Tolstoi's *War and Peace* (1869), depicted 1812 as the victory of the Russian soul over the false enlightenment of Europe. In Tolstoi's epic, Moscow symbolized Russian national identity, but it was a Moscow of aristocrats and peasants from which the middle strata and their Europeanized urban lifestyle were absent. In the 1860s and 1870s, when the modern collective memory of 1812 took shape in Russia, the Napoleonic occupation thus no longer provided ideological validation for the regime's urban policies.

Acknowledgements

My work on this project was supported by the National Endowment for the Humanities, the American Councils for International Education (ACTR/

ACCELS), the National Council for Eurasian and East European Research, the American Philosophical Society and the American Council of Learned Societies. My participation in the conference where this chapter was discussed was made possible by generous funding from the Institute for Scholarship in the Liberal Arts at the University of Notre Dame.

Notes

1. On Napoleon's Russian campaign, see: Dominic Lieven, *Russia Against Napoleon: The Battle For Europe, 1807–1814* (London, 2009).
2. I develop this argument in Alexander M. Martin, *Enlightened Metropolis: Constructing Imperial Moscow, 1762–1855* (Oxford, 2013).
3. John T. Alexander, 'Petersburg and Moscow in Early Urban Policy', *Journal of Urban History* 8/2 (1982): 145–169.
4. Jacques Casanova de Seingalt, *Mémoires*, 10 vols (Paris, 1833–1837), vol. 9, 290–291.
5. Catherine II, Empress of Russia, *The Memoirs of Catherine the Great* (New York, 2005), xxi.
6. On this topic, see John T. Alexander, *Bubonic Plague in Early Modern Russia: Public Health and Urban Disaster* (Baltimore, MD, 1980).
7. Marcus C. Levitt, *The Visual Dominant in Eighteenth-Century Russia* (DeKalb, IL, 2011), 196.
8. A. T. Bolotov, *Zhizn' i prikliucheniia Andreia Bolotova, opisannye samim im dlia svoikh potomkov*, 3 vols (Moscow, 1993), vol. 3, 143–144.
9. Martin, *Enlightened Metropolis*, especially chapters 2–4.
10. A. G. Tartakovskii, 'Naselenie Moskvy v period frantsuzskoi okkupatsii', *Istoricheskie Zapiski* 93 (1973): 356–379.
11. N. A. Troitskii, *1812: Velikii god Rossii* (Moscow, 1988), 193.
12. Martin, *Enlightened Metropolis*, 212.
13. K. V. Sivkov, 'Finansy Rossii pered voinoi 1812 goda', in *Otechestvennaia voina i russkoe obshchestvo*, ed. A. K. Dzhivelegov et al., 7 vols (Moscow, 1911–1912), vol. 2, 261.
14. Tsentral'nyi Istoricheskii Arkhiv Moskvy (Central Historical Archive of Moscow), fond (collection) 20, opis' (inventory) 2, delo (file) 2214, list (folios) 133–133v.
15. On Russian memoir accounts of 1812, see A. G. Tartakovskii, *1812 god i russkaia memuaristika: Opyt istochnikovedcheskogo izucheniia* (Moscow, 1980).
16. N. I. T–v, 'O 1812 gode: Vospominaniia iz razskazov sovremennikov i ochevidtsev', in *Bumagi, otnosiashchiesia do Otechestvennoi voiny 1812 goda*, ed. P. I. Shchukin, 10 vols (Moscow, 1897–1908), vol. 4, 331–46, 333.
17. [T. Tolycheva], 'Razskazy ochevidtsev o dvenadtsatom gode: Na Mokhovoi', *Moskovskiia Vedomosti* (1 March 1872): no pagination.
18. [V. I. Lebedev], 'Kratkoe opisanie proizshestvii, byvshikh pri Pokhval'skoi, chto v Bashmakove, tserkvi v 1812 godu', *Chteniia v Obshchestve liubitelei dukhovnago prosveshcheniia* 36 (1914): 54–76, 71.
19. J. A. Rosenstrauch, 'Geschichtliche Ereignisse in Moskau im Jahre 1812, zur Zeit der Anwesenheit des Feindes in dieser Stadt', in *Istoricheskie proisshestviia v Moskve 1812 goda vo vremia prisutstviia v sem gorode nepriiatelia*, ed. I. A. Rozenshtraukh (Moscow, 2015). The German original of this memoir of Moscow in 1812 is included in the book, see 169–220.
20. A. G. Khomutova, 'Vospominaniia A. G. Khomutovoi o Moskve v 1812 godu', *Russkii Arkhiv* 3 (1891): 309–328, 327.

21. 'Griboedovskaia Moskva v pis'makh M. A. Volkovoi k V. I. Lanskoi 1812–1818 gg.', part 1: *Vestnik Evropy*, kniga 8 (1874), 572–666, 613.
22. A. A. Smirnov, 'Moskva', in *Otechestvennaia voina 1812 goda: Entsiklopediia*, ed. V. M. Bezotosnyi et al. (Moscow, 2004), 476–479, 478.
23. [Tolycheva], 'Na Mokhovoi'.
24. 'Griboedovskaia Moskva', Part I, 592 and 615; F. P. Leont'eva, 'Zapiski F. P. Leont'evoi, 1811, 1812 i 1813 gody', (Part III), *Russkii Vestnik* 169/2 (1884): 670–721, 706–707; and Karolina Pavlova, 'Moi vospominaniia', *Russkii Arkhiv* 4/10 (1875): 222–240, 222.
25. Lebedev, 'Iz razskazov rodnykh', in Shchukin, *Bumagi*, vol. 3, 257.
26. Pavlova, 'Moi vospominaniia', 228.
27. See Rostopchin's memoirs of 1812, F. V. Rostopchin, 'Tysiacha vosem'sot dvenadtsatyi god v Zapiskakh grafa F. V. Rostopchina', *Russkaia Starina* 64 (December 1889): 643–725.
28. For examples of such charges, see 'Griboedovskaia Moskva', Part I, 619, 635 and 641; also Part II, *Vestnik Evropy*, kniga 9 (1874), 115–168, 117 and 141; and Anton Wilhelm Nordhof, *Die Geschichte der Zerstörung Moskaus im Jahre 1812*, ed. Claus Scharf and Jürgen Kessel (Munich, 2000), 240, 246, 253–254 and 263–264.
29. M. I. Makaruev, 'Zapiski M. I. Makarueva', in *1812 god v vospominaniiakh, perepiske i rasskazakh sovremennikov* (Moscow, 2001), 20–40, 40.
30. 'Rostopchin to Police Chief Ivashkin', 28 March 1813, in Shchukin, *Bumagi*, vol. 2, 214.
31. Martin, *Enlightened Metropolis*, 210–214.
32. 'Alexander I to S. K. Viazmitinov', 29 April 1813, Otdel Pis'mennykh Istochnikov Gosudarstennogo Istoricheskogo Muzeia (Division of Written Sources of the State Historical Museum, Moscow), f. 160, op. 1, d. 198, ll. 10–10v.
33. 'Otchet moskovskago ober-politsmeistera, za 1840 god', *Zhurnal Ministerstva Vnutrennikh Del*, chast' 41/7 (1841): 1–161, 2; and A. G. Rashin, *Naselenie Rossii za 100 let, 1811–1913 gg.: Statisticheskie ocherki* (Moscow, 1956), 93.
34. On this topic, see Albert J. Schmidt, *The Architecture and Planning of Classical Moscow: A Cultural History* (Philadelphia, 1989).
35. I. F. Rerberg, *Moskovskii vodoprovod: Istoricheskii ocherk ustroistva i razvitiia vodosnabzheniia g. Moskvy. Opisanie novago vodoprovoda* (Moscow, 1892); N. M. Bychkov, 'Istoricheskii ocherk osveshcheniia goroda Moskvy', *Izvestiia Moskovskoi Gorodskoi Dumy*, vypusk 1 (October 1895), otdel 2: 1–52; and M. P. Shchepkin, 'Istoricheskaia zapiska o raskhodakh goroda Moskvy po soderzhaniiu politseiskikh uchrezhdenii v 1823–1879 gg.', *Izvestiia Moskovskoi Gorodskoi Dumy*, vypusk 2 (1880), cols: 5–72.
36. Manfred Hildermeier, *Bürgertum und Stadt in Rußland, 1760–1870: Rechtliche Lage und soziale Struktur* (Cologne, 1986), 234–245 and 365; and M. Gastev, *Materialy dlia polnoi i sravnitel'noi statistiki Moskvy, chast' pervaia* (Moscow, 1841), 264.
37. See, for example: Alexander M. Martin, *Romantics, Reformers, Reactionaries: Russian Conservative Thought and Politics in the Reign of Alexander I* (DeKalb, IL,1997); Christopher Ely, *This Meager Nature: Landscape and National Identity in Imperial Russia* (DeKalb, IL, 2002); Alison K. Smith, *Recipes for Russia: Food and Nationhood Under the Tsars* (DeKalb, IL, 2008); and Elena Vishlenkova, *Vizual'noe narodovedenie imperii, ili 'Uvidet' russkogo dano ne kazhdomu'* (Moscow, 2011).
38. On these topics, see: Nicholas Riasanovsky, *Nicholas I and Official Nationality in Russia, 1825–1855* (Berkeley, CA, 1959); Andrei Zorin, *Kormia dvuglavogo orla ... Literatura i gosudarstvennaia ideologiia v Rossii v poslednei treti XVIII–pervoi treti XIX veka* (Moscow, 2001), especially chapters 5 and 10; Susanna Rabow-Edling,

Slavophile Thought and the Politics of Cultural Nationalism (Albany, NY, 2006); and Julie Grandhaye, *Les décembristes: Une génération républicaine en Russie autocratique* (Paris, 2011).

39. Richard Wortman, *Scenarios of Power: Myth and Ceremony in Russian Monarchy from Peter the Great to the Abdication of Nicholas II* (Princeton, NJ, 2013), 155.
40. V. Androssov, *Statisticheskaia zapiska o Moskve* (Moscow, 1832), 46. Pushkin made a similar observation in 1834 in 'A Journey from Moscow to St Petersburg', in Alexander Pushkin, *The Complete Works of Alexander Pushkin*, 15 vols (Norfolk, VA, 1999–2003), vol. 13, 234.
41. A. V. Zapadov, *Istoriia russkoi zhurnalistiki XVIII–XIX vekov* (Moscow, 1973), 159–160; Katia Dianina, 'The Feuilleton: An Everyday Guide to Public Culture in the Age of the Great Reforms', *Slavonic and East European Journal* 47/2 (2003): 187–210,188. See also Nurit Schleifman, 'A Russian Daily Newspaper and its Readership: *Severnaia Pchela*, 1825–1840', *Cahiers du monde russe et soviétique* 28/2 (1987): 127–144.
42. See for a comparison, Karen Hagemann, *Revisiting Prussia's Wars against Napoleon: History, Culture and Memory* (Cambridge, 2015), Chapter 12.
43. On this topic, see Elise Kimerling Wirtschafter, *Structures of Society: Imperial Russia's 'People of Various Ranks'* (DeKalb, IL, 1994); and Laurie Manchester, *Holy Fathers, Secular Sons: Clergy, Intelligentsia, and the Modern Self in Revolutionary Russia* (DeKalb, IL, 2008).
44. For examples of this literature, see: M. N. Zagoskin, 'Moskva i Moskvichi', in M. N. Zagoskin, *Sochineniia*, 7 vols (St Petersburg, 1889), vol. 5, 1–570; Faddei Bulgarin, *Peterburgskie ocherki F. V. Bulgarina*, ed. Al'bin Konechnyi (St Petersburg, 2010); [L'vov] M. Zh., 'Zhizn' v Moskve v Ianvare 1846 goda', *Moskvitianin*, chast' 1/2 (1846): 232–244; 'Zamechaniia o chisle umalishennykh, pol'zovannykh v bol'nitse Vsekh Skorbiashchikh v S. Peterburge 1832 goda', *Zhurnal Ministerstva Vnutrennikh Del*, chast' 8/2 (1833): 199–208; 'Zamechaniia na otchety Ober-Politseimeisterov po obeim Stolitsam', *Zhurnal Ministerstva Vnutrennikh Del*, chast' 6/2 (1832): 54–69; 'Zamechaniia o chisle krazh, sdelannykh v Moskve, S. P. burge i Londone', *Zhurnal Ministerstva Vnutrennikh Del*, chast' 8/3 (1833): 331–334; and 'Sravnitel'naia statistika prestuplenii v Parizhe i v Londone', *Zhurnal Ministerstva Vnutrennikh Del*, chast' 2, 'Smes' (1843): 443–457. This literature is discussed in Martin, *Enlightened Metropolis*, chapter 8. *tro*
45. On this subject, see Olga Maiorova, *From the Shadow of Empire: Defining the Russian Nation through Cultural Mythology, 1855–1870* (Madison, WI, 2010).

18

Creating Cultural Difference: The Military, Political and Cultural Legacy of the Anglo-American War of 1812–1815

Andrew Lambert

The Anglo-American War of 1812 was fought between two literate populations sharing a common language. It began in mid-1812, and although ended by a peace treaty signed on 24 December 1814, active operations continued until the treaty had been ratified in Washington, and news had reached the various theatres, including the Indian Ocean. While the British treated it as a mere sideshow to the Napoleonic conflict, to be quickly forgotten, for Americans it was the defining event of an era, one that generated numerous deeply partisan accounts to sustain domestic agendas long after the origins, aims and outcomes of the conflict had faded from memory. Above all, the Americans created the illusion of victory in a 'Second War of Independence' to sustain the Republican Party. This mythology would shape the development of divergent sectional and national cultures in the era before the Civil War.

Americans began to rewrite the war as a victory, exploiting the ambiguity of the diplomatic settlement achieved in the Treaty of Ghent on 24 December 1814, a *status quo ante* compromise that did not reflect the depth of America's defeat. The arrival of the draft treaty in Washington soon after reports of Andrew Jackson's victory at New Orleans, and the fact that it did not require any sacrifice by the United States, enabled President James Madison to link the battle and diplomacy. This artificial connection, reinforced by the concurrent release of a pamphlet, written by Alexander J. Dallas, Treasury Secretary under Madison, on the origins of the war, dominated the President's Message to Congress of 18 February 1815. Dallas's pamphlet had been written before news of the peace, as an attempt to defend the administration from the opposition Federalist critique of government incompetence being developed by the Hartford Convention. Peace ended the Federalist challenge, turning the pamphlet into a victory boast. Once the Senate had ratified the peace, Republican journalist Hezekiah Niles, editor of the Baltimore *Weekly Register,* claimed the war ended in 'a blaze of glory ... without a blot or blemish'.[1] Like all Republicans he preferred to ignore the fiery destruction of Washington DC in August 1814, the loss of the national flagship, the Hartford Convention of 1814–1815 and national insolvency. America had been beaten, but the Republicans needed a victory to retain control of the White House, and so the war

> ...passed from a sorrowful stalemate to a glorious myth—a triumphant contest, faintly remembered in the main for a handful of storied naval duels and for the one truly telling blow dealt to the enemy on land. Never mind that six months before, the republic had been on the ropes. With the country celebrating Jackson's feat and then rejoicing over the war's end, the Republican Party's earlier mistakes would soon fade from memory.[2]

When the frigate USS *Constitution* returned to New York, the Republican *National Intelligencer* claimed in May 1815: 'She has, literally become a *Nation's* ship, and should be preserved ... as a glorious Monument of her own, and our other naval Victories.'[3] In truth American naval victories 'had no direct effect on the course of the war', although they 'made Americans proud to be Americans'.[4] Why three frigate victories over markedly inferior opponents should be a source of such pride is hard to understand. While Republican Party propaganda elevated the *Constitution* to immortality, the loss of her sister ship, the USS *President*, was conveniently forgotten—the name has never been used again.

Victory was possible because Madison had abandoned his stated aims of 'Free Trade & Sailors' Rights', and the United States no longer suffered the land hunger that had led him to invade British territory. In October 1814, he declared that America's war aim was survival, and Americans were happy to collude in the deception. They were desperate for peace.[5] American 'victory' played a critical role in postwar domestic politics, contested ground which Republican partisans secured by creating a mass of words and pictures, transforming defeat into success. A common language ensured these products shaped English perceptions. The postwar decade witnessed both the high-water mark of American navalism, and the ultimate triumph of Republican continentalism: by 1830 open plains had replaced the high seas as the dominant cultural signifier.[6] The new reality manifested itself in high tariff barriers and coastal fortresses, to keep out the British in peace and war. Before 1812, the United States used low tariffs on imports, primarily to fund the Federal administration. In 1816, a 25 percent duty was imposed on imported British cotton and woollen goods, to protect American industries. Southern administrations were pro-agriculture and expansion, and low tariff, while Northerners protected their growing manufacturing sector.[7] Anxious to increase manufactured exports, British governments used reciprocity agreements to limit the impact of American tariffs, but they recognized the meaning of American policy. In 1861, British support for the

South was almost entirely a tariff question. A separate Southern state would reduce tariff barriers, because it had little industry.

However, that lay in the future when the Treaty of Ghent was signed. Before the Americans had even ratified the Treaty, Britain turned to the main issues, settling the future of Europe at Vienna, while British merchants dispatched fleets of merchant ships laden with manufactured goods to America. The war was quickly forgotten by all but a handful of interested participants. Having defeated and imprisoned the greatest warrior of the modern age, Britain had no reason to recall victory over James Madison.[8] Yet there were enough words, pictures and wooden trophies to undermine American claims of victory.

This chapter will examine how the evolution of distinctive British and American versions of the war, in the wider context of national cultures, reflected a fundamental sundering of a once coherent Anglophone Atlantic world view, with American continentalism and exceptionalism as a contrast to the older British maritime world view. The most important consequences were the emergence of a distinctive American identity in words and pictures, transmitted through the latest systems of mass production to a rapidly growing literate electorate. By the 1840s the politicians and publicists of 'Manifest Destiny' were using a distinctly unbalanced version of the War of 1812 to sustain demands for northward expansion, but the reality of the war was more accurately reflected in impressive American coastal defences.

American foreign policy, national identity and the legacy of the war of 1812

At the heart of America's war of 1812 lay a profound struggle for the culture of a new nation, a struggle that divided North from South, sea from land; and one in which the British played a relatively minor role.[9] In 1812 America remained a cultural dependency of Great Britain; art, literature, fashions, and manufactures flowed across the Atlantic unchecked by the caesura of 1782. Native literature and arts were considered second-rate. As historian Bradford Perkins observed, 'because' British critics 'came so close to the truth, they wounded American sensibilities'. British cultural superiority challenged national identity and self-esteem. Not that British arrogance was solely to blame. Republican hostility toward creative arts associated with monarchs and elites restricted the ambition of American artists and patrons to the simple 'Roman' naturalism of Gilbert Stuart's portrait of Washington. Ambitious American artists like Benjamin West moved to London. West even became President of the Royal Academy.[10]

Pre-war American literature remained equally derivative, echoing Republican concerns for social utility, local issues and land over individual expression. Stories were moral and improving, without much concern for merit, or originality. The market was dominated by imported British books, while three-quarters of all American publications were pirate editions. With no copyright protection for native authors, foreigners were fair game, either wholesale or by selection. The poverty of American cultural production, widely lamented at home, and not infrequently mocked abroad, constituted a critical challenge to American sovereignty. Without their own culture Americans were still in harness.[11] American culture reflected the deep divisions between the maritime, mercantile sector and the landed interests of plantation agriculture and westward expansion. America's first millionaires, shipowners in the Asian trade, lived in an Anglophone world; they fought alongside the British against French privateers in the West Indies between 1798 and 1800.[12] They backed John Adams' Federalist government and funded new warships, 'a compelling cultural expression' of Federalist America.[13] They agreed with Alexander Hamilton, member of the cabinet of President George Washington and founder of the Federalist Party, that a navy would be both the ideal cultural symbol of the nation, and the guarantee of their commerce.[14]

However, war in 1812 would be declared by another, larger, more dynamic America, a continentally minded nation of land hungry expansionists, anxious to push westward at the expense of Indians, Spaniards and Britons. These Americans did not share the pan-European cultural notions of the Republican leadership, the international commercial impulse of New England, or a taste for warships. In the South and West populist democracy, individualism and expansion would fight for land. Victory would provide more territory, and validate a new identity. Both would be free of Indians. The new identity reflected widely held anxieties about enervating sloth, factionalism, avarice and the loss of revolutionary fervour that transformed the war from a petty squabble about an ocean of legal niceties into the solution to existential angst. War would solve diseases internal to the American body politic; the unifying patriotism of war would soothe and bind, restoring older virtues. Internal concerns propelled the country to war, not British 'Orders in Council' and impressment. The 'War Hawks' grabbed the opportunity to impose protectionist economic policies and curb domestic dissent. On 9 May 1812, Hezekiah Niles, the editor and publisher of the Baltimore-based national weekly news magazine, *Niles' Register*, stressed, for example, that war would create 'a NATIONAL CHARACTER'.[15]

For a generation that had grown up in the shadow of the Revolution, war would be a moral tonic, vindicating the republican virtues of the Founding Fathers and a 'crusade for Union'. Precisely what kind of republic these men wanted was obvious, for many of the 'Founding Fathers' were land speculators.[16] They opposed naval increases because protecting American overseas commerce was 'a mere matter of calculation ... a question of profit and loss', and distinguished 'useful' exports of American agricultural produce from 'useless' carrying trades and re-exports, which were the primary drivers of maritime expansion after 1793. Although these trades made up more than half of national commerce, the Republicans would not tax farmers for their protection. They considered internal exchange the key to America's future, not external commerce. They did not need a navy, only gunboats to collect import duties.[17] After 1800, manufacturers joined farmers on the list of good Republican citizens; merchants remained outside the pale.

By 1810 domestic manufacturing had reached significant proportions, an unintended consequence of President Thomas Jefferson's Embargo Act of 1807 with which he responded to the Napoleonic Wars. Industrial protectionism added a significant element to war fever: ubiquitous British manufactured goods undercut domestic products. Catching the steady drift of Baltimore capital from ships to factories, Niles argued that war would end American dependence on foreign production. It was but a short step to postwar protectionism. Republican America sought internal self-sufficiency and continental hegemony behind the twin barrier of exclusive tariffs and coastal forts. By contrast, the British economic model relied on an ever-expanding network of maritime commerce, sustained by naval dominance.[18]

Thomas Jefferson, ideologue of Republican America, was obsessed by fears that treasonous New England Federalists would subvert the Union. After the Louisiana Purchase of 1803, he attacked their economic model and their cultural values. As America turned landward capitalists moved from shipping to industry. Between 1810 and 1820, American oceanic shipping fell by 40 percent, while inland shipping rose by 45 percent. Jefferson's search for internal self-sufficiency collided with a war that emphasized inland transport.[19] In 1817, coastal, riverine and lake routes became protected markets for American vessels. War and legislation would rebuild America along Republican lines, turning from oceanic commerce to overland expansion. British sea power had secured Canada, but the Hispanic West and the Southwest remained wide open. Bolstered by the mythic victory of 1814, successive United States' governments and their agents would push the expansionist agenda all the way to the Pacific, Puget Sound and the Rio Grande within four decades. After the war, 'Americans became more self-confident, more aggressive, and more determined to plot their own course'.[20] As America changed course it changed culture.

Although 1812 resolved little of substance between Britain and the United States, it proved a transformational experience for a young nation searching for an identity. In truth the real clash of cultures in 1812 was sectional, not international.[21] The postwar decades would be clouded by the complications of slavery in an expanding Union. War left the slave-owning South haunted by a nightmare combination of naval power, black soldiers and servile insurrection. Thomas Jefferson recognized that a slave revolt, backed by the British, could destroy America, but argued that the Southwest had earned the right to extend slavery at the Battle of New Orleans, while blaming New England abolitionists for sustaining the slave economy, as they profited indirectly from the proceeds of Southern agriculture.[22] The Civil War of

1861 to 1865 might have been 50 years in the future but the War of 1812 had already highlighted deep-rooted antipathies between the seafaring and commercial Northeast, landed societies in the middle states and the territorially expansionist South and West. The unifying issue for General Andrew Jackson's polyglot army in 1814 had been plantation slavery. After the battle they rounded up fugitive slaves, leaving the British army to retreat unmolested.[23] The Northeast did not share these concerns, nor did it share the Southern desire for free trade, preferring industrial protection.

Not that the process of cultural change was restricted to the western hemisphere. The Revolutionary and Napoleonic Wars created a British national consciousness to sustain the conflict. Two decades of war cut Britain off from the culture of Europe, hastening the creation of a truly British identity, complete with new cultural icons. In 1798, the figure of Britannia on British copper coins was subtly modified: the original bareheaded, voluptuous figure of a royal mistress bearing an olive branch acquired the helmet of Pallas Athene and more decorous attire, dropping the foliage the better to grasp and brandish the trident of sea power. Meanwhile J. M. W. Turner shifted his gaze from the Classical Mediterranean vistas of Claude and Vernet to the sublime native landscape, re-conceptualizing marine art to provide Britain with the cultural weapons of a great power.[24] With the mighty ocean and the genius of Nelson as the ultimate totems, Turner drove home his argument about the uniquely maritime nature of Britishness with powerful images that first anticipated and then celebrated the defeat of Napoleon by sea power.

The new British culture continued to cross the Atlantic, to a nation starved of heroes. Nowhere was American cultural dependence more obvious than in the case of Lord Nelson. After the Battle of Trafalgar in October 1805, the dead hero was re-imagined as a classical deity, the war god of the British state. His name and deeds became universal possessions. Americans avidly consumed eulogistic Nelson hagiographies during the War of 1812, especially Robert Southey's literary masterpiece, while Nelsonic rhetoric shaped the language of American naval heroism.[25]

The deification of Nelson emphasized the critical synergy of words and pictures in the creation of popular culture. If the technique, ambition and intellectual drive of American artists remained tied to the old world long into the nineteenth century, the evolution of a distinctive American pictorial tradition had been obvious from the early colonial era. American art expressed the expansive dreams of a new society. Seemingly endless 'open' land to the south and west challenged the maritime-Atlantic cultural orientation of port cities and merchant elites. While New Englanders commissioned art to represent successful lives, ships and ports, elsewhere artists tried to understand American land, people, animals and plants, seeking scientific rigour in sharp, hard-edged pictures and striking colours.[26]

War created an American art market dominated by aquatints and engravings, mass-produced works consumed by an audience primed by print media.[27] Before 1812, America consumed limited numbers of British and French prints, alongside a tiny domestic output. In 1812, American artists and engravers represented naval glory. Having captured HMS *Guerriere*, Captain Isaac Hull hired Michele Cornè to record his triumph.[28] Cornè's lively, colourful scenes were ideal for engraving. They became national possessions when Abel Bowen's *The Naval Monument* of 1816 included 21 engraved scenes based on Cornè's pictures, which were re-used as prints and tableware transfers.[29] The battles depicted were all American victories; they did not challenge the myth of victory. In the postwar years, the growing economic and political power of the middle class created an art market that privileged native subjects, images and artists. America became the subject of her own art just as the nation took a decisive step away from the sea.[30]

Although imported art and artists brought the high art of Europe to America, a truly original American form was emerging—the mass produced print. Thomas Birch, the first marine artist to achieve significant public recognition, created crisp, structured sea battles that were ideal for engraving. Many were available before the end of the war.[31] After 1815, Birch addressed the wider national seascape, an art largely consumed by Northerners.[32] The most popular naval subjects were American frigate victories and the action on Lake Erie.[33] They represented startling, even shocking events that reversed common expectations.

The American market also absorbed imported images. French artists produced some of the finest battle scenes, in oils and engravings, celebrating American naval success. Aquatints by British artist Thomas Buttersworth reached the United States in such numbers that many assume he was an American, even though he focused on British victories.[34] The stunning *Shannon–Chesapeake* action, fought in Boston Bay on June 1st 1813, when the British frigate HMS *Shannon* captured the American frigate USS *Chesapeake* following a battle of exceptional skill, ferocity and courage, generated 25 contemporary or near- contemporary images, reflecting both the brilliance of the engagement and its fundamental importance in reversing the run of American success.[35] The last word on the naval art of 1812 fell, appropriately enough, to *Shannon's* Captain, Sir Philip Broke. In 1830, Broke sent four new lithographs to the British Prime Minister. The Duke of Wellington recognized their deeper import as records of victory.[36] They appeared just as America turned away from the ocean, leaving Britain the unchallenged master of the Atlantic and the major consumer of marine art.

If the war created an American art it also empowered American literature. In America, the boundaries of reality were soft, and history had no professionals. The distinctions between truth and fiction were not allowed to spoil a good story. The American writers Washington Irving and James Fenimore Cooper combined the low business of making a living with the higher calling of grand narrative. Irving's subversive 'Knickerbocker' tales swept away the notion that literature should possess social utility.[37] As wartime editor of the *Analectic Magazine,* Irving pillaged British periodicals, eulogized American naval heroes and printed Francis Scott Key's patriotic anthem. His biographies were frequently reprinted: that of *Chesapeake's* ill-fated Captain James Lawrence reappeared six times in six years, exerting a powerful influence over subsequent studies, and exposing a fatal flaw in the construction of American culture.[38]

Although based on first-hand testimony, Irving's work was highly romanticized. The Lawrence essay contained serious errors that misled unwary authors for over a century, notably the romantic nonsense that the *Chesapeake* was an 'unlucky' ship, with a newly raised crew, led astray by a 'scoundrel Portuguese ... boatswain's mate'. This 'heroic' treatment elided past the awkward fact that the 'hero' was beaten in 13 minutes, by a ship of precisely equal force, with a significantly smaller crew. Irving's eulogy sent Lawrence into battle under 'disastrous and disheartening circumstances', effectively damning him as a brave idiot. A month after publication, Irving confessed his errors, but the damage had been done, and the essay would be reprinted many times.[39]

Irving's essay placed Lawrence at the heart of American popular culture, prompting an unseemly struggle for control of his mortal remains which resulted in three separate burials, the last requiring two tombstones. James Fenimore Cooper, who idolized Lawrence, sustained the heroic memory into the middle decades of the century, when Alonzo Chappell created the engraving 'Death of Captain Lawrence: Don't Give Up the Ship'[40] for Jesse Ames Spencer's illustrated *History of the United States* of 1858. Spencer claimed Lawrence's motto, 'consecrated in the eyes of his countrymen' has 'many a time since been used to animate the spirits of our brave seamen'.[41] Chappell deliberately followed the Nelson tradition, posing the dying hero as Christ's deposition from the cross. Little wonder that the reality of Lawrence's defeat remains troublesome.

Irving's nonsense would be revived, for very different purposes, by Theodore Roosevelt in the 1880s.[42] Although contemporary historian Rossiter Johnson dismissed such unworthy excuses,[43] Roosevelt chose to embellish the thick veneer of nationalist and racist hyperbole to overlay the evidence. He blamed Irving's fictitious Portuguese bosun's mate for deserting his post, an example followed by the 'mercenary' crew. He did not ask why an American warship needed a 'mercenary' crew. There was no need for excuses to explain Philip Broke's victory, nor any dishonour in Lawrence's defeat. The mercenary crew and 'evil' reputation, invented after the battle, were a crude attempt to preserve the propaganda value of earlier victories. That the United States Navy chose to take their defining motto from a man who had already lost the ship only adds to the confusion.

Irving made Lawrence 'one of those talismanic names which every nation preserves as watchwords for patriotism and valour'; his deeds constituted a naval legacy, 'the germ of future navies, future power, and future conquest', helping construct a national identity free from deference, facing the British as equals.[44] Shortly before the war ended, Irving moved to Europe to pursue a conventional literary career.[45] His 1819 essay 'The Voyage', a pioneering fictional treatment of the sea as a sublime romantic spectacle that influenced human imagination, inspired a generation of oceanic authors, including Herman Melville.[46] Although he brought American letters up to the European standard, Irving did not create a genuinely American literature. His output remained elitist, and derivative.

The way ahead had been charted by *The Port-Folio*, a journal of refined leisure that responded to the declaration of war by calling for 'a repository of every thing that may tend to give character to our country, and to cherish in the breasts of our fellow citizens, the holy flame of genuine patriotism'.[47] War opened the flood gates of euphoria: 'the glorious achievements of our navy' had 'kindled a new and holy spirit of nationality, and enabled the humblest citizen among us boldly to say to the world that he too has a country', while 'the remembrance of the old become the cause of future victories'. For the next 30 years one part of America would have a cultural frontier on the ocean, one that waxed and then waned in harmony with the glory days of deep-water commerce, whaling and travel, before giving way to continental visions in the railway age.[48]

Irving gave American literature a strong naval character, created a national hero, and made it difficult for literate Americans to avoid an encounter with the ocean.[49] He knew many leading naval officers, including his old friend and drinking companion Captain David Porter.[50] In July 1814, Porter returned to New York after losing his ship in the Pacific, and took a room in Irving's house. Portions of Porter's journal appeared in the *Analectic*, his book appeared in 1815 as *Journal of a Cruise to the Pacific Ocean by Captain David Porter in the United States Frigate Essex, in the years 1812, 1813, and 1814, Containing descriptions of the Cape de Verde Islands, Coasts of Brazil, Patagonia, Chile and of the Galapagos Islands*.[51] This energetic, ambitious, and occasionally unreliable account found a ready audience, and remains the outstanding first-hand narrative of the war.

While described as a 'Journal', a simple narrative of Pacific voyaging in the wake of Captain Cook, Porter's text was something rich and strange, mixing art, literature, history and travelogue. He created an American Pacific dreamscape, offering his countrymen boundless opportunities for whaling, trade and empire. In his wake sailed the whale ship *Essex*, Richard Henry Dana and Herman Melville. Contemporary British readers were unimpressed: the *Quarterly Review*, the house journal of Lord Liverpool's Tory ministry, published a scathing 31-page denunciation comparing Porter to a pirate.[52] The unsigned review, written by John Barrow, Second Secretary at the Admiralty, dismissed the central plank of Porter's romantic exoticism, sexual encounters and cannibalism on the Marquesas Islands as fantasy.[53] Historian William James reckoned it to be 'filth and falsehood'.[54] In reality most of Porter's exotic stories were true, providing Pacific literature with its defining metaphors—islands, sensual abandon, the cannibal and his feast.[55]

The British riposte

Although Scottish novelist Walter Scott put a few pungent lines in *Marmion*, mocking the ministers who fled the field of Bladensburgh in such hot haste,[56] and Barrow demolished David Porter,[57] the task of rebutting American claims of 'victory' was left to the lawyer and historian William James. Detained with his wife as Enemy Aliens at Philadelphia when war broke out, disgusted by their treatment and incensed by the sheer audacity of the American propaganda, James began collecting 'facts' about the naval actions of 1812. Despite his 'alien' status, he boarded American warships, and interviewed the crew. Escaping to Halifax in 1813, James continued collecting first-hand accounts. In the *Full and Correct Account of the Chief Naval Occurrences* of 1817, James stressed the fundamental importance of a mature historical understanding to the intellectual well-being of a nation:

> He who shall succeed in teaching American writers to venerate truth, as much as their readers idolize vain-glory, will have achieved, for the republic of America, ten-fold greater service than the whole pantheon of demi-gods, whose romantic feats, instead of being allowed to shine forth, bedezined ... as any other tale of 'fiction' or mock-heroic, are presented to the world under the specious garb of 'FAITHFUL HISTORY'.[58]

James focused on American accounts of the war that had reached the United Kingdom, including Washington Irving's biographical essays in the *Analectic Magazine*, which could mislead the public.[59] To counter this insidious literature, James developed a distinctive critical method, subjecting it to forensic cross-examination, well-directed mockery and robust criticism, to free the war from 'American dross'. His precise analysis of guns, tons and manpower confounded American claims that the three frigate actions of 1812 had been 'fair and equal', and he concluded: 'no American ship of war has, after all, captured a British ship of the same force; but the reverse has occurred, and might have occurred, again and again, had the Americans been as willing to fight as they still are to boast'. It hardly needs saying that James remained an advocate.[60] In 1826, James sent his work to British Prime Minister George Canning, to rebut American diplomatic bluster, along with a digest of American strategic geography and political prospects, as a guide for future conflict.[61] Creating an accurate record of the 'lessons' of the past, to assist planning and preparation, was the highest function of contemporary history. The following year the post-1815 American navalist impulse ended.[62]

James found fresh targets on land, ridiculing John Lewis Thomson's pretension that the outcome of the war 'ranked the United States among the first and most independent nations of the earth', as the 'climax of American gasconade'. That Thomson's hack work had reached a third edition by 1816, and T. O'Conner's *An Impartial and Correct History of the War* a fourth edition in 1817, indicated the relative levels of interest on either side of the Atlantic. James's works did not need second editions. When he reached the defining moment of America's mythic war, the Battle of New Orleans, James was scrupulously fair to Andrew Jackson, the better to eviscerate his panegyrists. Arsène Lacarrière Latour's widely cited history was shown to be consistently exaggerated, or ignorant. Latour served as Jackson's chief engineer during the Battle of New Orleans and published *Historical Memoir of the War in West Florida and Louisiana in 1814–1815* in 1817. Despite his initial focus on the tactical level, James recognized the underlying cultural realities, ending his work with a chilling prediction: 'It is in the interest of the United States to destroy, and they will in time destroy, either by the sword or debauchery, every Indian upon the American continent'.[63]

James's demolition of the American version, and his excoriating assessment of the standards and integrity of individual American authors, reflected the contempt of a legal practitioner who knew the difference between assertion and evidence that was credible in a court of law; his purpose was to remind his countrymen of the real outcome of the conflict. His potent combination of telling detail, official records, technical statistics and ringing phrases was equally effective in subverting American domestic agendas, posing a serious threat to the fragile cohesion of a nation building an identity on the myth of a victorious 'Second War of Independence'. His unblinking integrity made his work startlingly effective. Unable to challenge his findings, American authors subjected him to a sustained campaign of personal vilification long after his death in 1829.

In the 1830s, an American author contested James's arguments, if only obliquely, but only after he had created a truly American culture. Midshipman James Fenimore Cooper had served under James Lawrence, and engaged with the naval past throughout his life. The social structure of a sailing warship came close to the hierarchical ideal he imposed on the American past, noble leaders, loyal followers, men of character and talent, bound by a common task.[64] Although he resigned from the Navy in 1811, Cooper was swept up in Republican war-fever; the resolve and confidence of his old shipmates promised to lift the long shadow of colonial dependence.[65] The heroics of the next 12 months seemed to confirm such hopes, only to highlight the disasters that would follow. Stunned by the dramatic reversal of fortune that saw his hero cut down and the *Chesapeake* lost, Cooper took up *The Port-Folio's* call for an American literature and identity. War obliged artists to address their work to a distinctive national culture. Mixing Walter Scott's romantic nationalist agenda and a few of his plot lines with American history, Cooper set his stories in real American landscapes. Although he shared Irving's tendency to look back to better days, re-imagining history as mythic reality, his work found a large audience in the postwar decades. Cooper's novels demonstrated to 'American readers that their own country afforded a rich field for the writing of historical fiction'. It was 'patriotic service' to show that 'authentic works of art could grow in indigenous soil'. Cooper placed the personal drama of *Last of the Mohicans* against familiar historical backgrounds, and followed the same approach when he wrote 'serious and respectable' naval history, emphasizing the personal element in historic events.[66]

Yet his nationalism was not American; it was the sectional culture of the Northeast, of New England, New York and routes westward through the forested wilderness. In the South, other American authors were creating a very different literature, as they too built on Scott's romantic nationalism to sustain the peculiar institution, and much else that was out of step with the rest of the world.[67] In his naval history, Cooper treated British defeats as punishment for condescending treatment of America, while ignoring the loss of the USS *President* and the many political meanings that might be drawn from that disaster. Rather than attack Britain, he urged his countrymen to see the Navy as 'our chief defence against wrongs'. Past glories would encourage future achievement, hence the stress laid on Lawrence's motto. At a time when American commercial shipping dominated the Atlantic, he claimed the Navy would become an integral part of the national identity. America's manifest destiny would be oceanic. American enterprise and expansion would command the sea because America had demonstrated cultural as well as political independence from Britain.[68] Cooper's writing helped sustain cross-party support for the Navy 'as the prime instrument of nationalism' for two decades, but by the late 1820s the cultural tide had turned. Jacksonian America had become a continental power.[69] When an older, less confident Cooper produced his long-matured naval history in 1839, the glories of 1812 had faded, and he recognised that the frontier, which he had done so much to celebrate, was now the dominant theme. Claiming America's destiny lay in naval greatness reflected an emotional engagement with the past.

Nor had Cooper found an answer to William James's precise, number crunching critique. A quarter of a century had not healed the psychological injuries inflicted by Philip Broke's brilliant gunnery:

> Perhaps the capture of no single ship ever produced so much exultation on the side of the victors, or so much depression on that of the beaten party, as that of the *Chesapeake*. The American nation had fallen into the error of their enemy, and had begun to imagine themselves invincible on the ocean, and this without any better reason than having been successful in a few detached combats, and its mortification was in proportion to the magnitude of its delusion; while England hailed the success of the *Shannon* as a proof that its ancient renown was about to be regained.[70]

Cooper had shared the 'delusion'. Having been deified over his dinner in New York on 4 May 1813, Lawrence's defeat and death less than a month later coincided only too closely with Cooper's decision to abandon the sea.[71] This was the American journey, Cooper's journey, and it would be Melville's. Cooper must have realized that the ocean had been forgotten, along with his sea fiction. The frontier tales of the 1820s endured because continental concerns dominated politics, and culture. The Mexican War of 1846 emphasized the army, while sales of nautical fiction collapsed, leaving *Moby Dick* hopelessly beached.

Conclusion

The new expressive American secular literature published after the War of 1812 needed American pictures. Cooper's evocation of landscape and character through dress and appearance cried out for illustrations. Thomas Cole illustrated *The Last of the Mohicans* in 1827, while his 'American Sublime' became the dominant American artistic genre, a visual reference to the expansionist politics of Andrew Jackson and the dream of an American Empire.[72] This art directed the American gaze westward, making the frontier into the dominant theme across American culture.

Despite looking westward, the main items on the American defence budget between 1815 and 1861 were coastal defences, massive stone works along the Atlantic seaboard from Maine to Key West.[73] America lost the war, but secured cultural independence. It remained desperately vulnerable to sea power, and backed down when the British were serious.[74] The British retained a few relics of naval glory, including HMS *Shannon* and HMS *President*, to remind the Americans that Britannia still ruled the waves. When Anglo–American relations reached a particularly low point in 1833, the Admiralty despatched HMS *President*, carrying the flag of Admiral Sir George Cockburn. Cockburn, who set fire to the White House in 1814, had celebrated the event in his portrait.[75] These totems of power, backed by the compelling evidence assembled by William James, sustained British strategic hegemony in the Atlantic world into the late nineteenth century, without the need for war.

Notes

1. Paul A. Gilje, *Free Trade and Sailors' Rights in the War of 1812* (Cambridge, 2013), 277–279.
2. Pietro S. Nivola, 'The "Party War" of 1812', in *What So Proudly We Hailed: Essays on the Contemporary Meaning of the War of 1812*, ed. Pietro Nivola and Peter J. Kastor (Washington, DC, 2012), 22.
3. *National Intelligencer*, 23 May1815: cited in T. G. Martin, *A Most Fortunate Ship: A Narrative History of Old Ironsides* (2nd edn, Annapolis, MD, 1996), 206.
4. Ibid., 207.

5. Gilje, *Free Trade*, 259–261, for the triumphalist rhetoric of 1812 and early 1813, see 238–239.
6. Herman Melville's 'John Marr' of 1888 reflects this shift of identity. Marr, an old sailor finds himself isolated and alone among prairie dwelling Midwestern people who have no comprehension of the sea.
7. Gilje, *Free Trade*, 307–309.
8. Andrew D. Lambert, *The Challenge: Britain versus America in the Naval War of 1812* (London, 2012).
9. Alan Taylor, *The Civil War of 1812: American Citizens, British Subjects, Irish Rebels and Indian Allies* (New York, 2010), 40–42.
10. Bradford Perkins, *Prologue to War: England and the United States, 1805–1812* (Berkeley, CA, 1961), 96–99.
11. Ibid.
12. Alex Roland et al., *The Way of the Ship: America's Maritime History Re-envisioned, 1600–2000* (Hoboken, NJ, 2008), 101–102; Douglass C. North, *The Economic Growth of the United States, 1790–1860* (New York, 1966), 47–49; and Michele Felice Cornè Exhibition Catalogue, *Peabody Museum* (Salem, MA, 1972).
13. Frederick C. Leiner, *Millions for Defense: The Subscription Warships of 1798* (Annapolis, MD, 2000), 144–146, 161 and 236 footnote 5; Philip Chadwick Foster Smith, *The Frigate Essex Papers: Building the Salem Frigate, 1798–1799* (Salem, MA, 1974), 32–35.
14. Christopher McKee, *A Gentlemanly and Honourable Profession: The Creation of the U.S. Naval Officer Corps, 1794–1815* (Annapolis, MD, 1991), 106–107; and Leiner, *Millions*, 2–10.
15. Steven Watts, *The Republic Reborn: War and the Making of Liberal America, 1790–1820* (Baltimore, MD, 1987), 216 and 246–247; Roger Hamilton Brown, *The Republic in Peril: 1812* (New York, 1964); W. H. Earle, 'Niles' Register, 1811–49: Window on the World', http://nilesregister.com/NRessay.htm (accessed 27 January 2015); and for Baltimore's politico-economic interests, see Jerome R. Garitee, *The Republic's Private Navy: The American Privateering Business as practised by Baltimore During the War of 1812* (Middletown, CT, 1977).
16. Lawrence N. Powell, *The Accidental City: Improvising New Orleans* (Cambridge, MA, 2012), 340.
17. Gene A. Smith, *'For the Purposes of Defense': Politics of the Jeffersonian Gunboat Program* (Newark, NJ, 1995).
18. Sacvan Bercovitch and Cyrus Patell (eds), *The Cambridge History of American Literature, Vol. 1, 1590–1820* (Cambridge, 1994), 541–559.
19. A. T. Mahan, *The Influence of Sea Power upon the French Revolution and Empire, 1793–1812*, 2 vols (Boston, 1893), vol. 2, 204, and Roland et al., *The Way of the Ship*, 248, 428 and 439.
20. Frank Lawrence Owsley, Jr. and Gene A. Smith, *Filibusters and Expansionists: Jeffersonian Manifest Destiny, 1800–1821* (Tuscaloosa, AL, 1997), 141 and 181–192.
21. Taylor, *The Civil War of 1812* emphasizes inner divisions over international conflict.
22. Peter S. Onuf, *Jefferson's Empire: The Language of American Nationhood* (Charlottesville, VA, 2000), 118–131.
23. Peter J. Kastor, *The Nation's Crucible: The Louisiana Purchase and the Creation of America* (New Haven, CT, 2004), 172–200.
24. Eric Shanes, *Turner's Rivers, Harbour and Coasts* (London, 1981); and Linda Colley, *Britons: Forging the Nation, 1707–1837* (New Haven, CT, 1992).
25. For the cultural construction of Nelson, see Andrew D. Lambert, *Nelson: Britannia's God of War* (London, 2004); and R. J. Brockmann, *Commodore Robert*

F. Stockton, 1795–1866: Protean Man for a Protean Nation (Amherst, NY, 2009), 9–14 and 461–462.

26. John Wilmerding, *American Art* (London, 1976), chapters 1–9, esp. 31 and 38–50.
27. Edgar Newbold Smith, *American Naval Broadsides: A Collection of Early Naval Prints, 1745–1815* (New York, 1974), xvi.
28. Linda M. Maloney, *The Captain from Connecticut: The Life and Naval Times of Isaac Hull* (Boston, 1986), 200–202, 434 and 501–502; and Michele Felice Cornè Exhibition Catalogue, *Peabody Museum*, 18–20.
29. John Wilmerding, *American Marine Painting* (2nd edn, New York, 1987), xi and 69–72.
30. Ibid., 64–66 and 73, and Andrew Wilton and Tim Baringer, *American Sublime: Landscape Painting in the United States, 1820–1880* (London, 2002), 20–21.
31. Wilmerding, *Marine Painting*, 74–77, 80–83 and 110–111.
32. Kathleen A. Foster, *Thomas Chambers: American Marine and Landscape Painter, 1808–1869* (New Haven, CT, 2009).
33. Smith, *Naval Broadsides*, xiv.
34. Wilmerding, *Marine Painting*, 86–88; Smith, *Naval Broadsides*, 188–191; and Linda S. Ferber, *The Coast and the Sea: Marine and Maritime Art in America* (London, 2014), 24–28.
35. Suffolk Record Office, Ipswich (hereafter SRO), Broke collection: Broke MSS, HA93 13/18–26.
36. SRO, HA 9 9/330. 'Wellington to Broke', 17 July 1830.
37. Bercovitch and Patell, *American Literature*, 664–667 and 670.
38. Wayne R. Kime (ed.), *Washington Irving: Miscellaneous Writings, 1803–1859* (Boston, 1981), vol. 1, 295–309; and for Irving's enduring impact, see Albert Gleaves, *James Lawrence, Captain, United States Navy, Commander of the 'Chesapeake'* (New York, 1904).
39. Kime, *Washington Irving*, xxvii–ix, 69–70 and 73–78.
40. Smith, *Naval Broadsides*, 144.
41. B. J. Mitnick and D. Mewschutt, *The Portraits and History Paintings of Alonzo Chappell* (Pennsylvania, 1992), 51–52 and 58. The picture was bought by President Franklin D. Roosevelt, an enthusiastic War of 1812 collector. There is a print in Broke's papers probably placed there by one of his naval sons: SRO, HA 93 13/21.
42. D. L. Dennis, 'The Action between the Shannon and the Chesapeake', *The Mariner's Mirror* 45, (1959): 36–45, for an analysis of the historiography see 40.
43. Rossiter Johnson, *A History of the War of 1812 between the United States and Great Britain* (New York, 1881), 196–201; and Theodore Roosevelt, *The Naval History of 1812* (New York, 1882).
44. Kime, *Washington Irving*, 94–95 and 132.
45. Bercovitch and Patell, *American Literature*, 668.
46. George S. Hellmann, *Washington Irving Esquire* (London, 1924), 82 and 101, and Thomas Philbrick, *James Fenimore Cooper and the Development of American Sea Fiction* (Cambridge, MA, 1961), 39.
47. Kime, *Washington Irving*, xxix.
48. *The Port Folio*, 3rd series (1813), cited in Philbrick, *James Fenimore Cooper*, 1–2, 15 and 20–22.
49. *Washington Irving: A Bibliography*, compiled by William R. Langfeld (New York, 1933), 14 and 55.
50. Hellman, *Washington Irving*, 82, and David F. Long, *Nothing Too Daring: A Biography of Commodore David Porter, 1783–1843* (Annapolis, MD, 1970), 35–37 and 71–72.

51. David Porter, *Journal of a Cruise* (Philadelphia, 1815); *Second edition to which is now added an introduction, in which the charges contained in the Quarterly Review, of the first edition of this Journal and examined* (New York, 1822); Long, *Nothing Too Daring*, 71–72 and 331–332; and Bercovitch and Patell, *American Literature*, 763.
52. *The Quarterly Review*, vol. XIII, July 1815 (published early December 1815), art 4; and Long, *Nothing Too Daring*, 72–73 and 331–332.
53. H. Shine and H. C. Shine, *The Quarterly Review under Gifford: Identification of Contributors, 1809–1824* (Chapel Hill, NC, 1949), 48; and J. M. R. Cameron, 'John Barrow, the Quarterly Review's Imperial Reviewer', in *Conservatism and the Quarterly Review: A Critical Analysis*, ed. Jonathan Cutmore (London, 2007), 133–150.
54. William James, *A Full and Correct Account of the Chief Naval Occurrences of the late war Between Great Britain and the United States of America* (London, 1817), 73.
55. Long, *Nothing Too Daring*, 72.
56. C. J. Bartlett, 'Gentlemen versus Democrats: Cultural Prejudices and Military Strategy in the War of 1812', *War in History* 1/2 (1994): 140–159, 158–159.
57. D. Porter, *Journal of a Cruise to the Pacific Ocean by Captain David Porter in the United States Frigate Essex, in the years 1812, 1813, and 1814, [...]*, 2 vols (Philadelphia, 1815; 2nd ext. edn, New York, 1822). See Long, *Nothing Too Daring*, 71–72 and 331–332.
58. William James, *Full and Correct Account of the Military Occurrences of the late War Between Great Britain and the United States of America*, 2 vols (London, 1818), vol. 2, xxxii, Gilje, *Free Trade*, 283; and Andrew D. Lambert, 'Introduction', in *The Naval History of Great Britain, vol. 5: 1808–1811*, ed. W. M. James (London, 2002), i–iii.
59. James, *Military Occurrences*, xxxi–xxxii.
60. James, *Naval Occurrences*, 528.
61. 'James to Canning', 8 January 1827 and 'reply', 10 January 1827, in E. J. Stapleton, *Some Official Correspondence of George Canning, 1820–1827*, 2 vols (London, 1887), vol. 2, 340–334.
62. Craig L. Symonds, *Navalists and Antinavalists: The Naval Policy Debate in the United States, 1785–1827* (Newark, NJ, 1980).
63. James, *Military Occurrences*, Chapter 21, 387–394, on page 394 citing John Lewis Thomson, *Historical Sketches of the Late War Between the United States and Great Britain* (3rd edn, Philadelphia, 1816); Arsène Latour, *Historical Memoir of the War in West Florida and Louisiana in 1814–15, with an Atlas* (Philadelphia, 1816). Its modern edition: Gene A. Smith (Gainesville, FL, 1999).
64. Bercovitch and Patell, *American Literature*, 692–693; and Hester Blum, *The View from the Masthead: Maritime Imagination and Antebellum American Sea Narratives* (Chapel Hill, NC, 2008), 72– 84.
65. Wayne Franklin, *James Fenimore Cooper: The Early Years* (New Haven, CT, 2007), 160, quoting Cooper's *History of the Navy* (Philadelphia, 1839), vol. 2, 123.
66. Bercovitch and Patell, *American Literature*, 676–683, 680.
67. David Moltke-Hansen, 'The Fictive Transformation of American Nationalism after Sir Walter Scott', *Historically Speaking* 10/3 (2009): 24–27. Cooper was in Europe between 1826 and 1836, for this see Franklin, *Cooper*, 160–161, 483 and 519.
68. Franklin, *Cooper*, 298–290 and 402–403; and Philbrick, *James Fenimore Cooper*, 45–47, 54 and 58.
69. Philbrick, *James Fenimore Cooper*, 85; and Symonds, *Navalists and Antinavalists*, 234–235.

70. Philbrick, *James Fenimore Cooper*, 115, 121, 124–127 and 134; and Franklin, *Cooper*, 163–178.
71. J. F. Cooper, *History of the Navy*, vol. 2, 253–254, cited in Franklin, *Cooper*, 178–179.
72. Bercovitch and Patell, *American Literature*, 690, and Wilton and Barringer, *American Sublime*, 14, 20 and 23.
73. Mark A. Smith, *Engineering Security: The Corps of Engineers and the Third System of Defense Policy, 1815–1861* (Tuscaloosa, 2009) is the latest study.
74. Andrew D. Lambert, 'Winning without Fighting: British Grand Strategy and its application to the United States, 1815–1865', in *Strategic Logic and Political Rationality: Essays in Honour of Michael I. Handel*, ed. Bradford A. Lee and Karl F. Walling (Portland, OR, 2003), 164–195.
75. Roger Morriss, *Cockburn and the British Navy in Transition: Admiral Sir George Cockburn, 1772–1853* (Exeter, 1997), 210 and 222. HMS *President* has been the London Headquarters of the Royal Navy since the late nineteenth century, and commemorated the battle on the 200th anniversary. See http://www.royalnavy.mod.uk/news-and-latest-activity/news/2015/january/16/150116-historic-figure-head-returns-home (accessed 27 January 2015).

19

Creating National Heroes: Simón Bolívar and the Memories of the Spanish American Wars of Independence

Matthew Brown

In the half-century after 1826, when its Wars of Independence were largely concluded, Hispanic America struggled to recover from the economic dislocation and social upheaval of nearly two decades of intermittent warfare, which began in 1806 with the British invasions of Buenos Aires. The wars that ended up expelling Spanish colonial rule from the continental Americas (Cuba and Puerto Rico survived until 1898) ebbed and flowed, and were more intense and more destructive in some regions (in particular, Mexico and Venezuela) than others (what we now call Argentina escaped relatively lightly; and Brazil's transition from Portuguese colonial rule to becoming an independent empire itself was so peaceful relatively that it is often considered a case apart, and for reasons of space is not considered here).[1]

The individual whose words and actions in this arena of war had most global projection was Simón Bolívar (1783–1830). His feats of endurance in campaigning, the good fortune he enjoyed on the battlefield, his control of the print media during the key years of warfare and his maintenance of friendly international public relations contacts contributed to making him a *cause célèbre* in international liberal and radical circles from 1815 through to 1826.[2] In the last four years of his life, Bolívar's celebrity faded, besmirched by the political deals he cut and increased authoritarian tendencies, which resulted in his coups d'état and rule as a dictator from 1828 until 1830. Within a decade of his death, across Hispanic America and indeed across much of the world, Bolívar's memory became part of the everyday landscape of national imaginaries: Bolívar statues, squares, cities, bridges, cafés, political alliances and bus companies are common across the continent, not to mention the country, Bolivia, which has borne his name since its creation in 1826. Venezuela was renamed as the 'Bolivarian Republic of Venezuela' in 1999 after a referendum called by President Hugo Chávez.

Due to this broad appeal and relevance, this chapter explores themes of postwar legacy and memory through the story of Simón Bolívar. This does not mean that Bolívar was unique: far from it. Figures such as Hidalgo and Morelos in Mexico, Santander in Colombia, San Martín in Argentina, and O'Higgins in Chile have all been elevated to the rank of 'founding fathers' and 'secular saints', as many historians have shown in recent years.[3] There is scholarly consensus that the first half-century after independence was crucial in establishing national identities and reconstructing state institutions that had been blown down with the end of colonial rule.[4] What had been Spain's colonies in the Americas, dependent upon the viceroyalties established in Mexico City and Lima, became a disaggregated number of republics with relatively little interconnected trading or political relations. This was no longer 'Spanish America'. However, what to call these lands? For convenience this chapter uses the term 'Hispanic America' to refer to the republics that emerged from Spanish colonialism in North, Central and South America.[5] Nevertheless, even to speak of 'Hispanic America' is to neglect the extent to which indigenous peoples, Afro-Americans and mixed-race peoples were coming to have influence over what the new republics should be. An attempt to mould a shared 'Latin' American history was initiated in the 1850s, largely by Spanish-speaking intellectuals, Chileans and Colombians, who had travelled to Europe and discussed these matters in Paris. It was a collective construction which acquired meaning and allegiance during the next century.

Dislocation in Hispanic America after 1830

Economies and societies were profoundly dislocated after independence from colonial rule, and after the cessation of anti-colonial warfare. Though they were reconfigured, the continent's transatlantic economic, political and intellectual connections persisted. This created a need for the creation of revolutionary postcolonial histories, which could legitimize the new republics within the international order and maintain the hierarchical social orders at home.[6] The cult of Bolívar and other 'heroes' of independence was central to this. Before going on to discuss this in the central part of the chapter, the next section provides a general overview of the ways in which post-1830 Hispanic American legacies of war differed from those in Europe, which are discussed elsewhere in this volume. Independence was won by 1830: but the peoples who fought in those wars bore many scars.

First, and most importantly, the result of the Wars of Independence in Hispanic America was the end of formal Spanish colonialism on the continent. This marked the end of a significant political epoch which had lasted for three centuries, a break even more decisive than the famed end of the Ancien Régime in Europe after 1789. Social disorder, economic dislocation and political disputes were understood in the nineteenth century within the context of this shift from colony to nation/republic. This accounts for the fact that even in the twenty-first century, the histories of the Wars of

Independence continue to be used by regimes of varied political persuasions to justify contemporary political, social and economic programmes. Hugo Chávez was the most explicit of recent politicians in this sense, but his attempt to 'Bolivarianize' Venezuela was far from original. Postcolonial theorists across the continent are engaged in a project of trying to 'decolonize' knowledge and politics in the region, a task which is deemed to have begun with political independence in the 1820s, but that remains incomplete.[7]

Second, post-1830s Hispanic America was defiantly, resolutely republican. The propaganda battles that endured throughout the military and naval campaigning of the Wars of Independence ensured a legacy that equated monarchy with colony, and thwarted all of the attempts to reintroduce monarchy, as in Colombia in 1829, Ecuador in the 1840s and Mexico in the 1850s and 1860s. This was a profound and all-embracing consequence of the politicized Wars of Independence.

Third, the Wars of Independence left a legacy of unfinished regional and social conflicts whose abiding consequence was the continuance of violence for political ends. Soldiers may have been demobilized after 1826, but the weapons that had flooded into the continent during the Wars of Independence, as traced by Rafe Blaufarb in this volume, remained in soldiers' hands, and were repeatedly brought out during the civil wars that persisted throughout the nineteenth century. Mass mobilization during the Wars of Independence gave groups that had previously been excluded from political elites—whether on ethnic or class grounds—the sense that their voices had greater reason to be listened to, and they consequently made greater use of political negotiation as well as physical force to achieve this.[8] The persistence of civil wars largely within the newly-defined 'national' territories was an interesting variant on the spread of 'militarism' in Europe, as described by David Bell. In Colombia, Venezuela, Chile and Mexico, militarist and civilian factions competed for governmental control, and momentum ebbed and flowed at varying rates in different countries. Even so, it is clear that the links between military intervention and the providential 'saving' of the nation, established by Bolívar and others during the Wars of Independence, persisted into the twentieth century, when they were expressed in a wave of anti-democratic military coups d'état.

Fourth, new states had to fight hard to establish their legitimacy after the Wars of Independence. François-Xavier Guerra and Annick Lempérière have shown how new political spaces for sociability opened debates about the foundations of states and nations which took a long time to be worked out.[9] Similarly, the very gradual abolition of slavery through free-womb laws and manumission left questions of social and ethnic equality at the heart of political debate throughout the nineteenth century.[10] The attempts of elites to co-opt marginalized groups and incorporate them into their alliances have been a feature of Latin American politics, a phenomenon with its origins in the independence period. The Scottish adventurer Gregor MacGregor proclaimed himself as 'Inca' of South America, hoping to gain legitimacy through reference to the indigenous past. Simón Bolívar, in his famous 1815 Jamaica Letter, wrote that the Araucanian warriors of Chile, the Mapuche, should be the model for those elsewhere seeking to resist colonial rule.[11]

The cult of Bolívar

When President Hugo Chávez died in office in 2013, his funeral was used by his followers to safeguard his political reputation, and project an image of stability and statesmanship on the part of his designated successor, Nicolás Maduro, to the rest of the world. Suffused with references to Bolívar and their Bolivarian project, the service equated Chávez and Bolívar as the heroes and fixed points of the Venezuelan people's historical progress towards prosperity and equality. This was far from the first time that Hispanic American political leaders had been linked to the heroes of independence. In the case of Venezuela, as the historian Germán Carrera Damas showed a quarter of a century ago, the 'cult of Bolívar' was taken up by politicians and generals of all political ideologies from the mid-nineteenth century.[12] A church in central Caracas was dedicated to Bolívar and renamed the National Pantheon, where a statue to Bolívar occupies the space of the altar. This leaves *el Libertador* to physically take over the space formerly occupied by religion—this is as good an example as any of the way that nineteenth-century nation-states in Latin America tried, in the century after independence from Iberian colonial rule, to replace religious iconography of King and Spain with patriotic martyrs and new national identities.

The 'cult of Bolívar' has been a centrepiece of Venezuelan political and cultural life for over a hundred and fifty years, and a constant adjunct to moves towards South American or Latin American unification projects during the same time. As such, memories of Simon Bolívar and memories of the processes of the Wars of Independence have become absolutely entwined to the extent that as historian Michael Zeuske observes, it has become impossible to write a history of independence 'without Bolívar', despite historians' attempts—and their considerable successes—in uncovering the historical agency of subaltern actors in independence.[13]

The cult of Bolívar began during his lifetime and went into overdrive after his death, in 1830, after a drawn-out battle against tuberculosis that he lost under the care of a French doctor, Alexandre Próspero Reverend, on the Caribbean coast of Colombia, in Santa Marta. On 1 March 1830, Bolívar had resigned the presidency of Gran Colombia (the super-republic comprising the republics we know today as Colombia, Venezuela, Ecuador and Panama), later declaring that 'he who serves the revolution ploughs the sea'.[14] Sick, disenchanted and disillusioned, he prepared to go into exile, but on 17 December 1830 died before he could leave Gran Colombia. There is a long tradition, taken up by President Chávez, that Bolívar might have been the victim of poisoning; and that poisoning might have originated with Bolívar's political enemies—and those enemies might have been foreigners, like Dr Reverend.[15] It seems unlikely that this was the case.[16] Nevertheless, the section that follows demonstrates the way in which the repatriation of Bolívar's mortal remains took place within a determinedly international context, aimed at persuading the outside world of the country's modernity and order, in stark contrast to the repatriation of Napoleon Bonaparte's remains from St Helena to Paris two years earlier, the focus of which was resolutely domestic.[17]

Twelve years passed between Bolívar's death in Santa Marta and the repatriation of his remains to Caracas. In 1830, Bolívar's remaining allies, often loyalists-by-definition and hard-core reactionary conservatives by this stage, rather than radicals or liberals, had been distraught by the news, but were politically marginalized by the unpopularity of Bolívar's final dictatorship. Seething with anger and grief at the death of his friend and leader, the Italian-Colombian Colonel Carlo Castelli published a furious proclamation in which he blamed 'the envy, ambition and ingratitude' of Bolívar's rivals for pushing the *libertador* to his death. Castelli raged that 'the murder is consummated; it will be hard to forgive them!' The Irish-Colombian Daniel O'Leary cried that he had lost 'a chief, a father, a guide and a friend'.[18]

For ten years after Bolívar's death his friends were in exile across the Caribbean, or slowly reintegrating themselves into political and economic life through civil warfare and political violence. Their memories of Bolívar were generally shared in private, given the overwhelming public hostility to Bolívar's dictatorships of his final years. Yet in 1839–1842, Venezuela finally experienced a period of peace presided over by its dominant national *caudillo*, José Antonio Páez, the overwhelming victor in the presidential elections of late 1838. For political reasons, Páez's cabinet was stacked with former Bolívarians, despite his numerous run-ins with Bolívar in the 1820s. As the leader of a government representing what Venezuelan historians call oligarchic conservatism, Páez and his ministers proposed and enacted measures that they thought would integrate the republic into the modern, prosperous world, for example, private road-building schemes, national schools, immigration and repayment of the national debt. With a Scotsman, Guillermo (William) Smith, in the Finance (and later, also, Foreign Affairs) Ministry, Venezuela's progress was firmly tied to British power in these years. In Daniel O'Leary's words, 'General Paez has always shewn a desire to cultivate the friendship of England in preference to any other country'. The rehabilitation of the memory of Simon Bolívar was tied to the growing influence of the foreign powers, particularly Britain and France, during Páez's presidency. One of the last acts of Páez's administration, as he sought to ensure the election of his nominated successor, Carlos Soublette (O'Leary's brother-in-law), was to arrange the repatriation of the remains of Simón Bolívar.

The rehabilitation of the memory of Simón Bolívar came about alongside the consolidation of power in the early 1840s of conservative regimes in both Venezuela (under General Páez) and New Granada (under General Pedro Alcántara Herrán). The repatriation of Bolívar's remains provided an opportunity for the two governments to wallow in nostalgia for an apparently glorious past. The staging of the repatriation was notably and consciously Eurocentric. The Italian Agustín Codazzi was commissioned to design and build, in Paris, a carriage that would carry the urn containing Bolívar's remains, as well as 'a Victory Arch to adorn the solemn act'. It is possible that Codazzi, famous as the preeminent cartographer and geographer of the new republics, and resident in Paris in 1840, had witnessed the repatriation of Napoleon's remains, and communicated the idea that this might be emulated with Bolívar, to his friends back in Venezuela. No evidence for this connection has yet been found, and therefore it has to be assumed that the repatriation of Bolívar's remains was an independent event, though inspired by the same desire to legitimize political regimes through reference to the heroes of the recent past on both sides of the Atlantic.[19] On the whole, this study agrees with Charles Esdaile's summation that 'Napoleon and his wars were a European phenomenon that only impinged tangentially, if at all, upon many contemporary developments in the wider world'. Connection is not the same as causation.[20]

Bolívar's friend and historian, Daniel O'Leary, at the time working as a British diplomat in Venezuela, was charged with communicating with the Italian sculptor Pietro Tenerani, who was to create, in Rome, a marble monument where the remains would lie. Some of the friends who had been with Bolívar in his last days were also invited, including Alejandro Próspero Reverend, the French doctor who had treated Bolívar. A new urn was commissioned to be made in Bogotá to carry Bolívar's remains to Caracas, though Bolívar's heart was to be left in Santa Marta 'as a symbol of eternal friendship between the two countries'. Daniel O'Leary was at the time British consul in Puerto Cabello and acting consul in Caracas. It was O'Leary's idea that a British warship should be sent to Santa Marta to assist in transferring Bolívar's remains. A Venezuelan mission sailed for Santa Marta accompanied by the esteemed artist and El Santuario veteran Carmelo Fernández. Throughout the journey Fernández drew 18 sketches of the expedition's progress.[21]

The governor of Santa Marta in 1842 was Joaquín Posada Gutierrez. In his memoirs, he recalled that the Venezuelan commissioners arrived at Santa Marta not on their own ship, the *Constitución,* but in *La Circe,* the French corvette that had in theory been accompanying them. This was a suitable beginning for a multinational event where the British and French, especially, were ever-present. Posada Gutierrez welcomed the commissioners ashore with a speech evoking the memory of Bolívar, 'the man whose fame filled the world'. When the marble stone was lifted away from the grave, the foreign and national warships in the harbour (the Venezuelan *Constitución* and brig *Caracas*, HMS *Albatross*, the French corvette *La Circe*, the Dutch sloop *Venus* and the Danish sloop *Sainte Croix*) all began regular cannon fire to mark the occasion. The exhumation of the remains attracted interest from invited guests and locals alike, who all crowded for a glimpse. The funeral convoy to the port the next day was made up of 'all the honourable individuals, regardless of colour' who were in the town, and 'five or six thousand people' waved goodbye to the relics on 22 November 1842, when they began the 21-day journey from Santa Marta to the Venezuelan port of La Guaira. O'Leary joined the 'magnificent' cortege from La Guaira over the mountain to Caracas on 15 December, and he walked with the diplomatic community on 17 December when Bolívar's remains were taken into the San Francisco church. They lay there for seven days before moving on 23 December to the cathedral. Dreaming that even in death Bolívar would once again unite people despite their diverse origins or politics, O'Leary noted that 'every one seemed desirous that party spirit should be buried in the Tomb of Bolívar'. He reported to London that 'the British and Foreign naval officers who attended the funeral rites have been treated with great hospitality'.

From the moment of their arrival in Caracas, Bolívar's remains were subject to the most pompous and exaggerated accompaniment. The head of state, ministers, generals, the diplomatic community, and 'thousands of well-wishers' turned out on the streets. Rafael Urdaneta, at the time the governor of Guayana, recalled that 'the foreign residents of Caracas and La Guaira, filled with the same enthusiasm as the locals, had joined in the preparations and mixed in the lines wearing national uniforms'. President José Antonio Páez presided over the ceremonies in one of the last acts of his presidential term. As Elias Pino Iturrieta has shown, the intricate choreography of the return of Bolívar's remains was 'an important opportunity for the well-dressed sections of society to display how modern they were and to substantiate their claims that they deserved a place on the world stage'. The representatives of foreign powers, such as O'Leary, were to bear witness to Venezuela's modernity and the honours it paid to Bolívar.

Bolívar and Humboldt

The historian Michael Zeuske has attempted to situate the evolution of the official and popular Bolívar myths within their national and international historical contexts in *Simon Bolívar: History and Myth*. Zeuske's goal is 'to examine not only the myth's power to produce results, but also its *true* history and the *real* origin of the protagonists involved'.[22] Zeuske's indignation about the historical inaccuracies that fuel the Bolívar myth is rooted in his anger at the misrepresentation about the meeting(s) which are widely believed to have taken place between Bolívar and Alexander von Humboldt while

Bolívar was in Europe in 1805, which legend has it triggered a long-standing mutual respect and friendship between the two. The meeting with Humboldt is one of Bolívar's three famous encounters with other giants of 'Great Men's History'—the second being the 1822 Guayaquil Interview with José de San Martin, Liberator of the Andes, Chile and Peru, which occurred almost in secret and about which historians therefore continue to conjecture, and the third being with Napoleon Bonaparte, whom Bolívar claimed to have watched crown himself King of Italy in Milan in 1805, and in whose shadow Bolívar's reputation festered during his lifetime. The Bolívar–Humboldt meeting is certainly the least interesting of the three, given that Bolívar was a young frivolous traveller at the time of their meeting in Paris, and that any meeting was short and of little significance for either man, at the time or after. Most of the significance, as Zeuske archly shows, has been implied or created by later historians and myth-builders.

Nevertheless, Zeuske argues, 'in Germany, everyone, literally *everyone,* who is concerned with Simon Bolívar and the independence of Spanish America thinks first of the phrase "Humboldt and Bolívar"'.[23] He shows how many German thinkers liked the notion that Humboldt had given Bolívar the idea for independence, and that many Venezuelan myth-builders enjoyed the frisson of legitimacy and intellectual heavy-weight status that Humboldt lent to their Bolívar. Zeuske reveals the mistaken assumptions that have informed much of the scholarship, and argues that Humboldt's meeting with Bolívar was most likely invented by writers who so desperately wanted historical truth to mirror their imaginings of how history should or might have been. Linguistic analysis of the careful ambiguity of the phrasing in the few letters exchanged between Bolívar and Humboldt shows that it is indeed by no means certain that they did physically meet, rather than coincide in a place or exchange messages. Indeed, this important international dimension of the Cult of Bolívar is shown to hang on a series of factual and counter-factual memorializations and conscious myth-construction. Zeuske tells us as much as we need to know about the extent to which memories of the Wars of Independence in Spanish America have become significant political and cultural battlegrounds for nearly two centuries. His analysis reveals how myths have been grounded in and shaped by waves of Venezuelan cultural and political history, and by the place of Venezuela and its peoples in imperial and global systems since independence to today.[24]

The black legend of Simón Bolívar

Yet the heroic, liberating, emancipatory, enlightened Bolívar is not the only memory of this historic figure in Hispanic America. Alternative versions persist, demonstrating the continued ability of counter-narratives to live on even when dominant discourses push them to the cultural and media sidelines. German Carrera Damas and Elias Pino Iturrieta have both shown the way in which myths about Simon Bolívar and the 'founding fathers' of Venezuelan independence became absolutely central to the political and cultural activities of Venezuelan governments from the nineteenth century to the present. More than history, independence became a transcendental moment to be returned to again and again. Particularly because of the survival of his vast archive of documents, letters, speeches and reports, there was a Simon Bolívar for almost any Simon Bolívar myth that historians and politicians wanted to create. Conservative Bolívar was mirrored by Liberal Bolívar, Slave-owning Bolívar by Abolition of Slavery Bolívar, Capitalist Bolívar by Socialist Bolívar. As Rory Carroll showed in his recent, insightful book about contemporary Venezuela, Hugo Chávez's great skill was in adopting the People's Bolívar from provincial, oral culture, and wrapping his policies and his persona in the myths about the humble, brave, generous man on horseback who brought independence from Spain to life 200 years ago.[25]

In Colombia, however, a longer tradition of more critical Bolívar-worship has flourished in recent years. This tradition has a long trajectory all the way back to the Wars of Independence themselves, which this section traces forwards to the early twenty-first century, from the works of soldier-chroniclers to novelists Gabriel Garcia Marquez, William Ospina and Evelio Rosero. The alternative vision of Bolívar, what we might conveniently label his Black Legend, was first elaborated by his political enemies at home and abroad in the 1820s. Opponents who favoured alternative political strategies presented Bolívar as arrogant, vain and unprincipled. His will to power was often compared to that of Napoleon Bonaparte, and he was accused throughout his life of wanting to be crowned Emperor of Colombia, following Napoleon's example. Many of these negative representations were made popular in Europe by returning British and Irish mercenaries who had enlisted in Bolívar's armies in the 1810s, but had failed to realize their dreams of riches, El Dorado, land and glory in South America. In response, and to justify their own failures, they blamed conditions, treachery, foreigners and Bolívar. Dozens of memoirs were published along these lines in the late 1810s and 1820s which did a good deal to cement an image of South America in Europe as wild, exotic and different from Europe. The influence of demobilized soldiers turned memoir-writers in South America shares many similarities with the situation in Germany described elsewhere in this volume by Leighton James. When Karl Marx wrote an encyclopaedia entry on Bolívar in the 1850s, he drew on some of these critical sources, leading to a disjuncture that forever perplexed twentieth-century Hispanic American Marxist revolutionaries who wanted to enlist both Marx and Bolívar to their symbolic standards, and found the former lambasting the latter in print in terms that they struggled to comprehend.[26]

In his compendium of critical writing about Bolívar, Marcos Osorio Jimenez argues that the history of undocumented speculation and opprobrium heaped upon him was a story of partisan commentary and ignorant opinions. Nevertheless, his book spans over 400 pages and features otherwise well-respected commentators such as George Laval Chesterton, Germán Arciniegas, Clements Markham and William Miller, as well as Marx.[27] Many of these commentators have attempted to situate Bolívar's achievements alongside his everyday life, about which historians know quite a lot because of the thousands of pages of manuscript sources that have survived. Novelists have been much more successful than historians in tracing the personal dimensions of the heroes of independence. In 1981, Gabriel García Márquez published *The General in his Labyrinth,* a long, melancholy novel detailing Bolívar's last journey down the Magdalena River, away from power and towards exile. The book is rather sympathetic to Bolívar, drawing heavily on the published documents and tracing Bolívar's mental disturbances as he revisits his career, his battles, his friendships, his loves and his enemies. In doing so Garcia Marquez tried to create a more human-scale Bolívar, sometimes disillusioned, often petty, generally confused and unhappy, very different from the statue-like myth, brave and bold and liberating, which had loomed over his childhood and youth through patriotic history books and noble busts in squares. Carlos Alonso has argued that in doing so, García Márquez was attempting to move his readers 'from a melancholy relationship vis-a-vis the historical figure of Bolívar to a relationship that has the therapeutic qualities of mourning ... so that the phantom of the lost object of modernity [the symbolic figure of Bolívar] may cease to rule the libidinal economy of Spanish American discourse and historical life'.[28] The Colombian novelist William Ospina and the film-maker Jorge Ali Triana have both recently updated this vision of the human Bolívar, to popular and critical acclaim in Colombia and elsewhere.[29]

A recent and much more critical addition to this body of literature is a novel by Evelio Rosero, the Colombian author who is best known for his 2006 work *The Armies*. Having written in his first two novels about the devastating psychological effects of political violence in Colombian society, and on the legacy of a powerful Catholic Church in the institutional and social life of the nation, Rosero turned to the lengthy shadow of Bolívar cast across his nation's cultural life. Rosero, like García Márquez before him, immersed himself in the primary sources before venturing into Bolívarian territory. Rather than reimagining Bolívar in a historical novel, however, Rosero chose to present a group of friends in 1960s Pasto (southern Colombia) remembering Bolívar and debating his actions and historical legacy. The boldest gesture is to have one of the principal protagonists fighting to have Bolívar's personal flaws recognized as equally representative of his historical role as his military victories.[30]

Rosero makes some strident parallels with Colombian society today when discussing Bolívar's womanizing, an aspect of the Bolivarian Black Legend that is often acknowledged by historians and biographers before being swiftly skipped over. Rosero has no such scruples. The novel is savage in detailing and decrying Bolívar's bullying, his need to be presented with a dozen young girls on his victorious entry into every town. Rosero's characters, recalling oral histories from grandmothers who remembered anecdotes being passed down from their own grandmothers, discuss and accept allegations that Bolívar raped young girls, amongst other atrocities. As Rosero writes

> It is unbelievable how so many serious historians have fallen over backwards to justify every single one of Bolívar's actions, whether as a soldier or as a statesman. ... Every single historian has participated in the fabrication of the fraud [of the myth of the perfect Bolívar], from the most lucid to the most cretinous, with the exception only of José Rafael Sañudo.[31]

Catherine Davies and other scholars have shown how the Wars of Independence in Hispanic America made little immediate dent on gendered social structures in the continent; indeed it has even been persuasively argued that political independence set back the advances in gender equality that had been won by elite colonial women in the eighteenth century. Bolívar was widowed before his political career had even begun, and his military campaigning was punctuated by a brazen disrespect for women in his search for the fulfilment of his sexual needs. This aspect of Bolívar's everyday life has been overshadowed in the official historiography by the figure of Manuela Sáenz, one of Bolívar's lovers in the 1820s, who served in active military service and occupied an important position as a gatekeeper to Bolívar when he was resident in Bogotá. Sáenz, a heroine for Hispanic American twentieth-century feminists, has served as a cipher to hide the rather more tawdry reality of Bolívar's affairs, as described by Rosero.[32] It is clear from both sides of the story that Bolívar was a long, long way away from the image of the domesticated postwar patriarch.

In bringing 'popular images of Bolívar' back to centre-stage, Rosero follows Tristan Platt in showing the marked ambiguity of historical memory about Bolívar amongst low-status people in the Andes away from urban centres, and the resilience of orally-transmitted memories about Bolívar's activities during the years 1822–1825 when he was in the south of Colombia, Ecuador, Peru and Bolivia.[33] Principal amongst these, and the historical focus of Rosero's novel, is the siege and massacre of Pasto in 1822.

In remembering the massacre of the Pastusos, who had opposed Bolívar's rule and the liberating armies that sought to recruit them into its ranks and requisition their resources, Rosero draws on the work of the historian Sergio Elias Ortiz in *Agustín Aqualongo y su tiempo*. One of the characters comments, 'This was the first major example of barbarism in Colombian history, the first major massacre of the long, sad list that followed it'.[34] It is worth noting, given my comments above on the Irishman Daniel O'Leary's role in the first promotions of the myth of Bolívar, that the commander of the Rifles Battalion that carried out the massacre of Pasto in 1822 was another Irishman, Arthur Sandes. Rosero concludes his discussion of the massacre in Pasto by recalling that 'the massacre of men, women and children was carried out even when they were found hiding in churches, and the streets were left covered in corpses, so that the phrase *"at the time of the Rifles"* has remained in Pasto, signifying the horrific catastrophe of those days'.[35] Reference to the campaign in Pasto was obliquely removed from the service records of the Irishmen who served in it, with reference being made instead to the 'Campaign of the South', erasing the massacres of Pasto from the official, archived version of Colombian military history.[36] Rosero estimates that 400 civilians were killed on Sandes's orders, with Bolívar's support, in addition to the rebels killed in action in Pasto. The most recent history of the Wars of Independence, by the esteemed historian Anthony McFarlane, says that Bolívar found Pasto 'hard to crack', but makes no mention of the massacre.[37]

The massacre of Pasto is the centrepiece of Rosero's tour-de-force, a vivid and contentious representation of the revolutionary wars of the early nineteenth century. The novel goes on to link debates about historical memory from the independence era to the era of violence of the 1950s and 1960s, and into the present-day era of guerrillas and paramilitaries, which was the subject of *The Armies*. The novel is a stark attempt to reclaim the historical figure of Simon Bolívar, and the myth of a 'good' and 'progressive' independence, from the glorious nation-builders of the twentieth century as well as from the Bolívarian socialists of the twenty-first.

Conclusion

Like Bolívar, Hugo Chávez came as president to represent the hopes of the majority of the people he governed. Both were army officers who embraced democracy and recognized the importance of a country's history in shaping its contemporary identity and its relationship with the world. Chávez saw himself as building on the foundations constructed by Bolívar, which allowed him to redistribute wealth, build alliances across continents and globally, and work to reduce poverty in South America, long held to be the most unequal continent in the world. Casting Bolívar as his inspiration allowed Chávez to tap into the broadly-held, popularly-constructed myth of Bolívar as national redeemer. Memories of the Wars of Independence in Spanish America, their protagonists, victors and victims—though much debated in the street as well as in academia—continue to be one of the principal historical threads that link present-day societies to a sense of shared origins and common purposes.

Even as Hispanic American leaders look to the future, they ground their political discourse, and the way they look at the world, in their countries' historical pasts. This was as true in the half-century after the Wars of Independence, discussed above, as it was in what we might call the post-Cold War period, from 1990 to the present. One good example is the way the mortal remains of Simón Bolívar have been treated and debated in contemporary Venezuela. Bolívar's remains (excluding his heart, which stayed back in Santa Marta, Colombia, after his first exhumation in 1842) lie in what is now the National Pantheon in the centre of Caracas, which was consecrated as such in the 1870s under the watchful eye of the President General Antonio Guzmán Blanco. Guzmán Blanco is famed for his attempts to modernize Venezuela, to overhaul its urban planning following the model of Haussmann's Paris, and for his populist authoritarianism. Guzmán Blanco gave the definitive shift to the Bolivarian cult, erecting statues, renaming avenues, and orchestrating the publication of the 32 volumes of Bolivarian documentation. Yet whereas in the 1870s the National Pantheon occupied a secluded, rural setting in between urban Caracas and the northern mountain range separating it from the Caribbean—and with an awe-inspiring view of the city, combining peace and tranquillity with scope and horizon—the urban expansion that Guzmán Blanco shaped and encouraged has completely overrun the Pantheon, which now looks onto a concrete plaza and series of dual carriageway flyovers. Despite frequent architectural makeovers, on the inside and outside, the Pantheon feels like a hangover from another era that has been left behind by urbanization and development. The new architectural gesture of a mausoleum dedicated to Bolívar now stands behind it. Inside, Bolívar's remains have seldom been left to rest in peace. The need for historical origins to underpin political legitimacy has only got stronger over the last 200 years. The Wars of Independence in Hispanic America created dislocation and disorder, and a persistent need to ground present-day politics in memories of the past.

Acknowledgements

I am grateful to Amit Thakkar, Rebecca Earle, Rafe Blaufarb, Lloyd Kramer, Catherine Davies and the volume editors for their insightful comments on earlier drafts of this paper.

Notes

1. For a rejoinder to this interpretation, see Joao Paulo Pimienta, *Estado y nación al final de los imperios ibéricos, Rio de la Plata y Brasil, 1808–1826* (Buenos Aires, 2011).
2. John Lynch, *Simón Bolívar: A Life* (New Haven, CT, 2006); and Caitlin A. Fitz, 'Our Sister Republics: The United States in an Age of American Revolutions', PhD Dissertation (Yale University, 2010).
3. See Rebecca Earle, '"Sobre heroes y tumbas": National Symbols in Nineteenth-Century Spanish America', *Hispanic American Historical Review* 85/3 (2005): 375–416; and Matthew Brown, 'Soldier Heroes in the Wars of Independence in Gran Colombia', *Hispanic Research Journal* 7/1 (2006): 41–56.

4. Three new overviews of the Wars of Independence share this interpretation of the consequences: Jeremy Adelman, *Sovereignty and Revolution in the Iberian Atlantic* (Princeton, 2007); Anthony McFarlane, *Wars and Independence in Spanish America* (London, 2013); and Manuel Chust, *Tiempos de revolución: Comprender las independencias iberoamericanas* (Madrid, 2013).
5. Walter Mignolo, *The Idea of Latin America* (Oxford, 2005).
6. Matthew Brown and Gabriel B. Paquette (eds), *Connections after Colonialism: Europe and Latin America in the 1820s* (Tuscaloosa, 2013).
7. Arturo Escobar and Walter Mignolo (eds), *Globalization and the Decolonial Option* (London, 2013).
8. Clément Thibaud, *Repúblicas en armas: Los ejércitos bolivarianos en la Guerra de Independencia. Colombia–Venezuela, 1810–1821* (Bogotá, 2003); and Marcela Echeverrí, 'Popular Royalists, Empire and Politics in Southwestern New Granada, 1809–1819', *Hispanic American Historical Review* 91/2 (2011): 237–269.
9. François-Xavier Guerra and Annick Lempérière (eds), *Los espacios públicos en Iberoamérica: Ambigüedades y problemas, siglos XVIII–XIX* (Mexico, 1998).
10. Aline Helg, *Liberty and Equality in Caribbean Colombia, 1770–1835* (Chapel Hill, NC, 2004). This caution was triggered by fears about the nearby free black Caribbean republic of Haiti, from 1804.
11. Matthew Brown, 'Inca, Sailor, Soldier, King: Gregor MacGregor and the Revolutionary Caribbean', *Bulletin of Latin American Research* 24/1 (2005): 44–71; Bolívar, 'Jamaica letter', 1815, in *Simón Bolívar: The Bolivarian Revolution, introduced by Hugo Chávez*, ed. and trans. Matthew Brown (New York, 2009), 43; and Joanna Crow, *The Mapuche in Modern Chile* (Gainesville, FL, 2012).
12. Germán Carrera Damas, *El culto a Bolívar* (3rd edn, Bogotá, 1987, first edition: 1969).
13. Michael Zeuske, *Simon Bolívar: History and Myth*, (Princeton, NJ, 2013).
14. 'Bolívar to Juan José Flores, Barranquilla', 9 November 1830, in *El Libertador: Writings of Simón Bolívar*, ed. David Bushnell (Oxford, 2003), 150.
15. For a rebuttal of most of Chávez's theories about Bolívar, see Elias Pino Iturrieta, *El divino Bolívar* (Caracas, 2005).
16. Paul G. Auwaerter et al., 'Simón Bolívar's Medical Labyrinth: An Infectious Diseases Conundrum', *Clinical Infectious Diseases* 52/1 (2011): 78–85.
17. I am grateful to Alan Forrest for this observation.
18. The material in this section, including footnotes, is from Matthew Brown, *The Struggle for Power in Post-Independence Colombia and Venezuela* (New York, 2012), Chapter 7. When Castelli married in Villa de Leyva, Colombia, the invitations to the wedding featured engravings of his two heroes, Simón Bolívar and Napoleon Bonaparte. The invitations—one of very few documents in which Bolívar and Bonaparte are visually associated—can be seen in the Museo Antonio Nariño in Villa de Leyva, Colombia.
19. I am grateful to Alejandro Gómez for his suggestions on this matter. On Codazzi, see Giorgio Antei, *Los heroes errantes: Vida de Agustín Codazzi* (Bogotá, 1993); and also Giorgio Antei, *Guia de Forasteros, Viajes ilustrados por Colombia, 1817–1857* (Bogotá, 1995).
20. Charles Esdaile's review of Christophe Belaubre et al. (eds), *Napoleon's Atlantic: The Impact of Napoleonic Empire in the Atlantic World* (Leiden, 2010), in *Hispanic American Historical Review* 92/2 (2012): 384.
21. This paragraph draws on Brown, *The Struggle for Power*, Chapter 7.
22. Zeuske, *Simón Bolívar*, 5.

23. Ibid., 6. Italics are in the original.
24. Zeuske, *Simón Bolívar*, 87. My review of this book appeared in the *Journal of Latin American Studies* 45/4 (2013): 830–832.
25. Rory Carroll, *Comandante: Inside Hugo Chávez's Venezuela* (Edinburgh, 2013), 187–189.
26. A good review of the Marx–Bolívar conundrum is in James Dunkerley, *Americana: The Americas in the World, around 1850* (London, 2000), 232–238.
27. Marcos A. Osorio Jimenez (ed.), *Bolívar y sus detractors: Bibliografía crítica de la detracción bolivariana* (Caracas, 1979).
28. Carlos Alonso, *The Burden of Modernity: The Rhetoric of Cultural Discourse in Spanish America* (Oxford, 1998), 257–258.
29. William Ospina, *En busca de Bolívar* (Bogotá, 2010); Omar Porras, director, *Bolívar: Fragmentos de un sueno,* performed in Colombia and Europe, 2010; and María Elvira Villamil, 'Reflexividad y política en *Bolívar Soy Yo* de Jorge Ali Triana', *Romance Quarterly* 57/4 (2010): 245–246.
30. The analysis here reserves a lot of information about the plot. The English translation, by Anne McLean and Anna Milsom, will be published by MacLeHose Press in 2016.
31. Evelio Rosero, *La carroza de Bolívar* (Bogotá, 2012), 200, trans. by Matthew Brown. On Aqualongo, see Marcela Echeverri, 'Agustín Agualongo and the Royalist Cause in the Wars of Independence', in *The Human Tradition in Colonial Latin America*, ed. Kenneth J. Andrien (2nd edn, Lanham, MD, 2013), 289–304.
32. Catherine Davies et al., *South American Independence: Gender, Politics, Text* (Liverpool, 2006); and Pamela Murray, *For Glory and Bolívar: The Remarkable Life of Manuela Sáenz* (Austin, TX, 2008).
33. Tristan Platt, 'Simón Bolívar, the Sun of Justice and the Amerindian Virgin: Andean Conceptions of the Patria in the Nineteenth Century', *Journal of Latin American Studies* 25 (1993): 159–185.
34. Rosero, *La carroza*, 213.
35. Ibid., 217.
36. Hojas de Servicio [Service Records] are held in the Archivo General de la Nación in Bogotá, Colombia, and are discussed in detail in Matthew Brown, *Adventuring through Spanish Colonies: Simón Bolívar, Foreign Mercenaries and the Birth of New Nations* (Liverpool, 2006).
37. McFarlane, *War and Independence*, 393.

20

Celebration, Contestation and Commemoration: The Battle of Leipzig in German Memories of the Anti-Napoleonic Wars

Karen Hagemann

> It was one of the finest evenings of my life, when, on the 18th of October, I joined several thousand merry people to stand on the Feldberg, the peak of the Taunus, and saw the sky reddened all around for a great distance by more than five hundred fires. ... The news that came later, that on that evening flames glowed in the farthest reaches of the fatherland, was sweet as well.[1]

The well-known historian, political author and patriot Ernst Moritz Arndt wrote these words in the preface to the second edition of his work *On the Celebrations of the Battle of Leipzig*, which appeared in the summer of 1815. He expressed his sentiments on the first evening of the 'National Festival of the Germans', which was celebrated in hundreds of towns and villages across Germany on 18 and 19 October 1814 to mark the anniversary of the Battle of Leipzig. For Arndt, the experience of the widely visible fires linking the various regions of Germany must indeed have been remarkably moving. After all, the initiative for these 'joyful bonfires' (*Freudenfeuer*), as well as for the national festival as a whole, had come largely from him and a small circle of like-minded friends in Hesse. These included Friedrich Ludwig Jahn, known as the father of the gymnastics movement, who like Arndt worked at this time for the Central Administrative Department of the Allied Powers in Frankfurt am Main, and the Rödelheim Counsellor of Justice Karl Hoffmann. These German-national patriots had met in early May 1814 and made plans for the future. Among the topics of the meeting was the introduction of a 'Festival of the Battle of Leipzig', which Arndt had suggested shortly before in his pamphlet *Another Word on the French and Us*. He intended it to foster the 'preservation and invigoration of German nature and German thought', the 'awakening of German strength and discipline' and the 'revival of new and old memories' of German history.[2] Arndt summarized the results of the meeting in May 1814 in the first edition of his *A Word on the Celebration of the Battle of Leipzig*, which appeared in the summer of 1814.[3]

With their initiative for a 'National Festival of the Germans', the German-national patriots around Arndt, Jahn and Hoffmann took up suggestions that they and others had been making for some time. In the increasingly intense debate over 'national culture' and 'national manners', which had begun long before the Napoleonic Wars, patriots had repeatedly called for a national festival of all the Germans as a 'vivid means of uniting the entire people'.[4] But it was only after the victorious Battle of Leipzig in October 1813, which contemporaries already talked of as a 'Battle of the Nations', that this debate intensified, because now a central site of memory had been found, and with it a date to commemorate.

Between 16 and 19 October 1813, more than 171,000 men under Napoleon's supreme command, including many soldiers of his remaining German allies Baden, Saxony and Württemberg, faced a 301,000-strong Coalition force in Leipzig under the command of Austrian Field Marshal Prince Schwarzenberg. A substantial number of the forces on the European continent—more than 470,000 soldiers of many different nationalities—had massed in Saxony in the heart of German Central Europe. This made Leipzig the largest battle in history before the First World War. The 'liberation' of Germany, which had officially begun on 16 March 1813 with the declaration of war on France by Prussia and Russia, was not decided by this battle, to be sure, and it did not bring an end to the War of the Sixth Coalition. Napoleon was not deposed until April 1814, but the battle did represent a dramatic defeat for him. Following Leipzig, the remains of the Napoleonic army retreated to the Rhine to defend France's 'natural frontiers'.[5]

In this chapter, I will examine the construction of the collective memory of this battle, and with it the contested memories of the Anti-Napoleonic Wars in German Central Europe. The focus will be on the celebrations commemorating the 'Battle of the Nations' and on how they changed between 1813 and 1913. Celebrations and rituals play a central role in the construction of the collective memory of wars, since they were holistic experiences, which addressed all the senses and were strongly shaped by emotion.[6] Contemporaries were well aware that the experiences of events linked with strong emotions engrave themselves especially deeply in the memory. In his 1810 book *German Folkdom*, Friedrich Ludwig Jahn, for example, presents his extensive suggestions for the formation of a German 'folk culture' under the heading 'folk sensibility' (*Volksgefühl*).[7] For him, the 'language of signs' spoken by 'festivities, ceremonies and customs', was a 'language of the heart', a 'need of man, who recognizes the spiritual more purely in a mediating symbol'. This language comes 'to the aid of memory', because it creates a 'lasting effect of constant realization'.[8] Jahn understood perfectly the importance of emotions for the cultural construction of national memories, and the central role that ceremonies, rituals and symbols played in this process. He and many other patriots discussed intensely the development of a patriotic-national festival culture as part of the debate over the best forms of mobilization for war that began after the Prussian defeat of 1806–07.[9] Their suggestions for patriotic-national celebrations were widely adopted in German Central Europe during and after the Wars of 1813–1815. The largest celebration by far was the National Festival of the Germans, first held on 18 and 19 October 1814. Historians consider it to be the 'matrix of German national festivals in the nineteenth century'.[10]

The first celebrations of the 'Battle of the Nations' in October 1814

In *A Word on the Celebration of the Battle of Leipzig* Arndt succeeded in proposing a national festival of a kind that appealed to a wide public. The pamphlet had an impressive print run of 7,500 copies.[11] His idea for the 'Victory Festival' followed the thanksgiving and victory celebrations already practised across Germany before and during the Wars of 1813–1815, and sought to establish a German-national tradition of ceremonies to keep alive memories of the 'Wars of Liberty' more generally and the outstanding event of the 'Battle of the Nations' in particular, with an emphasis on the role of the people. For in his view, it had been the 'German people', in concert with the princes, who had achieved victory at Leipzig.[12] The National Festival should be 'strong and bind together all Germans', celebrated in a spirit of 'true and ancient German fraternity and honesty'.[13] For this purpose, Arndt offered concrete organizational suggestions. The first holiday, which would begin with the cessation of work at noon, should be a 'festive day for the people'. Therefore, he wanted to leave the detailed arrangements to local communities and associations. He merely recommended that, as soon as darkness fell, 'everywhere within Germania's borders' fires should be lit on mountain peaks, hills and towers, and kept burning until midnight. As 'signs of love and joy', these 'fiery messengers' were to proclaim to all the 'neighbours round about' that Germans now had but 'one sentiment and one thought': 'community and unity'. People should gather around these fires and celebrate in their Sunday best, if possible in the 'national costume'. The second day should be observed as a holiday by the 'authorities of every town'. Bells might already have been rung for events the evening before. For the morning, Arndt suggested 'splendid processions of the local authorities and officials', as well as of all 'men capable of bearing arms, without distinction'; there should also be thanksgiving services in the churches with 'collections for the poor'. The afternoon could be devoted to 'secular pleasures and festivities', contributing through speeches, songs, exercises and games to the 'invigoration and delight of the people and the refreshment and enjoyment of German virtue'. Among other things, Arndt envisioned events to honour the men and boys who had fought in 1813–1814, 'gala dinners' for the 'wounded and crippled warriors', and gymnastic exercises and sporting competitions for male youth. He also suggested turning the 18 and 19 of October into a 'children's festival' throughout Germany with games, 'pleasures and gifts', and combining it with information about the history and 'great significance of the festival', for 'what children and youth understand with soul and love' will 'never leave them in later years'.[14]

Arndt's suggestions combined such traditional and tested elements as the ringing of bells, services of thanksgiving, collections of donations, solemn processions and charitable banquets, with new ones such as mountaintop fires, gymnastic exercises and competitions, as well as the children's festival. This synthesis probably contributed significantly to the surprisingly rapid and widespread acceptance of the idea of the national festival and the programme of events, since it perfectly represented the mixture of underlying ideas. For Germans in the autumn of 1814, the model of Germany as a cultural nation and a unified federation of territorial states was still inextricably linked to religiosity, regional patriotism (*Landespatriotismus*) focused on one of Germany's territorial states, and the veneration of the monarch.

The idea of holding a national festival on 18 and 19 October 1814 was quickly taken up and disseminated. Among the periodicals already propagating it in September, shortly after Arndt's text appeared, were the *Rheinische Merkur,* the *National-Zeitung der Deutschen* and the *Zeitung für die elegante Welt.*[15] Press accounts consistently emphasized the idea that the festival could and must promote a national spirit and concord across regional borders and differences of rank and strengthen unity between peoples and princes, which is why they repeatedly invoke the image of the German 'nation as a *Volk* family'.[16] Even in the late summer of 1814, those in patriotic circles were still relatively hopeful that their rulers would prove accommodating and willing to recognize the people's achievements in the fight for liberation and grant them greater political liberties.[17]

The suggestion of a national festival was implemented across broad swathes of German-speaking Europe. The report on the festivities compiled by Hoffmann and entitled *The German People's Fiery Temple of Gratitude and Honour* was 1,146 pages long and covered 780 celebrations.[18] A glance at regional newspapers suggests that the total number was much higher, since many small towns and villages that mounted their own celebrations go unmentioned in the book. The report documents the festivities in central and western Germany in the greatest detail. This indeed appears to have been the centre of activity, which is not surprising since the initiators of the festival were located in the Rhine-Main region and their communication network was especially tight because of the many cities there. Moreover, the Prussian governors-general of Berg, the Lower Rhine and the Middle Rhine, installed after the victory over Napoleon, were strong supporters of the national festival. But the anniversary of the 'Battle of the Nations' at Leipzig was celebrated in other parts of Germany as well.[19]

In the Prussian monarchy, the 19 of October was officially declared a holiday on which a religious service of thanksgiving should be held.[20] The extent of other activities differed widely, however. Aside from the big cities of Königsberg and Breslau, the national festival was scarcely celebrated in East and West Prussia and Lithuania, and hardly at all in Silesia.[21] In Berlin, the Altmark and the Neumark as well as in western Pomerania, in contrast, the activities largely resembled those in western Germany. As for south Germany, the national festival was either merely tolerated, as was the case in Bavaria and Baden—though here it was nonetheless observed in many towns—or prohibited altogether, as in Württemberg. The national festival was celebrated almost nowhere in Austria, with the only report of festivities coming from Vienna.[22] In the General Government of Saxony, which was still under Russian administration, the celebrations were restricted to the major cities, Dresden and Leipzig.[23] In all, several hundreds of thousands of people participated in the national festival in 1814, especially in the middle-sized and large cities. From Siegen it was reported that 4,000 took part, from Heidelberg more than 5,000, from Marburg more than 8,000 and from Berlin well over 10,000.[24]

Regardless of the attitudes of their governments, the main organizers of the festivities everywhere were the 'district administrators, superintendents, school inspectors, local authorities, pastors, schoolteachers, commanders of the reserve forces, estate owners, church patrons and state and municipal officials'.[25] In short, these were the patriotically minded, middle- and upper-class men of the educated circles in town and countryside. Clergymen and teachers seem to have been especially involved.[26] At least in Prussia, then, the circle of organizers did not differ from that of other patriotic-national festivals during the Wars of 1813–1815, such as induction ceremonies for volunteers and militiamen, flag consecrations, thanksgiving and victory celebrations, and peace festivals and the homecoming festivities for volunteers and militiamen. It is unlikely, however, that the participants in the festivities were drawn from the same social groups, as scholars have often claimed.[27] To be sure, the movement for a national festival was rooted in the urban educated middle classes, and it is surely no coincidence that the 1814 national festival was marked with particular vigour in the large university towns.[28] But the many press accounts of the events suggest that the lower middle classes were also involved in the towns, and that the festivities were observed even in remote villages. Many accounts stress that men, women and children of all social classes took part.[29]

When we look at the many festival reports from all across Germany, it is striking that organizers everywhere took up not just the festival idea developed by Arndt and his friends, but also many of the specific elements they had recommended for the national festival. Regional differences were visible mainly in the political orientation of the festival. In southwest, west and central Germany, especially in the small and very small territorial states, the national festival seems to have had a stronger German-national orientation.[30] In Prussia and the rest of northern Germany, in contrast, regional-patriotic (*landespatriotische*) tendencies dominated.[31] The political differences are also evident in the arrangements for the festival, as the example of Berlin demonstrates. In the Prussian capital, the festivities for the anniversary of Leipzig had already begun on Sunday, 16 October, marking the start of the 'Battle of the Nations'. At ten o'clock in the morning there was a 'grand parade' on the central boulevard Unter den Linden. The infantry marched past the crown prince and the rest of the dignitaries who had gathered in the city.[32] On the morning of 18 October, the large garrison assembled again on Unter den Linden and marched to the parade ground in the Tiergarten, where an altar had been set up in the centre of the park. A service of public worship was held in the presence of the royal family, the court, the Governor of Berlin and the generals. This official thanksgiving ceremony by the court and military ended with the thunder of cannon and the usual hymn 'Lord God, we praise thee' (*Herr Gott, Dich loben wir*), before the orderly march of the troops back to their quarters.[33] At noon, a select company of men—the notables of the city, leading military officers and segments of the court and the government—attended a great banquet in the Stock Exchange.[34]

On the evening of 18 October two celebrations competed for the attention of the public in Berlin. In one, the local choral society, the *Singakademie,* celebrated the anniversary in the presence of the court, the venerated 'hero' General Gebhardt Leberecht von Blücher and 'a very numerous splendid assembly', by a performance of suitable choral music. The evening ended with a poem written by Johann Wolfgang von Goethe to honour Blücher and set to music by the local composer Carl Friedrich Zelter. In the other, the Berlin gymnasts organized their own 'Festival of the Glorious October Days' at their sports ground in the Hasenheide. The square and the surrounding buildings were festively illuminated. A beacon burned atop the ground's 22-metre high climbing frame. In addition, the gymnasts made a bonfire of whole oak trunks, around which they sang patriotic-national songs and shouted 'Vivas', 'first to the king, then to all the valiant men who had fought at Leipzig'. 'Hail to Thee in Victors Crown' (*Heil Dir im Siegerkranz*) was naturally among the songs. Inhabitants also lit similar bonfires at seven other elevated sites near Berlin between 7 p.m. and midnight.[35] On the morning of 19 October, all the church bells in the city called the inhabitants to services of thanksgiving. Afterwards, donations for the war wounded and the widows and orphans of the fallen were collected at the doors of the churches, and people gave generously.[36] In the afternoon the Berlin gymnasts staged public exercises in the Hasenheide in 'memory of the Battle of Leipzig that was our salvation'. The large audience from Berlin and the surrounding towns was estimated to contain more than 10,000 people, including 'princes and princesses of the royal family'—this at a time when the city had around 178,000 inhabitants, of whom 8 percent were soldiers. The festivities held on the evening of 19 October at the Royal Opera House included a premiere of a play written especially for the occasion by the popular author August von Kotzebue, entitled 'The Hundred-Year-Old Oak Tree, or 1914' with incidental music by Carl Maria von Weber. This performance had to be repeated 'by popular demand' on 24 October.[37] The official festivities in Berlin for the anniversary of the 'Battle of the Nations' show that the court, government and military leadership, while interested in emphasizing the significance of the battle, did not wish to go beyond the customary framework of thanksgiving and victory celebrations. In Berlin, the main competition came from the festivities organized by the gymnasts, which attracted broad segments of the population. Even here—in contrast to central and western Germany, where the 'October poetry' (*Oktoberlyrik*) composed especially for the occasion had a largely German-national flavour[38]—Prussian patriotism and veneration for King Friedrich Wilhelm III were unmistakeable, especially in songs, poems and 'Vivas'.[39]

This type of a regional-monarchic patriotism also influenced the character of the festivities in middle-sized and small towns and villages in Prussia. The many accounts of festivals published in the press suggest that the elements were the same everywhere and were merely adapted to local circumstances.[40] In villages, the festival programme was generally limited to a service of thanksgiving and a bonfire with 'festively dressed' participants wearing an oak leaf on their hats, jackets or dresses as a 'national emblem'.[41] A 'memorial oak' or even a 'memorial grove' was often planted as part of the festival ritual, to remind 'even the most distant descendants of the days of Leipzig'.[42]

Fire and oak trees were the central community-creating symbols of the national festival. With them, the inhabitants of even the smallest towns could observe the occasion without great material outlay. In speeches and sermons as well as 'October poetry', fire was largely interpreted as a symbol of German unity, 'fraternity' and valour, which, based on the absolute faith in God, had led to victory, and which in future would be essential for the defence of what had been achieved. In the guise of an altar and sacrificial flame, it was also interpreted as a symbol of the sacred aims of the war, which God had helped the people to secure because of their universal self-sacrifice. The oak, which was considered the German tree par excellence, was intended to symbolize honour, loyalty, love of liberty, Christian faith, steadfastness and permanence, in short, 'German qualities' and the 'German nation'.[43] Fire and oak trees alike had strongly masculine connotations. Both represented the nation primarily as a community of valorous men united in brotherhood. The 'Songs of Covenant' (*Bundeslieder*) that were composed for the national festival project a similar image. They are filled with brotherhood, fraternity, strength of arms, valour, honour and love of liberty.[44]

The sequence of events and symbolism of the 'National Festival of the Germans' thus represented the 'German nation' to the outside world as the genuinely masculine enterprise of a closed and combat-ready community of brothers. This external view included the internal imagination of the nation as a *Volk* family based on a clear gender-hierarchical division of labour. The tasks assigned to women and girls within the festival corresponded to this: they were responsible for embellishing the rooms and for performing caring 'good works'. As in all other patriotic festivals and celebrations, they were permitted to decorate houses, ceremonial halls and churches, prepare banquets, feed the poor, sick and wounded and collect donations, and they were most welcome as festively dressed spectators at processions, parades and performances as well as attendees at church, theatre and balls.[45] The preparation and events of the national festival thus reflected the model of the national gender order as a *Volk* family while at once reproducing and reinforcing it. Speeches, songs and poems regularly reminded women and men—frequently differentiated by age and marital status—of the roles expected of them. The October poetry in particular shows the marked efforts that were made not only to intensify the sense of unity and national belonging and shape the collective national memory through the national festival, but also to stabilize a gender order that had become 'disordered' during the crisis period of the war.[46]

The press reported extensively on the first national festival in October 1814, and there were unanimous calls for it to be repeated the next year. German-national newspapers and periodicals, above all *Deutsche Blätter, Nemesis* and *Rheinische Merkur*, strongly emphasized that the celebration 'had emerged in the true sense of the word from the people, from the most authentic and freest impulse of the people'.[47] In the foreword to his festival documentation, which appeared in September 1815, Hoffmann, too, spoke in favour of holding the festival annually.[48]

The national festivals of 1815–1817

The initiators' hopes that the national festival would be observed on the same scale in 1815 were to be disappointed. The public mood had turned in response to the politics of restoration that in many German states had already begun at the end of 1813.[49] Accordingly, while the press reported in 1815 that 18 and 19 October had been celebrated again in many parts of Germany, press accounts suggest that the number of celebrations was already significantly smaller than in 1814. As in the previous year, the celebrations were organized by German-national and regional-patriotic circles and many government agencies actively supported the events. Even the leadership of the Coalition armies celebrated the anniversary of the Battle of Leipzig in Paris, together with the troops still stationed there.[50] The celebrations were banned only in the kingdoms of Württemberg and Saxony, which did not, of course, prevent German-national patriots from holding them in private.[51] The form of events also appears to have remained largely the same, though, at least in early-liberal and German-national circles, the spirit in which the festival was conducted was very different. The *Rheinische Merkur* commented on this in a report published on 6 November 1815:

> For the second time, the day of the mountain fire has passed, and the German people observed it as festively as possible. However, it was not last year's bright silvery gleam of thrilling hope; the nation's inner sky appears quite overcast ... By the fires lit on lonely mountain peaks, the people considered what of the hopes that had been nurtured and expressed there a year before had come to fruition, and they realised that the flowers that had fallen were largely sterile...[52]

Given the increasing politics of a reactionary restoration by the monarchs and princes, in some places the 'joyful bonfire' had become a 'fire of wrath'.[53] For many patriots, the German Confederation founded by the Congress of Vienna on 8 June 1815 signalled the defeat of their 'struggle for liberty' in the Wars of 1813–1815. In their eyes, the founding document, the German Federal Act (*Deutsche Bundesakte*), represented the restoration of old, monarchical power relations.[54] Thus, it seemed all the more important to them to keep alive the memory of the Wars of 1813–1815 as 'People's Wars of Liberty' and thereby to continue to press their claims for more political liberties in recognition of the support they had given.

The altered sequence of events in Berlin illustrates the change of political mood. Officially, the 1815 'celebration of the anniversary of the Battle of Leipzig' was held in Prussia not on the 18 October, but on the following Sunday, the 22nd, when the victory festivities coincided with the 400-year jubilee of the Hohenzollern monarchy. In Berlin and elsewhere, the arrangement of these festivities took the same form as previous major thanksgiving celebrations.[55] In 1815, the Prussian-monarchic and regional-patriotic character of the official anniversary celebrations for the Battle of Leipzig was more marked in Berlin than it had been the year before. The change of date to fit in with the jubilee of the Hohenzollern monarchy is already evidence of this. In 1815, the Prussian government systematically sought to turn the 'National Festival of the Germans' into a regional-patriotic victory celebration. This was also intended to further suppress public perceptions of the Wars of 1813–1815 as 'People's Wars of Liberty' and to enforce their interpretation as 'Wars of Liberation'.[56] The comparatively modest celebration by the gymnasts on 18 October 1815 could do little to counter this. While they again provided 'a large bonfire and fireworks', only 700 people attended this 'commemorative celebration' on Hasenheide. This time, the press reports no further fires in Berlin and its environs.[57] On the afternoon of 19 October the gymnasts staged public gymnastic exercises as they had the year before, but here too the audience was significantly smaller than in 1814.[58]

These attempts to direct celebrations commemorating the Battle of Leipzig, and with it the Wars of 1813–1815, in a monarchical and regional-patriotic direction were part of postwar political conflicts over the legacy of these wars and the political consequences to be drawn from them. They further intensified in 1816, when even those governments that had still supported the festivities in 1814 and 1815 tried to put a stronger military stamp on them. In Prussia, apart from the obligatory thanksgiving services, parades by the regular army and even military manoeuvres were established as central elements of the celebration. Other states such as Saxony and Württemberg continued to ban the festivities altogether.[59] Part of the drive for a monarchical and regional-patriotic reinterpretation included shifting the date for the official celebration of the Battle of Leipzig following the Prussian example. That year, the events were held on the first Sunday after the anniversary of the 'Battle of the Nations' in other territorial states as well, separating the date of the festival from that of the event it commemorated, the 18 and 19 October, and therefore from the date propagated in German-national circles. The public perceived this change of date as a clear sign of the rejection of the national festival's German-national thrust, which is evident from the debates in Hamburg over the festival date. The Hamburg Senate had suggested observing the national festival on 20 October. Vehement protest and resistance from all sides forced the Hamburg government to drop their plans and return to the traditional dates of 18 and 19 October.[60]

In 1816, German-national patriots sought to counter this trend by mobilizing more vigorously for the national festival. Everywhere in 1816, the festivities were more spectacular than those of the previous year.[61] Two new elements already introduced in outline in 1815 now emerged more strongly. Both demonstrate the attempt to anchor memories of the 'Battle of the Nations' in the minds of future generations. First, there were various reports on the laying of cornerstones or the inauguration of local war memorials.[62] Calls for a national monument recalling the 'Battle of the Nations', which Arndt had already initiated in 1814, were repeated from various quarters.[63] Second, there were more frequent accounts of commemorative events held in educational institutions.[64] With the support of their teachers, educated young men, pupils of the *Gymnasien* (the academic secondary schools) and university students, members of gymnastic societies and student fraternities, sought to keep the national festival tradition with a German-national flavour alive the next year as well. This reflects the fact that during the Wars of 1813–1815 nearly half of all students volunteered to fight, and that after the war, gymnasts and fraternity members constituted the avant-garde of the German-national movement.[65] A year later, the greatest public attention focused on the Wartburg Festival, which the student fraternities organized on 18 and 19 October 1817 as a festival for the whole nation.[66]

Overall, however, in the course of the political restoration after 1816, the national festival appears to have been celebrated less often, and after 1819 only covertly among private circles of friends. The 'Battle of the Nations' faded more and more from memory. A fraternity member who, with his fellow-students, held a commemoration on the Leipzig battlefield on 18 October 1820 commented: '"Tis bleak and gloomy on Germany's mountaintops, and throughout the former German empire" tis deemed a sin to recall the past'.[67]

The anniversary celebrations of the battle of Leipzig in 1838, 1863 and 1913

In the first commemorations of the 'Battle of the Nations' immediately following the war, the focus was on the meaning of the battle and the Wars of 1813–1815 for the political culture of postwar society. The question of whether they were 'Wars of Liberation' or 'Wars of Liberty', which had already lead to intense discussions during the wars themselves, also remained important into the next century. It informed the highly contested construction of the memory of the wars in the German Confederation (1815–1866) and the German Empire (1871–1918). Two master narratives of the Wars of 1813–1815 proved most influential during the long nineteenth century. The monarchical-conservative Prussian narrative spoke of 'Wars of Liberation' fought by 'subjects' who were 'monarchical to their very marrow', followed the king's call to resist, and were led by his generals. Saxony and other German states shared a conservative interpretation of the wars, but downplayed the role of Prussia. The liberal German-national interpretation, in contrast, spoke of 'Wars of Liberty' conducted by 'the German people' as a 'free, autonomous movement' and a 'struggle for liberty' against external and internal forces. This debate on the name and meaning of the Wars of 1813–1815 was politically vital because their legacy was used to legitimate the German-national call for unification and liberal and democratic demands for more political rights on the one side, and to repudiate them on the other. The debate also led to questions about Prussia's role during the wars and its influence in any future German confederation. This dispute influenced constructions of memory up until the First World War, but after German unification by 'blood and iron' in 1871, which culminated in a German nation-state without Austria, the conservative-monarchical narrative became increasingly dominant and in the process shaped recollections of the Battle of Leipzig.[68]

The diverging histories of the different regions and states of Continental Europe between 1792 and 1815 were a second important factor that influenced memory creation. When constructing their collective memories, all 36 small and large German states that had joined the Confederation of the Rhine were forced to confront their time as Napoleon's allies and the fact that they had changed sides late in the game to support the struggle to free Germany and Europe from Napoleonic rule. For Saxony, which had been an ally of Napoleon until his defeat on 19 October 1813, memories of the war were even more contested than in most other German states within the Confederation of the Rhine, which had changed sides before the battle or at least before the defeat. Memories of the Battle of Leipzig and the Wars of 1813–1815 were complicated by the fact that Saxony had been one of the main battlegrounds and its population had suffered more than the inhabitants of other German territories. Instead of acknowledgment for these sacrifices, the Saxons experienced continued occupation, first by Russia and then by Prussia, and in May 1815 the Congress of Vienna ended up granting 40 percent of the territory of the restored Saxon monarchy to Prussia.[69]

Thus the memory of the Anti-Napoleonic Wars and the Battle of Leipzig remained highly controversial in the 1820s–1840s. The struggle over the orientation of memories, however, was no longer conducted in commemorative festivities in public space inviting broad participation, as had been the case in the immediate postwar period, but only in books and periodicals for a small circle of educated readers. The debate now took place primarily in the emerging popular, military, and later also academic historiography, in the rapidly growing numbers of war memoirs, and in novels, including, increasingly, historical novels.[70]

The 25th anniversary of the Wars of 1813–1815 was not celebrated widely in public with large festivals. The framework for recollections was now narrow and local. In Leipzig, for example, the city and its surrounding villages began to erect local monuments at the most important memorial sites of the battle in 1838. The initiator was the Leipzig Association to Celebrate the 19th of October, which had been in existence since 1814. The main aim of the initiative was to emphasize local contributions to the national history of the 'Wars of Liberty', to commemorate central personalities of these wars, such as military leaders and patriots, along with especially hard-fought battle sites, and to recall the region's great sacrifices. The local authorities, Protestant Church and middle-class associations always jointly organized the inauguration ceremonies for local monuments. A total of eight local memorials were established between 1845 and 1863. On the occasion of the 50th anniversary in 1863, the Leipzig Association installed another 44 'landmarks' on the battlefield.[71]

The 50th anniversary was celebrated on a far larger scale in 1863. Leipzig served as the central commemorative site for the first national celebration, for which a number of German cities, notably Berlin and Leipzig, had issued an invitation to all other cities with the agreement of the Saxon government. After the failed Democratic Revolution of 1848–49, the commemorative celebration was a clear political declaration of intent by the national-liberal middle classes to reclaim the unfulfilled demands for unity and liberty of 1813. Accordingly, they very consciously harked back to the ceremonial forms, images and symbols of the 'Wars of Liberty', integrated national movements such as the fraternities and the gymnastic and choral societies, which had already actively helped to shape the 'German national festivals' of 1814 to 1817, and used the October poetry of these years, which was now reprinted. The central procession in Leipzig gave pride of place to the surviving veterans of the Wars of 1813–1815, without regard to military or social rank, which was intended to symbolize that all of them had equally been 'comrades, fighters and victors in Germany's greatest battle'.[72] Some 20,000 people in all took part in the procession; the number of spectators has been estimated at around 100,000. At the close of the festivities the idea of a national monument was again raised and the foundation stone laid outside the city gates. It would be another 50 years, however, before this monument would be completed.[73]

The jubilee of 1913 was a different matter altogether.[74] Now, the focus was on the conservative monarchical myth of the 'Battle of the Nations' as the 'natal hour of the German people, which had unleashed the "noblest forces" of nationhood, of German national awareness', a myth that had become increasingly influential since the founding of the German Empire. It was now supported by broad segments of the national-liberal middle classes and was massively evident in the architecture of the 1913 Leipzig 'Monument to the Battle of the Nations'. Its construction was initiated by the 'League of German Patriots', founded in 1894, and was completed 20 years later. Even today, the 91-metre high colossus remains the tallest monument in Europe. During construction, 600,000 people already visited the site. The national monument was inaugurated with much pomp and a gigantic procession in 1913, in the presence of Kaiser Wilhelm II.[75]

Unconditional self-sacrifice for the nation was among the 'noblest forces' lauded in the many official speeches and the press on this occasion. This quality was very much in demand on the eve of the First World War. The 1913 celebrations conveyed an image of war calculated to put people in a frame of mind conducive to another great battle of the nations, and glorified war as a catalyst for national unity and renewal. This view of war met with broad approval even in educated middle-class circles. Thus in his *Die deutsche Erhebung von 1914* (translated into English as *The Warfare of a Nation*), which appeared shortly after the war began, the well-known Berlin historian Friedrich Meinecke consciously takes up the tradition of the Wars of 1813–1815 in a chapter entitled 'The National Crises of 1813, 1848, 1870 and 1914'. Here he emphasizes that 'death for the Fatherland, this most ancient sacrifice, has won for us a new and lasting meaning' and 'betokens a "sacred springtime" for all of Germany':

> In preceding years we were apparently irreversibly divided, often faint and discouraged at the unfortunate hostility of classes and confessions—the menace to our intellectual life. Now at a word we are raised above all barriers, one mighty, resolute community of the nation in life and death.[76]

And this closed the circle to the Wars of 1813–1815 for him and many other educated, national-liberal, middle-class men who now welcomed the new war in 1914. In fact, the First World War ushered in a new period of national heroic memory production, one in which recollections of the Battle of Leipzig and the Wars of 1813–1815 were once again used for present-day political—in this case mainly nationalist and militarist—ends, while the sufferings of soldiers and civilians in these wars and this mass battle were increasingly forgotten. Protests against the militarist and nationalist spectacle of the inauguration of the monument to the Battle of Leipzig by the youth movement and Social Democrats and warnings about the dangers of a new war faded away unheard.[77]

Conclusion

In an exemplary manner, the history of the celebration and commemoration of the Battle of Leipzig represents the contested and changing place of the Wars of 1813–1815 in German collective memory. The construction of these memories had already begun during the wars themselves and was politically highly contested from the outset. Conflicts over the interpretation of the history of the wars and one of its central battles continued until 1871, when German unification resolved at least one of the major political issues that lay at their heart. Critics continued to raise their voices, however, because in their eyes unification had been achieved without liberty. The anniversaries of the Wars of 1813–1815 marked the high points in commemoration. The 50th and 100th anniversaries in particular were celebrated on a large scale, but with very different political orientations, reflecting the two poles of representation and recollection of the wars and the Battle of Leipzig. In 1863, the battle was remembered as the turning point in the 'Wars of Liberty' fought by the people for both liberation from French occupation and oppression, *and* political unification and liberty within Germany. The educated and liberal-minded middle and upper classes in particular used the commemoration to remind monarchs and princes, after the defeat of the Revolution of 1848, that the political demands for unification and liberty were still not realized. In 1913, the battle was remembered quite differently, as a heroic act of 'great men'—monarchs, princes and generals—who had led subjects to victory in 'Wars of Liberation' against Napoleon. On the one hand, this change indicates how political events and periods such as the *Vormärz*, the failure of the Revolution of 1848, the Wars of German Unification and the founding of the German Empire left their mark on the narratives and their reception. On the other, it reflects the growing influence of the master narratives produced by a professionalizing academic historiography, which focused on a pro-Prussian, monarchic-conservative or national-liberal interpretation of the period of the Anti-Napoleonic Wars. These gained ascendancy in Imperial Germany and sought to legitimize German unification by 'blood and iron', under Prussian leadership and to the exclusion of Austria.

Acknowledgements

I would like to thank Pamela Selwyn for her translation. For more on this subject see: Karen Hagemann, *Revisiting Prussia's Wars against Napoleon: History, Culture and Memory* (Cambridge, 2015).

Notes

1. Ernst Moritz Arndt, *Ueber die Feier der Leipziger Schlacht* (2nd edn, Frankfurt/M., 1815), 3–4.
2. Ernst Moritz Arndt, *Noch ein Wort über die Franzosen und über uns* (n.p., 1814), 34.
3. Ernst Moritz Arndt, *Ein Wort über die Feier der Leipziger Schlacht* (Frankfurt/M., 1814).
4. Friedrich Kohlrausch, *Deutschlands Zukunft: In sechs Reden* (Elberfeld, 1814), 24 and 103–132. See also Hagemann, *Revisiting*, Chapter 10.
5. See Michael V. Leggiere, *Napoleon and Berlin: The Franco-Prussian War in North Germany, 1813* (Norman, OK, 2002), 256–278; Digby G. Smith, *1813: Leipzig. Napoleon and the Battle of the Nations* (London, 2001); and Andreas Platthaus, *1813: Die Völkerschlacht und das Ende der Alten Welt* (Berlin, 2013). For the civilian experience, see Karen Hagemann, '"Unimaginable Horror and Misery": The Battle of Leipzig in October 1813 in Civilian Experience and Perception', in *Soldiers, Citizens and Civilians: Experiences and Perceptions of the French Wars, 1790–1820*, ed. Alan Forrest et al. (Basingstoke, 2009), 157–178.
6. See Karen Hagemann, 'Celebrating War and Nation: The Gender Order of Patriotic Ceremonies and Festivities in the Time of Prussia's Wars against Napoleon, 1813–1815', in *Gender, War, and Politics: Transatlantic Perspectives, 1775–1820*, ed. Hagemann et al. (Basingstoke, 2010), 264–306.
7. Friedrich Ludwig Jahn, *Deutsches Volksthum* (Lübeck, 1810), 323–368.
8. Ibid., 337–338 and 342.
9. See Manfred Hettling and Paul Nolte (eds), *Bürgerliche Feste: Symbolische Formen politischen Handelns im 19. Jahrhundert* (Göttingen, 1993), 8–36.
10. Dieter Düding, 'Das deutsche Nationalfest von 1814: Matrix der deutschen Nationalfeste im 19. Jahrhundert', in *Öffentliche Festkultur: Politische Feste in Deutschland von der Aufklärung bis zum Ersten Weltkrieg*, ed. idem et al. (Reinbek, 1988), 67–88, 80.
11. Karl Heinz Schäfer, *Ernst Moritz Arndt als politischer Publizist: Studien zu Publizistik, Pressepolitik und kollektivem Bewußtsein im frühen 19. Jahrhundert* (Bonn, 1974), 257.
12. Arndt, *Ueber die Feier*, 3–4.
13. Ibid., 8.
14. Ibid., 16–17.
15. 'Die Feyer der Leipziger Schlacht', *Rheinischer Merkur* (RM), no. 124, 27 September 1814; see Düding, 'Das deutsche Nationalfest', 80.
16. 'Die Feier des neunzehnten Oktobers?', *Zeitschrift für die elegante Welt* (ZFeW), no. 202, 11 October 1814.
17. See Karl Hoffmann (ed.), *Des Teutschen Volkes feuriger Dank- und Ehrentempel oder Beschreibung wie das aus zwanzigjähriger französischer Sklaverei durch Fürsten-Eintracht und Volkskraft gerettete Teutsche Volk die Tage der entscheidenden Völker- und Rettungsschlacht bei Leipzig am 18. und 19. October zum erstenmale gefeiert hat,*

(Offenbach, 1815), 3–13; see also Karen Hagemann, *'Mannlicher Muth und Teutsche Ehre': Nation, Militär und Geschlecht zur Zeit der Antinapoleonischen Kriege Preußens* (Paderborn, 2002), 273–303.
18. Hoffmann, *Des Teutschen Volkes*, 1133–1146.
19. Ibid., 209–255, 545–549, 765–829, 1087–1092 and 1123–1131.
20. Ibid., 680–764.
21. See 'Ueber die Feier des Jahrestages der Leipziger Völkerschlacht', *Schlesisches Provinzialblatt* (SP), no. 9 (1815): 206–210.
22. See Brian E. Vick, *The Congress of Vienna: Power and Politics after Napoleon* (Cambridge, 2014), 90–95.
23. 'Das Fest aller Teutschen. Am 18. und 19. October 1814', *Nemesis* 3/1 (1814): 132–138. See also Hoffmann, *Des Teutschen Volkes*, 8–137, 138–208, 678–679 and 837–840.
24. Hoffmann, *Des Teutschen Volkes*, 55, 38, 669 and 691.
25. 'Der 18te October 1815 und der 18te Januar 1816', *Amts-Blatt der königlich kurmärkischen Regierung* (AB), no. 13, 29 March 1816, 122–123.
26. 'Nachlese zur Oktoberfeier', *RM*, no. 152, 22 November 1814.
27. Düding, 'Das deutsche Nationalfest', 69.
28. This was the case especially in Berlin, Halle, Heidelberg, Jena, Königsberg, Leipzig and Marburg. For more see Hagemann, *Revisiting*, Chapter 10.
29. See Hoffmann, *Des Teutschen Volkes*, 353, 680–670 and 732–733.
30. Ibid., 8–137, 258–275, 363–510, 814–829, 1124–1128.
31. Ibid., 297–299, 291–296, 545–249 and 550–554.
32. 'Sonntag, den 16ten, am ersten Jahrestage der eröffneten Leipziger Völkerschlacht', *Vossische Zeitung* (VZ), no. 125, 18 October 1814.
33. Hoffmann, *Des Teutschen Volkes*, 683; 'Berlin, den 20. Oktober', *VZ*, no. 126, 20 October 1814.
34. Hoffmann, *Des Teutschen Volkes*, 683.
35. Ibid., 685–686 and 690–691.
36. 'Berlin, den 20. Oktober', *VZ*, no. 126, 20 October 1814.
37. Hoffmann, *Des Teutschen Volkes*, 684–685.
38. See the songs reprinted in Hoffmann, *Des Teutschen Volkes* and the following examples: *Nachtrag zu den Volksliedern zur Jahresfeier der großen Errettungsschlacht am 18. Oktober 1813 bei Leipzig* (Frankfurt M., n.y. [1814]); *Volks-Lieder: Beim Siegesfeuer am 18ten Oktober zu singen* (n.p., n.y [1814]); and *Volkslieder zur Jahresfeier der großen Erretungsschlacht am 18. Oktober 1813 bei Leipzig* (Frankfurt/M., 1814).
39. 'Schlachtfeier, gesungen um Mitternacht an den Dankfeuern in der Hasenheide bei Berlin', in Hoffmann, *Des Teutschen Volkes*, 688–690.
40. 'Oderberg, den 20. Oktober', *Berlinische Nachrichten* (BN), no. 136, 12 November 1814; see also Hoffmann, *Des Teutschen Volkes*, 691–692 and 745–749.
41. Arndt, *Noch ein Wort*, 37.
42. 'Schreiben aus Anclam, den 20. Oktober 1814', *VZ*, no. 132, 3 November 1814.
43. See Hoffmann, *Des Teutschen Volkes*, 680–683 and 732–733; and Arndt, *Ueber die Feier*, 34–37.
44. See Hoffmann, *Des Teutschen Volkes*, 974–975.
45. Ibid., 264–267, 297 and 692–693.
46. Ibid., 454–464 and 729–731. See also Karen Hagemann, '"A Valorous Volk Family": The Nation, the Military, and the Gender Order in Prussia in the Time of the Anti-Napoleonic Wars, 1806–15', in *Gendered Nations: Nationalisms and Gender Order in the Long Nineteenth Century*, ed. Ida Blom et al. (Oxford, 2000), 179–205;

and Hagemann, 'Female Patriots: Women, War and the Nation in the Period of the Prussian-German Anti-Napoleonic Wars', *Gender & History* 16/3 (2004): 396–424.
47. 'Das Fest aller Teutschen: Am 18. und 19. October 1814', *Nemesis* 3/1 (1814): 132–138, 134; see also 'Nachlese zur Oktoberfeyer', *RM*, no. 152, 22 November 1814; and 'Das Fest aller Deutschen', *Deutsche Blätter* (DB), vol. 6, no. 226, 10 January 1815.
48. Hoffmann, *Des Teutschen Volkes*, 5.
49. Hagemann, *Mannlicher Muth*, 106–158.
50. 'Feier des achtzehnten Octobers in Paris', *Tageblatt der Geschichte* (TG), no. 216, 30 October 1815; and 'Paris, vom 18. October', *BN*, no. 132, 4 November 1815.
51. 'Vermischte Nachrichten', *BN*, no. 126, 21 October 1815.
52. 'Die zweyte Oktoberfeyer', *RM*, no. 325, 6 November 1815.
53. Ibid.
54. See Vick, *The Congress*, Chapter 6.
55. 'Berlin, den 24sten Oktober', *VZ*, no. 127, 24 October 1814; 'Berlin, vom 24. Oktober', *Schlesische Privilegierte Zeitung* (SPZ), no. 127, 28 October 1815; and 'Bekanntmachung, Berlin, den 6. Oktober 1815', *VZ*, no. 121, 19 October 1815.
56. See 'Der 18te Oktober 1815, und der 18te Januar 1816', *AB*, no. 13, 29 March 1816.
57. 'Feierlichkeiten vom 18ten Oktober', *VZ*, no. 119, 5 October 1815.
58. 'Beschluß der diesjährigen Turn-Uebungen', *BN*, no. 126, 21 October 1815. After the national festival, the two largest newspapers in the capital, the *Berliner Nachrichten* and the *Vossische Zeitung*, reported for quite some time on nearby and distant festivities under the special rubric 'Festivities of 18th October'.
59. 'Breslau', *SPZ*, no. 124, 19 October 1816; 'Königsberg', *VZ*, no. 130, 20 November 1816; 'Magdeburg, vom 20. Oktober', *SPZ*, no. 130, 2 November 1816; 'Mainz, vom 22. Oktober', *SPZ*, no. 131, 4 November 1816; 'Kassel, vom 19. Oktober', *SPZ*, no. 130, 2 November 1816; and 'Mannheim, vom 19. Oktober', in Ibid.
60. 'Hamburg, 18ten Oktober', *VZ*, no. 131, 31 October 1816.
61. 'Berlin', *SPZ*, no. 127, 26 October 1816; 'Berlin, den 22. Oktober', *VZ*, no. 127, 22 October 1816; and 'Potsdam, vom 20.10.1816', *SPZ*, no. 129, 30 October 1816; and 'Frankfurt a.M., vom 20. Oktober', *SPZ*, no. 130, 2 November 1816.
62. See 'Neisse', *SPZ*, addendum to no. 133, 9 November 1816.
63. See Steffen Poser, 'Soll es gesehen werden, so muss es groß und herrlich seyn...: Völkerschlacht-Erinnerung und Ideen für ein Völkerschlachtdenkmal', in *Völkerschlachtdenkmal*, ed. Stadtgeschichtliches Museum Leipzig (Altenburg, 2003), 44–63, 44–54.
64. See 'Feier des 18ten Oktober im königl. Joachimsthalischen Gymnasium', *VZ*, no. 126. 21 October 1815; and 'Königsberg', *VZ*, no. 130, 20 November 1816.
65. See Hagemann, *Revisiting*, Chapter 8.
66. See ibid., Chapter 10; also Klaus Malettke (ed.), *175 Jahre Wartburgfest: 18. Oktober 1817–18: Oktober 1992—Studien zur politischen Bedeutung und zum Zeithintergrund der Wartburgfeier* (Heidelberg, 1992).
67. Cited in Poser, 'Soll es gesehen werden', 53.
68. See Hagemann, *Revisiting*, Chapter 13.
69. Vick, *The Congress*, 278–320.
70. See Hagemann, *Revisiting*, Parts IV and V.
71. Renate Hartleb (ed.), *Die Zeit der Befreiungskriege und die Leipziger Völkerschlacht in Malerei, Graphik, Plastik*, exhibition catalogue (Leipzig, 1988), 36–39.
72. Stefan-Ludwig Hoffmann, 'Mythos und Geschichte: Leipziger Gedenkfeiern der Völkerschlacht im 19. und frühen 20. Jahrhundert', in *Nation und Emotion: Deutschland*

und Frankreich im Vergleich 19. und 20. Jahrhundert, ed. Etienne François et al. (Göttingen, 1995), 111–132, 117–118.
73. See Stefan-Ludwig Hoffmann, 'Sakraler Monumentalismus um 1900: Das Leipziger Völkerschlachtdenkmal', in *Der politische Totenkult: Kriegerdenkmäler in der Moderne*, ed. Reinhart Koselleck and Michael Jeismann (Munich, 1994), 249–280; idem., 'Mythos und Geschichte'; and Uwe Puschner, '18. Oktober 1813: "Möchten die deutschen nur alle und immer dieses Tages gedenken!"—Die Leipziger Völkerschlacht', in *Erinnerungstage: Wendepunkte der Geschichte von der Antike bis zur Gegenwart*, ed. Etienne François and Uwe Puschner (Munich, 2010), 145–162.
74. Siemann, 'Krieg und Frieden in historischen Gedenkfeiern des Jahres 1913', in *Öffentliche Festkultur*, ed. Düding et al. 298–320.
75. Ibid.
76. Friedrich Meinecke, 'Die deutschen Erhebungen von 1813, 1848, 1870 und 1914', in idem., *Die deutsche Erhebung von 1914* (Stuttgart, 1914), 9–38, 28–29.
77. Siemann, 'Krieg und Frieden', 298–320.

21
Contrasting Memories: Remembering Waterloo in France and Britain

Alan Forrest

For both Britain and France the Battle of Waterloo on 18 June 1815 held a particular significance, as the conflict that brought to an end the long series of eighteenth-century wars which have been called, with some justification, 'the second Hundred Years War'.[1] It was the last time they would fight over European and world hegemony, and it proved a turning point in the European balance of power, seeing France's political pretensions permanently halted, to Britain's advantage. Britain suffered, of course, both on the battlefield and on the home front. But the country could take pride in the quality of its soldiers and the prudence of their tactics, safe in the knowledge that, as a result of their sacrifices, France was no longer in a position to threaten her place on the world stage. As the Prussian general August Neidhardt von Gneisenau remarked, Britain should regard Napoleon as her benefactor, having 'no greater obligation to any mortal on earth than to this ruffian', whose aggressive behaviour lay at the root of Britain's subsequent greatness as an industrial powerhouse and a world empire. 'For through the events that he has brought about, England's greatness, prosperity and wealth have risen high. She is the mistress of the sea, and neither in this dominion nor in world trade has she now a single rival to fear'.[2]

Victories are, of course, better suited to commemoration than defeats, and easier to weave into the storyboard of a nation, as a glance at the contents of any national military museum shows. They find an echo in military parades and public acts of homage, in sports competitions and fireworks displays. But on such occasions commemoration and celebration are often confused: the nation not only remembers, but is encouraged to rejoice in the feats of its men in war. Artists record the deeds of victorious armies, portraitists paint their generals and their political leaders, and medals are struck and festivals held to impress the public at large. Those who lose are often forgotten, or are left to shoulder the blame for catastrophe. The battle, Napoleon believed, was lost by the smallest of margins; or, as he put it on Saint-Helena in his dictation to Baron Gourgaud, it had started so well, with the British and Prussians deceived, until some of the French generals, drained by the

1814 campaign, showed that they had 'lost something of that boldness, resolution and confidence which had brought them so much glory and had so contributed to the success of past campaigns'.[3] The French, moreover, had lost twice: after the *campagne de France* in 1814, when Paris fell and Napoleon was forced to abdicate; and again in 1815, after his ill-fated adventure in the Hundred Days, when his army was routed and he was left with no option but to abdicate for a second time. Two defeats; two sets of peace terms; two changes of regime—it all represented a bitter pill for any nation, and not least for a generation that had been weaned on the promise of military glory. In 1814 Napoleon had expressed the belief that the peace terms France was offered—essentially a return to the country's pre-revolutionary borders—would goad the French people into insurrection. He was wrong; and the terms imposed after Waterloo would prove harsher, and harder to bear.[4] This posed a huge challenge for those who sought to remember the wars in ensuing decades, to commemorate the sacrifice of their men without appearing to glory in the defeat of their nation.

Both nations had suffered in the wars, both had recruited unprecedented numbers of men for the army, and in both widows and orphans had to bear the consequences of war long after the guns were silenced. In both countries, too, the postwar years were marked by high rates of unemployment and often painful issues of reintegration into civilian life. For many soldiers and their families the years that followed the peace in 1815 were ones of hardship and rejection, and that was as true of Britain as it was of France. Private memories could be bitter on both sides. What did differ is to be found in public attitudes and official discourses. On the French side, there might seem to have been little to celebrate, or to remember with any relish: their army had been routed, their political system undermined, and the Restoration monarchy imposed at the behest of the victorious Allies. Public celebration was understandably muted. In Britain, in contrast, the government sponsored official celebrations of the victory and encouraged the public to wallow in a sense of national achievement. It actively encouraged an outpouring of popular patriotism that focussed, quite specifically, on Waterloo.

Britain's view of the battle

Britain, unsurprisingly, saw Waterloo as one of the great military turning-points of modern times and presented it as the victory of British arms and of a specifically British national character, of which steadfastness and stoicism were the salient characteristics. 'Nothing in ancient or modern history', claimed *The Times* on 29 June, 'equals the effect of the victory at Waterloo'.[5] Robert Southey, the Poet Laureate, placing the battle on a par with Charles Martel's victory over the Moors in 742.[6] Painters vied with one another to record the battle for posterity, with most portraying the excitement, the grandeur of the battle and the role of Britain's soldiers in the fighting.[7] It was a glorious moment that cried out for commemoration. But it was impossible to ignore the suffering and the cost in brave lives. The most famous painting to emerge from the battle, Turner's *The Field of Waterloo*, passed over the glorious fighting to linger on the dead, the bodies that lay heaped and entangled on the battlefield.[8] Walter Scott, in his poem on the battle with the same title as Turner's painting, likened the loss of Britain's heroes to the harvesting of wheat on nearby farms.[9] As a natural Tory Scott feared Napoleon, yet he admired him as a man of genius, whom he depicted as a flawed hero.[10] Wellington he saw as a true hero, later admitting that 'he had never felt awed or abashed except in the presence of one man—the Duke of Wellington'.[11]

If we are to believe their memoirs, many of those who served under him shared Scott's view, and their accounts did much to burnish Wellington's image for posterity. Among them was John Kincaid, one of six men from the Rifle Brigade—the 95th—to leave accounts of their war experiences. His book, *Adventures in the Rifle Brigade*, had all that it took to appeal to the mass market for military memoirs: a deeply patriotic tone and an exciting, if sparse, narrative of events as he had experienced them. Waterloo he presents as a hard-fought battle in which Britain's regiments had excelled where their Continental allies had failed. He gives little credit to the contributions of the Prussians, the Belgians or the Dutch. 'Our foreign auxiliaries', he writes,

> who constituted more than half of our numerical strength, with some exceptions, were little better than a raw militia—a body without a soul, or like an inflated pillow, that gives to the touch and resumes its shape again when the pressure ceases; not to mention the many who went clear of the field, and were only seen while plundering our baggage in their retreat.[12]

It was not a clear-cut victory from the start. But in the midst of the 'frightening carnage', his faith in Wellington remained undimmed. Indeed, he suggests,

> if Lord Wellington had been at the head of his old Peninsular army, I am confident that he would have swept his opponents off the face of the earth immediately after their first attack; but with such a heterogeneous mixture under his command, he was obliged to submit to a longer day.[13]

This was what his readers wanted to hear: a faith and a trust in a British military hero akin to that that had been expressed by French soldiers during Napoleon's earlier campaigns.

In reality, of course, their experience had often been grim, and the risks of death and injury unbearably high. Soldiers called upon to serve abroad had had plenty of time to contemplate the dangers that awaited them and to calculate the risks. Battles could be deadly. In a single day Waterloo cost thousands of lives on both sides: Wellington's army sustained over 16,000 casualties, and Blücher's more than 7,000, while Napoleon's in defeat suffered around 31,000 killed and wounded.[14] And the losses during the four days on the Waterloo campaign were far higher. But there were other causes of death and sickness. Chief among them was fever in the deadly climates of the Caribbean or the Indian sub-continent. At times, indeed, the odds against survival could seem overwhelming. It has been estimated that of the 45,000 officers and men in the British army who died in the Caribbean between 1793 and 1801 as many as 95 percent died of disease, not as a consequence of any enemy action. Even Europe could on occasion prove deadly, as with the 'Walcheren Fever' which in 1809 killed 4,000 men of the British expeditionary force.[15] Thomas Morris, on a ship to north Germany in 1813, told how he and his shipmates 'sat for hours together, meditating on my own folly and temerity, in thus rushing on to certain danger—perhaps to death'. They began to work out the odds of survival. 'Of our regiment', Morris asked, 'how many of them were destined never to return? And the question would arise—should I be among the first? or second?'[16] Theirs were bleak thoughts which drove some to despair or to God. Religion, especially in its evangelical variants, spread among the troops, often in response to fear and depression.[17]

The carnage of the battlefield played a prominent part in survivors' accounts of Waterloo. Some tried to minimise it, or to take comfort in the fact that enemy losses had been far greater. But the reality of death and mutilation could not be erased. William Tomkinson, in his *Diary of a Cavalry Officer*, does his best to sanitise the awfulness of the scene that he witnessed on 19 June when he surveyed the battlefield, dressing his account in the language of patriotism and claiming a somewhat spurious superiority for the medical care offered by his own side in the heat of battle. 'The wounded of a British army', he declared, without a great deal of supportive evidence, 'generally receive more attention than those of other nations'. In contrast, 'The French system is to run great risks with a man's life in hopes of saving a limb, from knowing that a soldier without a leg or arm is incapable of service, and probably a burthen to the state'.[18] Patriotism may have dictated that he presented the British army in a more favourable light than the French; though in practice there may have been little to choose between them.

Britain, of course, had every reason to put its victory to political use. As Linda Colley has pointed out, the British state that went into the Napoleonic wars was anything but united: indeed, the nature of British identity was still being argued over, with Scots, Irish and, to a more limited extent, Welshmen expressing Celtic doubts about their place in the supposedly united kingdom.[19] Scottish and Irish troops had played a full part in the battle, and artists never failed to note their presence, placing colourful and iconic images of kilted Highlanders in the front line of combat.[20] But divisions were not the monopoly of the Celtic fringe. England itself had been far from united against France in the 1790s, when many looked to the ideas of the French republic for an inspiration that the Hanoverian monarchy and its increasingly repressive justice system signally failed to provide. And there were many on the radical side of politics who regretted the restoration of the Bourbons and who soon transferred their sympathies from the French Jacobins of the 1790s to the Luddites and machine-breakers of industrial England. They saw Waterloo not just as the victory of the British over the French, but as a triumph for the Tory establishment which would keep the gentry and landowning classes in power for years to come. It was no semantic accident when the violent break-up of a radical demonstration at St Peter's Fields in Manchester in 1819 became known as 'Peterloo', and was depicted as yet another victory for the rich and privileged, as 'the climax of the prolonged postwar contest between governors and governed'.[21]

But the immediate response of the British public, especially in the capital, was one of jubilation at what they hailed as a victory for British arms and British virtues. Speaking for the government, Lord Castlereagh declared it 'an achievement of such high merit, of such pre-eminent importance, as had never perhaps graced the annals of this or any other country till now'.[22] He pointed to the youthfulness of the Allied army and to its comparative inexperience when faced by Napoleon's seasoned soldiers, and though he recognised the valiant part the Dutch and the Prussians had played in securing victory, he did not linger on their contribution. Throughout the nineteenth century the British authorities would continue to play down the part that Prussian, and more generally German, forces had played in Napoleon's defeat.[23]

Waterloo was greeted so passionately because it finally—for a second time in as many years—had brought the long war to an end. It was also the more remarkable in that it was a land battle; for Britain, so dependent on her navy, this was something of a novelty and was seen as evidence of total military supremacy. The immediate response to the victory was an outpouring of state-fuelled jubilation and thanksgiving. Both Houses of Parliament passed a vote of thanks for the outcome, and subscriptions were opened to help the victims of the war, not least the wounded servicemen who returned from the Continent and the bereaved families of those killed in action. Over 600 churches were built—known as 'Waterloo churches', and built under the Church Building Act of 1818—to provide Anglican worship in areas of the country where need was identified and to thank God for his intervention against the Usurper.[24] And across the land clergymen joined in the patriotic claim that this war had been fought in the cause of God and of all humanity.[25] They insisted that they wanted the deaths of their brave soldiers to serve some purpose, and therefore clung to the belief that the cause in which they had fought had been just. The British, one vicar assured members of the Westminster Waterloo Association, had been fighting a Manichean battle for good against evil, and it was God's battle, too. The French in their wickedness had been the instruments of God, 'who in his omniscience deriveth good from evil, hath permitted for more than twenty years anarchy and misrule in France, together with the extinction of the very forms and shadows of religion'. [26]

Wellington and Nelson

Wellington himself was a divisive figure, especially when he went on to have a political career in the post-1815 world, and he split opinion along partisan lines. For Tories he would remain a hero whom they would claim as one of their own. In the decades that followed they continued to hold anniversary dinners, where toasts were drunk to the great Duke and speeches made to mark Waterloo Day, which, declared an article in *Blackwood's Edinburgh Magazine* in 1835, 'is to more than one nation, and to many millions of beings, the anniversary of freedom and of independence'.[27] The article went on to attack the Opposition Whigs, whom it saw, in the image of Charles James Fox, as poor patriots and unrepentant apologists for France.[28] Twenty years on from Waterloo, the regard in which Wellington was held was the stuff of political point-scoring and party squabbles.

In any case, Britain already had its hero of the Napoleonic Wars, one who came closer to achieving consensus and uniting the nation. That honour continued to belong to Horatio Nelson, a naval hero for a nation that for generations had entrusted its defence to the sea, and who had outmanoeuvred and destroyed the French at Trafalgar. For Nelson, far more than Wellington, had the essential qualities to be a truly national hero, a man worthy of the patriotic myth that grew up around him. He is the one who takes his place, as the historian John MacKenzie reminds us, in 'the history books and compendia of heroic biographies that were such a feature of the late Victorian era'. He goes on to argue that heroic myths all have certain common characteristics which fit Nelson to perfection. The central character must be endowed with 'an unassailable conviction of rectitude'; he needs to have been martyred (in England's case 'Wolfe, Nelson, Livingstone and Gordon all shared this and their mythic power was much more potent as a result'); and 'the myth requires a striking and moving icon, invariably the moment of martyrdom', which in Nelson's case involved his prolonged drawn-out death on the deck of the *Victory*.[29] Nelson could be celebrated for both an exemplary life and a martyr's death, while Wellington's later career as a politician never again scaled the same heights of public admiration. In the nineteenth century it would prove an unequal battle for the nation's affections, as Nelson became, to appropriate Colin White's expression, 'apotheosised', as a hero for the nation, by the British establishment. Trafalgar Day was declared a public holiday; the famous column built on

Trafalgar Square in London and monuments commissioned in provincial towns and cities; Nelson's letters were edited and published; romantic prints were etched by leading artists of moments in the Great Man's life; and he was the centrepiece of the new Naval Gallery that was established in the Painted Hall at the Royal Naval Hospital in Greenwich.[30] As a final step in the process, his ship *Victory* was spared the breaker's yard when she was decommissioned in 1812. Instead she was moved to moorings off Gosport where she remained for almost 100 years as a tourist attraction and site of national memory. Queen Victoria herself visited the *Victory* on Trafalgar Day 1844, standing on the quarterdeck on which a laurel wreath marked the spot where Nelson fell.[31] The apotheosis of the hero was complete.

France and Waterloo

Whereas Britain and Prussia could celebrate a victory that brought deliverance from Napoleon—and in Prussia's case sweet revenge for the humiliation at Jena and Auerstedt in November 1806[32]—France had little to celebrate, apart from relief that the exhaustion of the Napoleonic years was over. A quarter-century of war and the loss of several million French lives had finally achieved little. The country had been invaded and occupied by the Allied armies. Though the occupation may not have been harsh, the army of occupation was a deliberate reminder by the Allied governments that France had been forced to surrender and that the people as well as their leader had suffered defeat.[33] But there were serious structural weaknesses to be addressed. The French economy was left weakened and distorted, with the consequence that the technological discoveries of the eighteenth century had not been put to industrial use and all except the war industries were seriously undercapitalised. France's first great empire, the Atlantic empire of the eighteenth century, was largely lost. It did not take the sight of what historian Jacques Hantraye has called the 'Cossacks on the Champs-Elysées' to bring home to ordinary people that the war had ended in disaster.[34] As France started to rebuild her commerce after 1815—to say nothing of her political ambition and public morale—the extent of what had been lost became clear. Several million soldiers had fought in these wars, and many returned to civilian life physically or psychologically damaged, without hope of employment. Many were refused the pensions to which they believed themselves entitled by a monarchy that regarded them with distrust.[35] It would not be possible to airbrush their experience out of national memory; the question was not whether these wars would be remembered in nineteenth-century France, but how.

A divided polity

There was another problem, too, which would colour the shaping of that memory—the fact that it was not just the Imperial army that had been defeated, but the political system created by the Revolution and Empire. In modern terminology 1815 was about regime change, the insistence by the victorious Allies that the French must abandon the institutions—and for many the ideals—for which they had sacrificed so much and accept the imposition of a restored monarchy that was agreeable to her conquerors, without regard for the feelings of the French people themselves. It was not only committed Bonapartists who resented this. Republicans also felt the Restoration as a humiliation, while Catholics and legitimists joined forces to exploit their good fortune. The Restoration Church, indeed, denounced the whole of the previous quarter-century, seeing the defeat as evidence of divine retribution and urging that France must atone by 'wiping out the crime that made it necessary or by prayer'.[36] It was a call to arms that goes far to explain the factionalism of the decades that followed.

For the politicians and army officers who had steered Napoleonic France, had shared the imperial dream of a new, modernised polity, and had taken their ideas of efficient administration, accessible justice and human dignity across Europe, often to peoples who enjoyed no individual rights, where justice was arbitrary or at the whim of a ruler, or where serfdom was still in force, it was this defeat that could seem most crushing. It was a defeat that blighted a whole generation, and it left nineteenth-century France a country bitterly divided against itself, a nation that might be sure of its national identity and proud of its collective culture, but which remained in a permanent state of political civil war. Not all Frenchmen had rallied to Napoleon, and not all saw 1815 as a defeat. For a minority of royalists and *émigrés*, this was a moment that called for celebration, an event which they greeted with ill-concealed relief. French painting during the Restoration largely reflected this spirit, with many works portraying the return of calm to France's public life. Jean Zippel, for instance, painted the entry of the Allied troops into Paris on 31 March 1814, through the triumphal arch that stood on the Boulevard Saint-Denis, dedicated to Louis XIV; Vergnaux chose to depict the entry of the Comte d'Artois on 12 April, crossing the Pont au Change to attend mass at Notre-Dame; and Martinet published prints of Louis mingling with the crowd in the Tuileries gardens after his return from exile in July 1815. All emphasised peace, public rejoicing and social harmony; and in all women, who were perceived as having opposed Napoleon's wars most fiercely, were given due prominence.[37]

Nostalgia and the Napoleonic legend

For those who had lived through the years of the Revolutionary and Napoleonic Wars and had contributed to the imperial adventure, the frustrations of the years that followed—when many were cast out of active service on half pay (*demi-solde*) or experienced trouble in finding employment in the depressed postwar economy—led them to look back on the war with unashamed nostalgia. That is not to say that the hardship and suffering were forgotten, as the ample evidence from memoirs and letters of the Moscow Campaign makes abundantly clear. Men had faced exhaustion and starvation and had been reduced to hacking slabs of meat from their dead horses to survive. They had in their wanderings across Europe witnessed, been the victims of and sometimes been party to acts of savagery and barbarism. They had lost friends and comrades and seen men horribly mutilated on the battlefield. War was not fun. But amidst the undeniable horror there were moments of warmth and companionship, and tales of adventure which lived with them for the rest of their lives. They had seen foreign lands, met exotic peoples and admired European capital cities as they would never have hoped to do in civilian life. These memories, too, stayed with them, and for many of the survivors it was these that came to dominate their recollections and colour their judgement on the Napoleonic years long after they had returned to civilian life. And if the 1820s were a period of unemployment and retrenchment for many, characterised politically by the values of monarchism and Catholicism, for thousands of Napoleonic veterans they were also years when it was still possible to dream. The growth of *charbonnerie* and secret societies was particularly strong among army veterans and those of Bonapartist sympathies, and the severity of government repression against anyone agitating for a return to the Empire only served to strengthen their resolve. The 1820s were punctuated with plots and conspiracies which, after the assassination of the Duc de Berri, made royalists apprehensive, and plots were rarely out of the headlines. Most notable, perhaps, was the conspiracy of the Four Sergeants of La Rochelle in 1822, whose youth and idealism played to the romantic imagination; the seeming inevitability of their condemnation and execution only helped ensure that they would live on in popular memory and inspire a new generation of loyalists to the cause.[38]

The most immediate recorded memories were those of contemporaries, the soldiers who had served and who now returned to life in civil society. Not all had done badly by the war: among officers especially, as historian Stéphane Calvet has shown in his study of the Charente, their years in uniform could form a socially-acceptable transition period in their lives, and they very often resumed the same kind of lifestyle and social status that they had enjoyed before they enlisted.[39] Young noblemen, especially, were often able to slip back into a comfortable lifestyle on their farm and chateau; it was the rural poor, farm workers and rural labourers, who had the greatest difficulty in reinsertion. Among them were many who lived out their lives in poverty and died in misery; at Ansouis in the Vaucluse, Natalie Petiteau calculates that ten of the 42 former soldiers who returned to their village from the Napoleonic Wars were at one time or another officially classified as 'indigent'.[40] But few of them left memoirs; few, indeed, had the level of literacy necessary to sustain any sort of correspondence with their families or do more than give them the most basic news about their whereabouts or their state of health. The stories that were passed on to postwar audiences were largely those of officers who had experience to share, whether with their immediate families or with a national readership. And what stories! They had been participants in great events; they had witnessed great moments of history and experienced the ravages of war. They spoke with the authority of men who had taken part in some of the most audacious campaigns of recent history, who had followed their Emperor to Poland or Portugal, who had suffered the extremes of climate of Russia and the Caribbean. However much they had suffered behind the Napoleonic eagles, they seldom dwelt long on these sufferings, preferring to talk of the good times, the joy of conquest, the pleasures of comradeship, their collective pride in the army, its victories, its Emperor. If the wars had ended in defeat—and they could scarcely try to deny that—defeat was not their central theme, and the final campaigns were often described with sadness rather than anger. Theirs were the voices that future generations wanted to hear; and the authors of war memoirs, conscious of the importance of what they were saying and eager to convey their sense of pride and adventure, rarely disappointed them.[41]

At key moments in the nineteenth century the popularity of these accounts soared, a living and communicative memory from the battlefront that provided later generations with a link to their Napoleonic past, and poets and novelists with a sense of the grandeur and pathos of the imperial adventure. Balzac, Victor Hugo and even Walter Scott were all dazzled by the person of the Emperor and by the scope of his military ambition, and through their writings a new generation would come to share the experiences of their elders. The fact that his career had ended in defeat, in exile and petty humiliations at the hands of his gaoler, Hudson Lowe, a man, said Napoleon, 'who never commanded or been accustomed to men of honour', added a certain pathos to his legend.[42] Politically, too, the memory of Napoleon remained alive and vivid, rekindled with almost predictable regularity across the nineteenth century. The July Monarchy played on Napoleon's memory in a bid to maximise popular support: four Napoleonic marshals flanked the new king at his coronation; the Vendôme Column was erected to Napoleon's memory in 1834; the Arc de Triomphe was inaugurated two years later as a memorial to the glories won by Napoleon's troops; and in 1840 the Emperor's body was returned from Saint-Helena.[43] The revolution of 1848 brought little relief, as Louis-Napoleon capitalised on his links to the Great Napoleon to seize political power. Under the Second Empire the government encouraged the growth of nostalgia for the Napoleonic age, the new emperor going so far as to reward every surviving veteran of his great-uncle's armies with the Médaille de Sainte-Hélène in 1857.[44] Napoleon III's reign would end, of course, in national disaster with the rapid defeat of the French army at Sedan in the Franco-Prussian War, a defeat which only demonstrated what many already knew to be true: how much the country's army—and with it, France's imperial ambition—had declined since the glorious days of Austerlitz and Jena.

For the faithful, the fact that the Napoleonic adventure had ended in failure and surrender—and in Napoleon's own abdication, a political failure to add to the military defeat—was as nothing when compared to the magnificence of the ambition and the vaulting imagination which had inspired his quest for Empire. Indeed, for the romantic nineteenth-century imagination, his defeat may even have added a certain pathos and sense of poignancy to Napoleon's legend, placing him alongside such national heroes and heroines as Duguesclin, Vercengetorix and Joan of Arc.[45] He had gone down fighting in a battle that he had come close to winning, as even Wellington had had the grace to admit, but which he and his generals lost through unforced errors. 'I sensed', Napoleon wrote later, 'that Fortune was abandoning me'.[46] It was a battle which was easy to depict as a 'glorious defeat', enshrouded in fog and mist yet illuminated by acts of outstanding courage: in particular, the heroic defence of the final square of the Old Guard, and the famous, if possibly apocryphal, verdict of General Cambronne that 'the Guard dies and does not surrender', would live long into the nineteenth century.[47] Likewise Victor Hugo's haunting poem made the battlefield into a nineteenth-century *lieu de mémoire* that was a tribute to French gallantry as well as to unquenchable ambition, and it is as such that it would be remembered and commemorated across much of mainland Europe. Hugo's was a romanticised image of a world France had lost, but it was a world to which many Frenchmen still aspired and a vision they would retain in their dreams and their prayers long after Napoleon's death on St Helena.[48]

Waterloo may have ended Napoleon's regime and destroyed any possibility of a return to power, but it did not destroy his reputation. He had his critics, of course; indeed, ever since the 1812 campaign in Russia there had been an increasingly loud chorus of critical voices, suggesting that Napoleon had taken unwonted risks, that he had lost his grip on reality, that his ambition had seduced him into pursuing impossible dreams. And after Waterloo, once more, some of his soldiers criticised his overconfidence, even his naivety, for trusting too readily the judgement of his marshals. Most famously, Marbot wrote somewhat contemptuously that 'we were made to manoeuvre like pumpkins' on the battlefield, while Blücher acted and Napoleon continued to wait for the arrival of Grouchy's reinforcements long after all communication with the Marshal had been lost, and that, as a consequence, he had needlessly handed the initiative in the battle to Blücher and Wellington.[49] But among senior officers there were few who expressed themselves so critically, even though they were realistic enough to recognise that the game was up, and that they had no choice but to sue for peace. Besides, in Louis XVIII's France this was not the moment to indulge in *Napoléomanie*. The years after 1815 were the high point of the black legend of Napoleon, with savage satires circulating in Paris presenting him as a tyrant, an ogre, an unrepentant terrorist and the devoted disciple of Robespierre. This image was fuelled by legitimist propaganda and by the missionaries sent out into the French provinces to re-impose Catholic worship on communities that had slumped into atheism or had become lax in their Dominican devotions. But significantly, even after all the misery and near-despair of the final campaigns, there were many, especially among his veterans, who remained loyal to the man they continued to regard as 'their' emperor.

A glorious defeat

For 1815 did not just spark a renewed cult of the person of Napoleon, significant as that would prove to be; it also created another mythology, especially in the military—that of the 'glorious defeat'.[50] The French troops who searched out the frontier and crossed the Ardennes in the wake of Waterloo knew that the war was lost; but they had no reason to see in their defeat any cause for reproach. They had fought well, with courage, against a series of coalitions and latterly against all the great powers of Europe. If they had made tactical errors, if there had been failures of communication, if they had misread Prussian manoeuvres, none of this besmirched their honour, for throughout they had fought with the courage and *élan* on which French military identity was based. Many of the soldiers were eager to talk of their experiences, which, in spite of the danger and the suffering, still counted among the most memorable of their lives. Some, indeed, were now so inured to a life of adventure that they could not bring themselves to accept the dull routines of village life, preferring to offer their swords to others, especially where they were fighting in some cause that could be identified with freedom or throwing off tyranny. And so French veterans would be found in significant numbers in the southern United States (where anti-British feeling could be mobilised), and in the liberation struggles in Mexico, Bolivia, Peru, Ecuador, and across central and south America. Their quest for blood and glory did not end at Waterloo.[51]

Besides, if Waterloo saw the rout of one army, it did not destroy France's military tradition, or undermine its efficacy. 1870, which saw the miserable collapse of the French army in the face of a Prussian invasion, was the exception rather than the rule, and historian Paddy Griffith rightly reminds us that still, in the middle of the nineteenth century, the French army was widely regarded as the best in the world. It was an army, he insists, 'which inherited not only Napoleon's odium but also much of his prestige—as well as many of his best generals and best ideas'.[52] Restoring France's prestige meant not only ending foreign occupation, something that was achieved ahead of time, but also rebuilding the country's military resources, a task which Louis XVIII handed (somewhat reluctantly) to Napoleon's former marshal, Gouvion Saint-Cyr, who was in the Emperor's service until November 1813, when he was taken prisoner at Dresden.[53] France was given a new army, which, in contrast to that of the Revolution, was to be 'long-service, professional and small'.[54] It went on to be involved in a succession of carefully-planned limited operations which served to consolidate its prestige: in Spain in 1823, Greece in 1827–1829, Belgium in 1831–1832, and Rome in 1849, besides its offensives into Africa, in Senegal, Madagascar and, most problematically, Algeria. Under Napoleon III, moreover, the French army fought valiantly against the Russians in the Crimea before the debacle of the Emperor's misguided expedition to Mexico. Though the army would not again be involved in campaigns of the size and ambition of Napoleon's, Waterloo should not be seen as ushering in a period of slump or disablement. In the Crimea the British did not hide their admiration for France's military endeavours. And the infant United States paid France the supreme compliment of modelling her army almost entirely on the French.[55]

Napoleon's battalions continued to have an assured place in nineteenth-century memory, in novels and history paintings, but also in the various media of popular culture, from the poetry of Pierre-Jean Béranger[56] to the brightly-coloured lithographs of Charles Pellerin.[57] In France and beyond, Romantic writers ensured that the wars of Napoleon would be remembered not just for individual acts of courage, but for the values they upheld, the civil liberties they offered, the grandeur of the imperial dream. In 1825 Stendhal described Marengo as the battle that had opened Italy to liberty and modernity and had launched liberal ideas, a revolution in culture that Napoleon's ultimate defeat had doomed to failure. 'The Italians are right', he wrote; 'Marengo advanced the civilization of their country by a hundred years, just as another battle has retarded it for a century'.[58] What he is suggesting is that Waterloo represented the end rather than the beginning: the end of an experiment in humanism, secularism, modern administration and accessible justice which France had come to represent and which through her victories she had offered to all of Europe. He was not alone in seeing things in this light. Nationalist writers in the nineteenth century turned increasingly to the Empire to exemplify the glory they so ardently craved. For Ernest Renan, in Robert Morrissey's words, 'a heroic past, great men and glory constitute the social capital on which to base an idea of the nation'.[59] Even in Britain, Philip Shaw can comment that 'it is a curious aspect of modern culture that Waterloo is best remembered as a tragic defeat rather than as a glorious triumph', a tragedy in which it is Napoleon, and not Wellington, who is cast in the leading role.[60] In the memorialization of the battle across Europe, as in the public presentation of the battlefield itself, the Emperor, even in defeat, remains the dominant figure, the reason why people, generations later, still visit the site of the battle. The famous Butte with its lion, which dominates the surrounding landscape now just as it has since its construction by the Dutch government in 1826, may commemorate an Allied victory. But the thoughts of the visitor are with Napoleon, and in the words of a tourist guide published in Brussels in 1907, they reflect not pity nor yet triumphalism, but 'the serenity and religious calm that comes from a destiny fulfilled'.[61]

Conclusion

Whereas nineteenth-century Britain was encouraged to wallow in a victory that Wellington claimed for his own, France remembered the battle as the epitome of a 'glorious defeat' that lent grandeur and a certain pathos to the Napoleonic legend. But it still remained a difficult moment to incorporate into France's national story. Two centuries on from Waterloo, indeed, and with a succession of bicentennial celebrations now behind us, it is hard to avoid the conclusion that it is not only the fact of defeat that is at issue here. Britain seems more comfortable remembering its military past, both commemorating and celebrating its triumphs at Trafalgar and in the Peninsula, whereas France has appeared far more reticent. There was little public celebration in Paris 200 years after Marengo, or Ulm, or Jena, or Wagram. We can only speculate on the reasons behind this. It may be that the French Republic is wary of heaping too much praise on the Empire; or that France, a founder member of a multi-national Europe, is reluctant to indulge in an orgy of nationalism at the expense of her European neighbours. It is, however, a salutary reminder that commemoration in the twenty-first century does not have to be an excuse for nationalistic triumphalism, especially when that commemoration is of wars in which so many died. We can also remember discreetly, and with dignity.

Notes

1. For a book-length account of the different memories of Waterloo in nineteenth-century Europe see my *Waterloo* (Oxford, 2015).
2. Cited after Robert and Isabelle Tombs, *That Sweet Enemy: Britain and France, The History of a Love-Hate Relationship* (London, 2007), 288.
3. Emmanuel de Las Cases, *Mémorial de Sainte-Hélène*, 2 vols (Paris, 1961), vol. 2, 236.
4. Munro Price, *Napoleon: The End of Glory* (Oxford, 2014), 250.
5. *The Times*, 29 June 1815, quoted in Philip Shaw, *Waterloo and the Romantic Imagination* (Basingstoke, 2002), 1.
6. Robert Southey, *The Poet's Pilgrimage to Waterloo* (London, 1816), 17–18.
7. Susan Pearce, 'The *matérial* of War: Waterloo and its Culture', in *Conflicting Visions: War and Visual Culture in Britain and France, 1799–1830*, ed. John Bonehill and Geoff Quilley (Guildford, 2005), 218.
8. Jenny Uglow, *In These Times: Living in Britain through Napoleon's Wars, 1793–1815* (London, 2014), 620.
9. Walter Scott, *The Field of Waterloo: A Poem* (Edinburgh, 1815), 14–15.
10. Thomas R. Dale, 'The Shaping of History: Scott's Life of Napoleon Buonaparte', in *Scott in Carnival: Selected Papers from the Fourth International Scott Conference*, ed. J. H. Alexander and David Hewitt (Aberdeen, 1993), 394.
11. Philip Shaw, *Waterloo and the Romantic Imagination* (Basingstoke, 2002), 59.
12. John Kincaid, *Adventures in the Rifle Brigade, in the Peninsula, France and the Netherlands, from 1809 to 1815* (London, 1929), 257.
13. Kincaid, *Adventures*, 258.

14. Jeremy Black, *Waterloo: The Battle that Brought Down Napoleon* (London, 2011), 31–32.
15. Michael Snape, *The Redcoat and Religion: The Forgotten History of the British Soldier from the Age of Marlborough to the Eve of the First World War* (London, 2005), 143.
16. Snape, *The Redcoat and Religion*, 142.
17. Ibid., 144.
18. William Tomkinson, *The Diary of a Cavalry Officer in the Peninsular and Waterloo Campaigns, 1809–1815* (Staplehurst, 1999), 319.
19. Linda Colley, *Britons: Forging the Nation, 1707–1837* (New Haven, CT, 1992), 6–9.
20. Ugo Pericoli, *1815: The Armies at Waterloo* (London, 1973), 47–50.
21. R. J. White, *Waterloo to Peterloo* (London, 1968), 16.
22. Parliamentary Papers, House of Commons, report of session of 23 June 1815.
23. See Peter Hofschröer, *Wellington's Smallest Victory: The Duke, the Model Maker and the Secret of Waterloo* (London, 2004).
24. Melvyn Thompson, *St George's (Kidderminster): a Waterloo Church* (Kidderminster, 2009), 14.
25. T. F. Bowerbank, *A Sermon Preached in the Parish Church of Chiswick, Middlesex*, July 30 1815.
26. Henry Cotes, *To the members of the Westminster Waterloo Association: A Sermon Preached in the Parish Church of Bedlington in the County of Durham, 20 August 1815* (Newcastle, 1815), 18.
27. *Blackwood's Edinburgh Magazine*, July 1835, 115.
28. Ibid., 114.
29. John M. MacKenzie, 'Nelson Goes Global: The Nelson Myth in Britain and Abroad', in *Admiral Lord Nelson: Context and Legacy*, ed. David Cannadine (Basingstoke, 2005), 144–146.
30. Colin White, 'Nelson Apotheosised: The Creation of the Nelson Legend', in *Admiral Lord Nelson*, 105–106.
31. Ibid., 109.
32. The classic German analysis of the battle is that of Carl von Clausewitz; for a useful synopsis see Bruno Colson, 'Clausewitz on Waterloo', *War in History* 19 (2012): 397–400.
33. See the chapter in this volume by Christine Haynes, 'The Allied Occupation of France, 1815–1818', 51–67.
34. Jacques Hantraye, *Les Cosaques aux Champs-Elysées: L'Occupation de la France après la chute de Napoléon* (Paris, 2005), *passim.*
35. Natalie Petiteau, *Guerriers du Premier Empire: expériences et mémoires* (Paris, 2011), 156–160.
36. Robert Gildea, *The Past in French History* (New Haven, CT, 1994), 227.
37. These images are reproduced and commented upon in Philip Mansel, *Paris Between Empires, 1814–52: Monarchy and Revolution* (London, 2001), plates between pages 208 and 209.
38. André Zeller, *Soldats perdus. Des armées de Napoléon aux garnisons de Louis XVIII* (Paris, 1977), 319–341.
39. Stéphane Calvet, *Les officiers charentais de Napoléon au dix-neuvième siècle* (Paris, 2010), 443–456.
40. Natalie Petiteau, *Lendemains d'Empire: Les soldats de Napoléon dans la France du 19e siècle* (Paris, 2003), 157.
41. Philip G. Dwyer, 'Public Remembering, Private Reminiscing: French Military Memoirs and the Revolutionary and Napoleonic Wars', *French Historical Studies* 33 (2010): 231–258.

42. Frank Giles, *Napoleon Bonaparte, England's Prisoner: The Emperor in Exile, 1816–1821* (London, 2001), 65.
43. Robert Gildea, *The Past in French History* (New Haven, CT, 1994), 96.
44. Sudhir Hazareesingh, *The Legend of Napoleon* (London, 2004), 243.
45. Christian Amalvi, *Les héros de l'histoire de France* (Toulouse, 2001), 68–71
46. Andrew Roberts, *Napoleon the Great* (London, 2014), 740.
47. For an account of the claims and counter-claims made about what Cambronne allegedly cried, see Pierre Larousse, *Le mot de Cambronne* (Paris, 1862).
48. Natalie Petiteau, 'Image des soldats de l'Empire dans l'œuvre de Hugo', in *Guerriers du Premier Empire*, 171–189.
49. *Mémoires du Général Baron de Marbot*, 3 vols, (Paris, 1891), iii, 403–404.
50. Jean-Marc Largeaud, *Napoléon et Waterloo: la défaite glorieuse de 1815 à nos jours* (Paris, 2006), *passim*.
51. Jean-Claude Lorblanchès, *Soldats de Napoléon aux Amériques* (Paris, 2012), *passim*.
52. Paddy Griffith, *Military Thought in the French Army, 1815–1851* (Manchester, 1989), 4.
53. Jacques Jourquin, 'Gouvion Saint-Cyr', in *Dictionnaire Napoléon*, 2 vols, ed. Jean Tulard (Paris, 1999), i, 886–888.
54. Gary P. Cox, *The Halt in the Mud: French Strategic Planning from Waterloo to Sedan* (Boulder, CO, 1994), 44.
55. Griffith, *Military Thought*, 191.
56. Pierre Brochon, *La chanson sociale de Béranger à Brassens* (Paris, 1961), 25.
57. Jean-Marie Dumont, *La vie et l'œuvre de Jean-Charles Pellerin, 1756–1836* (Épinal, 1956), 50.
58. Stendhal, *Voyages en Italie* (Paris, 1973), 83, in Michel Arrous (ed.), *Actes du colloque Napoléon, Stendhal et les Romantiques: l'armée, la guerre, la gloire* (Paris, 2002), 10–16.
59. Robert Morrissey, *Napoléon et l'héritage de la gloire* (Paris, 2010), 243.
60. Shaw, *Waterloo and the Romantic Imagination*, 1.
61. Fierens-Gevaert, *Figures et sites de Belgique* (Brussels, 1907), in Marcel Watelet and Pierre Couvreur (eds), *Waterloo, lieu de mémoire européenne, 1815–2000* (Louvain-la-Neuve, 2000), 159.

Part VI
Conclusion

22
Atlantic Revolutions, Imperial Wars, Post-Napoleonic Legacies, and Postcolonial Studies

Lloyd Kramer

The bicentennial historical analysis of the revolutions and wars that swept across the Atlantic world from the 1770s to the 1830s may well have generated more books and articles than appeared during all the years in which these great upheavals were actually taking place. Although some readers may assume that every significant historical issue has now been addressed, this collection of insightful essays shows that important new analytical perspectives can be added to the vast historiographical literature by examining the diverse personal experiences, social or political legacies, and cultural memories of both the Revolutionary and Napoleonic Wars in Europe and Wars of Independence in the Americas.

The bicentennial scholarship on this era might be compared to the expansive, territorial diversity of its far-flung conflicts because the study of these events has now carried historians into every country, culture, and society of the Atlantic world. Napoleon's life fascinates those who believe in the 'Great Man Theory' of history, but the ongoing study of his era suggests that we might also propose a 'Great History Theory' of Napoleon. The transitions and consequences of the transatlantic Napoleonic age constantly stimulate new historical approaches that now extend from biographical, military, and diplomatic studies into all the spheres of social, economic, cultural, and political history.

A concluding chapter for this impressive volume cannot possibly analyse all of the historical complexities that the authors have explored through their well-researched forays into the revolutionary/Napoleonic world. My response to these excellent essays will therefore simply offer some reflections on how the study of this revolutionary era in Atlantic history has evolved over several 'bicentennial historical generations' and how historians might possibly develop new perspectives by drawing on contemporary postcolonial studies. The long bicentennial era of the Atlantic Revolutions began with the imaginative, transnational work of historians such as Jacques Godechot (1907–1989) and R. R. Palmer (1909–2002), who argued in the early 1960s that revolutionary movements in North America and Western

Europe were connected parts of a transatlantic political transition to modern democratic societies.[1] The book you are now reading builds upon the early Godechot-Palmer project, but it shows how the study of the period of Revolutionary and Napoleonic Wars has expanded far beyond the largely political focus of their early transatlantic work.

A half-century of innovative social and cultural history—combined with new, critical-minded approaches to the history of race, gender, slave systems, nationalism, colonialism, empires, and revolutionary movements—has led to the kind of insightful historical work that appears in the preceding chapters. At the same time, however, other analytical themes and theories have emerged from the swirling currents of contemporary scholarship, which includes the critical perspectives of postcolonial theorists. This volume does not refer explicitly to the theorists or themes of postcolonial studies, but the insights of this burgeoning, interdisciplinary field could be brought more self-consciously into the study of Napoleonic systems and legacies.

Postcolonial theorists argue, for example, that the legacy of colonial hierarchies and social structures continued into later eras of national independence, that modern cultural identities have always been constructed through cross-cultural exchanges or the creation of multicultural 'hybridities', that knowledge and power were entangled in all colonial institutions, and that subaltern groups often resisted the daily demands of imperial administrative systems.[2] It could thus be productive for contemporary historians of Napoleonic imperialism to engage with such postcolonial themes as they continue to develop new analytical frameworks. Few historians of Napoleon's imperial system have explored the possibilities for this kind of theoretical engagement, with the exception of Michael Broers, who has discussed some parallels between the 'subaltern' society of Napoleonic Italy and British imperial possessions in India.[3] Establishing new dialogic connections between Napoleon scholars and postcolonial theorists would be a challenging project because these two intellectual camps probably have fewer cross-cultural exchanges than the opposing armies on early nineteenth-century battlefields. The chapters in this book nevertheless suggest that the more present-centred work of most postcolonial theorists could be enriched by exploring how specific Napoleonic conflicts and legacies confirm or complicate their theories. In short, a new phase of both historical analysis and postcolonial theorizing might develop through interdisciplinary dialogues about the Era of the Atlantic/Napoleonic Revolutions. These unlikely dialogues (have Napoleonic military historians and postcolonial literary theorists *ever* attended the same conferences?) may become more plausible if we briefly review earlier interpretations of the eighteenth-century democratic revolutions and then note how *War, Demobilization, and Memory* discusses recent historical themes that can be linked to contemporary studies of postcolonialism. This conclusion is therefore a postscript about 'post-history' as a current and future category of scholarly analysis.

Palmer and the 'Democratic Revolution'

R. R. Palmer's account of the transnational similarities of the American and French Revolutions (published in 1959 and 1964) offered provocative challenges to both American and European historians. Many Americans believed that the American Revolution was a 'war of independence' rather than a real revolution, but Palmer showed that the American revolutionary movement displaced thousands of people, confiscated the property of British Loyalists, violently repressed anti-revolutionary persons, and caused thousands of émigrés to flee the country (he pointedly noted the departure of 24 émigrés out of every 1000 people in revolutionary America versus only 5 émigrés per 1000 people in revolutionary France).[4]

Palmer's themes were also unsettling for many French historians who, to quote Palmer's own summary of their responses, believed he had downgraded the 'importance or uniqueness of the French Revolution by diluting it into a vague general international disturbance'.[5] Palmer's synthesis thus rejected both American and French national exceptionalism, but French historians were more inclined to ignore or condemn his argument. Palmer's *Age of the Democratic Revolution* described a transnational pattern in eighteenth-century conflicts that ranged from the British colonies in North America to France, Ireland, Germany, Italy, Switzerland, Holland and even Great Britain. Political mobilizations in all of these countries, as Palmer portrayed them, brought mostly middle-class and professional people into new oppositional campaigns that challenged the inherited legal and political privileges of aristocratic elites. These challengers based their demands for legal equality on Enlightenment ideas about inherent natural rights (to be restricted in practice to white men), but these ideas merged with social and political ambitions to produce the emotional passions of a violent revolution.

According to Palmer, a 'single revolutionary movement' spread across both sides of the Atlantic and denied that any person could exercise coercive authority simply by his own right, or by right of his status, or by right of 'history'. The general goal of the American and French revolutionaries was to open political institutions to social groups and persons who had been 'systematically excluded' from governing themselves and to make the 'people' as a whole sovereign within their own national states. Although he recognized that the concept of 'democracy' did not yet include modern principles such as the belief in universal suffrage, Palmer argued that the eighteenth-century revolution could be called 'democratic' because it was 'a movement which, however different in different countries, was everywhere aimed against closed élites, self-selecting power groups, hereditary castes, and forms of special advantage or discrimination that no longer served any useful purpose'.[6] This assault on inherited privileges led to the final dismantling of 'feudal' social and political hierarchies, and launched the modern era in which we still live. Palmer was by no means a Marxist, but his account of the transition to modernity emphasized the overthrow of a still-powerful, privileged aristocracy. Placed within an even wider historical context, his argument resembled 'modernization' theories in which the eighteenth-century Atlantic political transitions provided models for other societies that were still becoming 'modern' after the Second World War. Palmer thus called for a new transnational, comparative Atlantic history that would in fact emerge some two or three decades later.[7]

Transnational studies of the Atlantic world eventually became important and innovative, though critics noted numerous blind spots in Palmer's synthetic, pioneering work. Some Marxist critics complained that Palmer's view of Atlantic history simply offered historical justifications for the NATO alliance by positing a shared North Atlantic political history that differed from the communist systems of Eastern Europe. Later critics, by contrast, focused on other concerns that shaped the rapidly developing fields of global, social, and cultural history: Palmer did not discuss the critically important (authoritarian) Napoleonic era after 1799; he did not explain how new 'democratic' theories and institutions excluded women from political participation; he gave too little attention to the virulent racism and flourishing slave trade in America and the European colonies; he barely mentioned the Haitian Revolution and did not write about the early nineteenth-century Latin American revolutions and wars of independence; he did not analyse how the Western European revolutions affected Russia (except in brief discussions of the Polish partition); he did not explain the importance of art, literature or new cultural movements; and his emphasis on Enlightenment political theories did not adequately explain the powerful influence of economic interests, the growing significance of global capitalism, or the repressive aspects of democratic theory itself. Palmer was therefore an imaginative historical pioneer who called for a new kind of transnational, comparative analysis, yet the new Atlantic history that proliferated after 1990 mostly argued that the revolutionary/Napoleonic age was not really the democratic upheaval he had described.[8]

Recent histories of this era (and this volume offers good examples) have thus focused on the political exclusion of women and marginalized social groups, the oppressive racism of slavery, the transatlantic commodity trading systems, the cultural construction of nationalism, the historical significance of the Haitian and Latin American revolutions, and the vast social disruptions that the Revolutionary and Napoleonic Wars caused both within and beyond Europe. Palmer may have agreed that all these issues were important aspects of the revolutionary era, but his omissions (from a two-volume book that already reached 1100 pages) opened opportunities to develop new critical perspectives on the whole transatlantic revolutionary era. The Dutch historian Wim Klooster, for example, concisely summarized the criticism as he began his own comparative account of the Atlantic Revolutions: 'Palmer saw the age of revolutions as the triumphal march of democracy. But democracy is no appropriate prism through which to see these uprisings. It was hardly more than a temporary by-product of some insurrections'.[9] This summary distorts Palmer's use of the term 'democratic' (by which he mainly meant the opposition to inherited privileges), but Kooster's critique shows how historical analysis of the revolutionary/Napoleonic conflicts has evolved away from Palmer's important early books.

War and memory in current studies of Atlantic revolutions and the Napoleonic era

The meanings and legacies of the Revolutionary/Napoleonic era have been redefined through broader thematic frameworks, even when the research focuses on very specific places. These new themes include wider geographical coverage; more emphasis on the social, economic, and human costs of war; more analysis of civilian-military relations in warring and postwar societies; more discussion of how national identities and collective memories were culturally constructed; more critical attention to the ideologies and practices of gender exclusions and racism; and increasing recognition of how the legacies of warfare continued long after the wars apparently ended (a key theme of this entire book). Although many other issues appear throughout the recent historical scholarship and in this volume, I want briefly to note how these themes in *War, Demobilization, and Memory* broaden our understanding of the history of the period and lead toward possible new dialogues with the theorists of postcolonialism.

Geographical expansion

The wider global reach of contemporary historiography shows how this era's political and military conflicts spread far outside Western Europe. Russia has gained new prominence as one of the evolving national societies that must be included in transnational studies of the revolutionary and Napoleonic upheavals. Cold War-era historians may not have fully recognized Russia's significant participation in Atlantic world events between 1780 and 1825, but various chapters in this collection clearly demonstrate that Russia paid enormous costs in the Napoleonic Wars and that these costs long affected Russian society.[10] The financial expenses alone could not really be managed, and yet there may have been even greater cultural and political consequences as direct encounters with Napoleon's destructive Grande Armée made many Russians sceptical about all claims for the progressive development of post-revolutionary European culture.

But Russia is only one of the so-called 'marginal' societies that must now be included within a much wider context of Napoleonic conflicts and imperial expansion. Weapons, soldiers, and warfare flowed from Napoleonic Europe into South America, displacing government officials, transforming the lives of women who struggled to enter the public sphere (though some achieved notable influence) and even influencing the European-inflected memory of Simón Bolívar when he was honoured in Venezuelan national rituals.[11] From Latin America to the Caribbean to the North American 'War of 1812' the multicultural peoples of the New World were deeply involved in the revolutionary/Napoleonic maelstrom. Indeed, the widening analysis of the era's global transformations must now include Haiti, Egypt, North Africa, and the Ottoman Empire, where Napoleonic violence and imperialist interventions were very significant and where recent work has brought new geographical frameworks into historical studies of this era.[12] The Atlantic world, which now refers to more people, cultures, and conflicts than ever appeared in traditional histories of Europe's Revolutionary and Napoleonic Wars, seems to have become a too-narrow sphere for analysing the permanent global legacies of these conflicts.

Social, political, and economic impact of warfare

The new Atlantic history, as demonstrated in this book, has long since moved away from the traditional military history of battles. Battlefield strategies and events almost never appear in the preceding chapters, except when the authors refer to the huge number of casualties at Leipzig or Waterloo. Military history increasingly stresses that wartime experiences, for soldiers and civilians alike, mostly concerned the daily struggles to cope with environmental destruction, food shortages, diseases, displaced people, and the painful loss of family or comrades.[13] The violence affected non-combatants everywhere because urban populations were forced out of their homes, women were sexually assaulted, crops, forests and buildings were destroyed, and neither people nor animals could find enough food or safe environments. Economic exchanges were so disrupted that few people ever escaped from their wartime financial anxieties or recovered a commercial 'old regime'. This book provides no romantic narratives about the ennobling experiences of warfare, and it emphasizes that even the victors mourned their massive losses.

Civilian/military relations

The new history of revolutionary and Napoleonic warfare thus demonstrates the overlapping experiences (or deaths) of civilians and soldiers, despite the increasingly stark demarcation of these social categories in an age of large national armies. Soldiers moved back and forth between mobilizations and distant hometowns, veterans defined themselves through their military experiences long after they had left the army, and occupying troops regularly lived in the houses or neighbourhoods of city dwellers throughout Germany, Russia, France, and Italy. The military demanded conscripts and taxes from communities that could not avoid the social disruptions of war, no matter how far they were from the battlefields. The constant flow of people into and out of armies, occupied towns, veterans' groups, and port cities meant that the new kinds of warfare brought all social classes into the struggles.[14] Personal lives and public conflicts converged, which meant that women, children, and old people were swept into the chaos of enormous military deployments.

National identities and national memory

The new work on revolutions and Napoleonic warfare also shows that personal experiences or the memories of specific political and military events were far more important than political abstractions and national constitutions in creating collective national identities. Wars were remembered in memoirs, history books, public festivals, and local monuments that helped people define who was French, German, English, Italian, Russian, American or patriotic; but the 'memory work' was an ongoing cultural project. Military service and warfare became identity-shaping, international experiences, and yet the endless narratives about enemies or dangers or death encouraged the scapegoating of suspicious persons and a new hostility for allegedly disloyal groups, including Jews, religious outsiders, and anyone who may have supported the 'other side'. National identities were never simply fixed, however, so that emerging nationalist groups struggled to create or sustain an imagined national unity and shared national purpose. These nationalist aspirations show why historical studies of this era now include detailed analysis of collective memories and conflicting historical narratives.[15] This kind of cultural history explains persuasively how the memories of warfare and military participation often became more important than any event that actually happened. The cultural construction of national memories has thus become a salient theme in the historiography of the revolutions and wars of the period. Various authors in this volume also confirm (like other cultural historians) that nations were never united, homogeneous or fully coherent—which is why nationalists everywhere sought constantly to create mythical images of enduring national unity.

Gender and racial hierarchies

The classic military and political histories of this era often ignored women because they did not appear in military uniforms or government offices. Various authors in this book, by contrast, contribute to a major theme of the new Atlantic history as they show how women were actively involved in wars and constantly threatened by military occupations. Although they did not serve in armies, warfare displaced women from their communities, brought the deep grief of death to their families, gave them the difficult tasks of healing wounded or sick people, and required their participation in symbolic rituals of national remembrance. Such experiences offered new opportunities for autonomous action, but gender hierarchies still defined the social boundaries of women's and men's lives. This volume, like many other recent works, also demonstrates that analysing the history of gender means much more than bringing in women or studying constructions of femininity. It also helps us to understand the representations of masculinity and the ways in which conceptions of manhood contributed to political discourses, the creation of social hierarchies, the processes of political inclusion or exclusion, and the gendered meanings of military duties, political rights, and definitions of citizenship.[16]

Gendered hierarchies were also connected in many places to racial hierarchies, especially in the Caribbean and South American commercial systems that depended on enslaved labour. Several chapters in this volume explain how women challenged the gender or racial constraints on their public actions and also helped construct new social and national identities.[17] The much-desired return to 'normalcy' after the revolutionary upheavals, however, included strong reaffirmations of gender and racial hierarchies that may have been disrupted by warfare. The Napoleonic Wars thus left far-reaching social legacies in the gendered hierarchies of family life, the memory of deceased relatives, the continuing enslavement of Caribbean workers, and the economic vulnerability of displaced persons. Historians of the Atlantic world, as this book shows, are analysing all of these daily realities with careful attention to ideas about gender and race—and to the hierarchical structures that such ideas supported. Anxieties about the breakdown of patriarchal families or sexual seductions added to other fears about political subversions or betrayals, which suggests, in part, why the history of gender relations has also become an essential part of political and military history.

Legacies of warfare and the Longue Durée

Among the many issues that reappear often in this book, the most important overall theme emerges in the meanings of 'legacy'. Each essay ultimately poses a question that is evoked in the book's title: how do the legacies of revolutions and wars continue after all the specific public conflicts and battles *appear* to have ended? The answers to this question are complex and never complete, but an overall thesis emerges from the preceding chapters as the authors repeatedly show that people who survived the Revolutionary/Napoleonic upheavals could never go back to the 'normal' world in which they had lived before the wars. They continued to mourn the loss of parents and children; or they never returned to the house where they wanted to live; or they never resumed their previous work; or they never recovered their health; or they never forgot the traumatic violence they had seen; or they never lived again under the government they had once known. Although it is a historical cliché to say that 'nothing ever stays the same', this truism summarizes the general meaning of these great upheavals for the generations that lived through them and for the historians who now write about their experiences.

At the same time, however, the influences of these vast revolutionary conflicts endured for decades or centuries, so that it might also be truly said: 'the legacies of these wars never ended'. The authors in this book describe events and conflicts that continued to affect people long after the revolutionary/Napoleonic era supposedly came to a close in 1815 or 1825 or whatever date one might choose. Specific dates can serve only as semi-fictional end points, because the wars were never really over until the last persons who lost their parent or their home or their health finally died—and until the last ideological consequences had disappeared (which has not yet happened). Historians like to debate the causes of revolutions and wars, but this book provides a different kind of intriguing coherence by focusing on consequences that affected human lives far into the 'post-revolutionary' and 'post-Napoleonic' era. It therefore emphasizes the power of historical continuities as well as the power of historical changes; and it is this living legacy of the 'post' history that leads also to the key themes of postcolonial theory.

Postcolonial theory and the legacies of war in the era of Atlantic revolutions

Postcolonial theories emerged as a method for analysing how colonial conquests and systems continued to influence formerly colonized people after European empires officially withdrew from places they had once controlled. Postcolonial theorists have thus stressed the political, economic, social, and cultural legacies of earlier colonial hierarchies, all of which strongly influenced post-independence schools, economies, languages, collective memories, and personal identities.[18] The shaping forces of imperialism, as postcolonial theorists have described them, could never be completely effaced; and there could never be a return to pure, precolonial cultures (though independent nations also asserted their own cultural identities and broke free from many colonial structures). The postcolonial world outside of Europe, like the post-revolutionary and post-Napoleonic world within or beyond Europe, evolved out of previous imperial interactions between local populations and outside administrators, military forces, cultural institutions, and transnational economic systems.

These interactions were inherently hierarchical, but they shaped new, 'hybrid' personal and cultural identities that fused European cultures, languages, and education with cultures, languages, and educational traditions that had long existed among the colonized people. 'Hybridity' referred to this 'in-between' position that people experienced as they mediated between European impositions and their own cultural communities. The political and military occupations that resulted from the Revolutionary and Napoleonic Wars between the 1770s and 1815 did not last as long as most colonial systems, and yet the disorienting mediations with new political and military hierarchies, alien languages, and changing social systems pushed the people in post-Napoleonic societies (like those in postcolonial societies) toward different historical conditions and identities. There was no going back to pre-revolutionary, pre-Napoleonic cultures or social relations, though the nostalgia for semi-mythic old regimes flourished in almost every society.

Postcolonial theorists have criticized numerous colonial legacies, much as people in Germany, Spain, Italy and the Caribbean condemned the enduring consequences of Napoleon's Empire. Postcolonial analysis, however, recognizes that colonial inheritances are inescapable. These inheritances can be useful or creative sources of multicultural hybridity as well as oppressive carryovers, but in any case they remain influential forces in post-independence societies. As Robert J. C. Young explains in a wide-ranging discussion of the theoretical responses to these patterns, 'Postcolonial critique incorporates political and theoretical practices whose reach extends back into the history of the colonial past as well as the day-to-day realities of the postcolonial present, practices which seek to contest the legacies of that past as well as to challenge the priorities and assumptions of its political heirs'.[19] Similar patterns of remembering or challenging recent history and of criticizing reconstituted, post-independence states were also common among nationalist critics of the post-Napoleonic states in Prussia, Italy, Spain, and other nineteenth-century societies.

Postcolonial critics see imperial residues in the political, economic, and cultural power that governs their societies after the colonizing regime departs. 'Postcolonialism, therefore, operates through the dimensions of time or history and space'. Young goes on to explain that the critique of this time-space continuum requires a new sphere of 'cultural reconceptualization' in which knowledge and culture can be freed from previous power relationships. The complex 'practice of postcolonialism' thus 'produces a curiously fragmented and hybrid theoretical language' that reflects the complex historical experience it seeks to describe: 'conflictual cultural interaction'.[20] The intricacies of postcolonial theories may baffle empirical-minded historians, but those who study post-Napoleonic societies can find a familiar emphasis on the enduring influence of disruptive, traumatic experiences and comprehensible claims about the hybrid identities that emerged from evolving social hierarchies, new systems of power/knowledge, and difficult cross-cultural interactions.

It should be stressed that postcolonial analysis emerged with specific reference to colonial experiences outside Europe. Historians of Europe must therefore think comparatively and critically about how the highly racialized, demeaning social exchanges in Asia, Africa, and the Americas may have differed from French imperial interventions in other European societies. A simple Eurocentric appropriation of non-European experiences and ideas cannot be the starting point for new dialogues, but historians of Europe and North America can surely gain new perspectives when they explore how the 'empire writes back'.[21]

In the spirit of dialogical exchange, I would thus propose that the themes of postcolonial studies might enrich the field of post-revolutionary, post-Napoleonic Atlantic history because postcolonial theories push such historical analysis beyond the limiting frameworks of Eurocentrism; offer new perspectives on how colonial conquests resembled the disruptions of total war; stress the intricate connections between power, knowledge, and the control of subaltern populations; emphasize the hybrid, multicultural layers of national identities; examine the persistence of gender and racial hierarchies; and insist that the legacies of colonialism (like the legacies of war) never end on the day of independence or the date of a treaty. In short, there are postcolonial parallels for all of the themes that I noted in my earlier discussion of specific issues in this book, as I want to show through another brief summary of key concepts.

Eurocentrism

This volume exemplifies how recent historians of the period have gone far beyond the geographical focus of earlier scholarly generations in their work on the Caribbean, Latin America, and Russia, but future studies can move even further beyond the field's Eurocentric traditions. It would be good (as noted earlier) to learn more about the Napoleonic invasion of Egypt and the Ottoman Empire, to continue the discussion of French failures in Haiti, and to expand the research on how the colonial slave system was re-imposed in places such as Guadeloupe and Martinique. There is more work to be done on the ways in which French and British interactions with Muslims in North Africa and enslaved Africans in the Americas influenced post-revolutionary cultural identities on all sides and reshaped Napoleon's imperial ambitions. The further development of post-Eurocentric histories of Napoleonic legacies, for example, could respond to Sanjay Seth's description of postcolonial research as a 'challenge [to] the historical centrality accorded to Europe in most accounts of modernity'. Postcolonial perspectives, in other words, lead to alternative accounts of how 'modernity is not a tale of endogenous development in Europe, but of structural interconnections between different parts of the world'.[22] Taking up Seth's challenge, historians of the Napoleonic era and its legacies in the Atlantic world might better analyse the period's 'structural interconnections' by extending their research into the worlds of the Mediterranean and Indian Oceans too.

Disruptions and oppressions of colonial conquests

The new social and military histories of the Revolutionary and Napoleonic Wars emphasize the human and environmental destruction that armies caused as they confiscated crops and livestock, destroyed forests, burned houses, and pursued their enemies into cities and the countryside across Europe and the Americas. Anti-colonial theorists such as Frantz Fanon and Aimé Césaire wrote about similar violence when they explained how colonial interventions radically disrupted the towns, environments, and psychological wellbeing of colonized people. They also argued, however, that political activists and intellectuals could lead their colonized societies out of a cultural desolation that was as acute for Césaire as for the most fervent, anti-Napoleon nationalist in Prussia or Spain. Colonial occupations, Césaire explained in a twentieth-century critique that resembled the German philosopher Johann Gottlieb Fichte's angry response to the French occupation of Prussia after 1806, became a history of 'cultures trampled underfoot, institutions undermined, lands confiscated, religions smashed, magnificent artistic creations destroyed, [and] extraordinary *possibilities* wiped out'.[23] What, then, might be similar or different in the cultural responses to French imperialism among Spaniards in 1810, Prussians in 1813, and Algerians in 1960? There may also be intriguing overlaps in the strategies of anti-Napoleon theorists and the later leaders of modern anti-colonial movements. It is worth noting, for example, that Nelson Mandela read the Prussian military theorist Carl von Clausewitz's classic work *On War* as he began to define his own strategy to defeat the oppressive white-controlled regime in South Africa.[24] 'I read Clausewitz', Mandela once explained, because he provided insights into 'the rules of war' and the 'principles of war'.[25] A path toward new perspectives on the legacy of the Napoleonic era could well lead historians to the famous South African leader who used the theoretical 'principles' of an anti-Napoleon military reformer to think about the relation between politics and violence. Perhaps the two strategists were dealing with a common problem. 'As a theoretical critique', notes the literary critic Robert P. Marzec, 'postcolonialism confronts the oftentimes brutal, always questionable colonial activities of empire ... and [the] domination that affected the geopolitical development of people, communities, and cultures'.[26]

Power/knowledge and the control of subaltern populations

The administrative managers of Napoleon's imperial projects believed they were introducing advanced knowledge and scientific progress into every society they entered. Here, too, the postcolonial theorists have led the way in showing how colonial interventions were always linked to intellectual assumptions that devalued other cultures and justified the imposition of new laws and governing institutions. The influential cultural theorist Edward Said, drawing on the works of Michel Foucault, argued that colonizing forces relied on academic experts whose categorizing knowledge became useful contributions to the expansion of imperial social control. Social resistance to the colonizing experts soon emerged among the targeted, subaltern populations, however, which postcolonial historians have described by reconstructing the actions and identities of the most invisible groups in colonized societies. Historians of Napoleonic Europe have found similar patterns in the power/knowledge systems of imperial administrators (and in the local subaltern resistance), but postcolonial perspectives might add to the transnational analysis of these processes. As the historian Simon Gunn explains in a concise statement about Said's view of the power/knowledge connections in Orientalist discourses, 'Western academic, administrative and cultural knowledges were not viewed as in any sense neutral or disinterested'.[27] Such accounts of administrative knowledge in the colonial world provide a starting point for comparisons with French-imposed legal reforms or administrative systems that often survived the demise of Napoleon's Empire.

Nations, languages, and cultural hybridity

National identities evolve constantly through interactions between different national cultures, but these interactions become most hostile and intense during military conflicts. The wars in the Era of Atlantic Revolutions brought together multicultural armies in multicultural conflicts, so that both the military forces and their battles were sites of complex cross-cultural exchanges and collisions. The postcolonial conception of war (for which, as Mandela suggested, Clausewitz may be a highly relevant theorist) stresses that armed conflicts should be examined as open-ended political and cultural interactions. 'Fighting is an engagement with the enemy', the political analyst Tarak Barkawi writes in a perceptive discussion of military clashes, 'the nature and outcome of which lies outside of either side's control but which is jointly shaped by their interaction and context. At this most basic, "tactical" level war's main characteristic is evident: its ability to draw people into a violent embrace from which no one ever emerges the same'.[28] Barkawi thus explains how new identities emerge through wartime encounters, but the meaning of these clashes and exchanges are remembered in narratives that come from both sides of the battlefield. Although Waterloo meant something very different to the British and the French, both national cultures assimilated this event into self-affirming national narratives and enduring national identities.

The postcolonial interpretation of war as a protracted process of cross-cultural interactions thus offers intriguing perspectives with which to rethink the national and historical meaning of revolutionary and Napoleonic military conflicts. Postcolonial theorists nevertheless reject all claims for essential or innate national identities because no language or narrative can produce fully coherent nations. The citizens in every national society embody hybrid, fluid identities that change through cross-cultural conflicts and encounters with unfamiliar cultural languages. No society ever constructs complete national unity; and this cultural reality extended from the diverse conflicts of these years through the later memories of wartime experiences, and down to all modern postcolonial states.

Gender, race, and social hierarchies

Colonial systems on every continent reinforced gender and racial hierarchies that existed throughout the revolutionary and Napoleonic transitions within the Atlantic World. Recent historical scholarship (including this book) shows clearly how gender and racial ideologies entered revolutionary theories and policies, but postcolonial writers also emphasize that later national independence movements did little to alter the vulnerable, subordinate positions of women and marginalized racial groups. Robert Young's description of this postcolonial reality could apply almost equally well to the gendered social and political history of post-Napoleonic Europe. 'Whereas from a masculine perspective', Young writes, 'independence ushered in the defining new condition of postcoloniality, for women there was no such break: the struggle continued, now against a patriarchal sphere that no longer required women's support'. Although great collective efforts had been devoted to 'achieving national sovereignty', women soon found that another 'liberation struggle' would have to be waged to gain the political and social rights that men claimed mainly for themselves in postcolonial states.[29] Postcolonial studies have thus increasingly emphasized the gender hierarchies that sustained male privileges, much as historians of post-Napoleonic Europe and the post-revolutionary Americas have analysed the patriarchal systems that continued to control the lives of women after 1815.

At the same time, postcolonial theorists have critically examined the racism that was 'central to the growing power of imperial discourse during the nineteenth century' and the social 'construction of race' that was essential for 'the maintenance of imperial domination'.[30] This theme, which reappears throughout recent works on both colonial and postcolonial societies, also provides a framework for the less Eurocentric analysis of Napoleon's imperial policies and legacies in Caribbean and North African societies. Gender and racial hierarchies—and the cultural representations of such systems—thus offer another common theme for postcolonial and post-Napoleonic studies.

The colonial legacy continues

Although each of these issues could be used for future historical analysis, it is the overarching perspective of postcolonial theory that brings us back to the thesis of this volume on the legacy of the Atlantic Revolutions: the *post* era of great historical disruptions such as the American, French and Haitian revolutions, the Napoleonic Wars, the Spanish American Wars of Independence and later colonial conquests is best understood as a less violent continuation of ongoing conflicts, hierarchies, and ideologies by other means. This shared emphasis on long-term legacies provides an intellectual foundation for new dialogues between postcolonial theorists and historians of post-revolutionary and post-Napoleonic American and European national cultures. The preceding chapters of this book have examined many 'carry-overs' that connected the revolutionary/Napoleonic era to later cultures, and similar claims about structural continuities appear among the analysts of postcolonial history. Sanjay Seth summarizes this perspective in a paragraph that might be used to launch an open-ended conversation. 'The "post" in postcolonial theory does not signify the period or era "after" colonialism came to an end, but rather signifies the entire historical period after the beginnings of colonialism', Seth explains. 'The historical and theoretical claim signalled by the "post" in postcolonialism ... is that the world has been decisively shaped by colonialism, and that one cannot even begin to understand the contemporary situation if this fact is not acknowledged, taken into account, and explored in all its ramifications'.[31] Such assertions about the power of historical continuities should be completely persuasive to anyone who studies the legacies of the Atlantic world's revolutionary/ Napoleonic upheavals. We still live within institutions, ideologies, economic systems, and national states that were constructed in the era between 1770 and 1830, which suggests why historians are still exploring this legacy 'in all its ramifications'. This historical reality, along with many other overlapping analytical themes, opens the new possibilities for critical exchanges on the similarities and differences of post-revolutionary/Napoleonic and postcolonial history.

Conclusion

Amid all the vicissitudes of contemporary historical scholarship, the field of revolutionary/Napoleonic studies continues to thrive. This book affirms the intellectual vitality of a subject that constantly elicits new insights and leads historians into ever more diverse regions of the world. The legacies of this transitional period have been redefined with evolving, critical perspectives, and the subsequent historical memories of the whole era have become a major theme for creative research. The Atlantic revolutions, Napoleon's Empire, and their later, wide-ranging consequences remain both fascinating and endlessly controversial.

The end of the bicentennial commemorations is thus not a 'Waterloo moment' for revolutionary and Napoleonic historiography. New research methods, analytical problems, and theoretical arguments will surely continue to build the field's vast historical literature. I have proposed that the critical perspectives of postcolonial studies could offer imaginative frameworks for new dialogues about the global significance of the Atlantic revolutions and the Napoleonic imperial systems, but this is only one of the many possible ways in which studies of this era might move in new directions. Such dialogues could also provide creative new opportunities for postcolonial theorists and critics. They, too, might develop new perspectives on their specific concerns by reviewing the earlier Atlantic revolutions, the Napoleonic Empire, the resistance to that Empire, and the many after-effects of the wars of this era.

This book demonstrates the broad historical truth that 'nothing ever stays the same', and yet it also shows that certain historical structures, ideas, and legacies last for a very long time. These historical continuities can clearly survive the final defeat of Napoleonic Great Men and the collapse of great colonial empires. Historians of post-revolutionary/Napoleonic societies and postcolonial cultures therefore always come back to the same debatable, unresolved questions: what changes and what stays the same when vast historical upheavals inevitably give way to their long, multi-layered post-histories?

Notes

1. Jacques Godechot, *France and the Atlantic Revolution of the Eighteenth Century, 1770–1799*, (New York, 1965); R. R. Palmer, *The Age of the Democratic Revolution: A Political History of Europe and America, 1760–1800*, 2 vols (Princeton, NJ, 1959, 1964).
2. A brief overview of these themes can be found in Robert J. C. Young, *Postcolonialism: A Very Short Introduction* (Oxford, 2003).
3. Michael Broers, *The Napoleonic Empire in Italy, 1796–1814: Cultural Imperialism in a European Context?* (Basingstoke, 2005), 1–27, 275–299.
4. Palmer, *Age of the Democratic Revolution*, vol. 1, 185–190. Palmer's view of a 'real' American Revolution is confirmed by the valuable chapters of John R. Maass and Gregory T. Knouff in this book.
5. Robert Forster, R. R. Palmer, et al., 'American Historians Remember Jacques Godechot', *French Historical Studies* 16 (1990): 879–892, 883. For more on the responses to Palmer's work and his own views, see Marvin R. Cox, 'Palmer and Furet: A Reassessment of The Age of the Democratic Revolution', *Historical Reflections/Réflexions Historiques* 37 (2011): 70–85; and Lloyd Kramer, 'Robert R. Palmer and the History of Big Questions', *Historical Reflections/Réflexions Historiques* 37 (2011): 101–122.
6. Palmer, *Age of the Democratic Revolution*, vol. 1, 4–5 and 22–23 and vol. 2, 572.
7. For informative discussions of this expanding historiography, see Bernard Bailyn, *Atlantic History: Concept and Contours* (Cambridge, MA, 2005); and Jack P. Greene and Philip D. Morgan (eds), *Atlantic History: A Critical Appraisal* (Oxford, 2009).
8. For recent examples of the constantly expanding 'Post-Palmer' themes, see Joanna Innes and Mark Philp (eds), *Re-imagining Democracy in the Age of Revolutions: America, France, Britain, Ireland 1750–1850* (Oxford, 2013); Jeremy D. Popkin, *A Concise History of the Haitian Revolution* (Malden, MA, 2012); David Patrick Geggus and Norman Fiering (eds), *The World of the Haitian Revolution* (Bloomington, IN, 2009); and Karen Hagemann et al. (eds), *Gender, War, and Politics: Transatlantic Perspectives, 1775–1830* (Basingstoke, 2010).
9. Wim Klooster, *Revolutions in the Atlantic World: A Comparative History* (New York, 2009), 2.
10. Christine Haynes, Janet M. Hartley and Alexander M. Martin address such issues in their chapters for this volume.
11. These themes emerge in the diverse, insightful chapters by Rafe Blaufarb, Catherine Davies, Sarah C. Chambers, Cassandra Pybus and Kit Candlin, and Matthew Brown.
12. See, for example, Ian Coller, 'Egypt in the French Revolution', in *The French Revolution in Global Perspective*, ed. Susanne Desan et al. (Ithaca, NY, 2013), 115–132; Ian Coller, 'The Revolutionary Mediterranean', in *The Companion to the French Revolution*, ed. Peter McPhee (Malden, MA, 2013), 419–434; and Juan Cole, *Napoleon's Egypt: Invading the Middle East* (Basingstoke, 2007).
13. The chapters by Katherine B. Aaslestad, Alexander M. Martin, Christine Haynes, David Todd, and Alan Forrest examine these social and economic issues.
14. See the wide-ranging chapters by David A. Bell, Christine Haynes, Leighton S. James, John A. Davis, Rafe Blaufarb, and Cassandra Pybus and Kit Candlin.

15. Issues of national identity, collective memory and suspicions of 'difference' are perceptively examined in the chapters by Michael Rowe, Andrew Lambert, John Bew, Karen Hagemann, John A. Davis, and Alan Forrest.
16. See for example, Stefan Dudink et al. (eds), *Masculinities in Politics and War: Gendering Modern History* (Manchester, 2004); and idem. et al. (eds), *Representing Masculinity: Citizenship in Modern Western Culture* (Basingstoke, 2008).
17. Gender and racial hierarchies and ideologies receive detailed attention in the excellent chapters by Davies, Pybus and Candlin, Aaslestad, Hagemann, Hartley, Knouff, and Haynes.
18. For introductions to postcolonial theories and themes, see Robert J. C. Young, *Postcolonialism: An Historical Introduction* (Malden, MA, 2001); Dipesh Chakrabarty, *Provincializing Europe: Postcolonial Thought and Historical Difference* (1st edn, 2000, Princeton, 2008); Bill Ashcroft et al., *The Empire Writes Back: Theory and Practice in Post-colonial Literatures* (2nd edn, London, 2002); and Homi K. Bhabha, *The Location of Culture* (London, 1994).
19. Young, *Postcolonialism: Historical Introduction*, 66.
20. Ibid., 66 and 69.
21. This phrase comes from the title of the book by Ashcroft et al., *The Empire Writes Back*, who also emphasize the importance of critical, comparative analysis.
22. Sanjay Seth, 'Introduction', and 'Postcolonial Theory and the Critique of International Relations', in *Postcolonial Theory and International Relations: A Critical Introduction*, ed. Sanjay Seth (Abingdon, 2013), 1–13, 7 and 15–31, 19.
23. Aimé Césaire, *Discourse on Colonialism* (New York, 2000), 43. On Johann Gotlieb Fichte's development of a national philosophy to counter Napoleon's occupation of Prussia, see David James, *Fichte's Social and Political Philosophy: Property and Virtue* (Cambridge, 2011), 162–207.
24. For an English translation of Carl von Clausewitz's *On War* (published posthumously in German by his wife Marie von Clausewitz between 1832 and 1837), see Project Gutenberg: http://www.gutenberg.org/files/1946/1946-h/1946-h.htm (accessed 26 May 2015).
25. Nelson Mandela, *Conversations with Myself* (New York, 2010), 106. For an insightful discussion of Mandela's interest in Clausewitz, see Jonathan Hyslop, 'Mandela on War', *The Cambridge Companion to Nelson Mandela*, ed. Rita Barnard (New York, 2014), 162–181; and for an excellent, recent analysis of the military theorist himself, see Peter Paret, *Clausewitz in his Time: Essays in the Cultural and Intellectual History of Thinking About War* (New York, 2015).
26. Robert P. Marzec, 'The First Thirty Years of Postcolonial Literary Scholarship: The Continuing Importance of a Discipline', in *Postcolonial Literary Studies: The First 30 Years*, ed. idem. (Baltimore, MD, 2011), 2.
27. Simon Gunn, *History and Cultural Theory* (Harlow, 2006), 162; the passage refers to Edward Said's paradigm-shaping book, *Orientalism* (1st edn, New York, 1978).
28. Tarak Barkawi, 'War, Armed Forces, and Society in Postcolonial Perspective', in *Postcolonial Theory*, ed. Seth, 91. Barkawi also refers to Clausewitz; and (with Keith Stanski) he has co-edited a provocative book, *Orientalism and War* (Oxford, 2012).
29. Young, *Postcolonialism: Very Short Introduction*, 99.
30. Ashcroft et al., *Empire Writes Back*, 207.
31. Seth, 'Introduction', 1.

Bibliography: The Legacy of War in the Era of Atlantic Revolutions

Mark Edward Hay

The purpose of this bibliography is to offer a starting point for further reading on the topics of this volume. It focuses on the following six themes:

I: Rethinking the Legacy of Conflict in the Era of Atlantic Revolutions
II: Peace Making, Occupation and Military Demobilization
III: The Aftermath of War in Politics and Political Culture
IV: Restoring Economies and Reordering Societies
V: Postwar Cultures and Contested War Memories
VI: Atlantic Revolutions, Imperial Wars, Post-Napoleonic Legacies, and Postcolonial Studies

Aaslestad, Katherine B., *Place and Politics: Local Identity, Civic Culture and German Nationalism in North Germany During the Revolutionary Era* (Boston, 2005).
——— 'Paying for War: Experiences of Napoleonic Rule in the Hanseatic Cities', *Central European History* 39/4 (2006): 641–675.
——— 'Remembering and Forgetting: The Local and the Nation in Hamburg's Commemorations of the Wars of Liberation', *Central European History* 38/3 (2005): 384–416.
——— and Johan Joor (eds), *Revisiting Napoleon's Continental System: Local, Regional and European Experiences* (Basingstoke, 2014).
——— and Karen Hagemann (eds), 'Collaboration, Resistance, and Reform: Experiences and Historiographies of the Napoleonic Wars in Central Europe', special issue of *Central European History* 39/4 (2006): 547–705.
Adelman, Jeremy, *Sovereignty and Revolution in the Iberian Atlantic* (Princeton, NJ, 2007).
Alonso, Carlos, *The Burden of Modernity: The Rhetoric of Cultural Discourse in Spanish America* (Oxford, 1998).
Archer, Christon I. (ed.), *The Wars of Independence in Spanish America* (Wilmington, DL, 2000).
Armitage, David and Sanjay Subrahmanyam (eds), *The Age of Revolutions in Global Context, c.1760–1840* (Basingstoke, 2010).
Ascoli, Albert Russell and Krystyna von Henneberg (eds), *Making and Remaking Italy: The Cultivation of National Identity around the Risorgimento* (Oxford, 2001).
Ashcroft, Bill, Gareth Griffiths and Helen Tiffin, *The Empire Writes Back: Theory and Practice in Post-colonial Literatures* (2nd edn, London, 2002).
Aston, Nigel, *Christianity and Revolutionary Europe, 1750–1830* (Cambridge, 2002).
Auwaerter, Paul G., J. Dove and P. A. Mackowiak, 'Simón Bolívar's Medical Labyrinth: An Infectious Diseases Conundrum', *Clinical Infectious Diseases* 52/1 (2011): 78–85.
Bailyn, Bernard, *Atlantic History: Concept and Contours* (Cambridge, MA, 2005).
Bayly, Christopher, *The Birth of the Modern World, 1780–1914* (Oxford, 2004).
Beachy, Robert, *The Soul of Commerce: Credit, Property, and Politics in Leipzig, 1750–1840* (Leiden, 2005).

Belaubre, Christophe, Jordana Dym and John Savage (eds), *Napoleon's Atlantic: The Impact of Napoleonic Empire in the Atlantic World* (Leiden, 2010).
Bell, David A., *The First Total War: Napoleon's Europe and the Birth of Warfare as We Know It* (Boston, 2007).
Berghahn, Volker R., *Militarism: The History of an International Debate, 1861–1979* (New York, 1982).
Bertaud, Jean-Paul, Alan Forrest and Annie Jourdan (eds), *Napoléon, le monde et les Anglais: Guerre des mots et des images* (Paris, 2004).
Beskrovnyi, L. G., *The Russian Army and Fleet in the Nineteenth Century* (Gulf Breeze, FL, 1996).
Bessel, Richard, Nicholas Guyatt and Jane Rendall (eds), *War, Empire and Slavery, 1770–1830* (Basingstoke, 2010).
Bethan, Anika, *Napoleons Königreich Westphalen: Lokale, deutsche und europäische Erinnerungen* (Paderborn, 2012).
Bew, John, *Castlereagh: A Life* (Oxford, 2012).
Bew, Paul, *Ireland: The Politics of Enmity, 1789–2006* (Oxford, 2007).
Binhammer, Katherine, *The Seduction Narrative in Britain, 1747–1800* (Cambridge, 2009).
Black, Jeremy, *Waterloo: The Battle that Brought Down Napoleon* (London, 2011).
Blancpain, Marc, *La vie quotidienne dans la France du Nord sous les Occupations, 1814–1944* (Paris, 1983).
Blaufarb, Rafe, *The French Army, 1750–1820: Careers, Talent, Merit* (Manchester, 2002).
——— *Bonapartists in the Borderlands: French Refugees and Exiles on the Gulf Coast, 1815–1835* (Tuscaloosa, AL, 2006).
Blom, Ida, Karen Hagemann and Catherine Hall (eds), *Gendered Nations: Nationalisms and Gender Order in the Long Nineteenth Century* (Oxford, 2000).
Bolivar, Simon, *Simón Bolívar: The Bolivarian Revolution*, Introduced by Hugo Chávez, ed. and trans. Matthew Brown (New York, 2009).
Bonehill, John and Geoff Quilley (eds), *Conflicting Visions: War and Visual Culture in Britain and France, 1799–1830* (Burlington, VT, 2005).
Bouwers, Eveline G., *Public Pantheons in Revolutionary Europe: Comparing Cultures of Remembrance, c. 1790–1840* (Basingstoke, 2012).
Braun, Guido, Gabriele Clemens, Lutz Klinkhammer, and Alexander Koller (eds), *Napoleonische Expansionspolitik: Okkupation oder Integration?* (Berlin, 2013).
Brewster, Claire, 'Women and the Spanish-American Wars of Independence: An Overview', *Feminist Review* 79/1 (2005): 20–35.
Brière, Jean-François, *Haïti et la France, 1804–1848: Le rêve brisé* (Paris, 2008).
Broers, Michael, *Europe after Napoleon, 1814–1848: Revolution, Reaction and Romanticism* (Manchester, 1996).
——— *The Napoleonic Empire in Italy, 1796–1814: Cultural Imperialism in a European Context?* (Basingstoke, 2005).
——— Peter Hicks and Agustin Guimera (eds), *The Napoleonic Empire and the New European Political Culture* (Basingstoke, 2013).
Brown, Matthew, *Adventuring Through Spanish Colonies: Simón Bolivar, Foreign Mercenaries, and the Birth of New Nations* (Liverpool, 2006).
——— *The Struggle for Power in Post-Independence Colombia and Venezuela* (New York, 2012).
——— and Gabriel B. Paquette (eds), *Connections after Colonialism: Europe and Latin America in the 1820s* (Tuscaloosa, AL, 2013).
Brown, Roger Hamilton, *The Republic in Peril: 1812* (New York, 1964).
Bruyère-Ostells, *Walter, La grande armée de la liberté* (Paris, 2009).
Candlin, Kit, *The Last Caribbean Frontier, 1795–1815* (Basingstoke, 2012).

——— and Cassandra Pybus, *Enterprising Women: Race, Gender and Power in the Revolutionary Atlantic* (Athens, GA, 2015).

Cannadine, David (ed.), *Admiral Lord Nelson: Context and Legacy* (Basingstoke, 2005).

Castells, Irene and Gloria Espigado y María Cruz Romeo (eds), *Heroínas y Patriotas. Mujeres de 1808* (Madrid, 2009).

Cavanagh, John C., *Decision at Fayetteville: The North Carolina Ratification Convention and General Assembly of 1789* (Raleigh, NC, 1989).

Charters, Erica, Eve Rosenhaft and Hannah Smith (eds), *Civilians and War in Europe, 1618–1815* (Liverpool, 2012).

Chakrabarty, Dipesh, *Provincializing Europe: Postcolonial Thought and Historical Difference* (1st edn, 2000, Princeton, NJ, 2008).

Chambers, Sarah C., *From Subjects to Citizens: Honor, Gender, and Politics in Arequipa, Peru, 1780–1854* (University Park, PA, 1999).

——— *Families in War and Peace: Chile from Colony to Nation* (Durham, NC, 2015).

Chanet, Jean-François, Annie Crépin and Christian Windler (eds), *Le temps des hommes doubles: les arrangements face à l'occupation, de la Révolution française à la guerre de 1870* (Rennes, 2013).

Chappey, Jean-Luc, Bernard Gainot, Guillaume Mazeau, Frédéric Régent and Pierre Serna (eds), *Pourquoi faire la Révolution?* (Marseille, 2012).

Charters, Erica, Eve Rosenhaft and Hannah Smith (eds), *Civilians and War in Europe, 1618–1815* (Liverpool, 2012).

Chickering, Roger and Stig Förster (eds), *War in an Age of Revolution, 1775–1815* (Cambridge, 2010).

Chopra, Ruma, *Unnatural Rebellion: Loyalists in New York City during the Revolution* (Charlottesville, VA, 2011).

Clark, Christopher, 'The Wars of Liberation in Prussian Memory: Reflections on the Memorialization of War in Early Nineteenth-Century Germany', *Journal of Modern History* 68/3 (1996): 550–576.

Clark, J. C. D., *English Society 1688–1832: Ideology, Social Structure and Political Practice during the Ancien Régime* (Cambridge, 1985).

Cole, Juan, *Napoleon's Egypt: Invading the Middle East* (Basingstoke, 2007).

Cole, Laurence, *Military Culture and Popular Patriotism in Late Imperial Austria* (Oxford, 2014).

Colley, Linda, *Britons: Forging the Nation, 1707–1837* (New Haven, CT, 1992).

Cornell, Saul, *The Other Founders: Anti-Federalism and the Dissenting Tradition in America, 1788–1828* (Chapel Hill, NC, 1999).

Cowman, Krista, Nina Javette Koefoed and Åsa Karlsson Sjögren (eds), *Gender in Urban Europe: Sites of Political Activity and Citizenship, 1750–1900* (New York, 2014).

Cox, Edward, *Free Coloureds in the Slave Societies of St. Kitts and Grenada, 1763–1833* (Knoxville, TN, 1984).

Crouzet, François, 'Wars, Blockade and Economic Change in Europe, 1792–1815', *Journal of Economic History* 24/4 (1964): 567–588.

——— 'The Historiography of French Economic Growth in the Nineteenth Century', *Economic History Review* 56/2 (2003): 215–242.

Daly, Gavin, *The British Soldier in the Peninsular War: Encounters with Spain and Portugal, 1808–1814* (Basingstoke, 2013).

Damas, Germán Carrera, *El culto a Bolívar* (3rd edn, Bogotá, 1987).

Daniell, Jere R., *Experiment in Republicanism: New Hampshire Politics and the American Revolution, 1741–1794* (Cambridge, MA, 1970).

——— *Colonial New Hampshire: A History* (Millwood, NY, 1981).

Davies, Catherine, Claire Brewster and Hilary Owen, *South American Independence: Gender, Politics, Text* (Liverpool, 2006).

Davis, John A., 'Italy', in *The War for the Public Mind: Political Censorship in Nineteenth Century Europe*, ed. Robert Justin Goldstein (Westport, CT, 2000), 81–124.

——— *Naples and Napoleon: Southern Italy and the European Revolutions, 1780–1860* (Oxford, 2006).

——— *The Jews of San Nicandro* (London, 2010).

Desan, Suzanne, Lynn Hunt and William Max Nelson (eds), *The French Revolution in Global Perspective* (Ithaca, NY, 2013).

Devas, Raymund P., *The History of the Island of Grenada, 1650–1950* (St George's, 1964).

Dudink, Stefan, Karen Hagemann and John Tosh (eds), *Masculinities in Politics and War: Gendering Modern History* (Manchester, 2004).

——— Karen Hagemann and Anna Clark (eds), *Representing Masculinity: Citizenship in Modern Western Culture* (Basingstoke, 2008).

Düding, Dieter, Peter Friedemann and Paul Münch (eds), *Öffentliche Festkultur: Politische Feste in Deutschland von der Aufklärung bis zum Ersten Weltkrieg* (Reinbek,1988).

Duffy, Michael, *Soldiers, Sugar and Seapower: The British Expeditions to the West Indies and the War against Revolutionary France* (Oxford, 1987).

Dwyer, Philip G., 'Public Remembering, Private Reminiscing: French Military Memoirs and the Revolutionary and Napoleonic Wars', *French Historical Studies* 33/2 (2010): 231–258.

——— and Alan Forrest (eds), *Napoleon and his Empire: Europe, 1804–1814* (Basingstoke, 2006).

——— and Lyndall Ryan (eds), 'Massacre in the Old and New Worlds, c. 1780–1820', special issue, *Journal of Genocide Research* 15/2 (2013): 111–232.

Earle, Rebecca A., *Spain and the Independence of Colombia, 1810–1825* (Exeter, 2000).

Ely, Christopher, *This Meager Nature: Landscape and National Identity in Imperial Russia* (DeKalb, IL, 2002).

Espigado, Irene Castells Gloria and María Cruz Romeo (eds), *Heroínas y patriotas: Mujeres de 1808* (Madrid, 2009).

Fishman, Sarah, Laura Lee Downs, Ioannis Sinanoglou, Leonard V. Smith, Robert Zaretsky and David Lake (eds), *France at War: Vichy and the Historians* (Oxford, 2000).

Flynn, James T., *The University Reforms of Alexander I, 1802–1835* (Washington, DC, 1988).

Forrest, Alan, *Conscripts and Deserters: The Army and French Society during the Revolution and Empire* (Oxford, 1989).

——— *Napoleon's Men: The Soldiers of the Revolution and Empire* (London, 2002).

——— *The Legacy of the French Revolutionary Wars: The Nation-in-Arms in French Republican Memory* (Cambridge, 2009).

——— *Napoleon* (London, 2011).

——— *Waterloo* (Oxford, 2015).

——— and Peter H. Wilson (eds), *The Bee and the Eagle: Napoleonic France and the End of the Holy Roman Empire* (Basingstoke, 2009).

——— Karen Hagemann and Étienne François (eds), *War Memories: The Revolutionary and Napoleonic Wars in Modern European Culture* (Basingstoke, 2012).

——— Karen Hagemann and Jane Rendall (eds), *Soldiers, Citizens and Civilians: Experiences and Perceptions of the Revolutionary and Napoleonic Wars, 1790–1820* (Basingstoke, 2009).

Forster, Robert, R. R. Palmer, James Friguglietti and Emmet Kennedy, 'American Historians Remember Jacques Godechot', *French Historical Studies* 16 (1990): 879–892.

François, Etienne, Hannes Siegrist and Jakob Vogel (eds), *Nation und Emotion: Deutschland und Frankreich im Vergleich: 19. und 20. Jahrhundert* (Göttingen, 1995).
Frevert, Ute, *A Nation in Barracks: Modern Germany, Military Conscription and Civil Society* (Oxford, 2004).
Gaspar, D. B. and Darlene Clark Hine (eds), *Beyond Bondage: Free Women of Color in the Americas* (Chicago, 2004).
Geggus, David Patrick and Norman Fiering (eds), *The World of the Haitian Revolution* (Bloomington, IN, 2009).
Gilje, Paul A., *Free Trade and Sailors' Rights in the War of 1812* (Cambridge, 2013).
Glenthøj, Rasmus and Morten Nordhagen Ottosen, *Experiences of War and Nationality in Denmark and Norway, 1807–1815* (Basingstoke, 2014).
Godechot, Jacques, *France and the Atlantic Revolution of the Eighteenth Century, 1770–1799* (New York, 1965).
Grab, Alexander, *Napoleon and the Transformation of Europe* (London, 2003).
Greene, Jack P. (ed.), *The Reinterpretation of the American Revolution, 1763–1789* (New York, 1968).
——— and Philip D. Morgan (eds), *Atlantic History: A Critical Appraisal* (Oxford, 2009).
Griffith, Paddy, *Military Thought in the French Army, 1815–1851* (Manchester, 1989).
Guiomar, Jean-Yves, *L'invention de la guerre totale, 18e–20e siècle* (Paris, 2004).
Hagemann, Karen, 'Of "Manly Valor" and "German Honor": Nation, War and Masculinity in the Age of the Prussian Uprising against Napoleon', *Central European History* 30/2 (1997): 187–220.
——— *'Mannlicher Muth und Teutsche Ehre': Nation, Militär und Geschlecht zur Zeit der Antinapoleonischen Kriege Preußens* (Paderborn, 2002).
——— 'Female Patriots: Women, War and the Nation in the Period of the Prussian-German Anti-Napoleonic Wars', *Gender & History* 16/3 (2004): 396–424.
——— '"Be Proud and Firm, Citizens of Austria!" Patriotism and Masculinity in Texts of the "Political Romantics" written during Austria's Anti-Napoleonic Wars', *German Studies Review* 29/1 (2006): 41–62.
——— '"Heroic Virgins" and "Bellicose Amazons": Armed Women, the Gender Order, and the German Public during and after the Anti-Napoleonic Wars', *European History Quarterly* 37/4 (2007): 507–527.
——— 'Reconstructing "Front" and "Home": Gendered Experiences and Memories of the German Wars against Napoleon–A Case Study', *War in History* 16/1 (2009): 25–50.
——— *Revisiting Prussia's Wars against Napoleon: History, Culture, Memory* (Cambridge, 2015).
——— Gisela Mettele and Jane Rendall (eds), *Gender, War, and Politics: Transatlantic Perspectives, 1775–1820* (Basingstoke, 2010).
Handler, Jerome, *The Unappropriated People: Freedmen in the Slave Society of Barbados* (Baltimore, MD, 1974).
Hantraye, Jacques, *Les Cosaques aux Champs-Élysées: L'Occupation de la France après la chute de Napoléon* (Paris, 2005).
Harling, Philip, *The Waning of 'Old Corruption': The Politics of Economical Reform in Britain, 1779–1846* (New York, 1996).
Hartley, Janet, 'Russia in 1812: Part 1: the French Presence in the Gubernii of Smolensk and Mogilev', *Jahrbücher für Geschichte Osteuropas* 38/2 (1990): 178–198.
——— 'Russia in 1812: Part 2: The Russian Administration of Kaluga Gubernija', *Jahrbücher für Geschichte Osteuropas* 38/3 (1990): 399–416.
——— *A Social History of the Russian Empire, 1650–1825* (London, 1999).

——— 'The Russian Recruit,' in *Reflections on Russia in the Eighteenth Century*, ed. Joachim Klein, Simon Dixon and Maarten Fraanje (Cologne, 2001), 32–42.
——— *Russia 1762–1825: Military Power, the State and the People* (Westport, CT, 2008).
Hartmann, Anja Victorine, Malgorzata Morawiec and Peter Voss (eds), *Eliten um 1800: Erfahrungshorizonte, Verhaltensweisen, Handlungsmöglichkeiten* (Mainz, 2000).
Hay, William Anthony, *The Whig Revival, 1808–1830* (Basingstoke, 2005).
Hazareesingh, Sudhir, *The Legend of Napoleon* (London, 2004).
Helg, Aline, *Liberty and Equality in Caribbean Colombia, 1770–1835* (Chapel Hill, NC, 2004).
Heredia, Edmundo A., *Los vencidos: Un estudio sobre los realistas en la guerra de independencia hispanoamericana* (Córdoba, 1997).
Higman, Barry W., *Slave Populations of the British Caribbean, 1807–1834* (Baltimore, MD, 1984).
Hilton, Boyd, *Corn, Cash and Commerce: The Economic Policies of the Tory Governments, 1815–1830* (Oxford, 1977).
——— *The Age of Atonement: The Influence of Evangelicalism on Social and Economic Thought, 1785–1865* (Oxford, 1988).
——— *A Mad, Bad, and Dangerous People? England, 1783–1846* (Oxford, 2006).
Hippler, Thomas, *Citizens, Soldiers and National Armies: Military Service in France and Germany, 1789–1830* (New York, 2008).
Hoffmann, Christhard, Werner Bergmann and Helmut Walser Smith (eds), *Exclusionary Violence : Antisemitic Riots in Modern German History* (Ann Arbor, MI, 2002).
Hofschröer, Peter, *Wellington's Smallest Victory: The Duke, the Model Maker and the Secret of Waterloo* (London, 2004).
Hoock, Holger, *Empires of the Imagination: Politics, War and the Arts in the British World, 1750–1850* (London, 2010).
Horn, Jeff, *The Path not Taken: French Industrialization in the Age of Revolution, 1750–1830* (Cambridge, MA, 2006).
Hunt, Lynn, *The Family Romance of the French Revolution* (Berkeley, CA, 1992).
Innes, Joanna and Mark Philp (eds), *Re-imagining Democracy in the Age of Revolutions: America, France, Britain, Ireland, 1750–1850* (Oxford, 2013).
Isabella, Maurizio, *The Risorgimento in Exile: Italian Émigrés and the Liberal International in Post-Napoleonic Europe* (Oxford, 2010).
Iturrieta, Elias Pino, *El divino Bolívar* (Caracas, 2005).
James, Leighton S., *Witnessing the Revolutionary and Napoleonic Wars in German Central Europe* (Basingstoke, 2013).
Jardin, André and André-Jean Tudesq, *Restoration and Reaction* (Cambridge, 1983).
Jarrett, Mark, *The Congress of Vienna and its Legacy: War and Great Power Diplomacy after Napoleon* (London, 2013).
Jasanoff, Maya, *Liberty's Exiles: American Loyalists in the Revolutionary World* (New York, 2011).
Jensen, Merril, *The New Nation: A History of the United States during the Confederation, 1781–1789* (New York, 1950).
Kanter, Douglas A., *The Making of British Unionism, 1740–1848* (Dublin, 2009).
Kastor, Peter J., *The Nation's Crucible: The Louisiana Purchase and the Creation of America* (New Haven, CT, 2004).
Katz, Jacob, *Emancipation and Assimilation: Studies in Modern Jewish History* (Farnborough, 1972).
——— *From Prejudice to Destruction: Anti-Semitism, 1700–1933* (Cambridge, MA, 1980).
——— *Die Hep-Hep-Verfolgungen des Jahres 1819* (Berlin, 1994).

Kennedy, Catriona, *Narratives of the Revolutionary and Napoleonic Wars: Military and Civilian Experience in Britain and Ireland* (Basingstoke, 2013).
——— and Matthew McCormack (eds), *Soldiering in Britain and Ireland, 1750–1830: Men of Arms* (Basingstoke, 2012).
Kerber, Linda K., *Women of the Republic: Intellect and Ideology in Revolutionary America* (Chapel Hill, NC, 1980).
Kingston, Ralph, *Bureaucrats and Bourgeois Society: Office Politics and Individual Credit in France, 1789–1848* (Basingstoke, 2012).
Klein, Joachim, Simon Dixon and Maarten Fraanje (eds), *Reflections on Russia in the Eighteenth Century* (Cologne, 2001).
Klooster, Wim, *Revolutions in the Atlantic World: A Comparative History* (New York, 2009).
Knight, Roger, *Britain against Napoleon: The Organization of Victory, 1792–1815* (London, 2013).
Knouff, Gregory T., *The Soldiers' Revolution: Pennsylvanians in Arms and the Forging of Early American Identity* (University Park, PA, 2004).
Kraehe, Enno E., *Metternich's German Policy*, 2 vols (Princeton, NJ, 1963–1983).
Kramer, Lloyd, *Lafayette in Two Worlds: Public Cultures and Personal Identities in an Age of Revolutions* (Chapel Hill, NC, 1996).
——— *Nationalism in Europe and America: Politics, Cultures, and Identities Since 1775* (Chapel Hill, NC, 2011).
Kruse, Wolfgang, *Die Erfindung des modernen Militarismus: Krieg, Militär und bürgerliche Gesellschaft im politischen Diskurs der Französischen Revolution, 1789–1799* (Munich, 2003).
Kunisch, Johannes and Herfried Münkler (eds), *Die Wiedergeburt des Krieges aus dem Geist der Revolution: Studien zum bellizistischen Diskurs des ausgehenden 18. und beginnenden 19. Jahrhunderts* (Berlin, 1999).
Lambert, Andrew D., *Nelson: Britannia's God of War* (London, 2004).
——— *The Challenge: Britain versus America in the Naval War of 1812* (London, 2012).
Largeaud, Jean-Marc, *Napoléon et Waterloo: la défaite glorieuse de 1815 à nos jours* (Paris, 2006).
Lefler, Hugh Talmage and Albert Ray Newsome, *North Carolina: History of a Southern State* (Chapel Hill, NC, 1954).
Leggiere, Michael V., *Napoleon and Berlin: The Franco-Prussian War in North Germany, 1813* (Norman, OK, 2002).
——— *The Fall of Napoleon* (Cambridge, 2007).
Lentz, Thierry, *Le congrès de Vienne. Une refondation de l'Europe, 1814–1815* (Paris, 2013).
Lewis, Jan, 'The Republican Wife: Virtue and Seduction in the Early Republic', *William and Mary Quarterly* 44/4 (1987): 689–721.
Lieven, Dominic, *Russia against Napoleon: the Battle for Europe, 1807 to 1814* (London, 2009).
Linch, Kevin, *Britain and Wellington's Army: Recruitment, Society and Tradition, 1807–15* (Basingstoke, 2012).
Lorblanchès, Jean-Claude, *Soldats de Napoléon aux Amériques* (Paris, 2012).
Lynch, John, *Simón Bolívar: A Life* (New Haven, CT, 2006).
Mahan, A. T., *The Influence of Sea Power upon the French Revolution and Empire, 1793–1812*, 2 vols (Boston, 1893).
Main, Jackson T., *The Antifederalists: Critics of the Constitution, 1781–1788* (Chapel Hill, NC, 1961).
Manchester, Laurie, *Holy Fathers, Secular Sons: Clergy, Intelligentsia, and the Modern Self in Revolutionary Russia* (DeKalb, IL, 2008).

Martin, Alexander M, *Romantics, Reformers, Reactionaries: Russian Conservative Thought and Politics in the Reign of Alexander I* (DeKalb, IL, 1997).

——— *Enlightened Metropolis: Constructing Imperial Moscow, 1762–1855* (Oxford, 2013).

McCarthy, Matthew, *Privateering, Piracy, and British Policy in Spanish America, 1810–1830* (London, 2013).

McCluer Calhoon, Robert, *The Loyalists in Revolutionary America, 1760–1781* (New York, 1973).

McDonnell, Michael A., Clare Corbould, Frances Clarke and W. Fitzhugh Brundage (eds), *Remembering the Revolution: Memory, History, and Nation Making from Independence to the Civil War* (Amherst, MA, 2015).

McFarlane, Anthony, *Wars and Independence in Spanish America* (London, 2013).

Moores, John Richard, *Representations of France in English Satirical Prints, 1740–1832* (Basingstoke, 2015).

Morrissey, Robert, *The Economy of Glory: From Ancien Régime France to the Fall of Napoleon* (Chicago, 2014).

Muir, Rory, *Britain and the Defeat of Napoleon, 1807–1815* (New Haven, CT, 1996).

Mulligan, William and Brendan Simms (eds), *The Primacy of Foreign Policy in British History, 1660–2000* (Basingstoke, 2010).

Murray, Pamela S., *For Glory and Bolívar: The Remarkable Life of Manuela Sáenz* (Austin, TX, 2008).

Nicolle, André, 'The Problem of Reparations after the Hundred Days', *Journal of Modern History* 25/4 (1953): 343–354.

Nicolson, Harold, *The Congress of Vienna: A Study in Allied Unity, 1812–1822* (London, 1946).

Nivola, Pietro and Peter J. Kastor (eds), *What So Proudly We Hailed: Essays on the Contemporary Meaning of the War of 1812* (Washington, DC, 2012).

Norton, Mary Beth, *Founding Mothers and Fathers: Gendered Power and the Forming of American Society* (New York, 1996).

O'Shaugnessy, Andrew, *An Empire Divided: The American Revolution and the British Caribbean* (Philadelphia, PA, 2000).

Palmer, R. R., *The Age of the Democratic Revolution: A Political History of Europe and America, 1760–1800*, 2 vols (Princeton, NJ, 1959–1964).

Paret, Peter, *The Cognitive Challenge of War: Prussia 1806* (Princeton, NJ, 2009).

——— *Clausewitz in his Time: Essays in the Cultural and Intellectual History of Thinking about War* (New York, 2015).

Patriarca, Silvana and Lucy Riall (eds), *The Risorgimento Revisited: Nationalism and Culture in Nineteenth Century Italy* (London, 2012).

Paul G. Auwaerter, J. Dove and P. A. Mackowiak, 'Simón Bolívar's Medical Labyrinth: An Infectious Diseases Conundrum', *Clinical Infectious Diseases* 52/1 (2011): 78–85.

Perkins, Bradford, *Prologue to War: England and the United States, 1805–1812* (Berkeley, CA, 1961).

Peters, Lars, *Romances of War: Die Erinnerung an die Revolutions- und Napoleonischen Kriege in Grossbritannien und Irland, 1815–1945* (Paderborn, 2012).

Petiteau, Natalie, *Lendemains d'Empire: Les soldats de Napoléon dans la France du XIXe siècle* (Paris, 2003).

——— *Guerriers du Premier Empire: expériences et mémoires* (Paris, 2011).

Planert, Ute,. *Mythos vom Befreiungskrieg: Frankreichs Kriege und der deutsche Süden: Alltag, Wahrnehmung, Deutung 1792–1841* (Paderborn, 2007).

——— *Krieg und Umbruch in Mitteleuropa um 1800: Erfahrungsgeschichte(n) auf dem Weg in eine neue Zeit* (Paderborn, 2009).

Platthaus, Andreas, *1813: Die Völkerschlacht und das Ende der Alten Welt* (Berlin, 2013).

Popkin, Jeremy D., *A Concise History of the Haitian Revolution* (Malden, MA, 2012).

Price, Munro, *Napoleon: The End of Glory* (Oxford, 2014).

Pybus, Cassandra, Emma Christopher and Marcus Rediker (eds), *Many Middle Passages: Forced Migration and the Making of the Modern World* (Berkeley, CA, 2007).

Quataert, Jean H., *Staging Philanthropy: Patriotic Women and the National Imagination in Dynastic Germany, 1813–1916* (Ann Arbor, MI, 2001).

Rath, John, *The Fall of the Napoleonic Kingdom of Italy, 1814* (New York, 1975).

Rey, Marie-Pierre, *Alexander I: The Tsar Who Defeated Napoleon* (Dekalb, IL, 2012).

Riordan, Liam, and Jerry Bannister (eds), *The Loyal Atlantic: Remaking the British Atlantic in the Revolutionary Era* (Toronto, 2012).

Rivera, Raquel Rosario, *Los emigrantes llegados a Puerto Rico procedentes de Venezuela entre, 1810–1848* (Hato Rey, 1992).

——— *Real Cédula de Gracias de 1815 y sus primeros efectos en Puerto Rico* (San Juan, 1995).

Rodriguez O. and Jaime E., *The Independence of Spanish America* (Cambridge, 1998).

Rodriguez, Moises Enrique, *Freedom's Mercenaries: British Volunteers in the Wars of Independence of Latin America*, 2 vols (Lanham, MD, 2006).

Rogers, Clifford J. (ed.), *The Military Revolution Debate: Readings on the Military Transformation of Early Modern Europe* (Boulder, CO, 1995).

Roland, Alex, W. Jeffrey Bolster, Alexander Keyssar, *The Way of the Ship: America's Maritime History Re-envisioned, 1600–2000* (Hoboken, NJ, 2008).

Rowe, Michael, *From Reich to State: The Rhineland in the Revolutionary Age, 1780–1830* (Cambridge, 2003).

——— (ed.), *Collaboration and Resistance in Napoleonic Europe: State-Formation in an Age of Upheaval* (Basingstoke, 2003).

Sartorius, David, *Ever Faithful: Race, Loyalty, and the Ends of Empire in Spanish Cuba* (Durham, NC, 2013).

Scheina, Robert L., *Latin America's Wars*, 2 vols (Washington, DC, 2003).

Schroeder, Paul W., *The Transformation of European Politics, 1763–1848* (Oxford, 1994).

Serna, Pierre, Antonio De Francesco and Judith A. Miller (eds), *Republics at War, 1776–1840: Revolutions, Conflicts, and Geopolitics in Europe and the Atlantic World* (Basingstoke, 2013).

Shaw, Philip, *Waterloo and the Romantic Imagination* (Basingstoke, 2002).

Shepherd, Verene, Bridget Brereton and Barbara Bailey (eds), *Engendering History: Caribbean Women in Historical Perspective* (London, 1995).

Simms, Brendan, *The Struggle for Mastery in Germany, 1779–1850* (New York, 1998).

Sims, Harold Dana, *The Expulsion of Mexico's Spaniards, 1821–1836* (Pittsburgh, PA, 1990).

Sked, Alan, *Metternich and Austria: An Evaluation* (Basingstoke, 2008).

Smith, Digby G., *1813: Leipzig: Napoleon and the Battle of the Nations* (London, 2001).

Stoker, Donald, Frederick C. Schneid and Harold D. Blanton (eds), *Conscription in the Napoleonic Era: A Revolution in Military Affairs?* (London, 2008).

Symonds, Craig L., *Navalists and Antinavalists: The Naval Policy Debate in the United States, 1785–1827* (Newark, NJ, 1980).

Taylor, Alan, *The Civil War of 1812: American Citizens, British Subjects, Irish Rebels, & Indian Allies* (New York, 2010).

Thibaud, Clément, *Républiques en armes: Les armées de Bolívar dans les guerres d'indépendance du Venezuela et de la Colombie* (Rennes, 2006).

Todd, David, *L'identité économique de la France: Libre-échange et protectionnisme, 1814–1851* (Paris, 2008).

——— 'A French Imperial Meridian, 1814–1870', *Past & Present* 210 (2011): 155–186.

Thoral, Marie-Cecile, *From Valmy to Waterloo: France at War, 1792–1815* (Basingstoke, 2011).

Uglow, Jenny, *In These Times: Living in Britain through Napoleon's Wars, 1793–1815* (London, 2014).

Urquijo, Jesús Ruiz de Gordejuela, *La expulsión de los españoles de México y su destino incierto, 1821–1836* (Sevilla, 2006).

Vagts, Alfred, *A History of Militarism* (Westport, CT, 1981).

Valugera, Alfonso, *Bullón de Mendoza Gómez de, La Primera Guerra Carlista* (Madrid, 1992).

Veve, Thomas Dwight, *The Duke of Wellington and the British Army of Occupation in France, 1815–1818* (Westport, CT, 1992).

Vick, Brian E., *The Congress of Vienna: Power and Politics after Napoleon* (Cambridge, MA, 2014).

Wacker, Volker, *Die allierte Besetzung Frankreichs in den Jahren 1814 bis 1818* (Hamburg, 2001).

Wahrman, Dror, *Imagining the Middle Class: The Political Representation of Class in Britain, c.1780–1840* (Cambridge, 1995).

Waresquiel, Emmanuel de and Benoît Yvert, *Histoire de la Restauration, 1814–1830: Naissance de la France moderne* (Paris, 1996).

Watts, Steven, *The Republic Reborn: War and the Making of Liberal America, 1790–1820* (Baltimore, 1987).

Welch, Pedro, *'Red and Black Over White': Free Colored Women in Pre-Emancipation Barbados* (Bridgetown, 2000).

Whitaker, Arthur Preston, *The United States and the Independence of Latin America, 1800–1830* (New York, 1962).

White, Eugene N., 'Making the French Pay: The Costs and Consequences of the Napoleonic Reparations', *European Review of Economic History* 5/3 (2001): 337–365.

Wilson, Kathleen, 'Rethinking the Colonial State: Family, Gender, and Governmentality in Eighteenth-Century British Frontiers', *American Historical Review* 116/5 (2011): 1294–1322.

Wilson, Peter H., *German Armies: War and German Politics, 1648–1806* (London, 1998).

Wishon, Mark, *German Forces and the British Army: Interaction and Perceptions, 1742–1815* (Basingstoke, 2013).

Woolf, Stuart J., *Napoleon's Integration of Europe* (London, 1991).

Wright, Christine, *Wellington's Men in Australia: Peninsular War Veterans and the Making of Empire c.1820–40* (Basingstoke, 2011).

Zamoyski, Adam, *1812: Napoleon's Fatal March on Moscow* (London, 2004).

——— *Rites of Peace: The Fall of Napoleon and the Congress of Vienna* (London, 2007).

Zeller, André, *Soldats perdus: Des armées de Napoléon aux garnisons de Louis XVIII* (Paris, 1977).

Zeuske, Michael, *Simon Bolívar: History and Myth* (Princeton, NJ, 2013).

Note

I would like to thank the editors for their helpful cooperation in the work on this selected bibliography.

Index

Printed by Printforce, the Netherlands